Brandy Station, Virginia, June 9, 1863

Brandy Station, Virginia, June 9, 1863

The Largest Cavalry Battle of the Civil War

Joseph W. McKinney

McFarland & Company, Inc., Publishers
Jefferson, North Carolina, and London

The present work is a reprint of the illustrated case bound edition of Brandy Station, Virginia, June 9, 1863: The Largest Cavalry Battle of the Civil War, *first published in 2006 by McFarland.*

LIBRARY OF CONGRESS CATALOGUING-IN-PUBLICATION DATA

McKinney, Joseph W., 1948–
  Brandy Station, Virginia, June 9, 1863: the largest cavalry battle of the Civil War / Joseph W. McKinney.
      p.   cm.
  Includes bibliographical references and index.

  ISBN-13 978-0-7864-7723-4
  softcover : acid free paper ∞

  1. Brandy Station, Battle of, Brandy Station, Va., 1863.
  2. United States — History — Civil War, 1861–1865 — Cavalry operations.
  3. Virginia — History — Civil War, 1861–1865 — Cavalry operations.
  I. Title.
  E475.51.M3   2013
  973.7'455 — dc22   2006016738

BRITISH LIBRARY CATALOGUING DATA ARE AVAILABLE

© 2006 Joseph W. McKinney. All rights reserved

No part of this book may be reproduced or transmitted in any form or by any means, electronic or mechanical, including photocopying or recording, or by any information storage and retrieval system, without permission in writing from the publisher.

Front cover: *The Gray Comanches,* painting by Don Troiani; www.historicalartprints.com

Manufactured in the United States of America

McFarland & Company, Inc., Publishers
  Box 611, Jefferson, North Carolina 28640
    www.mcfarlandpub.com

To the officers and men who did
their duty at Brandy Station

Contents

List of Maps	viii
Introduction	1
1. A Real Virginia Winter *Stand-Off on the Rappahannock, December 1862–June 1863*	5
2. Every Private Was a General *Confederate Cavalry and Cavalrymen*	20
3. By Easy Marches *The Assembly of Stuart's Regiments in Culpeper County*	39
4. Pretty Well Used Up *Cavalry Corps Reorginization, May 1863*	55
5. Stirring Events *Grand Reviews in Culpeper County, May–June 1863*	79
6. What Dispositions Should be Made? *Union Preparations for Combat, May 23–June 8, 1863*	94
7. Success Was Dearly Bought *Beverly Ford to Saint James Church*	107
8. A Small Affair *The Advance of the Left Wing and the Fight at Stevensburg*	133
9. Fight Like Gentlemen! *Fleetwood Hill*	153
10. Hurrah for Hell, Wade In! *Yew Hills and the Union Withdrawal*	180
11. Few Will Exult *After the Battle*	198

12. Old Soldiers Never Die 219
    Life After June 9, 1863

Appendix A: Order of Battle and Casualties 253
Appendix B: West Pointers at Brandy Station 262
Notes 265
Select Bibliography 303
Index 317

List of Maps

1 — Pleasonton's Plan	105
2 — Stuart's Reaction	113
3 — Beverly Ford	118
4 — St. James Church	130
5 — Butler's Move to Stevensburg	142
6 — Duffié's Attack at Stevensburg	146
7 — Wyndham's Attack at Fleetwood	160
8 — Kilpatrick's Attack	174
9 — The Stone Fence	184
10 — Yew Ridge	190

Introduction

On May 23, 1863, Edwin M. Stanton, Lincoln's Secretary of War, sent a short memorandum to Major General Henry Halleck, the General-in-Chief of the Union Army. Stanton, ever fearful of an attack on Washington, asked for Halleck's assessment of the defenses of the capital. In addition, Stanton asked for Halleck's recommendations regarding the disposition of Union Cavalry forces. In his response, Halleck advised Stanton that Confederate cavalry was rumored to be massing around Culpeper Courthouse, seventy miles south and west of Washington. To counter the Confederate build-up, Halleck recommended that Union cavalry be either deployed to protect the Orange & Alexandria Railroad, a main supply route for the Army of the Potomac, or assigned the mission of "attacking and breaking up the enemy's cavalry."[1]

That exchange of memorandums set in motion a chain of events that led, just over two weeks later, to the largest cavalry battle of the Civil War. That battle was fought over a large part of eastern Culpeper County, and, not surprisingly, victory was claimed by both sides. The Confederates retained possession of the field at the end of the day and suffered fewer casualties. But the Union troopers were clearly the aggressors, and had for the first time taken the fight to their Southern counterparts in a major engagement. JEB Stuart officially named the battle Fleetwood, while most Union accounts referred to the engagement as Beverly Ford. Today, the battle is named for the nearest town, Brandy Station, at the time of the battle "a doulful looking place with two stores, a tavern, blacksmith shop, and no streets."[2]

Over the years, historians have attributed varying degrees of significance to that encounter of almost 16,000 mounted troopers on June 9, 1863. A popular modern view is that Stuart, humiliated at being surprised by Alfred Pleasonton's cavalry corps, embarked upon a raid into Maryland and Pennsylvania later that month to burnish his reputation. Stuart, while capturing wagons in Rockville and skirmishing with Union cavalry across Maryland and southern Pennsylvania, deprived Robert E. Lee of his eyes and ears. Upon rejoining the army at Gettysburg late on July 2, Stuart earned himself a rare rebuke from Lee, who caustically observed that the captured wagons were more an impediment than benefit.

On the other hand, many historians have largely ignored the battle at Brandy Station. Compared with bloodlettings at Chancellorsville and Gettysburg, Brandy Station almost shrinks to insignificance. The U.S. Military Academy's basic military history text, Vincent

Esposito's *West Point Atlas of American Wars*, devotes a single paragraph to the battle, as did Jefferson Davis in *The Rise and Fall of the Confederate Government*. Clearly, the battle at Brandy was not considered particularly significant.

Lately, more historians have shown an interest in the battle of Brandy Station. This perhaps reflects its unique nature. Engagements between large bodies of mounted cavalry were rare in the Civil War. Unlike many Civil War battles, the fighting at Brandy Station occurred over a relatively large area, roughly 70 square miles. Additionally, the battle was the first encounter between Stuart's Cavalry Division and the Army of the Potomac's Cavalry Corps, and it remains the largest cavalry battle fought in North America or by American soldiers. Also, the fighting around Brandy Station marked the opening of the Gettysburg Campaign, Lee's last offensive into the North. Finally, for many, Brandy Station was the harbinger of change — the rise to dominance of Union horse soldiers and the corresponding decline of Stuart's Southern cavaliers.

Naturally, my intent with this book is to describe what happened at Brandy Station and explain, when I can, why it happened. Some historians, particularly those with a strong affinity for strategy and tactics, occasionally lose sight of the fact that battles are fought by men (and today, women). Wherever possible, I have attempted to interject the human element into my description of events. Wars entail much more than the movement of units about a battlefield. For the leaders and troopers on both sides, the Civil War was characterized by long marches, short rations, worn-out horses, endless days drilling in camp, and tedious weeks on picket duty. So, I have included some discussion of those aspects of soldiering in this account.

While almost everyone accepts that leaders, both good and bad, affect the performance of their units, the art of leadership remains the most intangible element of combat power. In describing Stuart's cavalry division and Pleasonton's cavalry corps, I have identified the commanders, briefly described their backgrounds, and indicated the length of time each had been in command. Today our army's leaders are almost homogenous, molded by years of common education and training. In the Civil War, there was a vast diversity among the officers. James Lucius Davis, commanding the 10th Virginia, was fifty years old at Brandy Station. Pierce M.B. Young, commanding Cobb's Legion, had not yet reached his twenty-fourth birthday. Percy Wyndham, commanding a brigade, had fought for the French, British and Italians, and been knighted by King Victor Emanuel II before coming to the United States and offering his services to New Jersey. Contrast Wyndham's background with that of Lieutenant Colonel James Deems. Two years before leading the 1st Maryland in its charge up Fleetwood Hill, Deems had been a music teacher and composer in Baltimore. Many readers may not be surprised to learn that Stuart's division had the more experienced set of brigade and regimental commanders, many of whom — West Pointers — were more professionally qualified than their Northern counterparts. That said, the high turnover of leaders in Pleasonton's cavalry corps is astonishing by modern standards. Union commanders truly learned by doing.

When writing a nonfiction book about an aspect of the American Civil War, a prospective author is more likely to be challenged by an overabundance of resources than a shortage. Thousands of soldiers, both Rebel and Yankee, wrote letters to their loved ones recounting mundane activities as well as experiences in combat. Other soldiers recorded their military service in contemporaneous diaries. After the war, many soldiers realized that they had been participants in the defining event of American history. They formed fraternal organizations such as the Grand Army of the Republic and the United Confederate Veterans. They held reunions, discussed the war, gave speeches, and wrote papers recounting their experiences. Thousands of magazine articles and books, written by veterans and for veterans, provide eyewitness accounts of Civil War battles.

Additionally, the Government recognized the Civil War's significance to the Nation. Between 1880 and 1901 the War Department compiled and published the existing official documents relating to the Civil War, both North and South, in a series of 128 books. Voids exist, particularly with respect to Confederate records. However, a wealth of information is readily available. For example, the *Official Records* contain 13 Union and 28 Confederate reports of the Battle of Brandy Station. Finally, a prospective author can cull further detail from individual service records maintained by the National Archives and available elsewhere on microfilm.

However, not all that was written is necessarily accurate. Many commanders, when preparing their official reports, exaggerated their accomplishments while downplaying (or omitting completely) their failures. Personal accounts written after the war were frequently embellished to increase their entertainment value. Unit histories, published by many Union regiments after the war, frequently stray from strict factual accounting of events. The reader today should also approach popular series, such as those published in *Century Magazine* and the *Philadelphia Weekly Times*, with some skepticism. In 1886, J. A. Kidd, who served under George Custer and was himself breveted to brigadier general during the war, wrote to General Wesley Merritt, then serving as the Superintendent at West Point. Kidd asked Merritt to review "with conscientious care and scrupulous fidelity" an account of the battle of Cedar Creek that Kidd had drafted. Merritt, in his response to Kidd, wrote that he no longer read accounts of the war because "an officer writes one month what is to him a truthful account of events and the next month that account is contradicted by three or four in print with dozens of others who content themselves with contradicting it in talk." Although Merritt offered to discuss the war with Kidd, he stated that he was "sick of the fiction" being written about it.[3]

Just like Merritt, today's reader is faced with contradictory accounts of events, and distinguishing fact from fiction remains a challenge. Shortly before his death, Douglas Southall Freeman gave a speech to the Civil War Round Table in Richmond. Freeman told his audience that for his biography of Robert E. Lee, he revised his description of the battle of Gaines' Mill five times, but was still not sure that he got it right.[4] Like Freeman, I do not know if my account is entirely correct — it is probably wrong in many ways. I do believe, however, that I am reasonably accurate with respect to the facts, and I am confident that my analysis and interpretation of events is reasonably sound. Any errors are mine, alone, and hopefully will not detract from the enjoyment readers derive from the story of this unique battle.

Many individuals have earned my gratitude and deserve my thanks — far too many to name all individually. First, I am honored to have come to know the officers and men, both Union and Confederate, who fought at Brandy Station on June 9, 1863, and recorded their experiences in letters to loved ones and in diaries. I appreciate the efforts of research staffs at libraries throughout the eastern United States who have assisted me in finding and gathering those documents and first-hand accounts that provide the foundation for this book.

I also appreciate family and friends who read drafts of this work as it progressed, and freely offered me ideas and constructive criticism. Two in particular warrant mention: Judge Howard Rives of Bellaire, Florida, a family friend and infantry officer in World War II; and Colonel Arthur R. Marshall of Portland, Oregon, my uncle and, like many of the officers I have written about, a member of West Point's "Long Gray Line."

I also must thank Mrs. Rebecca Denny of Richmond, Virginia, for providing a copy of her early twentieth century photograph of Beauregard, the house from which Robert E. Lee watched the battle. Also, I greatly appreciate the assistance I received from Mr. William Rachal, Jr., of Vienna, Virginia, who found and provided a photograph of Jacob Kent Langhorne, a young man who did his duty on June 9, 1863.

One cannot fully understand a battle without walking the ground, and I owe a particular debt of gratitude to landowners in Brandy Station who have most graciously allowed me to examine the terrain over which this battle was fought. On the property of Mr. P. W. Stillwell, I spent a morning examining the banks of the Rappahannock up and downstream from Beverly Ford, where the battle began. Mr. Tony Troillo allowed me free access to Fleetwood Hill, where the most intense and prolonged fighting of the day took place. Finally, Mr. Jimmy Bowen welcomed me onto Beauregard Farm, where I spent days getting the lay of the land in the Yew Hills (and picking up poison ivy and a few ticks along the way). I also wish to thank both the Civil War Preservation Trust and the Brandy Station Foundation for preserving a large part of the Brandy Station battlefield, and making their holdings accessible to the public. The battlefield is today a pristine jewel because of those groups' determination and hard work. It is well worth a visit.

Without the support and assistance of my wife, Rose, this book would never have been completed. She cheerfully did my chores around our farm while I was away conducting research and during the hundreds of hours I spent cloistered in my study reading and writing. She also read and edited every draft, of which there were many, saving me from countless embarrassing errors.

Finally, I must acknowledge the contributions of my mother, Mrs. Alma McKinney. She helped spark my interest in the Civil War, reminding me many times that my middle name, Wade, was bestowed in honor of Wade Hampton — in the view of many of her generation and those that preceded it, the Carolinas' greatest hero. It also was my mother who first encouraged me — prodded is a more accurate expression — to write this book. Unfortunately, she passed away in June 2004, and did not see its completion. I believe she secretly wanted me to write a novel, but I feel she would be very happy with this true story.

Joseph W. McKinney
Brandy Station, Virginia

1

A Real Virginia Winter

Stand-Off on the Rappahannock, December 1862–June 1863

On December 13, 1862, Robert E. Lee's outnumbered Army of Northern Virginia handily defeated Major General Ambrose Burnside's Army of the Potomac at Fredericksburg. In the day's fighting, the Rebels inflicted more than twelve thousand casualties on the Yankees while suffering well less than half that amount. Viewing a Confederate counterattack, Lee remarked to the commander of his First Corps, Lieutenant General James Longstreet, "it is well that war is so terrible — we should grow too fond of it." In the North, however, people naturally perceived the results of the battle quite differently. News of the Union defeat and heavy losses was deeply demoralizing to both soldiers and civilians.[1]

After the battle, both armies settled in for the winter. Lee's men occupied the heights above Fredericksburg, blocking any Federal advance along the most direct route to Richmond. On the north side of the Rappahannock, Union soldiers set up their camps from Falmouth, opposite Fredericksburg, to Aquia Landing, a small port on the Potomac.

Lee's infantrymen were kept busy improving their fortifications while his cavalry, under the command of James Ewell Brown — universally abbreviated as JEB — Stuart, was tasked with patrolling the flanks of the army up and down the river. At the end of December the weather turned miserable. According to one Southerner the season became "a real Virginia winter, with a good deal of Northern thrown in. It snowed, froze, thawed and rained by turns, with here and there bright days."[2] The Confederates spent much of their time huddled in their crude huts, and, except for an occasional review, commanders suspended most drill. Snowball fights between regiments, a temporary relief to boredom and inactivity, were a popular pastime, as were religious services. Fire breathing chaplains were much in demand as evangelical fervor swept through the Rebel camps. Thomas J. "Stonewall" Jackson, dubbed a Roundhead by one officer, was certainly pleased with the men's new interest in spiritual matters.[3]

At the end of January, Burnside, who felt compelled to break the stalemate along the Rappahannock, attempted to turn Lee's army out of its fortifications. The Army of the Potomac marched west from its camps toward the upriver fords, but promptly bogged down in the sodden roads. The army, after two days of intense effort by both the men and their draft animals, failed to make much headway through the mire. Frustrated, Burnside gave up and ordered his army to return to its camps. In part because of this "Mud March," as the operation became known, Burnside was relieved and sent West where he could do less harm to the Union war effort. The hapless Burnside was replaced by a more aggressive and ambitious officer, Major General Joseph "Fighting Joe" Hooker.[4]

After the Mud March, and partly as a result of that fiasco, morale among the soldiers in the Army of the Potomac sank to an all-time low. Consequently, Hooker immediately set out to improve the attitude of his men. He ordered passes and furloughs to those deserving and issued better rations to all. Tobacco was distributed regularly and whiskey occasionally, usually when men had suffered from exposure. To overcome idleness, Hooker ordered that units drill more frequently. To foster unit pride and cohesiveness, Hooker implemented a system of distinctive corps and division badges, a small but effective step.[5] Hooker also issued a barrage of directives to his army addressing its various shortcomings. These included a prohibition on the use of soldiers as servants, limitations on the movement of civilians within the lines, guidance on the management of regimental funds, instructions on how to conduct outpost duty, restrictions on sutlers, instructions on distribution and use of new pack saddles, and a warning that the cruel or careless treatment of government animals would be punished.[6]

Hooker also devoted his attention to more weighty operational matters. His predecessors, Generals McClellan and Burnside, had used Pinkerton agents to collect and evaluate intelligence. The results were dismal. Hooker ridded the army of the Pinkertons and in their place established a Bureau of Military Information under the supervision of his Deputy Provost Marshal, Colonel George H. Sharpe. In short order, the accuracy of information provided Hooker regarding Lee's army improved greatly. In particular, estimates regarding the Confederate army's strength became much more accurate.[7]

Concurrently, Hooker attempted to restrict the flow of information regarding his own forces to the Confederates. During the winter hiatus, trade across the Rappahannock — coffee moving south in exchange for tobacco going north — was common, while gossip and newspapers flowed freely in both directions.[8] Hooker prohibited all contact between the Yankee and Rebel pickets. Additionally, Hooker curtailed the activities of the newspaper correspondents who accompanied the army and had before roamed freely through the camps. Not unexpectedly, such restrictions were unpopular with the press.

Hooker, like most of his predecessors, also reorganized the Army of the Potomac. He simplified the chain of command by eliminating the three "Grand Divisions" created by Burnside. Instead, Hooker elected to deal directly with his seven corps commanders.[9]

Significantly, Hooker completely reorganized the cavalry of the Army of the Potomac. Like many senior officers in both the Union and Confederate armies, Hooker held cavalry in disdain, once sarcastically asking, "Whoever saw a dead cavalryman?"[10] His quip was on the mark, at least with respect to Union horsemen. Burnside, and before him McClellan, had frittered away their mounted men, allocating cavalry out by brigade and regiment to the infantry corps and divisions. While JEB Stuart's troopers won fame in their rides around the Army of the Potomac and their raids deep into Union territory, Federal horsemen had been used almost exclusively as pickets, couriers, and escorts for senior officers. Union cavalrymen had simply not done much fighting and had earned no accolades.

Hooker, envisioning his cavalry as a viable complement to his infantry, created the Army of the Potomac's Cavalry Corps on February 5, 1863, and assigned most of the Army's cavalry regiments to that new organization.[11] The newly formed corps comprised more than five hundred officers and close to 10,600 enlisted men present for duty, along with twelve pieces of artillery. Of those present, roughly twelve hundred enlisted men were rated as ineffectively equipped, most probably due to the lack of fit horses.[12]

Hooker appointed Major General George Stoneman to command of the new Cavalry Corps. Stoneman, a New Yorker, graduated from West Point in 1846 where he had roomed with classmate Thomas J. Jackson. Stoneman had not seen action in the Mexican War, instead serving as the quartermaster of the Mormon Battalion on its march from Fort Leavenworth, Kansas, to San Diego. Afterward, Stoneman served with the dragoons and cavalry in the Southwest. By the eve of the war, Stoneman's longevity had earned him the position of senior captain in the 2d Cavalry. Stoneman's wartime career was not particularly impressive. McClellan, a West Point classmate, appointed Stoneman as his Chief of Cavalry in August 1861, at the time a staff position with no operational control over the army's cavalry regiments. Stoneman had seen some fighting, commanded an infantry division on the Peninsula, and had briefly commanded an infantry corps at Fredericksburg.[13]

Hooker left no doubt among his subordinates that he now expected his cavalry to fight. Anticipating hard campaigning, Stoneman ordered his officers and men to use every legitimate means to "fit and perfect themselves for the most vigorous and rapid movements."[14]

While Hooker was busy revitalizing his army, Lee was principally occupied with preserving the strength of his own forces. During the winter, the Confederate Quartermaster Department failed utterly in providing subsistence

Upon assuming command of the Army of the Potomac, Major General Joseph Hooker immediately set out to improve the fighting qualities of his cavalry. By the time his efforts began to bear fruit, Hooker was relieved of command (Library of Congress).

to Lee's army, and the shortages of food for both men and horses were almost constantly on Lee's mind.[15] After the first snowfall of January 1863, Lee wrote to his eldest son, Custis, "We have another snow storm this morning which promises to be deep. Our men and animals have suffered much from scarcity of food & I fear they are destined for more."[16] Fortunately, the men eked by, foraging in their spare time to supplement their meager rations. Additionally, occasional packages from home with dried vegetables and other treats were always a welcome addition to the soldiers' bland diets. Creative measures were also undertaken with mixed results. To help prevent scurvy, each regiment was directed to send out parties to gather sassafras buds, wild onion, lamb's quarter, and poke sprouts. As spring approached, those meager greens were totally consumed almost as soon as they began to appear.[17]

Lee's cavalry, artillery and draft horses had greater difficulty subsisting than did his men. The official Confederate ration for each horse was fourteen pounds of hay and twelve pounds of grain per day—close to six tons of hay and five of grain daily for each full strength cavalry regiment (although this logistics challenge was reduced, since by early 1863 most Confederate cavalry regiments were significantly under strength).[18] Because of the

In February 1863, Hooker selected Brigadier General George Stoneman (seated at center with his staff) as the first commander of the Army of the Potomac's Cavalry Corps. Stoneman was relieved in May, a scapegoat for the debacle at Chancellorsville (Library of Congress).

insufficient supply of hay and grain, it was necessary for the troopers to turn their horses out to graze whenever possible. As the winter progressed, the animals ate everything green for miles around the army's camps. Then the horses began to starve. Again, Lee expressed deep concern for the effect of inadequate rations and bad weather on the army's horses. Following a particularly deep snow in February, Lee wrote his wife that he feared the bad weather would kill many horses, observing that "The men can do very well but our animals suffer terribly."[19] Some men might have disagreed, since the weather and the inefficiency of the Confederate Quartermaster Department were hard on all. In that regard, the commander of a company in the 2nd North Carolina Cavalry noted in his official record that "During the month of March till April 4 the Company was camping in Essex County, Virginia, horses dying with starvation and the men doing but little better."[20]

To help alleviate the supply situation for both his men and the animals, Lee was forced to disperse portions of his army. Lee sent Longstreet and half his corps to North Carolina where they could subsist more easily while gathering supplies to help feed the troops left

Cavalry horses required a significant amount of care, even when not on campaign. In winter camp, men sometimes built crude stables for their mounts, such as those shown here. However, in many regiments the only shelter the animals received was that of trees (Library of Congress).

along the Rappahannock. Additionally, Lee ordered all artillery that could be spared moved off the line along the Rappahannock and sent south where more food for the horses might be found. At the end of March 1863, Lee's Chief of Artillery reported that despite that measure, the artillery remaining along the Rappahannock required twelve hundred horses to be fully ready for future operations.[21]

Lee also sent Brigadier General Wade Hampton and his cavalry brigade south of the James River near Lynchburg, an area that was thus far unmolested by Union forces or picked bare by encamped Confederates. There Hampton was directed to "recruit" in preparation for the coming campaign season.[22] In this context, "recruit" meant Hampton was to replenish his brigade with fresh supplies. This was a most necessary activity, since in Lee's view Hampton's brigade required "complete restoration" before it would be ready to fight.[23]

Despite the hardships, JEB Stuart and the two cavalry brigades remaining with the army—commanded by the two Lees, Fitzhugh and William Henry Fitzhugh, kept active during the winter. Between manning picket posts at fording sites along the Rappahannock and patrolling, the Rebel cavalry mounted occasional raids into the Union lines. While much drill was suspended, reviews of the regiments and brigades were occasionally conducted despite the weather. A review of Stuart's division by Robert E. Lee in January was particularly memorable for the misery it inflicted. The troopers trotted past Lee in a cold, driving rain, so heavy that they could barely see each other and likely were little seen by their commanding general. The march back to camp, up to thirteen miles for some regiments, added to the discomfort of the men.[24]

Without a doubt, JEB Stuart was the best-known cavalry officer, North or South—famous for both his flamboyance and as his military exploits. An 1854 graduate of West Point where his classmates had nicknamed him "Beauty," the thirty-year-old Stuart had a well-deserved reputation as a dandy. Stuart wore a full beard that hid a weak chin while accenting his bright blue eyes. He favored a distinctive plumed hat and thigh-length boots with gold spurs. Stuart, probably more than any other general officer, reveled in military pomp. When not on duty, he particularly enjoyed social activities. He liked music, kept a banjo player in his headquarters, and held dances even when campaigning.[25] Stuart enjoyed a good joke and was one of few officers who had the audacity to tease dour Stonewall Jackson. Stuart was an accomplished flirt who loved the company of young ladies, particularly those who were pretty. Stuart's flirtations, once publicized, became a concern to his wife, Flora. Later in the war, Flora questioned Stuart's conduct and in response Stuart chided: "As to being laughed at about your husband's fondness for Society & the ladies, all I can say is that you are better off in that than you would be if I were fonder of some other things, that excite no remark in others. *The society of ladies will never injure your husband*, & ought to receive your encouragement."[26]

While Stuart's frivolity was legendary, it was less well known that Stuart was devoutly religious, a devoted husband (despite his flirtatious nature), a loving father, and a teetotaler. Unfortunately, Stuart's flamboyance frequently overshadowed his considerable abilities as a cavalry commander. Stuart had shown that he was expert at gathering information about Union forces while protecting Lee's army from surprise. Further, Stuart had proven when it became time to fight that he was a highly effective and inspirational combat leader.

William Henry Fitzhugh Lee's brigade picketed the Rappahannock from Port Royal, where he had his headquarters, to the juncture of the Rapidan River and the Rappahannock, a point known locally as the "Great Fork."[27] W. H. F. Lee's friends called him "Rooney," a childhood nickname that his father, Robert E. Lee, had forsworn in 1852 (Lee referred to his son as Fitzhugh). Unlike many of his contemporaries, Rooney was not a West Pointer. He had been unable to obtain an appointment to the academy and instead attended Harvard where he distinguished himself more as an oarsman on the rowing team than in academics. Apparently an earlier

By 1863, James Ewell Brown Stuart, the epitome of a Southern cavalier, had earned his reputation as the war's most effective cavalry commander. He was skilled at screening, reconnaissance, and, when necessary, fighting (Library of Congress).

injury—in 1845 he caught his left hand in a hay cutter and lost the tips of two fingers—caused no lasting disability.[28] In 1857, after three years as a student in Cambridge, Rooney left Harvard to accept a commission as an infantry lieutenant. After serving two years in the army, Rooney resigned to take up farming at White House, a plantation on the Pamunkey River that he had inherited.[29]

Upon the secession of Virginia, Rooney entered Confederate service as a captain commanding Company H, 9th Virginia Cavalry. In April 1862 he was elected colonel of his regiment followed by promotion to brigadier in September of that year. Rooney Lee, at six feet four inches tall, towered over most of his contemporaries. Still, the young general tended toward corpulence, a trait most tactfully described by one of his lieutenants: "Though carrying more weight than was suitable to the saddle and the quick movements of cavalry service, [Rooney Lee] was, nevertheless, a good horseman and an excellent judge of horses. So well and wisely, did he select them, that when mounted there seemed an admirable harmony between his own massive form and the heavy build and muscular power of his steed."[30]

The second brigade under Stuart's immediate control, commanded by Fitzhugh Lee, was tasked with picketing the Rappahannock upstream from the Great Fork to Amissville, a hamlet in Rappahannock County. Lee established his headquarters in Culpeper Courthouse, a central location from which to oversee the activities of his brigade.

Fitzhugh Lee, known generally as "Fitz," was the son of Robert E. Lee's younger brother. Fitz graduated from West Point near the bottom of his class in 1856 and was commissioned in the cavalry. He saw service with the 2nd U.S. Cavalry in Texas where he earned a reputation as an aggressive Indian fighter. During an expedition against the Comanches in Kansas in June 1859, Lee and his men were advancing on foot against a party of Indians who had taken cover in a thicket. As the troopers neared the thicket, Lee was struck in the chest by an arrow. The wound was serious—blood was gurgling from Lee's mouth—but after a lengthy convalescence he returned to field duty.[31] Lee had apparently fully recovered when he fought his next skirmish in January 1860. While attempting to chase down an Indian on foot, Lee was surprised when the Indian unexpectedly turned to fight. The two grappled hand-to-hand for a few moments until Lee succeeded in throwing his larger opponent to the ground and killing him with two pistol shots.[32]

When Virginia seceded, Lee resigned from his position as a tactics instructor at West Point, accepted a commission in the Confederate army, and joined General Joseph Johnston's staff. After First Manassas, he was appointed lieutenant colonel of the 1st Virginia Cavalry. In April 1862, Lee was elected colonel of the 1st Virginia with only four dissenting votes, and then in July 1862, he was promoted to brigadier for his service during the Peninsular Campaign.[33] Besides being Stuart's favorite subordinate—both had the same taste for humor and frivolity—Fitz Lee had proven himself a competent cavalry commander.[34]

Without Hampton, only the two Lees and their ten haggard regiments remained on the Rappahannock to deal with the new feistiness exhibited by Hooker's cavalry. The first significant clash between the two groups occurred on March 17. While Hooker and most other senior officers in the Army of the Potomac attended Saint Patrick's Day celebrations hosted by Brigadier General Thomas F. Meagher and his "Irish Brigade," about two thousand Union cavalrymen under command of Brigadier General William W. Averell crossed the Rappahannock at Kelly's Ford.[35] The crossing was hotly disputed for over an hour by roughly two dozen Confederate pickets manning rifle pits, allowing time for Fitz Lee to bring forward his troops who were camped near Culpeper Courthouse. A daylong battle

Left: W.H.F. "Rooney" Lee was Stuart's youngest brigadier. Unable to obtain an appointment to West Point, Rooney attended Harvard for three years before accepting a commission in the infantry. *Right:* Brigadier General Fitzhugh Lee, Stuart's favorite subordinate, fought his friend Averell at Kelly's Ford. At the time, none of Lee's five horses — all worn down by short rations over the winter — was fit for a cavalry raid (Library of Congress).

between two thousand Federals and eight hundred Confederate horsemen followed.[36] The fighting was indecisive, and at the end of the day the Union troopers withdrew back to the north side the river. As was common when the outcome of an engagement was inconclusive, both sides claimed victory. In his report of the engagement, Averell noted, "The principal result achieved by this expedition has been that our cavalry has been brought to feel their superiority in battle; they have learned the value of discipline and the use of their arms."[37]

A popular story regarding the fight at Kelly's Ford is that a taunt from Fitz Lee instigated the Union foray. Averell and Lee had been cadets at West Point together, Averell graduating with the class of 1855. On February 24–25, 1863, Lee conducted a raid into Federal lines. Marching through deep snow, Lee's troopers surprised and routed the Federal cavalry manning picket posts around Hartwood Church, a road junction several miles from Falmouth. Union forces made a concerted effort to capture the rebel raiders, with Hooker offering a major general's stars to any of Stoneman's brigadier's who might bag Lee. Nonetheless, Lee and his men made their escape, taking about one hundred fifty prisoners along with them.[38]

Supposedly, Lee left a note at Hartwood Church for his old friend Averell: "I wish you would put up your sword, leave my state, and go home. You ride a good horse, I ride a better. [But] Yours can beat mine running [away]. If you won't go home, return my visit and bring me a sack of coffee." Averell apparently found the note galling and responded to Lee's taunt in kind. Near Kelly's Ford, the Confederates reportedly found a bag of coffee to which Averell had pinned a note, "Dear Fitz. Here's your coffee. Here's your visit. How did you like it?"[39]

No one in the Confederacy liked Averell's "visit." Among the casualties that day was Major John Pelham, the dashing Alabamian who commanded Stuart's horse artillery. Pelham, had accompanied Stuart to Culpeper the day before the battle so that Stuart could testify at the courts-martial of Lieutenant Colonel Henry Clay Pate, 5th Virginia Cavalry. Hearing the sounds of fighting from the ford, Stuart and Pelham rode out to take part in the action as individuals—Stuart left Fitz Lee in tactical command of the fighting and most of Pelham's guns were in Fredericksburg. Approaching Kelly's Ford, Pelham rode to the front and joined a group of troopers congregated behind a stone fence. A Union artillery round exploded close by and Pelham was struck at the base of his skull by a small piece of shrapnel. The gallant major fell

Brigadier General William Averell struck the Cavalry Corps' first blow against Stuart's horsemen. The all-day fight at Kelly's Ford on St. Patrick's Day, 1863, ended as a draw (Library of Congress).

to the ground unconscious, his eyes open and unblinking. Two troopers were detailed to carry Pelham to the rear over the back of a horse, the wounded officer's head hanging on one side of the saddle and his feet dangling on the other. Pelham was later shifted to an ambulance and taken to Culpeper where he died that night.[40]

Both Stuart and Robert E. Lee were deeply aggrieved at the loss of Pelham. In a letter to his elder brother, describing the fight at Kelly's Ford, Robert E. Lee wrote of Pelham, "I do not know how I can replace the gallant Pelham. So Young So True So Brave. Though stricken down in the dawn of manhood, his is the glory of duty done!"[41] Stuart, upon being notified of the birth of his daughter, asked his wife to name the baby Virginia Pelham in honor of the major—posthumously promoted to lieutenant colonel—whose loss was mourned throughout the South.[42]

By spring, which came late in 1863, the effective strength of the regiments along the Rappahannock had dropped significantly, greatly hindering operations. In a letter of March 28, 1863, Fitz Lee's father described the condition of his son's brigade at Kelly's Ford. "[Fitz] has I think five horses—and hardly one in order for a *raid*. His cavalry was in such bad condition for the want of food, he could only take about 800 men and the horses were so weak & thin they could hardly be got along. He is losing several horses a day from *starvation*...."[43]

What Stuart's cavalry needed for their horses were several weeks to rest and graze on fresh grass before active operations began. Unfortunately, their respite was of necessity deferred. Hooker had other plans.

Hooker intended to begin campaigning as early as weather permitted, his haste partly driven by the pending expiration of terms of enlistment in some of his veteran regiments. By early April, Hooker was satisfied that his army was prepared for battle, and he invited President Lincoln to Falmouth to see first-hand the improvements that he had made in the Army of the Potomac over the past two months. Lincoln traveled from Washington to Aquia Landing by steamer and from there to Falmouth by train, arriving at Hooker's headquarters on the morning of April 6, a Sunday. The next morning, Lincoln and his party, including wife, Mary, and youngest son, Tad, went by horse and carriage to the reviewing ground, a distance of about three miles. Drawn up on the field was the Cavalry Corps, almost ten thousand strong. The President and his party rode up and down the double-line of troops, accompanied by the senior cavalry commanders, and then the regiments passed in review for the President. One participant recorded, "I do not expect to ever again witness such an exhibition of 'war's magnificently stern array' as was here presented."[44] A similar opinion was expressed by one of Lincoln's official party, who thought the cavalry review was simply "the grandest sight I ever saw."[45]

While the cavalry review may have appeared splendid to observers, it was almost a disaster. On the day before the review, the two horses belonging to Brigadier General David McMurtrie Gregg, the commander of the 3rd Cavalry Division, came up lame. Gregg was faced with finding a new mount on short notice. At the review, Gregg was for the first time riding a fine-looking horse owned by an officer in the 1st Maine Cavalry. En route to the

Parades and ceremonies were common in both the Union and Confederate armies. This sketch by Edwin Forbes depicts President Lincoln reviewing the Cavalry Corps in April 1863. As a sign of respect, Lincoln removed his hat to salute the men in the ranks (Library of Congress).

reviewing grounds, the horse began to get nervous at the sounds of clinking sabers and martial music. When it became Gregg's turn to escort President Lincoln up and down the 3rd Division's line of troops, the general found that his mount had a "mouth of iron," meaning that the horse did not respond to pressure on the bit Gregg was using. The horse set a blistering pace, oblivious to Gregg's attempts to rein it in, while the President, not known as a particularly accomplished rider, struggled to keep up. At one point Lincoln implored, "General Gregg, I beg of you that you will not ride quite so fast." At the moment, Gregg most feared that the President would be thrown from his horse into one of the ditches that traversed the reviewing ground. Fortunately, President Lincoln kept his seat and completed the review without incident. Perhaps even more fortunate for Gregg, Lincoln believed that the general had intentionally set a true cavalryman's pace for the reviewing party. Obviously pleased that he had kept up, Lincoln leaned over to Gregg and remarked, "General, what a furious and exciting ride we have had."[46]

Tuesday Lincoln visited the Fifth Corps in its camps. Wednesday the Second, Third, Fifth and Sixth Corps— sixty thousand men — marched in review for the President. Thursday, Lincoln reviewed the First Corps. Friday the President concluded his visit to the army with a review of the Eleventh and Twelfth Corps. When reviewing the troops, Lincoln invariably returned the salutes of officers by lightly touching the brim of his stovepipe hat. Yet when the massed formations of enlisted men marched past, the President would remove his hat and uncover his head, a gesture of respect that was noticed and appreciated by the infantrymen in the ranks.[47]

Throughout his visit, the President was accompanied everywhere by a detachment from the 6th Pennsylvania Cavalry, better known as Rush's Lancers. The dapper troopers, armed with eight-foot lances, each festooned with a red pennant at the tip, added a touch of color to Lincoln's official party.[48]

The following week Hooker put his army into motion. He dispatched Stoneman and the Cavalry Corps to the west where they were to cross the upper fords on the Rappahannock and then swing to the south and east, destroying Robert E. Lee's lines of communication and supply depots. Hooker intended the raid as a prelude to a knock out blow that would be delivered by his infantry. Hooker planned for his infantry to cross the Rappahannock on pontoon bridges below Fredericksburg, and then fall upon Lee's rear and pursue the Rebel army to its destruction. The infantry's river crossing would be ordered only after Lee, responding to the incursion by Stoneman's raiders, moved his infantry from the earthworks about Fredericksburg. Thus, it was imperative that the Cavalry Corps present a credible threat to the Army of Northern Virginia. To ensure that the cavalry played its role correctly, Hooker issued Stoneman detailed orders in which he exhorted his cavalry chief to pursue and destroy Stuart's cavalry. The orders read in-part:

> If the enemy should retire by Culpeper and Gordonsville, you will endeavor to hold your force in his front, and harass him day and night on the march and in camp unceasingly. If you cannot cut off from his columns large slices, the general desires that you take small ones. Let your watchword be fight, and let all your orders be fight, fight, fight, bearing in mind that time is as valuable to the general as the rebel carcasses. It is not in the power of the rebels to oppose you with more than 5,000 sabers, and those badly mounted, and, after they leave Culpeper, without forage or rations, keep them from Richmond and, sooner or later, they must fall into your hands.[49]

Stoneman's raid got off to an inauspicious start. After a slow and halting march up the Rappahannock, the Union troopers were prepared to cross the river on April 15 near Rappahannock Station. Stoneman sent one brigade, under the command of Colonel Benjamin F. "Grimes" Davis, farther up the river to cross near Sulphur Springs in Fauquier County. Davis and his men were then to sweep back down the south bank, clearing away pickets so that the main body of the Cavalry Corps might cross unimpeded. However, as Stoneman waited near Rappahannock Station, heavy rains set in and the river began to rise. As the water running through the fords deepened and the current increased, Stoneman began to question the wisdom of immediately proceeding into rebel territory. Choosing caution over audacity, Stoneman elected to wait until the water dropped before sending more men across. Davis, stranded on the south bank and unsupported, withdrew by swimming his brigade through the fords, losing several men and horses in the process.[50]

Meanwhile, Hooker had advised Lincoln that his cavalry was in motion and assured the President of its success. Several hours later, an embarrassed Hooker was forced to notify Washington that his earlier optimistic report was not accurate and that all was not going well along the upper Rappahannock. Lincoln, perceiving that perhaps the fighting abilities of the Army of the Potomac were not much improved, was discouraged.[51] Since it was now evident to the Confederates that a raid had been in the making, Hooker ordered his horsemen back to their camps.

Hooker believed the basic concept behind his plan — coordinated cavalry and infantry operations to turn Lee out of the Fredericksburg fortifications — was sound, and he reset his timetable. For the second iteration, however, Hooker wisely decided to rely less on his mounted arm, instead advancing concurrently with both his infantry and cavalry. More significantly, Hooker planned to use the bulk of his infantry to turn Lee out of his positions by "stealing a march" on the Confederate Commander. Using stealth, Hooker planned to cross the Rappahannock at the upriver fords before the Army of Northern Virginia could react. Hooker's infantry would then march back down-river and attack Lee's left flank and rear. The cavalry raid would be merely a supporting operation.

After making major efforts toward security and concealment, Hooker put his infantry in motion on April 27.[52] On April 28, Hooker ordered Stoneman to have his entire force across the Rappahannock by 8:00 a.m. the following day. After crossing the river, Stoneman was to split his force into two columns. One column, commanded by Averell, was to strike toward Gordonsville. The second column, commanded by Stoneman, himself, was to strike toward Richmond.

Again, the plan quickly went awry. Stoneman and his men arrived at the ford well after the appointed time on the morning of April 29 — the infantry reached the fords ahead of the cavalry and were already crossing the river. Stoneman's troopers were forced to stand idly by as the long columns of blue-clad foot soldiers waded through the chilly water. Stoneman finally got his three divisions across the river late in the afternoon, hours behind schedule. The Union cavalry advanced only four miles beyond the river before halting for the night, having made no significant contact with Confederate cavalry. Over the following two weeks, Stoneman and his column ineffectually raided lines of communication in Robert E. Lee's rear while Rooney Lee with two of his haggard regiments contained Averell's column and permitted him to do virtually no damage.

While they did not do much damage of military significance, Stoneman's raiders did disrupt the personal plans of a young Virginian named Jacob Kent Langhorne. Langhorne, who had almost reached his eighteenth birthday, had been raised in Christianburg in the upper Shenandoah Valley. While Stuart's cavalry was suffering from shortages of food and forage along the Rappahannock, Langhorne was struggling through his "rat" year at Virginia Military Institute in Lexington. Langhorne had entered VMI the previous fall at the urging of his parents, and like most rats before and since, he was homesick, hazed by the upperclassmen, and having difficulty mastering algebra.[53] Like many of his fellow cadets, Langhorne was eager to leave VMI and go to war.[54]

Early in 1863, Langhorne's parents finally gave their son permission to leave the academy and enlist. After resigning from VMI, Langhorne and several friends set off from the Valley to "jine the cavalry" just as Hooker set the Army of the Potomac into motion against Lee. Crossing the Blue Ridge, the young men stopped for a short rest at the home of Langhorne's Aunt Bettie. To her, Langhorne made a remark that she found much different from those expressed by most young men traveling off to war. Langhorne told his Aunt, "I have no disposition to be in a fight, but if I ever am, I shall try to do my duty."[55]

Upon heading east from Albemarle County, Langhorne and his friends found their progress impeded by marauding Union cavalry. On May 1 near Orange Courthouse, they were chased through the woods for about two miles by a squad of blue-clad cavalry. On the following day, they encountered another party of Union cavalry tearing up the railroad tracks. The Yankees spotted Langhorne's white horse and two troopers pursued the young Rebels-to-be for about a mile before giving up the chase and turning back. That night Langhorne and his friends were riding along the tow path that paralleled the James River when they stumbled into a Union patrol. The young Southerners escaped by swimming with their horses to an island in the river and then crossing the rest of the way on a private ferry. On May 8, Langhorne wrote to his father that he had finally reached Ashland, Virginia, but had not found the regiment he was seeking. Reflecting on his trip, Langhorne told his father that he had "learned how to retreat but not advance."[56]

After Chancellorsville, Hooker placed Alfred Pleasonton, his senior cavalry brigadier, in command of the Cavalry Corps. Pleasonton, characterized by one officer as a "newspaper humbug," was not a particularly popular choice (Library of Congress).

Unfortunately for Hooker, Lee was unconcerned that Union cavalry were raiding in the rear of his army. Instead, Lee remained focused on the main threat to his army: Hooker's seven infantry corps. Consequently, while Hooker sent the bulk of his cavalry off on a sideshow, Lee kept Stuart with most of his available horsemen close at hand to conduct reconnaissance while screening the movement of Confederate infantry. History has judged Lee's choice to be the wiser. Of immediate significance, on May 1 west of Chancellorsville, Fitz Lee's troopers discovered that Hooker's right flank was unprotected, precipitating Jackson's covert flanking march and attack against the Union Eleventh Corps on the evening of May 2.

In contrast to Lee, Hooker retained immediate control of only a single cavalry brigade, that commanded by

Brigadier General Alfred Pleasonton. Pleasonton, originally from Washington, D.C., had graduated from West Point in 1844. A dragoon officer, he had served in the Mexican War where he was breveted for gallantry, against the Sioux on the northern Plains, and in Florida against the Seminoles. Pleasonton distinguished himself in the Peninsular Campaign and as a result had been promoted to brigadier general in July 1862. In the Maryland Campaign and at Fredericksburg he had commanded a cavalry division.[57] In two years of war, Pleasonton had also established a well-deserved reputation for self-promotion.

Pleasonton's small command — only four regiments— did not accomplish much during the fighting around Chancellorsville. However, the limited role played by his troopers did not deter Pleasonton from making expansive claims regarding his own accomplishments during the fighting. In his official report of the battle, Pleasonton wrote that he ordered the 8th Pennsylvania Cavalry to charge and blunt Jackson's attack "at any cost," a task that they "splendidly performed, but with heavy loss." In reality, Pleasonton had merely sent the 8th Pennsylvania to support Howard's Eleventh Corps. While en route, the Pennsylvanians found themselves on the Plank Road between the skirmishers and battle line of a Confederate infantry brigade. The 8th Pennsylvania charged through the gray ranks to escape, and in the process lost thirty-three men and eighty horses killed.[58] Pleasonton also claimed that he had personally supervised the employment of twenty-two pieces of artillery, and, moreover, that the fire from the guns had halted the flight of the fleeing Eleventh Corps and turned back Jackson's pursuing Confederates.[59] Other witnesses discounted both Pleasonton's personal involvement in directing the artillery and the effects of the artillery fire on Jackson's Corps.[60]

Pleasonton's cavalry did play a minor role in one of the most significant events of May 2. As darkness fell, Jackson ordered A. P. Hill's division, which had not yet been committed in the day's fighting, forward to conduct a night attack, a rare event in the Civil War. In preparation, Hill ordered Colonel James Lane's North Carolina brigade to move up. The Tar Heels felt their way forward in the twilight along the Plank Road, they engaged a few scattered bodies of Union infantry and passed by the dead horses and troopers of the 8th Pennsylvania. Rumors spread among Lane's men that Union cavalry was still actively patrolling in the area.

Jackson, unbeknownst to the advancing Confederate infantrymen, had gone forward with several staff officers to conduct a personal reconnaissance. The corps commander and his party attempted to reenter Confederate lines as Lane's men, nervously anticipating contact with Yankees at any moment, advanced. As Jackson and his mounted officers approached through the trees in the deepening gloom, the North Carolinians mistook them for Federal cavalry and fired a few shots. One of Jackson's party called out, "Cease firing, cease firing! You are firing into your own men." An officer in the 18th North Carolina responded, "Who gave that order? It's a lie! Pour it into them boys!"[61] And, pour it into them they did. The ensuing volley crashed through the trees. Jackson was struck three times. His horse, Little Sorrel, bolted into a tree, adding scrapes and bruises to Jackson's wounds. As Jackson's staff helped their wounded general to the ground, Little Sorrel, thoroughly spooked, ran away toward Union lines.[62]

While Jackson was being carried to the rear, A.P. Hill—the only remaining major general in Jackson's corps—was wounded by Federal artillery fire and unable to walk or ride his horse. In a surprising move, Hill, instead of turning over command to an infantry brigadier, called for Stuart to take charge of Jackson's Corps. Stuart, upon moving forward, sent a staff officer to find Jackson and ask for instructions. The staff officer, Lieutenant Colonel Alexander "Sandie" Pendleton, found Jackson shortly after doctors had amputated his shattered left arm. Jackson, whom the doctors had drugged for the operation, was only able to respond, "I don't know — I can't tell; say to General Stuart he must do what he thinks best."[63]

Stuart was in a difficult position. He had taken command in the middle of the night, several of the corps' generals and colonels were dead or wounded, his staff was scattered, the divisions and brigades intermingled, and information regarding the location of Union lines was vague. Lacking any guidance, Stuart spent the night sorting out his units, and when daylight came he resumed the attack against Hooker's right flank. In his first and only performance as an infantry corps commander, Stuart energetically and credibly orchestrated the movement of his infantry and the fires of his supporting artillery. Attacks by Stuart against the Union right and Lee against the Union front knocked the fight out of "Fighting Joe" Hooker.[64]

On the night of May 5, the Army of the Potomac slipped out of its positions around Chancellorsville and crossed back to the north bank of the Rappahannock, putting the river between itself and the Army of Northern Virginia. Hooker's attempt to steal a march on the Confederates had been successful, but in battle Hooker had proved himself no match for the audacity of Robert E. Lee and the determination of Stonewall Jackson. Although Hooker was clearly whipped, the bulk of the Union army managed to escape destruction. When Lee was advised that the Union army had abandoned the battlefield during the night, undetected and not pursued, he exhibited a rare display of frustration, exclaiming to the messenger, "Why General Pender! That is the way you young men always do. You allow those people to get away. I tell you what to do, but you don't do it!"[65]

Although the Army of the Potomac suffered more than seventeen thousand casualties at Chancellorsville, close to 119,000 officers and men remained present for duty.[66] Thus Edwin Stanton, the Union Secretary of War, was able to inform the governors of the Northern states and other army commanders that although Hooker's operation had failed, there had been "no serious disaster to the organization and efficiency of the army." Stanton predicted that Hooker would soon resume the offensive while proclaiming that one aspect of Hooker's operation, Stoneman's cavalry raid on Richmond, had been a "brilliant success."[67] In a separate message, Stanton advised Hooker that the Richmond newspapers were "full of accounts of the panic and destruction" resulting from the Stoneman's raid.[68]

Almost certainly Stanton's letter to the governors was intended to calm and reassure them. In reality, Chancellorsville, following Fredericksburg, was a second consecutive and equally embarrassing defeat for the Army of the Potomac. While Hooker agreed with Stanton that overall the defeat was not a disaster, he advised, accurately, that the cavalry raid failed to accomplish much.[69]

As Hooker and Lee pondered their next moves, each faced significant problems with respect to his cavalry. Lee's horsemen were widely dispersed and most of the horses were simply worn out by inadequate rations and hard campaigning. However, Lee had reason to be confident in the leadership of his senior cavalry officers and the quality of his mounted men. Hooker faced even more significant challenges than Lee. Although numerically superior, his cavalry was also worn out — Stoneman's raiders had been admonished not to "spare the horse" in their sweep behind Confederate lines. Hundreds of broken down horses had been abandoned — the standing order was that they were to be shot — leaving several regiments essentially dismounted. Further, the ability of the Union's cavalry leaders to effectively challenge their Confederate counterparts in battle was questionable. On the bright side, the Union troopers had displayed a willingness to fight.

Both Army commanders set to work repairing their cavalry in preparation for the upcoming campaign.

2

Every Private Was a General

Confederate Cavalry and Cavalrymen

If Stonewall Jackson had been a roundhead, JEB Stuart was a cavalier, and his regiments had more in common with the cavalry of England's Charles I in the 1600s than with military organizations of today. Stuart's regiments were filled with the youth of the South. Many were sons of planters accustomed to riding astride high-stepping thoroughbred horses, but even more were farm boys, more comfortable astride grade horses trained to pull plows as well as carry saddles. Common among Stuart's troopers was their devotion to their cause—perhaps more defense of home and hearth than the abstract concept of state's rights. Stuart's men were also proud of themselves and their companies and regiments. His troopers held a common belief that they were superior to Northerners as soldiers, and further, that they would ultimately prevail in battle. Thus far, events had validated those beliefs—Stuart and his men had beaten the Yankees almost every time they met, even when outnumbered. Nevertheless, by 1863, vulnerabilities were becoming evident as the Confederacy failed to supply the resources—men, horses, weapons, ammunition, food, and clothing—necessary to wage a modern protracted war.

Most Confederate cavalrymen came to the army from farms, with the more well-to-do listing their civilian occupation as "planter." Next after farming, most men had been laborers, although many were so young that they had not yet taken up an occupation. Some men were from the professions: engineers, lawyers, teachers, and even doctors served in the ranks. Other soldiers had been employed as clerks and shopkeepers or had worked in trades. Painters, stone cutters, bricklayers, coopers, and wagon makers were represented in the ranks, and at least one cavalryman had earned a living as a cigar maker before taking up arms. Some new troopers had been college students before they enlisted.[1]

While war was the domain of young men—the age of most troopers ranged from late teens to late twenties—occasionally a man in his forties or even fifties joined the ranks. Ephriam Crews, who enlisted in the Halifax Troop of the 6th Virginia Cavalry in 1861, admitted to being sixty-five years old and was perhaps even older. It is possible that Crews was a veteran of the War of 1812.[2] Although they possessed the will to serve, many older men were eventually discharged, their bodies unable to stand the hard life of a Confederate cavalryman.

Most Southern cavalrymen were literate, although a few validated their enlistments by making a mark. Almost all wrote home, and a plea for a note in return was a common closing to a soldier's letter. George Julian Pratt, a private in the 18th Virginia, was sufficiently frustrated with the lack of mail from his family that he began a letter of October 10, 1861, by scolding:

Dear Father,

I should like to know what in the name of common sense prevents you from writing to me. I look anxiously for each mail hoping to hear from home and am so sorely disappointed. If you are too busy to write why cannot Aunt Em, Grandma, brothers, and a host of others from whom I would be thankful to hear write to me. You all think it outrageous in me to keep you in suspense one week; yet seem to forget three days [without a letter] for a poor soldier far from home and its comforts is infinitely worse.[3]

Paper was sometimes scarce. To cram the most words on a sheet of paper, the enterprising trooper first filled the page horizontally, then rotated the page ninety degrees and continued writing. The lines of script, crossing perpendicularly, were undoubtedly difficult for the loved ones at home to decipher, as they are for historians and researchers today.

Many soldiers chronicled their military life in diaries. Some recorded the mundane, jotting in their journals simple entries such as "Cold today. In camp. Had drill." Other filled their diaries with a wealth of detail that today provides insights regarding camp life, military operations, and the emotional dimension of war.

The basic unit of cavalry was the company—a group of men under the command of a captain (it did not become common to refer to cavalry companies as "troops" until after the war). Companies were generally raised in a single locality. Some companies had been part of their state's militia with lineage going back to the early years of the century, and in a few cases even back to the Colonial era. Other companies, particularly in Virginia, were raised in reaction to John Brown's raid on Harpers Ferry in October 1859. Most companies, however, including those from the Carolinas and the deep South, were organized during the heightened martial ardor that swept the country immediately before and after secession.

Eventually, Confederate regulations codified a cavalry company as one captain, one first lieutenant, two second lieutenants, four sergeants, four corporals, and sixty privates. Each company was also authorized two musicians who might serve as buglers or be aggregated in a regimental band. Companies were also authorized one blacksmith and one farrier. The blacksmith, using his forge, hammer, and tongs, manufactured horseshoes, nails, and other small metal parts needed by the company. The farrier was responsible for trimming the horses' hooves to the proper length, for shaping the shoe to fit the hoof, and then nailing the shoe to the hoof. In addition, most farriers had some knowledge of the veterinary treatment of horse diseases and injuries.[4] The aggregate authorized strength of a company was seventy-six.

However, the reality differed considerably from that which was authorized in regulations. Companies were rarely at full strength. For example, the Little Fork Rangers of Jeffersonton, Culpeper County's only cavalry company, mustered into Confederate service on May 27, 1861, with one captain, three lieutenants, five sergeants, four corporals, and forty-four privates. No record was made of blacksmiths, farriers, or musicians.[5]

Companies were usually formed in an *ad hoc* fashion. The prominent members of communities generally took the lead in recruiting the men, usually for a one year enlistment in anticipation of a short war. It was not uncommon for a wealthy man to fully or partially offset the expenses of equipping a newly formed unit (often out of necessity since the states were lacking in means). Company officers were customarily chosen by popular election among the men of a company, and, quite naturally, those who aided in raising a unit were frequently rewarded with election to its leadership positions. Commonly, many family members—fathers, sons, brothers, cousins, and uncles—enlisted in the same company. For example, in April 1861, Dulany M. Ball raised a cavalry company in Fairfax County,

Virginia. Eight other Balls joined Dulany in the company and a ninth enlisted in 1864.[6] As expected, the new soldiers—all volunteers—brought with them a rather egalitarian attitude toward the military's formal grade structure. One soldier in the 12th Virginia later wrote that within his company, the Baylor Light Horse, "we bore the relation of brother, cousin, schoolmate, neighbor, and friend," and consequently "every private was a general and needed no guidance from his officer" to do his duty.[7]

A first item of business for a newly organized company was adopting a name. Some new cavalrymen gave their companies fanciful names such as the Wildcat Company, River Rangers, Governor's House Guards, and Maryland Exiles. A few companies were named to honor a famous personage. For example, the men of a company raised in Lynchburg, Virginia, named themselves the Wise Troop in honor of the then-governor of the state. However, most companies took either the name of their hometown or county, or the name of their first commander. The Prince William Cavalry, the Loudoun Light Horse, and the Newtown Light Dragoons were in the former category, while Mebane's Company, and White's Rebels fell into the latter.

Before the war, companies generally designed their own uniforms, which were then purchased by the members of the organization, furnished by prominent citizens, or funded though subscriptions solicited from the local community. Several units adopted particularly gaudy attire. Members of the Wise Troop outfitted themselves with red coats and "bright blue pantaloons with a gold cord down the sides, [with] the brightest scarlet horsehair tufts hanging down behind them."[8] The uniforms of the Little Fork Rangers featured blue caps, red cutaway jackets with yellow stripes, and white trousers.[9] Robert Thruston Hubard, Jr., of the Cumberland Light Dragoons, recalled: "We had very showy uniforms—silver mounted

This sketch by Alfred Waud presents a stylized view of the horsemen of the 1st Virginia Cavalry. By 1863, fancy dress had been replaced by plain—but practical—field garb (Library of Congress).

helmets—with long flowing hair—dark blue-cloth frock coats, with two rows of silver buttons, elaborate trimmings of white cord across the breast—between the buttons—and silver mounted epaulettes on the shoulders; and dark blue pants, with white on the outside seams."[10]

Most of the men realized that their uniforms were impractical for field service and donned some form of gray garb before marching off to war. In April 1861, the members of the Little Fork Rangers raised two hundred ninety two dollars through a subscription and purchased several bolts of gray cloth from a woolen mill at Waterloo, across the Rappahannock River in Fauquier County. The cloth was cut by a tailor in Warrenton, the Fauquier county seat, and sewn into jackets and trousers by the ladies in Jeffersonton and the surrounding area. The uniforms were ready when the Little Fork Rangers left Culpeper for Manassas on July 3 of that year.[11]

Eventually, Confederate regulations prescribed an official uniform for the regular army that served as a guide for state volunteer units in the Provisional Army: light blue trousers for regimental officers and enlisted men, cut loosely to spread well over the foot; a cadet gray frock coat with a skirt to extend midway between the hip and knee; and a *kepi*. Additionally, a light gray double-breasted blouse was authorized for enlisted men for fatigue use. Cavalry officers were to have yellow facings on their coats, yellow stripes down the seams of their trousers, and a raised "C" on the buttons of their coats. Enlisted men in the cavalry were to have the collars and cuffs of their coats faced in yellow and their regimental number in large figures on their buttons. *Kepis* for both officers and enlisted men in the cavalry were to have a dark blue band with yellow sides and crown. Authorized footwear for both officer and enlisted cavalrymen included boots and "Jefferson" boots, a style of low-cut, laced shoes.[12]

With respect to footwear, fashionable officers such as Stuart wore high boots of soft

The uniform and weapons of this group of Confederate cavalrymen in the west—slouch hats, short jackets, carbines, and sabers—are typical. There are a few photographs of Southern horsemen (Photographic History of the Civil War).

leather that extended midway up the thigh to protect the leg when riding. When dismounted, the officer could fold the boots down below his knee to allow flexion for walking or comfort while sitting. Modern English riding boots with brown leather cuffs are replications of the style of such boots. Enlisted men's boots commonly extended to the knee, with some cut higher in the front to protect the kneecap when riding but still allow the troopers' legs to bend. Most troopers wore their trousers outside their boots, although some tucked their trouser legs into their boots.

Initially enlisted men were responsible for providing their own uniforms for which they were compensated by the government, a process known as the commutation system. Early in the war, however, the Confederate government realized that the commutation system would not work and that it was necessary for the government to provide uniforms to the men. The Confederate government established a clothing allowance based on a three-year term of service and began purchasing clothing from local vendors, importing clothing from Europe, and manufacturing its own uniforms in government depots. Since clothing came from many diverse sources and specifications were vague, cloth, color, cut, and quality varied greatly.[13]

For a three-year enlistment, each soldier was authorized four caps, four coats, seven trousers, seven flannel drawers, nine flannel shirts and one overcoat. Each trooper was also authorized three pairs of boots, six pairs of bootees, twelve pairs of stockings, and one stable frock.[14] Obviously the clothing allowance was inadequate for hard service in the field. Regulations provided for a trooper to be issued additional items of clothing when necessary, but the trooper's pay was docked for the cost of the excess items. Many Confederate cavalrymen chose to provide their own clothing rather than rely on government issues. In

These Confederate troopers, captured at Aldie, Virginia on June 17, 1863, exhibit the usual variations in attire among Stuart's horsemen when on campaign (Gardner's Photographic Sketch Book of the Civil War).

their letters home, troopers asked their families to send them all manners of clothing, including boots, socks, drawers, trousers, shirts, jackets, coats and oilskins.

Because of the variations in issued uniforms and preference of many men for civilian clothing, the appearance of a regiment could be considered "uniform" only in the broadest sense. Perhaps the most common items of apparel among Southern cavalrymen were their ubiquitous slouch hats, much preferred to the prescribed *kepi*, which was rarely, seen in a formation of cavalry troopers.

Throughout the war, officers were required to outfit themselves at personal expense. In July 1862, Heros von Borcke, a German serving as Stuart's Inspector General, advised a prospective staff officer that he would be required to have:

> A good Horse wich can be bot in Richmond or among the Rgts, the cost will be 400–500 Doll
> A good Jenifer saddle and bridle, wich can be bot at the ordonance store for 62 Doll.
> Arms will be sabre & pistol, wich will cost from 80 to 100 Doll.
> A Uniform trimmed with yellow (Cav) or buff (Staff) either coat or jacket 80 to 100 Doll.
> Good Cavalry Boots with Spurs 50 Doll
> Grey or Black Hat 15 Doll.
> Saddle Blanket and other Blanket 20 Doll
> Oilcloth Coat 25–30 Doll
> Several little things not mentioned (little Vallise, Comb, brushe, etc etc)[15]

Thus the up-front cost for an officer to join Stuart's staff was roughly seven hundred to eight hundred fifty dollars. Costs were probably less for officers in cavalry companies where sartorial standards were not as high.

Weaponry among Stuart's troopers was as varied as their clothing. Most troopers were armed with saber, pistol, and carbine, and within a regiment various models of all three weapons could be found. A relatively few weapons were manufactured in the South, some taken from Union sources, and many imported from Europe.

Several types of carbines were in common use. Less fortunate troopers were armed with muzzle loading carbines, or musketoons, that were unwieldy and almost impossible to reload while mounted. About twenty-five hundred muzzle-loading carbines were manufactured at the Richmond Arsenal, though the weapons were clearly outdated by the time the war began. Breech-loading carbines in various designs were more popular among cavalrymen. These included the Hall's carbine, an early breech-loader adopted by the Army in 1838 and manufactured in large quantities through 1850. The original version of the Hall's was a flintlock, but those used by the Confederate army were converted to the standard percussion cap priming system. The Sharps carbine, the standard arm for the U.S. cavalry at the beginning of the war, was a more modern weapon and fairly common in the Confederate cavalry. Many Southern troopers equipped themselves by capturing Sharps carbines from their Union counterparts. Other Sharps were manufactured in Richmond, but the three thousand or so "Richmond Sharps" had a reputation, mostly unfounded, for poor quality.[16] Before the war, several Southern states purchased Maynard's carbines for their militias. The Maynard's, which came in two calibers, the standard .52 and a smaller .36 inch, was a popular and unique weapon. Unlike most carbines that featured hinged breeches, the Maynard broke open like a modern shotgun. Instead of percussion caps, the Maynard's primers were sealed on a strip of paper that advanced as the weapon was cocked, much like a roll of caps for a toy pistol of the 1950s. Additionally, instead of using a paper or linen cartridge like other carbines, the Maynard used a brass cartridge. The Confederate army also issued a little more than a thousand Burnside carbines, designed and patented by Ambrose Burnside, late of the Army of the Potomac.

A fair number of Southern cavalrymen were armed with Enfield rifles imported from England. The Enfield rifle was similar to the Enfield rifled musket, a good weapon that was a standard arm for Southern infantry. The rifle version of the Enfield was eight inches shorter than the rifled musket and thus slightly more suitable for cavalry use.

The Confederate cavalry was also armed with a variety of pistols. At the beginning of the war, equipping troopers with smoothbore muzzle-loading "horse pistols" was common (the name derived from the fact that the pistols were carried in holsters attached to the saddle, not the trooper's belt). Some horse pistols were still in use in mid–1863, although revolvers were naturally much more popular among the troopers. Colt revolvers in army and navy versions, .44 and .36 calibers, respectively, were common. Some were privately owned, many more were captured, and about ten thousand copies of the Colt designs were manufactured at various locations in the South.[17] The Confederate government also imported British and French revolvers in large quantities. One Confederate pistol, the Le Mat, was unique. This massive handgun, designed by physician from New Orleans and manufactured in England and France, featured a nine-shot cylinder in .40 caliber that revolved about .63 caliber shotgun barrel. When necessary, a trooper, by flipping down the hinged nose of the hammer, could discharge a load of eleven buckshot pellets through the center barrel. Stuart carried a Le Mat as his personal sidearm.[18]

Southern cavalrymen were issued swords from many manufacturers — quality, length, weight, and curve to the blade varied. However, given the proliferation of pistols, most troopers had little need for their swords as weapons. Many cavalrymen used their swords more frequently to suspend meat over the cooking fire than to slash at Yankees.

Instead of their issued weapons, some troopers preferred to arm themselves with shotguns. A sawed-off double-barreled shotgun was handy, reliable, and, charged with two loads of buckshot, devastatingly effective at close range. When mustered in, some twenty-five men of the Little Fork Rangers carried shotguns.[19]

The vagaries of armament within the Confederate Cavalry are perhaps illustrated by the records of a company commander in the 2nd North Carolina. In the spring of 1862, he took his company of about thirty-five men on picket near New Berne, North Carolina, armed with two Sharp's carbines, six Hall's carbines, five Colt's rifles (six-shot revolvers), four Mississippi rifles, twelve double barreled shotguns, and perhaps half-dozen horse pistols. The commander observed that his regiment "was armed with almost every kind of arms (except the newest patterns) known to the warrior or sportsman, and was never fully equipped with arms of modern warfare until it equipped itself with those furnished by the United States and taken by its troops in Virginia."[20]

Ironically, many Confederates held the view that they were better equipped by the Federal government than by their own. After the war, Colonel Thomas Munford, commander of the 2nd Virginia Cavalry, observed that at the outset of the war the men were armed with a variety of shotguns in various calibers and equipped with civilian bridles and saddles unsuitable for cavalry service. However, by the end of the war, the men of his brigade had "as complete an outfit" as they wanted, "all of which had been supplied by the United States Quartermaster Department." In Munford's memory, all that his men wanted or needed was "branded 'U.S.'"[21]

For most troopers, organized soldiering began when the states grouped their militia companies into regiments and offered the regiments to the Provisional Army of the Confederate

States, or PACS, for service. Confederate regulations prescribed that every cavalry regiment would consist of ten companies.

Companies were officially designated by the letters A through K — in keeping with tradition, there was no "J" Company — followed by their regimental designation. However, many companies continued to be known by their original, unofficial names. Thus, throughout the war D Company, 6th Virginia Cavalry, was called the Clark County Cavalry, while H Company, 4th Virginia Cavalry continued to be called the Black Horse Troop.[22]

Field grade officers of the regimental headquarters included a colonel in command, a lieutenant colonel, and a major. The headquarters also included a rudimentary staff. From among the lieutenants, the colonel would select his adjutant. Since the adjutant's primary duty was preparation of official correspondence, literacy and penmanship were important attributes, as was compatibility — of necessity, the colonel and his adjutant worked closely together. The commander was also charged with nominating an officer for assignment as regimental quartermaster. Because the quartermaster's responsibilities included the purchase of supplies, he was required to obtain a bond. As a result, quartermaster officers were frequently men of some means. Usually a surgeon and a chaplain were assigned to the regiment as well. From among the sergeants in the companies, the colonel selected his sergeant major, the senior noncommissioned officer in the regiment. The colonel also selected a sergeant who was given the honor of carrying the regimental colors.

Depending upon the manner in which a regiment was organized, its field grade officers could be either appointed by the governor of the regiment's home state, by President Jefferson Davis, or elected by popular vote among the regiment's company grade officers.[23] When appointing regimental commanders, governors and President Davis generally looked first to those who had professional military training. Twelve of the officers initially appointed to command in the first fifteen Virginia regiments to be organized were either West Point graduates or former cadets who had left the academy before their graduation. Additionally, one of the three non–West Pointers was Charles Thornburn of the 14th Virginia Cavalry, an 1853 graduate of the Naval Academy. Four of the officers initially appointed to command Stuart's eight non–Virginia cavalry regiments were also West Point graduates or former cadets.

In late 1861, the Confederate government began to grapple with an impending crisis in the Provisional Army — during the spring of 1862, the one-year enlistments of most its soldiers were due to expire. As a solution, in December 1861 the government passed a conscription act which, as modified in March 1862, gave the government authority to draft men for three years or the duration of the war. The act also contained an incentive for soldiers to voluntarily extend their enlistments: in regiments whose soldiers agreed to remain with the colors, the men would be permitted to elect new officers.[24] This plan was widely denounced by officers with professional experience. Distrustful of democracy in the ranks, "old soldiers" feared that the men would elect officers who were lax and reject those who were diligent and imposed discipline. In a letter to his wife, JEB Stuart denounced the pending legislation as "the most outrageous abortion of a bill ever heard of for the reorganization of our forces."[25] Nonetheless, in April 1862 the act was implemented and most serving soldiers reenlisted for their regiments. The resulting round of elections — with the men voting for company-grade officers followed by the officers voting for field-grades — were disruptive. As feared, several competent officers, including five West Pointers, were turned out. Perhaps those commanders' ideas of military discipline differed from the egalitarian views of the men in the ranks.

In the first two years of the war, turnover was high among cavalry regimental commanders. By the spring of 1863, the 1st Virginia was on its fifth commander: JEB Stuart and Fitz Lee had been promoted out of the position; William E. Jones had been voted out of command in the reorganization of April 1862; and one colonel had resigned. By the fall of 1862, the 7th Virginia was serving under Colonel Richard Dulaney, its fourth commander. The regiment's first commander, Angus MacDonald, an 1817 graduate of West Point, suffered from rheumatism and was unfit for field duty. MacDonald's successor, Turner Ashby, was killed in action in June 1862. William E. Jones, transferred to the 7th after being turned out of his position in the 1st Virginia, was promoted to brigadier general in September 1862, creating the vacancy filled by Dulaney. Three colonels had commanded the 6th Virginia Cavalry, and by the summer of 1863, the colonel's billet had been vacant for close to nine months. The men of the 2nd, 3rd, and 4th Virginia regiments had all served under two commanders. The 10th, 11th, 12th, and 13th Virginia regiments were in the minority, each having had only one commanding officer. Those regiments, however, were formed late: April 1862, February 1863, June 1862, and July 1862, respectively.[26]

Confederate cavalry regiments, particularly during the early years of the war, were accompanied by a host of servants, mostly black slaves. Many officers and well-to-do enlisted men were accompanied by their body servants, while other officers and men hired slaves to perform menial, but essential, duties. Servants set up and took down their masters' tents. While in camp, servants cooked, cleaned and mended. In camp and on the march servants cared for their masters' horses and foraged. Some cavalrymen had servants, known as "hostlers," whose specific duty was to care for horses. Servants cared for their masters when they were sick or wounded. On occasion, body servants took up arms and fought for the Confederacy. Generally, the master was responsible for providing his personal servant's sustenance and transportation.[27]

In January 1863, the adjutant and of the 3d Virginia Cavalry and a messmate decided that obtaining a cook would be beneficial for them. The adjutant, Robert Thruston Hubard, Jr., wrote to his father explaining the need for a cook and outlining the logistical details associated with supporting both a cook and a hostler.

> At present we have men detailed to cook for the company and [we] get our meals but twice a day — at Sunrise & Sunset. In consequence we eat too much when we do eat. We get nothing but meat (beef or bacon) and bread. Matthews [a messmate] will furnish a horse for our hostler to ride and I must furnish one for the cart. Our negroes have to be furnished with something to ride. As two of my riding horses are at present not fit for service and I do not desire to keep two of them in camp at once I wish you would look out for and buy at once an old horse *or mule* for me. Uncle Edmund had one or two old animals which he could n't sell when I was at home last. Probably you could get one from him. I think for from $25 to $50 you might buy a very good old horse or mule who could stand a march at a slow gait and the stunted fare we get for horses without dying on my hands this winter or spring. You will readily understand that "toughened" not "active" is the desirable quality for the pack horse. Robert and Thruston [two servants] brought a boy Jim Smith, of Ca Ira, as the negroe we will hire I suppose. Thruston is our hostler — the same who carried my horses home. An old saddle and bridle will be necessary. But if you can't get one readily, I can here in camp. Several of the boys [troopers] are about to get new ones on requisition. The boys [Robert, Thruston, and Jim Smith] will come on at once, as they have been written for and I want one of them to bring the horse. I will have to pay about $15 for them & $15 for the provisions (including primary outlays) per month. This will leave $60 to furnish uniforms etc.[28]

While one cannot excuse slave owners for their participation on the South's "peculiar institution," it is important to understand that close personal bonds, developed between master and slave before the war, most likely strengthened during service with the army.

Jim, the body servant of Robert S. Hudgins, II, a sergeant in the 3rd Virginia, contracted typhoid and died shortly after Lee's army returned to Virginia from Gettysburg. Hudgins, who kept a vigil at Jim's side as the slave died, recalled the event. "I reached down and took his parched hot hand and held it tightly. I was not ashamed at the tears that streamed from my eyes for I knew that I was witnessing the passing of not only a slave and servant, but a friend who could never be replaced. He gave my hand a quick clasp, gasped once, and was gone. We wrapped him in a blanket and laid him to rest at the foot of a giant pine overlooking the Shenandoah River."[29]

Most Confederate cavalrymen, unlike their union counterparts, were required to furnish their own horses.[30] Enlisted men were required to provide a single horse. Brigadier generals were authorized four horses, colonels through captains were authorized three horses, and lieutenants were authorized two.[31] For each authorized horse, the government provided shoeing and feed, and payed the owner a stipend of forty cents per day. Since a private's pay was twelve dollars per month, the trooper received as much money for his horse's service as he earned for his own.

Each cavalryman was responsible for the day-to-day care — mainly feeding and grooming — of his horse or horses. Obviously, an officer with two or three horses required a servant to help with their care. W. W. Blackford, the Engineer Officer on Stuart's staff, was authorized three saddle horses and was allocated a government cart for his engineering equipment. Blackford's arrangements were perhaps a little better than those of the average officer. "Gilbert was my body servant and on marches took charge of my two spare saddle horses—Comet, Magic and Manassas were my mounts—riding one and leading the other. In camp [Albert] the wagon driver became the groom of the five horses, so far as the hard work at the curry comb was concerned, while Gilbert was responsible for the important duty of feeding. Having the wagon to keep forage found on the road, and two excellent foragers in my interests, Gilbert and Albert, it was a cold day when my stable was entirely empty of food for my mounts."[32] Horses belonging to the enlisted men, most of whom did not have "excellent foragers" at their disposal, probably did not fare so well.

Horses of the time fell into three general categories. Horses bred to race, or "blooded" horses, were frequently descended from thoroughbred stock imported from England in colonial times. Such horses were popular mounts because of their speed and stamina. Most races of the era were conducted over longer distances than races today, although "Quarter-racing" had been popular in the Carolinas since the early 1700s.[33] Saddle horses, the precursor to modern-day walkers and pacers, had been bred to carry planters about their estates or transport gentry on trips to town. They were prized for their endurance and comfortable gaits. Draft horses were generally heavier and bred to pull plows or wagons. Consequently, drafts were considered less desirable as cavalry mounts.

The Confederate government's policy of requiring men to furnish their own mounts offered some advantages. The up-front cost of equipping cavalry regiments was reduced since the government had no need to purchase horses. Additionally, the men enlisting in the cavalry could be expected to be proficient riders and to provide themselves with reasonably suitable mounts (e.g., broken to saddle; sound; proper size; mature but not aged). Further, ownership provided an incentive for the men to take proper care of their horses. Southern cavalry rode hard and fought hard without resorting to the oft-heard Union cavalry exhortation, "Don't spare the horse."

Initially the Confederate system proved adequate. During the first years of the war, the average Southerner was generally acknowledged to be better mounted than his Northern counterpart who relied upon the Union Quartermaster Department to provide his

The Union Army established six major remount depots. The largest, at Giesboro Point in Washington, could accommodate 30,000 horses. Most horses were kept in large corrals, such as the one in this photograph, but Giesboro also had stables with 6,000 stalls. In contrast, Southern troopers were responsible for providing their own mounts, saving the Confederacy the expense of establishing a remount system. However, the Southern system was incapable of effectively sustaining Stuart's cavalry (National Archives).

horse. Complaints from the ranks were few. Most Southern cavalrymen were happy to furnish their own horses and unquestioningly brought them into the service. A good horse was a source of individual pride, and most men felt a genuine affection for their horses as well. For the Southern cavalryman, "his horse is his second self, his companion and friend, upon whom his very life may depend."[34] In countless letters home, troopers expressed concern over the well being of their horses, particularly with respect to the habitual shortage of forage. One soldier in the 9th Virginia, presented with a choice between his own comfort and that of his horse, chose comfort for the horse. On May 20, 1863, the trooper mailed home to his mother two new shirts and a pair of socks, explaining, "my horse gets so little to eat, I want to get rid of all the baggage I can."[35]

However, as the war progressed, problems with reliance on private ownership of horses became evident, and the Confederate army began to suffer from the lack of an organized remount system.

Each horse mustered into cavalry service was appraised. When a horse was killed in battle or died as a result of its service, the Confederate government reimbursed the owner at the appraised value. No reimbursement was made when a horse became lame or otherwise disabled, a source of great irritation to many cavalrymen, who ruined their personal mounts in the service of their country. Not surprisingly, appraisal values increased greatly during the war as the supply of suitable horses shrank and inflation ruined the Confederate economy.

At the beginning of the war, one trooper in the 1st Virginia informed his wife that the average value of the horses in his company was 175 dollars with one valued at 225 dollars. The trooper went on to add that "Col Stuart said about 40 of our men were the best mounted men he had ever seen."[36] Similarly, the June 1861 muster roll for the Little Fork Rangers listed fifty-seven officers and men with horses ranging in value between 75 and 150 dollars.[37] By 1863, prices for horses were much higher and even horses that were not particularly suited for cavalry service had increased greatly in value. In June 1863, one soldier in the 9th Virginia advised his father that he needed a new horse because his present horse, "Little Peep," which was valued at 690 dollars, was too small.[38] Fine horses were even more valuable. In June 1863, a soldier in the 18th Virginia wrote to his wife that he had captured a "superb" horse from Union General Robert Milroy's orderly and estimated that the horse would be "worth in 'dixie' about $1500."[39]

As the supply of horses diminished, even senior officers also had difficulty obtaining suitable remounts. In early 1864, four of JEB Stuart's horses become ill (two of which died). Stuart was forced to draw a loan from his brother to buy a new mount. Stuart assured his brother that the sum, fifteen hundred dollars, was the current market value of a good horse.[40] Later in the war it not unusual for soldiers to receive two or even three thousand dollars in compensation for horses killed in action.

Considering that a cavalry private was paid twelve dollars per month, later in the war it was virtually impossible for a trooper to save enough money to purchase a suitable remount. Well after the war, Colonel Thomas Munford, the commander of the 2nd Virginia Cavalry, wrote that it eventually cost a trooper five years' pay in Confederate money to purchase a good cavalry mount, and it would take weeks or months until the "all the papers had gone through the [red] tape of office in Richmond" allowing a soldier to be reimbursed for a horse that had been killed.[41] In that regard, Byrd Clapsaddle, a private in Company E, 7th Virginia Cavalry, lost his horse in a fight at Greenland Gap, West Virginia, on April 25, 1863. His company commander noted on the unit's muster roll "Private B. Clapsaddle is a good soldier but a poor man, and will not be able to remount himself unless paid for his horse killed in action." The government later paid Clapsaddle four hundred dollars for his horse.[42] Fundamentally, it was basically unfair that a Confederate trooper faced both physical and financial risk when defending his state.

Because of the vagaries of their quartermaster system, Confederate troopers were almost always concerned with obtaining sufficient feed for their horses. The supply of grain and hay, particularly the latter, was usually inadequate. During active campaigning—when grass was growing—the cavalry was frequently on the move with little time to allow the horses to graze. In winter, when the cavalry was in camp, there was little grass upon which to graze and the quartermaster utterly failed to deliver enough grain and forage. On April 4, 1863, William Corson, a soldier in the 3rd Virginia, wrote to his sweetheart, "We are faring badly now I tell you. Men only get one fourth rations and horses are starving. They are only allowed 8 pounds of corn and 1½ pounds of hay in 24 hours."[43]

Troopers also had to be concerned with keeping their horses properly shod to help prevent hoof damage and lameness. Periodic shoeing was (and is) necessary not only because iron horse shoes wear out, but because horse hoofs grow from one eighth to one quarter inch per month. To shoe a horse, a farrier must remove the old shoes, trim the horse's hoofs to the proper length, shape a new set of shoes to fit, and nail the shaped shoes to the hoof. An experienced farrier can shoe a cooperative horse in an hour or so. Horses generally go about six weeks between shoeing. The interval between shoeings, however, varies greatly depending upon the rate of hoof growth, the type of shoe, footing conditions (e.g.: mud; hard ground; macadamized roads), and the amount of work done by the horse. Occasionally horses will lose shoes, requiring immediate replacement by a farrier.[44]

Machines for manufacturing iron horse shoes were developed in the mid–1800s and by the 1860s machines were in use manufacturing horse shoe nails. However, the North benefitted most from this industrialization. In the cavalry of the Confederate Army, most

Farriers at work — a scene common in all cavalry camps. The mound at the left rear is perhaps horse manure. Its daily collection and disposal required continual effort (Library of Congress).

horse shoes were made in the traditional manner — the company blacksmith heated iron bars in a forge, cut the bars to shoe length, hammered the pieces into the shape of a shoe, and punched nail holes into each blank shoe with his pritchel.[45] For each shoe, the farrier also had to make eight nails from iron bar stock. This was obviously a time-consuming process and occasionally a regiment would detail several troopers with smithy experience to manufacture large quantities of shoes in anticipation of future needs.

Apparently horse shoes were scarce from time to time. Major Henry B. McClellan, Stuart's assistant adjutant general, recalled that "Horseshoes, nails, and forges were procured with difficulty; and it was not an uncommon occurrence to see a cavalryman leading his limping horse along the road, while from his saddle dangled the hoofs of a dead horse, which he had cut off for the sake of the sound shoes nailed to them."[46] In a similar vein, Colonel Thomas Munford, commander of the 2nd Virginia, noted that while on the march, shoes, nails, and blacksmiths were often not at hand. Consequently, like McClellan, he recalled seeing his men "many a time have[ing] the hoof of a dead horse strapped to their saddles, which they had cut off at the ankle with their pocket-knives, and would carry them until they could find a smith to take it off with his *nippers*, and thus supply their sore-footed steeds."[47]

However, the problem of unshod horses may have reflected more of a problem with organization than with supply. In an April 1864 letter to Brigadier General Thomas Rosser, Stuart directed that Rosser devote "special attention" to keeping his brigade's horses shod. Stuart ordered Rosser to immediately ensure that a farrier was assigned to each squadron and that the farrier with his tools and a small amount of shoes accompanied the squadron on the march. Stuart added that if Rosser's troopers "were habituated to carry extra shoes in their pouches, we will have succeeded in doubling the efficiency of the command."[48]

To help alleviate the chronic shortage of suitable horses, Stuart established a "horse hospital" in Albemarle County in November 1862. Horses that were ill, injured, or simply worn out were sent to Albemarle for recuperation while their now-dismounted owners were drilled as infantry skirmishers.[49] The horse hospital was staffed with troopers detailed from the regiments. While Stuart's initiative was helpful in returning some horses to service, it was minuscule in comparison to the remount depots established by the Union quartermaster department.[50]

Training for Confederate cavalry troopers was rudimentary. Training at the time consisted of a series of drills set forth in the tactics manual of each arm (e.g.: infantry; artillery; cavalry). The Confederate government never published a cavalry tactics manual, leaving officers to train their men as prescribed in various extant manuals. One widely-used cavalry manual was that promulgated by the Regular Army and commonly known as "41 Tactics" or "Poinsett Tactics," after Joel Poinsett, the Secretary of War in the administration of Martin Van Buren. Poinsett, better-known today for the holiday flower that bears his name than his service as a cabinet official, in 1839 dispatched several officers to France to study that nation's tactics. The officers returned with a copy of the French tactics manual — the French army being then considered the best in Europe. The War Department translated the French manual into English and in 1841 published it as its own. The manual remained in use over the next twenty years and many senior officers in Stuart's division were familiar with its provisions from their service in the "Old Army."[51]

Another manual in wide distribution was *A Concise System of Instructions and Regulations for the Militia and Volunteers of the United States*, better known as "Cooper's Manual," after its author, Samuel S. Cooper. Cooper, who graduated from West Point in 1815, wrote the manual as a captain in 1836. In 1852, Cooper was promoted to brigadier general and appointed as the army's Adjutant General. Although a New Yorker, Cooper had married a Virginia woman and in 1861 he resigned his commission to serve the South. He was promptly appointed as Adjutant General of the Confederate Army, a post he held throughout the war.[52]

Another tactics manual in use in the South was written by James Lucius Davis, an officer in the Virginia Militia. Davis' book, perhaps most distinguished by its lengthy title, *The Trooper's Manual: or, Tactics for Light Dragoons and Mounted Riflemen. Compiled, abridged and arranged, by Col. J. Lucius Davis, graduate of the United States Military Academy, West Point, formerly an officer of the United States Army; and for many years commander and instructor of volunteer cavalry*, was published in Richmond in 1861. Davis prefaced his book by opining that "No military work is in more demand at present than a cheap, plain, brief compendium of Cavalry Tactics." Davis' assessment regarding the need for a cheap and plain manual may have been accurate since the book was reprinted in 1862. However, at close to three hundred pages, the *Trooper's Manual* was hardly brief. Interestingly, in his introductory remarks, Davis set forth that "Fancy hats with plumes of ostrich or other feathers are only suitable for parades and reviews, but on campaign, they are a useless incumbrance."[53] Apparently JEB Stuart, noted for his extravagant plumed hat, chose to ignore Davis' admonition.

Following the execution of John Brown in 1859, Governor Wise asked the superintendent of VMI to prepare a tactics manual for the Virginia militia. In response, Major William Gilham, the commandant of cadets and tactics instructor at VMI, wrote the *Manual of Instruction for the Volunteers and Militia of the United States: With Many Illustrations* which was published in 1861. In preparation for war, VMI offered training for prospective officers while its cadets were detailed as drill masters at camps around Richmond. Consequently, many Virginians were exposed to Gilham's system of training.[54]

All of the manuals were similar in that they relied heavily on drill — the repetition of certain actions until the action could be done quickly, correctly, and without thought. Each manual set forth a progressive series of drills that, if followed, would hopefully produce a trained soldier in a trained unit. In theory, a new cavalryman would begin his military training in the school of the dismounted trooper, learning to march and practicing with his weapons afoot. Next, the new soldier would progress to the school of the mounted trooper, during which he would learn how to ride and handle his weapons on horseback. Finally, the new trooper would begin training as part of a unit, starting with the platoon, progressing through company and squadron, and ending with the regiment.

Immediately after secession, Virginia established a cavalry training center at Ashland, north of Richmond. Cavalry companies were directed to report to Ashland where, under the tutelage of Colonel Charles Field and a cadre of West Pointers and VMI cadets, they were drilled extensively.[55] As regiments were formed, they left Ashland for active service, and intensive periods of formal training became less frequent. Fields, an 1849 graduate of West Point and until recently a captain in the 2nd U.S. Cavalry, left Ashland himself in the fall of 1861 to take command of the 6th Virginia Cavalry.

Fortunately, the concepts of cavalry warfare were relatively simple. As Winston Churchill, who began his career in public service as lieutenant in the 4th Hussars and fought in the Sudan with the 21st Lancers, succinctly explained, "cavalry manoeuvre in column and fight in line ... [therefore] cavalry drill resolves itself into swift and flexible changes from one formation to the other."[56] Confederate troopers learned to form as a regiment, break from a line formation to a column, and march in a column. They also learned to form a line from a column to the front, right, or left, and to advance in line by squadrons, changing directions by wheeling to the right or left. The men also trained to use their weapons when either mounted or dismounted. Finally, troopers trained to fight dismounted, which required one man in four to hold horses.

Cavalry units, unlike infantry, were faced with a unique challenge because horses, as well as soldiers, had to be trained. Progressive training was necessary not only for new troopers, but for green horses as well. Many horses, although perfectly behaved when ridden alone or in a small group, become fractious when in ridden in a large group; kicking is common, biting less so. Some horses have the disconcerting habit of constantly sticking their head against the rump of the horse in front, frequently receiving a kick in return, particularly if the horse in front is a mare. Many horses have problems with their paces. Some horses, particularly those bred to race, have a strong urge to run in the front of the pack. Some horses walk more slowly than the horse in front, allowing a gap to develop. The lagging horse then breaks into a trot to catch up. In a long column formation, this results in what is sometimes called an "accordion effect" and tends to frustrate the riders at the rear of the column. Some horses prefer a slow canter to a trot, a habit that tends to disrupt a formation. Most irritating, many horses "jig" rather than walk, fatiguing both themselves and their riders. Finally, training was essential so that horses became accustomed their riders swinging sabers about their heads and flanks and firing pistols, carbines, and even sawed-off shotguns from the saddle.

Formal training, however, was much reduced when units became engaged actively in military operations. For most of Stuart's regiments, there was simply insufficient time to conduct rigorous individual and unit training, even had there been a strong inclination to do so. Therefore, training, as described by a sergeant in the 3rd Virginia in camp near Yorktown in the spring of 1862, was much less formal than the drills prescribed in the various manuals.

We spent the greater portion of each very cold day inside, reserving our military training for better weather. When the temperature permitted, our drill was sabre, carbine, and pistol practice. Targets were set up and we wagered over our respective scores. More difficulty was obtained by putting paper targets on fence posts to be fired at as we galloped past on our horses.... Sabre practice was also conducted on horseback. We would set up saplings and, as we charged past on our horses, we would undertake, with considerable success, to cut their heads off. Before the spring campaign began, our regiment had gotten in very fair shape. Our mounts had become accustomed to one another and the men had schooled them until they moved with precision and learned the commands. We had learned to stand to horse, mount, dismount, move in columns, charge, and etc. When our squadron drew our sabres and charged, giving the Rebel yell, we made quite an imposing sight.[57]

Doubtless, by 1863 the training for most new recruits consisted of learning-by-doing, with formal periods of drill conducted only intermittently.

Manpower shortages were a continual problem for Stuart's regiments. While each regiment was authorized more than forty officers and roughly seven hundred enlisted men, most had far fewer in the ranks. After the hard winter on the Rappahannock, Stuart's regiments averaged just more than seventy percent of their assigned enlisted strength present for duty, and many of those who were present had horses unfit for campaigning.[58]

While service in the cavalry was popular, recruiting efforts were rarely successful in filling units to their authorized level. Even with conscription, most units fell well short of their manpower goals.

Further reducing a regiment's effective strength was the need to provide soldiers to perform a variety of tasks. Within their regiment, soldiers were most commonly detailed

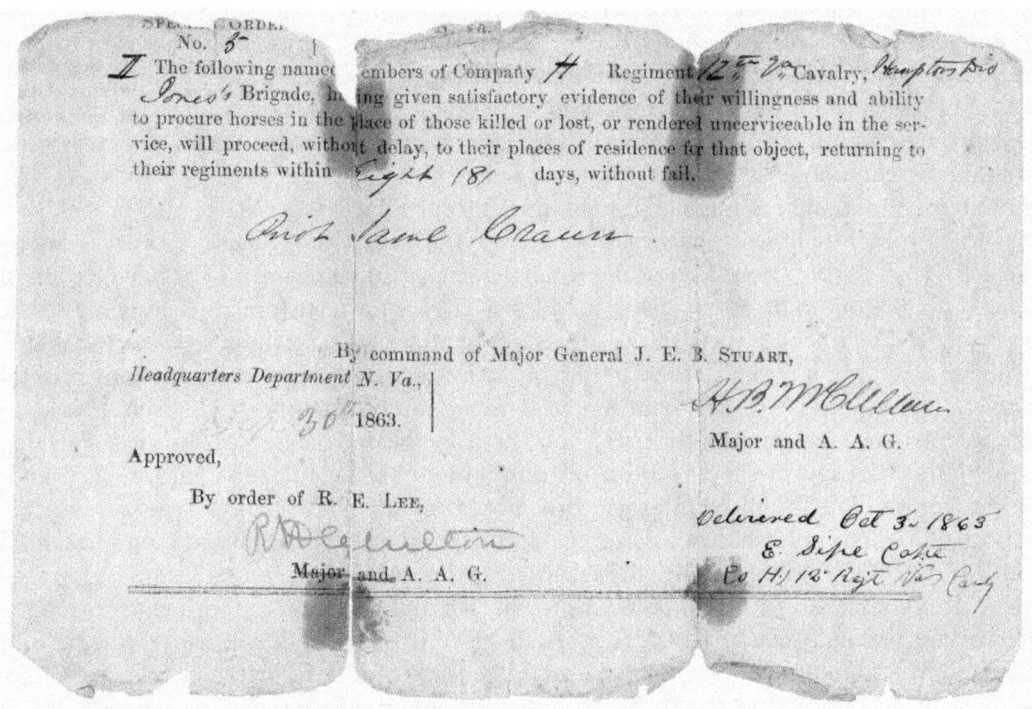

This "horse pass" authorized Private Samuel Craun, 12th Virginia Cavalry, eight days' absence to procure a remount. The pass was signed by Major H.B. McClellan, Stuart's Assistant Adjutant General (VMI Archives).

as teamsters to drive the regimental baggage and supply wagons. Soldiers were also assigned as couriers, medical orderlies, ordnance sergeants, artificers, and butchers. While regulations prohibited soldiers from acting as servants, troopers were selected to cook and wait in the officers' mess.

Soldiers were also detailed to duties that took them away from their regiment, although they remained on the regimental rolls for the duration of the detail. In the spring, if a regiment was near the mouth of a river, fishing parties were organized to catch and smoke shad as that species made its predictable run upriver to spawn. In the summer, details were dispatched to harvest hay. From time to time, parties were sent out to herd quartermaster cattle. Men were also sent off on recruiting duty, to tend worn out horses, and round up deserters. Finally, division and brigade headquarters always needed diligent men to serve as couriers and scouts.[59]

At any given time a few deserving men were on furlough visiting their homes. More men were always absent on "horse detail" or "horse pass," having been released for a few days or weeks to find remounts. This system was inherently inefficient and greatly reduced the effectiveness of the units. Toward the end of the winter of 1862–1863, a company commander in the 2d Virginia succinctly noted that "The company would be more efficient and report a larger number of men for duty if the horses could be properly fed, but they have suffered a great deal with hunger and are thus soon rendered unfit for service. The men whose horses are thus disabled for want of forage are detailed to go home and furnish themselves with fresh ones which diminishes our numbers and imposes a very heavy expense on the men."[60]

Troopers without mounts were temporarily assigned to an *ad hoc* organization known as "Company Q" for various and sundry duties that could be accomplished by men afoot. Assignment to Company Q, characterized by one trooper as a "quasi organization of dismounted men who followed the cavalry like a nightmare," was considered the ultimate indignity by many troopers.[61] However, a worse indignity — reassignment to the infantry — was the prescribed fate of cavalrymen who were unable to obtain a remount. As the anticipated start of summer campaigning in 1863 approached, nineteen hundred officers and men, approximately one quarter of Stuart's division, were reported as "not effectively mounted."[62] In many regiments the only unit at full strength was Company Q.

Within each regiment a few men were always absent without leave, known today by the acronym "AWOL." Southern soldiers had a casual attitude regarding the need to obtain official permission to be absent from the ranks. They were accustomed to enlisting in the company and regiment of their choice, and serving under officers whom they elected. Many men saw no reason not to visit their homes on occasion, particularly when the army was not actively campaigning.[63] Consequently, a certain amount of unauthorized absence was tacitly accepted and overlooked. Tom Garber, the color-bearer of the 12th Virginia Cavalry, wrote to his wife in April 1863 and included in his letter some advice for an AWOL friend: "I wish you would tell Sam Thomas if he does not hurry down here [to camp near New Market] that he will be published as a deserter [and] tell him he has been absent long enough."[64]

Most AWOL troopers eventually returned to their regiments, received minor punishment, and continued to serve. Some, however, left the ranks intending never to return. They were eventually classified as deserters, dropped from the rolls of their regiments, and reported to Richmond so that warrants might be issued for their arrest. It was customary to provide notice of a deserter in the local newspaper and offer a reward — generally thirty dollars—for the deserter's return. One company commander added a touch humor to the notice he posted regarding the desertion of Private William K. Kramer, 6th Virginia Cavalry:

Said KRAMER is about 5 feet 5 inches in height, has short frizzled hair, pop eyes, short arms, duck legs, squat body, big head and squeaky voice, fancies he can sing "Annie Laurie," and other sentimental songs.... I should have advertised said KRAMER sooner, but have been deliberating whether he would be worth thirty dollars to the Southern Confederacy, if recovered.[65]

In response to the newspaper notification, several people wrote letters to the Confederate War Department in Kramer's behalf, asserting that the AWOL soldier did not realize he had actually enlisted in the cavalry.[66]

A few deserters avoided returning to the ranks by surrendering to the Union army, taking the oath of allegiance, and moving to the North or the West. However, there was an inherent danger in attempting to desert to the North because Federal authorities held the view that Confederate spies habitually assumed the guise of deserters. Confederate soldiers who attempted to find safety in the North frequently found themselves in prison.

At every muster, many men were tallied as absent either in the hospital or convalescing at home. Most were suffering from illness and injury, fewer from wounds. Perhaps the most common affliction among the soldiers was chronic diarrhea, a reflection of the unsanitary conditions in the camps. Erysipelas, or streptococcus infection, was also a frequent cause for hospitalization. Other common ailments included dysentery, tonsilitis, mumps, measles, bronchitis, rheumatism, neuralgia, tuberculosis, pneumonia, smallpox and typhoid. Occasionally troopers were treated for venereal diseases. Many men's health problems were documented in terms that are today obscure, including scorbutus (scurvy), fistula (abscess), spermatorhea (seminal discharge), catarrh (inflamation of the mucous membranes), rubeola (measles), anascara (general edema, perhaps from heart disease), otaglia and otirrhea (eye and ear infections), and dyspepsia (chronic indigestion). Men were disabled by valvular disease of the heart, atrophy of the muscles, and preternatural mobility of the joints. Scabies was a common skin problem, and occasionally a man had to be hospitalized for "camp-itch," which was a pervasive, though less serious, medical condition.

Some hospitalizations resulted from the active lifestyle of a cavalryman. Occasionally a trooper was injured in a fall from his horse, and from time to time hospitalization was the result of an accidental gunshot wound.[67] In an unusual example of the latter, Captain Everton Shands, Company I, 7th Virginia Cavalry, was giving a patriotic speech to his men in their camp at Mack's Mill in Rockingham County when a trooper's weapon accidentally discharged. Shands was struck by the bullet and killed.[68]

Manpower shortages imposed a significant burden on the men in the ranks who day-in and day-out were required to scout and perform picket duty. Commanding skeleton companies also affected the morale of the officers. Captain Charles M. Blackford, commander of the Wise Troop from Lynchburg, wrote to his wife in November 1862 that "My company is becoming smaller and smaller through sickness, wounds, and lack of horses, chiefly the latter. It is, as you well know, difficult for a city company like ours to keep up in mounts. My men do not have farms, or relatives and neighbors with farms from whom they can draw when their horses get killed or disabled, but have to purchase their horses at prices even I hesitate to pay."[69] The following month a frustrated Blackford accepted a position as judge advocate on Longstreet's staff, explaining to his wife, "I would just as soon stay here if I could fill up my company, but I find that almost impossible. I can get the men enough — the difficulty is about the horses."[70]

Captain Henry Billings, the commander of Company H of the 12th Virginia was perhaps even more deeply disturbed by the low strength of his company. On May 29, 1863, he resigned his commission, explaining: "I consider it my duty to resign, as I feel it an imposition upon the service in having so many commissioned officers in so small a company, and would prefer being a humble private of cavalry." Billings reenlisted as a private in Company B, which was fortunate because Stuart's regiments needed privates as well as officers.[71]

Manpower shortages affected the more senior officers as well. Stuart had proposed that his division be reorganized into a cavalry corps by reducing the number of regiments per brigade to three. This would create additional brigades that could be grouped into two divisions. Stuart believed that the proposed organization would be more effective: smaller brigades being more maneuverable. Additionally, several new general officer billets would be created, allowing the promotion of worthy officers. Presumably, Stuart, as a corps commander, might be promoted to lieutenant general. Lee, however, disapproved Stuart's proposal, noting that in the cavalry's "depleted" condition, "a brigade of three regiments would be a very small command for a general officer." More to the point, Lee asked Stuart, "Cannot something be done to bring up [the strength of] your very small regiments?"[72] Unfortunately, not much could be done.

Despite the severe shortages of personnel, increasing difficulty in finding remounts, haphazard training, inferior weapons, and inadequate supplies, Southern cavalry was still considered superior to Union cavalry. On several occasions, Stuart's brigades had shown their ability to penetrate through Union lines and raid deep into Federally-held territory. Concentrated, Stuart's division would present a significant threat to the North.

3

By Easy Marches

The Assembly of Stuart's Regiments in Culpeper County

Shortly after Chancellorsville, Robert E. Lee instructed Stuart to gather his cavalry in Culpeper County, an action that served two purposes. First, any offensive move by the Army of Northern Virginia would likely be preceded by a shift from Fredericksburg to the west where the Rappahannock could be more easily crossed and Union defenses avoided. In Culpeper, Stuart's cavalry would be positioned to screen the anticipated movement of Lee's infantry. Second, and perhaps more important, Culpeper County was known for its abundant pasturage. Lee believed it was imperative that the cavalry's horses, debilitated after the hard winter, be well nourished before the coming campaign.[1]

Culpeper County was formed by an act of the colonial Virginia legislature in 1759 and named for Lord Thomas Culpeper, colonial governor of Virginia from 1680 to 1683.[2] The county is fairly flat in the east, rising toward the foothills of the Blue Ridge in the west. The county sits between the Great Fork of the Rappahannock and Rapidan rivers. Both rivers, although fordable at many locations, significantly impeded north-south movement. During the 1840's a series of locks and dams had been built along the Rappahannock to support barge traffic as far upriver as Waterloo in Fauquier County. However, with the coming of railroads in the 1850s, the barge system fell into disuse. The dams, however, remained, and along with mill dams, pooled the water at many locations along the river.

Not surprisingly, the county's largest community was its county seat. Originally named Fairfax after another colonial governor, by the mid–1800s the picturesque small town was known to locals as Culpeper Courthouse, or simply "the Courthouse." About six miles to the southeast of Culpeper Courthouse lay the small, sleepy village of Stevensburg, formerly the largest community in the county and once considered as a potential site for the University of Virginia. About six miles to the northeast of Culpeper Courthouse was a hamlet called Brandy. Initially the community, which grew around the intersection of the Old Carolina Road and the road leading from Fredericksburg to the Shenandoah Valley, was called "Crossroads."[3] The major attraction in Crossroads was a popular tavern that served a potent brandy to thirsty travelers (most taverns of the time limited their beverages to wine, ale or beer, and cider). The tavern's owners, Isaac and Hannah Herring, advertised their brandy with a large sign, and the tavern became known as the Brandy House. Eventually locals began referring to the community about the tavern as Brandy. In 1852 the Orange & Alexandria Railroad was extended into Culpeper County and the whistle-stop at Brandy was named Brandy Station. On the eve of the Civil War, Culpeper resident George Williams described Brandy in a letter to his sister as "a doulful looking place [which] has two stores, a tavern blacksmith shop and no streets."[4] While the town itself was insignificant, the land around was for the most part open pasture or in crops, and thus suitable for fighting, although streams draining into the Rappahannock presented an occasional obstacle to rapid cross-country movement. In August 1862 the fields to the northeast of Brandy Station had been the site of a brigade-sized cavalry engagement during Major General John Pope's withdrawal from the county at the beginning of the Second Manassas Campaign.[5]

Six miles east of Brandy Station on the south bank of the Rappahannock River sat Kellyville, where John P. Kelly had established Culpeper County's first industrial park. The centerpiece of the small community and the source of most of Kelly's wealth was a large grist mill which could grind one hundred barrels of flour per day.[6] Besides the grist mill, Kelly operated a saw mill, a blacksmith shop, a cooperage and wheel shop, a shoe shop, two ice houses, a bean house, a dairy, a sausage grinder, a smokehouse (Kelly slaughtered one hundred hogs per year), a cloth factory, and a retail store. John Kelly's seventy-one slaves, plus ten slaves owned by other family members, did the labor. Kelly's house and a few other modest dwellings completed the village. A toll bridge had spanned the river at Kellyville as early as 1848, but it had fallen into disrepair. Thus, travelers and wagon traffic were forced to cross the river through Kelly's Ford. In 1862 Kelly sent his moveable machinery to Lynchburg to prevent its destruction by Union troops, and by 1863 Kellyville had begun to fall into disrepair.[7]

At the beginning of the Civil War the population of Culpeper County was just more than twelve thousand, with a little more than half being slaves. The county was loyal to the Southern cause, its white males having voted unanimously in favor of Virginia's ordinance of secession in April 1861.[8] However, Culpeper did have one prominent Union man, John Minor Botts.

At the outbreak of the war, Botts, a former U.S. representative, lived in Richmond where his outspoken pro–Union views were unpopular. He was harassed by Confederate authorities and even briefly incarcerated in what he termed a "negro jail." To avoid further persecution, Botts requested a pass to allow him to move North with his family, but the Confederate government denied him permission to leave the South. Instead, in January 1863 Botts moved to Culpeper to "seek retirement and obscurity, to get out of the way of the world, and to follow for the balance of my life the peaceful pursuits of agriculture."[9]

Botts and his family settled at Auburn, an estate between the Courthouse and Brandy with a fine house and twenty-two hundred acres of land.[10] According to local gossip, Botts won Auburn in a poker game at Madden's Tavern, a popular inn along the road from Fredericksburg owned by Willis Madden, Culpeper County's most prosperous free black.[11] Botts, however, claimed to have purchased the property from James A. Beckham during a visit to Culpeper in the fall of 1862.[12]

JEB Stuart arrived in Culpeper County on May 20 and set up his headquarters in the yard at Afton, a farm owned by Samuel Bradford that lay about three miles northeast of the Courthouse.[13] With Stuart were about a dozen staff officers, a platoon of couriers, scouts, clerks, teamsters, and other assorted personnel, including Sam Sweeney, the headquarters banjo player.[14]

Most notable among the staff officers was Heros von Borcke, an immense Prussian who had come to America upon the outbreak of war and offered his services to the Confederacy. Von Borcke was well known for his wit and social graces, as well as the oversize sword he carried. The urbane Prussian had earned a reputation as an accomplished dancer, even when wearing cavalry boots and despite his size (he stood about six feet two inches tall and weighed about two hundred fifty pounds).[15]

New to Stuart's staff was his assistant adjutant general, Major Henry B. McClellan, whom Stuart had selected to replace the popular Channing Price, who had been killed at Chancellorsville. McClellan was originally from Philadelphia and a cousin to the Union general of the same name. He had studied to be a minister at Williams College, but after graduation in 1858, he instead accepted a teaching position in Cumberland County, Virginia. Upon the outbreak of the war, McClellan enlisted in the 3rd Virginia Cavalry, rose to the rank of captain and served as adjutant of his regiment before moving to Stuart's headquarters.[16] Also new to Stuart's staff, and to the army as well, was Lieutenant Robert H. Goldsborough, a junior *aide de camp*.

Fitz Lee and three of his regiments—the 2nd, 3rd, and 5th Virginia—had rested in Orange County for almost two weeks after the battle at Chancellorsville. They then made the easy march back to Culpeper where the brigade had been posted for picket duty during the late winter.

The 2nd Virginia Cavalry was formed from companies that mustered at Lynchburg in the spring of 1861. The first commander was Colonel Richard C. W. Radford, an 1845 graduate of West Point and a veteran of the Mexican War. In the April 1862 reorganization, Radford failed to be reelected colonel of the regiment, the officers instead selecting Thomas T. Munford, an 1852 graduate of the Virginia Military Institute, as their leader.[17] Munford began the war as lieutenant colonel of the 30th Virginia Mounted Infantry, a dragoon unit absorbed by the 2nd Virginia when the regiment was formed. Munford was well regarded as a leader and had been wounded twice. On several occasions he had temporarily commanded the brigade, and in that capacity he had done well. Consequently, Munford was considered qualified for promotion should a brigadier general's position become vacant.[18] As early as October 1862, and again in March 1863, Stuart recommended that Munford be promoted and placed in command of a brigade. However, no action was taken by the War Department on either of Stuart's requests.[19]

Jacob Kent Langhorne and his friends, after evading Stoneman's raiders along the James River, finally caught up with the 2nd Virginia while it was encamped in Orange County. Colonel Munford took Langhorne under his wing and arranged for the young man to visit the various companies of the regiment so that he might pick a company he liked. In the end, though, Munford convinced Langhorne to enlist in Company B—the continuously under strength Wise Troop—commanded by Captain William Steptoe. Munford emphasized to Langhorne the positive aspects of serving in a small company. In a letter of May 11, Langhorne informed his father that he had safely reached the regiment and that he was planning to join the Wise troop because "Col[onel] M[unford] & Judge say that they think it best for me to join the Wise Troop for three very good reasons. 1 that Capt. Steptoe is willing to take me in his mess. 2 you can get nearly twice as much for your horse to eat as a general thing in a small Company than you can in a large & when they issue corn you get a bag for each company and if the company is small you get as much more. 3 and best reason you will fare better in that line your self." Anticipating the coming campaign, Langhorne concluded his letter by asking his father to "Tell Ma I am a better hand to take care of my self than she thought. I flanked the Yankees until I got across the James R[iver] and please don't be so uneasy about me in the future."[20]

The companies of the 3rd Virginia Cavalry had been raised in May 1861 from counties on the James Peninsula east of Richmond, and the regiment was organized in July of that year. After a short period of training at the camp for cavalry instruction at Ashland, the regiment was posted back to Yorktown where it spent the first year of the war. The regiment's initial commander was Colonel Robert Johnston, an 1850 graduate of West Point.

For a brief period, another West Pointer, Major John Bell Hood, was assigned to the regiment and tasked with improving the troopers' proficiency at drill. Hood, however, quickly moved to a more senior position in the infantry.[21]

In April 1862, Johnston failed to be reelected colonel of the regiment, reverted to captain, and was assigned duties elsewhere in the Confederate army. The winner of the election and Johnston's replacement was the former lieutenant colonel of the regiment, Thomas Goode, a popular lawyer from Mecklenburg County, Virginia. Goode's tenure as colonel of the regiment was short. In November 1862, ill health forced him from field duty and he later resigned his commission.[22] Goode was replaced by Thomas Owen who was serving as lieutenant colonel of the regiment. Owen was an 1856 graduate of VMI who before the war had farmed and worked as a civil engineer.[23]

Thomas Rosser's 5th Virginia Cavalry had been formed in June 1862 by adding two independent companies to a battalion of seven companies raised earlier in the year by Lieutenant Colonel Henry Clay Pate.[24] Rosser, who began the war as a lieutenant of artillery, was appointed colonel of the 5th Cavalry when that regiment was organized. The young commander attended West Point, but along with classmate John Pelham had resigned in May 1861 just two weeks before graduation. Standing about six-feet-two-inches tall, Rosser was an imposing figure whose ambition matched his stature. He was a fearless and generally effective leader in battle, but was also self aggrandizing and quick to take offense. Stuart had recommended Rosser's promotion to brigadier, commenting that "no officer that I have met in the Confederacy combines in a more eminent degree the characteristics of the Cavalry Commander than Colonel Rosser."[25] However, Rosser privately believed that Stuart was impeding his advancement. At the time of the move to Culpeper, Rosser may have been looking forward more to his pending marriage — set for May 28 — than to the expected summer campaign.[26]

Rosser's appointment as commander caused some hard feelings within the 5th Virginia since many the officers and men believed that Pate deserved the colonel's billet. Those hard feelings were quickly exacerbated when Rosser preferred courts-martial charges against Pate. In August 1862, Pate had complained to Stuart that Rosser had been drunk on duty.[27] Stuart forwarded the allegations back to Rosser, and Rosser, perhaps in retaliation, charged Pate with leaving camp to visit his wife without proper authority. In March 1863, Pate was tried by courts-martial and acquitted.[28] It was not surprising that the working relationship between the two senior officers of the regiment remained tense.

In the spring of 1863, the 5th Virginia had the lowest strength of any regiment in Fitz Lee's brigade, with only about 30 percent of its personnel — a few more than 200 in number — present and effectively mounted.

Instead of resting in Orange after Chancellorsville, the 1st Virginia Cavalry had been posted to picket duty on the upper Rappahannock near Amissville, a small hamlet about thirteen miles northwest of the Courthouse. The regiment was formed in the summer of 1861 from companies brought together to support Jackson, and then Joseph Johnston, at Harpers Ferry. Ever since, the regiment had played a prominent role in the campaigns of the Army of Northern Virginia. Stuart had been the regiment's first commander, and Fitz Lee had also served in the regiment as lieutenant colonel and briefly as its commanding officer. Since October 1862 the regiment had been commanded by Colonel James H. Drake, an efficient but unremarkable officer. Unlike many of Stuart's regimental commanders, Drake had limited professional military experience. Before the war, he had worked as a mechanic and plasterer in Frederick County in the Shenandoah Valley. Drake began the war as the commander of the Newtown Light Dragoons, a militia company organized in

1858 at Middletown and later officially designated Company A of the 1st Virginia in July 1861.[29]

Williams Carter Wickham's 4th Virginia also did not make the move to Culpeper, having been assigned picket duty along the Rappahannock about six miles upstream from Fredericksburg. The regiment included Culpeper County's Little Fork Rangers and Fauquier County's Black Horse Troop. The Black Horse troop was perhaps the best-known cavalry company in the Army of Northern Virginia. The troop had distinguished itself at First Manassas when it pursued General Irving McDowell's retreating army, delivering the last blow of the day as the defeated Union Army crossed Cub Run. Among some Southerners, the Black Horse Troop was known as the "Bravest of the Brave," although Union sources more frequently referred to the men of the troop, who for the past two months had been independently scouting in Fauquier and Stafford counties, as horse thieves and bushwhackers.[30] Initially, the members of the company were required to ride dark-colored horses, but by mid–1863, they rode any colored mount available. As one trooper noted, "The black Virginia racers had been succeeded by animals of all hues as well as all sizes and breeds."[31]

Wickham, related to Rooney Lee by Lee's marriage to Charlotte Wickham, was a University of Virginia graduate who before the war had practiced law, been a planter, and served twelve years in the Virginia legislature. His military career began in November 1859 when he organized the Hanover Light Dragoons, later Company G of the 4th Virginia. Wickham was appointed lieutenant colonel of the 4th when the regiment was formed in September 1861. The regiment's first commander, Beverly Robertson, was considered a martinet by officers and enlisted alike, and was turned out of his position in the elections of April 1862. In his place, the officers elected Wickham colonel of the regiment.[32]

As a regimental commander, Wickham had proven himself competent. He had been wounded at Williamsburg, and while convalescing had been captured by McClellan's men and paroled.[33] Wickham, like Munford, was considered brigadier general material, and Wickham privately expressed dissatisfaction that he had not already been promoted. Even while campaigning, Wickham remained active in Virginia politics, and in 1863 he was seeking a seat in the Confederate Congress.

Rooney Lee's brigade, after three weeks of dogging Stoneman's raiders and protecting the Virginia Central railroad, spent a few days resting in Orange County before moving to Culpeper County in mid–May. The brigade consisted of five regiments, one of which remained on picket duty below Fredericksburg. That regiment, the 15th Virginia Cavalry, was ostensibly under the command of Colonel William B. Ball, a longtime militia officer. Ball, however, had been absent due to illness since December 1862. The lieutenant colonel of the regiment, John R. Critcher, while personally brave, lacked self discipline. Without authority, Critcher sneaked through the Union lines to visit his home — supposedly to attend a funeral — and was captured on May 23, 1863.[34] Fortunately for the regiment, the 15th's remaining field grade officer, Major Charles R. Collins, an 1859 graduate of West Point, was competent.

Collins, originally from Pennsylvania, graduated third in his academy class and was commissioned as a topographical engineer. He saw service map-making in Utah and as a staff officer in Washington, D.C., where he married a Virginia woman. Collins' wife apparently influenced his future, since after the outbreak of the war, he resigned from the army and offered his services to the South.[35] Collins was initially commissioned in the artillery but was quickly transferred to the engineers and employed supervising the construction of fortifications in North Carolina and Virginia. Colonel Ball, aware of Collins's good reputation, requested his transfer to the cavalry, which was approved.

Since it had been organized in the fall of 1862, the 15th had been used almost exclusively for picket duty and scouting. Some officers and men had become frustrated with the lack of action in their assignments. Consequently, the officers of four of the companies prepared a petition expressing their dissatisfaction. The petition was passed to Brigadier General Henry Wise, the former governor who had entered the army at the outbreak of the war, in early June 1863. In the petition, the disgruntled officers asserted that "We did not enter the service to *'play soldier'* but to *act* it.... Of course as soldiers we obey orders and serve where directed, but we command as good fighting men as ever 'Mounted a steed' and desire a bold dashing leader who will give us chances *in the field.*"[36]

No action was taken by the Confederate government in response to the petition, but obviously Collins faced a major challenge in restoring morale and turning his regiment into an effective fighting force.[37] But for the time being, the 15th Virginia remained on picket duty and well away from the action.

The 9th Virginia Cavalry, one of the strongest regiments in Stuart's division with more than six hundred men present and effectively mounted, was commanded by Colonel Richard Lee Turberville Beale. The regiment had been formed in January 1862 and was originally occupied in defending the lower Rappahannock. The earliest action seen by some of the 9th Virginia's soldiers was an engagement with Federal gunboats that plied the rivers and estuaries of eastern Virginia. The regiment's first serious combat occurred in early April 1862 as it withdrew from the Northern Neck as General George McClellan's forces moved up the Peninsula. Since then, the men of the regiment had become seasoned veterans, having participated in most of Stuart's exploits, including his ride around McClellan during the Seven Days campaign.

Colonel John E. Johnson, who attended West Point for two years before resigning in December 1832, commanded the 9th when it was first organized. However, Johnson, who was a successful architect, was not particularly popular. Additionally, he was usually at loggerheads with his popular and competent lieutenant colonel, Rooney Lee.[38] In the reorganization of April 1862, the officers of the regiment voted Johnson out of his position and selected Lee as his replacement.[39]

In the election that ousted Johnson, the officers chose Beale as Rooney Lee's lieutenant colonel. When Rooney Lee was promoted to brigadier and elevated to command of a cavalry brigade, Beale was given command of the regiment. The forty-four-year-old Beale was a prominent citizen of Westmoreland County, where before the war he had practiced law, represented his district in the U.S. Congress, and served in the Virginia State Senate. With the crisis of secession looming in 1861, Beale had been elected first lieutenant of a cavalry company known as Lee's Light Horse, after "Light Horse" Harry Lee of Revolutionary War fame. Beale's company was eventually mustered in to service as Company C of the 9th Virginia.[40]

The 10th Virginia Cavalry was commanded by Colonel James Lucius Davis, an elderly officer by contemporary standards. Davis graduated from West Point in 1833, but after three years' service as an artillery officer, he resigned his commission to take up farming. In 1839 Davis went west where he served for two years as a captain in the Texas Rangers. In the 1850s Davis, having returned to his home state, became active in the Virginia Militia. In 1861 he was breveted as a colonel of cavalry and published his cavalry tactics manual while serving as *aide de camp* to the governor.[41] Davis gained his first wartime experience as a cavalry leader in August 1861 when he was given command of the cavalry assigned to the Wise Legion during its abortive campaign in West Virginia. When the 10th Cavalry was organized in May 1862, Davis was appointed as its commander. Three of Davis' sons enlisted in the regiment and served under their father.[42]

The 13th Virginia Cavalry was formed in the summer of 1862. Seven companies that had been part of the 5th Virginia were combined with three newly formed companies to comprise the regiment. All ten companies had been raised around Petersburg and in the Tidewater area of Virginia. Colonel John R. Chambliss, an 1853 graduate of West Point and formerly the commander of the 41st Virginia Infantry, was appointed to command of the 13th. In the ten months of its existence, the 13th Virginia had seen only limited action — some skirmishing around Kelly's Ford and against Stoneman's raiders near Gordonsville.[43]

Rooney Lee's brigade also included the 2nd North Carolina Cavalry. The regiment had been formed in August 1861 when the state legislature authorized the "legion" of cavalry raised by Stephen Spruill to be increased from five to ten companies. Initially, the new regiment was known simply as Colonel Spruill's Cavalry Regiment after its commander.[44] Spruill, a resident of Bertie County in eastern North Carolina, had attended West Point as a member of the class of 1827, but resigned before graduating. In March 1862, Spruill resigned his commission and Matthew Davis, an 1852 academy graduate, was appointed colonel of the regiment. However, Davis, who had been serving in Richmond, died of pneumonia en route to take command. Meanwhile, the regiment's lieutenant colonel, William G. Robinson, a West Pointer from the class of 1858, had been captured in a skirmish at Jones, North Carolina. The officers of the 2nd North Carolina were apparently frustrated, and petitioned their governor to appoint Solomon "Sol" Williams to command of the regiment. Williams at the time was serving in the 20th North Carolina Infantry. Williams' transfer was approved in June 1862.[45]

Williams, also an 1858 graduate of West Point, had served with the dragoons before resigning in 1861 to enter his state's service.[46] As 1862 ended, Williams brought his regiment to Virginia. However, instead of commanding his troopers in action, Williams was promptly detailed to an extended period of courts-martial duty. Without both Williams and his lieutenant colonel (Robinson was still awaiting exchange), Lieutenant Colonel William Payne of the 4th Virginia was placed in temporary command of the regiment. Apparently, assigning a Virginian to command a North Carolina Regiment caused some disgruntlement among the officers. Williams rejoined his regiment on May 8, and after moving to Culpeper he took advantage of the lull in operations to depart on a short furlough to Petersburg to be married.[47]

Brigadier General Wade Hampton brought his brigade, fresh from its recruiting efforts at Amherst, Virginia, to Orange County after the battle at Chancellorsville. Hampton's brigade then moved from Orange to Culpeper in mid–May. Hampton, the scion of South Carolina society, was reportedly the largest landowner in the South with vast estates in both his home state and Mississippi. Before the war, Hampton occupied himself with politics — he served in both houses of the South Carolina legislature — and with such manly pursuits as hunting and fishing. Upon the secession of South Carolina, Hampton raised a legion — six companies of infantry, four of cavalry, and a battery of artillery — using his personal funds to pay for four hundred Enfield rifles for his infantry and four British Blakely rifled guns for his artillery battery.[48] When hostilities began in Virginia, Hampton, with a colonel's commission from his state, took his legion north and arrived in time to fight at First Manassas, where he was wounded for the first time.

Combined arms organizations were not popular in the Confederate army and Hampton's Legion was broken into its separate components. Hampton was promoted to brigadier and given command of an infantry brigade which he led through the Peninsular Campaign in the summer of 1862. Afterward, Hampton was given command of a cavalry brigade in Stuart's division. Hampton, whose promotion to brigadier was dated May 23, 1862, was

Wade Hampton, Stuart's senior brigadier, took umbrage with Stuart's favoritism toward Virginians. Hampton, who eschewed frivolity and fancy dress, was a no-nonsense commander and a determined and deadly fighter. Reportedly, Hampton personally killed thirteen Federals during the course of the war (Library of Congress).

Stuart's senior subordinate, but the two were not close. Hampton was older than Stuart by almost fifteen years, and unlike the other cavalry generals, had no collegial background from days in the "Old Army." Hampton, unlike Stuart, was reserved in both action and dress. While Stuart was identified by his plumed hat and gold spurs, Hampton was known for his four-foot, straight-bladed, double-edged sword, as well as his ability to wield it in battle.[49] Moreover, the difficulties between the two generals stemmed from Hampton's belief that Stuart showed favoritism toward both his Virginian subordinates and their Virginia regiments. To distance himself from Stuart, Hampton once proposed that he take a brigade of cavalry to Mississippi, but Jefferson Davis had not favored the idea.[50]

Of the six regiments in Hampton's brigade, five made the move to Culpeper: the 1st South Carolina; the 2nd South Carolina; the 1st North Carolina; the Cobb's Legion Cavalry; and the Jeff Davis Legion. The sixth regiment in the Brigade, the Phillips Legion Cavalry, was detailed to picket duty with the infantry near Fredericksburg.

The Phillips Legion, like Hampton's Legion had been initially composed of infantry, cavalry and artillery. It had been raised in Georgia in 1861 by Colonel William Phillips, a prominent lawyer and militia captain before the war. Phillips was given a brigadier's commission by the governor of Georgia, but he relinquished that grade to command the legion on active service.[51] The Phillips Legion participated in the Kanawha Valley campaign in West Virginia in late 1861, during which Phillips contracted typhoid fever. Illness forced Phillips to return to Georgia to recuperate.[52] In early 1862 the Phillips legion was sent to South Carolina, and in late summer of that year, the Phillips Legion Cavalry, a battalion of four companies commanded by Lieutenant Colonel William W. Rich, was transferred to the Army of Northern Virginia and assigned to Hampton's brigade.

Rich, a north Georgia lawyer and planter, had previous military experience. In 1847 he raised a company of mounted riflemen that saw service late in the war against Mexico. In 1861 Rich raised and commanded a company of cavalry, this time in the Phillips Legion.[53] In March 1863, the War Department officially separated the infantry and cavalry of the Phillips Legion, and two additional companies were assigned to the now-independent cavalry battalion bringing its strength up to six companies.[54]

The precursor to the 1st Regiment, South Carolina Cavalry, was the 1st Battalion South Carolina Cavalry which was organized on October 31, 1861, with six companies under the command of Lieutenant Colonel John Logan Black. Black, who had attended West Point from 1850 to 1853, resigning a year short of graduation, was a large, aggressive man who had a reputation for proficiency in the art of swearing. In early 1862, South Carolina added three additional companies to Black's battalion, and in June added a tenth company and officially created the 1st Regiment. Black was promoted to colonel and appointed to command. Thus far in the war, the 1st South Carolina had seen little action.[55]

The nucleus of the 2nd South Carolina was the four-company battalion that had been initially raised as the cavalry component of Hampton's Legion. In the summer of 1862, those four companies were combined with the 4th Battalion South Carolina Cavalry and three independent South Carolina cavalry companies to form the 2nd Regiment, South Carolina Cavalry.[56] The well-connected Matthew C. Butler, a lawyer, state legislator, and son-in-law to South Carolina's governor, was appointed colonel of the regiment upon its formation. Butler had begun his military career as captain of the Edgefield Hussars, a militia company, in 1859.[57]

The 1st North Carolina Cavalry was organized in August 1861 and mustered into Confederate service in October of that year. The regiment was immediately sent to Virginia, arriving at Manassas on October 22. In 1862, the regiment shifted back and forth between Virginia and eastern North Carolina, but saw considerable action with Stuart in Virginia and Maryland. The regiment's first commander was Robert Ransom, an 1850 graduate of West Point who resigned his regular commission on the eve of the war to serve the Confederacy. In March 1862, Ransom was promoted to brigadier general and appointed to the command of an infantry brigade. He was replaced by the lieutenant colonel of the regiment, Laurence Baker, an 1851 academy graduate.[58] Baker had performed well as a regimental commander and was considered by both Stuart and Robert E. Lee to be qualified for brigade command. Lee, in particular, desired to brigade together Stuart's North Carolina regiments and thought Baker the North Carolinian most suitable for its command.

Cobb's Legion had been raised in Georgia by Thomas Cobb, a well-respected attorney, in the spring of 1861. The Legion had six companies of cavalry, six of infantry, and an artillery battery. Cobb brought his legion to Virginia in July 1861 and was posted to Major General John B. McGruder's command on the Peninsula. The legion participated in the Seven Days battles and was then split, the cavalry being assigned as a battalion in Hampton's Brigade.[59] By February 1863, four additional mounted companies had been raised in Georgia and sent to Virginia, bringing Cobb's Legion cavalry up to regimental strength.[60]

The commander of Cobb's Legion Cavalry was Pierce Manning Butler Young, the son of a Georgia planter, who had resigned from West Point in May 1861, just a few weeks before his graduation.[61] Returning home, Young was offered commissions by both Georgia and the Confederate government. He accepted a position as lieutenant of artillery in the Confederacy's regular army, believing that it had greater potential for advancement. However, Young was posted to the staff of General Braxton Bragg in Pensacola, Florida, a backwater far from the seat of war. After First Manassas, Young, anxious to get into action, traveled to Richmond where he met Thomas Cobb. Cobb, impressed with the young officer, arranged for Young to be appointed major in Cobb's Legion Cavalry. Young, was subsequently promoted to command of the battalion and then the regiment. Young showed considerable *elan* as a cavalry leader. In Maryland he led his men into a melee during which he was shot in the calf and then pinned to the ground when his horse was killed. Fortunately, at the end of the fight Young's men held the field and he avoided capture. The leg-wound was not severe and

Young wrote his parents from Richmond that he was enjoying the treatment of pretty girls. In a more macabre vein, Young added that during the recent encounter, he had "peeled a Yankee's head in real trooper style."[62]

The Jeff Davis Legion was ostensibly a Mississippi unit, although two of the legion's six companies were from Alabama and one was from Georgia. A, B, and C Companies of the legion were raised in Mississippi in 1861 as independent companies. Those three companies moved separately to Virginia, and once there were organized into a Mississippi battalion under the command of Lieutenant Colonel William T. Martin, who had raised Company A at Natchez. Subsequently, three non–Mississippi companies were added to create a six-company battalion, with Martin remaining in command as its lieutenant colonel (unlike most other legions, the Jeff Davis legion never included infantry companies or an artillery battery).[63]

Martin, originally from Kentucky, had practiced law in Natchez before the war. He proved a competent cavalry commander and distinguished himself during Stuart's famous ride around the Army of the Potomac and during the Seven Days battles in the summer of 1862. In December 1862, Martin's abilities were rewarded with promotion to Brigadier General and he was sent to Tennessee, eventually rising to command of a division in General Joseph Wheeler's cavalry corps. Martin was replaced by his deputy, Joseph Frederick Waring, who began his military service as a "cornet" in the Georgia Hussars.[64]

The Georgia Hussars, a militia company with lineage dating back to colonial times, was accepted into Georgia service as a heavy artillery company at Fort Pulaski in January 1861. Apparently that mundane duty did not suit the members of the Hussars, because a month later they offered their services to the Confederate government as a cavalry company. The governor of Georgia, however, took issue with the Hussars leaving the state, and required them to return their state-owned equipment before leaving for Virginia. As a result, the men of the company were required to purchase their own weapons at a cost of about twenty-five thousand dollars. The company finally arrived in Richmond in September 1861, and shortly afterwards its members voted to join the 6th Virginia Cavalry as its Company E. The company moved with the regiment to Northern Virginia and served on outpost duty there until December, when it was transferred to the Jeff Davis Legion as the Legion's Company F.[65]

Robert E. Lee, intent on strengthening the cavalry of Army of Northern Virginia, arranged for Major General D. H. Hill, commanding Confederate forces in North Carolina, to transfer to Virginia a small cavalry brigade commanded by Brigadier General Beverly Robertson. Robertson had graduated from West Point in 1849 and served mostly with the dragoons in the regular army. His first posting was to the army's cavalry school in Carlisle, Pennsylvania, where he served under then-major Philip St. George Cooke. While at Carlisle, Robertson became romantically involved with Cooke's daughter Flora, but their relationship waned after Robertson was transferred to Socorro, New Mexico, with the 2nd Dragoons. Flora Cooke later married JEB Stuart, which perhaps served as a source of friction between the two Confederate cavalry generals.[66]

In 1861, Robertson was dismissed from the army for disloyalty, having accepted a commission from Virginia. Once exclusively in the service of his state, Robertson was appointed colonel of the 4th Virginia when that regiment was formed, served as commander of Jackson's cavalry in the Valley after the death of Turner Ashby, and was promoted to brigadier in June 1862.[67] He had performed credibly, first under Jackson in the Valley and then under Stuart during the 2nd Manassas campaign. However, Robertson was never fully in Stuart's favor, and he was not held in high regard by Lee, who thought him a good organizer and instructor, but less effective as a field commander.[68]

Lee sent Robertson to North Carolina in September 1862 and was not particularly anxious to have him return to the Army of Northern Virginia. Thus, Lee offered to send Robertson back to North Carolina if his services were required there. Additionally, Robertson's departure would give Lee the opportunity to create a North Carolina cavalry Brigade with Lawrence Baker as its commander. However, D. H. Hill declined to take Robertson back, cryptically responding, "I am much obliged to you for the offer of Brigadier-General Robertson, but he has once been in this department."[69] For the time being, Robertson remained in command of his small brigade and Baker remained in command of his regiment.

Robertson brought to Virginia the 4th and 5th Regiments, North Carolina Cavalry, commanded by colonels Dennis Ferebee and Peter Evans, respectively. Both regiments had been raised in mid–1862 and neither had seen much action, having spent most of their time picketing and patrolling in eastern North Carolina.

In August 1862, five independent cavalry companies were ordered to report to Colonel Ferebee, a forty-seven-year-old lawyer with Unionist sympathies from Camden County. Two other companies were added to Ferebee's command in September, and an eighth company was added in March 1863, leaving Ferebee's command, officially designated the 4th North Carolina Cavalry, short two companies. Ferebee's companies were originally designated as partisan rangers, but never used as such.[70] Instead the regiment was deployed as regular cavalry to help limit the incursion of Federal forces in eastern North Carolina. The first action for many of the men was an engagement against three Union gunboats— the *Hunchback*, the *Commodore Perry* (named after Colonel M.C. Butler's uncle), and the *Whitehead*— on the narrow Blackwater River on October 3, 1962. During the engagement, the three gunboats fired 491 shells and reported suffering 4 men killed and 15 wounded. Six Union sailors were later awarded Medals of Honor of the heroism they displayed during the fighting. No losses in Ferebee's regiment were reported, although two infantrymen whose regiments were also engaged fighting the gunboats were wounded.[71]

The 5th North Carolina was formed in October 1862 when two independent cavalry companies and eight companies from two partisan ranger battalions were combined. Peter Evans was appointed to the command of the new regiment. Evans had commanded a company in the 3rd North Carolina Cavalry, but failed to be reelected by his men in the April 1862 reorganization. Obviously, however, Evans, retained the confidence of the governor.[72]

Robertson's Brigade left North Carolina shortly after the battle at Chancellorsville had ended and arrived in Culpeper at the end of May. Both regiments, although not greatly tested in battle, were strong by mid–1863 standards, numbering more than five hundred officers and men each.[73]

The fifth brigade of cavalry en route to Culpeper was that commanded by Brigadier General William E. "Grumble" Jones. Most of the brigade's service had been in the Valley and many of its men had begun their service in Turner Ashby's "Valley Cavalry."[74] The brigade had first been commanded by Beverly Robertson, and after Robertson was sent to North Carolina in the fall of 1862, Jones assumed command. Jones, whose nickname reflected his irascible character, had graduated from West Point in 1848 and served in the dragoons on the frontier.

In 1852, Jones lost his new bride in a tragic accident. Jones had been posted to California, and the ship upon which he and his wife were traveling foundered in a storm along the Texas Coast. As the passengers and crew abandoned the ship, Jones' wife was swept from his grasp and drowned (some claimed that Jones' dour personality was a result of that event).[75]

In 1856 Jones resigned his commission, and after a lengthy tour of Europe, he returned to western Virginia and took up farming.[76] During the events leading up to secession, Jones helped organize a volunteer cavalry company — later Company D, 1st Virginia Cavalry — and was elected its captain.[77] When the 1st Virginia Cavalry was organized, Jones was appointed as its lieutenant colonel, and when Stuart was promoted to brigadier, Jones was elevated to colonel in his stead. Following in the ebullient Stuart's footsteps, Jones proved unpopular with the officers and men of the 1st Virginia, who voted against him and in favor of Fitz Lee in the reorganization of April 1862. However, Jones was not out of work for long. The death of Turner Ashby provided R. E. Lee the opportunity to transfer Jones to command of the newly-reorganized 7th Virginia. In that capacity, Jones acted credibly during the summer of 1862, earning his promotion to brigadier in September of that year.[78]

Stuart strongly opposed Jones' promotion to brigadier and, moreover, objected to giving Jones command of a brigade in his division. In his October 1862 reorganization plan, Stuart wrote to Lee: "With Brigadier General Jones I feel sure of opposition, insubordination, and inefficiency to an extent that would in a short time ruin discipline and subvert authority in that brigade.... I must beg the Commanding General to avert such a calamity from my division and if there are any who entertain different views in regard to General Jones, let such have the benefits of his services and his talents."[79]

Initially Stuart got his wish. Robert E. Lee left Jones' Brigade in the Shenandoah Valley to operate semi-independently. From fall 1862 until spring 1863, the main task facing Jones was to protect the lower Valley from depredations committed by Union troops under the command of Major General Robert Milroy. Milroy required Southern sympathizers — nearly the entire population of the counties surrounding his headquarters in Winchester — to guarantee the safety of Union resources. Severe penalties were levied upon the civilians following any rebel activity. The local citizens complained to the Virginia legislature that they were not being adequately protected and were dissatisfied with measures taken by Jones to ensure their safety and protect their property. The complaints were forwarded to James Seddon, the Confederate Secretary of War, who requested that Lee relieve Jones. Lee, who fully appreciated the tactical difficulties Jones faced, deferred taking action.

In April 1863, Jones, in concert with Brigadier General John Imboden and his command, led three of his regiments on an extensive raid into West Virginia (the 11th Virginia was left at Strasburg to guard the Shenandoah Valley). The purpose of the raid was to sever the Baltimore & Ohio Railroad, a key transportation link between Union theaters in the east and west. After a month of inconclusive action — the railroad line was cut but quickly repaired — Jones' men returned to the Valley and went into camp near Harrisonburg.[80] On May 23, Robert E. Lee ordered Jones to move his brigade east to join the rest of Stuart's cavalry in Culpeper. Lee, mindful that Jones' men and horses had been severely taxed by the just-completed raid, instructed Jones to make the move "by easy marches" so that he might give his men and horses "proper rest and refreshment."[81]

Jones began the march east on May 25, with the 7th, 6th, and 12th Virginia Cavalry regiments and the 35th Battalion, Virginia Cavalry. Again the 11th Virginia Cavalry was left behind at its posts near Strasburg, where Massanutten Mountain rises to split the Shenandoah Valley into two broad avenues of approach leading from the northeast to the southwest. In keeping with Lee's direction, the move was made at a leisurely pace, with a brief delay on the Blue Ridge in a mostly vain attempt to round up deserters believed to be hiding in the mountains.

The 7th Virginia had been raised in the Valley beginning in the Spring of 1861 by Colonel Angus McDonald. McDonald was an 1817 graduate of West Point who resigned from the army in 1819 to become a fur-trader, then in 1825 returned to Virginia to practice law.

As field operations commenced in the fall of 1861, strenuous duty was beyond the ability of the elderly Colonel McDonald, who suffered from rheumatism. McDonald resigned and was replaced by Turner Ashby.[82] Ashby was an aggressive and charismatic leader, but a lax disciplinarian and indifferent administrator. Consequently, the performance of his cavalry was inconsistent. Nonetheless, Ashby was greatly admired, and in May 1862 he was promoted to brigadier general over the objections of Jackson, his commander.

Recognizing the need for cavalry in the Valley, in the fall of 1861, the Confederate Government permitted the 7th Virginia to exceed the normal authorization of ten companies. By the spring of 1862, the 7th had expanded to 29 companies. On the June 6, Turner Ashby was killed near Harrisonburg — shot through the chest while fighting on foot after his horse was killed. Ashby's death provided an opportunity to dismantle the bloated 7th Virginia. The Regiment was reduced to the standard ten companies. Eighteen companies were distributed to other cavalry regiments, and one company, Chew's, was converted to an artillery battery. Grumble Jones, whose no-nonsense approach to soldiering had proved unpopular in the 1st Virginia, was appointed to the command of the 7th.

Following Jones' promotion to brigadier in October, Richard Dulaney was promoted to colonel of the regiment. Dulaney, of Welbourne in Fauquier Country, was best known locally as the founder of the Upperville Horse and Colt Show which had been held annually since 1853.[83] Dulaney had been wounded during the raid in West Virginia — shot during an assault on a Federal blockhouse — and was hospitalized in Charlottesville. In his absence, Lieutenant Colonel Thomas Marshall commanded the regiment. Marshall, also of Fauquier County, had attended the University of Virginia, studied law, and farmed before the war. In a skirmish the previous August at Orange Courthouse, Marshall had been struck by a saber blow, knocked senseless, and captured. After a month of imprisonment, he was exchanged and returned to duty with the regiment. The Marshall family was well represented in Jones' brigade. Thomas Marshall's older brother, James, was serving as a lieutenant in the 12th Virginia, and a nephew, Richard, had spent a year as a private in the 6th Virginia.[84]

One of Jones' regiments, the 6th Virginia Cavalry, had endured almost continual turmoil among its senior leaders. When the 6th Virginia was formed in September 1861, Colonel Charles W. Field was appointed as its commander. Field, a Kentuckian, graduated from West Point in 1849 and served continuously in the regular army until he resigned to join the Confederacy. His initial assignment for the South was to command the camp of cavalry instruction at Ashland. Unfortunately for the men of the 6th Virginia, in March 1862 the well-regarded Field accepted appointment as a brigadier general of infantry.[85] Julien Harrison, a wealthy farmer, was given command of the regiment, an appointment confirmed by vote of the officers of the regiment during the reorganization of April 1862. Harrison, however, suffered from hemorrhoids, a significant affliction for a cavalryman who must, of necessity, spend long days in the saddle. Harrison resigned his commission in July 1862, and the lieutenant colonel of the regiment, farmer and politician Thomas S. Flournoy was promoted in his stead.[86] In September 1862, Flournoy took leave of absence due to illness, and later resigned his commission citing "domestic affliction."[87]

Without a qualified officer, Flournoy was replaced temporarily by Lieutenant Colonel John Shackelford "Shac" Green, a farmer from Rappahannock County and first cousin to Turner Ashby.[88] A few days after Green assumed command, the regiment disgraced itself in a skirmish at Paris, Virginia. The 6th, guarding Ashby's Gap in the Blue Ridge, deployed to block a foray by a Union Cavalry brigade. Confronted by the superior Union force and mismanaged by Green, the men fled the field. The Union commander reported that the 6th "broke in great disorder.... [But] their horses were fresh and [they] could not be overtaken."[89] In a letter written the following day, Chaplain Richard Davis of the 6th Virginia told his wife that at Paris he had "a new experience incident to cavalry chaplaincy"—a "stampede." The chaplain related that "In such a case everything depended on your horse's keeping his feet — if he goes down you will hardly get up again directly. But old Bill, I knew, was to be depended upon, and amongst the crowd of rushing horses, he held his own place, & carried me out."[90]

During the skirmish, Green was wounded — two saber blows to the head — and captured. Green's wounds were thought so severe that a Union surgeon advised his immediately parole.[91] Consequently, Green was not imprisoned. A few hours later, Chaplain Davis, who had been sent under a flag of truce to tend to the 6th Virginia's wounded, found Green up and walking about despite his wound.[92]

The regiment's major, twenty-two-year-old Cabell Flournoy, the son of Thomas Flournoy, temporarily assumed command of the regiment while Green went home to convalesce and await exchange.[93] Cabell Flournoy was a fire-eater, who before the outbreak of the war had offered his services to South Carolina in the event Virginia did not secede. Once Virginia left the Union, Flournoy raised a cavalry company named the Pittsylvania Dragoons from the area surrounding Danville, Virginia. After the Georgia Hussars were transferred to the Jeff Davis Legion, the Pittsylvania Dragoons were assigned in their place as Company E of the 6th Virginia, and shortly afterward, Cabell Flournoy was promoted to major of the regiment. The younger Flournoy's reputation was, however, tarnished because of his actions in the skirmish at Paris. Flournoy, on Green's orders had gone to the rear to rally some of the men, and his movement away from the front line had sparked rumors among the officers and men that he had led the rout.[94]

Shac Green was exchanged in January 1863, and, having recovered from his wounds, returned to duty. Green was in command of the regiment as General Jones set out on his arduous raid into West Virginia. Meanwhile, Julian Harrison had recovered from his hemorrhoids and petitioned the Confederate government to reinstate his commission and reappointed him to command of the 6th Virginia. Both actions requested by Harrison required waivers of army policy. Consequently, a decision on who should be appointed to command the regiment could not be quickly made.

During the raid into West Virginia, the 6th did not perform particularly well. At Rowlesburg on April 26, Jones ordered Green to charge through the town and capture the Baltimore & Ohio Railroad bridge across the Cheat River. Upon making contact with a small party of Union infantry manning rifle pits, Green pulled his men back, dismounted skirmishers, and attempted to flank the Union positions. The attack bogged down and Jones' plan to burn the bridge — a major objective of his raid — was frustrated.[95] This display of indecision and lack of tactical acumen perhaps reflected Green's shortcomings as a commander. An officer in the 6th Virginia later wrote regarding Green that "there never was a more gallant man than he or one of more lovable disposition, but at the same time he was wholly unfitted to command the Regiment and no one realized it more than he."[96] Stuart held a similar view of Green, having earlier advised Robert E. Lee that Green would not make a good colonel, although he was undoubtedly gallant.[97]

After returning to Virginia, Jones preferred charges against Green for failing to obey orders. At the same time, Jones, as required by regulations, convened a board of officers to determine if either Green or Flournoy were qualified for promotion to fill the vacant colonel's billet. Over three days, the board interviewed the two field grade officers and most of the company grade officers. After closed deliberations, on May 29 the board announced its conclusions. The board recommended that Julian Harrison be reappointed to command of the regiment. Were that not possible in view of existing army policy, the board recommended that Green be promoted to colonel and appointed to command. The board apparently felt that Green, who was well-liked but not diligent, would make a better commander than Cabell Flournoy. With respect to Flournoy, the board recommended that he be relieved from all duties with the regiment "as soon as practical."

The board's harsh recommendation regarding Flournoy may have been a result of the rumors that he had exhibited cowardice during the fight at Paris in September 1862. Additionally, Flournoy's personal traits were probably counted against him by the board members. One trooper in the 6th Virginia observed that Flournoy was "a little too fond of the bottle, not choice in his language and rather reckless."[98]

While Jones pondered the problems of leadership in the 6th Virginia, the men were concerned with more mundane issues. Private John Opie's most pressing problem was his horse, a coal-black mare whose disposition — according to Opie — matched her color. Upon the outbreak of the war, Opie left his home in Staunton, enlisted in the infantry, and fought at First Manassas. Like Jacob Langhorne, Opie's parents insisted that he enroll at VMI. Opie only spent only a few weeks as a cadet before leaving Lexington to join the cavalry. In October 1861, Opie enlisted in Company D of the 6th Virginia, which had been raised in Clarke County. Opie had worn out his horse serving a short stint as a volunteer courier for Stuart, and hastily purchased the black mare as a replacement. The mare, while fast, was headstrong and ran away with him whenever the opportunity arose. In addition, the mare was sometimes vicious. Shortly before Jones' raid into West Virginia, she kicked Opie in the face with both hind feet, knocking him unconscious. A friend, believing that Opie was sure to die, ordered a coffin made to transport his body home. Fortunately, Opie regained consciousness the next day and returned to duty a few days later. Obviously, Opie needed a new mount, could one be found.[99]

The 12th Virginia was created in June 1862 with ten companies from the 7th Virginia when that oversized regiment was split. The 12th Virginia's commander, Asher Harman, was one of the few of Stuart's colonels who was not a professional soldier. Instead, the thirty-three-year-old Harman had operated a stage line in Staunton before the war. He enlisted in April 1861 in the 5th Virginia Infantry and had shown proficiency as an infantry company commander in the Stonewall Brigade.[100] Jackson undoubtedly influenced the selection of Harman, an infantryman, as the commander of the new regiment.[101]

Jones' Brigade also included the 35th Battalion, Virginia Cavalry, known as White's Battalion after its aggressive commander, Elijah V. "Lige" White. Lige White was originally from Montgomery County, Maryland. In 1855, after completing his education in New York and Ohio at the age of twenty-three, White had gone to the Midwest and fought with proslavery Missourians against abolitionists in Kansas. In 1856, he returned East and took up farming in Loudoun County, Virginia. White joined a volunteer company from Loudoun, saw service in the aftermath of John Brown's raid, and fought as an *aide* to Colonel Eppa Hunton at Ball's Bluff early in the war. In recognition of his valuable service, White was commissioned and authorized to raise a cavalry company.[102]

White's Rebels, as the resulting company was called, was formed in December 1861 and mustered into service in January 1862. The company was initially designated for border warfare service, an undefined phrase.[103] By the fall of 1862 the company had grown into a battalion and White was elected its lieutenant colonel.[104] Because of its unusual designation, some of White's men felt themselves to be more partisan rangers than regular cavalry troopers, and indiscipline was an occasional problem. In January 1863, when the battalion was assigned to Jones' brigade, the men came close to mutiny. Although the bulk of the battalion had served for the past four months in the Valley and on the raid into West Virginia, men were frequently sent back into Loudoun County on scouts and other details, which helped bolster morale.[105]

The 11th Virginia had been formed in February 1863 by combining a battalion of seven companies from Ashby's Cavalry with three independent companies. Lunsford Lomax was ordered east from the Army of East Tennessee to command the newly formed regiment. Lomax, the son of a regular army officer, had been born at Newport, Rhode Island, but spent much of his childhood in Virginia before entering West Point with the class of 1856. Commissioned in the cavalry, Lomax served in Kansas and Nebraska before resigning in April 1861 to offer his services to the South. Thus far in the war he had seen only staff duty, including service under Joseph Johnston and Earl Van Dorn.[106] The lieutenant colonel of the regiment was forty-six-year-old doctor and farmer Oliver R. Funsten, Sr. An enormous man, Funsten was affectionately called "Our big colonel" by the men of the regiment. Funsten had commanded the battalion that formed the nucleus of the 12th Virginia. Funsten and most of his officers believed that he — and not Lomax — was entitled to the colonelcy of the regiment. Funsten submitted his resignation to protest the appointment of Lomax, but it was not accepted by the War Department.[107]

As Brigadier General Albert Jenkins' brigade moved down the Valley in preparation for the upcoming campaign into Pennsylvania, the 11th Virginia was freed from its duties near Strasburg. On June 3, Lomax crossed the Blue Ridge and two days later joined the rest of the cavalry in Culpeper. On June 7, Colonel Williams Wickham's 4th Virginia was relieved of picket duty near Fredericksburg and began the one-day march to Culpeper the following morning.[108] On the afternoon of June 8, 1863, the largest concentration of Confederate cavalry — nineteen regiments plus White's Battalion — was complete. For the most part, Stuart's cavalry was composed of veteran regiments led by veteran commanders. While the winter had been difficult, the officers and men looked forward to the summer's campaigning with confidence.

4

Pretty Well Used Up

Cavalry Corps Reorganization, May 1863

Even as the battle at Chancellorsville was being fought, it became apparent to Joseph Hooker that neither the creation of a cavalry corps nor his exhortation for it to "fight, fight, fight" had produced an organization that could whip JEB Stuart's horsemen. More work was needed. Historically, senior military commanders have little toleration for subordinates who are unsuccessful in battle. Consequently, those subordinates who are not captured or killed in a losing effort, are frequently relieved from command. It is not surprising, then, that Hooker decided a change in leadership in the army's cavalry corps was an immediate necessity.

The first senior officer removed from command was Brigadier General William Averell. With more than two thousand men on the field at Kelly's Ford in March, Averell had been outfought by eight hundred Rebels under Fitz Lee. In May, Averell and his division had comprised one wing of Stoneman's raiding force, and had again crossed the Rappahannock at Kelly's Ford. This time, Averell advanced into Culpeper County almost without opposition. Nonetheless, he soon became convinced, incorrectly, that he faced significant opposition. Inexplicably, Averell halted for two days on the north bank of the Rapidan River.[1] Frustrated with Averell's lack of activity, Hooker ordered him to rejoin the army, thinking that the brigadier and his division might be put to better use supporting the Army of the Potomac's infantry, at the time decisively engaged in the woods and thickets about Chancellorsville. Averell continued to dither in southern Culpeper County until a second summons from Hooker prompted him to move.

The dilatory general and his troopers arrived at Ely's Ford on the evening of May 2 and promptly set up camp. Apparently believing that no Rebels were near, the Union troopers built fires and relaxed. Unbeknownst to them, JEB Stuart with a body of cavalry and infantry, positioned to guard Stonewall Jackson's flank, had Averell's camp under close observation. The Rebels fired three volleys into the camp and withdrew. Averell's troopers panicked. The commander of the 16th Pennsylvania fled for cover behind a nearby outbuilding, exhorting his regiment to "rally on the barn," behavior for which he was later ridiculed by his men.[2]

In five days of campaigning, Averell had lost one officer and two men killed, plus a handful of officers and men wounded — a casualty rate that was indicative, at least in Hooker's opinion, of a lack of aggressiveness.[3] Hooker was displeased, and on May 3 he ordered Averell relieved of command.[4] Averell's excuse for inaction — that he had received conflicting instructions from Stoneman, his immediate commander, and Hooker — did not wash with the Army commander. A week later, Hooker wrote to the Adjutant General in Washington, where Averell had been sent for reassignment, explaining the basis for his decision:

> It is no excuse or justification that he received instructions from General Stoneman in conflict with my own, and it was his duty to know that neither of them afforded an excuse for his culpable indifference and inactivity. If he disregarded all instructions, it was his duty to do something. If the enemy did not come to him, he should have gone to the enemy.
>
> It is unnecessary for me to add that this army will never be able to accomplish its mission under commanders who not only disregard their instructions, but at the same time display so little zeal and devotion in the performance of their duties. I could excuse General Averell in his disobedience if I could anywhere discover in his operations a desire to find and engage the enemy. I have no disposition to prefer charges against him, and in detaching him from this army my object has been to prevent an active and powerful column from being paralyzed in its future operations by his presence.[5]

Hooker next turned his attention to Major General George Stoneman, who was falling into disfavor even before he returned through Union lines after his raid. On May 7, Secretary of War Edwin Stanton sent Hooker a message advising him that the Richmond newspapers were "full of accounts of the panic and destruction accomplished by Stoneman."[6] Hooker, when he responded to Stanton three days later, advised that rail communications between Fredericksburg and Richmond were disrupted by Stoneman for only one day, that important bridges were "untouched" by the Union cavalry, and that except for Kilpatrick, who with part of his brigade had reached the outskirts of Richmond and then passed through Union lines to safety at Gloucester Point, the raid "did not appear to have amounted to much." Ominously, Hooker added that "my instructions appear to have been entirely disregarded by General Stoneman. I shall know the particulars soon."[7]

On May 8, Stoneman with his weary troopers, began to cross the Rappahannock and reenter Union-held territory near Rappahannock Station. If Stoneman were expecting a hero's welcome, he was mistaken. That day, Hooker's Chief of Staff, Major General Daniel Butterfield, sent the Cavalry Corps commander a message with wording that reflected Hooker's souring opinion. Responding to an earlier message in which Stoneman expressed concern that he might be attacked while south of the Rappahannock in Culpeper County, Butterfield wrote: "It is not clear to the general [Hooker] how any force of the enemy can reach you, having to cross the Rapidan when you cannot cross the Rappahannock. He thinks you need have no apprehension on that source. The major-general commanding desires to know, in reference to your remark—'Should these supplies not reach you, you would not be responsible for the consequences'—who you would consider responsible?"[8] Butterfield concluded his message by informing Stoneman that Averell had been relieved and sent to Washington.

On May 12, Butterfield further advised Stoneman that "The major-general commanding desires a full report of your operations—a prompt report of the condition of your command; its location and position, with all detachments; the number fit for duty; a copy of any and all orders issued to Brigadier-General Averell from yourself subsequent to his crossing the river at Kelly's Ford; the number and position of troops assigned to the duty of guarding the railroad from Rappahannock Station to Cedar Run." Additionally, Butterfield directed that Stoneman put his force in readiness for action, and asked what part of the Cavalry Corps was ready for immediate field duty.[9]

The following day, Stoneman replied to Butterfield. He informed the Chief of Staff that he had begun preparing his report on the raid, that "the horses were pretty well used up and the men pretty tired," and that he had forwarded separately the number of troops assigned to guard the railroad. Stoneman added that he would provide a full report on the readiness of his command after conducting inspections.¹⁰ On the same day, apparently before receiving Stoneman's message, Butterfield asked a second time for the report Hooker had requested. As before, Butterfield's message revealed that Hooker was not pleased. "The commanding general desires to know what steps have been taken by you to comply with the order in regard to the railroad from Rappahannock to Cedar Run. The bearer [of this message] will await your reply, which you will please communicate in writing. The commanding general directs me to remind you that no reply has been received to any of the inquiries in my communication of yesterday."¹¹

On May 15, Butterfield again wrote to Stoneman, again asking him what portion of the Cavalry Corps was ready for duty.

> The following extract of my letter of May 12 is furnished:
>
> He [Hooker] desires to know what force of those brought back with you can add to this number for immediate duty in the field. He is anxious that General Buford's brigade of Regulars should be of this number.
>
> The Commanding General does not understand why this has not yet been complied with.¹²

Brigadier General John Buford, a Kentuckian by birth, was considered by many officers to be the most capable cavalry commander in the Army of the Potomac. Buford, eight days junior in grade to Pleasonton, succeeded Pleasonton in command of the 1st Cavalry Division (Library of Congress).

Stoneman replied that same day, reminding Butterfield that he had promised a report after making inspections—which was probably not what Hooker wanted to hear—and estimated that he could field a mounted force of about two thousand men.¹³

Stoneman apparently discerned from Butterfield's messages that he had fallen out of favor with Hooker. On May 20, severely afflicted by his hemorrhoids and likely perceiving that he was being made the scapegoat for the fiasco at Chancellorsville, Stoneman requested a leave of absence. The leave was promptly approved by Hooker who, in keeping with convention of the time, selected his most senior brigadier, Alfred Pleasonton, to take command of the Cavalry Corps. Shortly after departing, Stoneman was officially relieved from his command and ordered to Washington for further assignment.¹⁴

Pleasonton's appointment to command of the Cavalry Corps was not met with much acclaim among either the officers or the men. In a letter to his wife on May 17, Elias Beck, Mexican War veteran and surgeon of the 3rd Indiana Cavalry, wrote, "Poor little pusilaneous Pleasonton wants to Command the Army Corps—to have Stonemans place—& he is about as fit for it as any 2d Lieutenant in the Command."¹⁵ Captain Charles Francis Adams, Jr., descendent of presidents and a company commander in the 1st Massachusetts, described his feelings regarding the change in commanders in greater length. In a letter to his mother, Adams wrote:

> Now Pleasonton is the *bête noire* of all cavalry officers. Stoneman we believe in. We believe in his judgment, his courage and determination. We know he is ready to shoulder responsibility, that he will take good care of us and won't get us into places from which he can't get us out. Pleasonton also we have served under. He is pure and simple a newspaper humbug. You always see his name in the papers, but to us who have served under him and seen him under fire he is notorious as a bully and toady. He does nothing save with a view to a newspaper paragraph. At Antietam he sent his cavalry into a hell of artillery fire and himself got behind a bank and read a newspaper, and there, when we came back, we all saw him and laughed among ourselves. Yet mean and contemptible as Pleasonton is, he is always *in* at Headquarters and now they do say that Hooker wishes to depose Stoneman and hand the command over to Pleasonton. You may imagine our sensations in prospect of the change.[16]

Bête noire or not, Pleasonton wasted no time in making an assessment of his new command and providing a report on its status to Hooker. Pleasonton pointed out that the strength of the cavalry corps—about 12,000 men and horses in March—had dropped to about a third of that strength, and that, overall, the corps was not fit to take the field. Pleasonton closed by absolving himself of any responsibility for the condition of his command, superfluously advising Hooker: "In taking this command, I cannot do myself such an injustice as to remain silent as to the unsatisfactory condition in which I find this corps. I shall use every exertion to bring it to a state of efficiency at the earliest possible moment, but the responsibility of its present state, it is proper that the major-general commanding should know, does not belong to me."[17] Hooker did not ask Pleasonton whom he would consider responsible, having already determined that it was Stoneman who had been at fault. Hooker, who at the time was trying to obtain a large number of remounts from the Quartermaster Bureau in Washington, forwarded Pleasonton's report to General Halleck, the army's General in Chief.[18]

Averell's relief and the elevation of Pleasonton to replace Stoneman created vacancies in two of the Cavalry Corps' divisional command billets. In an obvious move, Pleasonton transferred Buford, the next ranking brigadier, from command of the Reserve Brigade to command of the 1st Division, the largest division in the corps. Buford, a Kentuckian, had graduated from West Point in 1848, been commissioned in the dragoons, and spent his entire career in the West and on the Plains. At the outbreak of the war, he was a captain commanding a company in the 2nd Dragoons in Utah. Since moving east with his regiment, Buford had been a steady and reliable combat leader. He was promoted brigadier general of volunteers and appointed to command of a brigade in July 1862, and promptly afterwards been wounded at 2nd Manassas. When not in command of a brigade, Buford had served as the Chief of Cavalry for the Army of the Potomac, at the time a staff position.[19]

Colonel Benjamin Franklin "Grimes" Davis commanded Buford's First Brigade. Davis was an 1854 graduate of West Point and a classmate of JEB Stuart, had been commissioned in the infantry, and served in the Southwest and California with the dragoons. Davis also was a Southerner—born in Alabama and appointed to the military academy from Mississippi—and reportedly a cousin to Jefferson Davis. Nevertheless, upon secession of his home state, Grimes Davis remained loyal to the Union.[20]

The Federal government, unlike the Confederacy did not try to form brigades with regiments from a single state, a fact shown in the composition of Davis' brigade, which included regiments from four states.

Davis' brigade, as was common, included his own volunteer regiment, the 8th New York Cavalry. That regiment had been raised by its first colonel, Samuel Crooks in western New York beginning in the summer of 1861. The troops were mustered into the service in Rochester in late November 1861, and promptly departed for Washington.[21] Conditions in the regiment's camp in the nation's capital were poor, and many men reportedly died of "black measles" and fever. Another problem facing the regiment was indecision within the War Department. At the time, officials believed that the army had sufficient cavalry. Consequently they did not issue horses to the fledgling troopers. Instead the men were issued Hall's carbines and drilled as infantry. Crooks, not a particularly competent officer, resigned in February 1862 and the governor of New York offered command of the regiment to Alfred Gibbs, a captain in the regular army.[22] However, on July 8, 1861 Texas irregulars had captured Gibbs while he was serving with the dragoons in New Mexico. Although he was paroled, Gibbs was not exchanged until August 27, 1862. Perhaps because of that encumbrance on his duty, Gibbs declined the governor's offer to command the 8th New York.[23] In the spring of 1862, the 8th New York, still dismounted and led by its lieutenant colonel, Charles Babbitt, deployed to the Shenandoah Valley and fought as infantry under Nathaniel Banks against Jackson, a highly demoralizing experience for the men.[24]

In the summer of 1862, things began to improve for the regiment. Grimes Davis was appointed its commander in June and immediately tightened up discipline. In July, the regiment was finally issued its horses, and on August 29, the unit conducted its first regimental mounted drill. Immediately afterwards, the 8th New York moved to Harpers Ferry. Two weeks later, Davis distinguished himself by refusing to surrender his men to Stonewall Jackson with the rest of the Union garrison. Instead, on the night of September 14, Davis led his regiment, along with the 12th Illinois Cavalry and part of the 1st Maryland Cavalry, across the Potomac River on a pontoon bridge. The column made its way through Confederate lines to safety, capturing some supply wagons en route.[25] In the spring of 1863, Davis was elevated to brigade command and the 8th New York was placed under the temporary command of Major Edmund Pope, a twenty-six-year-old lumberman and real estate agent from Monroe County, New York.[26]

The 8th Illinois Cavalry was raised in the summer of 1861 by John Franklin Farnsworth, a lawyer and former two-term member of Congress.[27] When the regiment mustered into service at St. Charles, the ladies of the community presented the regiment its first flag, which they had made. As the color bearer ceremoniously unfurled the flag before the assembled men, a stiff breeze tore it to shreds. After that inauspicious beginning, the regiment moved to Washington with troops and horses on separate trains. En route the regiment suffered its first "casualty" when private James Macklin had his big toe crushed between the couplings of two cars. Amputation was required.[28] The regiment spent the winter drilling at its camps in Washington and Virginia before taking the field with the Army of the Potomac in March 1862. In November 1862, Farnsworth was promoted to brigadier general, a rank he held until March 1863 when he resigned to retake his seat in Congress. After Farnsworth's promotion, the regiment's lieutenant colonel, William Gamble, who had been severely wounded at Malvern Hill, was promoted to colonel. In January 1863, Gamble was appointed to brigade command. In May 1863, without more senior officers, Major Alpheus Clark, newly promoted from captain, commanded the regiment.[29]

The 3rd Indiana Cavalry was recruited from the southeastern part of that state in the summer of 1861. Shortly after mustering at Madison, the regiment, then consisting of eight companies, was issued its horses, and companies A through F were ordered east under the command of Colonel Scott Carter, a local lawyer.[30] The truncated regiment traveled up the

Ohio River by boat to Wheeling, Virginia (today West Virginia), and marched overland from there to Pittsburgh. While the men had been issued their horses before their departure, bridles and saddles had not been supplied. Consequently, the men traveled on foot, leading their mounts. Reportedly, some more enterprising troopers improvised saddles out of cloth sacks and rope scrounged from farms along the way. From Pittsburgh, the regiment traveled by train to Washington, arriving in early September 1861.

Once in Washington the men finally received the tack for their horses and their weapons. Initially the men were armed with sabers and obsolete horse pistols, the latter eventually replaced with revolvers. Carbines were scarce and were initially issued to only a few men in each company. The War Department attached the regiment to Hooker's division in March 1862, and active campaigning began. In the spring of 1863, Lieutenant Colonel George H. Chapman, a publisher and lawyer with three years' experience as a naval midshipman, replaced Carter in command of the regiment. The regimental surgeon characterized Chapman as "a conceity little upstart" who, nonetheless, had managed the regiment well and would fight.[31] After returning from Stoneman's raid, Chapman left on furlough, leaving the regiment temporarily in the command of Major William S. McClure.[32]

McClure was a twenty-six-year-old merchant from Madison, Indiana. He had helped recruit Company E of the regiment was rewarded for his efforts by election as its first lieutenant. However, McClure was mustered into the service as its captain because the elected captain resigned. McClure had performed competently, and in October 1863 was promoted to major.[33]

The 9th New York Cavalry was recruited in upstate New York in the summer of 1861 and completing mustering into the service in early November.[34] The regiment then traveled to Washington, by steamer down the Hudson and then by train from South Amboy, New Jersey. Upon boarding the train, the troopers became disgruntled when they were loaded into cattle cars while their officers were accommodated in a passenger coach at the end of the train. As the train was pulling out of the station, a trooper decoupled the coach, leaving the officers behind. The men arrived in Philadelphia at 1:00 a.m. and had an unsupervised—but short—night on the town before the car with the officers arrived just after daylight. United again, the regiment went on to Washington.[35]

No horses were available to mount the regiment, and, further, the War Department felt that the army did not need more cavalry. Consequently, one battalion of the 9th was trained as artillery while two battalions were drilled as infantry. The regiment was deployed in those roles to the Peninsula in the spring of 1862. Naturally, this caused much dissatisfaction among the men, many of whom had enlisted because of the glamour of cavalry service. Finally, in late June 1862, the 9th New York received its horses and began drilling as a cavalry regiment, although initially some men had to ride bareback due to a shortage of saddles.[36]

The 9th New York's first commander was Colonel John Beardsley, an 1841 graduate of West Point. Beardsley was commissioned in the infantry and saw service against the Seminoles and in Mexico, where he was breveted for gallantry. In 1853 he resigned his commission and took up farming in New York, his home state. In November 1861, the governor appointed Beardsley colonel of the regiment. Once the 9th New York was mounted, Beardsley was appointed to the command of a cavalry brigade, leaving the 9th New York under the supervision of its lieutenant colonel, William Sackett. Beardsley proved an ineffective leader, and additionally, charges of disloyalty, intoxication, and abandoning his regiment in the face of the enemy were preferred against him. In March 1863, Beardsley submitted his resignation, which was quickly endorsed by both Pleasonton, who was the division commander, and Stoneman.[37]

Sackett commanded the 9th New York through Stoneman's raid, which had been particularly hard on the regiment's horses. After returning from the raid, only five companies could be mounted.[38]

Rounding out Davis' brigade was a squadron consisting of companies A and C of the 3rd West Virginia Cavalry. Most of the troopers in the 3rd West Virginia enlisted with the understanding that they would only be required to serve for local defense near their homes. Consequently, nine companies from that regiment were dispersed across West Virginia. One company of the regiment was posted near Winchester to support Major General Robert Milroy, and two companies were assigned to the Cavalry Corps. The regimental commander, author and artist Colonel David Strother, remained in West Virginia. The squadron with the Cavalry Corps was commanded by Captain Seymour Conger, the commander of Company C.[39]

Buford's 2nd Brigade was commanded by Colonel Thomas Casimer Devin. Devin, born in New York in 1822, was older than most of his contemporaries, and, unlike many senior officers, he had not attended West Point and had no prewar experience in the Regular Army. Instead, Devin had worked as a house-painter while serving extensively in the New York Militia, rising to the rank of lieutenant colonel. Mustered into service as a captain in the 1st New York Cavalry in July 1861, Devin was appointed colonel of the 6th New York Cavalry four months later. Although not dashing, Devin was steady and well respected by both his men and his peers.[40] With the detachment of the 8th Pennsylvania to picket duty in King George County, Devin was left with only two regiments in his brigade — his own regiment, the 6th New York, and the 17th Pennsylvania.

The 6th New York, also known as the 2nd Ira Harris Guard, was organized in the fall of 1861, and while completing its mustering, conducted its initial training at Camp Scott

This sergeant of the 6th New York Cavalry is showing off his horse, a well groomed mount in good flesh. The long shank on the horse's bit helped a rider control his horse, even when holding the reins in one hand. The style of the sergeant's hat indicates that this photograph may have been taken later in the war (History of the Sixth New York Cavalry).

Major Charles Jarvis Whiting (seated at left), who graduated from West Point in 1835, was one of the oldest officers in the Cavalry Corps. Whiting succeeded Buford in command of the Reserve Brigade. In November 1863, Whiting was dismissed from the army for making disrespectful comments about President Lincoln. Standing is Captain James Harrison, a former marine revenue officer who commanded the 5th US Cavalry (Library of Congress).

on Staten Island.[41] Conditions in the camp were deplorable, resulting in a high rate of sickness and much dissatisfaction among the men. On December 6, 1861, the men rioted and burned down the camp's cookhouse in protest over being served rotten fish. Devin quickly quelled the rebellion by brandishing his pistol and chiding the angry protesters that now with no cookhouse, they would have to eat outdoors.[42]

On December 23 and 24, 1861 the regiment moved to a camp near York, Pennsylvania, for additional training, all of which was dismounted since no horses had been issued. The men celebrated New Year's, 1862 at York in style. Each company was issued a keg of beer, which undoubtedly raised the men's spirits, at least temporarily. In early March 1862 the regiment moved to camp in Perryville, Maryland, where four companies were mounted and sent to the Peninsula to serve with the Army of the Potomac. The remaining eight companies were transferred from Perryville to Washington. On July 1, 1862 as the regiment began to draw the remainder of its horses, a near-disaster occurred. A detail of 72 men was sent to draw 216 horses from the quartermaster. However, the horses were spooked by a passing train and stampeded, injuring many men and horses. Despite that setback, the 6th New York conducted its first mounted regimental drill on July 11, and two weeks later moved to Fairfax Courthouse to begin operations as a cavalry organization.[43]

After the battle at Fredericksburg, Devin had been given command of a brigade, leaving the regiment under the command of its lieutenant colonel, Duncan McVicar. During the early fighting at Chancellorsville, the regiment got into a sharp engagement with Fitz Lee's brigade in a field belonging to Hugh Alsop, a local farmer. During the engagement, the regiment was overwhelmed, losing about fifty officers and men killed, wounded, and missing. Among the dead was McVicar, leaving the 6th New York under the command of Major William E. Beardsley.[44]

The 17th Pennsylvania was organized at Harrisburg, Pennsylvania between September and November 1862.[45] Josiah Kellogg, a Pennsylvanian and 1860 West Point graduate, was selected to command the regiment. Before the war, Kellogg had served briefly with the 1st Dragoons in California, and then as adjutant of that regiment in Virginia.[46] As commander of the 17th Pennsylvania, Kellogg established a reputation as a demanding drill master. Unlike some cavalry regiments, the 17th Pennsylvania was quickly issued its horses, many of which had not been broken. Consequently, the men's early equestrian training was characterized by "rearing and kicking, running and jumping, lying down and falling down, men thrown by their horses, kicked and getting hurt in various ways." At the end of November, the regiment moved by train to Washington. Like the 9th New York, the men rode in box cars without seats or bunks while the officers were provided passenger coaches, and although those arrangements raised the hackles of some of the new soldiers, the trip was completed without incident. The 17th Pennsylvania's stay in the capital was brief. In December the regiment joined the Cavalry Corps at its camps in Stafford County, Virginia.[47]

With Buford's elevation to division command, Major Charles Jarvis Whiting, the senior officer serving in the Reserve Brigade, was appointed to its command. Whiting, born in Massachusetts and raised in Maine, was one of the oldest officers in the Cavalry Corps. He had graduated from West Point, standing second in the Class of 1835. Commissioned in the artillery, Whiting briefly served against the Seminoles in Florida. However, military life did not suit Whiting, at least initially. In May 1836 he resigned to take up surveying for a railroad in the Florida Panhandle.[48] Afterward, Whiting returned to Maine where he founded and was the headmaster of the Military and Classical Academy in Ellsworth. For a time, a later-famous youth named Joshua Chamberlain studied under Whiting.[49] After six years as a teacher, Whiting headed west to survey the boundary between the United States and Mexico established by the Treaty of Guadalupe-Hidalgo.[50]

After completing the boundary survey, Whiting remained in the West as the Surveyor-General of California. While in that position, the state legislature asked him to provide a plan for ridding the state of grasshoppers that frequently plagued its agricultural industry. Perhaps in jest, Whiting proposed that California buy and import turkeys from the East. The turkeys would eat the grasshoppers, and then—fattened-up by feasting on the grasshoppers—could be sold at a profit. Whiting appended charts with his proposal detailing the number of turkeys required and the associated costs. As expected, the legislature did not adopt Whiting's solution.[51]

When the army expanded in 1855, Whiting sought and received a commission as captain in the 2nd Cavalry. Since then, he served with the regiment almost continuously, and for much of the war had been its commanding officer, developing a reputation for railing against various politicians whom, he believed, were responsible for the war. Whiting had led the regiment in a disastrous charge at Gaines' Mill in June 1862. During the charge, Whiting's horse was killed and he was left on the battlefield and captured. Whiting spent two months in prison in Richmond before being exchanged.[52]

The Reserve Brigade consisted of four regular regiments of cavalry—the 1st, 2nd, 5th and 6th—and one regiment of volunteers, the 6th Pennsylvania. The army organized the

1st U.S. Cavalry in 1833 as the 1st Regiment of Dragoons. When the army was reorganized in August 1861, the regimental designation was changed to the 1st U.S. Cavalry. Similarly, the 2nd Dragoons, organized in 1836, became the 2nd Cavalry in 1861. The 5th U.S. Cavalry was organized in 1855 as the 2nd U.S. Cavalry and renumbered in the reorganization of 1861. In 1861 Congress authorized the army to raise the 6th U.S. Cavalry, and men for the regiment were recruited from around Pittsburgh in September of that year.[53]

The 1st, 2nd, and 5th Cavalry Regiments had seen extensive service in the west before the war. Following secession, they lost many of their Southern officers, who chose to resign and serve their states rather than the Federal government. Most of the enlisted men, however, had remained in the ranks, and competent sergeants had been promoted to fill commissioned vacancies.[54] However, because volunteer units provided greater opportunity for promotion, regular regiments experienced great difficulty retaining qualified officers. This was evident in the Reserve Brigade where captains commanded all of its regular regiments.

At the beginning of the war, the 1st Cavalry was stationed on the Pacific Coast and in New Mexico. Leaving D and G Companies in New Mexico, the regiment moved to the East, arriving in Washington in January 1862.[55] In the Peninsular Campaign the regiment had been commanded by its Lieutenant Colonel, William Grier, who had been a classmate with Whiting at West Point.[56] Grier was wounded at Williamsburg and replaced by Captain Richard S. C. Lord.

Lord, who graduated from West Point in 1856, had been in command of Company D of the 1st Cavalry during the battle at Valverde, New Mexico, in February 1862. The Union commander at Valverde, Colonel Edward Canby, questioned Lord's performance during the fight, asserting that a counterattack led by Lord had not been pressed aggressively, and that had contributed to the Union defeat on the banks of the Rio Grande. However, the subsequent board of inquiry exonerated Lord. Companies D and G were disbanded in the West, freeing Lord to travel east and rejoined the regiment. In January 1863, Lord was appointed regimental commander.[57]

The ranking officer in the 2nd U.S. Cavalry after Major Whiting, Captain Charles Norris, had been sent in November 1862 on extended detached service as a mustering and disbursing officer, first to Annapolis, and then to Indianapolis.[58] Captain Wesley Merritt, an officer who, although untested in battle, had exhibited much talent, was placed in the command billet vacated by Whiting.

Merritt, who graduated in the middle of the 1860 class at West Point, had served as a lieutenant in Buford's company of the 2nd Cavalry (then the 2nd Dragoons) in Utah. Upon the secession of the Southern states, Merritt marched east with his regiment, but thus far in the war he had done no actual fighting. Instead, Merritt had first served almost exclusively as an *aide de camp,* first to Phillip St. George Cooke and then to General Stoneman.[59] During Stoneman's raid, Merritt had been placed in charge of a small detachment and sent to destroy bridges along the South Anna River. That mission was Merritt's only leadership experience in a combat environment, although he and his men did not engage any Confederates.[60] After Stoneman left the Cavalry Corps for Washington, Merritt served for about two weeks on Pleasonton's staff. Merritt apparently impressed his new commanding general, since Pleasonton approved the young officer's transfer to command the regiment.[61]

The 6th Cavalry (originally to be designated the 3rd Cavalry) began recruiting men around Pittsburgh in May 1861. Two-thirds of the officers of the regiment were selected from among the officers of other regiments or from civilian life, and one-third were former sergeants in regular regiments. David Hunter, a major serving as paymaster at Fort Leavenworth, was initially appointed to command the regiment, but he arranged a promotion for himself to major general of volunteers with appointment to departmental command.[62] The regiment's lieutenant colonel, William H. Emory, was promoted to fill the vacancy created when Hunter declined the position. In September, Emory took the regiment—less Company L, which did not join until the following July—to Bladensburg, Maryland where the men were issued horses and weapons. Efforts were made to ensure that the horses were distributed fairly. Sergeants chose their mounts first in order of their rank. Each remaining horse was given a number, the privates drew numbers from a hat, and each man was assigned the horse corresponding to the number he drew. This horse "lottery" was a source of much amusement. Troopers who drew well jeered those less fortunate who drew the brutes of the lot.[63]

Shortly after the horses were issued, the regiment moved to camp in Washington, where began, in the words of one private, a "season of diversion" as the men and their horses began mounted drill. Like many Union cavalry organizations, the 6th U.S. had mostly inexperienced riders and its share of green horses. During drill, kicks, falls, and runaway horses were common. The troopers of the 6th, like those in all cavalry regiments, both Union and Confederate, had the most trouble executing wheeling movements. Trooper Sidney Davis recalled that "unless remarkably great care was taken, the men on the marching flank would move too fast or the men in the center would move too slow—both productive of the same results—and the inevitable consequence was the curving of the line instead of being kept 'well-dressed up' ... and when the wheel was completed the company or squadron would be crescent shaped, with the two wings projecting far beyond the center."[64]

Also, while in Washington, the men had difficulty obtaining uniforms. On November 27, Colonel Emory sent a memorandum to the Quartermaster General complaining of a shortage of pantaloons, reporting that "the men are suffering for [want of] these garments very much."[65]

In March 1862, Emory was appointed brigadier general of volunteers and left the regiment to take command of an infantry brigade.[66] The regiment took the field in Northern Virginia, then deployed to the Peninsula under the command of Major Lawrence Williams. Williams, a native of Washington, D.C., was related to Robert E. Lee and had been raised at Arlington. He was an 1852 graduate of West Point and had been serving as a captain in the 10th Infantry before being appointed major of the 6th Cavalry when that regiment was formed in 1861. While on the Peninsula, Williams was apprehended outside the Union picket lines after dark, placed under arrest, and accused of attempting to communicate with the enemy. Williams had been innocently, and naively, visiting Mary Lee, the wife of Robert E. Lee, who at the time was staying at White House on the Pamunkey, Rooney Lee's estate. Williams protested his treatment and was quickly released from arrest, but at the conclusion of the campaign he was transferred to New York. Once there, Williams went absent without leave for five months, resulting in his dismissal from the service.[67]

The next commander of the 6th U.S. was Captain William P. Sanders, who led the regiment through the Maryland campaign, then departed in February 1863 for duty as the colonel of the 5th Kentucky Cavalry.[68] Upon Sander's departure, Captain George C. Cram, took command. Cram was not a particularly popular officer, at least among the men in the ranks. He was described as a "curious, capricious man, seeming to be most delighted when the men most feared him." The men reciprocated, verbalizing their attitude toward their commander with the epithet "Damn Cram!"[69]

The 5th Cavalry, formerly the 2nd Cavalry, was a regiment with an illustrious pedigree. When the regiment was formed in 1855, its initial draft of officers from the Regular Army included Albert Sidney Johnston, Robert E. Lee, Earl Van Dorn, Kirby Smith, William

Hardee, John Bell Hood, George Thomas, and George Stoneman. After its activation, the regiment saw continuous service in the Southwest. With the secession of Texas in March 1861, the regiment moved to the East, leaving behind many of its horses, which, along with other public property, the regiment turned over to state authorities by order of the Departmental Commander, Brigadier General David Twigg, a successionist supporter.[70]

The regiment saw limited action at First Manassas, but was employed extensively during the Peninsular Campaign. Late in the day at Gaines' Mill, Brigadier General Phillip St. George Cooke, then commanding Union cavalry, ordered the regiment, then commanded by Charles Whiting, to charge Brigadier General George Pickett's advancing brigade. Cooke was at the time concerned that Pickett's men were about to overrun Major General Fitz John Porter's artillery—guns that had thus far kept Robert E. Lee's army at bay. Dutifully, Captain Whiting led his men across 300 yards of open ground and into the massed musket fire of Pickett's Virginians. The results of the charge were disastrous. Of the 250 cavalrymen engaged, the regiment suffered 58 casualties for no appreciable gain. Cooke was faulted for his decision to order the attack and shortly afterward he asked to be relieved from field command.

When Whiting was elevated to command of the Reserve Brigade, the ranking captain in the regiment, James E. Harrison, assumed command. Harrison, from Alexandria, Virginia began his public service as an officer on a revenue cutter, and in short order established himself as gallant and industrious leader. The citizens of Charleston presented him a silver goblet for attempting to rescue the crew of the revenue cutter *Hamilton* after that ship foundered in December 1853. While serving on the Pacific Coast in 1855, Harrison, as a volunteer, accompanied an expedition of the 4th Infantry against a local Indian tribe. During a fight with the Indians, the officer commanding the force was killed. Harrison took charge of the surviving fifty-one men and led their withdrawal to Fort Steilacoom. In reward for his gallantry, Harrison received a commission in the 2nd Cavalry where he continued to serve with distinction both before and during the war. Although efforts had been made to induce him to join the Confederate service, Harrison remained firmly loyal to the Union.[71]

The Reserve Brigade's volunteer regiment, the 6th Pennsylvania Cavalry, was one of the most colorful cavalry units in the Army of the Potomac. The regiment was better known as Rush's Lancers in honor of its first commander and in recognition of its distinctive arms.

The regiment, originally known as the First Philadelphia Light Cavalry, had been raised in later summer 1861. Many of the regiment's recruits were drawn from that city's upper classes, causing one trooper to characterize the regiment's officers as "Beardless Boys" belonging to Philadelphia's "Ginger Bread Aristocracy."[72] The regiment was raised by it's first commander, Richard Rush, the grandson of Benjamin Rush, a signer of the Declaration of Independence and confidant of John Adams. Rush was born in London while his father was serving there as United States Ambassador, graduated from West Point with the class of 1846, and fought in war with Mexico before resigning his commission as first lieutenant of artillery in 1854.[73]

At the suggestion of General George B. McClellan, also an 1846 Academy graduate, the 6th's troopers were armed with nine-foot lances capped with bright red pennants.[74] McClellan and other senior officers may have been impressed with the Napoleonic flavor imparted by the lances, and probably thought that the distinctive weapons would add a certain *elan* to the regiment. The troopers, on the other hand, considered the pig-stickers a nuisance. Even worse, the lances made the men of the 6th Pennsylvania the laughingstock of the army. Not surprisingly, lances proved totally unsuitable for combat in Virginia in the 1860s. Consequently, the men of the 6th Pennsylvania usually found themselves detailed to various headquarters as couriers and escorts.[75]

In the spring of 1863, the regiment underwent two major changes. On April 27, Colonel Rush, who had been in poor health for some time and on frequent sick-leave, was appointed Chief of the Invalid Corps—a desk-job in Washington. Rush, never a particularly popular leader, was replaced by Major Robert Morris, Jr. (the regiment's lieutenant colonel, C. Ross Smith, was on detached duty as Provost Marshal at Cavalry Corps Headquarters). Morris, the great-grandson of Robert Morris, a signer of the Declaration of Independence and "financier" of the American Revolution, had completed a three-month enlistment in the infantry before accepting a commission as second major in the 6th Pennsylvania. Morris, who had been wounded at Malvern Hill in June 1862, commanded the regiment on Stoneman's raid, although the Lancers did not see much action during that operation. Perhaps of greater significance than Rush's departure, on May 24 the troopers exchanged their lances for Sharps carbines.[76] No regrets were recorded regarding either the change in command or the change in weaponry.

David McMurtrie Gregg's 3rd Division was least affected by the changes in the Cavalry Corps. However, his division had seen the hardest recent service, having participated fully in Stoneman' raid. Consequently, his regiments were in poor condition.

Gregg was an 1855 graduate of West Point. Commissioned in the dragoons, Gregg had extensive experience fighting Indians in the Washington Territory and was assigned as a captain to the 6th U.S. Cavalry when that regiment was raised in Pennsylvania in May 1861. Although he was absent due to illness from October 1861 until January 1862, Gregg was appointed colonel of 8th Pennsylvania on January 24, 1862. After leading his regiment on the Peninsula and throughout the Maryland Campaign, Gregg earned a promotion to brigadier general of volunteers in November 1862. Since then, Gregg had served as commander of a cavalry division.[77]

Colonel Judson Kilpatrick commanded Gregg's 1st Brigade. A small, spindly man, during Stoneman's raid Kilpatrick had enhanced his reputation as a fighter by sweeping to the gates of Richmond and then continuing on to Federal lines at Gloucester Point.[78] Kilpatrick's men, pleased with their performance, submitted a petition requesting Kilpatrick's promotion to brigadier general. The promotion was endorsed by Kilpatrick's superiors and was working its way through the War Department bureaucracy in Washington.

Kilpatrick had led a busy life in the two years since he graduated from West Point in May 1861. He was married on his graduation day and one month later was in combat at Big Bethel, where he became the first Regular officer wounded in action (somewhat embarrassingly, Kilpatrick was struck by shrapnel in his buttocks).[79] Detailed to recruiting duty, Kilpatrick raised troops from his home state of New Jersey for service in the regiment that became the 2nd New York Cavalry, the Harris Light. In the process, Kilpatrick secured himself an appointment as lieutenant colonel of volunteers in that regiment. In December 1862 Kilpatrick was promoted to colonel and given command of the Harris Light.[80]

As a field officer, Kilpatrick had shown himself to be an effective trainer and an aggressive raider. Like many other officers, Kilpatrick also displayed a zeal for self promotion, blatantly overstating his own role in events.[81] Of greater concern, however, was Kilpatrick's evident lack of military judgment. He was derisively called "Kill Cavalry" by many, initially because he drove his regiment's horses to exhaustion, but later because some believed he needlessly squandered the lives of his men.[82] Also of concern was Kilpatrick's moral corruption. He spent three months under arrest in Old Capitol Prison in Washington after being accused of accepting bribes and kickbacks from sutlers. Although acquitted by courts-martial, the evidence left little doubt that Kilpatrick had lined his pockets by both taking bribes and selling horses his men had seized from Southern civilians. Kilpatrick also had a well-earned reputation

Brigadier General David McMurtrie Gregg commanded the 3rd Cavalry Division. His cousin, Colonel John Irwin Gregg, commanded a brigade in the 2nd Cavalry Division (Library of Congress).

as a womanizer. During the winter of 1862–3, the camp of the Harris Light was rife with stories of Kilpatrick's sexual activities with his two "cooks" who loudly and publicly squabbled over his affections.[83]

Kilpatrick's brigade was made up of his own regiment, the Harris Light, along with the 10th New York Cavalry, and the 1st Maine Cavalry. Additionally, Kilpatrick's brigade included Captain William C. Orton's cavalry company, a volunteer unit from the District of Columbia.[84]

As mentioned, in the fall of 1861, the Regular Army set about raising a seventh regular cavalry regiment. However, even though the troops enlisted as regulars, Congress failed to appropriate the necessary funds. To solve the problem, the War Department passed the regiment to New York as a volunteer unit. The state designated the regiment the 2nd New York Cavalry, called the Harris Light, after New York's popular Senator, Ira Harris. The regiment, reflecting its Regular Army roots, included companies from New York, Connecticut, New Jersey, Pennsylvania, and Indiana.

The first commander of the Harris Light was Colonel J. Mansfield Davies. Kilpatrick was lieutenant colonel of the regiment, and Davies' nephew, Henry Eugene Davies, was its major. Also on the regimental rolls was a dapper Frenchman, Captain Alexander Napoleon Duffié. Duffié had served several years in the French army as a sergeant — and for two months as a lieutenant — before deserting and immigrating to the United States. Because of his military experience, Duffié took up the role of the Harris Light's drill master. Duffié, although skilled at drill, was better remembered as a reliable source of amusement because of his broken English and twisted syntax.[85]

In the fall of 1861 the regiment moved to Washington, was issued horses, and after a short stint of training, moved to Virginia to participate in the defense of the capital. In 1862 the regiment deployed to the Peninsula and afterwards participated in the campaigns of 2nd Manassas and Antietam, although it did not see much actual fighting. In December 1862, Colonel Davies resigned his commission and Judson Kilpatrick was appointed colonel of the regiment in his place. Since Kilpatrick was acting as a brigade commander, the Harris Light was commanded by Henry Davies, who was promoted to lieutenant colonel. Davies was a twenty-seven-year-old New York lawyer who before August 1861 had no military experience.[86]

Eight companies of the 10th New York were raised by the regiment's first colonel, fifty-five-year-old John C. Lemmon, in upstate New York during the fall of 1861 (the remaining four companies were not recruited until the fall of 1862). The under-sized regiment, known as the Porter Guard after Peter B. Porter, the Secretary of War in the administration of President John Quincy Adams, undertook its initial training in camp near Elmira, New York. In the interest of efficiency, the officers of the regiment hired a retired Prussian officer named Bernstein to instruct them in drill and tactics. However, Bernstein, pompous and overweight, was a complete failure at training Americans. During its stay in Elmira, many men were issued uniforms, but unfortunately, all the uniforms were the same size — large. One trooper observed that had the cloth been cut more judiciously, there would have been sufficient material to outfit the entire regiment. Nonetheless, the sight of diminutive troopers drilling in their immense coats provided great amusement.[87]

In December 1861, the under-sized regiment was sent to Gettysburg, Pennsylvania, arriving there on Christmas Day. The move cost the Porter Guard its first "casualty." On December 28, Private John Congdon, the tallest man in the regiment at six feet five inches, arrived in Gettysburg by train, having been detained in Elmira for a few days because of illness. As the train approached the town, Congdon leaned out from the platform of his car to wave to his friends. His head struck a timber trestle on the bridge over Rock Creek. The blow knocked Congdon off the car and into the icy water below. He was dead by the time assistance arrived. The following day the regiment buried Congdon with full military honors.[88]

During their ten-week stay in Gettysburg, the men continued to drill on foot since no horses had been issued. On a more practical level, the troops set to work building barracks so that they need not be quartered in private homes scattered throughout the town. In early March 1862, just as the barracks were completed, the War Department sent the regiment to Maryland to guard bridges and ferries along the Susquehanna River. However, the regiment's effectiveness as bridge guards would have been limited had fighting been necessary since the men were not issued pistols and carbines until mid–June. Finally, in August 1862 the eight-company regiment drew its horses and began preparing to fight as a cavalry unit.[89]

Colonel Lemmon, a merchant from Buffalo, apparently did not have much aptitude for cavalry command. Perhaps because of the infirmities of age, he also preferred riding in an ambulance to riding a horse, and in October 1862 was injured when his wagon overturned. Lemmon, who left the regiment to convalesce and await his discharge, was replaced by his lieutenant colonel, William Irvine, a lawyer who before the war had represented his New York district in the U.S. Congress.[90]

The 1st Maine Cavalry was raised in the fall of 1861, the eleventh volunteer regiment raised by that state (ten infantry regiments had already been sent to Washington). The notion of a cavalry regiment from the Bay State proved popular and the ranks were quickly filled. As one Maine-man remarked "it makes common men look dignified and imperious to sit on a horse."[91] Supposedly, the first enlistee was Jonathan P. Cilley, whose father was killed in a duel in 1838 while serving as a member of the U.S. Congress.[92] The regiment's first commander was Colonel John Godard, who resigned in March 1862 because his lumber business was suffering during his absence. The regiment's lieutenant colonel was Thomas Hight, an 1853 graduate of West Point who had been serving as a first lieutenant in the 2nd Cavalry before he accepted a volunteer commission from Maine's governor. Hight, who had been overseeing most of the men's training, became disgruntled when the governor passed over him to promote Major Samuel Allen as colonel of the regiment. Hight resigned his volunteer commission.[93]

The regiment was initially billeted at the state fairgrounds in Augusta where it drew its horses on November 8, 1861 (a very long day, since representatives of the Quartermaster Department and the regiment could not agree on whether there were 1035 or 1036 horses on-hand). The arrival of the horses displaced the men from the wooden stables where they had been bunking. The men's move from the stables into tents caused complaints that the animals, costing real money, were more valuable to the army than the soldiers who came free. Mounted drill began in December. Perhaps of all 259 Union volunteer cavalry regiments, the 1st Maine best exemplified the notion that Union cavalry consisted of men who, by background and experience, were ill-suited to mounted service. The regiment's Company K, made up mostly of seamen, had a particularly difficult time mastering its mounted drill. One officer, when asked why his men had not maintained their proper alignment during drill, explained that he had "missed stays," a nautical term.[94]

Over the winter, the 1st Maine remained in Augusta, while in Washington the War Department considered disbanding the unit so that the horses might be transferred to the artillery, whose batteries were in dire need of animals to draw the guns. After intense lobbying from state officials, the War Department abandoned that notion. In March 1862, the regiment moved by a series of train and steamer connections to Washington, was issued weapons, and almost immediately ordered to Harpers Ferry to join the army of Major General Nathaniel Banks. The regiment was commanded in the field by Major Calvin Douty, a former sheriff from Piscataquis County, as Colonel Allen was absent sick.[95] Under Douty, who was eventually promoted to Colonel after Allen resigned, the regiment participated in the battles at Cedar Mountain, 2nd Manassas, Antietam, and from that time with the Army of the Potomac at Fredericksburg and on Stoneman's raid. Douty was a solid performer, and for part of 1863 he had acted in brigade command.

Gregg's 2nd Brigade was commanded by Colonel Sir Percy Wyndham, the thirty-year-old son of an officer in the British Army who had been born aboard the ship *Arab* in the English Channel. Wyndham was a true soldier of fortune, as a teenager had fought in the French revolution of 1848, then served in the French marines, the British army, and the Austrian army. He distinguished himself fighting for Garibaldi in Sicily, and King Victor Emmanuel II had knighted him for his service there. Wyndham, who was colonel of the 1st New Jersey Cavalry, was distinctive both in his dress (thigh-high boots and plumed hat) and his facial hair (moustaches extending ten inches past his cheeks). Despite his foppery, Wyndham was efficient. He had shown himself to be an effective trainer and disciplinarian, and he had performed creditably fighting in the Shenandoah Valley against Jackson (where he was captured and briefly held before being exchanged) and at 2nd Manassas.[96]

Although clearly competent by Union standards, Wyndham was a foreigner and thus many of his contemporaries resented him. An officer in another regiment dismissed Wyndham as "an Englishman, an alleged lord. But lord or son of a lord, his capacity as a cavalry officer was not great. [But] He had been entrusted with one or two independent commands and was regarded as a dashing officer."[97] With perhaps greater accuracy, Wyndham was known as an officer who on occasion ruined the horses of his regiment while zealously attempting to accomplish the missions he had been assigned. Partially because of the recognition he had gained and the zeal with which he carried out his orders, capturing Wyndham, termed an "unprincipled scoundrel" by Stuart, had been the objective of partisan commander Major John S. Mosby's March 9, 1863 raid on Fairfax Courthouse.[98] However, the British officer, whose regiment had been temporarily detailed to the defense of the capital, had unexpectedly gone into Washington for the evening. Mosby had to content himself with capturing Brigadier General Edwin H. Stoughton instead. Supposedly, Mosby woke the soundly sleeping Stoughton by pulling down the bed sheets and slapping him on his bottom.[99]

Wyndham's brigade consisted of the 1st New Jersey, the 1st Maryland, the 1st Pennsylvania, and the 12th Illinois Cavalry Regiments.

The 1st New Jersey Cavalry was informally known as Halsted's Horse, after William Halsted, the regiment's first commander. After five decades as a lawyer and politician, the elderly Halsted decided to embark upon a military career by raising a cavalry regiment in his home state. Though highly motivated, Halsted quickly proved unsuitable as a cavalry officer. In his six-month career, Halsted was twice tried by courts-martial. He was first charged with arresting his executive officer without filing any charges. Afterward, he was charged with falsely claiming forage for his five personal horses. Halsted was acquitted in the first trial, but found guilty of improperly claiming feed worth fifty-eight dollars in the second. Shortly after his conviction, a board of officers determined that Halsted was unqualified to serve as a cavalry officer and accordingly he was dismissed from the service.[100]

In Halsted's place, the governor of New Jersey appointed Wyndham to command. Wyndham had proved effective and popular with the men of the regiment, despite the widespread bias against foreign officers. When he was elevated to brigade command, the command of the regiment devolved upon Lieutenant Colonel Virgil Broderick. Broderick, who had served with the 1st New Jersey since it was organized, was well respected. As one man noted of Broderick, "though frequently lacking as a camp commander, he was never found wanting on the field."[101]

The 1st Maryland Cavalry was organized between August 1861 and June 1862. Although the bulk of the regiment was raised in Maryland, two companies were from Pittsburgh and two were from Washington, D.C. Part of the regiment had seen action in the Valley against Jackson, and the regiment had participated in the battles at Cedar Mountain and 2nd Manassas under Pope. Two of the 1st Maryland's companies had been assigned to the garrison at Harpers Ferry, and had evaded capture with Colonel Grimes Davis in September 1862. In 1863 the regiment participated in Stoneman's raid. The regiment's first commander, Andrew Miller, a West Pointer from the class of 1842, resigned his commission in May 1862. His successor, Eugene Kielmansegge, resigned in May 1863. This left the 1st Maryland under the command of Lieutenant Colonel James M. Deems, a forty-five-year-old music instructor and composer from Baltimore.[102]

The 1st Pennsylvania Cavalry was formed at Harrisburg on September 1, 1861. Seven companies were sent to Washington, where in September, the governor of Pennsylvania fortuitously selected a young New Yorker, George D. Bayard, as the regiment's colonel. Bayard had graduated from West Point in 1856, taken a commission in the cavalry, and served in the west, where he was wounded in 1860. Bayard proved a most energetic and competent commander and quickly brought the 1st Pennsylvania to an adequate level of proficiency. He was perhaps aided by the fact that most members of the regiment were from rural areas and, in the opinion of one officer, "were good if not properly trained riders."[103]

By December 1861, when the regiment saw its first action at Dranesville, three more companies had been added to the rolls, with the remaining two companies following in January 1862. The 1st Pennsylvania then fought against Jackson in the Valley and as part of Pope's army during the summer of 1862. Late in the day on August 9, 1862 at Cedar Mountain, Nathaniel Banks ordered a battalion of the 1st Pennsylvania, the only portion of the regiment present on the field, to charge Major General A. P. Hill's division. One hundred sixty-four troopers drew sabers and galloped forward through a wheatfield as ranks of Georgian, Virginian, and North Carolinian infantrymen took them under fire at close range. The charge, in which ninety-two saddles were reportedly emptied, had no tactical benefit, but it earned the troopers of the 1st Pennsylvania a reputation for steadiness and valor.[104]

Because of his recognized competence, Bayard was quickly appointed to brigade command with promotion to brigadier general following in May 1862. Owen Jones, a Philadelphia lawyer who had served a term in the U.S. Congress followed Bayard in command of the 1st Pennsylvania. Jones quickly tired of military service and resigned his commission at the end

A deserter from the French Army, Alfred Napoleon Alexander Duffié commanded the 2nd Cavalry Division. Duffié, known for his poor — but humorous — English syntax, was nominated for promotion to brigadier general after the battle at Kelly's Ford (Library of Congress).

of January 1863. He was replaced by Colonel John P. Taylor.[105] As a youth, the thirty-five-year-old Taylor had tried to enlist during the Mexican War, but had been prevented from doing so by his parents. In 1859, he joined a newly-formed Pennsylvania militia company as a lieutenant, and when the 1st Pennsylvania was organized he received a captain's commission. Taylor had been promoted to lieutenant colonel of the regiment in September 1862.[106]

The 12th Illinois was organized in the fall of 1861 at Springfield and mustered into service with nine companies in February 1862.[107] In its first four months of existence, the regiment was detailed to guard Confederate prisoners of war in its home state. In the summer of 1862, the regiment received orders to deploy to Virginia. Shortly after arriving in the east, the men of the regiment saw their first action near Martinsburg, West Virginia, at the opening of the Antietam Campaign. The 12th then joined the garrison at Harpers Ferry, where, as part of Colonel B. F. Davis's command, it escaped the night before the garrison was surrendered to Stonewall Jackson.

The regiment's commander, Colonel Arno Voss, was in poor health, and day-to-day command was generally left in the hands of Lieutenant Colonel Hasbrouck Davis, a competent officer who had taught school and served as a Unitarian minister before establishing a successful law practice in Chicago. Davis led the regiment during Stoneman's raid, and during that operation destroyed a significant amount of Confederate property and captured 175 horses and mules, while losing 2 officers and 33 men. Unable to return to Union lines along the Rappahannock, Davis had led his regiment to safety at Gloucester Point where he linked up with Kilpatrick. There the regiment remained, separated from its brigade.[108]

With Averell relieved, Colonel Alfred Duffié was appointed commander of the 2nd Cavalry Division. Duffié, although not the most senior colonel in the Cavalry Corps, had been recommended for promotion to brigadier general for his performance at Kelly's Ford, and the paperwork was making its way through the War Department bureaucracy.

Duffié, as previously discussed, had served as a sergeant in the French Army and compiled a good record, earning decorations for valor in North Africa and a commission as a second lieutenant. In 1859, Duffié met and fell in love with an American woman who was working as a nurse in Europe. Duffié submitted his resignation, but it was rejected by the French army, forcing the recently commissioned officer to desert. Duffié traveled to New York where he married the woman, the daughter of a prominent Staten Island couple. Upon the outbreak of the war, Duffié was commissioned as a captain, and then quickly promoted to major in the Harris Light. When he applied for service with the U.S. Volunteers, Duffié embellished his résumé, claiming that he was the son of a count and a graduate of the French military academy at St. Cyr. Duffié made no mention that he was a deserter.[109]

Duffié, despite his difficulties with English, had done well as a field grade officer in the Harris Light. In July 1862, Governor William Sprague appointed him commander of the 1st Rhode Island Cavalry when that regiment's original commander resigned his commission. At Kelly's Ford, Duffié had been in command of Averell's 1st Brigade, and had performed well, justifying the recommendation that he be promoted to brigadier.

Duffié's 1st Brigade was commanded by another foreign-born officer, a dapper Italian named Luigi diCesnola Palma. DiCesnola had been born in northern Italy in 1832, and enlisted in an infantry regiment at the age of fifteen. Shortly after that he was commissioned and served in the Sardinian Army during the war against Austria. Later, he served with the British in the Crimea.[110] DiCesnola emigrated to New York sometime around 1858 and there eked out a rather impoverished existence teaching foreign languages. His fortunes improved in 1861 when he married a woman with a modest inheritance. Upon the outbreak of war in the United States, diCesnola established a school for prospective cavalry officers, charging each pupil one hundred dollars, "payable in advance."[111] The school proved profitable for the enterprising new American.

In February 1862, diCesnola obtained a commission as lieutenant colonel of the 11th New York Cavalry. Although by the standards of the time he was a proficient officer, his introduction to military service in America did not go smoothly. The ambitious Italian resigned in frustration after the 11th New York was assigned to garrison duty in Washington instead of being sent into combat. Before leaving the regiment, however, diCesnola injudiciously encouraged a few of his men to seek service in more active units, an act for which he was promptly arrested, briefly imprisoned, and then charged for "calculat[ing] to produce a mutiny." DiCesnola appealed to higher military authorities and the charges against him were dropped.[112]

Upon being released from confinement, diCesnola was given a commission as lieutenant colonel of the 4th New York Cavalry, a regiment raised in New York City. The 4th New York was also known as Dickel's Mounted Rifles after its first commander, Christian Dickel. Dickel resigned in September 1862, allowing diCesnola to be promoted to colonel of the regiment.[113] The 4th New York was not a popular regiment with senior officers in the Army of the Potomac. Filled with immigrants, orders given in English were usually repeated in German and Italian before they were executed. Doubtless, diCesnola's linguistic skills proved helpful.

DiCesnola led the regiment on active service in Virginia for several months until, in February 1863, he was peremptorily dismissed from the army for larceny of public property. The provost marshal discovered six army pistols in a package that diCesnola had mailed to his wife and made the logical assumption that diCesnola was stealing the weapons. The Italian, however, claimed that he sent the pistols to New York that they might be used to guard a state depot, and that he used his wife's address merely for convenience. After five weeks in limbo, diCesnola's dismissal was revoked and he was reinstated in command of the 4th New York.[114]

As summer approached, diCesnola was unhappy. To a friend, he explained that things were not going well in the Cavalry Corps, in part because "everybody commands, but nobody wants to obey." The post–Chancellorsville reorganization further raised the ire of the Italian, who felt that native-born officers with fewer qualifications—whom he derisively called "shopkeeper Colonels"—were being favored. DiCesnola was perhaps surprised when on May 20, he was given temporary command of a brigade, leaving the 4th New York, which at the time had only 276 out of 731 men mounted.[115]

The 1st Massachusetts Cavalry was organized in September 1861 by assigning eleven independent militia companies to the newly authorized regiment (only H company needed to be raised). The governor appointed Captain Robert Williams as colonel of the regiment. Williams, a Virginian (born in Culpeper) and 1851 graduate of West Point, had been serving in the military academy's tactics department at the outbreak of the war.[116] The governor also selected Horace Sargent of his own staff as lieutenant colonel. The selection of these two officers caused a near-mutiny among the company officers, who had expected to elect the field grade officers from among their own ranks. Williams quickly quashed the incipient revolt. One enlisted man was wounded and a number of officers dismissed from the service, but order was restored.[117] Despite the dissension, Williams proved a popular commander and well-wishers purchased him a horse before the regiment left Massachusetts. The horse, an immense brown named Clodhopper, was considered the best steeplechase racer in Canada. However, Clodhopper's gaits were rough, making long periods in the saddle uncomfortable. Consequently, Williams seldom rode his gift horse.[118]

The regiment spent fall of 1861 at camp in Readville, Massachusetts, where the men were issued horses. The poor quality of the mounts provided caused some troopers to grouse that the regiment had received "nearly all the unruly beasts in New England."[119] On December 19, the regiment paraded through Boston. Unlike the dashing lancers and dragoons of the pre-war militia, the citizens of the city saw "dingy uniforms begrimed with mud and dirt and showing hard usage; untamed steeds, rough in their autumn coats; a redundant outfit of saddles, bridles, queer stirrups, and superfluous bits, all stiffened by the December cold."[120]

Beginning on Christmas day, the regiment moved via New York and Annapolis to Hilton Head, South Carolina. While some members of the regiment would have preferred to be sent immediately to duty in Virginia, Captain Charles Francis Adams, Jr. expressed a more a more prudent opinion in a letter to his father. "As for active service, it's just impossible. You could n't get our horses within a mile of firearms, and the drilling task before us is something terrible to contemplate. We are all green, officers, men, and horses, and long practice is absolutely necessary. But we can do, I imagine, picket and camp duty."[121]

After seven months in South Carolina, the 1st Massachusetts, leaving one battalion of four companies behind, moved to Virginia and joined the Army of the Potomac.[122] In November 1862, Colonel Williams resigned his volunteer commission for duty in the army's Adjutant General's office in Washington. Lieutenant Colonel Sargent was promoted to fill the vacant command billet.[123]

Colonel Sargent, before his appointment as lieutenant colonel of the regiment, had no military experience, his only qualifications being his horsemanship, his enthusiasm, and his personal study of military matters. Not surprisingly, some officers did not consider Sargent a particularly effective commander. Captain Adams wrote to his father in London:

> You've no idea what a nuisance such an ass as [Colonel Sargent] is at the head of a regiment. Ignorant to the last degree of his supposed profession, his ignorance is only surpassed by his conceit and vanity and his love of display. He has only two of the qualities of an officer of cavalry: he is a good and daring horseman and a man of great personal courage. At the same time he is the most cruel man on horses I ever saw in my life, and his courage, combined with his plenteous lack of judgment, only endangers the lives of those under his command. He prides himself on being a disciplinarian, knowing nothing of discipline, and so wears out his officers and men by an inordinate attention to useless trifles. He considers himself a tactician and yet he could not drill a corporal's guard without making ludicrous blunders. His mistakes on the drill ground, his theories of war and his absurdities in camp are, as John will tell you the laughing stock of the regiment. He is universally disliked as well as ridiculed.[124]

Sargent's promotion created a vacancy in the regiment's lieutenant colonel billet and Major Greely S. Curtis was promoted to fill it. During Stoneman's raid, Colonel Sargent acted as commander of the 1st Brigade, leaving Curtis in command of the 1st Massachusetts during Averell's aborted foray. Curtis, an engineer from Boston, was a disciplinarian, as strict on himself as on his men, and admired by some for his ability to say "no" to requests from his close associates.[125]

The 6th Ohio Cavalry was organized in the Western Reserve section of that state in October 1861. For the first seven months of its existence, the regiment remained in Ohio, conducting dismounted drill and guarding Confederate prisoners of war. Fortunately, the Confederate prisoners were docile, since the soldiers of the 6th Ohio were mostly without arms. In May 1862 the regiment, accompanied by a mascot dog named Paddy McManus, moved to Wheeling, West Virginia, was issued horses, and two companies were dispatched south to join Major General John C. Fremont who was campaigning against Stonewall Jackson in the Shenandoah Valley. The regiment first saw significant action at Cross Keys, losing several men killed and wounded.[126]

In September 1862, one battalion of the regiment was detached and sent west for service. Over the winter, two freshly recruited companies joined the regiment in Virginia, while recruiting for the final two companies continued in Ohio.[127] Thus, the regiment had present only ten of its authorized twelve companies.

Although the regiment participated in most of the Army of the Potomac's campaigns, it did little actual fighting until the battle at Kelly's Ford on March 17. In April, the regiment's first commanding officer, Colonel William R. Lloyd, was discharged, leaving Major William Stedman, a forty-eight-year-old merchant and farmer in command. Before the war, Stedman, a staunch abolitionist and temperance man from Portage County, had helped fugitive slaves on the Underground Railroad and been elected to a term in the state legislature where he established a reputation as a Radical. In May 1861, Stedman raised an infantry company and served for five months as a captain in that arm before accepting a commission as lieutenant of cavalry. With the rest of Averell's division, Stedman and the 6th Ohio played little role in Stoneman's raid or the fighting at Chancellorsville.[128]

The 1st Rhode Island, initially named 1st New England Cavalry, was recruited in the fall of 1861 with battalions from Rhode Island and New Hampshire. The regiment's first commander, appointed by the governor of Rhode Island, was Colonel Robert Lawton, a former captain in the Regiment of Mounted Rifles. As the regiment's companies were being filled, the officers contributed to defray the expenses of recruiting musicians for a regimental band, apparently in the belief that music would enhance morale.[129]

The regiment mustered into Federal service at a camp established in a riding park near Pawtucket in December 1861 and remained there until March 1862.[130] The weather was poor, military duties were boring, and the men chafed under the restrictions to their liberty (only three men per company per day were allowed out of camp on passes). In their pursuit of liberty, the more audacious recruits dressed in civilian clothes to sneak past the camp guards, some even disguising themselves as women.[131] On a positive note, early in the winter the regiment received its horses. Most were Morgans, which turned out to be excellent cavalry mounts. In March 1862 the regiment moved to Washington where it was assigned to the Army of the Potomac. Shortly afterward, Colonel Lawton resigned, and in July the Governor of Rhode Island appointed Alfred N. Duffié, then a major in the Harris Light, as Lawton's replacement.

The officers of the regiment took great umbrage at the appointment of an outsider, and particularly a foreigner, as their commander, and all but four of the Rhode Island officers submitted their resignations. Duffié, faced with a crisis in his command, called a meeting of the officers during which he asked them to withdraw their resignations and give him four weeks to prove himself worthy of his position. Most of the officers decided to give the Frenchman a chance. Over the next few weeks, Duffié showed that he was competent and most of the officers remained with the regiment.[132]

Duffié was an effective regimental commander and in March 1863 was placed in brigade command, leaving Lieutenant Colonel John L. Thompson in command of the regiment. After earning a degree from Harvard, Thompson, who had been born and raised in New Hampshire, studied for a year in Berlin, Munich, and Paris before moving to Chicago to practice law. At the beginning of the war he had enlisted as a private in the 1st Illinois Light Artillery, and then accepted a commission as a first lieutenant in the New Hampshire battalion of the 1st Rhode Island Cavalry.[133]

John Irwin Gregg, the cousin of David McMurtrie Gregg, commanded Duffié's 2nd Brigade. At the age of twenty-one, Gregg had volunteered as a private during the Mexican War. He was quickly commissioned as a lieutenant in the 11th Infantry and later breveted to captain. After the war, Gregg returned to civilian life, but remained active in the Pennsylvania militia, rising to the grade of lieutenant colonel. At the beginning of the Civil War, Gregg obtained a commission as a captain in the 6th U.S. Cavalry when that regiment was organized in Pittsburgh during the fall of 1861. In October 1862, Gregg left the regulars to accept an appointment as colonel of the 16th Pennsylvania Cavalry.[134] His brigade, unlike other brigades in the Corps, was made up exclusively of regiments from a single state — Pennsylvania.

The 3rd Pennsylvania Cavalry, known also as the Kentucky Light Cavalry, was raised in the spring and summer of 1861 by Colonel William Young. A later historian of the organization observed that "no sane reason" for the regiment's name could be determined, since eleven of the companies were from Pennsylvania (the twelfth was an independent company, known as the President's Mounted Guard, from Washington, D.C.). The companies of the regiment assembled in Washington in August 1861 and shortly afterwards Colonel Young resigned, allowing the governor of Pennsylvania to appoint William Averell, then a captain in the 5th U.S. Cavalry, as its commander. Initially the regiment served in the defenses around Washington where, on August 26, 1861, Private Peter Brennan of Company B was killed in an ambush, perhaps the first volunteer cavalryman killed in the war.[135] In the following months, the regiment participated in most of the campaigns of the Army of the Potomac.

When Averell was promoted to brigadier general in November 1862, John McIntosh, a Floridian who had served as a midshipman during the war with Mexico, was appointed to command the 3rd Pennsylvania. At the outbreak of the Civil War, McIntosh, who had been living in New Jersey, was commissioned as a lieutenant in the 2nd U.S. Cavalry and had then been breveted to major during the Peninsular Campaign. After Hooker formed the cavalry corps, McIntosh was moved up to brigade command, and command of the 3rd Pennsylvania passed to Edward S. Jones, the lieutenant colonel of the regiment.[136]

The 4th Pennsylvania Cavalry was raised from various counties and towns of that state in September and October 1861, with an initial enlistment of 1006 men.[137] Shortly after mustering-in, the regiment moved to Washington and served on provost guard duty in the capital. Horses were in short supply, and by spring of 1862 only six of the regiment's twelve companies were mounted. The regiment's company officers developed a scheme to secure horses for the half of the regiment without mounts. Each day, the commanders of the not-mounted companies would draw a few unserviceable horses for various camp details. Those horses would be traded to the mounted companies for serviceable horses. At inspection, the lame and broken down horses—now in the mounted companies—would be condemned and serviceable replacement horses drawn from the remount depot. Though unethical, the ruse, repeated through the following weeks and months, helped get the entire regiment mounted by the time it was assigned to the Army of the Potomac in late spring 1862.[138]

The regiment's first commander was Colonel David Campbell, who had commanded a three-month regiment that had completed its term of service and mustered out. Campbell resigned his commission in the 4th Pennsylvania on March 12, 1862 to take command of the 5th Pennsylvania Cavalry which the state had begun organizing. He was replaced by his lieutenant colonel, James Childs. Childs, in temporary command of a brigade, was killed at Antietam, hit in the hip and disemboweled by a solid shot from an artillery piece. Lieutenant Colonel James Kerr was promoted to command the regiment, but he resigned on May 17, 1863. Upon Kerr's resignation, Lieutenant Colonel William Doster was placed in command of the regiment.[139]

Doster was a man of great potential. Born in 1837, he had graduated from Yale, earned a law degree from Harvard, studied in Germany at the University of Heidelberg, and spent a year practicing law. With the onset of the war, he raised two cavalry companies, resigning from the first after it was converted to an infantry regiment. Doster, initially commissioned a captain, was promoted to major in October 1861. In February 1862 he was assigned as the Provost Marshal for the District of Columbia. While serving as the Army's top policeman in the capital, Doster was promoted to lieutenant colonel of the 4th Pennsylvania. He finally returned to the regiment in the spring of 1863 and shortly afterward assumed command.[140]

In this drawing, Edwin Forbes depicts one of the most common activities of all cavalrymen: waiting for orders. Note the small size of the horse, with the trooper's stirrups extending well below his horse's belly. Small horses were common in cavalry service, both north and south (Library of Congress).

The 16th Pennsylvania Cavalry was recruited from throughout that state in the fall of 1862. The regiment held its initial rendevous at Harrisburg on November 18, and John Irwin Gregg was appointed its first commander.[141] Gregg led his regiment in the fight at Kelly's Ford, and afterward was given command of the brigade.[142] Gregg's successor, Lieutenant Colonel Lorenzo Rogers, ridiculed for his order to "rally on the barn" near Ely's Ford, resigned his commission on May 16, leaving Major William H. Fry in command of the regiment.[143] Being part of Averell's division, the 16th Pennsylvania did not see much action during the Chancellorsville Campaign and the regiment was largely untested.

The Cavalry Corps had seen hard service in April and May. While the condition of many of the corps' thousands of horses left much to be desired, the confidence of the men had been strengthened by their experiences. Although Stoneman's raid may have not done much to damage the Army of Northern Virginia, the Union troopers found raiding much preferable to the boredom of continuous picketing and escort duty. Additionally, active service produced a "winnowing" effect on the leaders in the army's cavalry regiments. Admittedly, some good officers were disabled or killed, but others — impaired, weak, or unmotivated — resigned. As Pleasonton prepared his corps for the coming campaign, it was rare for a regiment to be commanded by a colonel, and ever more rare for a commander to have had six months tenure. However, for the most part, the colonels, lieutenant colonels, and majors commanding regiments were veterans with at least a year's experience in the field, albeit in positions of lesser responsibility. Still, it remained to be seen whether Pleasonton and his new subordinates were capable of whipping Jeb Stuart's division in major fight.

5

Stirring Events

Grand Reviews in Culpeper County, May–June 1863

By the third week of May, the brigades of Hampton and the two Lees had arrived in Culpeper County to begin preparations for the coming summer campaign. The regimental camps ringed Culpeper Courthouse with files of white tents dotting the green fields. In those fields, thousands of horses grew sleek and fat grazing on the late spring grasses. An idyllic spring—war or no war—had settled on the Virginia Piedmont and the spirits of the officers and men of Stuart's cavalry improved after their arduous winter and early spring fighting. In a letter to his brother, a captain in the 2nd South Carolina wrote of his new surroundings, "Culpeper, I think, has been more severely ravaged by the Yankees than any county I have seen. For miles and miles, the country is depopulated, fine mansions are standing untenanted and the fencing of the plantations are all destroyed. Yet, in its desolation it is beautiful. It smiles even in its tears. The number of fields everywhere, though unfenced, are covered over with the finest clover and timothy."[1]

The cavalry camps in Culpeper likely conformed to guidance contained in Confederate regulations, with allowances made for trees, streams, and other variables of terrain. The tents for the men in a company were set in a single file, establishing a "company street." Each man tethered his horse to a pin driven firmly into the ground at a distance of three to six paces in front of his tent. The length of the company street was naturally proportional to the strength of the company since more men needed more tents. The width of the street was also proportional. Sufficient space was left between files of tents to allow each company to form in two ranks when mounted at the head of the company street. Thus a company with fifty men would have a company street twenty-five yards wide, and a regiment of five hundred men would have a camp roughly three hundred yards wide, allowing for intervals between squadrons.

At the front of each company street the sergeants pitched their tents while company officers pitched theirs to the rear of the company street. Tents for the staff and field grade officers were aligned to the rear of the company grade officers, with the colonel's tent centered on the regiment and identified by the regimental colors placed at its entrance. Regulations stated that each company was to establish a kitchen at the front of its street, but by 1863 cooking had become more informal, with troopers habitually eating in a "mess" of four to six men, with cooking and cleaning chores shared among them. To avoid undue familiarity between the officers and the ranks, the men's latrines (known as "sinks") were placed at the front of the camp while officer's latrines were placed at the rear.[2]

In the camps, the troopers' daily lives were not particularly arduous. Each morning and evening details of men led the horses to nearby streams or ponds to drink. Other details policed the camps. Removal of horse manure, necessary to keep down flies, was probably the most laborious task. On most days the troopers were called out to drill, with the remainder of the time devoted to preparing for the upcoming summer campaign. Horses needed to be reshod, weapons repaired, ammunition and supplies restocked, and clothing and tack mended. The horses, accompanied by a detail from each company, were turned out to graze in nearby fields for as long as possible each day that they might put on weight and regain their energy, depleted during the hard winter. At night, while the men not on guard duty relaxed, the horses, picketed by the tents, ate their grain rations from feed bags attached to their halters.

For Jacob Kent Langhorne, the transformation from civilian to soldier in Steptoe's company of the 2nd Virginia continued. The new trooper's mare, Maggie, was appraised at $650, although Langhorne, obviously proud of his horse, claimed to have been offered $800 for her by several men. Apparently obtaining horses continued to be a problem for Steptoe's troopers, most of whom were from Lynchburg. In a letter to his mother, Langhorne asked her to "Tell uncle Archer if Pa is not at home to know what Mr. Billy Barwell will take for his brown horse and if he will take $500 for him to let me know as Capt Steptoe wants a horse and cannot get one at any price."[3] Additionally, Langhorne was issued weapons. He drew a pair of pistols from the ordnance sergeants to use until he could capture his own, and one of his company-mates gave him a rifle captured at Chancellorsville. To complete his kit, Langhorne purchased a saber for three dollars—the best one he had seen in his brief tenure with the regiment.[4] Thus equipped and having completed a few days of drill, Jacob Kent Langhorne was ready to fight.

On May 20, 1863, Stuart arrived in Culpeper County and set up his headquarters in tents at Afton, a farm owned by the Bradford family, to the east of the Court House. Stuart, a lover of military pomp and ceremony, promptly ordered a review.

Military organizations have held reviews and conducted ceremonies throughout history. Such activities had a practical purpose—they allowed senior officers to gauge the proficiency of their units and men at drill. Presumably, a unit that could march with precision on the parade ground could march from position to position on the battlefield. Likewise, men who could handle their weapons on parade would hopefully do the same under fire.

Reviews also served other purposes. Generals believed, with some justification, that reviews bolstered the morale of the men and fostered esprit de corps within units (a belief not universally held among the enlisted men, many of whom viewed such "foppery" as a needless interruption of their leisure). On occasion, a leader might conduct a review to impress enemies with the military might of his force. Finally, reviews provided entertainment for the local population whom were burdened with having thousands of soldiers camping in their fields. Although civilians were supposed to receive payment for goods and services provided to the army, chickens, pigs, eggs, pails of milk, and other sundry items disappeared from Culpeper farms each evening.

The review—the first of what became known as three "grand reviews"—was held near Brandy Station on May 22, with approximately four thousand five hundred men taking part.[5] On the night after the review, the officers held a dance in Culpeper, but that social festivity must have disappointed the convivial cavalier commander. In a letter to his wife, William Gaston Deloney, a major in Cobb's Legion, recounted that he had been relaxing in camp chatting with a fellow officer when their commander, Colonel P.M.B. Young summoned them to town to attend the ball. Upon entering the ballroom, Deloney found several ladies with "the room otherwise crowded with gray uniforms and incipient whiskers and everybody dancing." Deloney told his wife that he "talked a little while, sat down a little while, walked about a little while, and a little while after called out to get my horse and ride home." Unfortunately, a servant, apparently thinking that the major would party all night, had sent the horse back to the camp. Deloney, who had to walk back to his tent, claimed that the ball "would be my last as it was my first."[6]

The following week was busy. Beverly Robertson's small brigade arrived from North Carolina, further augmenting Stuart's division by roughly one thousand troopers. On Wednesday, May 27, Virginia's gubernatorial election was held. The Virginia regiments set up polling stations so that the eligible soldiers might cast their ballots. The winner in the election was former governor and Culpeper attorney, William "Extra Billy" Smith, then serving as a brigadier in command of one of Jubal Early's division.[7]

The arrival of Beverly Robertson's brigade and the pending arrival of William E. "Grumble" Jones' brigade, then en route from the Valley, would raise the strength of Stuart's division to about nine thousand men. So, naturally, Stuart believed that another, even larger review was necessary, and he set June 5 as its date. Stuart envisioned a succession of gala activities to show off the Cavalry Division. Consequently, the review on June 5 became an extraordinary spectacle that, measured against all criteria, earned the adjective "grand."

Once Stuart ordered the review, everyone in his headquarters "exert[ed] themselves to the utmost to make it a success."[8] One staff officer recalled that "all the commencement of the month [of June] we were busy preparing for that important event."[9] Invitations were sent out far and wide, with particular attention given to the young ladies of Culpeper and the counties to the south. One of Stuart's staff officers even arranged for a group of young women from Charlottesville, fifty miles to the south, to attend the festivities.[10] Unfortunately, the young ladies to the north in Warrenton and Fauquier County were under Union occupation and thus unable to attend.

Nothing was left to chance. The staff officers purchased new uniforms so that they would meet Stuart's high standard for personal dress. The staff also set about attending to the myriad of details associated with orchestrating the review and associated activities.[11] A special train was arranged to transport guests from the Court House to the site selected for the review near Brandy. The men in the regiments were inspected and rehearsed repeatedly in preparation for the main event. In that regard, the wife of a Confederate officer visiting with the Bradford family at Afton recalled that there were "many reviews that week, all of them merely by way of preparation and practice for that famous grand review."[12]

In the camps, the troopers were busy as well, responding to orders to prepare themselves for the review. Supervised by their sergeants, the men polished metal fittings and weapons, cleaned their uniforms, polished their boots, and oiled their tack. The men curried their horses to remove all dirt and any vestige of winter coat. Manes and tails were combed out to remove all tangles and burrs. One trooper recalled that everyone "did his level best in the way of rubbing down horses, blacking boots, cleaning sabres, pistols, belts, etc., for this grand occasion."[13] Sergeant Robert Hudgins of the 3rd Virginia recalled that in response to orders from his captain, he had spent several days cleaning, polishing, and grooming. Hudgins, from a well-to-do family near Hampton, was fortunate that he was accompanied by Jim, his body servant, who undoubtedly helped with the preparations. Because of their combined efforts, Hudgins' horse was "as slick as a peeled onion and [his] spurs and accouterments sparkled in the sun like a mirror." Additionally, Hudgins had just received a new uniform from home that, with his sergeant's chevrons, added to his splendid appearance.[14]

In anticipation of the arrival of many women who needed entertainment, as well as

Heros von Borcke, Stuart's urbane and witty staff officer, was charged with organizing a gala ball on the eve of a Grand Cavalry Review. Von Borcke, although a huge man, was renowned for his skill on the dance floor (Library of Congress).

for the pleasure of his officers and his own desire for gaiety, Stuart set Heros von Borcke to work organizing a ball for the evening before the review. Von Borcke's selection was most appropriate because of his Continental refinement and his skills as a dancer.[15]

Early on the morning of June 4, von Borcke was dispatched by horse to Gordonsville, a small town about thirty miles south of the Court House where the Orange and Alexandria Railroad intersected with the Virginia Central, the rail line between Richmond and Staunton. There von Borcke met George W. Randolph, the most distinguished guest attending the review. Randolph was a Richmond lawyer and grandson of Thomas Jefferson. He had organized the Richmond Howitzers, a celebrated militia unit, and served briefly in the Confederate Army as a staff officer before being appointed brigadier general in February 1862. The following month Jefferson Davis selected Randolph as his Secretary of War. However, Randolph's tenure as a cabinet officer was brief. Unhappy with restrictions on his authority imposed by Davis, Randolph resigned from the Cabinet in 1862. He did not return to active military service.[16]

Von Borcke and General Randolph returned to Culpeper by special train — about a three-hour ride — with Stuart's battle flag flying from the locomotive.[17] Other guests for the review were traveling to Culpeper as well. Von Borcke noted that every train arriving at the station in the Court House that afternoon brought people who were met by escorts and

Culpeper Courthouse, a scenic Virginia Piedmont town, fell early under the hard hand of war. In 1862, the town was occupied by troops under General John Pope. Confederate prisoners (visible in this photograph) were confined on the balcony of the courthouse building. On the evening of June 4, 1863, the courthouse was put to more pleasant use as Stuart's officers and local belles danced under candlelight. Von Borcke's ball was a great success (Library of Congress).

taken by wagon or ambulance to their accommodations. Many guests stayed in tents in the cavalry camps since the town's two hotels, boarding houses, and private homes were full.[18]

That night Stuart hosted his ball in the country court house building on East Davis Street. "Virginia belles" from the surrounding countryside flocked to the gala event for the pleasure of dancing with the "flower of the chivalry of the Army." Music was provided by Stuart's band, made up of cavalrymen detailed to his headquarters from the regiments for their musical ability.[19] Von Borcke recalled that the ball came off "pleasantly enough," but was not nearly such a "gay and dazzling scene" as reported in the newspapers. Amenities were in short supply in Culpeper after two years of war and, contrary to reports that chandeliers illuminated the dancers, von Borcke could find only a few tallow candles to light the ballroom.[20]

The next morning at about eight o'clock, Stuart and his staff emerged from their tents around Afton and, attired in their new uniforms, mounted their immaculately groomed horses for the short ride to Auburn, the site selected for the review. Captain William Downes Farley, a volunteer *aide de camp* to Stuart and one of his most capable scouts, was among those officers who purchased new uniforms. Farley was so pleased with his resplendent attire that he told his friends that should he die in battle, they were to dress him in his new coat and ship his remains home to his mother in Laurens, South Carolina.[21] Doubtless, no one at the time took Farley's request seriously.

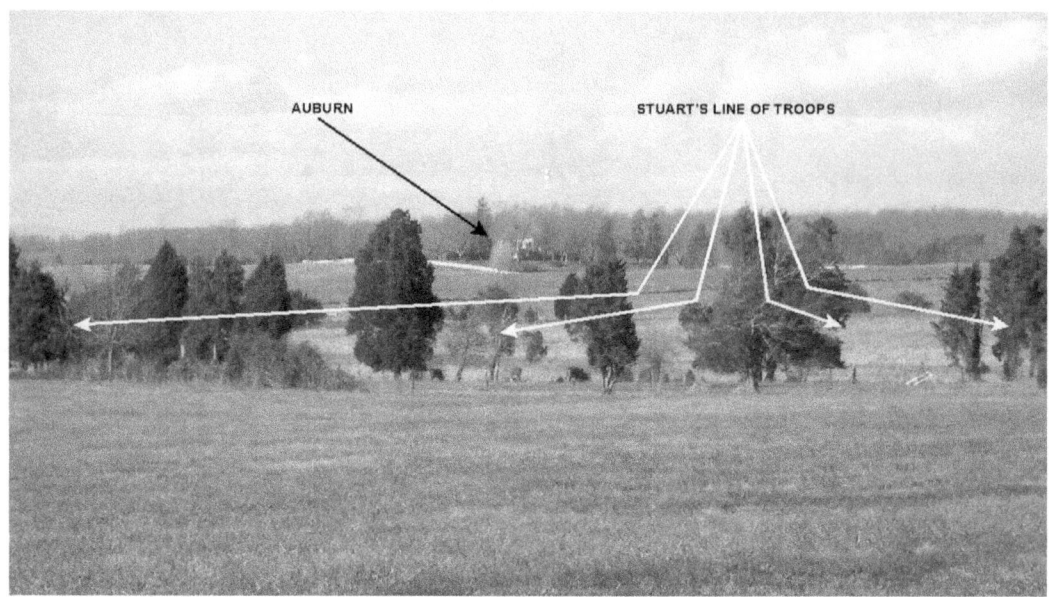

Stuart held his cavalry reviews on Auburn, a 2200 acre farm owned by John Minor Botts, Culpeper County's most prominent Union sympathizer. Stuart's troopers paraded from left to right on the flat ground between the Orange and Alexandria Railroad and Auburn's main house (center, in the trees) (Joseph W. McKinney).

Auburn in 1863. In the foreground is a typical Virginia rail fence. The fence rails were much-prized as firewood by both Union and Confederate soldiers. Note the slave quarters at the right (Library of Congress).

5 — Stirring Events

Today Auburn's main house appears much as it did during the Civil War (Joseph W. McKinney).

Auburn was an ideal location for a cavalry review. The terrain was open and flat — almost perfect for the assembled regiments to line up for the inspection and to march past the reviewing party. The land was in pasture or cultivation, consequently there were few trees to impede the movement of the troops or to block the views of spectators. Corn, planted in some fields, stood about a foot tall.[22] As an added benefit, the site lay next to both the Orange & Alexandria line and a parallel carriage road between the Court House and Brandy and easily accessible to spectators. Finally, Auburn was owned by a Union-man, John Minor Botts.

The exact site for the review was marked by Stuart's staff with a single plowed furrow, running straight and parallel to the Orange and Alexandria Railroad at a distance of about three hundred yards from the tracks. The regiments of the five brigades began assembling on the furrow at about eight o'clock and were ready for the activities to commence by about ten o'clock that morning.[23] The day was cloudy and cool — much easier on the horses and men than the weather during ceremony the previous month. May 22 had been unseasonably warm.[24]

It is impossible to determine exactly how many Southern troopers were drawn up on the field at Auburn that day. Estimates regarding the number of men participating in the review range from eight to twelve thousand.[25] The former number is certainly closer than the latter, which is far too high. Stuart's Assistant Adjutant General, the staff officer responsible for headquarters correspondence, later wrote that the total effective strength of the Cavalry Division on May 31, 1863, was 9,536.[26] Gains or losses in the week between May 31 and June 5 probably did not result in a substantial change in effective strength. Additionally, a few men would not have attended the review for various reasons (for example:

on picket duty; left in camp for fatigue detail; temporarily sick; horse unexpectedly lame). Several regiments were not present in Culpeper County. The 1st Virginia Cavalry had been sent to watch the upper Rappahannock near Amissville. The 11th Virginia had remained in the Shenandoah Valley near Strasburg, the 4th Virginia and 15th Virginia remained with the infantry around Fredericksburg, and the Phillips Legion was posted south of the James River. Discounting artillerymen, staff, and escorts, there were probably between seven and eight thousand "sabers" in the line of troops. In any event, it was the largest body of cavalry anyone present had ever seen assembled.

The troopers were drawn up along the furrow in two ranks, the standard cavalry formation.[27] Regimental, squadron, and platoon commanders positioned themselves centered on and to the front of their men. Other regimental officers and sergeants not in the ranks fell into the rear (those falling in at the rear were commonly called "file closers"). Brigade commanders and their staffs took positions to the front and center of their brigades.

Standard frontage for cavalry was calculated at one horse per yard, or about four inches between the boots of adjacent troopers. Intervals of ten yards between squadrons and fifteen yards between regiments were standard.[28] Thus, seven thousand officers and men in sixteen regiments and two battalions, drawn up in two ranks, would present a frontage of between two and two and one half miles.

The artillery battalion, with the arrival of Chew's battery from the Valley, consisted of five batteries and twenty guns under the command of Major Robert F. Beckham. As customary, the battalion formed on the extreme right of the line of troops, artillery being the senior arm of the service. Beckham, a Culpeper native, had graduated from West Point in 1859, standing sixth in the class of twenty-two.[29] In 1861 he resigned his commission as a topographical engineer in the "Old Army" and received a commission as an artillery officer in the Provisional Confederate Army. In April 1863 Beckham was appointed to the command of the cavalry division's artillery, replacing Major John Pelham who had been mortally wounded at Kelly's Ford on March 17.[30]

Beckham's artillery battalion was commonly referred to as the Stuart Horse Artillery. Horse artillery, considered elite among the "long" arm of the service, was so-named because all members of the battery were mounted on horses: some on the teams drawing the guns and caissons, some on limbers, and the remainder on saddle horses. This allowed the horse artillery to maneuver with cavalry. In standard light field artillery batteries, most gun-crew members were expected to march on foot at the side of the horse-drawn guns.[31]

Observers did not record the exact order in which cavalry brigades units were aligned along the furrow. While a commanding general had the authority to designate any order of alignment he desired, it was customary for the unit commanded by the most senior officer to occupy the position of honor on the right flank of the line of troops. Since most generals in the Confederate army were highly conscious of the prerogatives of rank, it is likely that Stuart followed tradition and thus placed Hampton's brigade on the far right of the cavalry.[32]

It is possible that within some regiments, commanders "sized" their companies, meaning that the troopers were arranged according to the height of their horses (ideally, larger troopers would be riding larger horses as well). Cooper's *Volunteer Manual* specified that the tallest horses should be placed on the right of the rank progressing down to the shortest horses on the left. The method of sizing was more complicated in Cooke's *Cavalry Tactics*. Cooke recommended that the tallest horses be positioned in the middle of the rank, progressing down to the shorter horses on both flanks. Either technique would present a more uniform appearance and provide a practical benefit — the gaits of equally sized horses might be better matched.[33]

Stuart and his staff took up their position upon a small rise near the railroad, centered on the line of troops with the crowd of spectators congregating to their rear. Many spectators observed the review from horse-drawn carriages parked nearby. Others remained aboard the special train—a locomotive with several flat cars filled with benches—that Stuart had arranged to run out from the Court House that morning.[34] Since there was no traffic on the Orange and Alexandria north of Culpeper, having the train to remain stationary for most of the day presented no problem to commerce.

Unexpectedly, and shortly before the review was to begin, Major General John Bell Hood arrived at the head of a long column of marching infantrymen. Fitz Lee had invited Hood to the review, and casually added that Hood could "bring a few friends." Hood brought with him seven thousand "friends," the men of his division who, to observe the festivities had that morning, marched six miles from their camps. Hood's veterans sat down in a long line to the right of Stuart's reviewing party and relaxed as they waited for the cavalry to put on its show.[35]

When all was ready, bugle calls signaled "Attention" and the regiments made final alignments to their ranks and drew their sabers. Stuart then began the review by inspecting the assembled units in the "usual way." Accompanied by his staff as the band played martial music, Stuart galloped to the right flank of the line of troops. There the party turned and galloped down the front of the line. Regimental commanders, in succession, commanded "present sabers" as Stuart passed to their front. In response, each officer in the regiment raised his saber from the "carry saber" position (saber held in the right hand, hilt at hip, blade resting on the right shoulder) to a vertical position, blade upward, with the hilt at chin level. After Stuart passed, the regimental commander commanded "carry sabers" and the officers returned their sabers to their shoulders with hilts held at waist level. Throughout, the troopers sat motionless.

As Stuart rode down the line of troops, Brigade commanders and their staffs fell in with his party as it passed by. Upon reaching the far left flank, the entire group—now grown to almost one hundred horsemen—turned and galloped up the rear of the line of troops. Passing around the right flank of the line, Stuart returned with the entire party to his original position on the hill near the railroad tracks.[36] In making his inspection, Stuart covered a distance of six to eight miles in probably a little less than an hour.[37]

Watching the procession, George Neese, the first sergeant of Chew's battery of the horse artillery, was impressed with Stuart's horsemanship. Neese later recalled that Stuart was "the prettiest and most graceful rider I ever saw. When he dashed past us I could not help but notice with what natural ease and comely elegance he sat his steed as it bounded over the field, and his every motion in the saddle was in such strict accord with the movements of his horse that he and his horse appeared to be but one and the same machine."[38]

Most of the young ladies who watched the activities were more impressed with Stuart's resplendent appearance than his horsemanship. Years later, one of them wrote that "He wore a fine new uniform, brilliant with gold lace, buff gauntlets reaching to his elbows, and a canary-colored silk sash with tasseled ends. His hat, a soft, broad brimmed felt, was caught up at the side with a gold star and carried a sweeping plume; his high, patent-leather cavalry boots were trimmed with gold. He wore spurs of solid gold, the gift of some Maryland ladies—he was very proud of those spurs—and his horse was coal black and glossy as silk. And how happy he was—how full of faith in the Confederacy and himself!"[39]

After Stuart and the party of generals and staff officers returned to the reviewing position, a bugle call directed that the "pass in review" begin, and it became the turn of the regimental commanders to demonstrate the proficiency of their units and their men. First the horse artillery, with its six-horse teams and mix of guns passed in front of Stuart and took up a firing position on a nearby rise. After the artillery got underway, in succession each cavalry regiment broke from the line, wheeling to the right into a column of fours with the squadrons of each regiment following one another—a squadron being two companies, or roughly 80 to 120 men commanded by the more senior captain. After passing what had been the right end of the line of troops (at a point most likely marked by a flag), the head of the column executed a left turn and, remaining in fours, marched a short distance toward the spectators aligned along the Orange and Alexandria Railroad. On command, each squadron successively executed a "Platoon Left Front."[40] This maneuver brought each regiment, still in a column of squadrons but the troopers in each squadron in two ranks, back toward Stuart and the other general officers of the reviewing party.[41]

At Auburn, the Southern cavalry first passed in front of Stuart and the reviewing party at the walk, giving the generals ample opportunity to observe each unit's skill at moving in a properly aligned, or "well dressed," formation. According to one observer, it was easy to tell the regiments apart according to their style as they passed Stuart and the spectators. The Carolinians rode with "military primness and were mounted on steeds of delicately-shaped limbs with glistening eyes and full of fire and motion." The lower Virginians rode with "graceful nonchalance" presenting a "steady front of veterans." The "strong, well-limbed horses" of the men from Virginia's Shenandoah Valley and the Piedmont region "gave their squadrons an impression of massive and warlike strength."[42] Not surprisingly, the observer in this instance was from Jones' brigade, which consisted of regiments that were raised mostly in the Valley and the Piedmont.

As a whole, most of the troopers were less brilliantly mounted than described. By the summer of 1863, the army's demand for horses had begun to outstrip supply and cavalrymen rode what they could get. At that point, even within the renowned Black Horse Troop of the 4th Virginia, "The black Virginia racers had been succeeded by animals of all hues as well as all sizes and breeds."[43]

After passing Stuart at a walk, the long column of regiments circled to pass in review a second time.[44] This iteration, however, was far more animated. After making its final left turn and starting back toward the reviewing party, each regiment went from the walk to a trot. A short distance before reaching the reviewing party, each regimental commander ordered his men to the gallop and as the pace increased, then ordered the charge. When the troopers passed Stuart, they were at galloping at full speed, brandishing their sabers and shouting the rebel yell. Beckham's horse artillery, firing blanks and galloping to new firing positions about the field, added realism to the cavalry's simulated charges.[45]

No review is ever flawless, nor was this one. Several horses fell as the regiments charged past the reviewing party—fortunately no riders were injured, although those who "lost their seats" in front of the crowd were probably embarrassed.[46] When it came time for the 6th Virginia to pass in review the second time, Private Opie's black mare, as was her nature, became greatly excited. Despite Opie's "caresses and expostulations" and pressure from the severe bit he was using that day, the mare "shot out like an arrow" from Opie's squadron, then overtook and passed through the squadron to his front. Fortunately, the private's "rear attack" on the leading squadron of his regiment went unnoticed by the spectators. Opie did not record whether his mare's antics resulted in any rebuke for him.[47]

Most of the spectators were greatly impressed with the "sham battle." One female guest recalled that each time the artillery fired, she and her friends would leap out of their carriage, worried that its team of horses would bolt at the sound of the guns.[48] An officer on Stuart's staff observed that the excitement overcame some young ladies and they "clasped their hands and sank into the arms, sometimes, of their escorts, in a swoon." However, the officer wryly noted that the young ladies only swooned when their escorts were nearby and thus available to catch them.[49]

Hood's infantrymen had been admonished not to taunt or jeer at the cavalrymen as they passed in review — there being considerable rivalry between foot soldiers and horse soldiers. Nonetheless, any time a trooper's hat flew off, an infantryman would dash onto the field "to immediately gobble it up, never to be returned, — which according to wartime ethics, was perfectly proper."[50]

Apparently activities along the sidelines of the reviewing ground were also amusing for the infantrymen. One of Hood's soldiers noticed several young women accompanied by their officer escorts riding up and down the road at full speed. The infantryman observed that the local "girls" were "great riders" who rode more swiftly than the men.[51] Although the day was an amusing diversion from camp-life, one Texan probably expressed the view held by many when he wrote to his wife that he saw a "grand display," but marching six miles to Auburn and six back to camp, arriving there after dark, was a lot of effort just "for fun."[52]

Stuart's troopers trampled John Minor Botts's crops under the hooves of their horses. Botts, perhaps correctly, believed he was being persecuted because of his political beliefs. He complained to the Confederate Government, but Richmond ignored his requests for monetary compensation (Library of Congress).

More critical observers were impressed with the review as well. The officers and men of the Cavalry Division were almost universally pleased by the display that they put on that day. In the words of Stuart's assistant adjutant general, "It was a brilliant day, and the thirst for the 'pomp and circumstance' of war was fully satisfied."[53] Even Private Opie, despite his difficulty controlling the black mare, concluded that the review was a "brilliant affair and that it was a grand sight to behold this splendid pageant."[54]

Festivities for the day continued after the troops finished their sham battles, marched off the field, and settled back into their camps. That evening Stuart hosted a second ball for the entertainment of the officers and their ladies. Less elaborate than the previous evening's soiree, this event was held outdoors on the lawn at Afton, Stuart's headquarters. Couples danced on the grass while light provided by several large fires "gave the whole scene a wild and romantic effect."[55]

Meanwhile, the Grand Review did not go unnoticed in the Union camps to the north of the Rappahannock. On the afternoon of June 5, General Meade notified Hooker that he heard firing from up the river at about 8:00 a.m., and opined—incorrectly—that it was from Colonel Duffié's division, then posted near Rappahannock Station.[56] On June 6 Buford notified Pleasonton that his men had heard cannon firing from the vicinity of Culpeper on the previous day. Buford accurately added that he believed the firing was a salute, having been told that Stuart had scheduled an inspection of his entire force on that day.[57]

One aspect of the Grand Review caused some notoriety both at the time and in later years. As noted by Private Opie, the review was held "regardless of the growing crops of corn, wheat, and oats, which we heedlessly trampled under the iron heels of our galloping chargers."[58] Some Southerners took delight from the fact that the Confederate cavalry destroyed a Union man's crops.[59] In that regard, a woman who was present for the review later recalled:

> It was while I was [staying] at Mr. Bradford's that one of the most stirring events in Confederate history occurred. This was the trampling down of John Minor Botts's corn. Very good corn it was, dropped and hilled by Southern negroes and growing on a large, fine plantation next to Mr. Bradford's; and a very nice gentleman Mr. Botts was, too; but a field of corn, however good, and a private citizen, however estimable, are scarcely matters of national or international importance. The trouble was that John Minor Botts was on the Northern side and the corn was on the Southern side, and that Stuart held a grand review on the Southern side and the corn got trampled down. The fame of that corn went abroad into all the land. Northern and Southern papers vied with each other in editorials and special articles, families who had been friends for generations stopped speaking and do not speak to this day because of it, more than one hard blow was exchanged for and against it, and it brought down vituperation upon Stuart's head. And yet I was present at that naughty grand review ... and I can testify that General Stuart went there to review the troops, *not* to trample down the corn.[60]

Naturally, John Minor Botts was not happy that his crops were destroyed, no matter Stuart's intent. Botts perceived, perhaps with some justification, that he had been singled out for persecution and complained directly to Stuart, who failed to show much concern over the trampled corn. A servant who overheard the encounter between the two recounted that "Mr. Botts ripped and rarred and snorted, but Genrul Stuart warn't put out none at all." Reportedly Stuart even burst into laughter during the altercation with the apoplectic Botts.[61]

Botts next sought satisfaction by writing to the Confederate War Department, asserting that Stuart's cavalrymen did as much damage as a "hostile army." However, the War Department failed to take any action and provided Botts no relief.[62] Further, it is doubtful that Botts received much sympathy from his neighbors given the general devastation that Culpeper had endured the previous summer when the county had been occupied by forces under Major General John Pope.[63]

Unfortunately for Stuart's ego, as well as the comfort of his men, Robert E. Lee was unable to attend the Grand Review.[64] Obviously Stuart anticipated that Lee would be present when he selected June 5 as the date for the event. However, it does not appear that Lee ever seriously considered altering his schedule to be in Culpeper on that date. In response to a memorandum from Stuart, Lee on May 31 advised his cavalry commander that while he would take great pleasure in seeing Stuart's assembled division, he saw "no prospect" of attending the review because of pressing business in Fredericksburg.[65] Also, on June 3, Lee wrote to his wife from Fredericksburg that he would be unable to attend the review.[66]

Lee's time in Fredericksburg was well spent supervising the withdrawal of his infantry from the fortifications on the south bank of the Rappahannock River and beginning the march that would ultimately take them to Pennsylvania. On June 5, as Stuart and his staff were heading from their camp to Auburn for their review, the Union Army began showing signs of offensive intent along the lower Rappahannock. That morning engineers from General John Sedgewick's corps began laying pontoon bridges across the river and Federal infantry began deploying to the south bank east of Fredericksburg. Since only Lieutenant General A. P. Hill's corps remained in the lines, the direct route to Richmond was vulnerable to Federal attack.[67]

Lee spent the June 5 and the morning of June 6 observing the operations of the Union forces around Fredericksburg. Becoming convinced that Sedgewick's action was merely a demonstration and thus did not pose a serious threat to his plans, Lee left Fredericksburg on the evening of Saturday, June 6, and arrived in Culpeper the following day.[68] Shortly after his arrival, Lee notified Stuart that he wished to review the cavalry and June 8 was set as the date.[69]

While Stuart and his men were preparing to parade in front of General Lee, Lee concentrated on orchestrating the pending invasion of Pennsylvania. On June 7, Lee sent a message to Brigadier General Albert Jenkins, directing that he have his brigade ready to concentrate at either Strasburg or Front Royal by June 10. He admonished Jenkins to "Keep your horses as fresh as you can and have your whole command prepared for active service."[70] Lee also sent a message to Brigadier General John Imboden directing that he "attract the enemy's attention in Hampshire County" by moving toward Romney, West Virginia or another similar location. After completing his feint, Imboden was to cooperate with Lee's Army as it moved north through the Valley.[71]

On the morning of June 8, a cool day, the Cavalry Division assembled at Auburn. In form, the review that day was much like the review conducted three days earlier. The regiments lined up along the furrow with their commanders and the brigade commanders and staffs to their front. Stuart took his position in the center front of the assembly, taking care to ensure that all was in order among his troops. Noticing that the first sergeant of Chew's horse artillery battery was riding a mule with enormously long and flopping ears, Stuart ordered both man and mule from the ranks.[72] The first sergeant, George Neese, felt that Stuart's action was an unjustified indignity for himself and his mule.

When all was ready, Lee, accompanied by Lieutenant General James Longstreet, other general officers from Longstreet's infantry corps, and officer's from Lee's staff, rode onto the field and joined Stuart. As before, the review began with an inspection of the troops. This time General Lee led the party and set a smart pace on his favorite horse, Traveler.[73] Three days earlier, Stuart had been the focal point of attention. On this day, the men in the ranks most noticed Lee, riding with "easy posture and soldierlike mien," pointing occasionally to parts of the line of troops as he rode by.[74] On this occasion, the party was not joined by the brigade commanders and staff, who remained in their positions in the front of the line of troops. After passing around the ranks, Lee, Stuart, and the others in the party returned to their position on the small hill.

About to order assembled units to make their pass in review, Stuart noticed that Jones' brigade appeared unready, apparently standing "at ease" in the ranks. Jones was the junior brigadier general, and consequently his brigade may have been positioned on the left flank of the line of troops. If so, he would have had a wait of roughly an hour between when Lee passed by and when the Laurel brigade would have to march off to pass in review. Jones had a reputation for detesting ceremonies and flamboyance, and it would have been in character for him to have allowed the troopers to relax while they waited. Stuart thought otherwise and ordered a young lieutenant on his staff to ride to Jones and ask about the situation. The lieutenant found General Jones lounging on the ground next to his horse, dutifully made his inquiry, and in return received a tongue-lashing from "Grumble." Nonetheless, as the lieutenant turned away to return to Stuart's reviewing position, he heard Jones' bugler sound "boots and saddles" and the brigade quickly mounted-up and prepared to march.[75]

The regiments' pass in review on June 8 was a much more subdued affair than that of three days earlier. General Lee, being concerned about the condition of the men and horses, directed that the regiments not gallop. Thus, the cavalry made no simulated charges for his benefit. Additionally, Lee prohibited the horse artillery from exercising their pieces.[76] The lack of action may, in part, have led one member of General Lee's entourage to grumble that they required him to sit on his horse "in the dust for half the day for the squadrons to march in display backward and forward near us."[77] However, General Longstreet's adjutant spoke for most when he later recalled that "It was a magnificent day, befitting the superb body of cavalry that, under Stuart, marched rapidly in review for the Commander-in-Chief. A sight it was not soon to be forgotten. The utmost order prevailed. There could be no doubt that the cavalry was as ready for the work before us as was our matchless infantry."[78]

The Chaplain of the 6th Virginia contrasted the two reviews from the perspective of a participant. He observed that both were "grand affairs," but while the earlier review had been "graced by the presence of a large crowd of citizen spectators and ladies," their absence at the latter was "more than compensated by the generals who were close & observant onlookers."[79]

After the review, Lee recorded his personal impressions of the event in a letter to his wife. Apparently the days spent in "green and pretty" Culpeper had proved beneficial to Stuart's cavalry, as Lee noted: "It was a splendid sight. The men & horses looked well. They had recuperated since last fall. Stuart was in all his glory. Your son [Rooney] & nephews well & flourishing." However, Lee added that their nephew, Fitz Lee, was afflicted by rheumatism in his knee and was not mounted. Instead, during the review Fitz Lee was "sitting by some pretty girls in a carriage."[80]

Additionally, the review prompted some official business on Lee's part. After returning to his headquarters that afternoon, Lee wrote to Colonel Josiah Gorgas, the Confederate Army's Chief of Ordnance, informing him of complaints he had heard about equipment from Stuart's officers.

Lee informed Gorgas that he was told that the saddles manufactured in Richmond ruined the horses' backs, referring to the Jenifer, a style that had been adopted by the Confederacy and was manufactured at various locations in the South.[81] Lee also advised Gorgas that the cavalry's carbines were "so defective that they demoralized the men," referring to the Confederate version of the Sharps carbine. The barrels of several of the "Richmond Sharps" weapons had burst during field testing, a problem that was reported in the newspapers. Also, gunpowder leaking from the paper cartridges supplied by the Confederacy tended to accumulate under the breech of the Richmond Sharps. When a subsequent round was fired, the powder would occasionally ignite, flashing in the face of the shooter. Although not particularly dangerous, a flash-in-the-face was disconcerting to the man firing the weapon.[82]

Lee, who earlier in the war had served as Jefferson Davis' military advisor, advised Gorgas that he was aware of the difficulties in manufacturing arms and equipment, and that he thought it would be better "to make fewer articles and have them serviceable."[83] No response from Gorgas to Lee was recorded.[84]

After the review, most of the cavalry shifted to new camps nearer the Rappahannock

5 — Stirring Events

to be better positioned for supporting the pending movement of the army to the Shenandoah Valley. Fitz Lee's brigade, less the 4th Virginia Cavalry which was detached, crossed the Hazel River with a section of horse artillery and took up camp near Oak Shade, picketing the upper fords on the Rappahannock. Since Fitz Lee was unable to ride, the brigade was under the temporary command of Colonel Thomas T. Munford of the 2nd Virginia, its senior colonel.[85] Rooney Lee's brigade and a section of artillery encamped near the Wellford house to the south of the Hazel River. Elements of Jones' Brigade were positioned along the road between Brandy and Beverly's Ford and was responsible for picketing that crossing site.[86] Robertson's Brigade moved to camps to the west of Brandy between Auburn and the Barbour House. The Barbour family had recently renamed their farm Beauregard, in honor of General P.G.T. Beauregard after the Confederate victory at First Manassas.[87] Robertson was assigned responsibility for picketing the lower crossing sites on the Rappahannock, principally Kelly's Ford.[88] Farther to the south, Hampton's Brigade occupied its old camps between Brandy and Stevensburg.[89] Beckham and the bulk of his horse artillery battalion camped at the side of the road leading to Beverly Ford, a little over a mile back from the river.

On the previous day, June 7, Stuart had shifted his headquarters from Afton to the east end of Fleetwood, a long ridge rising above the plain on the south side of the Rappahannock. Stuart and his staff pitched their tents about one half mile north of Brandy Station near the Miller House. At that point, Fleetwood was occasionally called Miller House Hill.[90]

Returning to the camp on Fleetwood from the review, von Borcke learned that two of his horses and his small gray mule, Kitt, were missing. While von Borcke was at that day's review, his servant had turned von Borke's animals out to graze, but had failed to keep a watchful eye on them. Von Borcke immediately assumed that the three missing animals had been stolen. Good horses were in short supply and in each regiment there were a number of troopers who were unmounted. Consequently, theft of unattended horses was a persistent problem when regiments were camped near each other.

For von Borcke the loss of the animals was a particularly severe blow. Because he was so large, the average horse was unsuitable. Consequently, von Borcke bought only exceptionally large, strong, and (therefore) expensive mounts. Von Borcke and his servant spent the remainder of the afternoon and evening searching the surrounding camps for the missing horses and mule, but their efforts were fruitless. That night around the fire, von Borcke's messmates teased him unmercifully about his loss.[91]

Elsewhere Stuart's troopers, much "worried out by the military foppery and display," rolled into their blankets for a night of well-deserved rest.[92] Unfortunately, their sleep would be disturbed before sunrise the following morning.

6

What Dispositions Should Be Made?

Union Preparations for Combat, May 23–June 8, 1863

JEB Stuart made no particular effort to conceal the movement of his brigades to Culpeper, and Union scouts and spies quickly detected the concentration of Confederate cavalry well to the west of Hooker's army. In Washington, fears arose that Stuart might be preparing to embark on a raid of particularly grand scale. After all, in December 1862 Stuart had penetrated Union lines and ridden all the way to Burke Station in Fairfax County with only eighteen hundred troopers. While at Burke Station, Stuart had even taken the time to send a telegram to the Union army's Quartermaster General, Montgomery Meigs, complaining about the poor quality of Union mules he was capturing.[1] At the head of his entire division, Stuart might be tempted to maraud throughout Maryland, into Pennsylvania, or even to attack Washington, although the Capital was well defended by a strong garrison occupying a ring of more than 60 forts.

On May 23, the day after Stuart reviewed the three brigades then present in Culpeper, Edwin. M. Staunton, Lincoln's Secretary of War, sent a memo to Major General Henry Halleck, the army's General in Chief, asking:

> In view of the possibility of an early raid by the enemy, I desire you to state—
> 1. What provision, in the present condition of the Army of the Potomac and the forces around Alexandria, Baltimore, and Washington, should be made to guard against such raids.
> 2. Whether proper precautions have been taken to guard against such raids.
> 3. What dispositions of our cavalry forces should be made under present circumstances.
> 4. Any other suggestions you deem proper to make in respect to the above-mentioned forces for offense or protection. You will also state what cavalry force now belongs to the Army of the Potomac, where it is, and on what duty engaged.[2]

Later that day Halleck responded. He gave Stanton a status report on the Army of the Potomac, and told Stanton that the army had already undertaken several actions to protect Washington better. These included felling trees along routes toward the capital, nightly removal of the wooden planking on the Chain Bridge over the Potomac, frequent inspection of the city's fortifications by officers, and the establishment of a cavalry screen beyond the line of fortifications. Brigadier General Julius Stahel's division manned the cavalry screen.[3]

In his memorandum, Halleck noted that Confederate cavalry was rumored to be massing around Culpeper. He recommended that Hooker's Cavalry Corps be employed either protecting the Orange & Alexandria Railroad, an important supply route for the Army of the Potomac, or "attacking and breaking up the enemy's cavalry."[4] However, Halleck, more clerk-in-chief than general-in-chief, closed his memorandum by reminding Stanton that he had no authority over the Army of the Potomac, and that Hooker reported directly to President Lincoln.

The following day, Stanton forwarded Halleck's memorandum to President Lincoln. By that time, Hooker had certainly learned of the contents of Halleck's memorandum, including Halleck's recommendation regarding the employment of the Army of the Potomac's Cavalry Corps. While Halleck was writing his response to Stanton, Hooker's chief of staff, Brigadier General Daniel Butterfield, was visiting the War Department on business, and the two generals had conferred regarding how best to protect Washington from a Confederate raid.[5]

On May 25, Hooker traveled from his headquarters in Stafford County to Washington for meetings with Stanton and the President.[6] While no record of their discussions was maintained, they doubtless talked about the ominous massing of Confederate cavalry in Culpeper, and the proposals made by Halleck regarding options for the employment of Hooker's cavalry. Hooker obviously recognized the need to protect the Orange and Alexandria and prevent its interdiction — train transportation was essential for supplying that part of his army guarding the upper Rappahannock.[7] By temperament, however, Hooker was offensive minded and he probably wanted to strike a blow south of the Rappahannock if he could be assured of success.

Nonetheless, before Hooker could again launch his horsemen with exhortations to "fight, fight, fight," it was necessary that he get the Cavalry Corps — worn down after Stoneman's Raid — back into shape. The men could be restored and ready for action after only a few days' rest. The horses were another story. Many horses were worn out from being overworked and underfed. Other horses were afflicted with sores on their backs from not being unsaddled for days and weeks while behind Confederate lines. To recover, horses in such poor condition needed a lengthy period of rest and proper feed.

The day before Hooker's meetings with Stanton and the President in Washington, Brigadier General Rufus Ingalls, the Army of the Potomac's Quartermaster, sent a message to Brigadier General Montgomery Meigs, the army's Quartermaster General, advising that the Cavalry Corps' need for horses "has never been so severely felt as at this moment." Ingalls asked that Meigs provide three to four thousand serviceable animals as soon as possible, and added that Meigs should that week send as many horses as his officers could procure.[8] Given the poor condition of his cavalry, Hooker undoubtedly followed up on Ingall's message by personally voicing his need for horseflesh in person during his discussions with Stanton and the President.

Hooker's need for several thousand horses placed Montgomery Meigs in a quandary — horses were in great demand everywhere and, in obedience to the laws of supply and demand, prices for horses had risen as quality had dropped. Also, the previous month Meigs had endured a spat with General William Rosecrans, commanding a Union army in Tennessee. Although his army had received more than 14,000 horses since November 1862, Rosecrans claimed that he was receiving far too few remounts and that most of those he did receive were unsuitable for cavalry service. To alleviate Rosecrans' problems, E. M. Stanton had directed that no effort be spared to provide horses to the Army of the Cumberland.[9] Now, it would be necessary to redirect the priority from Tennessee to Virginia.

While General Ingalls was prodding the Quartermaster Department for more horses, newly-installed Cavalry Corps Commander, Brigadier General Alfred Pleasonton, was more concerned with the welfare of the horses on hand. Upon assuming command, Pleasonton conducted an inspection of his corps and estimated that he had 6,677 serviceable mounts with a requirement for roughly 12,000. In actuality, Pleasonton's estimate of serviceable horses may have been overstated. Many commanders, holding the belief that a poorly mounted trooper was better than an unmounted trooper, had failed to condemn and return to the quartermaster horses that were incapable of standing up to hard service.[10] Thus, it is likely that many of Pleasonton's men, though mounted, were only marginally so.

To help prevent horses from being abused, Pleasonton issued an edict prohibiting the men from overburdening their mounts. Union cavalrymen were frequently accused of carrying too much superfluous equipment. The classic account — told repeatedly for its humor — was of a strapping Irish recruit preparing for his first campaign. The recruit packed his entire kit — extra clothing, bedding, rations, ammunition, pots and pans, etc.— into an immense knapsack. The well-meaning trooper then hoisted the pack on his back before mounting-up that he might share the load with his unfortunate horse. There may have been a kernel truth in the tale, for on May 24, Pleasonton directed that "Hereafter no enlisted man of cavalry will be permitted to take upon his horse anything except his arms, the rations of forage and subsistence ordered, one blanket besides the saddle blanket, and that under the saddle, and an overcoat."[11] The response to the new guidance among the men was not recorded.[12]

At the same time, Hooker instructed his cavalry commanders to send as few troops as possible on picket duty, consistent with the Army's need for security. The remainder of the men were to be kept in their camps where the men and animals could be "recruited" as much as possible. Although many men may have remained in camp, all was not rest and relaxation. Throughout history, military leaders have looked upon idleness among the men as a threat to efficiency and discipline. Consequently, energetic Union cavalry commanders initiated a rigorous round of inspections to ensure that the men and their weapons were clean, and that discipline was maintained.[13] In some units the results of the inspections added little to combat readiness, at least in the short run. In the 16th Pennsylvania many troopers' saddles were condemned and turned into the quartermaster along with many older horses.[14] Now suffering from a shortage of both saddles and horses, the regiment's ability to fight was significantly impaired, at least temporarily. In a letter dated May 24, Captain Charles Francis Adams, Jr. probably spoke for many members of the Cavalry Corps when he complained of "a camp life of monotony, varied only by ham and hard bread."[15]

Although many men were kept in camp, operations did not cease completely. Active picketing along the Rappahannock continued, and patrols were sent into Rebel-held territory. On May 22, a squadron from the 3rd Indiana Cavalry was sent by boat to the Northern Neck for two days of raiding, during which the Hoosiers captured one officer, a few Confederate deserters, and fifteen horses. The raiders were accompanied by Lieutenant George A. Custer, one of General Pleasonton's *aides de camp*. Custer ordered one captured horse — quite likely the best of the lot — turned over to General Pleasonton. The young lieutenant also profited from the raid, personally capturing two horses, which he kept for himself.[16]

Consistent with Halleck's recommendations to Stanton, patrolling the Orange and Alexandria Railroad was an important mission for Hooker's cavalry. The O&A's trains, traveling through the woods and fields of southern Fauquier County, were tempting targets for Mosby's men. Because of their irregular style, Federal authorities invariably referred to Mosby and his followers as thieves and bushwhackers. Officially, they were "partisan rangers," although even Stuart acknowledged that the title "partisan" implied a certain amount of lawlessness. Stuart, in his initial instructions to Mosby on March 25, 1863, advised the then-captain to avoid calling his men "partisan rangers" because the term was "in bad repute." Instead, Stuart recommended Mosby refer to his organization "Mosby's Regulars."[17] Initially, David McM. Gregg, commanding both his and Duffié's divisions, was responsible for picketing the upper Rappahannock and patrolling the railroad from Rappahannock Station to Catlett's Station.

Concurrently, it was necessary to have Kilpatrick's brigade, at the time camping across the York River from Yorktown at Gloucester Point, rejoin its division. Hooker directed Kilpatrick to make a thirty-mile sweep through Gloucester and Middlesex Counties to Urbanna, a hamlet on the south bank of the Rappahannock, with his 800 mounted men, while leaving his 200 dismounted men behind. At Urbanna, Kilpatrick was to rendezvous with ferries and gunboats from the navy's Potomac Flotilla, and cross the river to the Northern Neck. Once on the Northern Neck, Kilpatrick was to sweep up the peninsula to the Union lines near Falmouth. Since there were only guerillas and spies in the areas that Kilpatrick was to traverse, Hooker anticipated that Kilpatrick would meet no serious opposition. Instead of fighting Confederates, Hooker hoped that Kilpatrick would bring in a large number of contrabands and horses. The river crossing was scheduled for June 1 at 8:00 a.m. Hooker ordered Kilpatrick to be on time.[18]

As a backdrop to the army's routine activities, concern among Union officials regarding Stuart's presence in Culpeper continued to grow. On May 27, Hooker's Bureau of Military information issued a report on the concentration of Stuart's cavalry, advising that "There are three brigades of cavalry 3 miles from Culpeper Court House, toward Kelly's Ford. They can at present turn out only 4,700 men for duty, but have many dismounted men, and the horses are being constantly and rapidly recruited by the spring growth of grass. These are Fitz. Lee's, William H. Fitzhugh Lee's, and Wade Hampton's brigades. General Jones is still in the Valley, near New Market, with about 1,400 cavalry and twelve pieces of light artillery."[19] The information was remarkably accurate, but three days out of date. Apparently Colonel Sharpe's scouts, deserters, and network of Union sympathizers had not yet detected the arrival of Beverly Robertson with his thousand troopers, or the start of Jones' march from the Valley with roughly fifteen hundred more men.

In view of the buildup in Culpeper, Hooker became increasing concerned that Confederate troopers might cross the Rappahannock either to cut his supply lines or raid in the rear of his army. On the day following Sharpe's report, May 28, Hooker ordered a division from Meade's V Corps to defend Banks' Ford, United States Ford, Richards' Ford, and Kelly's Ford, all upriver from Fredericksburg. To further impede a possible Rebel advance, Pleasonton ordered David McM. Gregg, whose division was protecting the Orange & Alexandria Railroad from the Rappahannock to Catlett's Station, to destroy the rail bridge over the river at Rappahannock Station.[20]

On May 28, Pleasonton advised Hooker that he had received reports that many Rebel scouts were around Warrenton, and that the Confederate force there was reported to be large. Pleasonton recommended that Hooker release Buford and his brigade from their security mission near Dumfries on the Potomac in Prince William County, and send them to reinforce Gregg near Bealeton. Gratuitously, Pleasonton advised his superior that "The rebels always mean something when their scouts become numerous."[21]

Upon receiving Pleasonton's message, Hooker concurred with Pleasonton's recommendations and directed Pleasonton to order Buford with the Reserve Brigade from Dumfries to Bealeton. Hooker also provided explicit guidance to Pleasonton regarding what he wanted done. Once at Bealeton, Buford, as the senior general officer, was to take charge of all cavalry in the area and drive any Rebels he found back across the Rappahannock. Additionally, Hooker also gave Buford the discretion to cross the Rappahannock and drive Stuart out of Culpeper if he thought he had sufficient forces to accomplish that mission. Finally, Buford was to spare no effort to learn the purpose for the concentration of Confederate cavalry in Culpeper. Upon receiving Hooker's orders, relayed through Pleasonton, Buford replied laconically, "Your dispatch (instructions) has been received. I'll do my best."[22]

On May 30, Buford arrived in Bealeton and took command. He was welcomed by Mosby and a party of his men whom that day ambushed a train near Catlett's Station. The Rebels loosened a rail, but left it in place so that alert train crewmen would not detect the damaged track. The partisans then hid in a nearby thicket and awaited the approach of a southbound train. As the locomotive drawing a morning supply train neared the loosened rail, the partisans pulled the rail away from the track with a concealed rope, creating a gap. The locomotive ran over the gap and derailed, along with its following cars. Mosby and his men took the train under fire with their mountain howitzer before fleeing at the approach of a detachment of Stahel's cavalry. Buford, responding immediately, moved with part of his command up the tracks from Bealeton to Catlett's Station but found no sign of Confederates. He then set his men to work clearing the tracks of the train wreckage.[23] Buford, finding that the countryside north of Bealeton was more amenable for camping — with abundant fresh water readily nearby — shifted his headquarters to Warrenton Junction, a small hamlet a few miles south of Catlett's Station.[24]

The following day, Buford advised Pleasonton that reports of a Rebel build-up near Warrenton were greatly exaggerated. Based upon the results of reconnaissance missions to Sulphur Springs, Waterloo, and Orlean, Buford reported that the only Confederates in Fauquier were those that had been there all winter.[25]

Although the Confederates were not in Fauquier, they were nearby, and Stuart could not resist taking some offensive action. On June 3, the calm along the Rappahannock was broken by a sharp skirmish at Sulphur Springs. On that day Colonel Thomas Owen of the 3rd Virginia led a detachment of about three hundred men of Fitz Lee's brigade on a sweep along the river. Seeing a few pickets from the 1st Massachusetts Cavalry on the road leading from Sulphur Springs to Bealeton, Owen sent a squadron across the river to try to capture the Union troopers. Surprisingly, the Yankees, commanded by a lieutenant with "more spirit than discretion" put up a stiff fight, charging twice and inflicting saber wounds on a half-dozen Confederate troopers, while losing three men killed and two captured. The lieutenant, Daniel Gleason, was wounded by a saber blow to the head and then thrown to the ground when Dixie, his out of control horse, stumbled. Left behind as his men retreated, Gleason made his way into the woods and hid.

Upon hearing of the fighting, Captain Charles Adams Jr., whose company was camped nearby, ordered his men to mount. Once his company was in the saddle, Adams led them forward to aid their beleaguered comrades. After galloping about one half mile, Adams and his men met the withdrawing pickets "flushed and hatless from their rapid retreat, but all steady and quiet under the command of Sergeant Jimmy Hart, an old rough and fighting man, and evidently there was lots of fight in them yet." Expecting to meet advancing Rebels at every bend in the road, Adams and his company, now reinforced by the pickets, pushed ahead to Sulphur Springs, arriving only after the Confederates had withdrawn to safety on the south side of the river. That a Union detachment of only two officers and thirty-three men had fought so aggressively against a much larger body of Rebels was an encouraging omen to Adams, who had witnessed first-hand the havoc wreaked on Federal cavalry by Fitz Lee's men at Hartwood Church only three months earlier.[26]

In the days after his meeting with Stanton and the President, Hooker mulled over Halleck's proposal and began voicing an interest in striking a preemptive blow against Stuart. In a message on May 28, he advised Stanton that Stuart now had five brigades in Culpeper and Jefferson[ton], and that had Stoneman not "almost destroyed" half his cavalry, he would "pitch in" to Stuart. In a bid to gain control of Major General Stahel's cavalry division assigned to the defense of Washington, Hooker added that he would attack Stuart immediately if he were augmented by Stahel's cavalry for a few days.[27] The following day, Stanton responded, informing Hooker that his proposal had been forwarded to the President, but that General Halleck had advised against releasing Stahel's cavalry to the Army of the Potomac, as it was committed to the defense of Washington.[28] Hooker's response to the rebuff was not recorded.

On May 29, the army's remount system finally began to respond to Hooker's request for horses. On that day, Montgomery Meigs sent Hooker a telegram advising the army commander that he had just discussed the shortage of horses in the Army of the Potomac with Secretary Stanton. Meigs told Hooker that he hoped to be able to provide the Army of the Potomac 2,500 horses within a week. In way of excuse, Meigs explained delays in satisfying Hooker's request were the result of a rise in the price of horses and the need to supply Rosecrans. However, Meigs assured Hooker that remounts were again arriving in Washington in large quantities, including 340 that very morning.

In his message, Meigs also chided Hooker regarding the need for his army to better conserve its stock of horses. He recommended that Hooker not allow officers, who were permitted to purchase horses from the quartermaster at fixed prices, to buy horses and then send them home for future personal use. Meigs recommended that if an officer no longer needed a former quartermaster horse to perform his military duties, he should be required to return the horse to the government. Meigs also warned Hooker that sutlers and camp followers, perhaps with the assistance of soldiers, were smuggling captured horses to the North. Finally, observing that "a horse is as much contraband of war as a barrel of gunpowder, and, being used by a guerrilla, a spy, or a messenger, more injurious to us [and] even in the plow they relieve the men from the necessity of digging for a living," Meigs recommended that Hooker leave no horse, whatever its condition, in Rebel territory.

Noting that the Army of the Potomac had 31,000 horses and 14,000 mules, Meigs closed his message by suggesting that Hooker mount a body of infantry and together with his cavalry and light artillery strike a blow against Stuart. Meigs opined that Hooker might capture or destroy whatever Rebel force was encountered, disrupt Rebel plans, and improve the morale of Hooker's men.[29]

Hooker's response to Meigs' message is not recorded. Undoubtedly, he was pleased with the news that he would soon be receiving remounts in large quantities. It is equally likely that he did not appreciate receiving gratuitous advice from a Washington bureau chief. Hooker, however, might have pondered over Meigs' suggestion that he conduct a preemptive strike into Culpeper. Perhaps Stanton had mentioned that course of action in his discussions with the Quartermaster General. If so, Meigs' comments might be a hint to Hooker that he was expected to take action.

The situation regarding what to do about Stuart's cavalry came to a head on June 5 and 6. On June 5, against a backdrop of alarming reports that Stuart was within three days of starting on a raid with 15,000 to 20,000 troopers—including mounted Texan infantrymen—Hooker advised President Lincoln that he anticipated Lee would soon begin moving his infantry to the west and north. Hooker recommended that he attack into the rear of Lee's army, but cautioned the President that if he did so, he might temporarily leave Washington and Harpers Ferry unprotected.

In conjunction with his plans for taking the offensive, Hooker ordered Pleasonton to dispatch a large body of cavalry against Stuart to disrupt the Confederate commander's plans. Accordingly, Pleasonton sent a message to Buford directing that he "make a strong demonstration without delay upon the enemy in your front toward Culpeper, and push them as far as possible without jeopardizing your command. The enemy are in motion in front of Fredericksburg; a portion have gone toward Orange Court-House. Keep me fully advised."[30] In response, Buford assigned the mission to Duffié, who with his division was ordered to cross the Rappahannock at Sulphur Springs and approach Culpeper Courthouse from the north.

Lincoln responded to Hooker's telegram on the afternoon of June 5. The President, who had good reason to doubt Hooker's ability to best Lee in battle, provided the general with some practical advice. Lincoln cautioned Hooker to avoid becoming entangled by the Rappahannock and there be "like an ox jumped half over a fence and liable to be torn by dogs front and rear, without a fair chance to gore one way or kick the other." General Halleck, following up on the President's advice, opined that it might be wiser for Hooker to fight Lee's army once it moved north of the Rappahannock and perhaps presented a flank that was vulnerable to attack. Halleck again suggested to Hooker that the most immediate threat was from Stuart's cavalry, not Lee's infantry.[31]

Finding little support for his plans in Washington, Hooker made modifications. Instead of attacking across the Rappahannock into Lee's rear, Hooker decided to conduct a demonstration to feel out the Confederate strength remaining at Fredericksburg. Accordingly, on June 6 Hooker sent Sedgewick's corps across the river on pontoon bridges. Additionally, Hooker decided to take action against Stuart. That afternoon, Hooker sent a message to Halleck outlining his plan for dealing with the threat presented by the Confederate cavalry in Culpeper County:

> As the accumulation of the heavy rebel force of cavalry about Culpeper may mean mischief, I am determined, if practicable, to break it up in its incipiency. I shall send all my cavalry against them, stiffened by about 3,000 infantry. It will require until the morning of the 9th for my forces to gain their positions, and at daylight on that day it is my intention to attack them in their camps. As many of my cavalry are still unserviceable from the effects of Stoneman's raid, I am too weak to cope with the numbers of the enemy if as large as represented. It would add much to my efficiency if some of Stahel's forces could advance, and hold the fords at Beverly and Sulphur Springs some time during the forenoon of the 9th. If this should be done, I desire that the officer in command should not be informed of the object of his march, but merely to hold these fords. It is next to impossible to confine information to its proper limits.
>
> I have 2,500 sabers on a reconnaissance to-day in the vicinity of Jefferson[ton]. Jones' brigade, which has been hovering about Milroy all winter, numbering 1,600, is among them; also an additional brigade from North Carolina.[32]

Having decided upon a course of action, Hooker set about organizing his attack, a task made more difficult by his insistence that information regarding his plans not be disclosed prematurely. While Hooker was secretly making his plans, Pleasonton, most likely advised that a major mission was imminent, reorganized the command structure of the Cavalry Corps. On June 6, he formed the 1st Division and the Reserve Brigade into one command under Buford, and combined the 2nd and 3rd Divisions into a single command under Gregg.[33] This restructuring provided several advantages. First, it relieved Pleasonton of the responsibility of commanding both the 1st Division and the Cavalry Corps. Second, it formally provided Buford, considered by many to be the most competent cavalry commander, with increased responsibility. Finally, by subordinating Duffié to Gregg, it decreased the authority and responsibility of the Frenchman, a desirable outcome in view of Pleasonton's prejudice against foreigners. Because of the reorganization and the need to position the forces for an attack into Culpeper, it was necessary for the 1st Cavalry Division to move from its camps near Stafford Courthouse and Brooks' Station, midway between Falmouth and Aquia Landing, to Catlett's Station and Warrenton Junction, where Buford was located with the Reserve Brigade. The division's regiments made the move on June 7.[34] In a mix-up, the 12th Illinois Cavalry did not make the move. The 12th Illinois had been assigned to Wyndham's brigade of the 2nd Division, but during Stoneman's Raid, it had linked up with Kilpatrick's column at Gloucester Point. Once the regiment had returned with Kilpatrick to Falmouth during the first week of June, it had been reassigned to the 1st Cavalry Division. The Regimental Commander, Colonel Arno Voss, was instructed by Kilpatrick to join his new division as "soon as practicable," but no time was specified. Consequently, the regiment remained in camp near Stafford Courthouse while the Division moved to Warrenton Junction. The loss, however, was not great, since the 12th Illinois could muster only 120 effectively mounted troopers.[35]

While Hooker was corresponding with Washington and mulling over his plans, and Pleasonton was reorganizing, Duffié was conducting the "demonstration" to Jeffersonton. Initially, the regiments were formed-up to move from their camps at Bealeton at 9:00 p.m. on June 5, but then the departure was postponed until 2:00 a.m. on the following day, The long columns finally got under way about 2:30 a.m. and crossed the Rappahannock near Sulphur Springs about noon. The division reached Jeffersonton without meeting any opposition and then turned South toward the Hazel River and Rixeyville. To Captain Charles Adams, it appeared as if the only purpose of the operation was "to pick a fight," but instead of cooperating, any Rebels they met immediately fled.[36]

While Duffié was making his uneventful sweep through the Little Fork, Hooker received a false report that three brigades of Stuart's cavalry were at Jeffersonton, prompting the army commander telegraph Buford directly and ask "Can you tell me how this is?" Buford responded that Hooker's information was incorrect since Duffié was then near Jeffersonton with his division. Additionally, Pleasonton, probably relaying orders from Hooker, notified Buford that the previous day's order to conduct the demonstration was cancelled. Buford, doubtless frustrated with the indecision at higher headquarters, advised Pleasonton that it was too late to cancel the mission, but that he had sent a rider out to recall the French colonel and his men.[37]

Upon receiving orders from Buford to pull back, Duffié turned his division about and the troopers—"dirty, hungry, tired, and with weary and unfed horses"—crossed back into Fauquier County at Sulphur Springs as the sun was setting.[38] After halting for an hour to feed the horses, the division marched through the night to Bealeton, arriving about 3:00 a.m. During the march, officers and men slept in their saddles as their horses trudged along the dark trails. A few riders—sleeping soundly—were carried off by their horses as the hungry animals left the column and wandered off into fields to graze. On the morning of June 8, Duffié cancelled Reveille, allowing his men to sleep until 9:00 a.m.[39]

Meanwhile, since Hooker had determined that the Cavalry Corps would require infantry support to effectively destroy Stuart's cavalry, it was necessary to organize a suitable force. Instead of simply tasking a corps to provide a unit of the appropriate strength, Hooker took the unusual step of forming two "picked" brigades, each to consist of fifteen hundred infantrymen plus an artillery battery.

As a first step, it was necessary for Hooker to select an appropriate commander for each brigade. Hooker chose newly-promoted Brigadier General Adelbert Ames, a sailor-turned soldier, to fill one position. After a stint as mate on a clipper ship, Ames entered West Point, graduating with the Class of May 1861 and receiving a commission in the artillery. Ames saw his first action at Manassas two months later where, although shot in the thigh and suffering from a shattered femur, he continued to lead his gun section while sitting atop a limber. For that act, the Army breveted him to major and later awarded him the Medal of Honor.[40] Ames commanded an artillery battery in the Peninsular Campaign and afterwards transferred to the infantry, accepting a promotion to colonel of volunteers and appointment as commander of the 20th Maine. Ames led his regiment at Fredericksburg and at Chancellorsville with distinction and, having proven himself an effective combat leader, was promoted to brigadier general on May 20, 1863.[41] This was Ames' first command as a general officer.

Initially Hooker chose Alexander Shaler, who had been promoted to brigadier on May 26 to fill the second brigade command billet. Before the war Shaler had served in the New York militia, rising to the grade of major. Since the beginning of the war, the New Yorker had served with the Army of the Potomac and participated in most of its battles. For his gallantry in command of a regiment at Fredericksburg he was later awarded the Medal of Honor.[42] At the last minute, however, Shaler was replaced and Brigadier General David A. Russell was appointed to command the picked brigade. Russell had graduated from West Point in 1845 and served in Mexico and the Pacific Northwest as an infantry officer. By 1861, after sixteen years' service, he had risen to the grade of captain in the 4th Infantry. In January 1862 Russell, like many of his regular officer contemporaries, joined the volunteers and was appointed colonel of the 7th Massachusetts Infantry. He did well as a colonel and was promoted to brigadier general in November of that year.[43]

After selecting commanders, mustering the troops was necessary. Accordingly, on June 6 Hooker sent dispatches to the commanders of the III, XI, XII Corps, ordering each to provide a command of five hundred men ("one or two regiments") to General Ames. The units were to rendezvous that night at Spotted Tavern, near Hartwood Church. Hooker provided detailed guidance for the organization of each corps' detachment.

> The command to go prepared to be absent a few days from camp, say five or so; 150 rounds of ammunition by pack-mules and on the person; no wagons, knapsacks light, for purposes to be made known. It is desired that the command sent should be one well disciplined and drilled, capable of marching rapidly, and of endurance; that the officers should be noted for energy and efficiency. Two ambulances, properly supplied to accompany them. You will report here the name of the commanding officer and the regiments assigned for this duty. The destination of these men will be confidential with the commanding officer. The pack-mules for the ammunition and the officer's shelter tents and rations should come from the reserve mules supplied by the chief quartermaster for contingent uses, to avoid, if possible, taking any from the wagons. The pack masters, ambulance attendants &c., should be supplied, so that the effective fighting command reached the number specified above.[44]

Hooker sent similar dispatches the following day to the commanders of the I and VI Corps, directing each to provide six hundred men, and to the commander of the II Corps, who was to detach a command of three hundred men. Those detachments were to report that night to General Russell at Hartwood Church. The dispatch to those three corps commanders also requested that they "please instruct the commander of the expedition to select such a route as will prevent the enemy on the opposite side of the river from observing his movement, and to take into custody all citizens he may meet with on the way, to prevent them from informing against us."[45]

The affected corps commanders quickly set about organizing the detachments they were to send to General Ames and General Russell. Concurrently, Hooker directed his Chief of Artillery to task the commander of the Army of the Potomac's artillery reserve to provide a battery of horse artillery to each of the picked brigades.[46]

By gathering regiments from three different corps to form each brigade, Hooker added to the complexity of the task. Most regiments in the Army of the Potomac did not have sufficient strength to meet a corps quota of five or six hundred men. Consequently, most corps commanders found it necessary to task two or more regiments for the mission. For example, General Sickles, commanding III Corps, detached the 86th New York and the 124th New York from the 2nd Brigade of General Birney's division. General Slocum, commanding the XII Corps, provided troops from 2nd Massachusetts and the 3rd Wisconsin, both assigned to the 3rd Brigade of General Williams' division. The 3rd Wisconsin was apparently a last-minute addition, made at the request of the 2nd Massachusetts (the officers of the two regiments messed together over the winter's encampment).[47] The brigade was rounded out the 33rd Massachusetts from 2nd Brigade of General Steinwehr's division, General Howard's XI corps. All totaled, General Ames' picked brigade consisted of men from five regiments.

Similarly, General Russell's brigade was put together with men from seven regiments. General Reynolds, whose I Corps was tasked with providing six hundred men, selected the 7th Wisconsin, augmented by two companies from the 2nd Wisconsin, both regiments from the renowned "Iron Brigade" of Wadsworth's division, and the 56th Pennsylvania from the 2nd Brigade of Wadsworth's division.[48] General Hancock, commanding the II Corps, made his quota by tasking the 5th New Hampshire and the 81st Pennsylvania from the 1st Brigade of General Caldwell's division.[49] General Sedgewick, the VI Corps commander, chose the 6th Maine and the 119th Pennsylvania from the 3rd Brigade—conveniently commanded by General Russell—of Wright's division.[50]

While the troops were en route to their rendevous at Spotted Tavern and Hartwood Church, Hooker sent separate messages to Generals Ames and Russell directing them to report to General Pleasonton for orders. Both brigade commanders were admonished to conceal their movements, to apprehend any "guerrillas, spies, or wanderers" they might meet, and to keep their commands ignorant of their destination.[51] Ames and his brigade left Spotted Tavern on the morning of June 7 and had an easy day's march to Bealeton, where they went into camp to await the arrival of Pleasonton's cavalry.[52] Along the way, the Union troopers arrested any men they found, leaving behind weeping women and children.[53] Reportedly, during the march General Ames was much interested in a novel, which he pulled from his pistol holster to read at halts.[54] Russell's brigade assembled at Hartwood Church at around midnight on June 7 and on the morning of June 8 the men commenced their march toward Kelly's Ford, reaching that location about 5:00 p.m. The march went without incident, but reportedly the men suffered from a lack of water along the way.[55]

As an added measure, General Hooker informed General Meade, commanding the 5th Corps, that he had ordered Pleasonton to make an attack into Culpeper. Hooker ordered Meade, whose corps was picketing the Rappahannock, to provide any assistance that Pleasonton might need. Meade, through his division commander, directed that Colonel Jacob Sweitzer, whose infantry brigade guarded the north bank of the Rappahannock at Kelly's Ford, cooperate with Pleasonton in any manner requested.[56]

On the morning of June 7, Pleasonton arrived at Warrenton Junction to personally begin directing the operations of the Cavalry Corps. The cavalry general was under the impression that the infantry brigades would be in-place for an attack on the following morning, June 8. However, about noon, General Butterfield wired Pleasonton that Russell's infantry would not arrive at Kelly's Ford until the evening of June 8, consequently, the attack could not begin until June 9.[57]

Not trusting the telegraph's security, at 4:15 p.m. on June 7, Hooker dispatched one of his most trusted *aides de camp*, Captain Ulrich Dahlgren, to Pleasonton's Headquarters with orders for the pending strike into Culpeper. Dahlgren, the son of Admiral John Dahlgren, commander of the Washington Naval Yard, had recently proposed that a regiment or two of cavalry make a raid to burn the bridges over the James River, and then "dash through Richmond." Hooker wisely turned down the ill-conceived scheme.[58] Hooker ordered Dahlgren to remain with Pleasonton after delivering the orders, perhaps so that he might later give Hooker an objective assessment of the attack on Stuart.

Leaving as little as possible to chance, Hooker's orders—written by his chief of staff, Daniel Butterfield—to his cavalry commander were detailed and specific.

> I am directed by the major-general commanding to inform you as follows:
>
> Brigadier-General Ames left here yesterday and Brigadier-General Russell marches to-day, and it is expected that their brigades, consisting of 1,500 men and a horse battery, will be in position tomorrow night. The latter marches with rations for three days, and will require to be replenished before they cross the river from Bealeton. As they march without wagons, it will be advisable to have them sent to Kelly's Ford, in season to be distributed to-morrow night. Two boats have also been forwarded, to facilitate the passage of the last-named ford. As it is held by the enemy's pickets it may be advisable to throw over a small party above or below the ford, to knock them away, without resorting to the use of artillery, as the first gun would be heard by the enemy at Culpeper and vicinity.
>
> From the most reliable information at these headquarters, it is recommended that you cross the Rappahannock at Beverly and Kelly's Fords, and march directly on Culpeper. For this you will divide your cavalry force as you think proper, to carry into execution the object in view, which is to disperse and destroy the rebel force assembled in the vicinity of Culpeper, and to destroy his trains and supplies of all description to the utmost of your ability. Shortly after crossing the two fords, the routes you will be likely to take intersect, and the major-general commanding suggests that you keep your infantry force together, as in that condition it will afford you a moving *point d'appui* [point of support] to rally on at all times, which no cavalry force can be able to shake. It is believed that the enemy has no infantry. Should you find this to be the case, by keeping your troops well in hand, you will be able to make head in any direction.
>
> The general also recommends that you make use of the forest and the cavalry to mask the movements of the infantry from the enemy's forces, and keep the enemy ignorant of their presence as long as possible, in order that at the proper time you may be able to cut off and destroy great numbers of them.
>
> The general further suggests that you throw out strong pickets in the direction of the Ely and Germanna Fords, and that you hold Stevensburg with not less than a regiment and a section of artillery, with special instructions to look after Raccoon Ford. All the fords on the Rappahannock below Kelly's, and including it, are held by our forces.
>
> If you should succeed in routing the enemy, the general desires that you will follow him vigorously as far as it may be to our advantage to do so.
>
> The officer in command holding Kelly's Ford will be instructed to lend you such aid as may be in his power, and it is hoped will be able to throw out on to the Culpeper road a sufficient force, in conjunction with your cavalry at Stevensburg, to secure your flank from any force in that direction.
>
> Captain Dahlgren, aide-de-camp, will deliver this to you, and it is desired that he should remain until you recross the river, and that you communicate with headquarters as often as practicable. He will hand you some maps of the direction in which you are operating. Having received no reply from Washington as to the force to be sent to your assistance from General Heintzelman's command, you will not be able to count upon any assistance from there.[59]

Hooker's orders to Pleasonton reflected a Napoleonic flair: the force to advance along multiple routes for speed and deception; the wings to concentrate before battle to better overwhelm any opposition; the enemy relentlessly pursued and destroyed. Hooker's plan

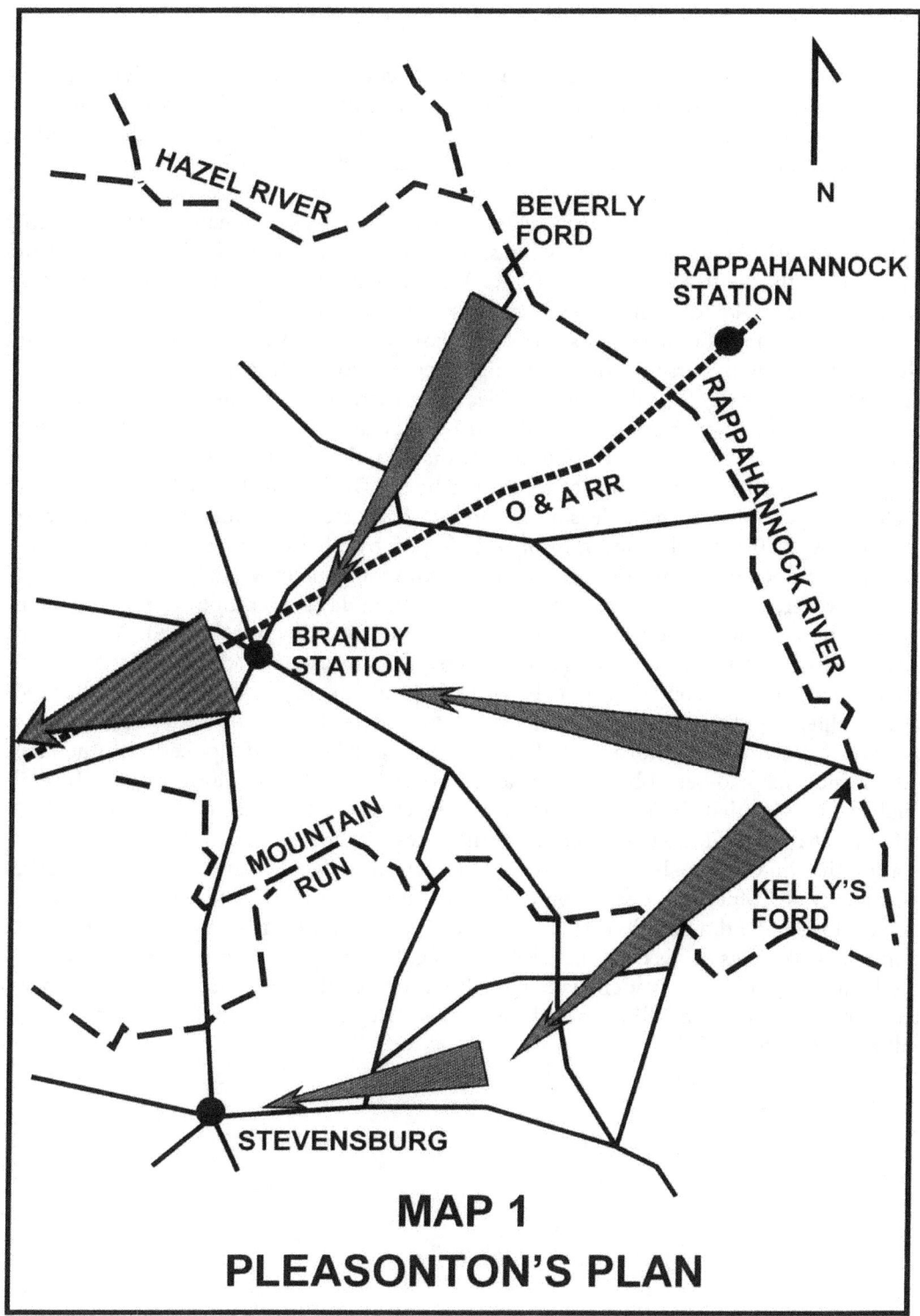

**MAP 1
PLEASONTON'S PLAN**

Alfred Pleasonton's Cavalry Corps was to cross the Rappahannock at first light on June 9, with Buford's wing at Beverly Ford and Gregg's wing at Kelly's Ford. After uniting at Brandy Station, Buford and Gregg were to march toward Culpeper Courthouse where Stuart's division was believed to be camped. Duffié's division was to move to Stevensburg to protect the Corps' left flank.

also reflected his lack of confidence in the ability of cavalry to achieve a decisive victory—infantry, concealed and kept close, would cut off Stuart's men and destroy their supplies. Pleasonton, who had been anxiously awaiting his orders and concerned that they might be too directive, found that little had been left to his discretion. Essentially, the only decision left to Pleasonton was to designate which "wing" of his corps would cross at each ford.

Nonetheless, June 8 was a busy day for the Cavalry Corps commander. That morning General Stahel had marched with between sixteen and seventeen hundred cavalrymen from Fairfax Courthouse to Kettle Run in Prince William County. Pleasonton arranged for the Hungarian general and his men to secure the railroad as far south as Bealeton, freeing the Cavalry Corps from that responsibility.[60] Pleasonton issued his orders to Buford and Gregg—probably in person—that they might begin repositioning their divisions to commence the attack early the following day. Pleasonton arranged for Buford to relieve Duffié's pickets along the Rappahannock with the 1st U.S. Cavalry, and ordered the Frenchman to move his division to Morrisville. Duffié was instructed that he was to take with him all baggage and least fifteen pounds of forage per horse. Duffié was directed to arrive before nightfall, if possible.[61] Finally, Pleasonton conducted a personal reconnaissance of the crossing sites. At 8:30 p.m. Pleasonton informed Hooker by telegraph that "things look favorable. At 4 o'clock in the morning [June 9] everything will be moving."[62]

However, when looking forward to the following day's operation, General Pleasonton may have privately had some doubts that everything would go as planned. When Duffié returned from his demonstration through Jeffersonton, Pleasonton advised Hooker that the Frenchman had only scouted the road between Sulphur Springs and Culpeper, not the roads from Culpeper to Stevensburg and Brandy Station where the bulk of Stuart's cavalry were reported.[63] Early on the morning of June 8, Pleasonton provided Hooker with the latest intelligence that had been obtained by General Gregg: "The scout, Yager, sent me by Colonel Duffié, says that the two Lees are at Culpeper. Hampton's Legion and almost 1,000 infantry at Brandy Station. Artillery at both places. Yager says that he has reliable information that infantry are being sent to the Valley from Lee's army, and that there is a force of infantry at Culpeper." Pleasonton did not comment on the fact that the presence of a cavalry brigade and a sizable infantry force at Brandy Station might make it difficult to unite the two wings of his corps before becoming decisively engaged with Stuart. Nor did the Union cavalry commander make any alterations to the plan formulated by General Hooker. Pleasonton, and all his people, as he had telegraphed to Hooker on June 7, were "all ready to pitch in."[64]

7

Success Was Dearly Bought

Beverly Ford to Saint James Church

While General JEB Stuart was busy displaying his command to Robert E. Lee, General Alfred Pleasonton was making final preparations for executing General Hooker's orders to cross into Culpeper and there "disperse and destroy" the Rebel cavalry.

In conformance with General Hooker's plan, Pleasonton organized the Cavalry Corps into two "wings." The right wing, under the command of General John Buford, was to cross the Rappahannock at Beverly Ford, two miles upstream from the Orange and Alexandria Bridge.[1] The left wing, under the command of General David McM. Gregg, was to cross at Kelly's Ford, four miles downstream from the railroad bridge. Both attacks were to commence just at first light, hopefully catching Stuart's horsemen by surprise and unable to react before the two wings united at Brandy Station, where roads from Beverly and Kelly's fords converged. From Brandy Station the combined force would advance toward Culpeper Courthouse, most likely paralleling the railroad line where the terrain—which included the site used by Stuart for his Grand Reviews—was favorable for cavalry fighting.

Hooker anticipated that Pleasonton would meet Stuart's cavalry somewhere between Brandy Station and Culpeper Courthouse and, augmented by two brigades of picked infantry, fully expected Pleasonton to crush the Rebels. Thus far in the war, cavalry—even Stuart's—had shown little inclination or ability to stand and fight against infantry. Additionally, morale was high among the blue-clad troopers of the Cavalry Corps, prompting Pleasonton to boast to Hooker that his men were ready to "pitch in" to the Confederates.[2]

On June 8, General Gregg moved his 3rd Cavalry Division south from Warrenton Junction to camp for the night near Kelly's Ford. There Gregg met his supporting infantry brigade, commanded by Brigadier General David A. Russell. The infantry regiments had marched on the previous day from their camps to a rendevous at Hartwood Church, and that day completed their movement to the ford. Some regiments had marched close to thirty miles over both days, and a lack of drinking water along the route in southern Stafford and Fauquier counties had plagued the men. During the march, Russell's infantry had used back roads, keeping to the "hollows and behind woods" in a successful effort to conceal their movement from Rebel scouts and spies.[3]

Meanwhile, Colonel Alfred N. A. Duffié moved his 2nd Cavalry Division from its positions around Catlett's Station to Morrisville, a hamlet a few miles north of Kelly's Ford. Some of Duffié's regiments arrived at Morrisville as early as 7:00 p.m. However, the movement of other regiments was much delayed, and many troopers did not go into camp until close to midnight. At Morrisville, Duffié awaited further orders from General Gregg, who would command both the 2nd and 3rd Divisions during the next day's operation.

Also on June 8, General Buford and the cavalry of his wing, the 1st Cavalry Division and the Reserve Brigade, broke camp around Warrenton Junction and marched to Bealeton. There an infantry brigade commanded by Brigadier General Adelbert Ames awaited their arrival. On the previous day, the infantry had marched to the whistle stop on the Orange & Alexandria from Spotted Tavern near Hartwood Church, a distance of about eighteen miles. After dark on the evening of June 8, Buford's combined force of infantry and cavalry quietly moved a few miles farther south, going into camp shortly before midnight approximately one half mile from the Rappahannock River.[4] As Buford had hoped, the Confederates did not detect his wing's approach march to the river.

General Pleasonton, who chose to accompany Buford's wing, and his staff moved south from Warrenton Junction and camped for the night about a mile from Beverly Ford at the home of William Bowen, Sr., a prominent local citizen. Bowen's son was at the time serving with the Black Horse Troop, Company H, 4th Virginia Cavalry, and other members of the Bowen family lived throughout the area. The nearest town, Rappahannock Station, had been known as Bowenville before the railroad pushed through the county in 1853.[5]

The Union soldiers settled down for a short, uncomfortable night. No fires were allowed, so the men went without warm meals. Light discipline was strictly enforced, at least in some units. Captain Daniel Oakey, 2nd Massachusetts Infantry, was placed under arrest when one of his men was caught with a fire.[6] However, in some units the desire for coffee overcame discipline, and men kindled small fires to brew their favorite drink.[7] Most of the cavalry troopers stretched out on the ground and napped, reins in hand, as their horses grazed about them. After a few hours' rest, the men were quietly awakened in preparation for the day's activities. The men mounted-up in silence. Bugle calls were prohibited, so "boots and saddles" was passed through the ranks in a low voice or whisper.

At 4:00 in the morning of June 9, the men of the Cavalry Corps' right wing began to advance quietly through the darkness toward Beverly Ford.[8] The way to the river had been scouted earlier that morning by a company of thirty men from the 2nd Massachusetts Infantry and found to be clear of Rebels, so the approach was uneventful.[9] Leading the way was an advance guard of two squadrons from the 6th New York Cavalry. Their mission was to quickly overwhelm the Confederate pickets expected to be guarding the south bank of the river, allowing Buford's main body to pass through the river without delay. Buford designated Colonel Benjamin Franklin "Grimes" Davis with his 1st Brigade to lead the main body, and Davis, with his reputation as an aggressive, hard-fighting officer was a good choice to spearhead the attack. Characteristically, Davis selected his own regiment, the 8th New York, to lead his brigade. Major Whiting's Reserve Brigade and Brigadier General Ames' infantry were to follow Davis through the ford, with the 2nd Brigade, commanded by Colonel Thomas Casimir Devin scheduled to cross the river last.[10]

The two squadrons of the advance guard arrived at the river just as it was beginning to get light and entered the water about 4:30 a.m.[11] A slight mist rose from the water, which was running stirrup-deep through the ford.[12] A few yards upstream there was a small dam, built in the 1840's to support barge traffic on the Rappahannock. Fortuitously for the advancing Federals, water rushing over the dam muffled the sound of the horses as they splashed through the river.[13] Most likely, given the depth of the water, the troopers and their horses crossed the river at a walk. Only with difficulty can horses move rapidly through water that is up to their chests. Further, going faster would increase the risk that one's horse would stumble over an unseen obstacle on the river's bottom. No trooper wished to risk a dunking just before a

7 — *Success Was Dearly Bought*   109

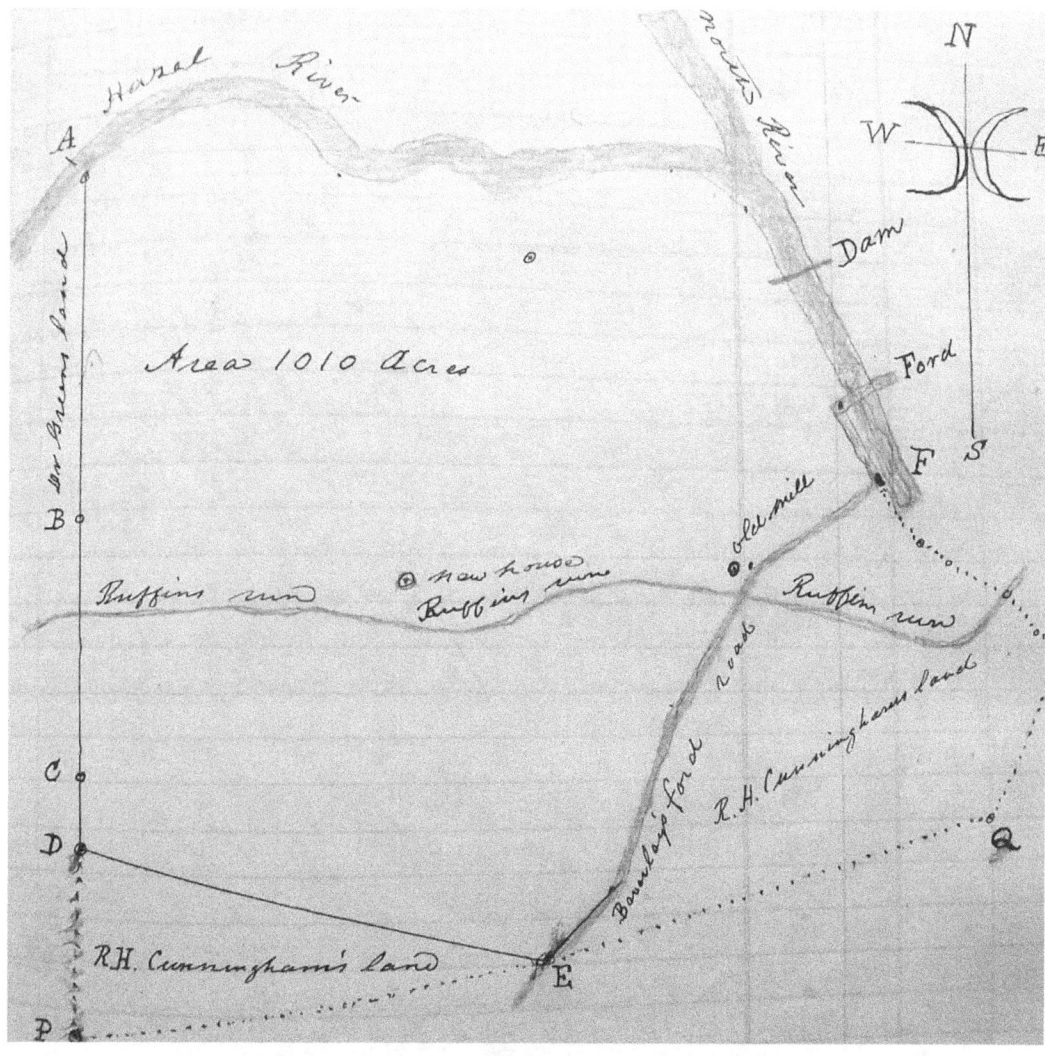

This 1866 plat shows the route of the Beverly Ford Road, along with the relative positions of Beverly Ford, a dam across the river, and the Little Fork. Much of the ground that was fought over on June 9 was owned by R.H. Cunningham, a major landowner in the county. The "new house" on Ruffins Run was probably built to replace Cunningham's original home, burned by Federals later in the war (Culpeper County Deed Records, photograph by Joseph W. McKinney).

battle. The crossing was further delayed since the banks of the river were steep and entrance and exit from the ford were narrow — the men were unable to enter the water four abreast, the normal width of a cavalry column.[14] In all likelihood, there was some confusion at the river with troopers held up on the north bank waiting to cross. As troopers waited in silence to enter the ford, the long column approaching the river naturally ground to a halt.

Buford was at the ford early, riding his favorite horse, Gray Eagle, and calmly smoking his pipe as the first of his troopers entered the water. Right behind Buford, General Pleasonton and his entourage arrived to observe the operation — thus far undetected by the Confederates.[15] Among Pleasonton's straphangers — he traveled with ten *aides de camp* — were several young, soon to be famous officers, including Captain George Armstrong Custer, one of Pleasonton's favorite *aides*. At the time Custer was actively promoting his own

Top: Beverly Ford today. Most of the river bed is silt, but at the ford, stones were placed on the bottom, most likely to prevent wagons from bogging down while crossing the river (Joseph W. McKinney). *Bottom*: The north bank of the Rappahannock at Beverly Ford. When the ford was in use, workers would have excavated the banks, which run roughly ten feet in height, to allow wagons to enter the river. Nonetheless, Union troopers commented about the steep banks they encountered as they rode their horses into the water on the morning of June 9, 1863 (Joseph W. McKinney).

Ripples in the water mark the site of the "crib" dam above Beverly Ford. Over time, the timbers in the dam rotted away and stones, placed between the timbers, sank into the river bottom. Water, rushing over the dam, concealed the sound of the Union cavalry approaching the river (Joseph W. McKinney).

advancement in the volunteers, an activity in which he would soon be successful.[16] Reportedly, also present as an *aide de camp* to Pleasonton was Ranald Slidell MacKenzie, who the previous year had graduated first in his class from West Point, been commissioned in the engineers, and served with distinction at Second Manassas and Fredericksburg.[17] Captain Ulrich Dahlgren, General Hooker's *aide de camp* whom the previous day had given Pleasonton his orders, was also present at the ford as an observer for the army commander.[18]

About the time Pleasonton arrived at the river, the cracking of pistol and carbine fire could be heard above the noise of the water rushing over the dam. The troopers of the 6th New York had made contact in the trees on the south bank of the river, surprising the Confederate pickets. The Battle of Brandy Station had begun.

Unexpectedly, the ford that morning was guarded by only two Confederate troopers, Privates Fleet and Bob James of Company A, 6th Virginia Cavalry. The James brothers failed to detect the New Yorkers' approach to the river because of the low-hanging mist and the sound of the rushing current, but they reacted quickly as the Union troopers emerged from the flowing water. Since resistance was hopeless, the two brothers immediately fled, firing their pistols into the air to alert the other men of their company.[19] The rest of Company A, about two dozen in all, were on "picket guard," camped a short distance back from the river. While the men of the picket guard were permitted to dismount and relax, they kept their horses saddled and bridled. Upon hearing the James brothers' fire, the company commander, Captain Bruce Gibson, ordered his men into their saddles. Gibson dispatched

This 1863 photograph shows Wellford's Ford on the Hazel River, about two miles upstream from Beverly Ford. A crib dam, similar to the one at Beverly Ford, obstructs the flow of the river just above the ford. Above the dam, a Union pontoon bridge spans the river (Library of Congress).

two couriers to warn his regiment of the advancing Union column, and formed the remaining men in a line at the edge of a stand of trees. A small cedar hedge to the front of the Confederates concealed their thin line and offered some protection, more psychological than physical, since a cedar bush will not stop a bullet.[20]

Meanwhile, at the river, Davis pressed ahead. He immediately sent the 8th New York Cavalry through the ford and once on the south bank, that regiment passed through the advance guard and moved south along the Beverly Ford Road. The 8th Illinois followed immediately behind the 8th New York. The dense woods near the river hampered the movement of both regiments. For security, Davis ordered a few men from the 8th New York to dismount and go forward as skirmishers to flush out any rebels who might be hiding among the trees.[21]

Meanwhile, as Gibson and his men prepared for action, the two pickets came galloping up from the river with Federals following close behind them.[22] Gibson steadied his men, passing up and down the line, encouraging the troopers to keep calm and telling them that when the time came, to "shoot to kill." A rank of mounted blue-clad troopers emerged from the trees in front of the Rebels, and Gibson ordered his outnumbered men to open fire.[23] In the first volley, twenty-three-year-old Lieutenant Henry Clay Cutler, the commander of Company B, 8th New York Cavalry, was struck in the neck by a bullet and fell dead, the first casualty of the day.[24] Cutler's men immediately charged at the Virginians. The Rebels, who had delayed the Union attack only momentarily, fled for their lives, lying over the necks of their horses to present smaller targets as Union carbine balls hissed past their heads. Gibson had several men wounded and left two men dead on the field.[25]

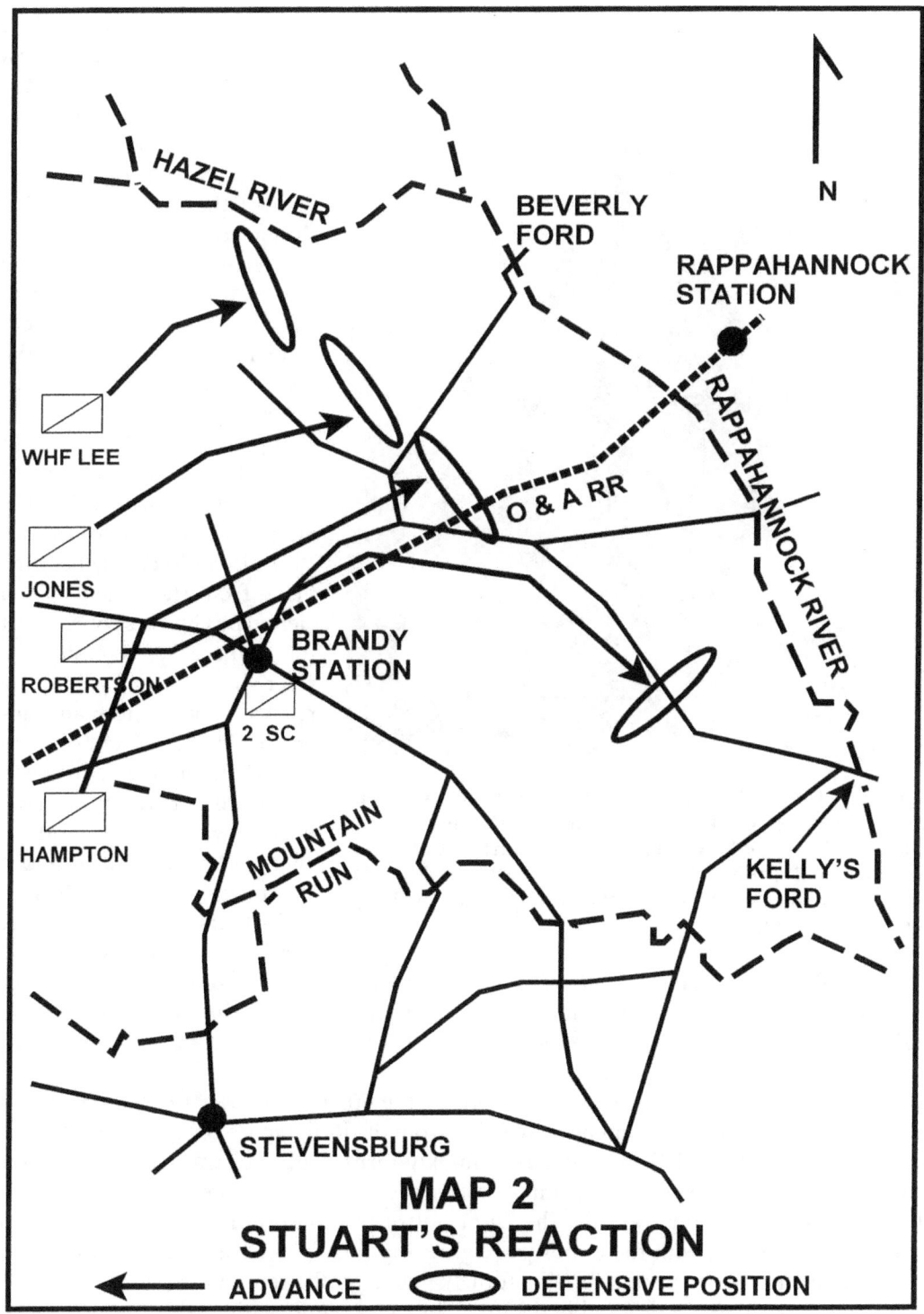

Upon receiving word of the Union attack, Stuart ordered his brigades forward to block the approaches from the fords. He also ordered Colonel Thomas Munford, commanding Fitz Lee's brigade (off the map north of the Hazel River) to move toward the developing battle. Initially, Stuart posted the 2nd South Carolina Cavalry in Brandy Station as a reserve.

Lieutenant Henry Clay Cutler, commanding Company B, 8th New York Cavalry, was killed — shot through the neck — in the opening volley of the battle. It is almost certain that Cutler was the first casualty of June 9 [New York State Military Museum and Veterans Research Center (courtesy US Army Military History Institute)].

Davis next ordered the 8th Illinois to move up abreast of the 8th New York. Once the regiments were aligned, he continued his movement south with the New Yorkers to the west of the road and the 8th Illinois to the east.

With the issue of his fitness to serve as major of the 6th Virginia unresolved, Cabell Flournoy made the most of the opportunity presented by the Federal attack. Camped around the Gee House beside the road leading from Beverly Ford to Brandy Station, the soldiers of the 6th Virginia could clearly hear the firing from the pickets. Then alerted by Gibson's courier that the Yankees were crossing the river in strength, Flournoy reacted immediately and aggressively. He ordered his men into their saddles, and when about half were ready, led them north toward the river and the enemy. At the head of about 150 men, some half-dressed and others reportedly riding bareback, Flournoy charged through Gibson and his pickets, who were fleeing as fast as possible from the horde of blue-clad attackers. Flournoy and his small party of Virginians struck the two leading Union regiments head-on and after a brief, sharp fight drove the surprised Union troopers back a short distance into the woods.[26]

The rush down the road to Beverly Ford by the 6th Virginia was the last charge for Private Opie's black mare. Upon hearing firing from the ford, Opie's company, led by lieutenants R. O. Allen and G. G. Shumate, quickly formed-up and galloped with Major Flournoy toward the river in a column of fours. Opie's black mare remained true to her character, and, according to Opie, she "shot out of the column like a thunderbolt and rushed down the road with the rapidity of lightening." The mare passed the other horses, taking Opie on a one-man charge as he futilely pulled on the reins and shouted "Whoa!" Opie briefly considered trying to kill the mare, but armed only with a saber (someone had stolen his pistol several days earlier), he had no means to do so. Opie also considered leaping off the mare, but given her speed he decided that was not a good alternative. Rounding a curve, Opie and the mare ran abruptly onto a party of advancing Union cavalrymen. As Opie later recalled that moment: "My hope was that, seeing a single horseman, they would understand my situation and not fire; but I suppose they thought it was the devil, as my horse was black as night, and was running at the rate of about forty miles an hour. At any rate, I saw them raise their carbines, then a line of smoke, then a crash; when, heels over head, both horse and rider tumbled through the air and fell, head long, in a pile on the side of the road." The mare, hit by four bullets, had died instantly. Opie was unhurt, although a ball had struck the sole of his boot. The now-horseless cavalryman jumped up, saber in hand, as his comrades charged past and began fighting the line of Union cavalry. Fortunately for Opie, he was quickly able to catch another horse, this one belonging to a lieutenant who had been shot dead, and remount.[27] Once back in the saddle, Opie rejoined his comrades as they began withdrawing back up the road toward Brandy Station. As Opie recalled, "quicker than some of us came up, we went."[28]

Not all men of the 6th Virginia were as fortunate as Opie. In the dust and confusion of the melee, Second Lieutenant Isaac Coles, the acting adjutant, could not tell friends from foe. He found himself surrounded by Yankees with his route of escape cut off. As Coles attempted to ride through the Yankee line, his horse was shot and he was thrown into a ditch as the horse fell. Coles arose, unhurt except a bloody cut on his nose, and he was promptly taken

Private John Opie, 6th Virginia Cavalry (shown here as a Virginia Military Institute cadet), rode his black mare in a one-man charge down Beverly Ford Road on the morning of June 9. Opie survived, the mare did not (*A Rebel Cavalryman*).

prisoner by an "Irishman." Coles later recalled that his captor asked if he were wounded. "I replied, 'No.' I sometimes wonder what my fate would have been had I answered, 'Yes.' He might have left me, or he might have shot me [just] 'to make sure.'"[29] In any event, Coles was marched to the rear and into captivity.

Flournoy's counterattack, though not delivered in great strength, was unexpected, and as a result the Union advance faltered. Colonel Grimes Davis, the senior Union officer south of the river, immediately set about regaining the momentum of his attack. To rally his men who were scattered in the woods, Davis trotted up the road past his front line, saber in hand, exhorting the troopers from New York and Illinois to follow him. Meanwhile, Lieutenant R. O. Allen and a few other men from the 6th Virginia had concealed themselves in the woods at the side of the road to further observe their enemy's actions. Upon seeing Davis

YOUNG PARSONS AVENGING THE DEATH OF COLONEL DAVIS AT THE BATTLE OF BEVERLY FORD.

This engraving of the death of Colonel Benjamin F. "Grimes" Davis mistakenly shows the troopers of the 6th Virginia fighting dismounted. Additionally, Davis's nemesis, Lieutenant R.O. Allen, survived the encounter only to be seriously wounded later in the day on the slopes of Fleetwood Hill (*Kilpatrick and Our Cavalry*).

alone and exposed in front of his lines, and noticing that the Union troopers' view of their commander was blocked the trees at a bend in the road, Allen decided to strike a blow. He rode out of the trees and trotted up the road toward the Union colonel. Davis, his attention on the New Yorkers to his rear, failed to notice Allen until the Confederate lieutenant was only a few paces away. Davis took a swing at Allen with his saber, but Allen, an excellent horseman, dodged the blow by ducking away behind his horse's neck. Allen was armed with a pistol — the weapon of choice among Confederate cavalrymen — and he fired once at Davis. The ball from Allen's pistol struck Davis in the head, killing him almost instantly. As Davis fell, Allen and his party beat a hasty retreat, but one of Allen's men was killed by the New Yorkers who charged forward to avenge their fallen commander.[30]

Shortly after Davis was mortally wounded, and perhaps prompted by that event, General Pleasonton sent his first report of the unfolding battle to General Hooker. In a message timed at 6:00 a.m., Pleasonton wrote to his superior: "Enemy has opened with artillery and shows some force of cavalry. Had a sharp skirmish. Colonel Davis, commanding Second Brigade [sic], First Division, led his column across and is badly wounded."[31] Regarding the death of Davis, Buford later wrote that his division's "success was dearly bought, for among the noble and brave ones who fell was Colonel B. F. Davis, Eighth New York Cavalry. He died in the front, giving examples of heroism and courage to all who were to follow."[32] Like most tough commanders, Davis, although widely respected, was not universally loved by his men.[33] Nevertheless, despite his lack of popularity, Davis was an experienced and effective commander and his loss, coming at a critical time in the operation, was a serious blow to the Federal effort.[34]

Private Opie was not the only soldier having problems with his horse that morning; so was Captain George Custer, who, anxious to get into the fighting, had crossed the river that morning with Davis' brigade. Custer was accompanied for the day by his orderly, Private Joseph Fought. As the battle commenced, Custer's and Fought's horses spooked, jamming themselves against a fence. As the 6th Virginia attacked up the Beverly Ford Road, the two horses stood at the fence whinnying and refusing to move. With great effort, Custer and Fought got their mounts turned about and began a dash to rear, but a stone fence blocked their path. Fought's horse cleared the fence easily, but Custer's horse jumped awkwardly. Custer lost his balance and was thrown to the ground; fortunately he was unhurt. After remounting, Custer and Fought continued to the rear where Custer delivered the news to General Pleasonton that Colonel Davis had been killed.[35]

Upon Davis's death, command of the 1st Brigade devolved upon Major William S. McClure of the 3rd Indiana Cavalry. McClure, a twenty-six year old riverman and merchant from Madison, Indiana, had no military experience before the war (Roger D. Hunt Collection at the U.S. Army Military History Institute).

Leadership losses early that morning were not limited to Grimes Davis. In the melee with the 6th Virginia, the 8th Illinois Cavalry's commander, Major Alpheus Clark, was shot in the hand, requiring his evacuation. Almost immediately, the next ranking officer in the 8th Illinois, Captain George Forsyth, was shot in the thigh. As the men carried Forsyth to the rear, he quipped that it was unfortunate they had wounded him at sunrise rather than sunset, causing him to miss most of the battle to come.[36] At about the same time, Captain Benjamin F. Foote, commanding Company E, 8th New York, was shot and killed.[37] Lacking leaders, the Federal attack stalled as the troopers at the front fell back to regroup. "Under those most unfavorable circumstances, and while considerable confusion prevailed," Buford decided that it was necessary to make changes to his chain of command.[38]

After receiving word that Davis had been killed, Buford crossed the river to see the situation for himself. Pressing to the front, he found that the attack had bogged down with his remaining leaders experiencing great difficulty controlling the deployment of their units in the woods.

Buford ordered the senior officer in the 1st Brigade, Major William S. McClure, commanding the 3d Indiana Cavalry, to move forward and take charge. At the same time, Buford called forward Colonel Devin, the most experienced officer remaining in the division. Buford ordered Devin, known to his men as "Old Tom," to assume command of the

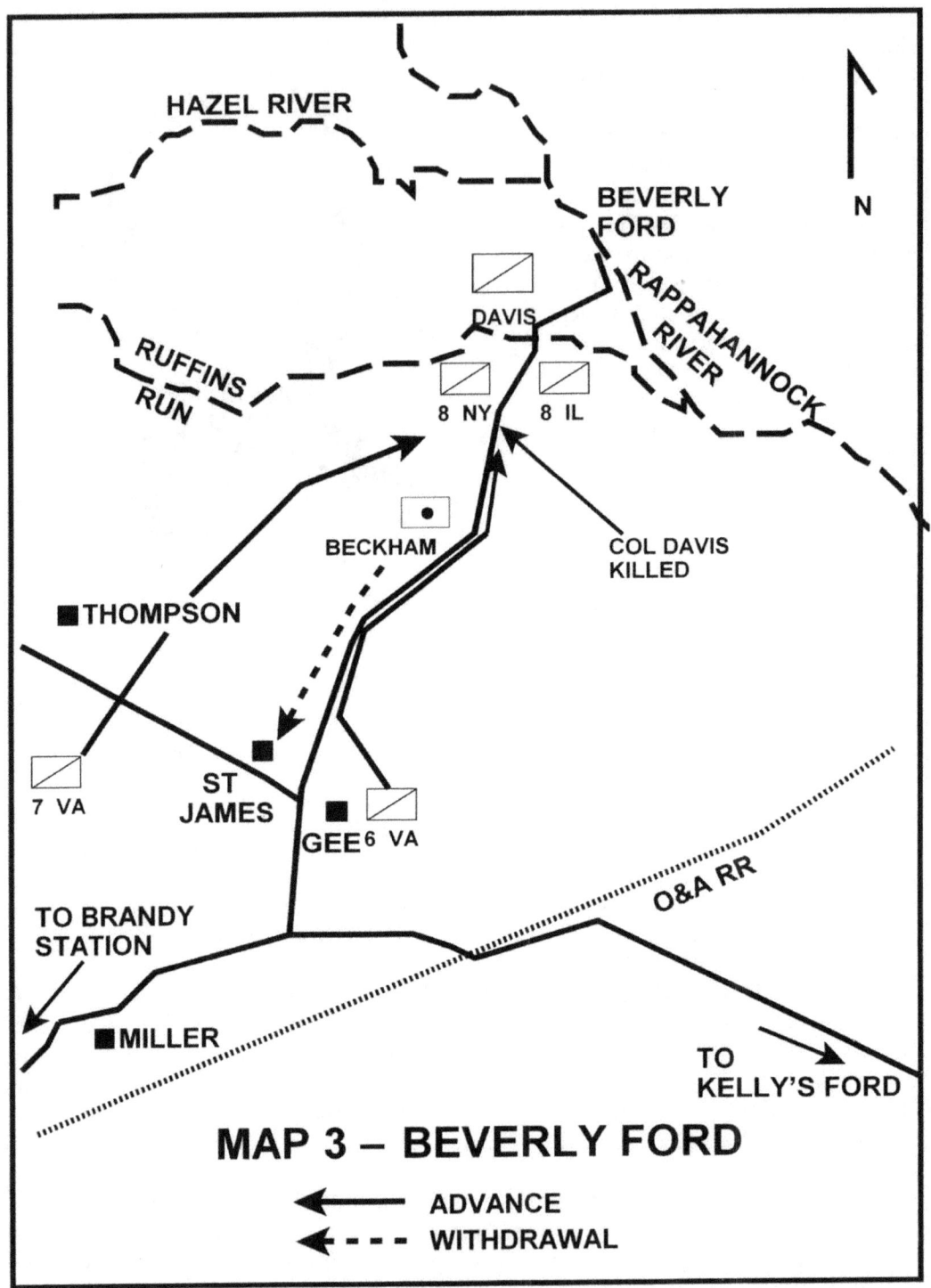

General Buford began crossing Beverly Ford at 4:30 a.m. with Colonel Benjamin F. "Grimes" Davis's brigade in the lead. Unexpected counterattacks by the 6th and 7th Virginia Cavalry regiments slowed Buford's advance, allowing Stuart's artillery, commanded by Major Robert Beckham, to escape. Colonel Davis was killed in the fighting.

division and to personally direct the operations of Davis' brigade.³⁹ Undoubtedly, putting Devin in charge helped restore order and confidence among the Union troopers at the line of contact. It also freed Buford to better manage his three major units (e.g., the 1st Division; the Reserve Brigade; and Ames' infantry brigade). However, altering the chain of command took time—an hour or so—while the new commanders came forward, received orders, examined the terrain, and acquainted themselves with the tactical situation. All the while, the advance down the Beverly Ford road was halted, leaving the Confederates free to react and prepare.

A little more than three miles to the south, Stuart, by now well aware that the Federals had crossed the river in force, was also busy trying to determine the enemy situation and position his forces accordingly. Stuart and his staff had spent the night camped at the Miller House on Fleetwood Hill, about one half mile northeast of Brandy Station. The Miller House was a modest dwelling that stood in a grove of trees at the southern end of the ridge, and Fleetwood was at that point known locally as Miller House Hill.⁴⁰ Fleetwood, the first prominent terrain feature south of the Rappahannock, rises from the plain near the Orange and Alexandria roadbed and extends in a northerly direction for close to two and one half miles. The height of the ridge, relative to the surrounding countryside, increases from about seventy feet near the Miller House to just more than two hundred feet in the north at the Wellford's Ford Road.

The men of Stuart's headquarters—sleeping on the ground about the Miller House—were awakened that morning by the sound of small arms and cannon fire from the ford. Shortly afterward, a courier arrived from William E. "Grumble" Jones, with word that a large Union force had crossed the river and driven back the pickets, prompting Stuart's volunteer *aide de camp* and scout, Captain William Farley, to throw his hat in the air and shout "Hurrah, We're going to have a fight."⁴¹ A flurry of activity followed the arrival of Jones' courier, as Stuart immediately dispatched his own couriers to alert his brigade commanders to the threat and assigned various tasks to his staff officers.

The cannon fire referred to by Pleasonton in his 6:00 a.m. message to Hooker and heard by Stuart on Fleetwood came from Beckham's horse artillery. On the evening of June 8, four batteries—Hart's, Chew's, Moorman's, and McGregor's—camped beside the Beverly Ford road about one and one half miles south the river.⁴² Beckham had apparently positioned his artillery that it might get an early start toward the fords on the morning of June 9, the day the Army of Northern Virginia was to begin its movement from Culpeper to the Shenandoah Valley. However, so positioned, the artillery battalion was unprotected. Other than Gibson's company, no Confederate forces stood between Beckham's campsite and the river.

Before sunrise the artillerymen were awakened by the sound of gunfire at the ford and a few minutes later Major Beckham received word that the pickets were being driven back. The twenty-six-year-old West Pointer knew immediately that his guns were in jeopardy and ordered his batteries withdrawn from their exposed position. As Flournoy and his troopers were beginning their gallop north toward Beverly Ford, Beckham's gunners were frantically at work packing personal belongings, loading equipment into wagons, and hitching up their limbers in preparation for galloping off in the opposite direction. To cover the withdrawal of his battalion, Beckham ordered Hart's gunners to manhandle one piece into a firing position at the side of the road leading to the ford.⁴³ Beckham ordered his other battery commanders to withdraw their pieces to a more secure firing position about one half mile south near Saint James Church, a small Episcopal chapel beside a road linking the roads to Beverly Ford and Welford's Ford on the Hazel River.⁴⁴

Left: After Colonel Davis was killed, General Buford called forward Colonel Thomas Devin and placed him in command of 1st Cavalry Division. A former house painter from New York City, Devin had served for many years in the New York State Militia and was highly respected by his men, who called him "Old Tom" (Library of Congress). *Right*: Major Robert Beckham, commanding the Stuart Horse Artillery, camped beside the Beverly Ford Road with four batteries of guns. Beckham's camp was almost overrun by Buford's men early on the morning of June 9. The artillerists were saved by the 6th Virginia Cavalry's audacious counterattack (*Long Arm of Lee*).

Union musket balls were whizzing overhead and striking the ground in the artillery park as Beckham's gunners completed hitching their teams, hooked guns and caissons to limbers, and began to move. Instead of only one gun, Hart had wisely placed two pieces into position, and their crews began firing shell down the Beverly Ford Road at Union troopers as they emerged from the woods about four hundred yards to the north.[45] About that time, Flournoy and his men—in a column about one hundred fifty yards long—galloped past. Off to their left, Beckham and his gunners also saw the 7th Virginia Cavalry galloping across the fields toward the Union position. Beckham must have felt a great sense of relief.

Upon his arrival in Culpeper in May, Stuart had directed that each brigade daily designate a regiment as its "grand guard" whose mission was "to move promptly to the front in case of the enemy's advance, in order to give time for the other regiments to bring in their horses from grazing and prepare for action."[46] The troopers of the grand guard were required to have "horses near at hand, arms and accouterments ready for use, and everything prepared to mount at short notice." While other regiments began their day with work details and breakfast, a brigade's grand guard began its morning with a five-mile march. On the morning of June 9, the 7th Virginia was the grand guard of Jones' Brigade. Consequently, the 7th Virginia was ready to march as soon as word was received of the Federal attack, and, unlike the 6th Virginia, the 7th was prepared to move with all its men in good order.

As Flournoy was leading his men up the road to Beverly Ford, Lieutenant Colonel Thomas Marshall led the troopers of the 7th Virginia from their camp cross-country at the

After withdrawing from his exposed position beside the Beverly Ford Road, Major Robert Beckham placed his 16 guns in a "line of metal" at Saint James Church. From there the guns dominated the battlefield (Joseph W. McKinney).

gallop. Shortly after the 6th made contact with the Federals, the 7th closed upon that regiment's rear, then moved up on its left to get into the fight. However, by that time the 7th closed with Davis' brigade, the woods were "swarming with the enemy's horsemen" and the 7th, like the 6th, was quickly forced to retire.[47]

The quick reaction that morning by the 6th and 7th Virginia slowed Buford's advance, providing enough time for the horse artillery to complete its withdrawal with Hart's guns, one covering the other, falling back by bounds to Saint James Church. As it turned out, Beckham's battalion reached their new position almost unscathed — Federal fire wounded only a few horses. The only equipment lost was Beckham's field desk — dropped from a wagon en route to Saint James Church. The desk was found later that day by Buford's men, providing a basis for Pleasonton's later claim that his force had "captured" the camp of the horse artillery finding "important papers" in the process.[48] At Saint James, Beckham positioned his sixteen guns in a "line of metal" extending roughly four hundred yards from east to west. The right end of the line was anchored on high ground just to the east of the Beverly Ford Road while the left end of the line was on high ground about two hundred yards beyond the church. From the position, Beckham's gunners had good fields of fire to the north and east. The morning could have turned out much worse. Major Beckham had come close to losing his guns to the enemy, the ultimate indignity for an artilleryman, and an event that would have had a profound effect on the outcome of the battle.

Although the preemptive Confederate attack delayed the Federal advance, the men from the 6th and 7th Virginia regiments could not long remain in contact as more Federal units moved through the ford and joined the fight. In its brief encounter near Beverly Ford, the 6th Virginia lost about 30 men killed, wounded, and missing. Flournoy withdrew his men back down the Beverly Ford Road about one half mile beyond the Gee House to the Orange & Alexandria Railroad tracks.[49] The 7th Virginia withdrew about two hundred yards to the southwest into a stand of trees that provided the men some cover. There, Lieutenant Colonel Marshall halted for a time while his sharpshooters, protected by a fence, took under fire any Union troopers who emerged from the trees. After withdrawing farther, Marshall received orders from General Jones to move forward and regain contact. After advancing a short distance, Marshall ordered a charge upon a party of Union cavalry that had emerged from the trees. However, by that time, Devin had the situation under control and had brought forward his artillery. Fire from a section of Lieutenant Vincent's guns prompted Marshall to break off his attack and fall back. Marshall eventually withdrew the 7th Virginia to a position on the far left flank of Jones' brigade, and for most the remainder of the day, Marshall took his orders from General W.H.F. "Rooney" Lee whose brigade was occupying that part of the battlefield. Casualties from the morning's fight were light in the 7th Virginia, with two men killed. The number of wounded in the morning's fighting was not recorded.[50]

According to Pleasonton, within less than an hour after first crossing the river, his "entire line was formed covering the ford," implying that the bulk of the right wing was on the south bank of the river.[51] However, that was probably an optimistic assessment of the situation at the time. Considering the conditions on the south side of the river, it was most unlikely that Buford could have moved his four thousand cavalrymen, one thousand five-hundred infantrymen, and three batteries of horse artillery through the ford and into position in just an hour.[52] Nonetheless, Buford had continued to steadily bring forward his units, spread out to the right and left of the Beverly Ford Road, and prepare to resume his attack.

By 6:00 a.m. General Ames' infantry, following most of the cavalry, began to cross the river.[53] Some soldiers, reluctant to get wet, began constructing a foot bridge over the waist-deep water. Their officers quickly put a stop to that time-consuming activity, and the men waded through the river, taking caution to keep their weapons and ammunition dry. Once on the south bank, the column of foot soldiers continued up the road toward the sounds of the battle, passing wounded headed to the rear, and seeing several dead cavalrymen — Rebel and Yankee — lying at the side of the road, all indications that hard fighting might lie ahead.[54]

As Devin and McClure were taking charge of their new commands, Buford began repositioning his forces. He ordered Ames to move his infantry forward and to take up concealed positions in the edge of the woods on each side of the road leading from the ford toward Saint James Church, thus securing the center of the Union line. Buford moved cavalry regiments of the 1st Division into the woods to the left of the infantry and sent the cavalry from the Reserve Brigade, consisting mostly of Regulars, to the right of the Infantry.[55] On the far right, the regular cavalrymen reached Elk Wood, a substantial home, part of a "very wealthy, splendid estate"built by Carter Beverley and later sold along with the adjoining property to Richard Cunningham. In 1862, the Cunningham family had sought safety from General Pope's incursion by moving farther south in Virginia, leaving the main house abandoned. They left the estate in the charge of Mr. Wiltshire, their overseer, who lived about one half mile southwest of the main house. Before leaving, Cunningham ordered Wiltshire to burn the house and furnishings if the Yankees should approach. For some reason, however, the overseer had not followed those instructions and the house still stood.[56]

While Buford reorganized and continued to push more units forward, Grumble Jones with the remainder of his brigade — the 11th Virginia, 12th Virginia, and White's Battalion — moved into position to the right and left of Saint James Church in support of Beckham's Artillery. The ground around Saint James provided some cover for the defenders and in the center and on the right afforded good fields of fire across the open fields to the north and east.[57] Colonel Lunsford Lomax's 11th Virginia, on the far left of Jones' line, was confronted with a belt of woods to their front. Consequently, Lomax sent forward a strong party of dismounted skirmishers while the 12th Virginia and White's Battalion remained mostly mounted. Riding back and forth along the line of troops at Saint James, Jones supervised his regiments' deployment in shirt sleeves with stocking feet showing from his stirrups. In his haste to respond to Buford's attack, Jones had left camp without his jacket and boots.[58]

Irascible Brigadier General William E. "Grumble" Jones checked Buford's advance at Saint James Church. Jones and Buford both graduated from West Point with the Class of 1848 (Library of Congress).

Meanwhile, other Union and Confederate forces were moving into action. Colonel John Logan Black with his regiment, the 1st South Carolina, had camped overnight near Stuart's headquarters. Upon hearing the firing, Black had mounted his horse and rode to Fleetwood. Stuart, not standing upon the formality of the chain of command, ordered Black to move his regiment forward to block any enemy that might approach Brandy Station from Rappahannock Station.[59] Black's regiment, Hampton's grand guard, moved out almost immediately, guided by one of Stuart's *aides*, Captain Chiswell Dabney, to a position about two miles east of Brandy where the Orange and Alexandria Railroad, the Old Carolina Road, and the most direct road from Kelly's Ford converged. There Black and his men found Cable Flournoy and the already-bloodied 6th Virginia and a squadron from his own regiment that Stuart had ordered forward the night before to reinforce the pickets. Upon recommendation from Flournoy, Black sent forward parties of dismounted sharpshooters on each side of the Orange and Alexandria tracks.[60]

Wade Hampton also rode to Fleetwood to confer with Stuart and receive his orders. Having anticipated that he would be told to bring his regiments forward, the South Carolinian had already mounted his men and begun moving them north from their camps between Brandy Station and Stevensburg. At Fleetwood, Hampton was confronted by a flurry of activity. Stuart, by now fully aware that a major fight was developing at Beverly Ford, had ordered his headquarters struck and moved to safety. In response, orderlies and servants were bustling about tearing down tent flies and loading baggage onto wagons.

Stuart directed Hampton to leave a regiment at Brandy Station as a reserve, and with the rest of his command fall-in on Jones' right flank. Hampton, ever sensitive to his prerogatives as a brigade commander, was piqued to learn that Stuart had issued orders directly to Black regarding the employment of the 1st South Carolina. Nonetheless, Hampton sent the 2nd South Carolina to Brandy Station and proceeded toward Saint James with his three remaining regiments — the Jeff Davis Legion, Cobb's Legion, and the 1st North Carolina.

Receiving word that Gregg was crossing the Rappahannock at Kelly's Ford, Stuart sent a courier to Beverly Robertson with orders that Robertson move his brigade forward to counter Gregg's expected movement up the road between Kelly's Ford and Brandy Station. Stuart also sent couriers to Rooney Lee and Munford with orders that they move their brigades toward the fight at Beverly Ford.[61]

Perhaps as an afterthought, Stuart sent his assistant engineer officer, Lieutenant Francis "Frank" Robertson, to Brandy Station with orders to take charge of the dismounted men of Hampton's brigade, thought to be assembled at that location, and to post them along the road leading from Brandy Station to the southeast toward Carrico's Mill and thence to Kelly's Ford.[62] Afterwards, having done all he could from his headquarters, Stuart left Fleetwood for Jones' position to observe the action for himself.

Hampton, in response to Stuart's orders, put his three regiments into positions to the east of Beckham's artillery and Jones' Brigade, running roughly west to east from the Gee House to the Orange & Alexandria Railroad. After Hampton's regiments moved into their positions and Robertson's Brigade moved forward, Black's regiment served little purpose to their rear astride the railroad tracks. Hampton ordered Black to shift to the west and fall in on the left of his brigade. In response, Black recalled his sharpshooters and moved to Hampton's left flank near the Gee House. Once there, he again dismounted his sharpshooters, armed a few days earlier with new Enfield rifles, and sent them forward into the woods.[63] Hampton, who had been given control of the 6th Virginia — now widely separated from Jones — left Flournoy and his men in-place near the railroad, perhaps because the Virginians were in need of rest and reorganization after their sharp early-morning fight.

Initially, Hampton had ordered one hundred sharpshooters — roughly a company from each regiment — to engage dismounted Union soldiers that could be observed to his front. Those hundred men were reinforced by Black's sharpshooters once the 1st South Carolina got into position near the Gee House.[64]

Regiments practiced fighting dismounting as part of their drill. The troopers in cavalry platoons were organized into "fours." Upon being ordered to fight dismounted, the Number 4 men remained in the saddle while the other three men dismounted. Number 3s passed their reins over their horse's neck to Number 4s. Number 2s tied their reins to the bridles of the Number 3s' horses. Number 1s tied their reins to the bridles of the Number 2s' horses. The dismounted men then hooked their sabers to their saddles, the saber being useless to a soldier when afoot, and moved off to fight. Under the direction of a sergeant, the Number 4s, riding their own horses and leading three, would move to a position out of the line of fire. However, this drill was more easily executed on the drill field than the battlefield with noise, confusion, balky horses, and casualties among the fours.[65]

Although tactically essential, most troopers probably did not care much for dismounted skirmishing — it was hard work. The men had to rush forward at the double-quick (wearing bulky boots), take up covered firing positions, and move almost constantly as battle lines shifted. As the sun rose, the day began to heat up, adding to the discomfort of both Union and Confederate troopers, all of whom were clad in wool jackets and trousers. Some Confederates were, of necessity, armed with muzzle-loading rifles instead of much-preferred breach-loading carbines. In the dismounted fighting between the railroad tracks and the Beverly Ford road, the rifles, with their increased range, provided a slight advantage to the dismounted Confederate troopers. Moreover, many Union troopers, observing that their enemies were armed with rifles, assumed that they were fighting Rebel infantry.[66]

To Hampton's north, Major McClure observed the Rebel sharpshooters advancing through the fields and woods. In response, he ordered up most of the 1st Brigade (less the 8th Illinois which had been detached). McClure sent squadrons from the 3rd Indiana and the 9th New York to extend his front line toward the railroad tracks to prevent it being flanked. He then ordered a second squadron from the 3rd Indiana to dismount and move forward to confront Hampton's sharpshooters in the center. Hampton responded by ordering an additional hundred sharpshooters into the growing fray. McClure countered by bringing forward the last of his regiments, the 8th New York, to thicken the line already occupied by the 3rd Indiana and the 9th New York, and to further strengthen his threatened left flank. Concurrently, Buford ordered Ames to move the bulk of his infantry forward along the Beverly Ford Road.

A Union artillery section moved into position to support McClure, but the gunners could not find a suitable firing position in the flat and wooded terrain so they quickly withdrew.[67] As the pressure from advancing Rebel skirmishers increased on McClure's left, Major William Martin charged with a squadron of the 9th New York (the other three companies of the regiment on the field were dismounted). Martin and his troopers forced the Confederates to fall back, but Martin was shot in the shoulder and evacuated, leaving the regiment in the command of the senior captain present.[68]

In the Union center, the men of the 124th New York Infantry, raised in Orange County and known as the "Orange Blossoms," found themselves in a thick band of woods. Ordered to defend at the tree line, but remain concealed if possible, the infantrymen formed into a single rank with a four-foot interval between each man. The commanders then ordered each man to conceal himself behind the nearest tree that could provide cover. Thus hidden and protected, the Orange Blossoms watched as strong party of sharpshooters — perhaps Black's — approached through the open field to their front. Just before the order was given to fire, the Rebel sharpshooters disappeared from view, appearing to sink into the earth. The line of Confederates had walked into a ravine. For several minutes, the New Yorkers waited, weapons raised, for the Rebels to emerge from the ravine. But instead of continuing ahead, the Confederate sharpshooters had turned and filed down the ravine which enfiladed the Union line.

Once on the Union flank, the Confederate sharpshooters emerged from the ravine, gave a Rebel yell, fired a volley, and rushed toward the New Yorkers. The New Yorkers, protected by trees and concealed by the powder smoke, shifted their positions and returned fire. Then began, in the words of a company commander, "an almost hand to hand Indian fight," with Rebels and Yankees shooting at each other from behind trees only a few feet apart. The arrival of a company from the 86th New York Infantry forced the Rebels to withdraw, a movement that was hastened by orders, shouted above the sound of the fighting, for a Union cavalry regiment to charge through the trees. As the Confederates fell back across the open field leaving several dead behind them, the cavalry "regiment" was found to be the commander of the 124th, Colonel A. Van Horne Ellis, accompanied by a captain, a lieutenant, three couriers, and a color bearer, all on horseback. The 124th New York lost two men killed and several wounded in the "Indian fight."[69]

By 8:00 a.m., it appeared that a stalemate was settling in east of the Beverly Ford Road with most of the fighting being done by dismounted troopers. Meanwhile, WHF "Rooney"

Lee, in response to orders delivered by a courier from Stuart, moved his regiments from their camps around the Welford House in a northeasterly direction to menace Buford's right flank.[70] Colonel Munford, in temporary command of Fitz Lee's Brigade, at Oak Shade several miles from the developing battle was, slow to react. About 10:00 a.m., Munford received an order that Fitz Lee had written at 7:00 that morning. Lee informed Munford that Union troops had crossed at Beverly Ford and directed Munford to "pack up your train, and keep everything ready to move; to bring your command a little farther in this direction, and keep up communication with [Fitz Lee] and to look out well to your picket line."[71] Almost immediately, one of Stuart's *aides de camp* arrived with orders that Stuart "wishes all of Colonel Munford's regiments but one brought this way, leaving a guard for the baggage, which can be sent toward Culpeper."[72] Munford, unsure what "this way" meant, began moving the brigade cautiously toward Wellford's Ford.

Once Rooney Lee's brigade made contact, Buford found it necessary to strengthen his right flank to prevent it from being rolled-up by the Confederates, now advancing through the woods along the bank of the Hazel River led by parties of dismounted skirmishers. To counter this new threat, Buford ordered his 2nd Brigade, now commanded by Colonel Josiah Kellogg to cross the Beverly Ford Road, move to the right of the Reserve Brigade, and take up positions near the Cunningham House. The 2nd Brigade was weak, consisting only of Kellogg's regiment, the 17th Pennsylvania, and the 6th New York. For good measure, Buford transferred the 8th Illinois from the 1st Brigade to the 2nd Brigade to further protect the threatened right flank.

The 8th Illinois, with its two ranking officers—Major Clarke and Captain Forsyth—wounded and evacuated, was in need of a commander. General Pleasonton sent one of his *aides de camp*, twenty-five-year-old Captain Elon Farnsworth, to take charge of the regiment. Farnsworth and Pleasonton had served together before the war with the 2nd Dragoons in Utah. Pleasonton, then a captain, was the regimental adjutant, while Farnsworth was employed as a civilian forage master. When the war broke out, Farnsworth obtained a commission as adjutant of the 8th Illinois, the regiment having been raised by his uncle, Brigadier General and former Congressman John F. Farnsworth. The elder Farnsworth had resigned his commission to resume his seat in Congress, where he was a confidant of President Lincoln. Consequently, it is not surprising that Pleasonton took an interest in the young and well-connected Farnsworth, choosing him as an *aide*, then placing him into command of a regiment when the opportunity arose.[73]

Anchoring his right flank along the Hazel River, Kellogg sent forward parties of dismounted skirmishers to meet those from Rooney Lee's brigade. During the dismounted fighting, an unusual incident occurred. Troopers from the 17th Pennsylvania noticed that a black man was fighting for the Confederacy among Lee's sharpshooters, and that further, he was "making some excellent shots." The Pennsylvanians devised a ruse to counter the black man. One trooper exposed himself as a target. When the black Rebel emerged from cover and drew a bead, another Pennsylvanian shot him dead.[74]

About the time Jones was setting up his defense around Beckham's guns at Saint James, Heros von Borcke arrived, sent there by Stuart to learn the state of affairs. While riding from Fleetwood, von Borcke passed through the wagons and baggage trains of Jones' brigade headed in great haste for the rear and safety. Fortuitously, von Borcke spotted a teamster riding to the rear on Kitt, his missing gray mule. The teamster pleaded with von Borke to allow him to keep the mule that he might ride to safety, and promised to return the mule later. However, von Borcke, having once lost his mule, would not hear of it. He ordered the teamster to dismount and make his way to the rear on foot. Von Borcke then dispatched a courier accompanying him to lead Kitt to the rear for safe keeping. After visiting Jones's position, von Borcke continued to the north to where Rooney Lee's brigade was skirmishing.[75]

Jones, from his position near Saint James detected that Buford was no longer pressing his attack. Although many blue troopers had earlier been seen in the woods to Jones' front, any that had moved forward had been driven back into the cover of the trees by the fire from Beckham's guns. Jones determined that a Confederate attack was "expedient" and ordered Colonel Asher W. Harmon with his 12th Virginia Cavalry to move forward to develop the situation.[76]

Harmon's regiment passed around Beckham's guns in a column of squadrons, with the lead squadron commanded by Captain Charles O'Ferrall. Harmon, with the next squadron trailed a few hundred yards behind. To O'Ferrall, it seemed eerily quiet as he and his men, dispersed as mounted skirmishers, advanced steadily through the open field. The waiting Union troopers, concealed and sheltered in the woods at the far side of the field, held their fire until O'Ferrall's squadron was almost to the wood line. They then opened with a "galling" fire that killed or wounded several men and horses. Almost simultaneously, mounted Federals charged out of the woods and were upon the two lead companies "as thick as angry bees from a hive when stirred." Fortunately for O'Ferrall and his men, Harmon quickly bought the main body of the regiment forward to their support and for a few minutes, the fight at the wood line remained "close, fast, and furious."[77]

Buford, just like his West Point classmate Jones, had judged offensive action necessary. Even before Jones ordered Harmon forward, Buford had sent instructions to Major Charles Whiting to charge Saint James with the Reserve Brigade and overrun Beckham's guns. Whiting set about organizing the attack, a task made difficult since his regiments were strung out in the woods between the Beverly Ford Road and Elkwood.

At the time, the Reserve Brigade had four regiments on the field: the 2nd U.S.; the 5th U.S.; the 6th U.S.; and the 6th Pennsylvania, although five of its companies had been delayed on the north side of the river. The 1st U.S. had just been relieved from picket duty by Stahel's cavalry and was making its way south, but was still miles away from the river. As Whiting was assembling his regiments in preparation for executing his orders to attack, General Pleasonton, unbeknownst to Buford, ordered the 2nd U.S. off to support a battery of artillery that was being pressed by Rooney Lee's brigade.[78] This left Whiting with a force of roughly two and one half regiments to break Jones' position.

From the start, the attack of the Reserve Brigade did not go well. Assembling in the thick woods took time, and when the advance began the column lengthened as the men picked their way through the trees. As a result, instead of a coordinated attack with several massed regiments, the attack was made piecemeal, with the bulk of the fighting falling to the lead regiment of the brigade, the 6th Pennsylvania, supported at a distance by the 6th U.S.[79]

As Harmon's attack was running out of steam at the wood line, Major Robert Morris led the five companies of the 6th Pennsylvania in a memorable but futile attack. The former lancers emerged from the trees with one company leading as mounted skirmishers, and two squadrons following, one trailing behind the other. Seeing Harmon's regiment to their immediate front, the Pennsylvanians immediately charged, and yelling like demons with sabers drawn, drove into the Virginians. Harmon's troopers, surprised and unprepared for the onslaught, were driven back in disorder. The screaming Pennsylvanians pursued closely, with Ulrich Dahlgren, Hooker's dashing *aide de camp*, riding among their ranks.[80]

However, the charging lancers immediately ran into problems. Once they emerged

The 6th Pennsylvania Cavalry, better known as Rush's Lancers, charged Beckham's guns at Saint James, but failed to overrun the defenders' position. Two weeks before the battle, the regiment turned in its lances (several are stacked at left) and drew carbines. Seated at the left is Alfred Waud, a noted Civil War artist (Library of Congress).

from the shelter of the trees, the troopers came under effective small arms and artillery fire and casualties began to mount. The terrain, which appeared flat, was actually drained by three deep ditches that ran perpendicular to the regiment's axis of advance. Horses that did not jump — and only few did — piled up as their riders attempted to pick their way through likely crossing sites. At one ditch, Major Morris was thrown to the ground when his horse fell. The horse, uninjured, ran away leaving Morris afoot in no-man's land.[81]

Despite those impediments, the 6th Pennsylvania continued to drive their charge home, almost reaching Beckham's guns. Beckham's gunners stood at their pieces in "silent awe" while to their immediate front the Pennsylvanians and Harmon's Virginians engaged in a running melee, trying to kill each other with saber blows and pistol shots.[82] General Jones, able to observe Harmon's plight, ordered Lieutenant Colonel Elijah H. "Lige" White's 35th Battalion, Virginia Cavalry, forward to support the 12th Virginia. The 35th, mostly Loudoun County men with some Marylanders, advanced at the gallop for about two hundred yards beyond Beckham's line of metal, passed through Harmon's disorganized troopers, and struck the Pennsylvanians. According to White, his men met "a confident and fiercely pursuing enemy," but the reality was far different. The Pennsylvanians were few and considerably disorganized after their long dash under fire. The Lancers' attack had simply run out of steam, and it was now their turn to retreat in disorder.[83] White's men pressed after the Pennsylvanians, yelling like Indians, the source of the battalion's nickname, "The Comanches."[84]

As the Lancers' attack was faltering, the 6th U.S. finally emerged from the woods to their left and made an equally futile foray against the Confederate positions around Saint James. The eight companies of the 6th U.S.—two were on detached duty and Major Whiting had sent two off as a flank guard—were also driven from the field by White's Comanches.[85]

In a letter to his sister written two days after the battle, Philadelphian Major Henry C. Whelan described what became for him a "race for life" as he and his comrades fought their way across some "full two miles of ground covered with dead and wounded men and horses" to Union lines. At one point, Whelan found himself closely pursued by a pack of rebel "blood-hounds" who alternated between shooting at him and calling upon him to surrender. Fortunately, Whelan was well mounted. His horse, a sorrel named Lancer, cleared the ditches like an antelope, allowing Whelan to keep ahead of his pursuers. Ahead, an imposing stone fence blocked Whelan's route of escape, but Lancer "topped [it] like a bird" leaving the bloodhounds stymied on the far side and allowing Whelan to make his getaway.

After negotiating a creek, two ditches and a second stone fence, Whelan joined a group of regulars who were also fleeing in the face of White's attack. Attempting to ride simultaneously through a narrow gate, the men's horses became jammed in a "horrid, kicking mass" with Lancer's head and neck stuck between the hind legs of a gray horse to his front. Fortunately, Whelan stayed in his saddle while Lancer persevered. After much "kicking, groaning, and rolling about," Lancer, bruised and bleeding, squeezed through the gate, allowing Whelan to continue his ride to safety.[86]

After the Lancers returned to the Union lines and regrouped, Whelan found that most of the men who made the charge failed to return. The survivors of the five companies were equivalent to only a small squadron.[87] Major Morris, left on the field without a horse, was among the missing.[88]

Arriving at Saint James, probably a little after 9:00 a.m., Stuart found "the enemy checked and his advance apparently abandoned."[89] Shortly afterward, Lieutenant Frank Robertson, who had been sent to Brandy to organize a blocking force with Hampton's dismounted men, arrived at Saint James and informed Stuart that none of Hampton's dismounted troopers were in Brandy, and consequently, he had been unable to post them on the road leading to Kelly's Ford. Stuart, apparently believing Robertson was suited to dismounted combat, ordered the lieutenant to take charge of a nearby party of skirmishers and advance through a section of woods until he made contact with the enemy. Robertson dismounted and set off on his new mission.[90]

By midmorning, the Confederates had established parity, if not superiority, in combat power on the Saint James front. With the brigades of Jones, Hampton, and Rooney Lee on the scene—Munford was still across the Hazel River—there was more Southern cavalry on the field than Northern, roughly the equivalent of fifty-nine squadrons to fifty-three. Additionally, Jones' and Hampton's men had taken up defensive positions. While surrendering some initiative and giving up some numeric strength to horse-holding, their regiments had gained the advantage of fighting from stationary positions that offered good fields of fire and some protection from Union small arms and artillery fires.

Although Beckham, with his four batteries, did not have a significant numeric superiority over the three batteries supporting Buford, the Stuart Horse Artillery dominated the field. Beckham's guns were well-placed to cover the Confederate front, and more important, Beckham had all his guns under his personal control and could mass his fires whenever necessary. Union artillery, on the other hand, was under decentralized control with batteries allocated to the support of Devin, Whiting, and Ames. Consequently, the Union artillery fires were never effectively massed.

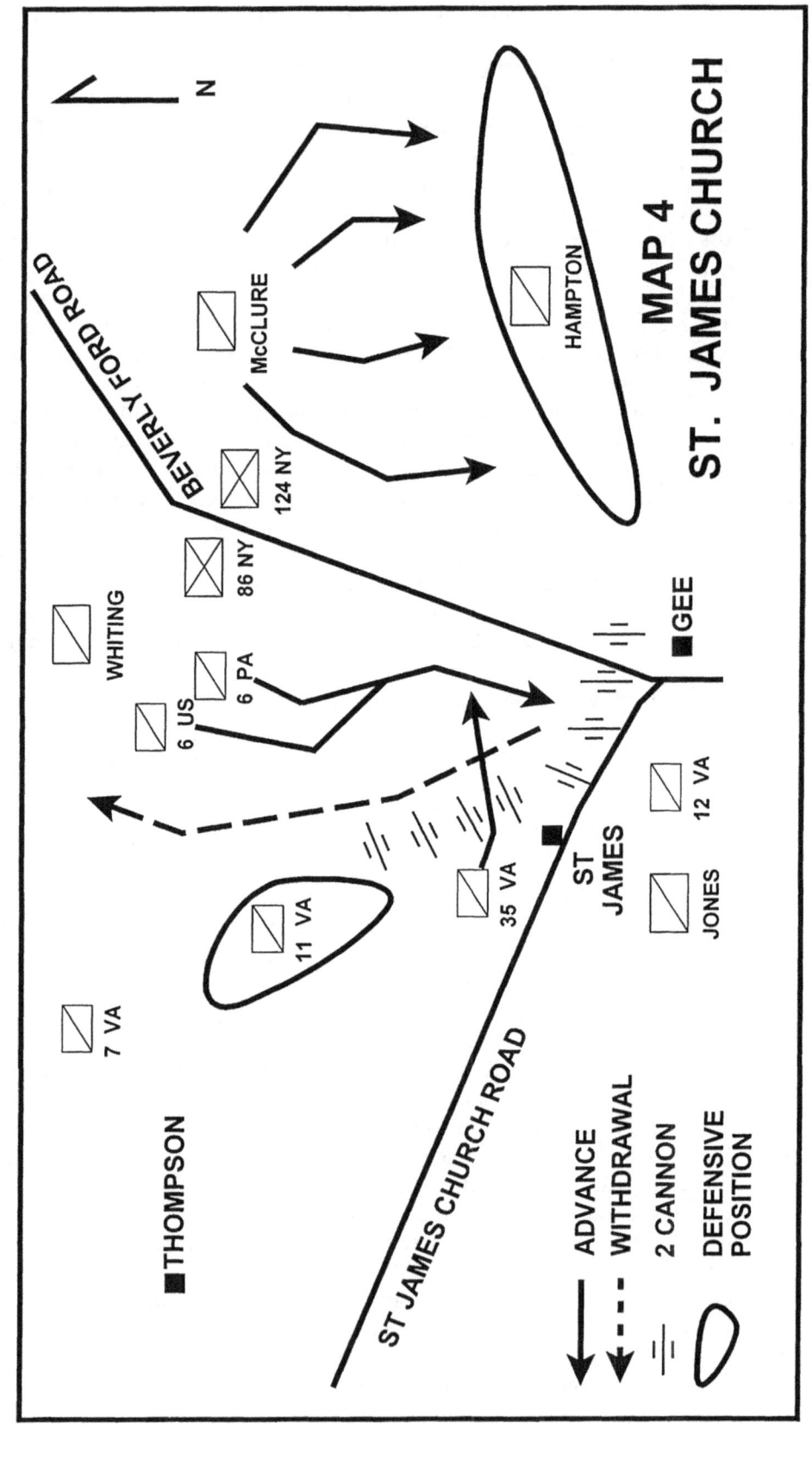

Opposite: Jones's and Hampton's Brigades, supported by Beckham's guns, halted Buford's attack at Saint James Church. A charge by Major Charles Whiting's Reserve Brigade failed to penetrate the Confederate line, and the exposed Federals were then routed by the 35th Battalion Virginia Cavalry's counterattack. ***Above:*** Saint James Church survived the battle only to be torn down the following winter by Union soldiers who used its brick and timbers as building materials for their winter huts. Today all that remains at the site are a few headstones in the graveyard and the outlines of the church's foundation. There are no known photographs of the church (Joseph W. McKinney).

However, Buford still had Ames' infantry brigade — thus far mostly uncommitted — and rarely had any cavalry, even Stuart's, withstood an infantry assault. Additionally, several of Buford's cavalry regiments had remained protected from observation and fire in the woods and had yet to be brought into battle. The presence of fresh infantry and cavalry provided Buford the flexibility and the potential for him to regain the initiative.

For Pleasonton, the old military axiom that the best plan lasts only until the first shot is fired proved true that morning. Apparently anticipating no major contact until his right and left wings converged at Brandy Station, Pleasonton was surprised at the speed and strength of the Confederate response. Sometimes in battle, the results of an unexpected blow can be disproportionate to that blow's actual strength. Such was the case with Flournoy's attack early that morning. The 6th Virginia landed only a jab to the nose of the Union right wing. While the 6th and later the 7th Virginia had insufficient strength to defeat Buford, they succeeded in upsetting the timing of his advance, allowing Beckham to escape and Stuart to organize an effective defense. Moreover, the quick Confederate response destroyed Pleasonton's confidence. Earlier Pleasonton had told Hooker that he was anxious to "pitch in." Now, as the battle unfolded, a less confident Pleasonton advised: "The enemy is in strong cavalry force here. We have had a severe fight. They were aware of our movement, and were prepared."[91] With the battle just three hours old, Pleasonton had drawn the wrong conclusion, a mistake that would influence his decisions for the remainder of the day.

However, the stalemate south of Beverly Ford did not last long. Within about an hour, artillery fire to the east signaled to all — Union and Confederate alike — that Gregg's left wing had finally swung into action near Brandy Station.[92] Soon Buford and Pleasonton could observe columns of gray troopers moving out of their positions around Saint James and hurrying to the southeast as the sounds of battle in that direction intensified. For Buford, this was perhaps another opportunity to do his part to disperse and destroy Stuart's cavalry.

8

A Small Affair

The Advance of the Left Wing and the Fight at Stevensburg

About 11:00 p.m. on the night of June 8, Colonel Alfred Duffié and his 2nd Cavalry division arrived at the small hamlet of Morrisville in souther Fauquier County. The men, much fatigued after their long afternoon and evening's march, promptly set up rudimentary camps and began preparing supper. Duffié's orders had directed that if possible he arrive at Morrisville before dark, but a conflicting requirement — that he move with his entire wagon train and all divisional materiel — had delayed his departure from Catlett's Station and had slowed his rate of march.[1]

Shortly after midnight, a staff officer sent by Brigadier General David McMurtrie Gregg, the commander of both the 3rd Cavalry Division and Pleasonton's left wing, arrived at Duffié's headquarters. The officer instructed Duffié immediately to march his division from Morrisville to Kelly's Ford, a distance of about five miles. Duffié knew the way, having led his brigade through that same ford against stiff rebel resistance on the morning of March 17. Once at the ford, Duffié was to report personally to Gregg and receive his orders for the coming day. To maintain tight security, General Pleasonton had not yet disseminated General Hooker's plan to "disperse and destroy" Stuart's cavalry to anyone other than his two immediate subordinates, Gregg and Brigadier General John Buford.

To the simultaneous sounds of boots and saddles, reveille, and assembly echoing from the various regimental camps, Duffié's tired troopers mounted and began preparing for the march forward. At 2:00 a.m. the regiments began moving down the narrow trails through the scrub pine and rolling hills toward the ford. For the third consecutive night, Duffié's men marched through the darkness.

Since the Confederates had hotly contested the Union crossing at Kelly's Ford on March 17, Hooker was reluctant to rely upon cavalry to secure the south bank of the river.[2] Instead, he provided Pleasonton with two folding canvas pontoon boats from the Army of the Potomac's engineers, along with a five-man crew for each. Gregg, after conferring with Pleasonton on the plan, organized an infantry "forlorn hope" — fifteen men from the 5th New Hampshire and a like number from the 81st Pennsylvania — who would cross the river with their muskets unprimed and with a bayonet charge overwhelm any enemy they might find. The infantry would then hold their position until the cavalry could cross the river, pass though the position, and continue the advance in a southwesterly direction.

About midnight, the engineers erected their two boats and placed them in the water a short distance upriver from the ford. There, unobserved, they and the thirty infantrymen of the forlorn hope waited anxiously through the night for orders to cross the river.

Kelly's Ford today. On the eve of the Civil War, John Kelly's ford was the site of a thriving industrial park with flour mill, textile factory, wheelwright shop, cooperage, slaughter house, and retail stores. By 1863, Kelly had moved much of his machinery south, and "Kellyville" was falling into ruin (Joseph W. McKinney).

Just before first light, Gregg sent word to launch the assault. The engineers and infantry clambered into the boats, pushed off into the river, and paddled downstream. Aided by the current, they were able to bring the two boats to the far shore without being detected. While the engineers remained with the boats, the infantrymen leaped into the water, climbed the steep bank and surprised a few Confederate pickets from Beverly Robertson's brigade. The unprepared North Carolinians promptly mounted their horses and fled without offering any resistance. The only loss on either side was a single straw hat, dropped by a fleeing Rebel, a trophy that one of the Union foot soldiers immediately "captured."[3] The way was clear for Gregg's wing to begin its advance toward Culpeper.

Yet, as frequently occurs during military operations, Gregg's plan quickly went awry. Duffié's division inexplicably got a later start from their camps than expected, and then encountered, in Gregg's words, "unexpected difficulty in following the direct route to the ford." In plain language, Duffié's division got lost. Stories surfaced that a guide, perhaps a spy for Stuart, directed Duffié down the wrong road. Whatever the reason, for the men of the 2nd Cavalry division, the march to the ford was a nightmare. They spent several hours of "hard marching," before eventually reaching the river, a distance of only five miles by the most direct route.[4]

Once at the ford, Duffié, as directed, reported to Gregg and received his orders for the day. By then, it was evident from the sound of artillery fire to the west that Buford was heavily engaged upstream, a fact that was quickly confirmed when a courier arrived with a message from Pleasonton. The Cavalry Corps Commander advised Gregg that he believed Buford to be fighting Stuart's entire cavalry division.[5] Obviously, haste was necessary.

Gregg ordered Duffié immediately to cross the river and then to march directly on Stevensburg, protecting the left flank of the Cavalry Corps' left wing. Once at Stevensburg, Duffié was to communicate with Gregg, who, it was anticipated, would by then be in Brandy Station. If all was going well, Duffié would leave a cavalry regiment supported by a section of artillery at Stevensburg in conformance with Hooker's instructions. Then with the bulk of his division, Duffié would continue toward Culpeper Court House where he would hopefully fall upon the unsuspecting right flank of Stuart's cavalry division.[6]

At the battle of Kelly's Ford in March 1863, a few dozen Confederate troopers fighting from rifle pits delayed Averell's division for more than an hour. To ensure that there was no delay on June 9, Brigadier General David Russell's infantry were assigned the mission of securing the south bank of the river. Five months later, Russell gained fame when his division seized Confederate works at Rappahannock Station, just four miles upstream from Kelly's Ford (National Archives).

As Gregg explained to Duffié, Russell's infantry brigade would follow Duffié across the river and then march upstream along the south bank. Russell and his men were to protect Gregg's right flank and his avenue of withdrawal, should it be necessary for the cavalry to fall back. Gregg would cross with his division after Russell, initially follow Duffié, and then turn toward Brandy Station, there to unite with General Pleasonton and General Buford. Together, the combined force of two cavalry divisions, the Reserve Brigade, and perhaps infantry would march toward Culpeper Courthouse, and fight Stuart's division as the opportunity arose. Finally, Gregg informed Duffié that infantrymen from Colonel Jacob

A "forlorn hope" of 30 infantrymen crossed the Rappahannock in two canvas pontoon boats crewed by engineers. The infantrymen seized the ford without firing a shot. The only casualty was a straw hat, left behind by Confederate pickets and captured by the Union troops. Unfortunately, Colonel Duffié and his division became lost en route to the ford, delaying the operation by close to two hours (Library of Congress).

Sweitzer's brigade, which was responsible for guarding the north bank of the Rappahannock at Kelly's Ford, would cross to the south bank of the river and provide additional protection for the rear of the wing.

Ordered earlier to be prepared to cross the river at 3:30 a.m., Duffié's men finally entered the water about 6:00 a.m. Leading his column was the 1st Brigade, commanded by the colorful Italian, Luigi Palma diCesnola, and consisting of the 1st Massachusetts, 1st Rhode Island, and 6th Ohio Cavalry Regiments.[7]

Following diCesnola's brigade was Duffié's supporting horse artillery, Battery M, 2nd U.S. Artillery. The battery was commanded by Captain Alexander C. M. Pennington, an 1860 graduate of West Point. Bringing up the rear of Duffié's division was his 2nd Brigade, commanded by Pennsylvanian John Irwin Gregg, a cousin to General David Gregg, and consisting of three Pennsylvania cavalry regiments, the 3rd, 4th and 16th.

After an easy crossing—the water was only about two and one half feet deep—Duffié swung his division to the southwest, guiding on the road toward Paoli Mill on Mountain Run, a creek that rises near Culpeper Courthouse, flows east and then south toward Stevensburg, and from there meanders east until it empties into the Rappahannock about a mile below Kelly's Ford. In anticipation of contact with the rebels, the French colonel placed the 1st Rhode Island and the 6th Ohio on the right of the road with the 1st Massachusetts to the left of the road. Duffié apparently elected personally to direct the regiments of diCesnola's brigade, leaving the Italian colonel with little actual responsibility.[8]

Hooker had suggested that Pleasonton send a strong picket — at least a regiment and a section of artillery — to Stevensburg to protect his flank from any Confederates that might try to approach Culpeper Courthouse from Richards Ferry, Germanna Ford, or Ely's Ford. By allocating an entire division with an artillery battery to that secondary mission, Gregg complied with Hooker's guidance, but risked frittering away the striking power that he and Pleasonton might need once the main fight with Stuart began.

Russell's infantry brigade followed Duffié's division across the river. In typical hurry-up and wait fashion, the officers awakened their men at daybreak with instructions to draw three days' rations and be prepared to march on a moment's notice. After making preparations to march, the infantrymen waited several hours while Duffié's division found its way to the ford and crossed the river. Russell's troops were finally ordered down to the water about 7:00 a.m. The infantrymen were not particularly hurried along their way. Regarding the crossing itself, Private William Ray of the 7th Wisconsin recalled that the infantrymen had time for a short frolic in the water. "Some [men] takes off shoes and socks, some roll up pants only. Most of them just wade in as they are, hollowing & yelling &c. We get across. Being the last regt today so we were the last infantry to cross."[9]

On the south bank of the river, the infantrymen swung to the right into Kellyville, a little farther than one hundred years upstream from the ford. There, Russell halted his column until the remainder of Gregg's cavalry crossed the river. While waiting, the infantrymen amused themselves by exploring the now-shabby hamlet. Kellyville, however, was a disappointment as the men found little of interest. The shelves of the store were bare and the troopers had to content themselves with picking through a few old ledger books that revealed John Kelly's prewar prosperity.

Gregg and his division crossed the river after the infantry and then followed the route taken by Duffié, now a mile or two ahead — toward Paoli Mill. Gregg's leading brigade, the 2nd, was commanded by the flamboyant Englishman, Colonel Sir Percy Wyndham, and consisted of the 1st New Jersey Cavalry, along with the 1st Maryland Cavalry and the 1st Pennsylvania Cavalry. Following Wyndham was Gregg's 1st Brigade, commanded by Colonel Judson Kilpatrick with the 2nd New York Cavalry, the 10th New York Cavalry, and the 1st Maine Cavalry. The Division was supported by the 6th Independent Battery, New York Light Artillery, commanded by Captain Joseph Martin. Sections of Martin's battery were interspersed among the cavalry regiments in the long column.

After Gregg's division cleared the ford, Colonel Sweitzer's infantrymen waded through the river and followed the two divisions of cavalry down the road toward Paoli Mill. As agreed upon with Gregg, Sweitzer followed the cavalry column toward Mountain Run, there to wait until ordered to withdraw. Along the way, Sweitzer posted squads of men from the 1st Michigan Infantry at each road and trail junction and every prominent terrain feature. Reaching Mountain Run at around 10:00 a.m., Sweitzer halted and prepared to defend against any Confederate forces that might approach from the east.[10]

Once Gregg was en route toward Paoli Mill, Russell marched his brigade, accompanied by Company L, 10th New York Cavalry, out of Kellyville along a road that paralleled the Rappahannock, heading in a northwesterly direction toward Newby's Shop. Before leaving Kellyville, however, Russell's men engaged the gears of Kelly's gristmill, probably with the malicious intent of ruining the great stones by having them grind, one directly upon the other.[11]

The infantry column advanced at a leisurely rate for about five miles. The only difficulty encountered by the men was the rising temperature as the day wore on. From time to time, parties were sent down to the river to fill canteens. Nonetheless, the men complained of thirst. Shortly after noon, the column reached the Orange and Alexandria Railroad about two and one half miles northeast of Brandy Station. Russell took the precaution of forming his men into line of battle and advanced across the tracks. It was evident to the infantrymen that a major fight was then underway in Brandy Station. Russell's troops could hear the sound of artillery and small arms fire to their front and see formations of cavalry charging back and forth in the distance as clouds of dust rose in the air. Russell halted his brigade and sent out pickets from the attached cavalry company along the roads to his front and flanks. Then Russell and his men settled down to await developments or further instructions. Thus far, Russell's men had not fired a shot.

The movement of the infantry is perplexing in view of Hooker's recommendation that Pleasonton use his cavalry to screen his infantry so that at the proper time the infantry might serve as a point of support, and then be used to "cut off and destroy great numbers" of Stuart's command.[12] Obviously Hooker was of the same mind as General William T. Sherman, who once remarked that he "had not seen a cavalry command of 1,000 that was not afraid of the sight of a dozen infantry bayonets."[13] Although Russell's brigade was positioned to protect Gregg's prospective routes of withdrawal, it was hardly close enough to the action to engage any of the cavalry that either Gregg or Pleasonton expected to meet between Brandy Station and Culpeper, or to participate in the ongoing battle. It is also strange that Gregg, obviously decisively engaged at the time, did not send word to Russell to bring his brigade forward and join the fight.

Although the Confederates did not oppose the movement of Pleasonton's left wing, it had not gone undetected. At the first indication of hostilities on the morning of June 9, Stuart had ordered Robertson's brigade forward to block the direct approaches from Kelly's Ford to Brandy Station. Meanwhile, Stuart ordered the 1st South Carolina, which was nearby, to check any Union advance until Robertson could move his two regiments forward. When later that morning Hampton arrived at Fleetwood Hill for orders, Stuart

Brigadier General Beverly Robertson was sent by Stuart to check any Union incursion at Kelly's Ford. Robertson, inexplicably, watched the Federals advance across his front — cavalry moving right and infantry moving left — without firing a shot (Library of Congress).

directed Hampton to place Matthew Calbraith Butler's 2nd South Carolina in reserve at Brandy Station while Hampton, with his remaining three regiments (Cobb's Legion, Jeff Davis Legion, and the 1st North Carolina) moved to Saint James and joined Jones in the fight against Buford.

As Robertson led his brigade past Brandy Station, Black's 1st South Carolina was released to join Hampton in the fight at St. James. This left three regiments, Robertson's 4th and 5th North Carolina and Butler's 2nd South Carolina, to oppose Gregg and Duffié with twelve cavalry regiments, fifteen hundred infantrymen, and three artillery batteries.

As Robertson approached Kelly's Ford by the road from Brandy Station, he observed Gregg's and Duffié's long column of cavalry moving past his front from left to right toward Paoli Mill. He also took note of Russell's infantry column approaching his brigade from the left front. Robertson promptly reported developments to Stuart and fell back toward Brandy Station as Russell's infantry advanced. In response to the report from Robertson, Stuart dispatched Butler's regiment from Brandy Station to Stevensburg. Stuart also ordered Williams Wickham's 4th Virginia, which had arrived late the day before from Fredericksburg and had fortuitously spent the previous night camped near Fleetwood, to move to Stevensburg and support Butler.[14] Stuart also ordered one artillery piece to Stevensburg to support the two regiments.[15] Stuart's volunteer *aide de camp* and scout, Captain Will Farley went ahead of Wickham's column to act as a liaison and guide.

Robertson's reaction to the Union advances—cavalry across his front from left to right; infantry along his left flank—was perplexing. In contrast to Jones's subordinates, who pitched into Buford's division without hesitation when the opportunity arose, Robertson deployed skirmishers, observed, and then withdrew without risking any engagement. Throughout the day, Robertson ensured his men stayed out of range of the muskets of Russell's infantrymen. Additionally, Robertson did not try to hinder Gregg and Duffié's columns as they moved away to the south. This behavior was uncharacteristic for a Southern cavalryman, who would be expected to try to find and exploit a vulnerable flank, or probe into the rear of the Union column. Robertson attempted neither. As Robertson passively watched and waited, Duffié and Gregg continued their advance unmolested.

About a mile beyond Mountain Run, Gregg with his division closed upon the rear of Duffié's division. Gregg, having received messages from Pleasonton regarding the severity of the fight at Beverly Ford, was apparently moving with greater haste than Duffié. Gregg ordered Duffié to press ahead toward Stevensburg, and turned the 3rd Division to the right onto the old Fredericksburg Plank Road. Brandy Station was about four and one half miles ahead of Gregg's division to the northwest.[16]

Why Gregg elected to take such a circuitous route to Brandy Station has never been fully explained. Gregg's route of march was about nine miles in length, while Brandy Station lies less than six miles from Kelly's Ford as the crow flies (and seven miles by more direct roads). The terrain between Kelly's and Brandy is flat with open fields interspersed with bands of trees, and presents few obstacles that impede cross country movement by cavalry. Perhaps Gregg thought that his division could move to Brandy more rapidly by going around Robertson's Brigade than through it. Or, possibly, Gregg chose an indirect route in hopes of making contact well in Stuart's rear. Regardless, Gregg failed to follow the well known Napoleonic axiom: when in doubt, march to the sound of the guns. While the left wing spent the morning crossing the river and indirectly approaching the battlefield, Stuart had been left free to deploy three brigades to Saint James Church where they, along with Beckham's artillery had fought the cavalry corps' right wing to a standstill.

Upon crossing Mountain Run near Paoli Mill, Duffié ordered a battalion of the 6th

Ohio forward to seize Stevensburg as rapidly as possible. In response, the regimental commander, Major William Stedman, sent four companies under the command of Major Benjamin C. Stanhope galloping ahead. Stanhope and his men approached Stevensburg from the northwest, and cresting the high ground at the south end of Hansbrough Ridge, they found the sleepy hamlet stretched out below them with houses on each side of the road leading from the Rappahannock and Rapidan fords in the east toward Culpeper Courthouse in the west.

Stanhope and his men swept past a church and down the hill into town without opposition. By courier, Stanhope reported to Duffié—still two miles short of the village—that there were no enemy to be seen. Reassured, Duffié sent Stanhope contradictory orders. The Frenchman instructed the courier to tell Stanhope to hold Stevensburg at all hazard, but "if pushed too hard, to retreat slowly." As the courier galloped back toward Stevensburg, Duffié resumed his methodical approach toward the small town, apparently indifferent to the tactical opportunity he had been given.[17]

Stevensburg, located on a ridge above Mountain Run, had a commanding view toward Brandy Station in the north and to the Blue Ridge in the west. The town had been sited at the intersection of the Old Carolina Road and Kirtley Road, both of which had been major transportation routes, north-south and east–west, respectively. In colonial days, Stevensburg, originally named "York," had been Culpeper County's largest community, and Thomas Jefferson had even considered the town a potential site for the University of Virginia. However, Jefferson settled on Charlottesville as the location of the state's university, perhaps because there was a lack of potable water around Stevensburg. In 1853, the railroad bypassed Stevensburg several miles to the west, and the community went into decline. Before the war, Stevensburg consisted of 26 homes, two merchants, two blacksmiths, one saddler, one wheelwright, one tailor, and one doctor, with a population of 96.[18]

Colonel Matthew C. Butler led the 2nd South Carolina Cavalry from Brandy Station to Stevensburg to block Colonel Duffié's division. In the fighting, Butler was struck by an artillery projectile and lost his left leg at the ankle. Four months later he returned to duty as brigadier general of cavalry (Library of Congress).

The Confederates, learning of the Union foray into Stevensburg, reacted with much more speed than the dilatory Duffié. At the time Stanhope and his men rode into the town, Colonel Matthew Calbraith Butler and the 2nd South Carolina, about 240 strong, were in their saddles and riding rapidly down the road from Brandy Station to Stevensburg, a distance of

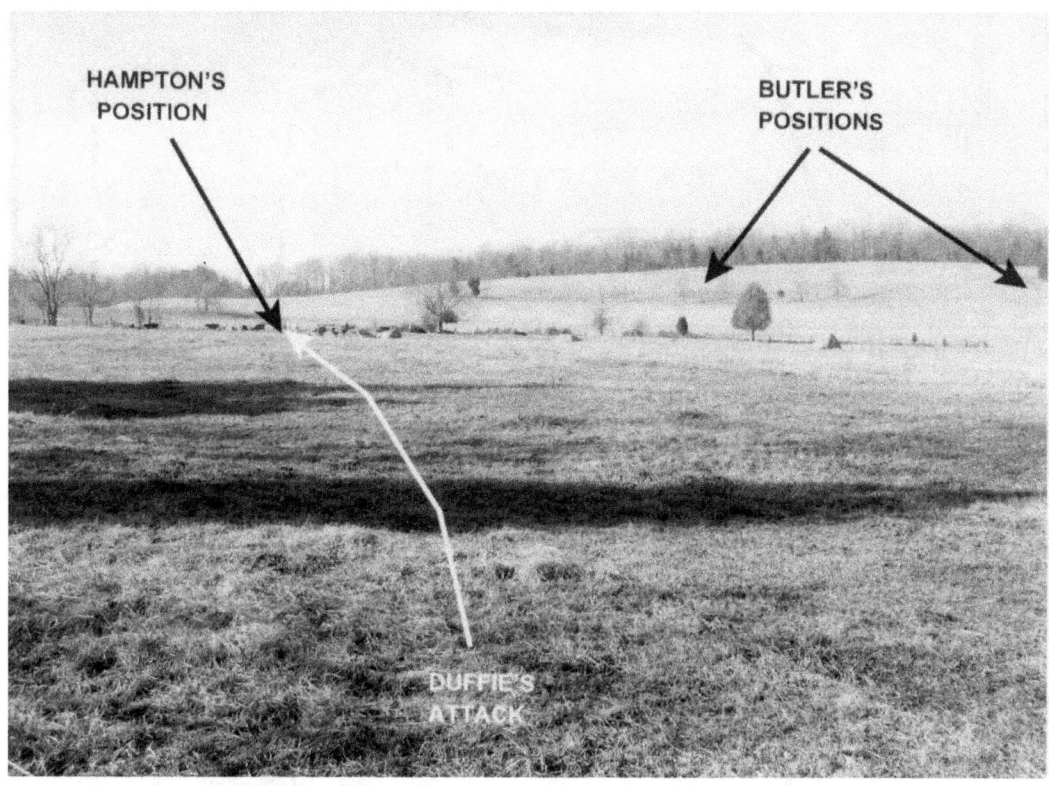

Butler chose to defend east of Stevensburg on the slopes of Hansbrough Ridge. Fighting dismounted, his men easily repulsed Duffié's initial attack. The Federals' second effort, a charge against Lieutenant Colonel Frank Hampton's small detachment on the south end of Butler's line, penetrated the Confederate line. Hampton was carried off the field, mortally wounded (Joseph W. McKinney).

about four miles. About a mile north of the village, Butler dispatched his major, Thomas J. Lipscomb, with forty troopers to swing east, cross Mountain Run at Cole's Hill, and approach Stevensburg from the north.[19] Concurrently, Butler ordered his lieutenant colonel, Frank Hampton, to lead a small party ahead of the main body of the regiment and enter the village from the west. Hampton, the younger brother of General Wade Hampton, dashed ahead with roughly two dozen men. Butler's intent was to attack any Union forces that may have reached Stevensburg from their front and right flank simultaneously, using the advantage of surprise to compensate for the small number of men available to him. With any luck, Lipscomb would cut off any Federal withdrawal.

However, Major Stanhope, either did not receive Duffié's order to hold the town "at all hazard," or considered the approach of Hampton and his platoon a precursor to being "pressed too hard."[20] Upon detecting the small party of Confederate horsemen riding south, Stanhope withdrew his battalion, avoiding any contact with the advancing South Carolinians. By the time Lipscomb and his men came sweeping down Hansbrough Ridge, Stanhope was out of the bag and withdrawing to the east. Lipscomb and his detachment pursued the retreating Yankees, but were unable to overtake them. Stanhope and his battalion fell back upon Duffié's division without having exchanged fire with the South Carolinians.

While Lipscomb was chasing Stanhope, Butler arrived in Stevensburg with the main body of his regiment and began preparing to receive the Union attack that he expected to

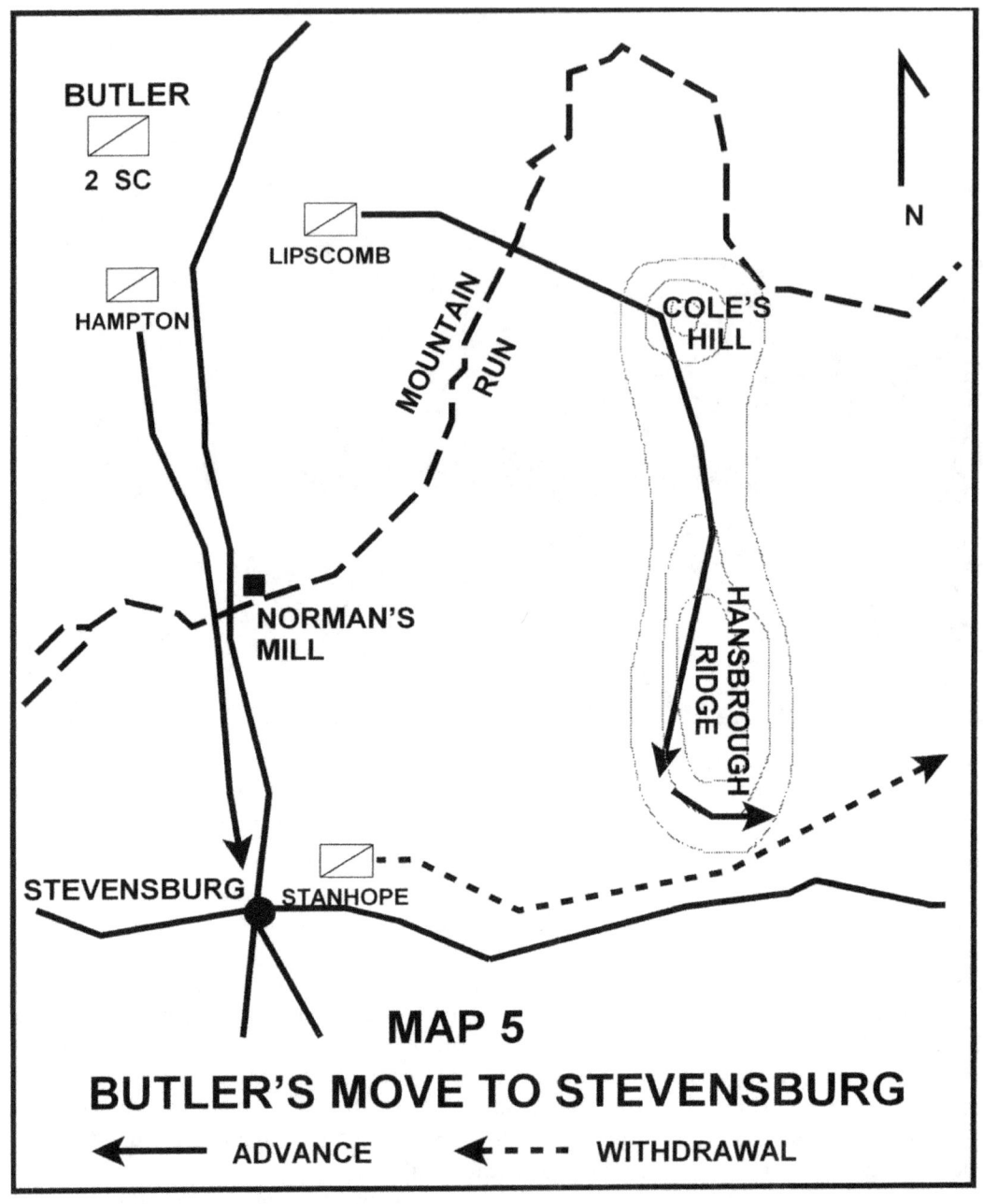

MAP 5
BUTLER'S MOVE TO STEVENSBURG

As the battle began, Colonel M.C. Butler and the 2nd South Carolina Cavalry were posted at Brandy Station as a reserve. Detecting Duffié's movement toward Stevensburg, Butler shifted south. Finding Stevensburg occupied by Union Cavalry, Butler sent Lieutenant Colonel Frank Hampton and two dozen men galloping ahead, while ordering Major T.J. Lipscomb with forty men to the left to block any Union withdrawal. Major Benjamin Stanhope withdrew his battalion of the 6th Ohio Cavalry before Lipscomb could spring Butler's trap.

begin at any moment. Butler moved a mile east from Stevensburg to terrain more favorable for defense, dismounted the bulk of his men, and established a defensive line along the military crest of the eastern slope of Hansbrough Ridge. The line extended almost a mile from the Doggett House in the south to the Hansbrough House in the north, passing through an area now known locally as the Devil's Jump, after a rock outcrop where supposedly Satan struck his heel when leaping from the Blue Ridge to the Chesapeake Bay.[21] Butler perceived that his position was most vulnerable on the far right where the terrain was fairly open and the road from Ely's Ford provided a good avenue of approach for the Union Cavalry. Butler placed Hampton, his most trusted subordinate, in charge of supervising defensive preparations there, and Hampton dismounted his men about the Doggett House. Butler ordered Lipscomb, who by then had returned from his futile chase after Stanhope, to take charge of preparations on the left, or north of the line. Butler himself took charge in the center of his line where a thick stand of trees offered some protection to his dismounted troopers (which also concealed the fact that there were only a few defenders).

The South Carolinians were well positioned and ready for a fight. Additionally, many were armed with Enfield rifles, a highly effective weapon in the hands of dismounted troopers. Nonetheless, Butler's regiment was stretched thin and presented little more than a skirmish line to check Duffié's advance. However, help was on the way. Williams Wickham and the 4th Virginia, having been dispatched by Stuart, were hurrying to Butler's support.

The 4th Virginia was the strongest Regiment in Fitz Lee's Brigade with close to six hundred men on the rolls as present and effectively mounted.[22] As the 4th Virginia approached Stevensburg, Wickham sent his lieutenant colonel, William Payne, forward to coordinate his actions with Colonel Butler's. However, the first order of business for Payne was to sort out which colonel would be in charge. Both Butler and Wickham had approximately the same seniority, each having been promoted to colonel in August 1862, but Wickham was senior by a few days.[23] Consequently, Butler advised Payne that he would "cheerfully" take orders from Wickham. Payne carried that word to Wickham and shortly afterward returned to inform Butler that Wickham preferred for the South Carolinian to remain in command, a smart decision since Butler had seen the ground and his regiment was already deployed and prepared to defend itself. The command issue having been settled, Butler asked that Wickham send a squadron to support Lipscomb on the left, move up two mounted squadrons to support Hampton along the road on the right, and dismount two squadrons farther to Hampton's right in an area that was still undefended.[24] In compliance, Wickham sent a squadron off to Lipscomb and continued moving the main body of his regiment forward, guided by Captain Will Farley.

Although a South Carolinian, Farley attended the University of Virginia and while a student there had traveled widely. He had taken time out from his studies to make a walking tour through northern Virginia and had become very familiar with the roads and trails in that part of the state. An ardent secessionist, Farley enlisted at the beginning of the war as a private in Maxy Gregg's South Carolina regiment, but he did not see much action as an infantryman. After his six-month enlistment expired, Farley continued to serve the Confederacy in a volunteer capacity, accepting no pay from the government. In May 1862, Farley joined Stuart's staff where his audacity and detailed knowledge of northern Virginia proved invaluable. Farley was renowned for equipping himself from the enemy. The sword he carried was captured from a captain in the 47th New York Infantry. The horse he was riding as he led Wickham's men forward, a fine bay, had been taken from a Union major. As an exception to his practice of subsisting off the enemy, Farley had recently purchased a splendid new uniform coat so that he would be properly attired for the reviews and balls of the previous week.

Farley was familiar with the Stevensburg area and knew the dispositions that Butler had made with his regiment. Farley advised Wickham to avoid moving forward on the main road leading east from the town. Instead, he guided the 4th Virginia down a side road that ran from Norman's Mill on Mountain Run through a thick copse of pines along the north side of the village, and then swung to the south where it intersected with Kirtley Road leading east from the town.[25]

As the 4th Virginia moved forward, Duffié initiated his attack with a probe against Butler's line. The Frenchman sent a party of skirmishers forward against Butler's center, but the dismounted South Carolinians, concealed by the trees, easily held their ground. Duffié then shifted his main effort to the right where, as Butler had anticipated, the defenses were most vulnerable.[26]

Wickham's Virginians broke into the open to the east of Stevensburg a short distance to the rear of the 2d South Carolina about the time fighting commenced. At that location, the trail the 4th Virginia was following turned to the south. Leaving the column under the control of junior officers, Wickham rode ahead of his regiment to reconnoiter the ground and find out the situation for himself. Wickham took with him a company to place in position to Hampton's right, as had been requested by Butler. At that moment — with Wickham separated from his regiment, and his troops emerging from the trees in a column, their flank to the enemy, with limited space for maneuver — Duffié launched his main attack. The Frenchman sent three regiments abreast — the 1st Rhode Island to the right of the road, the 6th Ohio on the road, and the 1st Massachusetts on the left of the road — against Hampton and his detachment now about three dozen men. Initially, a wooden fence to front of the 1st Massachusetts impeded the Union attack. Eight or ten troopers dismounted and went forward to tear down the fence. As the men went to work, Hampton's men, concealed behind several buildings and stone walls at Dogett's, took them under fire. Bullets rattled off the fence rails, but, miraculously, none of the Union troopers was hit. With the fence down, Duffié's regiments surged forward, with the 1st Massachusetts in the lead, charging through the gap in the fence.[27]

Stuart sent Colonel Williams Wickham and the 4th Virginia Cavalry to reinforce Butler. As the Federals overran Frank Hampton's position, the Virginians panicked and fled (Library of Congress).

Since Wickham had not yet moved up in support, Hampton and his three dozen men were facing overwhelming odds as the Union brigade bore down on their position. Hampton, in accordance with his instructions from Butler, ordered his men to mount in preparation to withdraw. However, before the small party of South Carolinians could fall back, they were overrun by the Federals and a melee on the road began. During the melee, Hampton, fighting with his saber, was slashed across the face and then disabled by a gunshot to the stomach. The South Carolinians, now leaderless, scattered, as one of Hampton's men led their wounded officer to the rear.[28] The Federals, no longer impeded, pressed their attack toward Stevensburg.

Describing the action from the Federal perspective, Sergeant A. A. Sherman, the guidon bearer of Company G, 1st Massachusetts Cavalry, recalled:

> We drew sabres and started on the charge, and there were only between eighty and ninety men altogether in the Squadron. The rebels stood until we got within a few yards of them. I thought we had got into a bad fix; but before we got to them, they broke and ran like a flock of sheep toward the village, and we among them using the sabre. I followed one man and called on him to surrender, but he took no notice of it. I soon reached him and struck him between the shoulders with the staff of the guidon. It knocked the breath out of him and he surrendered....[29]

The main body of the 4th Virginia, still in a column to the rear of the 2nd South Carolina, was physically and, moreover, mentally, unprepared to meet the Union attack. The Virginians panicked and ignominiously fled to the rear, or as one soldier characterized the event in a letter to his wife, "our regiment gave way with confusion."[30] Wickham attempted without success to overtake and rally his men. About half way to Stevensburg, he gathered up about thirty troopers and attempted to lead a counterattack. However, only a half dozen men followed him back toward the action, the rest resuming their flight in the opposite direction. Wickham and the few men with him were forced to flee as Union troopers, mostly from the 1st Massachusetts, pursued them through the town. As the Federals broke off their pursuit, Wickham finally halted at the gate to Jack Barbour's property, about a mile west of Stevensburg with just three or four officers and five or six men. Most of the men from the 4th Virginia had fled farther west, only stopping after they passed through an artillery battery that General Longstreet had ordered drawn on the slopes of Mt. Pony as a precaution. The Virginians excused their conduct for the debacle at Stevensburg by telling all who would listen that their formation had been broken up by a panic in the 2nd South Carolina.[31] In the panic, Duffié's men captured twenty-six Virginians.[32]

In one odd incident of battle, as they advanced up the road toward Stevensburg, several men from the 1st Massachusetts recalled seeing the body of a strikingly handsome dead Confederate at the side of the road. He was "tall, slim and athletic, with regular sharply chiseled features, he had fallen flat on his back, with one hand upraised as if striking, and with his long light hair flung back in heavy waves from his forehead." Captain Charles Francis Adams recalled, "It was curious, no one seems to have passed that body without the same thought of admiration...." Nonetheless, there was no time for the men to stop and linger over the dead Confederate.[33]

Duffié's lead brigade continued its advance. Sergeant Sherman recalled: "Going through the town, the women were abusive. The rebels made two or three attempts at making a stand, but it was no use. We went through them like a whirlwind. Captain Tewksbury got knocked off his horse once, and remounting shot the man that struck him."[34] In Stevensburg, Sherman and a comrade had the good fortune to chase down and capture a hospital wagon that was full of supplies, including liquor, tea, and coffee. After helping

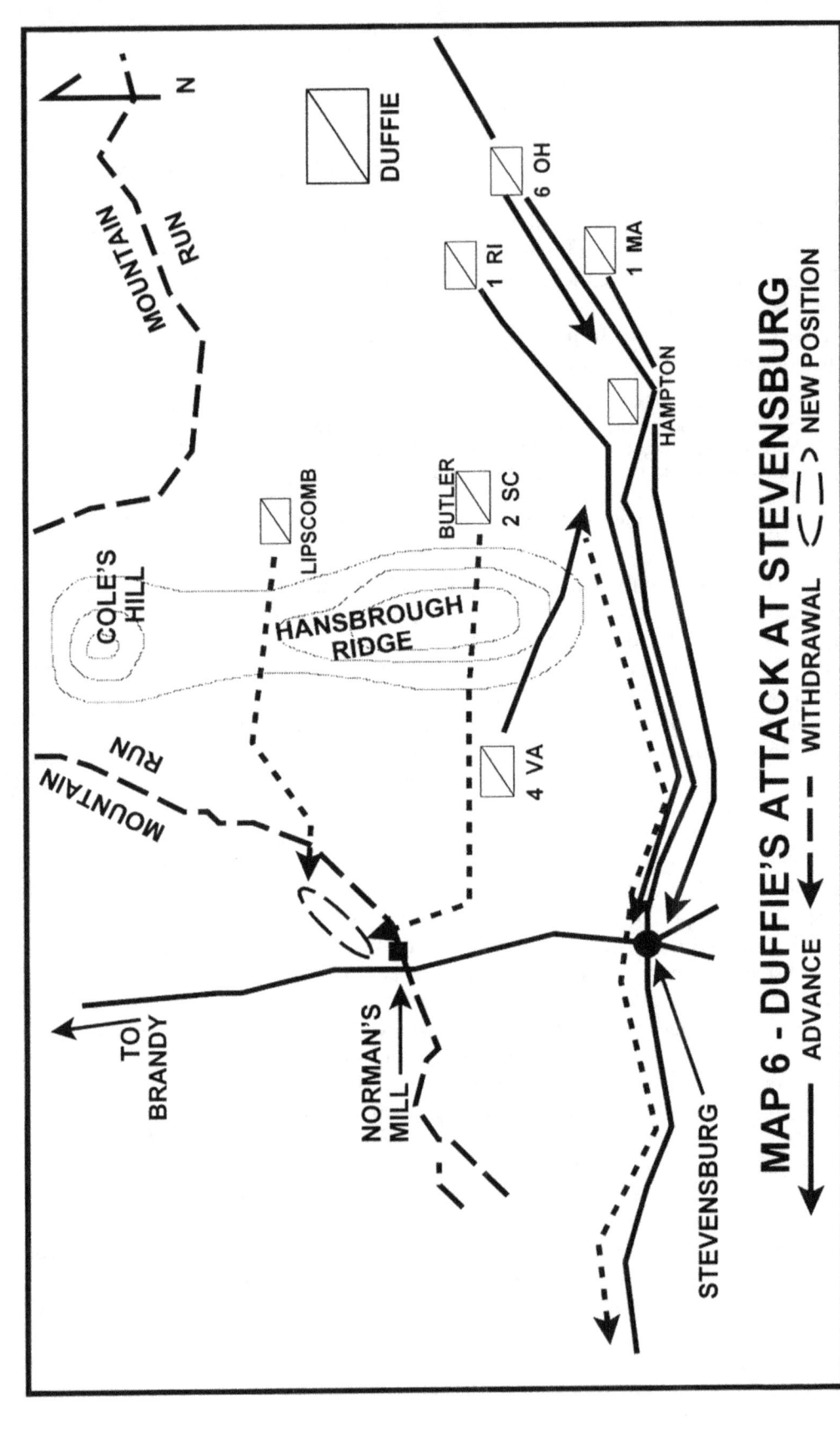

8 — A Small Affair   147

Opposite: After initially being repulsed by Colonel Butler on Hansbrough Ridge, Duffié sent his 1st Brigade against Frank Hampton's small detachment blocking the road to Stevensburg. Hampton was overrun as the 4th Virginia Cavalry, moving forward to reinforce the 2nd South Carolina, panicked and fled west. As the men from Rhode Island and Massachusetts dashed into Stevensburg, Butler and Major Lipscomb withdrew their detachments safely across Mountain Run. *Above*: Ignoring Wickham's orders to rally, the troopers of the 4th Virginia galloped through Stevensburg, not stopping until they reached the slopes of Mt. Pony (Joseph W. McKinney).

themselves to the contents of the wagon (and probably some libations since it was a hot and dusty day) the two troopers went back through Stevensburg. They were surprised to find that the women in the town refused to take Confederate wounded into their homes, saying that Wickham's Virginians had "disgraced the Confederacy by allowing so small a force to drive them through the town."[35]

Meanwhile, Butler and Lipscomb continued to hold their positions on the east slope of Hansbrough Ridge. Nevertheless, with Duffié now in their rear, it was imperative that they withdraw to safety. Butler withdrew the men under his control directly to the west across Hansbrough Ridge, skirted to the north of Stevensburg, and crossed Mountain Run. Once on the north side of the stream, the South Carolinians, dismounted and fanned out in a long arc from the southwest to the northeast. The trooper's line paralleled the sweeping bend of Mountain run about two hundred yards back from the banks of the stream. There, the Southerners prepared meet the Union attack when it resumed.[36] Butler sent his regimental adjutant to Fleetwood to advise Stuart that he had been forced to withdraw from Stevensburg.

To the rear of the line of troops the ground rose gently, with the road from Stevensburg to Brandy Station running almost directly north–south up the slope. A short distance up the slope the lone gun from Moorman's battery—sent earlier by Stuart to support Butler and Wickham—took up a firing position at the side of the road.

Meanwhile, Lipscomb, who had not received word to withdraw, remained back on the east slope of Hansbrough Ridge. As Duffié began his attack, Lipscomb had received orders from Butler—delivered by Captain Farley—to hold his position on the left of Confederate line, and Farley had brought with him a squadron from the 4th Virginia to reinforce the position. Since Duffié had made his attack against the south end of the Confederate line, Lipscomb had no difficulty maintaining his ground in the north, and he had not noticed

Captain William D. Farley, Stuart's volunteer *aide de camp* and scout, was struck by the same projectile that mauled Butler. Farley lost his right leg at the knee. He died in Culpeper that night (Virginia Historical Society, Richmond).

Top: Duffié's artillery battery was equipped with 3" rifled guns, such as the one shown in this photograph. The battery was commanded by Captain Alexander C.M. Pennington (right). Pennington's gunners were probably aiming at a lone Confederate artillery piece supporting the South Carolinians, and hit Butler and Farley by chance (Library of Congress). *Bottom*: Today a small monument marks the spot where Farley and Butler were wounded. The monument is about 100 yards north of the bridge over Mountain Run at the site of Norman's Mill (Joseph W. McKinney).

Butler pulling back with the rest of the regiment. About thirty minutes after he crossed Mountain Run, Butler became concerned over Lipscomb's absence. In response, he sent a courier to Lipscomb with orders to retire across Mountain Run "with rapidity." That task proved more difficult than anticipated because Lipscomb's party included sixteen dismounted troopers who could not be left behind. As Lipscomb and his men withdrew — some mounted and some afoot — toward Norman's Mill, they were spotted by two columns of Union troopers, each about three hundred yards away. The Federals gave pursuit. As Lipscomb's party and the two federal columns approached Mountain Run, Moorman's gunners opened fire. Either mistakenly, or possibly a result of poor gunnery, the first two rounds from Moorman's gun landed nearer to Lipscomb than the Federals. Nonetheless, the Federals broke off their pursuit and fell back toward Stevensburg, allowing Lipscomb to cross Mountain Run safely. While it is possible that the Federals were concerned about being brought under Confederate artillery fire, Lipscomb believed close strikes of the rounds convinced the pursuers that he and his men were Union troops attacking Butler.[37]

With his command now safely across Mountain Run, Butler settled down to await Duffié's next move. On the road a short distance down the slope from Moorman's gun, Butler sat astride his favorite war-horse, a sorrel his troopers called "Old Bench Legs" because of its crooked hind legs. From his position, Butler could observe the disposition of his troops and any activity by Duffié. Mountain Run, although shallow, was deeply eroded and presented a significant obstacle to the movement of cavalry, and a resumption of the attack by the Union force did not seem imminent. Captain Farley rode up to Butler and the two sat on their horses next to each other, the nose of Farley's horse next to Old Bench Legs' tail. Butler and Farley chatted about inconsequential matters, Butler recounting how one of his men had nonchalantly killed a Yankee officer on a gray horse with a lucky shot earlier in the day (Butler had initially chided the trooper for missing his target).

As the two officers chatted, Moorman's gunners, spotting a section of Alexander Pennington's battery on the heights near the church at the east end of Stevensburg, began firing across the valley.[38] Pennington's gunners returned fire and for a few minutes artillery projectiles went back and forth without much effect.[39] Neither Butler nor Farley paid any attention to the artillery fire going back and forth over and around them.[40]

The sight of two exposed mounted officers may have been too tempting a target, prompting one of Pennington's gunners to adjust the aiming point of his gun slightly to the left, or one gun may just have shifted slightly during recoil. In any event, a round from Pennington's section unexpectedly struck the ground about twenty yards down the slope from Butler, skipped, and continued on its trajectory a few feet above the ground. The projectile struck Butler's right leg, almost severing it at the ankle. After passing through Butler's horse, the round passed through Farley's horse and cleanly severed Farley's right leg at the knee.[41]

Butler's horse bounded into the air, throwing the colonel, saddle and all (the projectile severed the saddle's girth), onto the road. Old Bench Legs then ran off, his intestines trailing, to die in a field about one and a half miles away. The impact of the artillery round knocked Farley's horse over onto the road where it began thrashing about. Butler, who remained conscious, ordered several of his men to pull Farley away from the horse's kicking hoofs, and to administer first aid while he applied a tourniquet to his own ankle. Farley, ever the gentleman, protested to the men that they should treat their colonel's wound first.[42]

Farley, the more severely wounded of the two, was evacuated from the battlefield first, carried to an ambulance in a horse trough. As Farley was being carried away, he asked one

Duffié, ordered to move to Brandy Station and support Gregg, has been criticized for not crossing Mountain Run, fighting through the 2nd South Carolina, and taking the most direct route. However, as shown in this photograph the banks of Mountain Run near Norman's Mill are severely eroded in most places. A forced crossing by cavalry, opposed by roughly 200 Confederates, would have been difficult (Joseph W. McKinney).

of Butler's officers to bring him his severed leg. When the officer brought him the limb, Farley grasped it to his chest, remarking, "It is an old friend, gentlemen, and I do not wish to part from it."[43] The two "friends," Farley and his leg, were carried off the field together and taken to the home of Charles Ashby in Culpeper, then occupied by a Doctor Jones. Farley died there later that evening from shock and loss of blood.[44]

Butler turned over command of the regiment to Major Lipscomb and was carried off the field. Initially his men bore him off on a blanket with one man at each corner. Although the four bearers were careful, Butler was in excruciating pain as the shattered bones in his ankle grated against each other. To try to relieve Butler's suffering, the men placed the colonel in a water trough and carried him a short distance farther before an ambulance finally arrived. They then drove Butler to a nearby farmhouse belonging to Mrs. Fitzhugh where a field hospital had been established. Surgeons amputated Butler's leg at the ankle about 5:00 that afternoon.[45]

Shortly after Lipscomb assumed command, the regimental adjutant informed him that Brandy Station was full of Yankees, Gregg's division having finally arrived at that location. The news was alarming since the enemy was now in strength to both the regiment's front and its rear. Lipscomb decided that his men were in danger of being cut off and began retiring west toward Culpeper.[46]

Meanwhile, Duffié had consolidated at Stevensburg in preparation of resuming his attack toward Culpeper. However, about noon — before the attack was resumed — a staff officer from General Gregg arrived with orders for Duffié to bring his division to Brandy Station by the same road that Gregg had taken. Duffié, in compliance with his orders, reversed his division and withdrew by the same road he had used to approach Stevensburg earlier that morning. As before, diCesnola's brigade led the march. Colonel Gregg's brigade remained at Stevensburg for about an hour to cover the withdrawal, and then followed diCesnola's brigade, leaving the 4th Pennsylvania to act as the division's rear guard. The march was numbing for the troopers who had been in the saddle since 2:00 a.m. without dismounting, and had spent the two previous nights marching to and returning from the Jeffersonton reconnaissance.[47]

Later, Duffié was criticized for not fighting through the outnumbered Confederates along Mountain Run and proceeding to Brandy Station by the most direct route. That course of action would have reduced the distance he needed to travel from roughly six miles to a little more than three miles. Additionally, by moving on Brandy Station directly from the south, Duffié might have been better positioned to attack Stuart's flank or rear. However, Duffié and his division would likely encountered difficulty trying to force a crossing over Mountain Run and driving through the 2nd South Carolina defensive position. The South Carolinians, with a squadron from the 4th Virginia, had withdrawn in relative good order from the debacle east of Stevensburg earlier that morning, and they were well positioned to contest a crossing over Mountain Run. Additionally, Duffié had to be concerned that the bulk of 4th Virginia, had rallied and might be capable of striking the flank of his division from the west should he move directly north. Finally, Duffié did not know if additional rebel regiments were blocking the direct route to Brandy Station. All-in-all, the safer course of action was to backtrack as he had been ordered to do. While Duffié may not win praise for his lack of initiative or reluctance to accept risk, it is difficult to fault him for following his orders, the course of action that was expected of him.[48]

Lipscomb, after withdrawing about two miles toward Culpeper, made contact with Colonel Wickham. Wickham, who by then had made some progress in gathering his scattered regiment, had received word that Duffié was withdrawing. Wickham ordered Lipscomb to move back to Stevensburg and from there to follow Duffié. Lipscomb turned his regiment around and backtracked to Stevensburg. After passing through the town, Lipscomb sent out videttes to his right and left, and cautiously followed the Union division, eventually making light contact with the 4th Pennsylvanian which was covering Duffié's movement.

The fighting at Stevensburg was over for the day. The reported losses in the 2nd South Carolina were small, only one killed and one wounded. However, unofficial tallies suggested that the casualties were higher and that perhaps about forty men had been lost during the day's fighting.[49] Regardless, the blow to the leadership of the regiment had been heavy — Frank Hampton was dead and Butler would be out of action for months. In the 4th Virginia, the main casualty was a serious wound to the unit's pride. The loss of roughly two dozen men captured was small when compared to the shame resulting from the regiment's disgraceful rout. On the other hand, Duffié's men had done well. Although the Union strength was far superior at Stevensburg, only three blue regiments had gotten into the fight, and they had prevailed over the Confederates in a convincing manner. As one officer from the 1st Massachusetts somewhat laconically observed, "Nothing could have improved our attack, but it was a small affair."[50]

9

Fight Like Gentlemen!

Fleetwood Hill

By midmorning, activities had quieted down at Stuart's headquarters on Fleetwood Hill. Stuart had left to personally observe the action at Saint James Church, staff officers had been sent off with messages or on other details, the tents had been struck and the baggage wagons were on their way to safety at Culpeper Courthouse. All that remained near the Miller House on the low ridge to the northeast of Brandy Station were Stuart's assistant adjutant general, Major Henry B. McClellan, and a few couriers—left there to relay messages to Stuart if the need arose. The only out of the ordinary event since Stuart's departure was the unexpected arrival of a howitzer under the command of Lieutenant John Carter of Captain Preston Chew's battery. The crew parked their gun at the base of Fleetwood, having been withdrawn from the line of metal at Saint James when they exhausted their ammunition.[1]

Major McClellan was new to Stuart's staff, having been selected in May to succeed Major Channing Price, who had been killed at Chancellorsville. McClellan was a Pennsylvanian by birth and a cousin to the former commanding general of the Army of the Potomac of the same name. McClellan had studied divinity, and in 1858 at age seventeen earned a degree from Williams College in Massachusetts. However, instead of going into the ministry, he accepted a teaching position in Virginia. When hostilities broke out in 1861, McClellan sided with his newly-adopted state and he enlisted as a private in the 3rd Virginia Cavalry. After eleven months of enlisted service, McClellan's talents were rewarded with a commission and appointment as adjutant of his regiment. Although McClellan had been highly recommended by Fitz Lee to fill the vacancy left by the death of Price, he was untested on the division staff and the quality of his military judgment was unknown.[2]

Unbeknownst to McClellan, Gregg's 3rd Cavalry Division was approaching Brandy Station from the southeast on the Fredericksburg Plank Road. Wyndham's Brigade was leading and Kilpatrick's brigade trailing in the long column of hot, dusty troopers. The three sections of Captain Joseph Martin's battery, the 6th Independent New York Light Artillery, were dispersed among the column.[3] Although Stuart had dispatched Beverly Robertson with his brigade to block the way, Robertson had misunderstood his orders and watched passively as two divisions of Union cavalry moved around him to the right. The 2nd Division had marched to Stevensburg while the objective of the 3rd Division was Brandy Station, there to combine with Buford's wing of the Cavalry Corps. Gregg's advance had been essentially unopposed—the only impediment encountered by the Union troopers were occasional felled trees, dropped across the road by Confederate videttes to slow the Union

Brandy Station, Virginia, June 9, 1863

Top: This sketch by Alfred Waud depicts Brandy Station in 1863. The two-storey building in the center of the sketch may be the building known today as the "Graffiti House." The small building at the far right of the sketch may be the train depot (Library of Congress). *Bottom*: The Graffiti House was built in 1858 by John Stone, Brandy Station's postmaster. Confederate wounded were treated in the building on June 9. The upstairs walls are covered with Confederate and Union graffiti. The one-storey wing on the left is a more recent addition to the building (Joseph W. McKinney).

This drawing by Edwin Forbes shows Federal artillery in front of the Brandy Station Depot. The depot sat on the north side of the Orange and Alexandria tracks (Library of Congress).

advance.[4] The only Confederate force positioned to oppose Gregg, Colonel M.C. Butler's 2nd South Carolina, had earlier left Brandy Station to block Duffié's advance on Stevensburg. Butler had sent one company of thirty men to picket the roads near Carrico's Mill. However the company commander, who had deployed against Duffié, found himself bypassed by Gregg. Confronted by a Union regiment as he attempted to withdraw, the commander led his men into the woods where they hid for the remainder of the day.[5]

Shortly after 10:00 a.m., General Robertson's Assistant Adjutant General, Captain William N. Worthington, rode up Fleetwood Hill and advised McClellan that Union cavalry was approaching Brandy Station in great strength, and worse, that there were no Confederates to block their way. McClellan, knowing that Robertson had been dispatched just to prevent such an occurrence, was skeptical of the report. He ordered Worthington to go back through Brandy Station and verify the identity of the advancing column, thinking that it was probably Confederate. In about five minutes, Worthington galloped back up the hill and told McClellan that he could look for himself if he wished to verify the identity of the approaching horsemen. McClellan, looking to the southwest, observed Wyndham's brigade, still in a column, approaching the railroad station in the small hamlet. It was evident to the young major that a crisis was at hand. Fleetwood Hill, the dominant terrain feature in Stuart's rear, was undefended and in danger of being occupied by Union forces in a matter of minutes. Should that occur, the main Confederate position at Saint James Church would be untenable — the brigades of Jones and Hampton would have strong enemy formations to both their front and rear.[6]

McClellan immediately sent off his remaining couriers with orders to find Stuart and apprise him of an imminent disaster at Fleetwood. Meanwhile, the lead elements of Wyndham's brigade crossed the railroad tracks and swung to the right, approaching Fleetwood from the west. McClellan, with no real means to defend the position, decided to bluff. He ordered Carter to advance his howitzer from its concealed location on the east side of the hill and take up a firing position on the crest in full view of the advancing Union troops. Carter and his men were game. They boldly ran their gun forward and, having found a few defective rounds of ammunition in their caisson, engaged Wyndham's brigade with a slow fire.[7]

In the winter of 1863, Brandy Station was the main supply depot for the Army of the Potomac. The line of cedar trees in the distance at the left rear of the photograph sits atop Fleetwood Hill (Library of Congress).

Wyndham fell for McClellan's ruse, incorrectly perceiving that the Confederates were "strongly posted" on Fleetwood with "batteries planted on the heights."[8] In response to what he believed was significant opposition, Wyndham halted his brigade and ordered forward his section of Martin's artillery battery, commanded by Lieutenant Moses Clark. At the same time, Wyndham ordered the 1st Maryland Cavalry to move up abreast and to the right of the 1st New Jersey Cavalry, his lead regiment. Clark passed through the columns of cavalry troopers, wheeled his two three-inch rifled guns into position in a field near the railroad station but on the south side of the tracks, unlimbered, and took Carter's lone gun, by now almost completely out of all ammunition, under fire.[9] After enduring Clark's counterfire — termed a "fierce cannonade" by McClellan — for about fifteen minutes, Carter prudently withdrew his gun back into defilade on the reverse slope of Fleetwood Hill.[10] Wyndham, meanwhile, prepared to make a coordinated attack on the hill with his brigade.

While McClellan and Carter were playing their charade, JEB Stuart was with Grumble Jones' brigade at Saint James Church where, to all appearances, Buford's attack had lost its momentum. Stuart's sanguinity, however, was soon broken as he became aware of the new threat in his rear. First word of Gregg's advance came from Beverly Robertson who, though inactive, was efficient. Earlier, Robertson had promptly dispatched a courier to report the movement of Union cavalry across his front from left to right. Robertson's courier found Grumble Jones who relayed the news to Stuart, advising Stuart that his right flank was threatened. Stuart, piqued at receiving tactical advice from Jones, whom he detested, sent the courier back to the brigadier with a tart rejoinder, "Tell Gen. Jones to attend to the Yankees in his front and I'll watch the flanks." Upon receiving Stuart's response, Grumble Jones supposedly quipped, "So he thinks they ain't coming, does he? Well, let him alone; he'll damned soon see for himself."[11] And Stuart soon did.

Shortly after receiving Robertson's message, the first of McClellan's couriers arrived at Saint James with news that Federals had entered Brandy Station in strength. Stuart was incredulous, and ordered Captain James Hart, whose battery was positioned nearby, to go to Fleetwood and verify the report. As Hart made his departure, a second courier — Frank Deane, a trusted headquarters clerk — galloped up. Deane informed Stuart that the Yankees were, indeed, in Brandy, a fact verified by the sound of artillery as Carter's gun opened fire on Wyndham and then as Clark's section responded.[12]

Stuart, instantly recognizing the gravity of the situation, ordered Jones immediately to send two regiments to Fleetwood. Stuart also ordered one of his nearby staff officers, Lieutenant Frank Robertson, who had returned from his mission placing out sharpshooters, to "go fast" to Hampton with orders that the South Carolinian also send a regiment to Fleetwood at the gallop. Robertson did not know where Hampton was, but rode off rapidly in the direction Stuart had pointed.

In response to Stuart's directive, Jones ordered Colonel Asher Harmon to take his 12th Virginia Cavalry to Fleetwood. Jones also ordered Lieutenant Colonel Elijah White to follow and support Harmon with his battalion. Major Beckham ordered a section of William McGregor's battery to accompany the column from the Jones' Brigade. Since both the 12th Virginia and White's Comanches had been fighting mounted, neither organization had dismounted significant parties of skirmishers. Consequently, they were each able rapidly to get underway toward Fleetwood. As the column moved out, Stuart fell in behind them, intent on personally directing the fight for the hill.

Colonel Percy Wyndham, at the head of Gregg's division, reached Brandy Station in mid-morning on June 9. Wyndham, an English soldier of fortune who had been knighted by King Victor Emanuel of Italy, mistakenly thought Fleetwood Hill was strongly defended. Wyndham called forward a section of artillery and ordered the hill taken under fire (Library of Congress).

Frank Robertson, riding to the east from Saint James to find Hampton, soon ran up against a deep, apparently impassable ditch, and began searching for a location at which to cross. On the opposite side of the ditch, Robertson hailed a party of Confederates, and after a few minutes, one of them rode out to meet him. Fortuitously, the man who rode out was one of Hampton's staff officers. Robertson, shouting across the ditch, relayed Stuart's orders. Hampton's staff officer dashed off, and a few moments later Robertson saw a regiment pulling out of Hampton's defensive line and galloping toward the rear. The young lieutenant,

Today the approach from Brandy Station to Fleetwood looks much as it did in 1863. After his artillery had shelled Fleetwood for a few minutes, Wyndham ordered his brigade to attack. The 1st Maryland Cavalry moved directly toward the Miller House, where Stuart had his headquarters the night before. Wyndham, at the head of the 1st New Jersey Cavalry, charged to the left of the Old Carolina Road (Joseph W. McKinney).

considering his task accomplished, turned around and headed back toward Saint James in hopes of finding Stuart.[13]

Fleetwood, just over a mile to the southwest of Saint James across open, rolling country and a little farther by road, was about a fifteen minute ride for the troopers of the 12th Virginia and White's Battalion. As Colonel Harman and his regiment approached Fleetwood at a trot, McClellan, who could see that a charge by Wyndham's brigade was imminent, sent a courier to the colonel asking that he please hurry. Harmon, trusting that the situation was urgent, ordered his regiment to the gallop, and the column of troopers lengthened as the pace increased.[14] With no time to deploy, Harmon and his men ascended Fleetwood in a column of fours. At the bottom of the hill, White halted his battalion and ordered his men to form into the standard battle formation, a column of squadrons, each in two ranks.

On the opposite side of Fleetwood, Wyndham had ordered his brigade to attack Fleetwood with 1st Maryland — a regiment that was significantly under strength — on the right and the 1st New Jersey on the left. Wyndham ordered his remaining regiment, the 1st Pennsylvania, to be prepared to follow and support the 1st Maryland.[15] Wyndham, the colonel of the 1st New Jersey, rode at the head of his own regiment.

The two Union columns moved out of Brandy Station at the trot, passed Clark's now-silent guns, and advanced across one half mile of open and rolling ground to the base of Fleetwood. There, an intermittent stream impeded the progress of the columns only slightly.

The blue troopers negotiated the ditch in good order and swept up the slope, taking up a gallop as they approached the crest. Clark with one gun—the other was disabled with a projectile wedged in its bore—crossed the railroad tracks and followed the cavalry. Clark stopped about three hundred yards short of Fleetwood Hill, but before he could unlimber, Wyndham ordered him to a more forward position. Unknown to Clark, his battery commander, Captain Joseph Martin, was also hurrying forward to support Wyndham's attack with a second section of guns.[16]

Under those circumstances, one of the most confused and unique engagements of the Civil War began.

The modern perception of cavalry combat is generally inaccurate. Many people today, unfamiliar with the behavior of horses and misled by overblown written accounts and fanciful artwork, envision a battle with two extended formations of riders, each galloping forward boot-to-boot in straight, even ranks. In this imagined battle, the converging formations make contact at high speed with an audible crash, and the momentum of one group "breaks" the other and achieves victory. The reality in the Civil War was far different.

Cavalry was expected to attack mostly at the walk, only going to the trot when within about two hundred yards of the enemy, and then taking up a controlled gallop about one hundred yards from the enemy. At roughly 50 yards out, the commander would order the charge, and the buglers would echo his command. At the sound of the bugles, the troopers were expected to raise their sabers, loosen their reins and put their spurs to their horses, increasing their speed while still maintaining control. Those techniques would, hopefully, allow a squadron to maintain its formation at speed to generate the "shock action" that senior officers believed would result in victory.[17]

As a standard practice, regiments attacked in a column of squadrons with squadrons drawn up in two ranks (although Cooke in his *Cavalry Tactics* promulgated a single rank formation). Thus a ten-company regiment of 250 men would usually attack with a frontage of 25 men (five squadrons with two ranks per squadron). Commanders maintained sufficient distance between squadrons so that the trailing squadrons could, at least in theory, maneuver as they advanced. For example, a commander might order trailing squadrons to echelon right or left and enter a fight on the flank of the squadron to their front.

Maintaining order in a rank as it advanced was a challenge, particularly if the distance to be covered was great, the terrain difficult or turning movements—known as "wheelings"—were required. Ranks easily became ragged with gaps opening between horses as riders moved right or left to dodge stumps, brush, trees, holes, and rocks. Ditches and fence lines presented significant obstacles that caused troopers to queue up at crossing points and gaps. Commonly, attacks were abruptly halted at fence lines while several troopers dismounted to take down rails or pull down stones to create an opening (alternatively, attackers would detour down a fence line in a column until they found an open gate). Often during a charge, and despite the best efforts of their riders, stronger and faster horses surged ahead while weaker or slower horses lagged behind, further degrading the desired alignment of the ranks. Frequently, and especially when under fire, men tended to take up the gallop while too far away from the enemy. This invariably resulted in tired horses and ragged formations.

Additionally, as two ranks of opposing cavalry closed upon one another, either both in motion or one in motion and one stationary, each man in the front rank usually selected an opponent to fight. As ranks of horsemen converged, the pace slowed, and the charge devolved into a mass of men fighting one-on-one and two-on-one with pistols and sabers. Some men, instead of charging "home," might halt a few yards from their adversaries and

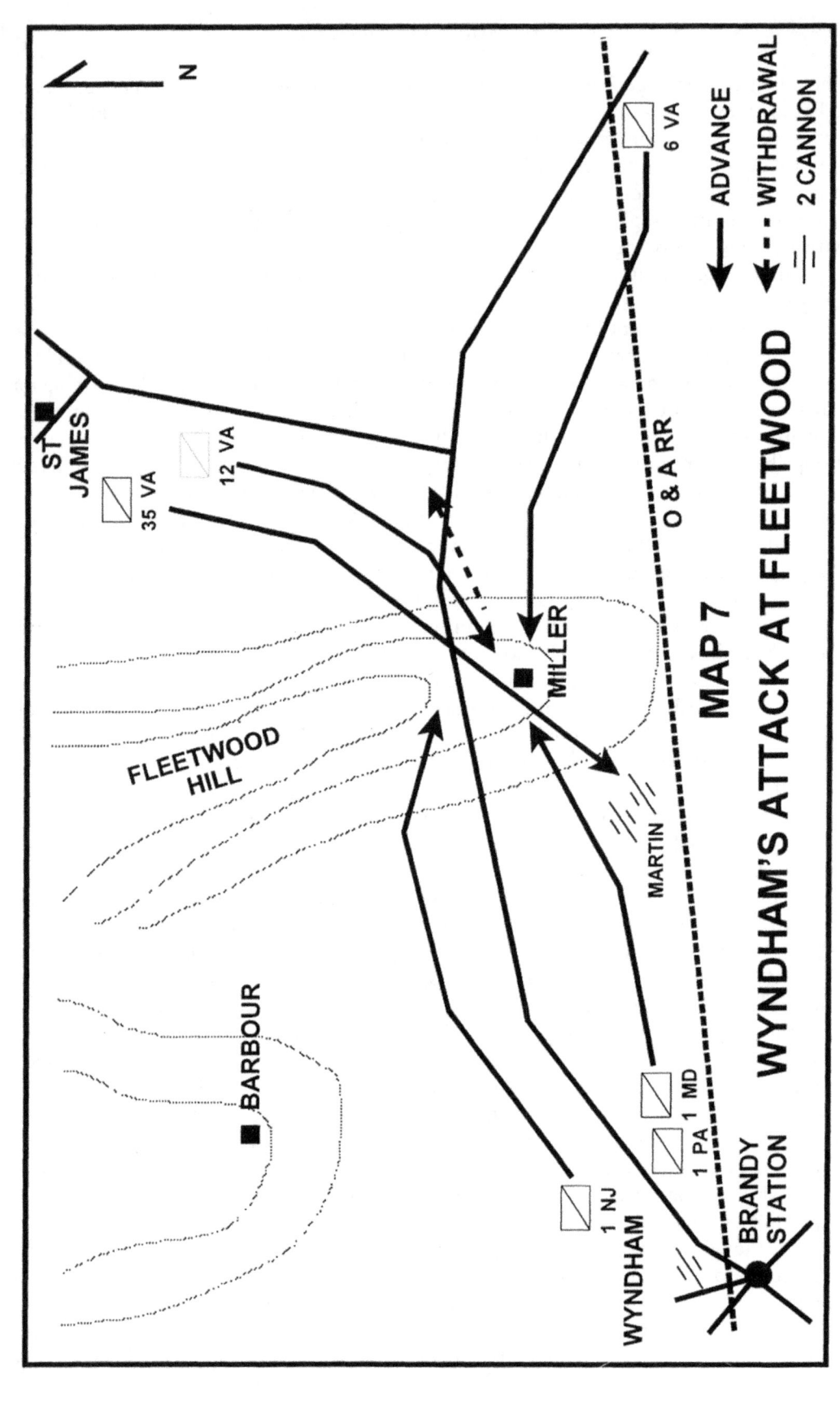

empty their pistols at close range. Others might move aside creating gaps in their ranks that allowed their opponents to pass through unmolested. A few men, electing not to fight at all, might even turn and run. Instead of victory through shock, cavalry against cavalry fighting was more likely a disorganized melee.

For a Civil War infantryman, it was usually more dangerous to flee than to stand and fight. On foot, a soldier needed several minutes to retreat beyond the range of a rifled musket, and during that time he was most vulnerable, unable to fire his own weapon while his back was turned to his enemy. However, in a melee, cavalry fought mostly with short range weapons — six feet for an arm extended with saber; perhaps ten yards (if lucky) for pistol fired from horseback. Additionally, mounted troopers could more quickly withdraw beyond the range of their opponent's weapons, including carbines. Thus, cavalrymen possessed the option of retreating to safety if they felt overmatched by their enemy.

Because of the dynamics of battle, when formations of infantry closed with one another, bloody, decisive combat usually ensued. However, when mounted cavalry clashed, the fighting frequently exhibited a different pattern: an initial engagement followed by a series of retreats, rallies, and follow-on engagements.[18] Eventually, one side or the other would become worn down, and quit the field. That pattern was followed for the next two hours as Stuart and Gregg fed their regiments into the struggle over Fleetwood Hill, considered by each general to be the most key terrain on the battlefield.

To begin, Asher Harmon's 12th Virginia, disorganized after its dash from Saint James, rode onto Fleetwood in a strung-out column of fours with Company B, the Baylor Light Horse, in the lead. When the gray-clad horsemen crested the hill, they met the 1st Maryland immediately to their front, approaching in a column of squadrons with its 2nd Squadron, under the command of Major Charles Russell, in the lead.[19] To their right, the Virginians could see the 1st New Jersey advancing, also in a column of squadrons. Without hesitation, Company B charged down the slope into the Marylanders. The remainder of the 12th Virginia entered the fight piecemeal as they crested the hill. Meanwhile, Wyndham led the better organized 1st New Jersey into the right flank of the 12th Virginia on the top of the hill.[20] Along with the two Union regiments, Moses Clark and his lone gun crested Fleetwood. The crew went into action, but only fired off one or two rounds before Clark withdrew the piece to a safer position at the base of the hill.[21]

Harmon's outnumbered Virginians fought the Union troopers from Maryland and New Jersey individually and in groups of two or three. The Virginians, disorganized at the outset of the engagement, were quickly overwhelmed by the superior numbers of their opponents and began withdrawing, galloping back the way they had come — over the crest of Fleetwood toward safety. As the troopers of the 12th fled down the east slope of the hill, they broke through the ranks of the 35th Battalion. The flight of the 12th impeded Lige White, who, under orders from Stuart to attack immediately, was attempting to bring his Comanches forward in battle order. After a delay of a few minutes to reform the ranks of the Comanches, White ordered his first squadron, led by Captain George Ferneyhough, to charge directly toward the Miller House, while White led the remaining two squadrons against Union troopers that had come into view to the left of the house. The Comanches,

Opposite: General David McMurtrie Gregg approached Brandy Station from the southeast, with Colonel Percy Wyndham's brigade leading his division. After passing through Brandy, Wyndham paused to allow his artillery to shell Fleetwood Hill at the Miller House, formerly the site of JEB Stuart's headquarters. By delaying his assault, Wyndham gave Stuart time to send regiments from Saint James to Fleetwood, and a two-hour contest for control of the hilltop began.

shouting and whooping their distinctive Rebel yell, swept over Fleetwood, bypassing some Union troopers and driving others before them. The momentum of the charge carried White and his two squadrons about two hundred yards beyond Fleetwood toward Brandy Station. However, the Union troopers remaining on Fleetwood threatened to overrun Ferneyhough's squadron, which had become involved in the melee on the top of the hill. Reluctantly, White, left twenty men to continue pursuing the Federals fleeing toward Brandy, and turned the rest of his men around and attacked the Union forces on Fleetwood from the southwest.[22]

Meanwhile, on the north side of Fleetwood Hill, Harmon was frantically attempting to halt the panic within his regiment. Riding back and forth shouting repeatedly, "For God's sake form! For my sake form!" he eventually regained control of most of his men. After forming into now somewhat depleted ranks, Harmon ordered his regiment back onto the hill to join the much-outnumbered Comanches.

As Harmon was rallying his men, the 1st Pennsylvania, under the command of Colonel John P. Taylor, had entered the fight. The Pennsylvanians advanced on an axis to the left of that followed by the 1st Maryland and upon reaching the top of Fleetwood, hooked to the right and charged the Miller House from the rear, overwhelming the Confederates remaining about the house. The onslaught of Taylor's saber wielding men prompted one beleaguered Rebel to shout at the Pennsylvanians, "Put up your sabres, draw your pistols, and fight like gentlemen." The Pennsylvanians, however, continuing to press forward slashing with their sabers, drove the Confederates from the hill and claimed for themselves the honor of capturing Stuart's headquarters.[23]

However, the Pennsylvanians' victory was short-lived, as the 12th Virginia reentered the fight. Around the site of Stuart's headquarters, evacuated earlier that morning, Rebels and Yankees fought each other individually or in small groups with little apparent order. Close to five regiments were now involved in the confused fighting. One Confederate trooper later wrote: "Round and round it went; we would break their line on one side, and they would break ours on the other. Here it was pell mell, helter skelter—a yankee and

Lieutenant Colonel James Deems, a Baltimore composer and music teacher before the war, commanded the 1st Maryland. As he and his men crested Fleetwood, they were met by the 12th Virginia, charging the hill in a column of fours from the opposite direction (Library of Congress).

there a rebel — killing, wounding, and taking prisoners."[24] Another trooper of the 12th Virginia recalled being captured twice and twice escaping during the back-and-forth fighting atop the hill.[25] Captain Charles O'Ferrall, commanding Company I, 12th Virginia, went man-to-man with a Union officer who, until that time had been leading his men in "magnificent style." O'Ferrall shot and wounded the Union officer who, as he was falling from his saddle, grabbed O'Ferrall by the coat. To break free, O'Ferrall hit the officer over the head with his pistol. Knocked senseless, the wounded Yankee fell to the ground while O'Ferrall rode off to rejoin his men.[26] Meanwhile, Harmon, in the thick of things, took a saber blow across the neck. Though seriously wounded and bleeding profusely, Harmon stayed in the fight.[27]

As the fighting continued on Fleetwood, Cabel Flournoy received orders from Hampton to move the 6th Virginia toward Brandy Station. Since the 6th was not engaged, Flournoy was able quickly to get his regiment on the move. Stuart, who had by that time taken a position where he could observe the fighting on the hill, saw the 6th Virginia moving down the south side of the railroad tracks. Recognizing that Harmon and White needed help on Fleetwood, Stuart sent a courier to Flournoy with orders that he attack the hill to cut off three hundred Yankees (his estimate of Wyndham's strength) near the Miller house. In response, Flournoy crossed to the north side of the tracks, and with six companies numbering about 200 men (the remainder of his regiment being either casualties or detached), charged up Fleetwood Hill from the east.[28]

Lieutenant Colonel Elijah Viers White and the men of the 35th Battalion Virginia Cavalry, the "Comanches," distinguished themselves on June 9. After routing the 6th Pennsylvania Cavalry at Saint James Church, they made several charges over the top of Fleetwood. The battalion suffered more casualties than any of Stuart's regiments (Library of Congress).

Flournoy's attack was unexpected, and he and his men succeeded in driving Wyndham's men from the area around the Miller House. However, while regrouping on the hilltop, the 6th Virginia was taken under fire by three guns from the 6th New York Independent Light Artillery (Captain Martin with his section of guns had joined Clark at the base of the southwest slope of Fleetwood). Flournoy ordered a charge on the guns, and he and his men galloped down the slope. Martin and his gunners opened fire on them with cannister, and Lieutenant R. O. Allen, who that morning had been the victor in his duel with Grimes Davis, was hit in the shoulder and severely disabled.[29] The 6th Virginia swept through the artillery position as Martin's gunners and drivers resorted to pistols and sponge staffs to defend themselves. Recalling the fighting among the guns, one trooper from the 6th Virginia wrote of Martin's men, "I must say that they were the bravest cannoneers that ever followed a gun. As we shot their men and horses down, they would fight us with their swabs, with but few of them left."³⁰

Although its charge was successful, the 6th Virginia was in an untenable position, isolated and pressed by Union cavalry from several directions. Flournoy's Virginians retreated toward the Miller House in confusion, and continued on past the Miller House as the retreat turned into a rout.

As the 6th Virginia withdrew, Private Opie, his black mare lying dead on the Beverly Ford Road, found that the stray horse he was now riding was "perfectly worthless." Despite Opie's efforts to encourage the horse with his spurs and repeated whacks on its rump with the flat of his saber, the animal refused to keep pace with the fleeing regiment. As the rout continued, Opie fell farther and farther behind his comrades and became a prime target for the pursuing Federals. With bullets whizzing past, Opie expected to be shot at any moment and recalled feeling as if "lizards and snakes were crawling up my spine." Opie's horse was so slow that three Federals—a captain, a sergeant, and a private—overtook Opie and passed by him in their haste to catch up with the main body of the 6th Virginia (probably presuming that Opie would be "gobbled-up" by other Union troopers following behind). To escape almost certain capture, Opie pulled hard on his reins, abruptly turning his horse off the trail to the right. The horse "bulged" through a scrub cedar hedge running parallel to the road, and Opie fled obliquely cross-country.³¹ The pursuing Federals continued up the road allowing Opie to escape.

Lieutenant Colonel Virgil Broderick commanded the 1st New Jersey Cavalry. During the fighting atop Fleetwood, the 35-year-old officer was unhorsed twice before being killed (John W. Kuhl Collection at the U.S. Army Military History Institute).

The hard fighting was also taking effect on the Union forces engaged, particularly the 1st New Jersey. The regimental commander, Lieutenant Colonel Virgil Broderick, was unhorsed early in the melee, but was able quickly to get back into the action when his bugler, Private James Woods, offered up his mount. Soon afterward, as White's men swept back over Fleetwood from the southwest, Broderick was killed, and command of the regiment passed to Major John Shelmire. However, because of the confusion of the battle, Shelmire could only exercise effective control only over those men nearby.³²

The regimental adjutant, Lieutenant Marcus Kitchen, took a hard fall when his galloping horse was shot in the head and killed instantly. Although bruised and dazed, Kitchen had the sense to take cover behind his horse's carcass as the battle flowed around him. As a Rebel approached, intent on capturing or killing the downed and vulnerable Union officer, Kitchen brandished his pistol from his protected position. Kitchen apparently presented a credible threat since the Rebel turned about and rode off. Afoot, Kitchen made his way without incident to a small knoll immediately to the southwest of the tip of Fleetwood Hill. There, Captain Martin, who had reinforced Clark's artillery section, had three guns in action, all firing at Rebel formations swarming on Fleetwood. Among the artillerymen, Kitchen found bugler Woods, who, having given up his horse to Broderick, had also withdrawn down the hill on foot. The resourceful bugler quickly found a horse captured from the Rebels and presented it to Kitchen, who promptly mounted. However, as the remounted adjutant prepared to return to the fight, the fight came to him.[33]

On the opposite side of Fleetwood, Lige White was struggling to regain control of his battalion, now much disorganized from its two-pronged attack on the Miller House, subsequent pursuit, withdrawal, and continual fighting for control of the hill. White's battalion had also suffered significant casualties both in the charge it made earlier in the morning at Saint James and in the fighting at Fleetwood. Fortunately, White received an infusion of relatively fresh manpower in the form of a company of the 6th Virginia sent to his support.[34] Thus reinforced, White ordered an attack on Martin's guns that, with their fire, had proved a considerable nuisance to the Confederates on the hill. The Comanches and the supporting company of the 6th Virginia charged down the hill through a hail of cannister fire and swept into the artillery position. Martin's gunners again attempted to man their pieces while defending themselves with pistols and sponge staffs.[35] Adjutant Kitchen fought with the gunners to defend the position as a squadron of the 1st Maryland, posted to support the artillery, and other Union troopers nearby joined the fight among the guns. During the melee, Kitchen admired a Rebel who was an accomplished rider mounted on a "splendid" horse. The Rebel would dash in among the guns, saber a gunner, dart away, and then sweep back and saber another gunner in almost a "supernatural" manner. Kitchen gave chase to the Rebel, and he and a few other men finally drove him away. However, neither Kitchen nor his comrades could inflict any injury upon the dashing Confederate.[36]

Stuart's staff had also been swept up in the ebb and flow of the battle for Fleetwood. Earlier, Heros von Borcke had been sent by Stuart to Rooney Lee's brigade on the far left of the line at Saint James. Von Borcke and Lee were watching the skirmishers to their front when the cannon fire opened from Fleetwood. Von Borcke, assuming his place of duty was there, mounted and hurried south, arriving at Fleetwood just as the rout of the 12th Virginia was beginning. The large Prussian posted himself at a gap in a fence and attempted to halt the stampede by threatening to shoot any man who did not return to the fight and encouraging others by striking them with the flat of his immense saber. However, von Borcke's efforts were in vain, and he, too, was soon forced to flee when a party of about ten Yankees led by a "hulking corporal" approached the gap. After jumping his horse over a fence to evade his pursuers, von Borcke came upon Captain Benjamin White, one of Stuart's *aides de camp,* making his way slowly to the rear. White had been shot through the neck and was having difficulty holding his head erect. Von Borcke slowed to help his comrade reach safety. Eventually, von Borcke left White with a courier and made his way back toward Fleetwood to rejoin Stuart.[37]

Frank Robertson, after leaving Saint James and relaying Stuart's orders for Hampton, headed for Fleetwood to find Stuart. Robertson that day happened to be riding Bostona, a long and tall thoroughbred mare that his father had bred and raised. In his months on Stuart's staff, Robertson had found that Bostona was not a particularly suitable cavalry mount. While fast, she took about one half mile to get fully up to speed. Also, she was an awkward horse. Roberston recalled that she was more difficult to turn than a six-horse wagon, and that when he needed to turn about to deliver a message, "she generally manages to sweep the road clear of both staff officers and couriers and always produces a laugh."[38]

Assuming that Fleetwood was in Confederate hands, Robertson trotted up the hill toward the fighting with his pistol holstered. Upon reaching the crest of the hill, Robertson rode "very composedly" into the head of a Federal charge. Robertson struggled to turn the horse about, and then rode for his life, a Yankee sergeant close behind, aiming his pistol over his horse's ears and "popping away" at Robertson's back. Robertson attempted to draw his pistol to defend himself, but every time he took his hand off a rein, Bostona began "blundering," forcing Robertson to regrip the reins to steady her. Fortunately for Robertson, the timely arrival of Confederate reinforcements caused the Yankee sergeant to break off his pursuit. Afterwards, Robertson was amazed that he had not been shot — the only injury was a slight furrow along one of Bostona's legs.[39]

First Lieutenant Chiswell Dabney, another of Stuart's *aides de camp*, had attached himself to White's battalion at Saint James. He had participated in the Comanche's charges over Fleetwood and into Martin's battery, and their precipitous retreat, coming through unscathed, although a bullet has passed between his hat and his ear. Nevertheless, as Dabney later nonchalantly advised his father, "a 'miss' is as good as a 'mile.'" At the time, Dabney was unaware that one of his horses had been captured. When Dabney had left Stuart headquarters that morning to guide Colonel John Black's 1st South Carolina, his servant, Dilbert, had taken Dabney's two spare horses into Brandy Station, apparently thinking that they would there be safe. Surprised when Wyndham's troops swept through the town, Dilbert, abandoned the horse he was leading but managed to escape on the horse that he was riding.[40]

Major William W. Blackford, Stuart's Engineer Officer, unlike several others on the staff, did not attach himself to any particular unit during the fighting over Fleetwood. Instead, Blackford found himself galloping back and forth across the field delivering orders. However, he managed to participate in the fray, later recalling that "friend and foe were so mixed together and all so closely engaged that I had some capital pistol practice, and emptied every barrel of my revolver twice at close range." While claiming to be a good marksman — pistol practice from the saddle at the gallop was his favorite amusement — Blackford was unable to tell if any of his shots struck home.[41]

For Robert Goldsborough, Stuart's new *aide*, the day's activities proved most unfortunate. Goldsbrough, a handsome twenty-two-year-old from Maryland, had served briefly in the artillery and then for a year in the 39th Battalion, Virginia Cavalry, a unit organized to serve primarily as scouts and escorts. This was Goldsborough's first action with the Cavalry Division. Stuart, concerned about his flanks, sent the young officer galloping off with a message for Williams Wickham. The inexperienced lieutenant, without taking any precaution, rode up to a body of Federal cavalry, mistaking them in their dusty uniforms for Confederates. Goldsborough was promptly taken prisoner and led off the battlefield.[42]

While Stuart was directing his troops from the east side of Fleetwood, David McM. Gregg was directing his division from Brandy Station. Gregg, observing Wyndham and his brigade struggling with the 12th Virginia and White's Battalion for control of Fleetwood, ordered Judson Kilpatrick to bring up his brigade and attack to Wyndham's right. Gregg, apparently sensing that he might need additional help to defeat the Confederates, also sent couriers galloping to Stevensburg with orders for Duffié to bring his division immediately to Brandy Station to join the fight.

Upon receiving Gregg's orders, Kilpatrick swung his brigade, with the 10th New York leading, off the road and proceeded through the woods to a position a little farther than three quarters of a mile to the east of Brandy Station. From that location, Kilpatrick's brigade was positioned to attack the nose of Fleetwood almost directly from the south, instead of from the west as Wyndham's brigade had done. As the troopers waited in the woods, they made last minute preparations for battle: tightening girths; unslinging carbines; arranging their ammunition for easy access in the fighting to come. One member of the 10th New York likened their actions to Roman gladiators preparing to enter the arena.[43]

As Wyndham and his men were struggling for control of Fleetwood, Colonel Judson Kilpatrick was moving to their support with his brigade. Kilpatrick's reputation was mixed. He presented himself as a fierce raider, but was considered by some to be too casual with the lives of his men. Additionally, his personal conduct revealed a streak of moral corruption (Library of Congress).

While remaining hidden in the woods south of the railroad tracks, Kilpatrick repositioned his regiments for the attack. Kilpatrick planned to move on Fleetwood with his regiments in echelon, the 10th New York on the left and leading, the Harris Light in the center, and the 1st Maine on the right and trailing. Kilpatrick's plan was sound. Moving toward Fleetwood in an echelon to the right would, in theory, protect his right flank should Confederates approach from that direction.

To comply with Kilpatrick's orders, the regiments moved from their march order— regiments one behind the other in a column of fours— and aligned themselves for the attack. The regimental commanders ordered their men to form into columns of squadrons in preparation for their movement across the open fields to the east of Brandy and over the railroad tracks, culminating with a charge up the hill. Unfortunately, their preparations took time. While Kilpatrick was getting ready, Wyndham and his men were taking a beating around the Miller House. However, a more significant development was that Wade Hampton had by then withdrawn his brigade from contact with Buford's division and with four regiments was bearing down on Kilpatrick's right flank.

Hampton, in his haste to respond to the threat in his rear, had left his dismounted sharpshooters behind as he pulled his mounted men back from the line to the east of the Beverly Ford Road. From their positions, the regiments moved south to the Orange & Alexandria Railroad. At the tracks, Hampton's force had turned to the left and was approaching Fleetwood and Brandy Station from the east.[44]

The approaching column was observed by the Federal commanders but caused little alarm. The dust of the battlefields at Saint James and on Fleetwood, as well as dust rising along the routes of march, had coated the uniforms of the troopers. The blue and gray of

Kilpatrick attacked Fleetwood from the south. His two leading regiments, after crossing the railroad tracks, were struck in their flanks and routed (Joseph W. McKinney).

Union and Confederate uniforms were obscured by a thick coating of dust making it difficult to tell friend from foe. General Gregg, observing Hampton's brigade approaching "well alligned (sic), at a rapid gait," thought it was part of Buford's division coming to his support.[45] Very quickly, however, Gregg learned of his error.

Meanwhile, Kilpatrick launched his attack. On Kilpatrick's order, the 10th New York emerged from the woods in a column of squadrons and took up a trot until reaching the railroad tracks. After crossing the tracks at the walk, the men of the regiment realigned their ranks and drew their sabers. On command, the regiment then resumed a trot toward the hill. As the 10th was moving forward, Kilpatrick ordered his section of the 6th New York Light Artillery, commanded by Lieutenant Wade Wilson, to move to their support. Wilson and his gunners were "compelled to cross a morass, several immense ditches, and a fence" to get into a position from which they could fire upon a column of rebels—Hampton's brigade—whom they observed approaching from their right front.[46]

With the top of Fleetwood only three hundred yards ahead, Kilpatrick ordered the 10th New York to charge. The regimental commander, Lieutenant Colonel William Irvine, ordered his men to the gallop, and the New Yorkers swept up the slope toward the fighting, clearly visible, at the top of the hill. Wade limbered up his guns and moved 150 yards farther up the slope to better support the New Yorkers.

The 2nd New York, the Harris Light, emerged from the woods following to the right rear of the 10th New York. For some reason, the leading squadron of the Harris Light, upon reaching the railroad tracks, veered to the left and went some distance down the tracks toward Brandy Station. Eventually the 2nd New York's commander, Lieutenant Colonel

Left: Colonel P.M.B. Young and the Cobb's Legion fought and defeated the 10th New York Cavalry. Young, who resigned from the West Point Class of June 1861, was Stuart's youngest colonel in command of a regiment (Library of Congress). *Right*: Lieutenant Colonel William Irvine, a former Member of Congress, commanded the 10th New York. Irvine was unhorsed and captured on the slope of Fleetwood. After he was exchanged, Irvine became an advocate for the better treatment of prisoners of war (Library of Congress).

Henry Davies, redirected his wayward squadron back to the right and then up the slope of the hill.

As the Harris Light began moving up Fleetwood Hill, the 1st Maine emerged from the woods to the right rear of that regiment and began its movement toward the railroad tracks. Misdirection by the Harris Light and delay by the 1st Maine had upset Kilpatrick's plan. Instead of attacking in an echelon, Kilpatrick's brigade moved toward contact in a column of regiments. Instead of fighting a coordinated battle, each of his three regiments was committed piecemeal and would fight Hampton's force on its own.

Hampton, perceiving from the distance that Fleetwood was for the most part in Union hands, ordered his lead regiment, the Cobb's Legion Cavalry, to take up a gallop and attack the hill. For good measure, Hampton ordered the 1st South Carolina, which was second in his march column, to follow the Cobb's Legion.

The commander of the Cobb's Legion Cavalry, young Colonel P.M.B. Young, led his men forward. The Georgians, who had been advancing parallel to the Orange & Alexandria roadbed, swung to their right front and picked up their pace, galloping the final mile to their objective. As the regiment closed on the hill, a courier arrived from Stuart with orders for Young to clear Fleetwood of Yankees. Seeing a regiment of Union troopers moving toward his front, Young immediately ordered a charge. Captain Hart, who had been paralleling Hampton's column with his battery, swung his four guns about, unlimbered, and put three rounds into the Federal column at a range of only few hundred yards before Young's regiment closed with the Federals and masked his battery's fire. Hart, with three of his guns—one having become disabled for the second time that day—limbered up and raced to the top of Fleetwood, taking up a firing position next to McGregor's battery that had arrived earlier in support of the regiments from Jones' brigade.[47]

The Georgians struck a heavy blow on the advancing Union column, completely disorganizing the 10th New York and taking Lieutenant Colonel Irvine, unhorsed in the melee, prisoner. The 10th New York's adjutant, Lieutenant B. B. Porter, recalled that both the Union and Confederate regiments were advancing toward each other in good order, but as the opposing ranks were about to close, the Confederates opened a rapid fire, "then followed an indescribably clashing and slashing, banging and yelling.... We were now so mixed up with the rebels that every man was fighting desperately to maintain the position until assistance could be brought forward." The 10th's trailing squadrons entered the fight, but to no avail, for "in an instant everything was mixed up and confused and Irvine [was] a prisoner."[48]

Captain Frederick Poughkeepsie, a twenty-three-year-old Englishman commanding Company H, had a particularly difficult few minutes on the south slope of Fleetwood. First he was struck in the right hand by shrapnel, probably by the fire from Hart's guns. Next, Poughkeepsie was shot in the right thigh, lost his balance, and fell to the ground. Poughkeepsie grabbed his horse, but the animal, undoubtedly excited, stood on the captain's right foot, crushing his big toe. Finally, as Poughkeepsie clambered back into the saddle without the use of his right leg, he suffered a hernia. Somehow, the hapless captain avoided capture.[49]

The fighting was equally intense and confusing for the Georgians of Cobb's Legion. Wiley Howard, a trooper from Company C, recalled that his regiment swung from a column into line and began their charge about two hundred yards from a line of Yankees on the crest of the hill. The route of attack for some men of Cobb's Legion led through a small orchard. Upon closing with the Union force, the Georgians "mixed with them ... each man fencing and fighting for the time with his individual foe." For his own part in the melee, Wiley, recalled:

> My man, having at the first slash, deftly wheeled to the rear, I rushed to the aid of one of my comrades, who being tangled in the limbs of a peach tree, was being chopped over the head by his adversary, when with a fortunate swing of the arm my blade touched his neck and the blood flowed, much to the relief of my friend, who dashed after his man and I was carried *nolens volens* right amid the confused mass of jumbled up retreating Yanks by my unruly mare, never stopping until she ran up against a piece of artillery they were trying to save, drivers and others jumping down and running for dear life.[50]

After a short melee, the Georgians prevailed and the New Yorkers retreated in disarray. Their withdrawal to safety was impeded by cuts along the Orange & Alexandria roadbed. Some daring troopers—those with bold horses—leapt the ditches and scrambled over the roadbed to safety. Other troopers attempted to pick their way though the ditches where, slowed and canalized, they made easy targets for their pursuers. A few troopers fled down the railroad tracks until they found a more suitable location to cross. Discipline broke down, and the regiment offered little resistance as all—officers and men alike—attempted to make their way to safety.[51] At the roadbed, Lieutenant B. B. Porter's horse leaped the cut and Porter escaped with minor injury—a Rebel bullet grazed his lip. Porter had overheard a Confederate officer shouting at his men to not kill Porter's horse, so perhaps to his good fortune the Rebels were aiming high. Lieutenant William J. Robb was less fortunate. Robb's horse failed to clear the cut and fell. As Robb struggled to his feet, he was run through with a saber and mortally wounded. Reportedly, the lieutenant's last words were "Left about wheel. Every man for himself."[52]

Three squadrons of the 1st South Carolina Cavalry (two squadrons of dismounted sharpshooters had been left behind) followed closely behind the Cobb's Legion. Colonel John Black, the regimental commander, observed part of a Union regiment, probably the Harris Light, turn to its left and move parallel to the railroad tracks, presumably to avoid Young's onslaught, then in progress.[53] Black ordered the head of his column to make a half-left and charged. The South Carolinians caught the Harris Light in the flank and broke up the New Yorker's attack before it could get fully underway. After a short fight, the regiment fell back in disorder. As Black and his men pursued, one squadron of the Harris Light separated and veered off around the west side of Fleetwood, and there

Colonel Calvin Douty, a former county sheriff, commanded the 1st Maine Cavalry in its first charge of the war. Douty was killed a week after Brandy Station at Aldie, Virginia (Maine State Archives).

for a time helped to secure Martin's guns, still in their exposed position at the base of the hill.[54] The bulk of the regiment fled across the railroad tracks where a cut checked the South Carolinians' pursuit. However, many of Black's men had recently been armed with Enfield Rifles and they kept up an effective fire on the retreating Union troopers.[55]

As the Cobb's Legion and the 1st South Carolina charged by them, Lieutenant Wilson and his men frantically limbered up their guns to withdraw. In their haste to wheel about, a limber tipped over on its side. Wilson halted his section and ordered the gun's crew to dismount and right the limber. As the men were manhandling the limber back onto its wheels, the section was attacked by a squad of Confederates (including, perhaps, the out-of-control Wiley Howard of Cobb's Legion) who rode up firing their pistols and carbines. Wilson's men defended themselves with their own pistols and drove off the party of Rebels. Afterward, Wilson and his men withdrew to safely, wheeling about occasionally to fire a few shells at any column of Confederates that they observed.[56]

While Young and Black were leading their charges, Hampton was attempting to turn the right flank of Gregg's division. To that end, he moved his two remaining regiments, the 1st North Carolina and the Jeff Davis Legion, across the railroad tracks and advanced through the open fields on the south side of the railroad toward Brandy Station. Hampton's intent

Top: The 1st Maine charged more than half a mile up the valley between Fleetwood and Beauregard, the home of James Barbour (Joseph W. McKinney). *Bottom*: Robert E. Lee observed the 1st Maine charge from a cupola on the roof of Beauregard. The cupola was removed during a renovation of the house early in the 20th Century (Mrs. Rebecca Denny).

Although enlarged, today Beauregard appears much as it did in 1863 (Joseph W. McKinney).

was to cut off and destroy Gregg's division, thereby harvesting the "fruits of victory," a much sought after but elusive goal for most Civil War commanders.[57]

The first few minutes of fighting had been disastrous for Kilpatrick's brigade. Two regiments had been sent forward, and each had been routed. Only the 1st Maine Cavalry remained uncommitted. Kilpatrick, with few options left, ordered Colonel Calvin Douty, the fifty-year-old former sheriff from Dover, Maine, to sweep with his regiment to the right and then charge the rebels fighting on the face of Fleetwood in their flank.[58] The 1st Maine, fighting as a regiment for the first time, moved forward briskly in a column of squadrons. The advance was briefly slowed as the troopers negotiated the railroad tracks and then reformed their ranks. To the troopers' front "the whole plain was one vast field of intense, earnest action ... a scene to be witnessed but once in a lifetime."[59]

Douty's men drew their sabers and galloped toward the fight, making their first charge ever. Their charge was perhaps one of the most memorable of the war, at least in appearance if not in effect. The regiment's axis of attack took them through a seam in the Confederate regiments. As they surged forward, the men from Maine swept portions of the Cobb's Legion and the 1st South Carolina from their path while chasing small parties of Rebels before them. The men of the 1st Maine galloped across the face of Fleetwood and continued up the up the west side of the ridge in a northerly direction. Confederate gun crews on Fleetwood fled, leaving their pieces as Douty and the Maine men galloped past their positions. Several Confederate troopers, swept up in the charge, for a time galloped along in the ranks of the 1st Maine. One trooper from Maine recalled that the wayward Rebels acted as if they belonged in the Union ranks. For some reason, it did not occur to the Union troopers to shoot the Rebels who had joined their charge.[60]

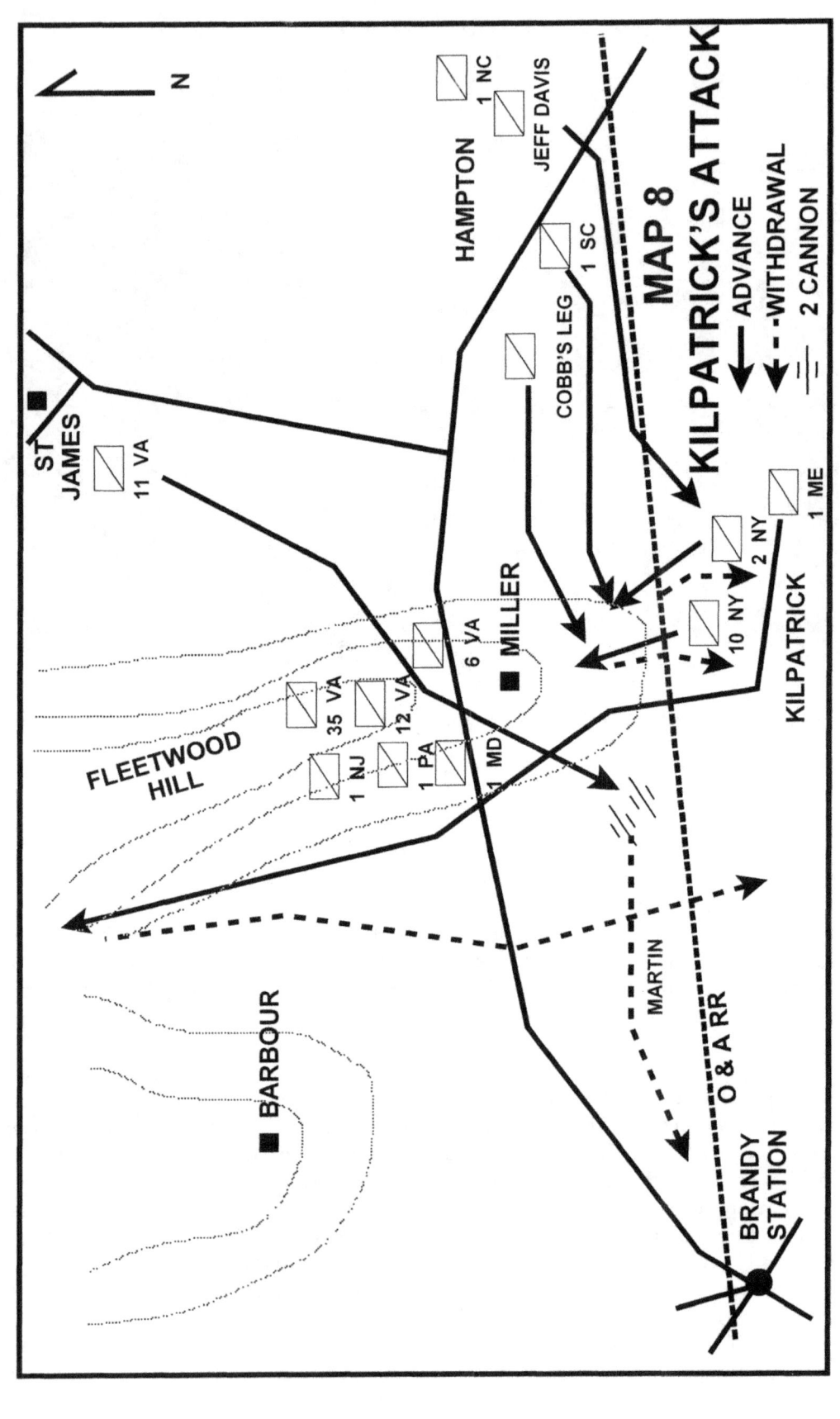

The success of 1st Maine's effort certainly exceeded everyone's expectations. The regiment galloped—unscathed—for almost a mile through the Confederate lines, halting a short distance from the Barbour House. At that point, the regiment was scattered, Colonel Douty was missing, and no other Federal units were within supporting distance.[61] The 1st Maine's second-in-command, Lieutenant Colonel Charles H. Smith, took charge and began reforming his men. Once Smith had gathered what he estimated was a sufficient force, he ordered the depleted unit again to charge, this time back toward their own lines. Skillfully obliquing right and left to avoid fire from Beckham's guns, whose crews had returned to man their pieces, the regiment galloped back to the railroad tracks without significant contact. Smith, recalling the charges into and out of Confederate lines in a letter to his fiancee, remarking, "Bully for the First Maine!"[62]

Military operations are normally oriented on the accomplishment of a clear objective, such as seizing prominent terrain or defeating an enemy formation. Colonel Douty focused on neither. Consequently, the 1st Maine did not secure Fleetwood, which was Kilpatrick's objective, nor did they drive off Hampton's regiments, which had continued their attack into Gregg's flank. However, the 1st Maine's charge, although misdirected, was almost the critical event of the day. Unknown to the men of the 1st Maine, their attack was likely observed by Generals Robert E. Lee and Richard Ewell from the Barbour House. Had the Union troopers pressed their attack a little farther, the outcome of the engagement at Fleetwood might have been significantly altered the course of the war.

Earlier that morning, about the time that the advance guard of Gregg's division was approaching Brandy Station, Lee mounted his horse and rode from his headquarters in Culpeper Courthouse to Ewell's headquarters at the Cooper House, a deserted home just north of the town.[63] Ewell, new to command of the II Corps, had arrived with his men in Culpeper on June 7 and gone into camp about three miles north of the Courthouse on the Rixeyville Road, positioned to lead Lee's advance to the Valley and beyond. Ewell's Corps had enjoyed the luxury of spending June 8 resting in camp.[64]

On the morning of June 9, Lee received messages from Stuart regarding the fighting. Additionally, Lee had certainly heard the artillery fire from Saint James, and was aware that a significant battle was underway. Upon arriving at Ewell's headquarters, Lee directed Ewell to deploy some infantry to support Stuart's cavalry division should the need arise. Ewell assigned the mission to Major General Robert Rodes, who ordered Brigadier General Junius Daniel and Colonel Edward. A. O'Neal to deploy their brigades.[65] Daniel started four regiments of North Carolinians moving at the double-quick toward Brandy while O'Neal did the same with his Alabama regiments. In keeping with guidance from Lee, both commanders took care to conceal their infantrymen from Union observation.

Meanwhile, Stuart had become aware that Pleasonton was supported by infantry and sent his Engineer Officer, Major W. W. Blackford, to General James Longstreet's headquarters. Blackford, who had spotted Russell's brigade through his powerful field glasses, made a "hot ride of six miles" and found Longstreet and his I Corps camped about the base of

Opposite: As Wyndham's brigade struggled with regiments from Jones's brigade on top of Fleetwood, Colonel Judson Kilpatrick attacked the hill from the south with three fresh Union regiments. Kilpatrick's two lead regiments, the 10th and 2nd New York, were routed by the Cobb's Legion and 1st South Carolina from Wade Hampton's brigade. As Robert E. Lee watched from the Barbour House, the 1st Maine charged up the valley between Fleetwood and Barbour House Hill, then charged back to safety. The charge, while spectacular, accomplished little, and Gregg ordered his division to withdraw.

Mount Pony. Blackford relayed a request from Stuart for infantry to support the Cavalry Division if the need arose. Longstreet, who had already received word from Lee that Stuart might require assistance, ordered Lafayette McLaws' division to move north toward Brandy Station.[66]

As O'Neal's and Daniels' troops began their march down the road from Chestnut Forks toward the Botts farm and Brandy Station, Lee and Ewell, with their staffs, rode ahead to observe the fighting first-hand.[67] Nearing Brandy Station, the two generals took up position in the cupola on the roof of the Barbour House. From there they had a clear view of the fighting raging across the top of Fleetwood, just ½ mile away. The staffs of the two generals, considerable in number, held horses and lounged in the yard of the elegant house, built six years earlier as a present from Coleman Beckham to his daughter on the occasion of her wedding to James Barbour.[68] As the generals watched the action on Fleetwood, the 1st Maine Cavalry made its intrepid charge across the face of the hill and up the valley between Fleetwood and the hill upon which the Barbour House sat. For a time it appeared as if the Barbour House might be the objective of the Federal troopers, a cause for some concern among the gaggle of staff officers. An alarmed subordinate dashed into the house and asked Ewell what should be done. Apparently unperturbed, Ewell replied that if the Yankees came, the Confederates would barricade the doors and defend the house to the last man.[69] Fortunately for Lee and Ewell, the men of the 1st Maine did not realize the prize they could have won had they slightly altered the direction of their attack.

By the time the 1st Maine completed its charge in reverse and reached Union lines, the 1st New Jersey had accomplished about all that it could in the fight on Fleetwood. The commander had been killed, and close to thirty troopers—heavy losses for a cavalry engagement—were also killed or wounded. Many other men had been unhorsed and captured, including Captain Henry Sawyer, the commander of Company K. Other unhorsed troopers, more fortunate, made their way on foot down the hill and evaded being taken prisoner. The horses of the troopers still in the fight were blown, having charged back and forth over the hill for almost two hours. Major Shelmire, the ranking officer in the regiment, recognized that it was necessary to withdraw to avoid defeat, and gave the order for the men of the regiment to fight their way toward Brandy. Leading a party of nearby troopers, Shelmire began a charge through groups of Confederates, some milling about and other still fighting, atop the hill. The route taken by Shelmire passed through a Confederate artillery position consisting of guns from McGregor's and Hart's batteries. McGregor's guns, a section commanded by Lieutenant Charles Ford, had accompanied the troopers from Jones' brigade. Hart's crews, having supported the Cobb's Legion Cavalry, had just reached the top of the hill and were in the process of wheeling their three guns about and unlimbering as the New Jersey men swept into the position, shooting and slashing. The gunners from the two batteries defended themselves as best they could, and with good effect. Lieutenant Ford killed one Yankee with his pistol. One of McGregor's men, Private Edward Sulley, unhorsed a Union trooper with his sponge staff and took the man prisoner. Major Shelmire was shot by Private LeGrand Guerry of Hart's battery and went down among the guns, fatally wounded.[70] The men from New Jersey who made it through the artillery position fell back toward Brandy Station fighting a rearguard action against pursuing Confederates.

Back at Saint James, Grumble Jones was in a quandary, left with only two regiments to contain Buford's reinforced division. Near the church, Jones had the 11th Virginia, commanded by Colonel Lunsford Lomax. The regiment had been fighting mostly dismounted since early morning and had strong parties of skirmishers deployed forward. Jones directed

Lomax to extend his line right and left as his other regiments left for the fighting on Fleetwood. About one and one half miles to the north, the 7th Virginia had fallen in on the flank of Rooney Lee's brigade after its early-morning fight on the Beverly Ford Road. Jones, concerned about the disparity of forces and his unguarded flanks, had coordinated with Rooney Lee, proposing that both brigades extend their lines to connect with each other and with Stuart. However, before he could shift his position, a courier arrived from Stuart with orders for Jones to bring his remaining regiments and artillery to Fleetwood. Jones ordered Lomax to immediately mount his men and move out with the guns to follow. Jones also sent couriers to Lieutenant Colonel Marshall, directing him to move the 7th Virginia, and to Rooney Lee notifying him of the situation. Jones, with nothing left to command at Saint James, followed the 11th Virginia for Fleetwood.

By the time Jones and the 11th Virginia arrived, Wyndham's brigade had been pushed off the hill and had withdrawn toward Brandy Station. Martin, with three guns, still occupied the low knoll to the southwest of Fleetwood, supported by a small body of dismounted cavalry. Stuart, seeing an opportunity, ordered Lomax to attack and seize the guns. The 11th Virginia rode down Fleetwood and swung to the left, crossing the Old Carolina Road and overrunning Martin's position. The cavalry supporting Martin were caught while mounting-up and offered little resistance.[71]

Captain Joseph Martin's artillery position had already been overrun twice before during the day. This time, however, there were no Union cavalrymen to come to his assistance. Since nearly all their horses had been killed or wounded, Martin ordered his men to abandon their guns.[72] Before withdrawing on foot, the New Yorkers attempted to spike their pieces and disable all remaining ammunition. In the two sections, thirty-three men entered the battle. During the day's fighting, Martin lost eight men wounded, thirteen men missing, and twenty horses killed.[73]

Lomax continued to press his attack, pushing the disorganized Union troopers back into and through Brandy Station. As Gregg's troopers withdrew from Brandy, Percy Wyndham was wounded, shot through the calf. Although bleeding, the British soldier of fortune remained in command until he had regrouped his brigade on the outskirts of the village. Afterward, Wyndham, much weakened from the loss of blood, turned over command of the brigade to Colonel John Taylor of the 1st Pennsylvania and left the field.[74] Meanwhile, Lomax, in response to orders from Stuart, sent 200 men toward Culpeper Courthouse and with the rest of his regiment pressed down the Stevensburg Road to establish communications with the 2nd South Carolina and the 4th Virginia.[75]

The success of Confederate attacks, both across Fleetwood and around its base were beginning to affect the men of Gregg's division, many of whom had been fighting for close to two hours. Some men, individually and in groups, believed that the battle was lost, and began to flee the fighting. Many withdrew to the southeast down the Fredericksburg Plank Road, the route on which they had advanced earlier that day. Colonel Duffié, moving to Gregg's aid with his division, encountered a squadron of the 10th New York "fleeing in the greatest disorder." Duffié claimed that the confusion caused by the fleeing New Yorkers added a half hour to his movement from Stevensburg.[76] Other "skulkers" made better time when fleeing from the battle. Well toward Kelly's Ford, Colonel Sweitzer and his infantry pickets could hear the sound of the fighting at Brandy Station. "Then clouds of dust were seen approaching from the same direction; then down the road, at full speed, came the usual crowd of mounted contrabands, camp—followers, and stragglers, *et id genus omne* that should be in—rather than with the army, shouting, 'We are all cut to pieces; the rebels are coming, &c.' We halted them until the road was choked up, and then, to get rid of them, allowed them to pass on."[77]

Meanwhile, Hampton, now south of the railroad tracks with two regiments—1st North Carolina followed by the Jeff Davis Legion—continued his advance toward Brandy Station. Advancing parallel to the tracks, Hampton's brigade engaged elements of Kilpatrick's brigade as they attempted to flee, in the process capturing the colors of the 10th New York. Unfortunately for Hampton, however, the head of his column came under a "heavy and well-directed" fire from Confederate artillery positioned on Fleetwood about one half mile to the north.[78] Apparently Beckham's gunners had as much difficulty telling friends from foes as did General Gregg earlier in the day.

Hampton halted his movement while he arranged for the friendly fire to be lifted, providing time for the Union regiments to his front to withdraw into the woods to the south of Brandy Station. Preparing to resume his attack, Hampton sent orders for Colonels Young and Black to rejoin him with their regiments. Word came back from the two colonels that Stuart had ordered them to remain at Fleetwood in support of the artillery positioned there. In Hampton's view, without the Cobb's Legion and the 1st South Carolina, he had insufficient combat power to overwhelm the Union force near Brandy Station, and in frustration he called off his attack. When Hampton's two regiments were eventually returned to his control, Stuart directed the South Carolinian to take up positions to protect Fleetwood.[79] Stuart, having fought hard to regain the hill, apparently was not willing to risk its loss.

After roughly two hours of fighting, Wyndham ordered his brigade to withdraw to Brandy Station. Captain Joseph Martin, with 20 of his horses dead, was forced to abandon his three guns at the foot of Fleetwood Hill. His battery, the 6th New York Independent Light Artillery, took 33 men into the battle at Fleetwood. At the end of the day, 8 were wounded and 13 were missing (U.S. Army Military History Institute).

By this time, Gregg did not believe that it would be productive to resume the attack on Fleetwood. He had committed all of his regiments and their attacks had been beaten back. Hours earlier, he had summoned Duffié, but the Frenchman and his division had failed to arrive. Even more ominously, Gregg had received reports that Confederate infantry were arriving in Brandy Station. Initially, Gregg had been told that Confederate infantry were being transported from Culpeper to Brandy by train, and he had sent out a party to delay their arrival by resetting a switch on the track. Subsequently, Gregg's scouts reported a large column of Confederate infantry moving toward Brandy Station on foot.[80] In Gregg's view, his division, even if reinforced by Duffié's division, could not defeat a sizable body of Confederate infantry. Consequently, Gregg began withdrawing his division to the east to link up with Russell's infantry and draw within supporting distance of Pleasonton's right wing.

This engraving depicts the fighting for Fleetwood. Many of the troopers fought with sabers, an uncommon practice during the Civil War (*Kilpatrick and Our Cavalry*).

With respect to the fighting that had occurred on and around Fleetwood, General Gregg later wrote: "if anyone failed on this day to get all the fighting he wanted his appetite for fighting must indeed have been prodigious."[81] Most of those who participated in the fighting, both Union and Confederate, would have agreed with Gregg's sentiments. As the Union cavalry withdrew toward the Rappahannock, Stuart made no effort to pursue, and the fighting around Brandy Station and atop Fleetwood ended.

10

Hurrah for Hell, Wade In!

Yew Hills and the Union Withdrawal

Late in the morning on June 9, Colonel Thomas Devin, who early in the day had been placed in command of the 1st Cavalry Division, closely watched the action on the left flank of the right wing of the Union Cavalry Corps. There, the 1st Division's 1st Brigade, now under the command of Major William McClure, 3rd Indiana Cavalry, was being pressed hard by a large body of Confederate sharpshooters, whom General Wade Hampton had ordered dismounted and sent forward from the main Rebel defensive line. Attempting to blunt the momentum of the advancing Rebel skirmishers, Devin had ordered a charge by the 9th New York Cavalry. That regiment, with only five companies present on the field, had valiantly launched the attack, only to be repulsed by Hampton's Carolinians, many of whom were armed with rifles and fighting from cover. During the attack, the 9th New York's ranking officer, Major William Martin, was shot through the shoulder and carried from the field.[1]

Next, Devin noticed the Confederate skirmishers unexpectedly withdrawing on foot and then mounting their horses, apparently in preparation for making a charge against his front. In response, Devin formed up a small force of three squadrons of the 8th New York Cavalry under the command of Major Edmund Pope, and called for his artillery to move forward. Instead of attacking, however, the Rebels wheeled into a column and moved off to their left. Devin, unsure of what was happening, sent a courier to General Pleasonton, advising the Union corps commander that either General David McM. Gregg, had finally brought his 3rd Division into action against the Confederate rear, or that the Confederates were massing to attack the center of John Buford's 1st Division from the vicinity of Saint James Church.[2]

General Buford, supervising the fighting on the right of his lines, also noticed Confederates withdrawing from their positions around Saint James. From that, and the sound of artillery in the Confederate rear, Buford correctly deduced that Gregg's division had finally entered the fight. Buford saw this development as a new opportunity for his wing — the 1st Division and the Reserve Brigade — to regain the initiative that he had lost several hours earlier when the charge by the Reserve Brigade against Saint James had failed.[3]

Thus far in the day, General Pleasonton had been discouraged with Buford's lack of progress, which Pleasonton attributed — erroneously — to Stuart's foreknowledge of the Union plans. For most of the morning, Pleasonton had stayed near the center of Buford's lines, and kept himself busy making trivial changes in the disposition of Buford's troops. Earlier, Pleasonton had ordered Wesley Merritt's 2nd U.S. Cavalry to support an artillery battery, thereby weakening the charge—previously ordered by Buford—of the Reserve Brigade. As the morning progressed, Pleasonton repositioned a few infantry companies from the left to the right, and did the same with the 8th Illinois Cavalry. Additionally, with the two ranking officers of the 8th Illinois wounded, Pleasonton had placed Captain Elon Farnsworth, one of his favorite *aide de camp*, in command of the regiment.[4] Hearing Gregg's artillery fire from the vicinity of Brandy Station, and anticipating an improvement in the tactical situation, Pleasonton went to Buford and ordered him to advance his entire line.[5] Pleasonton also sent his chief of staff, Lieutenant Colonel A. J. Alexander, to find Gregg, and then to bring back a report on the situation facing Gregg's command, the left wing of the Cavalry Corps.[6]

At 12:30 p.m., Pleasonton sent a message to General Hooker, advising "General Gregg has joined me, and I will now attack the enemy vigorously with my whole force. Prisoners report that Stuart has 30,000 cavalry here. Both Lees, Jones, and Hampton are with him. We have had a sharp fight, and have lost heavily, as we had the whole force in front of one-half of my command." Further, Pleasonton erroneously informed Hooker that Buford, supported by Brigadier General Adelbert Ames' infantry brigade, had driven the Confederates out of their strong positions around Saint James Church. Considering his optimistic projections, Pleasonton inconsistently concluded his message with a request that Hooker send a body of infantry from General George Meade's V Corps to Brandy Station if it could be spared.[7]

Hooker, meanwhile, had apparently become exasperated with the information he was receiving—delayed by several hours—from the battlefield. Writing for the commanding general at 12:10 p.m., Hooker's chief of staff, General Daniel Butterfield, advised Pleasonton: "Dispatch 7.40 [a.m.] received. If you cannot make head against the force in front of you, return and take your position on the north bank of the river, and defend it. At this distance it is impossible for the general [Hooker] to understand all of your circumstances. Exercise your best judgment, and the general will be satisfied."[8] Later that afternoon, Butterfield advised Pleasonton that in Hooker's estimation, Stuart had no more than 10,000 cavalry available, a remarkably accurate assessment of Confederate strength. In a follow-on message, Butterfield further hinted at Hooker's frustration: "General says, if enemy say they have 30,000, you give out you have 60,000." Despite his doubts regarding the accuracy of Pleasonton's estimate of Confederate strength, that evening Hooker arranged for Meade to send forward one thousand infantrymen to support Pleasonton, should they be needed.[9]

As Gregg pressed his attack at Fleetwood, Buford, under orders from Pleasonton to advance, looked for an opportunity to gain an advantage over the Confederates still facing his force. As the pressure on Buford's front and left diminished—due to the movement of the bulk of Jones' and Hampton's brigades toward Fleetwood—the Union division commander turned his attention to his right flank.[10] There, Rooney Lee, who had deployed strong parties of men as sharpshooters, had created considerable difficulty for the blue horsemen throughout the long morning's fighting. And unlike Jones and Hampton, Rooney Lee seemed to be staying put, at least for the time being.[11]

Lee had deployed his brigade across Mr. R. H. Cunningham's farm, known as Elkwood. Cunningham's extensive holdings lay immediately to the south and west of the Rappahannock and Hazel Rivers (the Hazel River was sometimes called the Elk River by locals). Originally Elkwood was a four thousand acre tract granted in Colonial times to Carter Beverly. Over the years various owners, including Cunningham, had sold several parcels of land, leaving the farm with about fifteen hundred acres.[12]

Immediately to the west of Elkwood lay the property of Dr. Daniel S. Green, who had purchased 474 acres from Cunningham in 1849. Dr. Green's house lay just over a mile to the southwest of the Cunningham house, on ground rising from Ruffins Run, an easily fordable stream that ran generally parallel to the Hazel River and flowed into the Rappahannock below Beverly Ford.[13]

To the south of the Green farm and the southwest of the Cunningham farm was Appleton, a farm owned by Mr. George G. Thompson. Like Green, Thompson had bought his property, a tract of 252 acres, from Cunningham in 1849. The southern boundary of Appleton was bordered by the Saint James Church Road, which ran roughly southeast to northwest from the church to the Wellford's Ford Road, a distance of almost one and a half miles.[14]

To the northwest of the Green Farm along both sides of the Wellford's Ford Road was the Wellford's farm (the second "l" was consistently omitted from place names in accounts of the battle and on Civil War era maps). The farm's imposing two-story house, 126 feet long, was built around 1800 by William Carter, an early major land owner in Culpeper County. The mansion, which was occasionally called Farley after the family name of Carter's wife, was a local landmark. William Wellford bought the property from the Carter family in 1843, and besides farming, operated a mill on the Hazel River. Wellford sold his farm in February 1863 to Franklin Stearns, a wealthy Vermonter who moved to Culpeper before the war, but the farm continued to carry Wellford's name throughout the war.[15]

To the south of Ruffins Run the terrain rises in a series of ridges running generally northwest to southeast. The Green and Thompson houses both sat upon ground rising toward the first ridge. The Wellford House was built upon the second ridge. The northern

Unlike the fighing at Fleetwood, much of the fighting between Buford and Rooney Lee was dismounted — one Southern trooper likened it to bird hunting. This Alfred Waud drawing shows troopers of the 1st Maine skirmishing afoot at Aldie. Inexplicably, these troopers are still carrying their sabers, a useless impediment to a dismounted trooper (Library of Congress).

end of Fleetwood Hill formed the third and highest of the ridges. The ridge lines were all gently sloping and easily traversed, either from north to south or east to west. The ground was mostly open farmland, although there were a few stands of woods. Stone fences, the result of years of cultivation, bordered many fields. Most of the fences, however, were not "dressed," such as those found in Britain or northern Fauquier County. Nonetheless, the stone fences were impediments to mounted movement and provided cover for soldiers fighting afoot. Collectively, the ridge lines between Ruffins Run and Fleetwood were known as either the Yew Hills or Yew Ridge.[16]

As fighting broke out on the Beverly Ford Road early in the morning of June 9, Rooney Lee's brigade advanced rapidly across the Wellford and Green farms and threatened Buford's right flank on Elkwood. There, the combat had thus far been almost exclusively between dismounted men on

Top: Two companies of Brigadier General Adelbert Ames's infantrymen finally cleared the stubborn Southern sharpshooters from the stone fence. Ames, who was awarded the Medal of Honor for valor at First Manassas, later became a Reconstruction governor of Mississippi (Library of Congress). *Bottom*: With the fighting at Fleetwood drawing Confederate strength from Saint James Church, Buford decided to try and turn JEB Stuart's left flank. There the way was blocked by sharpshooters from Rooney Lee's brigade. The sharpshooters, protected by a stone wall and supported by a section of artillery, repulsed attacks by the 6th Pennsylvania Cavalry and the 2nd U.S. Cavalry (Joseph W. McKinney).

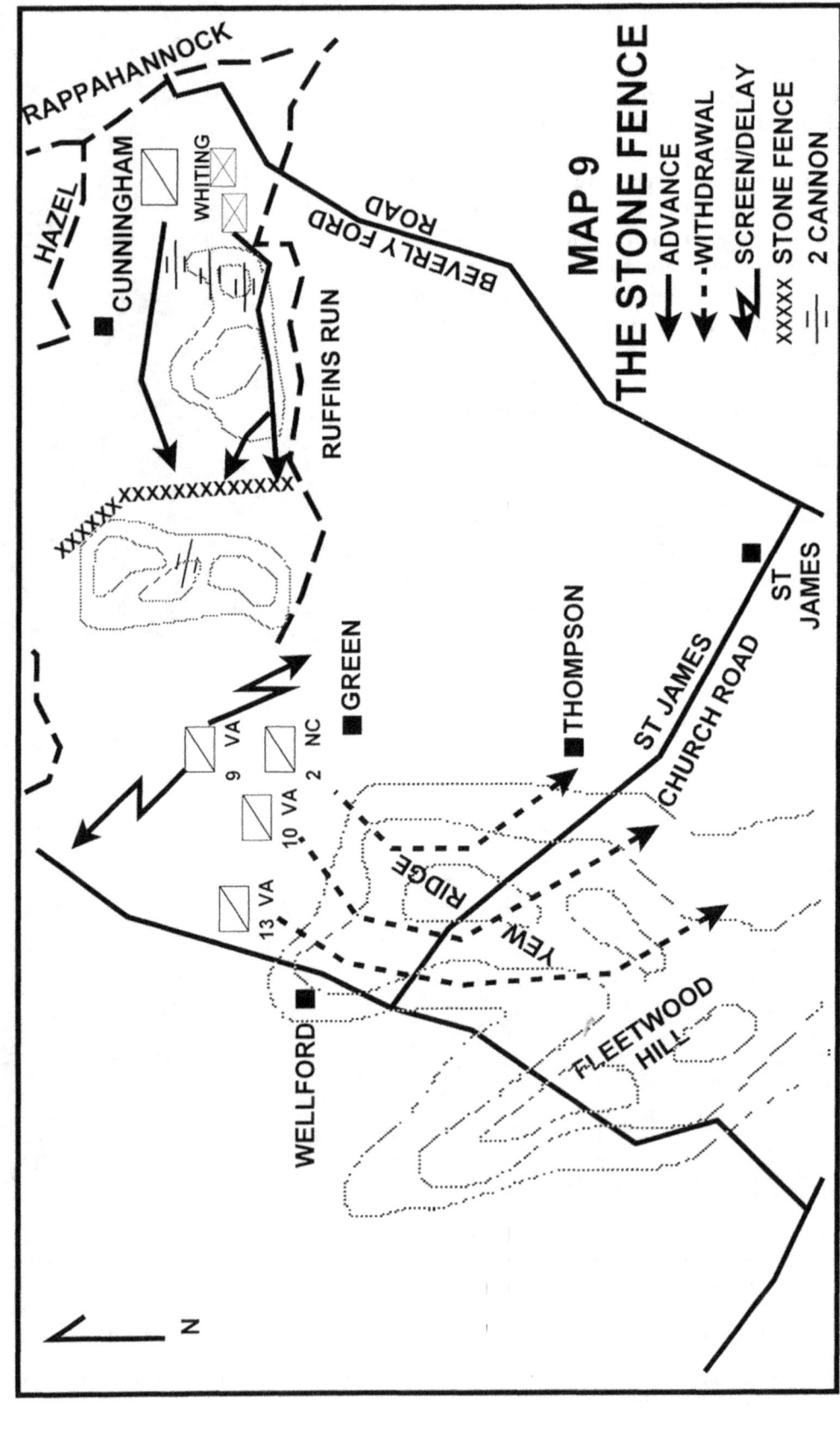

each side. The dismounted troopers, commonly called "sharpshooters" regardless of their marksmanship skills, skirmished back and forth from cover, and the results were inconclusive. The fighting experienced by the men of 2nd North Carolina Cavalry was typical. Hastily roused from their camp and unaware of the situation, the regiment galloped toward the Rappahannock in a column of fours until they reached the Green farm. There, taken under fire by Union artillery, Colonel Solomon Williams dismounted all of his men who were armed with rifles or carbines, and sent them forward as skirmishers. The Carolinians were almost immediately taken under fire by Union skirmishers concealed behind a stone fence. Charging the fence, Williams' men killed and wounded a few Yankees and captured eighteen. Among the Confederate casualties was one company commander mortally wounded, and another company commander seriously wounded. Having taken the stone wall at significant cost, the men of the 2nd North Carolina settled in to defend it.[17]

Charles Hoskins, a trooper in the 9th Virginia, provided a unique and personal characterization to the fighting in Rooney Lee's brigade. On the day after the battle, he wrote to his father that "It reminded me more of Bird hunting than any business I was ever engaged in, both parties hiding behind tree stumps & any place suited & firing on each other when ever a head was left uncovered. I am almost certain I killed one [Yankee] & probably more. Poor Chas Ward killed one and started to him when he [Ward] was killed. Whenever a Yank would show himself someone would draw a bead on him and he would fall dead as a wedge."[18] Although there may have similarities to bird hunting, hours of skirmishing on a hot June day was undoubtedly more hard work than sport.

The experience for Union troopers was much the same. A party of men from Buford's division, occupying a stone fence to the front of Battery E, 4th U.S. Artillery, commanded by Lieutenant Samuel S. Elder, were hard pressed by advancing Confederates from Lee's brigade. Buford ordered the 6th Pennsylvania Cavalry — now reinforced by its five companies that had been delayed north of the Rappahannock — forward to help defend the fence line. The Lancers advanced under intense fire through an open field to the stone fence. Once there, their situation did not improve. According to Major Henry Whelan, now commanding the regiment since Major Robert Morris Jr. was missing, the position behind the stone fence was "decidedly the hottest place I was ever in. A man could not show his head or a finger without a hundred rifle shots whistling about."[19] To perform his duty, it was necessary for Whelan had to ride back and forth along the fence directing his men (who could take cover behind the fence) as musket balls whizzed past on his right and left. Remarkably, Whelan was unscathed.

Hard pressed by the Rebels and nearly out of ammunition, Whelan ordered the Pennsylvanians to withdraw from the wall. As they fell back across the open field, Whelan's horse, Lancer, who had carried him to safety during the rout at Saint James, was struck in the flank by a rifle ball and fell, mortally wounded. Whelan, in shock, walked slowly away with his eyes filled with tears. Fortunately, Whelan's orderly, Private George Ward, retained his wits. Ward rode up to Whelan, dismounted, and told the captain to take his horse. As Whelan mounted and turned to head to the rear, Ward shot and killed a Rebel who was busy stealing Lancer's saddle and blanket.[20]

Opposite: In the early afternoon, Buford decided to turn Stuart's left flank by advancing through the Yew hills. Initially his movement was stalled by Confederate sharpshooters fighting from the cover of a stone fence on the Cunningham farm. After two infantry companies cleared the Rebels from their position, Buford ordered Whiting's Reserve Brigade forward. Concurrently, W.H.F. "Rooney" Lee bagan withdrawing his brigade. The 9th Virginia Cavalry covered the rearward movement, delaying the Reserve Brigade north of the Saint James Church Road.

Now in possession of the fence, Rooney Lee's sharpshooters proved particularly annoying to the Federals. From their covered position, and supported by two guns from Lieutenant Philip Johnston's section of Breathed's battery, the dismounted Confederates spent their time actively plinking away at long range with their rifles and carbines at gunners from Elder's battery. Although Elder's gunners, engaged in a duel with Johnston's section, were fully exposed to the Confederate small arms fire, none were killed or wounded.

Nonetheless, Buford sent a dismounted squadron from the 8th Illinois forward to clear the Rebels out of the fence line. Their attack was unsuccessful, even though the troopers exhausted their supply of carbine ammunition. Buford next sent forward a squadron from the 2nd U.S. Cavalry, but it also failed to dislodge the Rebels from the stone fence.[21] Since it appeared unlikely that cavalry could rout Lee's men, Buford, who was observing the action from among Elder's guns, summoned two infantry company commanders, one from the 3rd Wisconsin and the other from the 2nd Massachusetts, and ordered them to drive the Rebels away from the stone fence.

The captains, Stevenson and Oakey (the latter had been released from his arrest of the night before that he might take part in the battle), examined the terrain and withdrew their men, who had been lolling about on the ground behind the Union artillery, smoking their pipes and relaxing. The infantrymen, concealed initially behind the hill occupied by Elder's guns, worked their way forward through woods, brush, cornfields, and cedar hedges. Hoping to avoid detection, the Union infantrymen crouched as they moved forward, carrying their rifles low to prevent their barrels from glinting in the sunlight. At a wheat field near the stone fence, the two captains halted their companies and sent ten picked marksmen crawling forward. Once the marksmen had gained a flanking position on the Rebels, they delivered an enfilading volley down the fence line. Immediately, Stevenson, Oakey, and the rest of their men charged across the wheat field and over the wall. Once the Union foot-soldiers were among the Rebels, the fighting did not last long. One Badger recalled, "The poor wretches were taken by surprise. Some crawled off on their hands and knees; others fell dead or writhed in wounds; and a number surrendered." One or two of the Confederates were shot down as they attempted to flee, discouraging further attempts to escape. In

With the way clear, Buford ordered the Reserve Brigade forward. The 2nd U.S. Cavalry, commanded by Captain Wesley Merritt, led the way. Merritt was promoted to brigadier general three weeks later (Library of Congress).

the end, Stevenson and Oakey claimed that they had killed and captured more Southerners than they had present for duty in their two companies.[22]

With the Confederate sharpshooters dislodged from the stone fence, the way was now open for Buford to advance against Rooney Lee's brigade. About the same time, Lee had received word from Stuart that the Confederate right flank at Fleetwood was threatened. Additionally, the movement of Grumble Jones's regiments from Saint James Church to Fleetwood had uncovered Rooney Lee's right flank, leaving Lee's brigade to face Buford's reinforced division alone. In response to these developments, Stuart directed Lee to reposition his brigade to protect the left flank of the Cavalry Division.[23] To comply with Stuart's instruction and to protect his own exposed flank, it was necessary for Lee to withdraw his brigade roughly two miles to the southwest and occupy new positions on the upper reaches of Fleetwood Hill. Thus, as Buford was preparing to push forward, Lee was preparing to pull back.

Buford, hoping to turn Stuart's left flank, ordered Major Charles Whiting to move the Reserve Brigade forward. In response, the 2nd U.S., the 6th U.S., and the 6th Pennsylvania (the 5th U.S. was detached to support artillery at a different place on the battlefield) began to advance generally from east to west toward Rooney Lee's line. About the same time, Lee ordered his regiments to withdraw back across the Green farm. Lee ordered Colonel Richard L. T. Beale and the 9th Virginia Cavalry to cover the withdrawal of the brigade by delaying any Federal advance.

The Union troopers moved forward into a small valley where they were halted by their

When Merritt crested a long hill known today as Yew Ridge, he saw below "three fresh regiments of horse" moving quietly forward. Rooney Lee ordered his regiments, then formed in line on the Thomson Farm, to charge. In the ensuing fight, Rooney Lee was shot in the thigh (Joseph W. McKinney).

commanders as artillery fire from Elder's battery and the section from Breathed's battery screamed back and forth over their heads. This position was uncomfortable for the men, since inaccurate fusing frequently resulted in shells exploding prematurely.[24] After a few tense minutes, the artillery fire lifted as the Rebels withdrew their guns. The Regulars again moved forward, their leading squadrons driving back Beale's regiment and capturing many skirmishers, whom, dismounted, were unable to outpace the Union advance.

The Reserve Brigade's movement was not completely free of difficulty. Several stone fences caused the leading squadron to detour right and left in search of gaps. At one point, the advancing troopers encountered a steep ravine, thick with blackthorn shrubs. Finding a path down and up the steep banks and through the vegetation caused further delay. Nonetheless, the Regulars kept the pressure on the 9th Virginia as that regiment withdrew past the Wellford House.

Upon crossing the Saint James Church Road, Lee's withdrawing regiments began swinging to their right toward Appleton. Defending there would protect Stuart on Fleetwood by denying the Confederate left flank. To allow the regiments to withdraw unmolested, Beale halted the 9th Virginia at the Saint James Church Road and deployed for a fight. On the rolling fields of the Wellford Farm, the lead squadrons of the 6th Pennsylvania and the 2nd U.S. closed with the Virginians and a fierce mounted melee began. The commander of the lead squadron of the 2nd U.S., Captain Theophilus Rodenbough was slightly wounded in the hand-to hand-fighting. A second squadron commander, Lieutenant Charles Leoser, was more seriously wounded. One of Buford's *aides de camp*, Captain Joseph O'Keefe, who had obtained permission from the general to fight with the reserve brigade, fell wounded and was taken prisoner.[25]

Merritt's advance was delayed by Colonel Richard L.T. Beale and the 9th Virginia Cavalry. As Beale delayed, Rooney Lee withdrew his other three regiments and regrouped (Library of Congress).

After a succession of charges and counter-charges, the 9th Virginia was pushed back a few hundred yards to the upper reaches of Fleetwood Hill. The Reserve Brigade, with the 2nd U.S. leading, then swung to the left. Hoping to find the Confederate flank unprotected, the Federals advanced parallel to the Saint James Church Road to the heights of the Yew Hills, about one-half mile to the southwest of the Wellford House. Crossing the crest of the southernmost ridge, Captain Merritt observed three Confederate regiments drawn up in line of battle in the low ground on the Thompson farm, about one-half mile farther to the southeast. As Merritt watched, the Confederates began to advance up the slope toward his regiment.[26]

A few minutes earlier, about 3:00 p.m., Rooney Lee decided that to protect Stuart's flank, it was necessary for him to blunt Buford's attack and then drive the Federals back. Consequently, he ordered the three uncommitted regiments of his brigade to attack up the slope of the Yew Hills in a northwesterly direction from their position on the Thompson farm. Lee issued the attack order directly to Colonel Solomon Williams, 2nd North Carolina, who, in his first battle as a regimental commander, had gone to Lee to urge the general to permit the North Carolinians to ride to the aid of the beleaguered 9th Virginia. As Williams returned to his regiment, he passed Lee's order to Colonel James Lucius Davis, commanding the 10th Virginia, and that regiment began to advance up the slope. The men of the 2nd North Carolina on the right of the Rooney Lee's line, saw their colonel returning at the gallop, and noting the movement of the 10th Virginia, anticipated that they, too, would soon be in the thick of the fighting. As they expected, Williams rode to the front of his regiment and ordered the men to form in a column of squadrons. As soon as the squadrons were aligned, Williams commanded, "Gallop; March" and the 2nd North Carolina began its first regimental charge.[27]

The Union troopers, who had been fighting for close to an hour, waited on the high ground to receive Lee's brigade, now galloping up the slope with the 10th Virginia in the lead. At the head of the Virginians rode Major Joseph Travis Rosser, a lawyer from Petersburg. As the line of Confederate cavalry closed with the 2nd U.S., Rosser impulsively spurred his horse toward an officer from the regulars who had taken a position forward of the Union line. Observed by all, Rosser and the Union officer engaged in one-on-one combat. Inspired, and apparently with his adrenalin flowing, twenty-year-old Private John Smith, Company F, 10th Virginia, shouted to his comrades, "Hurrah for Hell, Wade in," and the Virginians surged forward, most immediately emptying their pistols at the Union troopers, despite Colonel Davis' earlier exhortation that they fight with their sabers.[28]

As with most cavalry-on-cavalry engagements, a general melee quickly developed, with the blue and gray clad troopers shooting and slashing at each other across the top of the hill. James Scott, the 10th Virginia's right guide, was drawing his saber back to take a cut at a Yankee to his front, when his blade was struck by a saber-blow from a Union officer to his rear. Scott's right arm went numb from the force of the blow, but he recovered in time to stab the man to his front. Meanwhile, a comrade wounded Scott's assailant, Lieutenant Thomas Dewees of the 2nd U.S. Cavalry.[29]

During the melee, Wesley Merritt emptied his pistol at the Confederates fighting to his right and left. Holstering his sidearm and drawing his saber, Merritt rode at a Confederate officer who was fighting with a nearby Union trooper. As he drew up, Merritt brandished his saber and demanded, "Colonel, you are my prisoner." Instead of submitting meekly, the Confederate officer slashed at Merritt's head with his own saber, knocking Merritt's hat to the ground. Lieutenant Paul Quirk, fighting nearby, shouted to Merritt that the two were alone and surrounded. Quirk and Merritt turned their horses about and rode to safety through a hail of Confederate pistol fire. The two officers rejoined the regiment, then regrouping farther up the ridge. Later, an Irish private lent Merritt his hat, which Merritt wore for the rest of the day.[30]

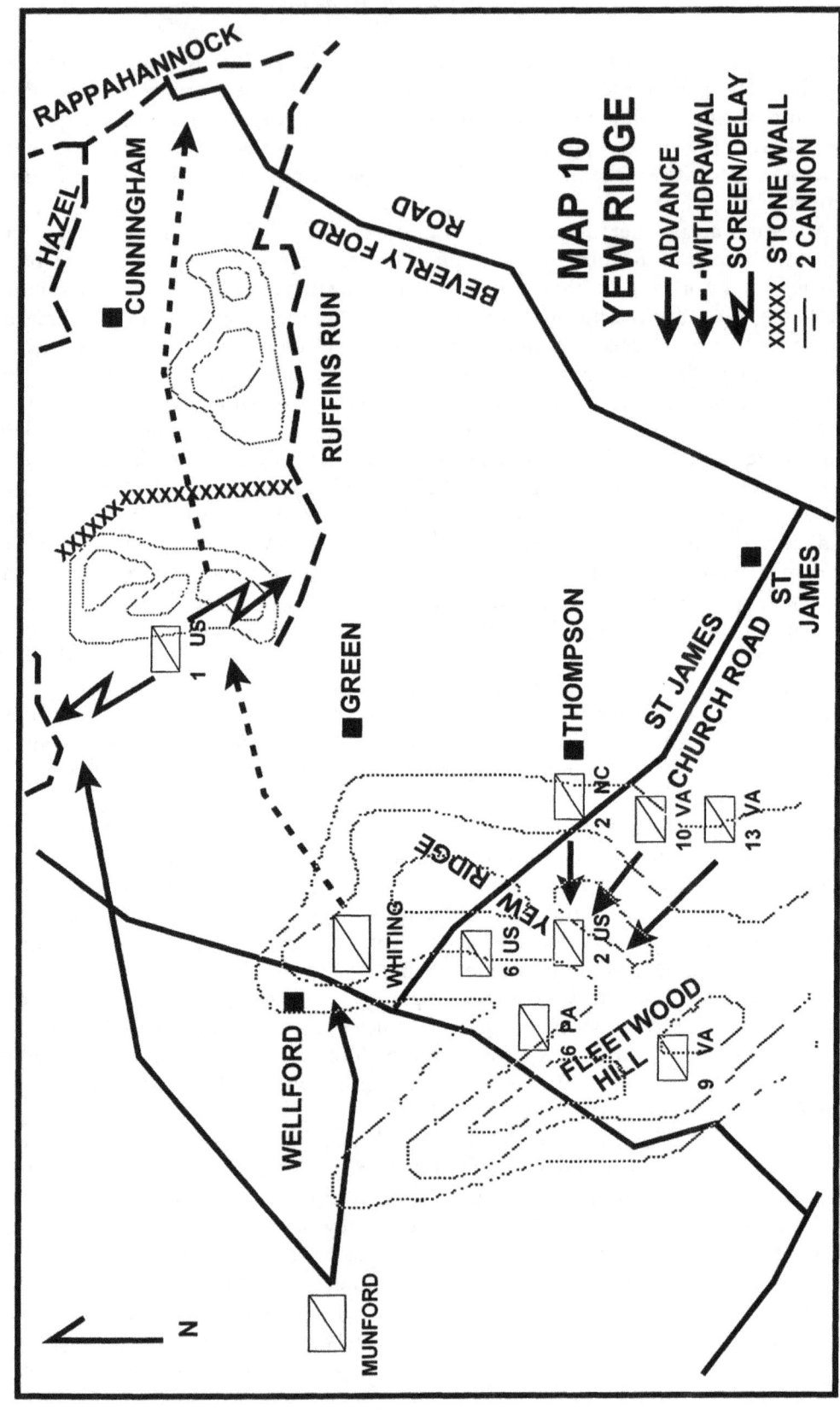

As the 2nd North Carolina advanced up the hill, Colonel Williams ordered his regiment to move obliquely to the right to avoid piling into the melee between the 10th Virginia and the 2nd U.S. Once the lead squadron of the regiment had cleared the 10th Virginia, Williams ordered his men to draw sabers and charge. The Carolinians let out the Rebel yell, and moving past the 10th Virginia on the right, engaged the now-beleaguered Yankees. Captain Pinkney A. Tatum, the commander of Company F, entered the fight with a disadvantage. Earlier, Tatum had been charged with not showing proper respect toward Lieutenant Colonel William H. Payne, 4th Virginia, who had been detailed to command the 2nd North Carolina while Colonel Williams was serving on courts-martial duty. Because Tatum was under arrest, he was prohibited from carrying arms or wearing spurs. Nonetheless, Tatum rode into the fight at the head of his company and was wounded during the melee.[31]

The 2nd North Carolina's attack was successful in breaking the Union line. With Williams in the lead, the Southerners drove the regulars back roughly one-half mile and onto Major Whiting's reserves. At that point, the Union troopers made a stand behind the intersection of two stone fences. Williams, who was about fifty yards in front of his leading squadron, turned to reform the ranks of his regiment, now much disorganized after their long gallop. Shouting for the men to rally on the regiment's colors, Williams was shot — struck between the eyes by a pistol ball — and killed instantly.[32] The regiment's adjutant and William's new brother-in-law, Lieutenant John Pegram, took his colonel's body to the rear as the regiment withdrew under Union artillery fire and in the face of Union counterattacks. The 2nd North Carolina lost heavily in their only charge of the day, but their efforts had allowed many of their comrades who had been captured by the Federals to escape.[33]

Rooney Lee's remaining regiment played only a minor role in the fighting on Yew Ridge. Two squadrons of the 13th Virginia fought alongside and to the left of the 10th Virginia, but the bulk of that regiment had been dismounted to fight as sharpshooters. The commander of the two mounted squadrons, Lieutenant Colonel Jefferson Phillips, was seriously wounded in the fighting on the hill.[34]

Rooney Lee, like many senior officers, was unable to resist personally joining the fight, and he took a carbine bullet in his thigh because of his impetuosity. As Lee was being carried to the rear, he summoned Colonel John Chambliss, the commander of the 13th Virginia and the next senior Confederate officer on the field, to take command of the brigade. By the time Chambliss, who had been busy supervising the employment of his three squadrons of sharpshooters, could take charge, the fighting on the Yew Hills was beginning to taper off.[35]

Eventually, Buford, pressed hard by repeated charges from Rooney Lee's regiments, ordered skirmishers in the wood lines to help anchor his position. As mounted men continued to fight back and forth on the open ground atop the ridge the situation stabilized. However, Buford was unaware that about an hour earlier, before the heaviest fighting between the Regulars and Rooney Lee's brigade even began, General Pleasonton had decided to break off the battle and withdraw across the Rappahannock.

Opposite: As Captain Wesley Merritt, commanding the 2nd U.S. Cavalry, crested Yew Ridge, he found three of Rooney Lee's regiments below on the Thompson farm. As Merritt watched, Lee ordered a charge and the regiments galloped up the slopes of the ridge. In the melee that followed, Rooney Lee was shot through the thigh and carried from the field. About that time, Buford received orders from Pleasonton to withdraw across the Rappahannock. As the Reserve Brigade was falling back, Colonel Thomas Munford brought Fitzhugh Lee's Brigade into the battle. However, Munford's Virginians were too late to do much damage to the Federals.

After being driven off Fleetwood Hill, David McM. Gregg rallied his 3rd Division in the fields about a mile to the southeast of Brandy Station, where he was finally joined by the tardy Colonel Alfred Duffié and the 2nd Division. Believing, correctly, that Buford was not moving toward Fleetwood, Gregg decided to try to move his force toward Buford. Unmolested by Hampton, who after being mistakenly fired upon by Confederate artillery from Fleetwood had broken off his advance toward Brandy Station, Gregg fell back to the east until his division closed upon Russell's infantry brigade, then located about one-half mile to the left of Buford's left flank. Stuart, apparently content to hold Fleetwood, did not pursue.

With the two wings of the Cavalry Corps now within supporting distance of one another, Gregg rode to Pleasonton's field headquarters near Saint James Church, arriving shortly after 2:00 p.m. The two generals conferred briefly regarding the situation. Gregg informed Pleasonton that his attack on Fleetwood, unsupported by Duffié, had been repulsed by Stuart's horsemen. He also advised Pleasonton that the Confederates were reinforcing Stuart with infantry, who had reportedly been seen arriving at Brandy Station by train from Culpeper Courthouse. This last bit of information, which later proved to be false, alarmed the Union Cavalry Corps commander. Although Duffié's division had been barely committed, Russell's infantry had not fired a shot the entire day, and Buford was finally making headway to the right, Pleasonton decided that it was prudent to withdraw.[36]

Gregg left Saint James Church with orders to withdraw his division across the river near the railroad bridge at Rappahannock Station while Buford's division withdrew through Beverly Ford. Pleasonton also instructed Gregg to direct Duffié's division to cover the withdrawal of both Gregg's and Buford's divisions. As Gregg rode off, Pleasonton sent one of his *aides*, Captain Frederick C. Newhall, to find Buford with orders that he begin to withdraw the troops then under his control. As Newhall galloped off, Pleasonton sent word to Devin and the detachments of infantry left near Saint James Church to prepare and pull back once Duffié was in place to cover their crossing.

Newhall had trouble delivering Pleasonton's orders to Buford. As Newhall headed to the front, he passed a steady stream of wounded heading back toward Beverly Ford, evidence of the hard fighting that was taking place on the Yew Hills. Close to the fighting, Newhall came upon a body of troopers drawn up at the base of a hill, apparently awaiting orders to attack, but none of the officers present knew of Buford's whereabouts. Newhall next came upon his own regiment, the 6th Pennsylvania, and again inquired regarding Buford. The regimental adjutant, Lieutenant Rudolph Ellis, responded that he had not seen the general, and was almost immediately afterward shot out of his saddle by a Confederate sharpshooter.[37] Continuing on, Newhall met Merritt, hatless after his encounter with saber-wielding Rebels. Like the others Newhall had met, Merritt did not know Buford's location.

Newhall then spied Major Charles Whiting a short distance to the rear. Newhall rode to Whiting and asked if he, as the second-ranking officer on the field, would accept Buford's orders and act upon them. Whiting, reluctant to order a retreat, refused. Fortuitously, at that moment Newhall saw Buford and a few of his staff officers siting on their horses atop a bare hill a little farther forward. At last, the *aide* could deliver Pleasonton's instructions, which Buford received without comment. Newhall waited a few minutes while Buford issued orders to break contact, then made his way back to Pleasonton to report that the withdrawal was underway.[38]

The timing of Newhall's meeting with Buford was probably fortuitous for the Reserve Brigade. Buford at best had little better than parity of strength with Rooney Lee's brigade, and it is likely that at the point of contact on Yew Ridge the Confederates outnumbered him. Of greater significance, and unknown to Buford, about the time Newhall was delivering Pleasonton's orders, Colonel Thomas T. Munford was belatedly bringing Fitzhugh Lee's brigade—three fresh regiments—into the battle against the Reserve brigade's flank and rear.[39]

On the night of June 8, Munford with the 1st, 2nd, and 3rd Virginia had camped at Oak Shade, across the Hazel River about seven miles from Saint James Church.[40] On the morning of June 9, Munford received messages from both Fitz Lee and Stuart. Lee's message, written by an *aide*, arrived first. It read, "General Lee desires me to inform you that the enemy have crossed at Beverly Ford, and are now fighting around the church. He desires you to pack up your train, and keep everything ready to move; to bring your command a little farther in this direction, and keep up communication with him, and look well for your picket line." A few moments later, at 10:15 a.m., a courier from Stuart delivered orders that were somewhat contradictory with those from Lee: "General Stuart wishes all of Colonel Munford's regiments but one brought this way,

Late in the afternoon, Colonel Thomas Munford brought Fitzhugh Lee's Brigade into the battle near the Wellford House. Buford, who had already received orders to fall back across the Rappahannock, conducted an orderly withdrawal. Munford was criticized by Stuart for not getting into the fight earlier in the day (Library of Congress).

leaving a guard for the baggage, which can be sent toward Culpeper."[41] Munford, confused over the contradictions in the orders and uncertain about which direction "this way" was, began moving deliberately east toward the sound of the battle which could then be heard in the distance. The brigade began crossing the Hazel River at Starke's Ford about 11:00 a.m., and then moved along the south bank of the river toward Wellford's Ford and the Wellford House.[42]

Munford, aware that he was nearing the battle as the sounds of small arms fire and artillery grew louder, intended to bring his brigade into the fight against the Union right flank. If he remained undetected and found the flank exposed, he might strike a devastating blow to the invaders. The challenge for Munford was to determine where the Union flank was located—a task made difficult by the woods and hills along the Hazel River. Further complicating the issue, the front line was not stationary. Instead the line moved back and forth over the ridge as the Reserve Brigade attacked and the 9th Virginia withdrew, then as Rooney Lee's brigade attacked and the Reserve Brigade withdrew.

As he moved his brigade cautiously forward, Munford missed the Union flank. Instead

Top: The Wellford House, one of the oldest and largest mansions in the local area, had been recently purchased by Franklin Stearns, a wealthy Vermonter who moved to Culpeper County before the war. The house served as Major General Sedgewick's headquarters during the winter of 1863–4 (Library of Congress). *Bottom*: The Wellford House today is known as Farley, the family name of the original owner's wife (Rosetta A. McKinney).

his column collided with the 9th Virginia, which at the time was attempting to mount a counterattack from Fleetwood Hill. After taking about thirty minutes to sort out the mingled regiments and find the left flank of Rooney Lee's brigade in the Yew Hills, Munford ordered the sharpshooters from his three regiments forward to dislodge what he believed were infantry and cavalry skirmishers fighting from a well timbered section of woods and a pine thicket. As the sharpshooters of his brigade were beginning to push back the Union skirmishers, who had by then already started to withdraw toward the Rappahannock, Munford brought forward his artillery, a section of Breathed's battery, which took any exposed Union troopers under fire. Believing that he might be able to cut off part of Buford's force, Munford then sent most of his mounted men along the high ground toward the Wellford House, while two mounted squadrons of the 2nd Virginia Cavalry pressed forward along the Hazel River toward Wellford's Ford.[43]

Moving with the mounted squadrons, Private St. George T. Brooke, a new recruit in the 2nd Virginia, found himself about one hundred yards forward of his regiment and separated from its front line by a stone fence. Brooke was unfazed by the obstacle since he was riding "Romeo," the finest horse his father could buy. Brooke rode Romeo at the fence and the horse cleared it easily, but Brooke's girth broke in mid-flight. Upon landing, Brooke, still in the saddle, was thrown over Romeo's head to the ground. Fortunately, the new recruit was not injured in the fall. Brooke placed the saddle on the horse's back, and standing Romeo next to the stone wall mounted without putting weight in his stirrups. Riding gingerly to keep his unsecured saddle centered on Romeo's back, Brooke rejoined his squadron. A company-mate lent Brooke a surcingle to secure the saddle, allowing Brooke and Romeo to continue advancing with the squadron for the rest of the day.[44]

As Munford moved forward with mounted detachments on the right and left and dismounted men skirmishing through the woods in the center, Buford's regiments continued their steady withdrawal. Munford, mistakenly believing he was outnumbered two-to-one, advanced cautiously, and consequently failed to inflict any significant damage on the Union force. Nonetheless, the fighting was deadly for some of those involved. Advancing steadily through the woods against only limited resistance from the Federal regulars, Munford's sharpshooters suffered twenty-one men wounded, three mortally. Former VMI cadet Jacob Kent Langhorne, a soldier for less than a month and in the first fight of his young life, was shot while skirmishing forward of his company. Langhorne, one of the final casualties of the day, died that evening.[45] As he had hoped, young Jacob Kent Langhorne had done his duty.

While Newhall was searching for Buford and delivering the orders for him to withdraw, Captain Richard S.C. Lord with the 1st U.S. Cavalry was crossing the Rappahannock. Lord's regiment, detailed to picket duty, had at 9:30 that morning been relieved by a regiment from Stahel's division. Lord had gathered his men, scattered along sixteen miles of river line, and marched south to join his brigade. However, Lord and his men arrived after most of the fighting for the day was over. When Lord reported to Buford, the general took advantage of the arrival of fresh troops by ordering Lord forward to cover the withdrawal of the rest of the Reserve brigade and Ames' infantry. Lord's men skirmished briefly with Munford's as the battle wound down, losing one man killed and one wounded.[46]

Meanwhile, several miles to the east, Gregg had made his way back to his command, issued his orders to Duffié, and began pulling the 3rd Division back toward the river. The movement and crossing were conducted without any significant incident. Duffié, ordered to cover the withdrawal of the Cavalry Corps with his 2nd Division, followed Gregg's division toward the river. Once well to the east of Brandy Station, the Frenchman posted one

of his brigades on the road leading from Brandy Station to Rappahannock Station to cover the withdrawal of Gregg's division. With the remaining brigade Duffié moved about two miles northwest to block the Beverly Ford Road, thereby protecting Buford from any Confederates that might approach from the south. After Buford's and Gregg's divisions had crossed the river, Duffié pulled his division back across Beverly Ford "without molestation" to safety.[47]

The withdrawal, however, was not completely uneventful. Upon reaching the river, the men of the 119th Pennsylvania Infantry were ordered to cross on the railroad bridge, which for some was the most frightening event of the day. The bridge was about six hundred feet long and its height was estimated at

Top: Jacob Kent Langhorne, a soldier for less than a month, was killed in his first fight. The eighteen-year old Langhorne was perhaps the last casualty of the day (Rachal Family Album). *Bottom*: As the day drew to a close, Pleasonton's forces made their way safely back across the Rappahannock. Some of the infantry balked at crossing the river on the Orange and Alexandria bridge at Rappahannock Station, preferring to get wet instead of stepping from tie-to-tie far above the water (Library of Congress).

ninety feet above the water. No planks had been laid across to the railroad ties to provide a footpath. Consequently, the infantrymen had to cross the bridge by stepping from tie to tie, with an unobstructed view of the water flowing by far below. Some men, not trusting their balance, crossed on all-fours. An officer berated one scrambling trooper, "Stand, up, walk upright ... where's your nerve, where's your manhood, never mind the depth below, you can't fall through." Despite raising doubts about his manhood, the soldier crawled off the bridge, climbed down the bank, and waded through the ford with the cavalry.[48]

When the 7th Wisconsin Infantry reached the river, the regiment was halted for a few hours to support an artillery section that was covering the rearward movement of the cavalry. About dark the regiment was ordered to the ford, which the men found was steeper and deeper than Kelly's where they had crossed to the south bank roughly fourteen hours earlier. Upon entering the water, the Badgers, who had suffered throughout the day from heat and a lack of water, stopped to drink and fill their canteens. An officer standing on the bank, wanting quickly to complete the crossing, began shouting at the infantrymen to move along, but most of the troops ignored his exhortations. After drinking their fill, the men emerged from the ford, marched about a mile, and went into camp near Rappahannock Station about 10:00 p.m. After a long, hot day, the men, lying on the ground and wet up to their waists, were chilled by the cool night air.[49]

The Battle of Brandy Station was over.

11

Few Will Exult

After the Battle

Immediately after the battle, the armies turned from fighting to other immediate and necessary tasks. The top priority for both Federals and Confederates was tending to the wounded, followed by burying the dead. Since the Confederates owned the battlefield, those tasks fell mostly to Stuart's troops. General Pleasonton sent Stuart a note through the lines requesting to retrieve the Union dead, provide medical supplies for the wounded, and send ambulances and surgeons to evacuate those whose wounds were severe. Stuart declined the offer, curtly informing Pleasonton that he had already seen to those matters.[1] As they tended to the wounded and the dead, the ever-needy Confederates sent out details of men to scour the battlefield for abandoned arms and equipment. Concurrently, both Union and Confederate commanders—or their adjutants—set pens to paper drafting official reports.

As a matter of pride, Stuart initially directed the activities of his division from his former headquarters at Fleetwood, a site fought over at great cost to both sides. However, the carcasses of horses littering the area, rotting under the hot Virginia sun, drew swarms of blue bottle flies. After a day, the flies and the stench of decaying flesh drove Stuart and his staff to move to a more pristine site—a grove near the reviewing ground on Auburn. Stuart named his new headquarters Camp Farley in honor of his trusted scout who had been mortally wounded near Stevensburg.[2]

Rooney Lee, the only general officer wounded on either side, was taken by wagon to a home in Culpeper Courthouse belonging to the brother of Lieutenant General A. P. Hill. The house, near the train depot in the Courthouse, was one of the more elegant mansions in the small town. Robert E. Lee spoke with Rooney as he was being carried from the battlefield and visited him at the Hill home later that evening. The elder Lee found Rooney comfortable and cheerful—the ball that struck his thigh injured neither femur nor artery. In a letter written the next day, Lee advised his wife, Mary, that he expected their son to heal quickly.[3] Mary Lee, however, was not so sanguine. At the time, she was renting rooms in Richmond in the home of Mr. and Mrs. James Caskie. Upon hearing from her husband that their son had been wounded, she sent for Mary Chesnut, a friend whose husband, Colonel James Chesnut, was an aide to Jefferson Davis. Mary Chesnut found Mary Lee distraught and taken to bed (Mary Lee suffered from arthritis and was frequently in poor health). Anticipating that her daughter-in-law, Charlotte, would take Rooney to convalesce at Hickory Hill, her family's plantation in Hanover County, Mary Lee lamented that she was a "poor lame woman [who was] useless to her children." Mary Chesnut recalled that Mrs. Caskie attempted to comfort Mary Lee, observing that General Lee had written that Rooney's wound was not severe, and "even Yankees believe General Lee."[4] After a day at the Hill mansion, Lee was taken, as Mary Lee had anticipated, to Hickory Hill.

Most of the wounded, including both Confederates and those unfortunate Union troopers who were left on the field, received less attention. The wounded from both North and South were taken to hospitals, hastily established in homes throughout the local area, where regimental surgeons plied their trade. Most of the wounds were gunshots, a few were shrapnel punctures, and, uncharacteristically for the Civil War, many were saber slashes. Initially, some believed that saber wounds would prove more severe and difficult to treat, assumptions that were quickly discounted by the *New York Times*.[5]

The Glebe Farm, about a mile west of the battlefield, served as a Confederate hospital during the battle. Mrs. Charles Wagner, who was living alone in the house with her children — her husband was away serving as captain of the Brandy Rifles — fled at the height of the battle to seek safety with relatives a few miles away. Although Mrs. Wagner escaped the fighting, she could not escape being vividly reminded of the day's events. Returning to the Glebe after dark on June 9, she stumbled over two dying Confederate troopers in her front yard and found two more laying on her front porch.[6]

In Brandy Station, a two-story frame building next to the railroad tracks belonging to John A. Stone, the Brandy postmaster, was also used as a hospital.[7] Being close to Fleetwood Hill, the building was quickly filled with wounded, including James Marshall, a lieutenant in the 12th Virginia and brother of the acting commander of the 7th Virginia. While convalescing, Marshall inscribed his name on the plaster wall of the house with charcoal, a popular pursuit among the young men treated there.[8]

Union medical services were generally superior to those of the Confederates, and fortunately for the Union wounded, most were evacuated from the battlefield before Pleasonton withdrew his force across the Rappahannock on the evening of June 9. Some of Pleasonton's wounded were transported that day by train from Rappahannock Station to hospitals in Alexandria.[9] Union wounded who were evacuated across Kelly's Ford were treated overnight at a field hospital established in a local church. The following day they were taken by wagon to Rappahannock Station, and from there moved north by train.[10] However, some wounded Union troopers were left on the battlefield and fell into Confederate hands. They not only faced treatment in the less-robust Confederate medical system, but also confinement as prisoners of war.

One such unfortunate was the officer who had been shot and then pistol-whipped by Captain Charles O'Ferrall on Fleetwood Hill. On the day after the battle, O'Ferrall went to a hospital in Brandy Station to visit several of his soldiers who had been wounded. While there, he was accosted by the wounded Union officer, who had recognized O'Ferrall as his nemesis. The Union officer, head bandaged, told O'Ferrall that he did not mind being shot, but he took great umbrage with being struck over the head after being wounded and thus unable to defend himself. The Union officer asserted that a "brave man" would not have done such a ungentlemanly thing. O'Ferrall was chagrined, and his explanation — that he was only trying to keep himself in the saddle — failed to mollify the wounded prisoner. The Union officer also claimed to have suffered the indignity of having had his watch — a gift from his father — looted as he lay wounded on the field. By chance, O'Ferrall had overheard one of his men boasting that after the battle he had taken a fine watch from the body of a dead Yankee. Once back in camp, O'Ferrall accosted the trooper, and upon examining the watch, found an inscription "From Father" inside the cover of the case. That evening, O'Ferrall returned the watch to its owner, an act that assuaged the Yankee's bad feelings. The two parted, according to O'Ferrall, as "good friends."[11]

The Officers' Circle around the flagpole at Culpeper National Cemetery contains the graves of three Union Officers killed at Brandy Station: Virgil Broderick and John Shelmire of the 1st New Jersey Cavalry and Isaac Ward of the 6th U.S. Cavalry (Joseph W. McKinney).

As was the practice, most of the dead—both Confederate and Union—were buried where they fell, or nearby.[12] Appropriately, and conveniently, some dead were buried on the grounds of Saint James Church.[13] Soldiers who lived in the local area were naturally taken home for burial in family plots. The remains of some, usually those more senior in grade or well-to-do, were returned to their more distant homes for burial.

The Adjutant of the Second North Carolina, Lieutenant John Pegram, arranged to have Colonel Sol Williams' remains tended in Culpeper and then taken to Petersburg where his body was given to his bride of only two weeks. Williams was buried next to his mother.[14]

Union soldiers carried Colonel Grimes Davis' body off the field during the battle. The disposition of his remains may have caused the Federal Government some consternation, since Davis was a Southerner and it would likely prove difficult to ship his body back to Alabama or Mississippi. In any event, Davis was buried at West Point on June 20, 1863, where he had earned his commission eight years earlier.

Frank Hampton's body was taken initially to Richmond where Colonel James Chesnut, a South Carolinian, arranged for its shipment home. While in Richmond, Hampton's remains lay in state in the Confederacy's Capitol. Before the coffin was sealed for transit to Columbia, South Carolina, Mary Chesnut chose to view the body—a choice she immediately regretted. She later wrote that when she had last seen Frank Hampton alive, he had been "all in the pride of his magnificent manhood," but now, "He died of a saber-cut across the face and head, and was utterly disfigured." She reflected, "There must have been hard hitting, the day Frank Hampton was killed — hand to hand. That ghastly cut across his head still haunts me."[15]

Inexplicably, and contrary to his wishes, Will Farley's remains were not sent home to his mother in South Carolina. Instead, he was hastily buried under a grape arbor in the yard of the Ashby House.[16]

The remains of a few enlisted men were also sent home for burial. On the day after the battle, Lieutenant Charles Phelps of Moorman's battery wrote to his aunt that he had arranged for the body of Corporal Anthony Dornin, the only soldier in the Stuart Horse Artillery to have been killed in the fighting on June 9, to be placed in the best coffin available and sent home to Lynchburg.[17] The men of the Wise Troop sent Jacob Kent Langhorne's remains home to his family, and he was buried in the Crockett-Kent graveyard in Shawsville, Virginia.[18]

The men of the Wise Troop, 2d Virginia Cavalry, apparently felt a personal loss from the death of young Jacob Kent Langhorne. As Lee's army moved north, Captain Steptoe and his men took time to prepare a resolution for Langhorne's parents:

> At a meeting of Co B (Wise Troop) 2d Va Cavalry held at Hillsborough on the 23d day of June 1863 the following preamble and resolutions were unanimously adopted.
>
> Whereas in the late battle of Brandy Station on the 9th of June 1863 our fellow Soldier J. Kent Langhorne received a mortal wound whilst gallantly battling against the enemy of which wound in the dispensation of Devine Providence he that day died.
>
> Therefore, Resolved that while we bow in submission to God in the dispensation of his Providence we can but give vent to our Sorrow that one so young, so brave, so gentle and wining in his manners, so beloved by his comrades should have been taken from us just as we began to know his worth. He died as Virginians can only be spared fighting the foe. He died without a stain upon his youthfull escutcheon, fell bravely, died calmly and passed away with the breeze that bore the notes of Victory his life was given to Win.
>
> 2nd That we tender to his afflicted Parents in their sad bereavement our heartfelt sympathy. Their gallant boy was beloved by all his comrades and our loss is second only to theirs.
>
> 3rd. That a copy of the above preamble and resolutions be published in the Lynchburg Papers and a copy sent to his family.[19]

Confederate officers and sergeants were also busy with other administrative and logistical activities. The belongings of the dead were inventoried and arrangements made for the return of their personal property to next of kin. Details of men scavenged the battlefield for anything that could be of future use, mainly weapons. Stuart's chief of ordnance reported that the Cavalry Division captured 142 carbines, 223 pistols, 56 rifles, and 155 sabers. Ten saddles and bridles were also reported as captured.[20] Those numbers were probably highly inaccurate. Troopers were required to turn over captured arms to their ordnance sergeants for accounting. Nonetheless, many soldiers undoubtedly helped themselves to a new Colt revolver or Sharps carbine. It is also likely that many troopers helped themselves to abandoned Union saddles, the McClellan being much preferred to the Confederacy's Jenifer.

Also, not fully accounted were horses captured by the Confederates. Several commanders noted that unspecified numbers of horses had been sent to the rear with prisoners or turned over to quartermaster officers (captured horses were either used by the army or appraised and sold, usually to troopers or officers in need of mounts). While it was later estimated that Stuart's men captured about one hundred horses, it does not appear that near that number were entered into the quartermaster system.[21] In any event, the battle provided a small windfall for the ill-equipped Cavalry Division. As Grumble Jones noted in his official report, his brigade had more horses and more and better weapons at the end of the day on June 9 than at the beginning.[22]

Rebels who were captured by Pleasonton's men were sent by rail to Washington and from there to Federal prison camps to await exchange. Union soldiers taken by the Confederates were sent to Richmond, where officers—two field grade officers and ten lieutenants and captains—were held in Libby Prison, and enlisted men—a total of 322 according to the *Richmond Examiner*—were sent to the pen on Belle Isle. Also taken to Libby prison was a correspondent from the *New York Herald* who fell into Rebel hands. The *Examiner* did not exhibit much collegial respect for Northern journalists. The Richmond paper opined that *Herald* correspondents were actually spies who "turn up like 'bad pennies'" and noted that two "pimps" from the *New York Tribune* were already being held at Libby. The *Examiner* urged that the correspondents be held as hostages to secure the release of Southern men and women held in Northern prisons.[23]

Not all persons who were captured were treated according to the customs of war. Tom and Overton, two body servants for officers of the 12th Virginia Cavalry, captured the black servant of a Union officer. Instead of turning the captured servant over to Confederate authorities, Tom and Overton kept him as their personal slave.[24]

Many Confederate troopers were faced with the problem of obtaining compensation for their horses killed and finding suitable new mounts before the army moved north, an event expected to occur shortly. On the day after the battle, Private John Opie made his way back down the road to Beverly Ford to recover his saddle and bridle. He discovered that his black mare, whose disposition matched her color, had been struck by four balls from the volley that abruptly halted his one-man charge. The next day Opie left the regiment on a horse pass. At his home in Staunton, Opie picked up a remount, a fine young horse he had purchased a year earlier as a "skeleton" for only one hundred fifty Confederate dollars. After only four days, Opie was back with the 6th Virginia, having avoided the ignominious fate of being assigned to the 6th Virginia's Company Q. Three months later, the Confederate government paid Opie $475 for the loss of his black mare, a sum that he probably considered a bargain considering her temperament.[25]

Heros von Borcke had less difficulty obtaining a remount. The evening after the battle, his servant, Henry, rode into camp on the Prussian's bay that had been stolen a day earlier. Although the thief had disguised the horse by cutting its mane and tail, Henry, through "cunning and adroitness," had found and recovered the animal, a feat for which he was justly proud.[26]

On both sides of the Rappahannock, men made arrangements for the care of lightly wounded horses. In Union regiments, horses that might recover from their wounds were returned to the Quartermaster Department and sent back to a remount depot for care. Since horses in Confederate cavalry regiments were personal—not government—property, the officers and men usually made their own arrangements. Some sent their wounded horses home with servants. Others left their horses in the care of local farmers.[27]

While policing the battlefield, Confederates were faced with the grisly job of destroying the more seriously wounded horses. At the time, a horse was "put down" by firing a bullet into its brain. This was a task more easily said than done. To kill a horse cleanly, it was important that a soldier aim his weapon perpendicularly to the horse's forehead, precisely at a point where imaginary lines from the horse's left ear to right eye and right ear to left eye intersected. Should the soldier miss by just an inch or two, he would fail to kill the horse instantly, as Lieutenant Frank Robertson learned. Robertson, returning to Stuart's Headquarters after the battle, came upon a fine looking sorrel that had lost a foreleg at the knee to an artillery shell. Desiring to put the horse out of its misery, Robertson rode up to within about eight feet of it, and fired his pistol at its forehead. The horse leapt forward, knocking over

Bostona and covering Robertson with blood which was gushing from its mouth. When Robertson finally got to camp, limping from his fall and with a bloody uniform, his comrades initially feared he had been seriously wounded.[28]

As details of soldiers scoured the battlefield and buried the dead, both Confederate and Union commanders began preparing their reports of the battle. As customary, successes were highlighted while failures were omitted, downplayed, or mitigated by exculpatory information. Most commanders also used their reports to praise subordinates who were — hopefully — deserving.

Rooney Lee, incapacitated by his wound, was unable to submit a report. In his place, Colonel Chambliss filed a report that consisted of a single paragraph. Chambliss noted that only a few shots were fired after he took command in the Yew Hills, and stated that he did not feel it was proper to report on what he saw before assuming command because "General Lee will make a detailed report as soon as his very painful wound will permit."[29] Unfortunately, circumstances prevented Lee from ever filing his report.

Beverly Robertson was faced with the daunting task of explaining his brigade's inaction. He rose to the occasion by deftly characterizing the role played by his North Carolinians: "My command, although opposed to the enemy during the entire day, was not at any time actively engaged." Robertson went on to explain that had he pursued Duffié and Gregg moving off to his right, the road he was ordered to defend would have been "utterly exposed." Robertson did not address other options, such as sending one regiment to harass Gregg's flank while blocking Russell's infantry with his second regiment. Stuart, after considering Robertson's explanation, concluded that the brigadier should have done more, and in his own report criticized Robertson for failing to conform to the movement of Gregg, and thus not "check[ing] or thwart[ing]" Gregg's advance on Brandy Station.[30]

Robertson's caution during the battle stemmed perhaps from awareness that his tactical judgment was questioned by both Stuart and Robert E. Lee. In a supplement to his report, Robertson wrote that "I came to this army [of Northern Virginia] resolved that my official conduct should meet the approbation of my military superiors, and whenever in their opinion I deserve censure, I shall most cheerfully submit to official investigation." Stuart put the matter to rest in his final endorsement to Robertson's report by stating, "It is very clear that General Robertson intended to do what was right."[31]

Thomas T. Munford felt compelled to explain his delay in getting Fitz Lee's brigade into the fight, citing first his confusion upon receipt of two orders that directed him to move to an unspecified location ("this direction" and "this way"). Munford further implied that once he arrived at the battlefield, the deployment of his brigade was delayed to avoid a collision with the 9th Virginia, and then in finding the flank of Rooney Lee's brigade. Stuart remained unconvinced, and in his report commented that Munford did not adequately explain his delay in bringing up Fitz Lee's brigade "as the distance [to travel] was not very great."[32]

Regarding the engagement, Munford praised his sharpshooters and the section of guns from Breathed's battery that supported them. However, it was apparent from the few casualties (three killed and eighteen wounded among the three regiments engaged under his command) that the brigade had not done much fighting. Munford, who had few acts of heroism to cite in his report, commented that officers in the 2nd Virginia praised the spirited conduct of Privates James K. Preston and Jacob Kent Langhorne, who were both killed at the front of their companies.[33]

The tense relationship between Hampton and Stuart was evident in Hampton's official report. The South Carolinian pointed out that three times Stuart — without informing Hampton — had issued orders directly to Hampton's regimental commanders. In a criticism of

Stuart's management of the battle, Hampton wrote that he was unable to pursue the enemy fleeing from Fleetwood and thereby "reap the fruits of the victory" because Stuart had "deprived" him of two regiments.[34] Hampton's men, however, had fought well against both Buford's division and Kilpatrick's brigade, a fact reflected in both Hampton's and Stuart's reports.

Regarding the fight at Stevensburg, both Major Lipscomb and Colonel Wickham filed reports explaining their regiments' roles in the engagement. Lipscomb wrote a detailed chronological account from his perspective, provided his report to the wounded Colonel Butler for review, and attached Butler's comments as a postscript. Butler provided several insights. First, according to Butler, Wickham assumed command of the Confederate force at Stevensburg as he moved his regiment forward to support the 2nd South Carolina. Additionally, Butler claimed he received no effective artillery support since the piece that Stuart had sent to his aid never crossed Mountain Run, despite his repeated requests that it occupy the high ground in Stevensburg. Butler also noted that following the Union attack against Frank Hampton's detachment at Doggett's, he had been able to quickly rally his men because the Union troopers mainly occupied themselves by pursuing the 4th Virginia through Stevensburg.[35]

It must have been difficult for Colonel Williams Wickham to describe the panic and resulting rout of his regiment, the 4th Virginia. Wickham laid some blame for the debacle at Stevensburg on the 2nd South Carolina, which he claimed broke and fled before meeting the Union charge at Doggett's. By way of excuse, Wickham reported that the fleeing South Carolinians (few that there were) frustrated his attempt to dismount sharpshooters. Wickham also claimed that the flight of the South Carolinians demoralized his Virginians, who were in the midst of deploying from their march column into line. Nonetheless, Wickham found it impossible to completely excuse the poor performance of his regiment, concluding: "I regard the conduct of my regiment, in which I have heretofore had perfect confidence, as so disgraceful in this instance that I have been thus minute in my report, that the major-general commanding, to whom I request that this [report] be forwarded, may have the facts before him on which to base any inquiry he may see fit to institute."[36] Stuart, perhaps because of the 4th Virginia's past performance or as a sign of confidence in Wickham, chose not to conduct an inquiry.

Jones, whose troopers had seen much hard fighting on June 9, was justifiably proud of the performance of his brigade. In his official report, Jones wrote that his brigade "bore the brunt of the action both in the morning and evening, and lost severely in killed and wounded, but had the satisfaction of seeing the enemy worsted in every particular more than ourselves." Jones indirectly credited himself with saving Stuart's artillery, indicating that the 6th Virginia and the 7th Virginia "were ordered" forward to gain time for the artillery whose park was without protection, and its safety doubtful. Jones closed his report by expressing appreciation for his staff, one of whom, Lieutenant W. M. Hopkins, joined in a charge at St. James and "killed his man" in the encounter.[37]

Stuart wrote a lengthy report — more than three thousand words — to describe in great detail the "battle of Fleetwood," his chosen name for the events of June 9. By design, Stuart disguised the closeness of the battle and downplayed the threats faced by the cavalry division at various points during the day's fighting. For example, the only hint that the horse artillery came close to being overrun in its camp were brief, easily overlooked comments. Stuart wrote that Jones' brigade had to "extricate" the artillery from its "exposed position" while the artillery was "hastily hitched up." Similarly, Jones was "hotly engaged" for a time at St. James, while the "contest" over Fleetwood Hill was "prolonged and spirited." Regarding the fighting at

Stevensburg, Stuart wrote that the force sent there was sufficient to check Duffié's advance, but the two regiments "failed to resist the enemy effectually." Significantly, the word "surprise" does not appear in Stuart's report.[38]

Stuart's version of events most diverges from the facts with respect to the fight over Fleetwood Hill. Placing a positive spin on events, Stuart claimed that the terrain and Union dispositions led him to determine that "the real stand" would be made on Fleetwood Hill. Thus, Stuart wrote that he ordered a section of artillery to Fleetwood and posted Major McClellan there to watch for Union columns. Stuart further wrote that his intention was to keep his force concentrated, except those troops necessary to delay the enemy, and then to strike with his whole force, presumably at Fleetwood. In reality, Moorman's gun was at Fleetwood purely by happenstance, McClellan was at Fleetwood to relay orders, not observe, and the arrival of Gregg's column — which should have been checked by Robertson — was not expected. Finally, instead of striking with his whole force, Stuart fed Jones' and Hampton's regiments into the fight piecemeal.[39]

As customary, Stuart concluded his report by singling out several subordinates for praise. The only brigadier to receive praise for his personal conduct was Rooney Lee, a "gallant officer" who led his brigade in a "handsome and highly satisfactory manner," and was severely wounded leading a "brilliant" charge. On the other hand, Stuart wrote that Hampton and Jones were merely "prompt in the execution of orders, and conformed readily to the emergencies arising."[40] To his report, Stuart appended an accurate map, prepared by his engineer, Captain William W. Blackford.

Robert E. Lee endorsed Stuart's report on June 16, commenting: "The dispositions made by you to meet the strong attack of the enemy appear to have been judicious and well planned. The troops were well and skillfully managed, and, with few exceptions, conducted themselves with marked gallantry."[41]

Concurrently, on the north side of the Rappahannock Pleasonton and his subordinates were also preparing and filing their reports of the action. Perhaps the officer with the most difficult task was Captain Joseph W. Martin, commander of the 6th New York Independent Light Artillery Battery, who was faced with explaining the loss of three of his pieces. Martin wrote that when ordered forward to his advanced position, he had been assured that support would be provided to him by Wyndham's brigade. However, no support was provided, and he and his thirty-six men were left to defend themselves against repeated Confederate charges. Of his men, Martin wrote: "Once [the Confederates were] in the battery, it became a hand-to-hand fight with pistol and saber between the enemy and my cannoneers and drivers, and never did men act with more coolness and bravery, and show more of a stern purpose to do their duty unflinchingly, and, above all, to save their guns; and while the loss of them is a matter of great regret to me, it is a consolation and a great satisfaction to know that I can point with pride to the fact that of that little band who defended the battery not one of them flinched for a moment from his duty."

Martin also reported that his crews had completely and effectually disabled the three guns before they were abandoned. Exhibiting attention for detail, Martin accounted for the horse tack and other equipment lost, and tallied the ammunition fired by his battery (122 Schenkl percussion shell, 126 Hotchkiss case shot, and 15 Hotchkiss cannister).[42]

Colonel Duffié faced two challenges when drafting his report. First, by getting lost, his division had delayed the advance of the left wing across Kelly's Ford. Duffié simply chose not to address that shortcoming. Second, as for his slow response in moving from Stevensburg to Brandy Station to support Gregg, Duffié pointed out that he had been ordered "return and join the Third Division, on the road to Brandy Station." Thus Duffié implied

that the option of fighting through the 2nd South Carolina and taking the more direct route to join Gregg's fight was not available to him. Duffié added that en route to Brandy Station, he came upon a squadron of the 10th New York with pack mules "fleeing in the greatest disorder" shouting that their flank had been turned by the Confederates. Duffié claimed that the encounter with the 10th New York delayed him for a half hour. Duffié concluded his report by noting that when his division arrived at Brandy Station, the fighting was over, leaving him to cover the withdrawal of the Cavalry Corps toward the fords on the Rappahannock.[43]

In his report, David McMurtrie Gregg documented Duffié's substandard performance on June 9, beginning with the Frenchman's "late start and unexpected difficulties" in arriving at Kelly's Ford on time, and concluding with his failure to bring up the 2nd Division in support at Fleetwood, despite twice being directed to do so. Left unstated, was why Gregg, faced with the tardy Frenchman and the sounds of fighting from Beverly Ford, failed to alter his order of march, cross his 3rd Division immediately, and enter the battle to relieve pressure on Buford.[44] As a West Point graduate and professional soldier, Gregg had studied the campaigns of Napoleon, and was certainly aware of the Napoleonic principle that a general can usually do little wrong by choosing to march to the sound of the guns.

Regarding the battle itself, Gregg recounted that his entire division was engaged at Brandy Station and the fight was "everywhere most fierce" against a force he estimated to be three times larger than his own. Gregg also inaccurately reported that rail cars loaded with Confederate infantry were sent to Brandy Station from Culpeper. To impede the arrival of the Rebel infantry, Gregg reported that he sent a party to obstruct the tracks, a task they accomplished by reversing a switch on the line. The basis for this episode is not clear. No trains with Rebel infantry were sent to Stuart's support. Nonetheless, "the field having been well contested and the enemy being reinforced with infantry from Culpeper that could be thrown in any force upon us," Gregg broke off the fight and pursuant to orders from Pleasonton, began to withdraw toward Rappahannock Station.

Gregg exonerated Captain Martin in the loss of the three guns, noting that the officers and men of the battery had defended their pieces with "the highest degree of soldierly character." Gregg concluded his report with praise for his staff, including his younger brother, T. J. Gregg, who was detailed to the Division Headquarters from the 6th Pennsylvania Cavalry and reportedly provided efficient service carrying orders during the battle.[45]

Buford began his report by effusively praising the late Colonel Grimes Davis as "A thorough soldier, free from politics and intrigue, a patriot in its true sense, an ornament to his country, and a bright star in his profession" who "died in the front, giving examples of heroism and courage to all who were to follow." Buford singled out his artillery and its battery and section commanders for praise, commenting that "they fought their guns with coolness, skill, and judgment, and often where they were in hot places." This last was perhaps an understatement, given the superiority of Confederate artillery around Saint James Church. For the most part, Buford described the engagement in a matter-of-fact manner, noting that his force was engaged for nearly fourteen hours and that his casualties were heavy, a reflection of the hand to hand fighting by the cavalry and extensive skirmishing by dismounted troopers and infantry. Unfortunately, Buford's report fails to shed much light on any influence Pleasonton may have exerted on the fighting at Beverly Ford and Saint James Church.[46]

Opposite: Stuart's Engineer Officer prepared a remarkably detailed map of eastern Culpeper County to accompany Stuart's official report of the battle (Official Records).

On the evening of June 9, General Pleasonton got a head start on his official report by sending a message to Hooker in which he summarized the day's fighting. In the message, Pleasonton praised both Buford and Gregg for their performance against what he believed to be superior Confederate forces. Pleasonton also claimed to have "crippled" Stuart's division and predicted that the Confederate commander would no longer attempt a raid into Maryland, initially planned to start on June 10.[47] At 5:30 the following morning, Pleasonton sent Hooker a second message summarizing the battle.

> We had splendid fighting yesterday, and I think it will prevent Stuart making his raid, which he was to have commenced this morning. Toward night, they opened 20-pounder Parrott guns at a long distance, showing they were re-enforced. They did not attempt to follow us with any vigor. My old division and the regulars have covered themselves with glory. We captured Stuart's camp, with his orders, letters, &c. He was to move to Maryland with 12,000 cavalry and twenty-five guns, and he was camped at the ford we crossed, a perfect hornet's nest, but we drove them over 2 miles before Gregg came up, and, when I found out he had had as hard a time as ourselves, and no fresh troops to call on, I returned to the north bank of the Rappahannock. The enemy lost very heavily.[48]

Predictably, in his report, written five days later, Pleasonton, provided skewed view of the battle. Regarding the fighting at Saint James, Pleasonton wrote that since Buford's wing was outnumbered at least three-to-one, he ordered it to hold its positions until Gregg's wing joined the fight. Pleasonton recounted that once he heard the booming of Gregg's guns at Fleetwood he ordered a general advance, capturing the camp of the Stuart Horse Artillery and important papers. Afterward, a junction was made with Gregg's force, who had meanwhile seized Stuart's headquarters with all its documents. Preparations were underway to continue the advance when "it was discovered" that Rebel infantry was moving to Brandy Station very rapidly on rail cars while a column approached on foot from Culpeper. Consequently, Pleasonton ordered both Gregg and Buford to withdraw. Before beginning to pull back, however, Buford conducted a "grand attack" on his right which featured the "finest fighting of the war" with regiments charging brigades, rallying and charging again, "never yielding, and always crushing the mass opposed to them." Pleasonton reported that Confederate officers "were seen to saber and shoot their men to keep them up to the fight."[49]

Pleasonton recommended that the government promote Buford and Gregg for their gallantry, and he devoted the last half of his report to citing the services of thirty-one other officers, including ten of his *aides de camp*.[50] Unfortunately, Pleasonton failed to describe his own activities during the long day's battle in any detail. Other than ordering Buford to advance upon hearing, Gregg's guns, Pleasonton was silent about where he was, what he saw, and what he did to influence the fighting.[51] Like Stuart, Pleasonton appended a sketch map of the battlefield to his report. The map, prepared by Captain von Koerber, an officer of the 1st Maryland Cavalry detailed to Pleasonton's staff as the topographical engineer, was much less accurate than that prepared by Blackford, Stuart's engineer. This was to be expected, since von Koerber had no opportunity to walk the terrain in the days after the fighting was over.[52]

One aspect of the battle that received only cursory attention in the reporting was the use made of the two picked infantry brigades. Neither Buford nor Gregg employed their infantry as suggested by Hooker: as a moving *point d'appui*, available always, which no Confederate cavalry could shake. On the contrary, Buford had frittered away his infantry on regimental and company missions in support of his cavalry. Gregg's infantry, positioned to protect his lines of withdrawal, played almost no part in the battle, except, perhaps, to confuse Beverly Robertson. Ames' brigade unquestionably would have had difficulty breaking Grumble Jones's line at Saint James, supported as it was by Beckham's battalion. However, the outcome of the day's fighting may have been quite different had Russell's foot soldiers, rather than Kilpatrick's mounted troopers, moved to Wyndham's support atop Fleetwood.

The cavalry, both Union and Confederate, had little time to dally after the battle on June 9. On June 10, Ewell's corps marched from Culpeper for the Valley, followed five days later by Longstreet's Corps. Coinciding with Longstreet's departure, Stuart's Cavalry Division moved north from Culpeper, paralleling the infantry and screening the passes through the Blue Ridge. As the commanders finished their reports, hoping to shape the official version of events, the public, led by the press, formed their own opinions regarding the encounter at Brandy Station. In the North, a general opinion emerged that Pleasonton and his troopers had done well. With respect to the Southern cavalry, public opinion was less favorable.

In the North, the consensus was that Pleasonton's operation had been successful in disrupting Stuart's anticipated raid into Maryland. On the morning of June 10, Secretary of War Stanton advised Major General Robert Schenk, commanding the middle department at Baltimore, that Pleasonton believed Stuart had been "too much crippled" to soon launch the raid into Maryland that the War Department had expected.[53] However, in his diary for that day, Brigadier General Marsena Patrick, Hooker's provost marshal, more accurately noted that "my fear is that Pleasonton does not pitch in strong enough to break up the expedition entirely."[54]

Northern newspapers began providing notice of the battle on June 10, and provided more detailed coverage over the next few days. The most thorough accounts of the battle were filed by correspondents for the *New York Times*, who were present on the field and witnessed some of the fighting.[55] The Northern press, like Secretary Stanton, expressed a positive view of the Union cavalry's performance and termed the battle as a victory. For example, the *New York Times*, on the front page of its June 12 edition, preceded its coverage of the battle with a dozen headlines:

> GREAT CAVALRY FIGHT.
>
> The Engagements at Beverley's Ford and Brandy Station.
>
> Full Details from Our Special Correspondents.
>
> Desperate and Gallant Fighting by Our Forces.
>
> THE REBELS DRIVEN BACK THREE MILES.
>
> THEIR CAMPS CAPTURED AND OCCUPIED.
>
> Two Hundred Prisoners and One Stand of Colors Taken.
>
> Highly Important Information Gained.
>
> Stuart Proposing to Start on his Great Raid Yesterday Morning.
>
> His Force 12,000 Cavalry and 16 Pieces of Artillery.
>
> Our Losses About 400 Killed, Wounded and Missing.
>
> THE REBEL LOSS MUCH HEAVIER.

The correspondent began his description of the battle by stating that "This [June 9] has been an exciting day" and ended with the assessment that "though our force was not large enough to thoroughly defeat the rebels, yet they received a sound thrashing, and it will result in postponing their 'grand raids' into the North for some time, if not indefinitely; for besides chastising them, we have gained full information of their strength, character and designs."[56] The *New York Herald* and the *American and Commercial Advertiser*, a Baltimore newspaper, relying upon an account by an officer who was present, published stories about the battle in their June 11 editions. The eye witness described the fighting at Brandy Station was of the "bloodiest character — hand to hand with sabre and pistol," and that "our own loss was considerable, and the slaughter of the Rebels was fearful." The article concluded with the assessment that "by this sudden and brilliant dash of our cavalry into the enemy's lines their plans have been frustrated, and the intended raid by Stuart's forces prevented."[57]

Also on June 11, the *Herald* published an editorial regarding the battle, which the newspaper's staff termed a "brilliant and successful cavalry fight." The editorial staff concluded that the battle "was undoubtably a desperate and bloody combat; but it succeeded in thwarting the plans of General Lee to get into the rear of the army on the Rappahannock, and lay waste to the fertile counties of Maryland and Pennsylvania."[58]

In contrast to the Northern press, Southern newspapers were critical of the performance of their cavalry. On June 10, only hours after Pleasonton withdrew his force to the north side of the Rappahannock, the *Richmond Examiner* informed its readers of the battle fought the day before. The newspaper apparently had excellent sources within the Confederate Government — it obtained and printed General Lee's telegram regarding the battle that he had sent to the War Department the night before. Although no details of the battle were provided, the *Examiner's* staff could not resist editorializing, "As General Lee is cautious in his language, we are justified in regarding the battle which he relates, as having been a very serious affair."[59]

The following day, under a headline "THE BATTLE IN CULPEPER" the *Examiner* provided a brief, inaccurate account of the cavalry engagement. As a cautionary note, the *Examiner* had prefaced the article with the disclaimer, "There are fifty conflicting accounts of this battle."[60] According to that Richmond paper, fifteen thousand Union troopers crossed the Rappahannock at a point believed unfordable and arrived "suddenly and unexpectedly" in the rear of Stuart's camp.[61] Stuart's division was saved only by the "gallantry and courage" of the men. According to the *Examiner*, the battle at Brandy Station "narrowly missed being a great disaster to our army," with the Union losses considerable fewer than those on the Confederate side.[62]

By June 12, the staff of the *Examiner* had obtained sufficient information on the battle to form an editorial position regarding the efficiency and effectiveness of the leadership — particularly that exercised by JEB Stuart — in the cavalry division of the Army of Northern Virginia. While the *Examiner's* account of the battle was indirectly unflattering to Stuart, the editorial position taken by the paper was scathing.

> The more the circumstances of the late affair at Brandy Station are considered, the less pleasant do they appear. If this was an isolated case, it might be excused under the convenient head of accident or chance. But this much puffed up cavalry of the Army of Northern Virginia has been twice, if not three times, surprised since the battles of December, and such repeated accidents can be regarded as nothing but the necessary consequences of negligence and bad management. If the war was a tournament, invented and supported for the pleasure and profit of a few vain and weak-headed officers, these disasters might be dismissed with compassion. But the country pays dearly for the blunders which encourage the enemy to overrun and devastate the land, with a cavalry which is daily learning to despise the mounted troops of the Confederacy. It is high time that this branch of the service should be reformed.

The surprise on this occasion was the most complete that has occurred. The Confederate cavalry was carelessly strewn over the country, with the Rappahannock only between it and an enemy who has already proven his enterprise to our cost. It is said that their camp was supposed to be secure, because the Rappahannock was not believed to be fordable at the point where it was actually forded. What ! do Yankees then know more about this river than our own soldiers, who have done nothing but ride up and down their banks for the last six months? They knew, at least, that the weather was dry, the water low, and that fifteen or twenty thousand horse, confident from impunity and success, were on the other side. They could not have failed to know this much, and they were surprised—caught at breakfast, made prisoners on foot, with guns empty, and horses grazing. Although the loss was insignificant, the events of that morning were among the least creditable that have occurred. Later, some of the best officers sacrificed their lives to redeem the day. A very fierce fight ensued, in which it is said, for the first time in this war, a considerable number of sabre wounds were given and received. In the end the enemy retired, or was driven, it is not yet clearly known which, across the river. Nor is it certainly known whether the fortunate result was achieved by the cavalry alone or with the assistance of Confederate infantry in the neighborhood. As the Southern troops remained masters of the field, and as they are believed to have taken at least as many prisoners towards the close of the day as they lost in the morning, they may be considered victors.

But it is a victory over which few will exult. It resembles that other victory won at Kelly's Ford on the 17th of March; both would have been well merited defeats if valour had not paid the price of conceit and carelessness. The ease with which the enemy outwitted the guard of the river on the first occasion, was the prompter of Stoneman's incursion at the head of ten thousand horse into the heart of the State, which he accomplished without the slightest interference from the Confederate cavalry. It is with pain that these reflections are made. They occur at this moment, not only to the present writer but also to the whole public, and and [sic] their utterance may have a wholesome effect. Events of this description have been lately too frequent to admit of the supposition that they are the results of hazard. They are the effects of causes which will produce like effects while they are permitted to operate, and they require the earnest attention both of the chiefs of the Government and the heads of the Army. The enemy is evidently determined to employ his cavalry extensively, and has spared no pains or cost to perfect that arm. The only effective means of preventing the mischief it may do is to reorganize our own forces, enforce a stricter discipline among the men, and insist on more earnestness among the officers in the discharge of their very important duty.[63]

On June 14 and 15, the *Examiner* reprinted accounts of the battle that had been originally published in the *New York Times*. Reading articles written from a Northern perspective and for a Northern audience must have been a bitter experience for Richmond readers.

News of the battle spread quickly throughout Virginia and the Carolinas. In Lynchburg, the *Daily Virginian* picked up on the themes expressed in the *Examiner* and stated that "Making all due allowance, however, for the defects in judgment in ourselves, we repeat the fear that we were taken at great disadvantage in the late affair and that we lost by the non-observance of proper precaution." The *Daily Virginian* concluded by expressing the hope that "Gen Stuart will be wide awake the next time [Union cavalry] come into his lines."[64] The *Charleston Mercury* notified its readers of the battle in its June 12 edition. It advised that the attack by Union forces was unexpected, but that after "desperate and sanguinary" fighting, the enemy was driven from the field. In its edition three days later, the *Mercury* eulogized the prominent South Carolinian casualties, Frank Hampton and Will Farley killed, and M. C. Butler wounded.[65]

Publicly, Stuart kept silent on the criticism in the press, but privately he fumed at accounts he considered inaccurate and ill motivated. In a letter to his wife on June 12, Stuart wrote, "The *Examiner* of the 12th *lies* from beginning to end. I lost no papers—no nothing—except the casualties of battle." Cryptically, Stuart added, "I understand the spirit and object of the detraction and can I believe trace the Source."⁶⁶ Stuart ended his comments on the subject by informing his wife that he would "take no notice of such base falsehood."⁶⁷ On June 15, Stuart wrote at length on the issue to an unnamed friend in Richmond:

> I am amazed as well as mortified that our papers should persist in declaring the greatest triumph southern Cavalry as yet achieved. The Richmond press owe my Cavalry an apology which it is hoped it will be willing to make when the truth is at their reach. The yankees give no more credit than our friends (?) for no claim is made in the north that it was a surprise.
>
> The remarkable co-incidence of statement produces the belief that some detracting puppy has made it his business to lie and misrepresent the matter to the press. Is there any way by which the fact can be ascertained as to the real source of the information can be made known to me. I send a copy of my congratulatory order—which if published will go to some extent towards a contradiction of the Slander. My official report is now sent in, & but for lack of time I would send you a copy. Every word is a base lie about capture of my order book plans of campaign &c. I lost nothing whatever of baggage or papers.
>
> I sincerely trust that you will never believe such lies. My cavalry has not been surprised since I commanded it which is from the beginning of the war—the *Richmond press to the contrary notwithstanding*—I *know some* of those editors to be gentlemen—the informant is I think the man to get at.
>
> Give much love to all. I sincerely hope the country will not be left without the benefit of your counsel.⁶⁸

While Stuart refused to respond openly to criticism, his supporters were less reluctant to do so. On June 13, a letter writer to the *Richmond Sentinel*, attributed erroneous accounts of surprise and disorder to "alarmists" in the rear as justification for their not being in the front, where their duty lay. The writer commented "That the Union attack was unexpected is true, but nothing more," and added that Jones' brigade checked the Union advance.⁶⁹ On June 17, The *Richmond Sentinel* published a lengthy letter from *Veritas*, apparently a member of the 1st South Carolina Cavalry. *Veritas* wrote that on the evening of June 8, Stuart reinforced his pickets with a squadron from the 1st South Carolina because he had received information that the Federals were planning to make an incursion into Culpeper County in strength. *Veritas* also challenged the assertion that Jones' brigade had been attacked in its camps, unmounted and with weapons unloaded.⁷⁰ On June 18, the *Examiner* printed excerpts from a letter written by a participant in the battle who wished to "correct the erroneous accounts of the affair that have heretofore been published." The letter writer asserted that Stuart had not been surprised and that the Union advance on Brandy Station had been "expected and provided for."⁷¹

The *Richmond Examiner*, did not relent from its editorial position regarding Stuart. Citing the Richmond correspondent for the *Charleston Mercury*, the *Examiner* informed its readers that Stuart had been holding large cavalry reviews and that at the last review Stuart had "bouquets pinned plentifully on his person to the disgust of General Lee."⁷² Further, the *Examiner* repeated a remark reportedly overheard "on the [railroad] cars": "If anyone asks you about the cavalry fight in Culpeper, tell 'em we were whipped." Surprisingly, considering its earlier published opinions, the *Examiner* commented that Stuart's cavalry had not been whipped, just "disgracefully surprised." Nonetheless, the editorial staff excoriated Stuart for attending balls instead of remaining vigilant, and for holding reviews "for the benefit of ladies and the enemy." In a biting comment, the *Examiner* staff stated that "Cavalry were intended to decide and complete victories—not to ride around."⁷³ Stuart obviously did not need such basic advice from the press.

The facts of the battle and criticism by the press—whether fully deserved or not—tarnished the reputations of Stuart and his command. Based in a large part upon what they read, both Southern civilians and members of Lee's army began to question the fighting capabilities of the cavalry division and Stuart's effectiveness as its commander.

John B. Jones, the Rebel War Clerk in Richmond, first heard of the battle on June 10, recording in his diary simply that the Federals had attacked, but been driven back. In the following day's entry, Jones was more skeptical of Stuart's performance. Besides copying into his diary Lee's June 9 message to General Cooper, Jones noted that while he had received no details of the battle, the Union attack was a "surprise, not credible to our officers in command." Jones' opinion was more critical on June 12 when he wrote in his diary, "The surprise of Stuart, on the Rappahannock, has chilled every heart, notwithstanding it does not appear that we lost more than the enemy in the encounter. The question is on every tongue — have our generals relaxed in vigilance? If so, sad is the prospect!"[74] Probably, the editorial in that day's newspaper influenced Jones' opinion.

On June 11, Joseph Waddell, an army quartermaster clerk in Staunton, recorded in his diary that accounts indicated Stuart's men "got rather the worst of it, losing 600 men taken prisoner, although capturing 300 of the enemy.... Our troops under Gen. Jones, late of the valley, were surprised!" Two days later, apparently after having read additional accounts of the battle, Waddell corrected the record in his diary, noting that while Stuart suffered heavy losses, "we had the advantage in the end" and that Jones' brigade had not been any more surprised than the other brigades of the Cavalry Division.[75]

In a letter to his wife dated June 12, Charles Blackford, formerly the commander of the Wise Troop, 2nd Virginia, and since detailed to Longstreet's Corps as judge advocate, expressed opinions similar to those presented in the *Examiner*. Blackford wrote, "The cavalry fight at Brandy Station can hardly be called a *victory*. Stuart was certainly surprised and but for the supreme gallantry of his subordinate officers and the men in his command it would have been a disaster and disgrace." In fairness, he added, "Stuart is blamed very much, but whether or not fairly I am not sufficiently well informed to say.[76] Since Captain Blackford had just arrived in Culpeper, having spent the day on the march from Orange County, it is unlikely that he had opportunity to read the Richmond papers. Instead, it seems more likely that his views reflect what he overheard upon arrival at Longstreet's Headquarters.

In a letter to his sister written on June 12, Colonel Thomas Rosser, who was on picket duty with the 5th Virginia Cavalry and missed the battle, wrote that "the fight was something like the Kelly's Ford fight. I think we were not benfited by it. The Yankees got rather the better I suspect and retired after the object of the expedition was accomplished."[77]

On June 12, Susan Caldwell, a housewife, wrote from Warrenton to her husband in Richmond. "I was sorry to learn that Genl. Stuart permitted himself to be surprised by the yankees and suffered such a heavy loss—tis true his loss was small compared to the yankees, but then he would not have suffered so heavily had his men been ready for action—but tis said that had it not been for the bravery of his men — his loss would have been much greater. Capt Farley of So. Ca.— was killed — he was a brave soldier. I deeply deplore his untimely end."[78]

That same day, Catherine Ann Devereaux Edmondston, of Halifax County, North Carolina, read the local newspaper's account of the battle. In her diary, she recorded "They surprized two of our Regiments at breakfast, the horses grazing, the men unarmed. Three companies of the third and one of the first Virginia were captured & about 600 horses and some horse artillery. They then fell on Jones Brigade which was in the act of forming with guns & pistols not loaded.... Our men recovering came forward & threw themselves sabre in hand on the enemy & they in turn were driven back with the loss of many prisoners and a battery, we recapturing our guns but not our prisoners."[79]

On a more personal level, Mrs. Edmondston lamented the death of fellow Carolinians, Lieutenant Colonel Frank Hampton ("a *gentleman and a gallant officer,* one drop of whose blood is worth a regiment of our opponents") and Colonel Sol Williams. Mrs. Edmondston's husband had perhaps been considered for command of the 2nd North Carolina, but was not appointed due to a lack of political influence. Recalling her disappointment when her husband had not received the commission, Mrs. Edmondston in her diary thanked God for sparing her the anguish and misery of widowhood. She concluded her comments on the battle with a more practical observation. "The enemy seem to be improving in their Cavalry management. I suppose they are learning how to ride, a pity of us, for all our best horses are exhausted, victims of bad management and no forage."[80]

By the time of her next diary entry on June 15, Mrs. Edmondston had learned more of the battle, prompting her to write, "The more we hear of the battle at Brandy Station, the more disgraceful is the surprise & the more glorious the courage of our men tho' thus taken at advantage." She noted that Union casualties included Colonel Grimes Davis, "who boasted that he was a kinsman of our President & had foxhunted over every inch of ground between Hanover & Richmond," and Sir Percy Wyndham, "who bears too good a name to be associated thus with such scoundrels."[81]

On June 13, Tally Simpson, a corporal in Kershaw's brigade wrote to his mother in South Carolina, "A few days ago our cavalry had a very severe engagement both at Brandy Station and Stevensburg. They were badly routed at the latter place, because they were both overpowered and completely surprised."[82]

In a letter to his father on June 14, William Hartwell Perry, an officer commanding an artillery battalion in Longstreet's corps, expressed an equally unflattering view of the Southern cavalry. Observing that any cavalryman riding past an infantry camp was subject to derision, he explained that "The affair [at Brandy Station] was an unfortunate one. Notwithstanding what the newspapers say our cavalry fought badly with some exceptions. There is no dismissing the fact that our cavalry will not fight except perhaps some times against yankee cavalry which is even worse that ours."[83]

Finally, an irate woman from Culpeper County aired her dissatisfaction with Stuart directly to the Confederacy's head of state. In an undated letter to Jefferson Davis, the woman, signing herself "Southern Lady," wrote:

> I have assumed a privilege which in no doubt will seem strange to you but I have deliberately premeditated over the matter & the true love I have for the Confederacy have dared to address our, President, allow a lady who deeply wishes our Confederacy success to say if General Stuart is allowed to remain our Commanding General of Cavalry we are lost people, I have been eye witness to the maneuvering of General Stuart since he is been in Culpeper & do know the whole of our unsuccess is his fault, General S loves the admiration of his class of lady friends, to much to be a Commanding General. He loves to have his repeated reviews immediately under the Yankees eye too much for the benefit & pleasure of his lady friends for the interest of the Confederacy & citizens who deeply suffer for his pleasure, I have also been eye witness to General Hampton during this winter campaign in Culpeper do plainly say he is the General he knows his place as a Gentleman & officer does not devote his military life seeking the admiration of ladys as General S does But for General H yesterday in the fight we never would of been surprised by hordes of those miserable creatures Yankees, Oh, what a life to endure then to see our Commanding General in fault, disgrace. President allow a true Southern lady to say General S conduct since in Culpeper has been perfectly ridiculous having repeated reviews for the benefit of his lady friends he riding up & down the line thronged with those ladys he decorated with flowers apparently a monkey show on hand & he the monkey in fact. General S is nothing more or less than one of those fussed up fops devoting his whole time in his lady friends company, President, I shall send a copy of this to

our Chief Commander, General Lee as I feel confident you or him are not posted with with [sic] General S conduct. Hoping a change may take place & more success may attend our army is my sincere pray[er] to God.[84]

Davis' reaction to the letter, if in fact he saw it, was not recorded. Custis Lee, probably amused, endorsed the letter for Davis and forwarded it to Stuart.[85] Although Stuart's reaction is unknown, he could not have been pleased with the Southern Lady's opinion regarding his personal conduct and her assessment of the recent battle. Additionally, the Southern Lady's high regard for Hampton must have been particularly galling to Stuart.

Without question, Stuart deserved some of the criticism, both public and private, directed toward him. Despite his protestations to the contrary, Stuart was surprised by the Federal incursion into Culpeper County on the morning of June 9. However, the press and other critics were off-base with their implication that the surprise occurred simply because Stuart's attention was focused on gala balls and reviews. The Cavalry Division of the Army of Northern Virginia was surprised for two reasons. First, the Federals carried out effective measures (today known as "operations security" or OPSEC) to conceal the pending attack. Second, General Stuart failed conduct proper and prudent reconnaissance and security measures.

The security measures employed by Hooker deserve considerable credit for protecting the Federal plan from compromise. Hooker distributed his orders for the attack—hand carried by trusted staff officers—on a strictly need-to-know basis. Corps commanders, for example, were directed merely to send infantry regiments to Spotted Tavern or Hartwood Church for an unspecified mission that would require hard marching. Further, Hooker delayed issuing his complete plan for as long as possible to prevent compromise. Pleasonton did not receive his orders until the evening of June 7, and his division commanders did not receive their instructions until the eve of the battle.

Hooker also provided specific guidance to his subordinates regarding how to conceal the movement of the two infantry brigades from their camps to the fords. Commanders were cautioned to avoid high ground where their men might be observed. They were also instructed to arrest potential spies and scouts that might carry news of the movement to Stuart. While it is not clear if Hooker provided such specific instructions to Pleasonton, the cavalry divisions exercised a great degree of caution during their movement. Commanders did not commence their movement south from camps near Catlett's Station until the afternoon of June 8, and they delayed approaching the river until after dark that evening. Once they neared the river, they imposed strict noise and light discipline. Troopers were prohibited from building cooking fires, and orders were disseminated verbally instead of by bugle call.

However, Union efforts to conceal the move to the south would have been in vain had Stuart established an effective screen of scouts or aggressively patrolled north of the Rappahannock. During much of the spring, Company H (the Black Horse Troop), 4th Virginia, had conducted independent scouting missions in Fauquier County. Since that company was raised in Warrenton in 1859, most of the men were welcome in the community and were familiar with the terrain, both factors which undoubtedly enhanced their ability to gather intelligence. After Chancellorsville, however, the company was withdrawn to the south bank of the Rappahannock where it rejoined its regiment. With the Black Horse Troop withdrawn, Stuart possibly intended to rely upon Mosby's partisans to provide information regarding Union troop movements north of the river. However, if arrangements were made for Mosby to feed intelligence to Stuart, neither recorded them in writing. Additionally, Mosby, who had been busy interdicting the Orange and Alexandria Railroad in southern Fauquier County through the end of May, shifted his operations north to Middleburg during early June. Consequently, he was probably not in position to detect the movement of the Cavalry Corps on the afternoon and evening of June 8.

South of the river, Stuart's pickets were organized to provide only early warning. Two troopers were posted at Beverly Ford, and only a handful at Kelly's Ford. Unlike the morning of March 17, when reinforced pickets from the 2nd Virginia delayed General William Averell's attack for an hour, the Confederates at the fords on the morning of June 9 were incapable of offering any real resistance. Nonetheless, they fulfilled their assigned duty. In keeping with established practices, the pickets were mounted and thus able to flee from the Union advance guard and carry word of the attack back to their commanders.

As news of the Union attack was carried to the rear, the Confederate response was mixed. Grumble Jones' Virginians reacted aggressively, consistent with their training and drill. Captain Bruce Gibson, on picket guard with his company, attempted to delay Davis' brigade. Flournoy, reacting instinctively, rode immediately with the 6th Virginia to the aid of Gibson. Marshall, whose 7th Virginia was Jones's "grand guard" and ready to deploy on short notice, brought his men into the fight soon after the alarm was sounded. On the other hand, the reaction at Kelly's Ford, where elements from Beverly Robertson's brigade were posted, was less effective. Robertson's pickets escaped Gregg's infantry "forlorn hope" and provided warning, but the picket guard offered no resistance. This perhaps reflects a different standard of training, as well as lower combat proficiency, within Robertson's two regiments. Recently arrived from North Carolina, neither the 4th nor the 5th North Carolina had seen much action. As previously described, once on the scene Robertson failed to engage either Duffié's or Gregg's division, an example of questionable tactical judgment. Significantly, however, the most serious criticism against Stuart—that his men had been caught in their camps with horses grazing and weapons unloaded—was a complete fabrication. All of Stuart's cavalry deployed from their camps before entering the battle.

The sole Confederate unit to be surprised in its camp was the Stuart Horse Artillery Battalion. Both Stuart, and Major Robert Beckham, the battalion commander, may be fairly criticized for the placement of the artillery on the night of June 8. Clearly, it was imprudent for artillery to bed down nearer the fords than the cavalry, and but for Flournoy's rapid reaction on the morning of June 9 (and Lieutenant R.O. Allen's good aim), the bulk of the guns would likely have been lost before the battle began. Unfortunately, it is not clear who actually selected the artillery's position (written orders have not been discovered, and both Stuart and Beckham were silent on the subject). It appears that since neither Stuart nor Beckham seriously contemplated a Federal attack, security was not a consideration when selecting a spot for the artillery to camp on the night of June 8. Nonetheless, although Stuart may not have picked the position for Beckham's camp, he, as the division commander was responsible for the error, whether it was his own or Beckham's.

Because Stuart's grand reviews of June 5 and June 8 were followed almost immediately by the battle on June 9, it was easy for observers to assume that there was a cause-and-effect relationship between the events—that the Federals could surprise the Confederates because Stuart was devoting his attention more to military pomp than to war fighting. There is some justification for that observance. It appears that during the first days of June, the priority of effort for Stuart's staff (and by extension, Stuart himself), was preparation for the review on June 5. As described, that review was a flamboyant affair, and while reviews were common, its extravagance exceeded the norm. The review on June 8, while large, was consistent with many other reviews conducted by both Union and Confederate units. Further, the review on June 8 was held at the request of Robert E. Lee—a request that Stuart could not refuse.

In the 1930's the Daughters of the Confederacy erected a modest monument atop Fleetwood Hill. Today many consider the battle a draw, but the Daughters of the Confederacy, in their plaque on the monument, left no doubt that they viewed the battle as a victory for JEB Stuart (Joseph W. McKinney).

Interestingly, the contemporaneous complaints about Stuart's reviews stem from relatively few sources. The "Southern Lady," being from Culpeper, likely had first-hand knowledge of the reviews (although she did not claim to be in attendance). Therefore, her letter to President Davis lends credence to an assumption that some people in Culpeper were dissatisfied with Stuart's behavior. It appears that most other critics based their opinion on what they read in newspapers, and much reporting was based upon accounts in the *Richmond Examiner*, perhaps the most influential newspaper in the South. Much of the *Examiner*'s reporting on the battle was factually inaccurate, and the editors of the paper clearly exhibited a bias against Stuart. Privately, Stuart believed that the *Examiner* was spouting malicious information obtained from one of his enemies (and he had a few). Although the motivation of the *Examiner*'s editors will probably never be known, upon objective review, one can easily conclude that the *Examiner* had an ax to grind.

Significantly, there was little criticism of Stuart — either for his extravagant reviews or his management of the battle — among senior Confederate commanders. Moreover, there is no evidence that Robert E. Lee was critical of Stuart's grand reviews. Finally, there is no indication that Lee found Stuart remiss in any way regarding the battle on June 9. With regard to Stuart's performance of duty, Lee's judgement must be weighted most heavily.

Interest in the battle at Brandy Station quickly diminished as Southern hopes and Northern fears shifted to Lee's invasion of Pennsylvania. A few hundred cavalry casualties in an inconclusive fight along the Rappahannock faded to insignificance when weighed against the twin Union victories at Vicksburg and Gettysburg three weeks later. However, after June 9, commanders, particularly Union commanders, altered the manner in which they employed cavalry, and hard fighting between mounted forces became the norm, not the exception. During the Gettysburg campaign, Union and Confederate cavalry faced off in pitched engagements at Aldie, Middleburg, and Upperville Virginia, at Hanover and Fairfield, Pennsylvania and at Gettysburg itself. By the end of the year blue and gray horsemen had fought three more times on the plains about Brandy Station. The trend toward hard fighting between cavalry, much of it with troopers dismounted, continued through 1864 with General Philip Sheridan's aggressiveness complementing that of his mentor, U. S. Grant. After the battle at Brandy Station, dead cavalrymen were a common sight. The era of the cavaliers had been supplanted by industrial age warfare.

12

Old Soldiers Never Die

Life After June 9, 1863

The Civil War continued for almost two years after the battle at Brandy Station. The pastures and fields of eastern Culpeper County were the scene of several more sizeable cavalry fights, most notably in August and October 1863. In November 1863, after an embarrassing defeat at Rappahannock Station, Lee withdrew his army south of the Rapidan River. Brandy Station became the main supply depot for the Army of the Potomac and the fields about the village became home to 120,000 of General Meade's soldiers. The following May, the armies again began to move, this time south instead of north, leading to the stalemate at Petersburg and eventually to the destruction of the Confederacy and the surrender at Appomattox.

As the conflict continued, most of the officers and men of the cavalry—both Union and Confederate—remained with their colors. Many officers progressed in grade as they displayed improved skills and as vacancies at the top opened. Others met a different fate: many were killed or felled by disease; more were disabled by wounds and invalided out of the service; and some fell into enemy hands as prisoners of war. A few of the men who fought at Brandy Station on June 9, 1863 went on to truly distinguished military careers, many more were noteworthy, and almost all did their duty.

As the Civil War ended, most of the officers and men of the cavalry returned home to take up the lives they had left more than four years earlier. This was naturally a much more difficult task for Southerners than those from the North. Much of the South's industry had been destroyed, the farms neglected, and the social system shattered. Instead of returning to their prewar lives, many former soldiers, their perspectives forever altered by their experiences during the war, sought new paths for their futures. A few shifted from volunteer to regular military service during the army's postwar reorganization. A few entered politics, some with great success. Some obtained patronage positions—who better to be a postmaster or United States consul than a distinguished veteran?

For most of the senior leaders who fought at Brandy Station and a few of their men, this the rest of their stories.

Immediately after the battle at Brandy Station, Brigadier General Alfred Pleasonton began again to reorganize the Cavalry Corps. He merged the 2nd Division with the 3rd, eliminating Duffié's billet (Gregg, as the senior officer, remained in command of the new 2nd Division). Pleasonton also merged the Reserve Brigade into the 1st Division and broke up diCesnola's brigade, sending the Italian colonel back to the command of the 4th New York Cavalry, while distributing that regiment and the two other regiments of the brigade to other brigades. By these moves, Pleasonton marginalized two of the three senior foreign-born officers under his command (the third, Wyndham, had been evacuated to Washington to recover from his leg wound and was replaced in brigade command by Colonel John McIntosh, of the 3rd Pennsylvania Cavalry).[1]

Pleasonton also made efforts to promote a few of his favorites. He arranged for the promotion of Merritt and Custer to brigadier general, each with a date of June 29, 1863 (Merritt, who was senior and had demonstrated competence in regimental command on Yew Ridge, ranked ahead of Custer on the list). Additionally, Pleasonton secured a general's star, also effective on June 29, for Captain Elon Farnsworth, who took command of the 8th Illinois upon the wounding of more senior officers Alpheus Clark and George Forsyth at Beverly Ford.[2] At news of the promotions, Buford reportedly quipped that he would no longer send captured Confederate spies to Cavalry Corps headquarters for fear that Pleasonton might pin stars on their shoulders and make them brigadier generals of cavalry.[3]

As the Army of Northern Virginia made its way north toward Pennsylvania, Pleasonton's Cavalry Corps fought a series of pitched engagements in Fauquier County against Stuart, whose division screened the movement of Lee's infantry up the Shenandoah Valley. Pleasonton, never very adept at reconnaissance or intelligence gathering, wrote on June 18 to his former subordinate and confidant, Congressman John Farnsworth, "The raid into Pennsylvania appears to be a fizzle — & some of the negroes say it is reported that Gen. Lee is moving his troops back to Culpepper — at any rate — the valley between this and the Blue ridge has no rebel infantry in it as far as I have been able to find out & my scouts are near Snickers Gap this eve. From this I begin to think this whole business on the part of the rebels had been a grand reinforcement to Vicksburg from their Army here."[4] Pleasonton added that his assessment was confirmed (at least to him) by the Richmond newspapers and asked that Farnsworth, who had resigned his brigadier general's commission to take a seat in the US. Congress, advise President Lincoln. Despite his ineptitude as a scout, Pleasonton secured for himself a promotion to major general on June 22, 1863.

During the battle of Gettysburg, the cavalry of the Army of the Potomac was actively engaged daily. However, Pleasonton positioned himself near Meade's headquarters and left the actual fighting to his brigadiers.

After the war, Pleasonton resigned from the Army, unhappy that he was offered only a major's commission in the ensuing reorganization. A life-long bachelor of some means, Pleasonton passed the time regaling friends and acquaintances with stories of the war (Library of Congress).

Pleasonton remained in command of the Cavalry Corps until March 1864, when Meade, embarrassed by the failure of the Dahlgren raid on Richmond, and angered that Pleasonton's testimony before the Joint Congressional Committee on the Conduct of the War was critical of his performance as commander of the Army of the Potomac, arranged Pleasonton's transfer to Missouri. In the West, Pleasonton performed credibly, defeating Stirling Price in the battle of Westport and again at Marais de Cygnes in October 1864. Although Pleasonton was breveted to brigadier general in the regular army for those actions, his victories went mainly unnoticed in the East and did little to improve his reputation.[5]

After the war, Pleasonton was scorned by the army establishment. As the volunteer units were disbanded, Pleasonton was offered a commission as a lieutenant colonel of infantry, which he turned down, preferring to remain in the cavalry. However, the War Department only offered Pleasonton a major's billet in the mounted service, and worse, the former major general would be forced to serve under a colonel and lieutenant colonel who were once junior to him.[6] An indignant Pleasonton requested to be retired at his volunteer grade. However, the War Department did not approve the request and the disgruntled general resigned instead.

Custer, by death at the Little Big Horn in 1876, gained fame that far exceeded that of his wartime contemporaries. His wife, Elizabeth, recalled that Custer, shown here as a lieutenant with his dog, loved animals (Library of Congress).

Afterward, Pleasonton held several minor civilian appointments, and served briefly as Commissioner of Internal Revenue. In his tenure there, he became embroiled in a controversy with the Secretary of the Treasury and was suspended. For two years Pleasonton was employed as the president of the Terre Haute and Cincinnati Railroad, after which he retired in Washington, D.C. In Washington, the confirmed bachelor lived a strange life, sleeping during the days and spending his nights in a bar entertaining patrons with his reminiscences of the war. Pleasonton died, perhaps of throat cancer, on February 17, 1897. In accordance with his wishes, Pleasonton was buried in Congressional Cemetery without military ceremony. His body was dressed in civilian clothing, not the natty uniforms he preferred as a cavalry commander.[7]

Joseph Hooker's *aide*, Ulrich Dahlgren, who delivered to Pleasonton the plan for the battle at Brandy Station and who had joined the charge of Rush's Lancers at Saint James Church, continued his quest for glory. At Hagerstown on July 5, Dahlgren, still a supernumerary, was shot in the leg while leading two squadrons of the 18th Pennsylvania cavalry. The wound was severe, requiring the leg to be amputated. Nonetheless, seven months later the newly promoted Colonel Dahlgren returned to duty. Dahlgren, who in May 1863 had recommended that Hooker launch a cavalry raid on Richmond, apparently retained his fixation on the Rebel capital. In February 1864, he was killed — shot five times — on the outskirts of Richmond during an unsuccessful raid to free Federal prisoners held in Libby Prison. Papers allegedly found on Dahlgren's body advocated burning the city and killing Jefferson Davis — "unchristian and atrocious acts," in the words Robert E. Lee.[8] The raid was an embarrassment to all who were involved.

Captain and *aide de camp* George Armstrong Custer was praised by Pleasonton in his official report for "conspicuous gallantry" on June 9, and rewarded, as mentioned, with a general's star later in June. In the lore of the battle at Brandy Station, Custer's role in the fighting grew. It was later commonly recounted that after Grimes Davis was shot dead, Custer assumed command of Davis' 1st Brigade. Although he did not personally make that claim, it is likely that Custer did not discourage such exaggeration. As a general officer, Custer showed that he was an aggressive fighter. However, at times Custer's military judgment was questionable, as evidenced by events at the Little Big Horn thirteen years later. Elizabeth Custer later wrote of "Autie," her husband: "He reverenced religion, he showed deference to the aged, he honored womankind, he was fond of children and devoted to animals. His domestic life was characterized by a simplicity, joyous contentment, and fondness for home that is surprising when it is remembered that, out of the thirty-seven years of his brief life, fourteen were spent in active warfare."[9]

Three weeks after he withdrew across the Rappahannock ending the Battle of Brandy Station, Brigadier General John Buford earned his place in history. Leading his division through Gettysburg in advance of Major General John Reynolds's corps, Buford made the fortuitous decision to dismount his cavalry and fight it out with Harry Heth's Confederate division, then approaching down the Chambersburg Pike. Since that day, armchair tacticians have speculated on the result — had Buford's troopers not delayed Heth, thereby allowing Federal infantry to initially defend west of Gettysburg, then to fall back and occupy positions on Culp's Hill and Cemetery Ridge, the outcome of the battle may have been dramatically different.

After Gettysburg, Buford continued to lead his cavalry division throughout the fall campaigns in Virginia, including two more engagements around Brandy Station. During that time Burford suffered much from fatigue and intermittent bouts of illness. Finally, in November 1863 Buford was incapacitated by typhoid. He took leave from his division, having been assigned to command of the cavalry of the Army of the Cumberland, and traveled to Washington where he convalesced in the home of his former commander, General George Stoneman. However, Buford failed to recover and he died on December 16, having that day been promoted to major general of volunteers. Supposedly Secretary of War Stanton approved the promotion only after being assured by President Lincoln that Buford was, in fact, dying. Buford, who was delirious much of that day, when told of his promotion reportedly whispered "I wish I could have lived now." One of Buford's aides signed the acceptance form since the General was unable to do so for himself.[10]

Buford's funeral in Washington was attended by many dignitaries, including President Lincoln. His remains were then transported to West Point where he was interred. Buford was the consummate professional among the cavalry generals, and his passing was much mourned by the troopers of the First Cavalry Division.

Colonel Thomas Devin, continued in brigade command through the Gettysburg Campaign, and in 1864 participated in the Dalgren raid on Richmond and in Sheridan's Valley Campaign against Jubal Early. Devin was belatedly promoted to brigadier in March 1865 and breveted to major general for meritorious service at the end of the war. Afterwards, Devin remained in the army, appointed as lieutenant colonel of the 8th Cavalry in 1866, and promoted to colonel of the 3rd Cavalry in 1877. However, Devin was in poor health, and in early 1878 he returned home to New York where he died on April 4 of that year.[11]

Almost immediately after the battle at Brandy Station, Major Charles Jarvis Whiting was removed from command of the Reserve Brigade and reassigned to command the recruit depot in Portland, Maine, his home state. On November 5, 1863, Whiting was dismissed from the service for "using contemptuous and disrespectful words against the President of the United States." (Whiting had a reputation for railing against politicians whom he believed were responsible for the war.)[12] However, on May 28, 1866, Whiting was restored to his former grade and appointed to fill the first major's billet that became vacant in the cavalry. From December 1866 until May 1869, Whiting served with the 3rd Cavalry in New Mexico. He was then promoted to lieutenant colonel in the 6th Cavalry and served in Texas with that regiment until January 1871. That year the War Department reduced the size of the army, and Whiting was placed on a list of "supernumeraries," or excess officers, and mustered out of the service. Whiting returned to Castine, Maine, where he lived quietly, content to show off his Indian artifacts, collected on duty in the west. Whiting died in Castine on January 1, 1890.[13]

After Brandy Station, Brigadier General Adelbert Ames continued to serve the Union with distinction, rising to brevet major general and command of an infantry division by the war's end. Following the war, Ames took a year's leave to tour Europe. Upon returning to the United States, Ames reverted to his regular rank — lieutenant colonel — and duty in the 24th Infantry, one of the army's two black infantry regiments. Ames was posted to the Reconstruction South as an assistant inspector general and then as the military commander at Vicksburg. In June 1868, Ames left the army for a political career — an appointment as provisional governor of Mississippi conferred by U.S. Grant, then the Secretary of War. In 1870, Ames married Blanche Butler, the daughter of Benjamin Butler, former Major General and then-Congressman from Massachusetts. Six hundred guests attended their wedding. That same year, the Mississippi legislature, in which the Republicans held a majority, elected Ames to the U.S. Senate for a term ending in 1875.[14]

In 1873, Ames ran for governor of Mississippi as a Republican and was elected. His tenure as chief executive of the state was marked by racial violence and civil unrest. Ames favored deploying Federal troops to regain order, but the nation was by then tired of "reconstructing" the South. In the elections of 1876, the Democratic Party took control of the Mississippi legislature and promptly began impeachment proceedings against Ames. In a deal worked out in advance, the legislature dropped the articles of impeachment on March 28, 1876, and Ames resigned the next day.[15]

Afterwards, Ames lived quietly and privately as a businessman in Massachusetts and Florida, broken only by a brief stint as a brigadier general of volunteers during the Spanish-American War. Ames died in 1933, the last surviving general officer of the Civil War.[16]

Brigadier General David McMurtrie Gregg continued in command of a cavalry division, earning a brevet to major general of volunteers during Grant's Overland Campaign in 1864. However, in February 1865, Gregg, citing a need to attend to personal affairs, resigned from the army, confirming for many in the cavalry that he wanted to go home to his attractive wife. Perhaps, also, he was disappointed that he had received no promotions in the Regular Army and was still carried on the rolls as a captain in the 6th U.S. Cavalry. Alternatively, Gregg may have chafed at serving under Sheridan, whose favorite subordinates — Merritt and Custer — were much junior to him in grade and experience.[17]

After the war, Gregg farmed in Pennsylvania until 1874 when U.S. Grant appointed him U.S. Consul to Prague. However, neither Gregg nor his wife was happy in Prague, and after a short stint, they returned to the United States. Gregg retired again to private live, broken by a term as the Auditor General of Pennsylvania, a post to which he was elected in 1891. He remained active in veteran's affairs, wrote accounts of the Gettysburg Campaign, was a sought-after speaker, and, upon the death of Winfield Scott Hancock, became the commander of the Pennsylvania Commandery, Military order of the Loyal Legion. Gregg died on August 7, 1916, having never publicly explained the reason for his resignation from the army in 1864.[18]

After Brandy Station, Colonel Percy Wyndham went to Washington to recuperate from his wound. During Lee's invasion into Pennsylvania, Wyndham briefly commanded the roughly three thousand cavalry assigned to the defense of the capital. Afterwards, he commanded the cavalry remount depot at Giesboro until he was mustered out of the army in July 1864.[19]

For a short time, Wyndham ran a military school in New York. However, in 1866 the lure of combat drew him back to Italy where he served on Garibaldi's staff. After that war ended in 1867, Wyndham returned to the U.S. and went into the fledgling petroleum business, only to be financially ruined by an explosion at his refinery. Next Wyndham went to South Asia where he married a rich widow and engaged in several ill-conceived ventures. In Calcutta he started a comic newspaper and organized an Italian opera. He speculated in lumber in Mandalay. He then attempted to induce the Burmese government to grow cotton. In his financial endeavors, Wyndham was spectacularly unsuccessful. He lost his wife's fortune, was forced to pawn his jewels and awards to pay his debts, and was reduced to being a hanger-on at the court in Mandalay.[20]

In 1879, Wyndham embarked upon a scheme to recoup his fortunes by conducting balloon ascensions. On his first flight, and before a large crowd drawn by extensive advertising, Wyndham's balloon reached an altitude of about three hundred feet. At that point his balloon burst open, collapsed over the wicker gondola, and fell into a lake. Wyndham was killed in the crash The Rangoon *Gazette* reported that the balloon had been made of "flimsy white shirting" that when inflated showed several rents. When the rents were pointed out to Wyndham before he ascended, he cavalierly remarked that they were "nothing" and that he had ascended before in balloons with "holes the size of a man's head."[21]

Five days after Brandy Station, Colonel Judson Kilpatrick was promoted to brigadier general. Unfortunately, his performance continued to be inconsistent at best. At Gettysburg he ordered the 1st Vermont Cavalry to make an unnecessary charge across broken ground unsuitable for horsemen. Newly-promoted Brigadier General Elon Farnsworth was needlessly killed in the effort along with many of his men.

During the Bristoe Campaign in October, Kilpatrick was routed by JEB Stuart in a fiasco thereafter known as the Buckland Races. Confederates took great satisfaction from the event. The lieutenant colonel of the 3rd Virginia Cavalry recorded in his diary, "This was quite a successful affair & particularly gratifying as the braggart Kilpatrick was completely outgeneraled and badly defeated."[22]

In February 1864, Kilpatrick commanded Ulrich Dahlgren's raid to Richmond to free Union prisoners of war. The raid, an utter failure and a political embarrassment, led to Kilpatrick's transfer to Sherman's army. Advised that Kilpatrick was not reliable, Sherman supposedly quipped, "I know that Kilpatrick is a hell of a damned fool, but I want just that sort of man to command my cavalry in this expedition [the march through Georgia]."[23]

In Georgia, and the Carolinas, Kilpatrick's men established more of a reputation for looting and pillaging than for fighting. Kilpatrick, ever the lecher, was accompanied by a succession of female companions, some of whom dressed in men's clothing to disguise their sex. Early in the morning of March 10, 1865, the Confederate cavalry under command of M. C. Butler attacked Kilpatrick's camp near Fayetteville, North Carolina. Surprise was complete and Union losses were nineteen men killed, sixty-eight wounded, and one hundred three missing. Reportedly, Kilpatrick, who had been spending the night in the plantation house with his mistress, came out onto the porch where he was accosted by a Confederate officer. The Confederate, waving his pistol, demanded to know who was in charge. Thinking quickly, Kilpatrick pointed to one of his troopers and responded, "There he goes, [the one getting away] on the black horse." As the Confederate spurred his horse after the fleeing trooper, Kilpatrick, clad in his nightshirt and drawers, jumped over the porch railing and hid in the bushes until the Confederates withdrew.[24] Despite his failings, Kilpatrick was breveted to major general and promoted to major general of volunteers at the end of the war.

After the war, Kilpatrick resigned his regular commission as captain of artillery, became active in politics, and served as ambassador to Chile in the Johnson and Garfield administrations. Between postings, he earned his living giving lectures on Sherman's March to the Sea. Kilpatrick died in Chile in December 1881 and was later buried at West Point.[25] Kilpatrick had two daughters by his second wife. Unfortunately for historians, the younger daughter destroyed Kilpatrick's personal papers and letters shortly before her death in 1955.[26]

Pleasonton, prejudiced against foreign-born officers and dissatisfied with Colonel Alfred N. A. Duffié's performance on June 9, removed the Frenchman from division command in the reorganization that immediately followed the battle of June 9. In further humiliation, Pleasonton did not assign Duffié to brigade command, although he was pending promotion to brigadier. Instead, Duffié reverted to command of his regiment, the 1st Rhode Island Cavalry.

On June 17, Duffié was ordered to march with his regiment from Manassas through Thoroughfare Gap to Middleburg, where he was to camp for the night. On the 18th Duffié was to proceed to Purcellville, and from there continue north through Loudoun County. Unfortunately, Stuart's cavalry was in strength between Aldie and Upperville. Upon reaching Middleburg, Duffié came upon Stuart's headquarters, which he drove from the town. Duffié sent messengers to Kilpatrick in Aldie asking for help, but none was sent. After a few hours of skirmishing, Duffié withdrew his men from Middleburg into some nearby woods, there to hide for the night — horses saddled, no fires, and no talking allowed. On the following morning, Duffié attempted to extricate his regiment, but as the troopers moved onto the road they found themselves surrounded by Confederate cavalry. Duffié ordered a charge, but "in tone and manner [he] implied no hope of success. The men wavered, broke, and jumped their horses over a stone wall into a wheat field on the east side of the road, and, through the wavering wheat the regiment rushed in confusion with the rebels close after them." During the pursuit, the 1st Rhode Island was virtually destroyed. Duffié made it to Centreville with four officers and twenty-seven enlisted men. He reported losses from the regiment at twenty officers and two hundred forty-eight men. Over the next several days, a few other officers and men straggled into Union lines, leaving a total loss in the regiment of six killed, twenty wounded, and one hundred seventy captured.[27]

On June 23, Duffié was promoted to brigadier and transferred to the Department of West Virginia where he effectively commanded a cavalry division through the remainder of 1863. In 1864 he participated in campaigns in the Shenandoah Valley and operated against Early during that Confederate's raid into Maryland. On October 25, 1864, Duffié, while returning to his headquarters from a meeting with Sheridan, was captured. The circumstances were particularly ignominious. Duffié was accompanying a large, heavily escorted wagon train down the Valley Pike. He became impatient with the slow pace of the wagon train, and near Bunker Hill, about five miles north of Winchester, went on ahead in his "two-horse light spring wagon" with an escort of about a dozen cavalrymen. Unbeknownst to Duffié, John Mosby and a party of his partisan rangers were observing. As the rangers swept onto the Pike, the Union cavalry escort fled and Duffié's wagon went into a ditch. Mosby and his men seized the Frenchman and hustled him off to Richmond. Sheridan, highly displeased, wrote to Halleck, "I respectfully request his [Duffié's] dismissal from the service. I think him a trifling man and a poor soldier. He was captured by his own stupidity."[28]

From Richmond, Duffié was transferred to a prison camp near Danville, Virginia, where he attempted to organize an escape. However, Duffié's plan failed and he remained a prisoner until paroled in February 1865. After his exchange in March, Duffié was posted to Arkansas, then sent to Kansas where, on June 5, 1865, he was mustered out of the service.

Immediately after the war, Duffié lived on Staten Island where his wife had family. In 1869, Duffié was appointed by President Grant as the U.S. Consul at Cadiz, Spain, where he served until his death from tuberculosis in November 1880. Duffié's body was returned to the United States and buried on Staten Island. Later, the veterans of his regiment took up a collection for a monument to their former commander. Over time they raised $1,129.96, mostly in small donations. In July 1890 the veterans of the 1st Rhode Island Cavalry dedicated a modest monument to Duffié at the North Burying Ground in Providence.[29]

Colonel John Irwin Gregg continued to command a cavalry brigade in the Army of the Potomac until the end of the war. He was wounded seriously at Deep Bottom in 1864, and was breveted to major general of volunteers, but was never appointed to a position in that grade. After the war he served first as the Inspector General of Freedmen in Louisiana, and in July 1868 he was promoted to colonel in the 8th Cavalry. Gregg served mostly on the Pacific Coast until he was retired for disability in April 1878. He died in Washington, D.C. in January 1892.[30]

Less than two weeks after Brandy Station, Colonel Luigi diCesnola, who may or may not have participated in the battle, was again arrested, this time for insubordination. DiCesnola, easily slighted, had publicly expressed dissatisfaction that junior officers were promoted

Alfred Duffié was appointed U.S. Consul to Cadiz, Spain, a post he held until his death in November 1880. Although Duffié is buried on Staten Island, New York, the men of the 1st Rhode Island dedicated a monument to him in the North Burying Ground in Providence, Rhode Island (John E. McKinney).

over him. However, soon after diCesnola was placed under arrest, the 4th New York became hotly engaged with Stuart's cavalry at Aldie, Virginia. DiCesnola was released from arrest that he might lead his regiment in a charge against a Confederate artillery position.

DiCesnola led several charges, all of which failed to drive the Confederates from the field. During the final charge of the day, diCesnola was wounded — saber blow to the head and gunshot wound to the leg — and pinned under his horse that had been shot and killed. DiCesnola was left on the battlefield and after dark was taken prisoner by Confederates scavenging for weapons. He spent ten months as a prisoner of war, an experience which prompted him to write a book about his life in Libby Prison.[31] After being exchanged, diCesnola returned to command of the 4th New York and remained in that position until he was mustered out with his regiment in September 1864.[32]

DiCesnola later claimed that President Lincoln had promised him a brevet to brigadier general, an action for which there is no known documentary evidence, and which would have been unlikely (the ever-disgruntled Italian had supported McClellan in the election of 1864). After the war, diCesnola eventually secured himself an appointment as the American consul to Cyprus where he spent most of his time and energy digging up and amassing a vast quantity of antiquities. By 1872 he had exported more than thirteen thousand artifacts from the island.[33]

Following his return to the United States in 1873, diCesnola sold the bulk of his remaining collection — other antiquities had been sold in Europe — to the New York Metropolitan Museum of Art. In 1879, after another trip to dig in Cyprus, diCesnola was appointed director of the museum, a position he held until his death. Eventually the provenance of many of diCesnola's artifacts were challenged and he was accused of "faking" some of his antiquities. DiCesnola, ever ready for a fight, denigrated his main accuser, a French coin collector, calling him a "charlatan, ignorant of archaeology." The Frenchman in-turn sued DiCesnola for libel. At the conclusion of the three-month trial, a major source of entertainment in New York in late 1883, the jury concluded that the Italian's remarks about the Frenchman were not libelous.[34]

In later life, diCesnola continued to assert that he was rightfully a general, but his claim was never legitimized by the Federal Government. DiCesnola had greater success documenting his gallantry, and in 1897 he was awarded the Congressional Medal of Honor for his valor at Aldie on June 17, 1863.[35] DiCesnola died in New York in on November 20, 1904, two days after attending the annual dinner of a veteran's organization. The cause of his death was listed as acute indigestion.[36]

David A. Russell, whose pick-up infantry brigade did little during the battle at Brandy Station, was even less engaged at Gettysburg. There his brigade, 3rd Brigade, 1st Division, VI Corps, suffered only two men wounded. In November 1863, however, Russell returned to the Rappahannock and distinguished himself when, in division command, he made a daring night attack to seize the fortified Confederate bridgehead on the north bank of the river near Rappahannock Station. Russell's men inflicted more than sixteen hundred casualties (mostly captured) on Major General Jubal Early's division, while losing just more than three hundred.[37] In the spring of 1864, Russell commanded his division through the Wilderness to the investment of Petersburg. In the summer, he and his division were recalled to Washington and then sent to the Valley after Early. Russell, personally leading one of his brigades, was killed instantly by a shell fragment at Opequon Creek near Winchester on September 19, 1864. He was posthumously breveted major general of volunteers for his gallantry on that date.

Of the Union officers who commanded cavalry regiments at Brandy Station, none had a more lengthy and successful career than Captain Wesley Merritt, 2nd U.S. Cavalry. Less than three weeks after the battle Merritt was promoted to brigadier general of volunteers and assumed command of what had been the Reserve Brigade. Merritt continued in command of cavalry—first at brigade, then at division level—throughout the remainder of the war. He was commanding Union troops on the field at Yellow Tavern when JEB Stuart was shot and mortally wounded.

Merritt developed a close and enduring social and professional relationship with Philip Sheridan, who had been brought east by Grant in the spring of 1864 to command the Army of Potomac's Cavalry. With respect to the social aspects of their relationship, Merritt had an advantage over some officers. Temperance was in vogue, and many officers in the Union Army, including George Custer, had pledged to abstain from alcohol. Sheridan, however, had a reputation as a hard drinker, and he and Merritt, who also shunned the temperance pledge, would share a bottle of liquor from time to time.[38]

As the war ended, Merritt was promoted to major general, but due to administrative error, George Custer's promotion to that grade predated Merritt's. Sheridan intervened with the Secretary of War, amending Merritt's promotion to maintain Merritt's seniority over Custer in the shrunken postwar army.[39] Immediately after the end of the war, Merritt took an extended leave of absence to visit Europe, the first of many trips he would make to that continent over the next forty years. Upon his return to duty, Merritt reverted to lieutenant colonel of the 9th Cavalry, one of the regiments of "Buffalo Soldiers," and was posted with his regiment to Texas. While with the 9th, Merritt helped his youngest brother, Charles,

In 1898, Wesley Merritt, shown here at the center of his staff, commanded the expedition to the Philippines to seize Manila from the Spanish (National Archives).

obtain a commission as a lieutenant in the regiment. Unfortunately Charles was not suitable as an officer and developed a drinking problem. He was convicted by courts-martial in 1879 for being drunk on duty, neglect of duty in the face of the enemy, and conduct unbecoming an officer. In Santa Fe, two weeks after being dismissed from the army, Charles killed himself.[40] Wesley Merritt, who had been promoted and assigned to command of the 5th Cavalry, was campaigning against the Ute Indians in Colorado at the time.

Merritt was again promoted to brigadier in 1887 and to major general in 1895. Troops under his direction managed the Oklahoma land rush in April 1889, and later that fall conducted the army's first large scale training maneuvers—seventeen hundred officers and men took part—in Kansas.[41] During the Spanish-American War, Merritt commanded the U.S. troops in the Philippines that captured Manila. He also served as a member of the peace commission in Paris that followed the Spanish defeat.[42]

After his retirement as second-ranking officer in the army in 1900, Merritt lived in Washington. Daniel Butterfield, Hooker's chief of staff, made a concerted effort to have Merritt awarded the Congressional Medal of Honor in recognition for his for his actions at Yew Ridge on June 9, 1863, but was not successful. Merritt, whose health failed late in life, died while visiting a spa at Natural Bridge, Virginia on December 3, 1910. He was buried at West Point.[43]

The careers of the commanders of the other regular regiments did not match Merritt's. Captain George Cram, 6th U.S. Cavalry, reverted to command of a squadron in his regiment during the Gettysburg Campaign, supplanted in regimental command by Major Samuel H. Starr. In the disastrous fight at Fairfield, Pennsylvania on July 3, Captain Cram was captured, one of 232 casualties suffered by the 6th Cavalry out of roughly 400 men engaged on that day. Cram was quickly paroled to await exchange, a fate that was preferable to that suffered by many of the others who were taken by the Confederates. After the war, Cram — still a captain — remained in the army, eventually rising to the grade of major in the 4th Cavalry.[44] Captain James Harrison, of the 5th U.S. Cavalry, suffered a bout of sunstroke immediately after the battle at Brandy Station. Unfit for active service, Harrison was transferred to the depot at Portland, Maine for six months. While there he volunteered to command troops manning a gunboat — reprising his days as a marine revenue agent — in pursuit of a steamer that had been seized by pirates. Afterward Harrison served in the Cavalry Bureau in Washington and as an inspector in Arkansas. In June 1867, while he was on duty in Mississippi, Harrison's health failed and he returned to Washington where he died that December. He had been breveted for his actions at Hanover Courthouse, again for his actions at Antietam, and cited for gallantry at Beverly Ford.[45] Captain Richard S. C. Lord, whose 1st U.S. Cavalry covered Buford's withdrawal across the Rappahannock on June 9, was breveted to major for gallantry at Gettysburg where he was severely wounded. After two months' convalescence and five months duty in Washington, Lord returned to command of the 1st U.S. Cavalry. In April 1865, he was breveted a second time for gallantry at Five Forks. After the war, Lord served briefly on recruiting duty and for three months on garrison duty in California. In June 1866, Lord took leave to travel home to Ohio where he died of consumption that October.[46]

The only regular officer commanding a volunteer cavalry regiment at Brandy Station, Colonel Josiah Kellogg, 17th Pennsylvania, did not enjoy a long career, a consequence of poor health. Kellogg, a classmate of Merritt's at West Point, resigned his volunteer commission in December 1864, and on February 6, 1865, was retired for disability resulting from "disease contracted in the line of duty." After the war, Kellogg served as a civilian instructor at West Point, and then worked as a professor of civil engineering and tactics at Rutgers University. Despite his disabilities, Kellogg lived to the age of 82, dying in Illinois in 1919.[47]

Two cavalry commanders died as a direct result of their participation in the fighting at Brandy Station. Major Robert Morris, Jr., whose horse fell at a ditch during the charge of Rush's Lancers at Saint James Church, was captured and taken to Richmond where he was confined in Libby Prison. He died there of disease on August 12, 1863. He was twenty-seven years old at the time of this death.[48] Major Alpheus Clark, who was shot in the left hand on the Beverly Ford Road while leading the 8th Illinois, was evacuated to Washington. Although the wound did not appear particularly serious, complications developed. Clark died of his wound July 5, 1863.[49]

Two cavalry commanders were killed in action later in the war. Colonel Calvin Douty, who at Fleetwood led the men from Maine in their first regimental charge, was shot and killed at Aldie a week later. At the time, he was at the head of his regiment leading it in its second charge. Captain Seymour Conger, of the 3rd West Virginia, returned with his squadron to West Virginia in November 1863. He was promoted to major before he was killed leading a charge at Moorefield on August 7, 1864. William Averell, Conger's commanding general, wrote that the young major "found death as he had always wished, in the front of battle, with heart and hand intent upon the doing of his duty."[50]

Of the volunteer officers who commanded cavalry regiments at Brandy Station, only one served as a general officer during the course of the war. Lieutenant Colonel Henry Davies, whose 2nd New York was driven off the slopes of Fleetwood by Wade Hampton's charging regiments, was promoted to colonel of the regiment shortly after the battle. In September 1863 Davies was promoted to brigadier and served in brigade and divisional command until the end of the war, when he was promoted to major general. Davies resigned in January 1866 and returned to his law practice in New York City, serving several years as the assistant district attorney for the Southern District of New York. Davies was a prolific writer and authored a biography of his former commander, Philip Sheridan.[51]

In 1865 the Federal Government recognized the meritorious and faithful service of more than one thousand three hundred officers, rewarding them with brevet promotions to brigadier general (in contrast, there were only 583 general officers, brevet or otherwise, who served in-grade during the war). While the thirteen hundred breveted officers never served as brigadiers, and earned no additional pay, for the remainder of their lives, they could be correctly addressed by the honorific title, "General."

Included in the group of officers honored with brevets to brigadier were eight men who commanded cavalry regiments at Brandy Station. Major Edmund Pope, 8th New York, was promoted to colonel of his regiment before being breveted. After the war he moved to Minnesota where he died in 1906. Lieutenant Colonel Greeley Curtis, 1st Massachusetts, returned to Boston after the war to continue his career as an engineer and architect. Additionally, he served for two years as the city's Fire Commissioner. Curtis died in Boston in 1897. Major William Stedman, 6th Ohio Cavalry, was promoted to colonel of his regiment on January 1, 1864. Stedman, who made it through the war unscathed, had a close call on June 24, 1864. In fighting near Charles City, a bullet struck Stedman's boot heel just as his horse, "Putman" was shot in the nose. Reacting to the pain of his wound, "Old Put," as the horse was called, wheeled about several times, almost throwing Stedman to the ground. Fortunately, Stedman was uninjured and the horse recovered. In October 1864, Stedman mustered-out of the army at the end of three years' service due to poor health. Both he and Putman returned to Ohio. Once home, Stedman returned to farming and politics, accepting an appointment in 1868 to fill a vacant seat in the Ohio Senate. In 1869, President Grant appointed Stedman as U.S. Consul to Santiago, Cuba. Unfortunately, Stedman contracted Yellow Fever and died on July 6, just a week after assuming his post. Despite the fact that Stedman's remains were buried in Cuba, his funeral was held in Randolph, Ohio on August 6, 1869. Fellow politician, former general, and personal friend James A. Garfield delivered the lengthy oration.[52] Stedman's remains were never returned from Cuba. Lieutenant Colonel John Thompson, 1st Rhode Island, was appointed colonel of the regiment two weeks after Brandy Station. In March 1864 he resigned his commission to accept the colonelcy of the 1st New Hampshire Cavalry when that regiment was formed. After the war Thompson returned to Chicago and resumed the practice of law. He died there in 1888. Lieutenant Colonel William Doster, 4th Pennsylvania, led his regiment effectively during the Gettysburg Campaign. However he contracted typhoid fever and his debilitation led him to resign his commission in October 1863. Again a civilian, Doster returned to the practice of law, initially in Washington where he had served as a provost marshal. While there, he was appointed defense counsel for Lincoln conspirators Lewis Payne and George Atzerodt. After that trial Doster returned to his hometown of Bethlehem, Pennsylvania, married, and with his wife traveled extensively, making at least thirty-four visits to Europe.[53] Between his travels, Doster practiced law, was active in banking, and intermittently worked on a book, *Lincoln and Episodes of the Civil War*, which he completed four years before his death in 1919.[54] Lieutenant Colonel James Deems, 1st Maryland, was mustered out of the service in November 1863 at the end of his three-year term, although he later served as inspector general for cavalry on the staff of Major General Franz Sigel. After the war, Deems returned to his music career and composed several patriotic songs. He died in Baltimore in 1901.[55] Colonel John Taylor, 1st Pennsylvania, continued to serve with the cavalry until he was mustered out of the service. After the war he took up farming and livestock trading in his home state. He died in 1914.⁵⁶ Lieutenant Colonel William Irvine, who was captured by the men of Cobb's Legion on the southern slope of Fleetwood was eventually paroled and exchanged. Afterward, having experienced the rigors of captivity first-hand, he became an advocate for the better treatment of prisoners held in the South. Irvine was promoted to colonel in February 1864, but never mustered in that grade, being on courts-martial duty or absent sick. He was mustered out of the army at the end of his three-year term of service in December 1864, four months before being breveted to brigadier. After the War, Irwin served two years as the Adjutant General of New York. He then moved to San Francisco and returned to the practice of law. He died in San Francisco in 1882.⁵⁷

Two of Pleasonton's cavalry commanders ended the war as brevet colonels. In October 1864, Major William Beardsley, 6th New York, completed his three years of service and was mustered out as a major. Six months later, in March 1865, Beardsley was commissioned as lieutenant colonel of the 26th New York Cavalry, a regiment raised for duty on the border with Canada. Only five companies of the regiment were mustered into service before the regiment was disbanded in the summer of 1865. Nonetheless, Beardsley earned himself a brevet to colonel of New York Volunteers for his service.⁵⁸ Lieutenant Colonel Edward Jones, 3rd Pennsylvania, was promoted to colonel of his regiment in August 16, 1864, but never served at that grade. He was mustered out with his regiment as a lieutenant colonel on August 24, 1864.

Three cavalry officers who commanded at Brandy Station failed to be officially promoted to the grade of colonel. Major William Martin, who commanded the five companies of the 9th New York that fought at Brandy Station and was wounded by a ball to the shoulder during the battle, resigned his major's commission on December 8, 1863.⁵⁹ Major William Frye, 16th Pennsylvania, was breveted to lieutenant colonel before being discharged at the end of the war. Major William S. McClure, 3rd Indiana Cavalry, who was given command of the 1st Division's 1st Brigade after Davis was killed, led his regiment through the Gettysburg Campaign. Later in the war, the governor of Indiana appointed McClure as colonel of a newly raised cavalry regiment, the 9th Indiana. McClure resigned his commission in the 3rd Indiana to accept the more senior position in the 9th. However, upon learning that the governor had appointed all the officers of the regiment, including its adjutant (customarily the prerogative of the commander), McClure resigned. Since McClure had never mustered as a colonel, he was officially considered to have declined the appointment, and was discharged from the volunteers as a major. McClure returned to Madison, Indiana where he served four years as a revenue collector, engaged in private business, and was active in veterans' affairs and local politics. He died on January 11, 1900.⁶⁰

Major Henry Whelan, who led Rush's Lancers after its commander, Major Robert Morris Jr., was unhorsed and captured, continued in command through the summer. He was promoted to lieutenant colonel in September 1863, but never mustered in that grade. Always in poor health, Whelan left the regiment on sick leave after the Mine Run Campaign in November 1863. He never returning to the regiment, and died of pulmonary disease in Philadelphia on March 2, 1864. The regimental historian noted that Whelan "was distinguished in the regiment for his soldierly qualities, his manly preference, and courteous manners; he was a strict disciplinarian in camp and a brave and judicious leader in the field, a man in whom the war developed great thoughtfulness of character and earnestness of purpose."⁶¹

Major Benjamin Stanhope of the 6th Ohio, who led the advance guard of Duffié's Division into Stevensburg, only to be run out of the town by Frank Hampton and the South Carolinians, was wounded at Aldie on June 17. Stanhope, whose arm was shattered by a ball, died on June 25.⁶²

Captain Henry Sawyer, the commander of Company K, 1st New Jersey Cavalry, who was unhorsed and captured on Fleetwood Hill, was taken by train to Richmond and placed in Libby Prison. Unfortunately for the captain, before he could be exchanged, General Ambrose Burnside, in department command in Ohio, ordered the execution of Confederate Captains William Corbin and T. G. McGraw, who had been caught recruiting men in Kentucky. In response, Confederate authorities conducted a lottery among the Union captains being held at Libby Prison and selected two, Sawyer, and John Flynn, of the 51st Indiana Infantry, to be executed in reprisal. Sawyer and Flynn were allowed to write home, and Sawyer's description of his plight made him a *cause celebre* in his home state. The Federal government responded by holding Rooney Lee and the son of Brigadier General John Winder, the provost marshal of Richmond hostage, both to be hanged if Sawyer and Flynn were executed. The situation was eventually defused, and in March 1864, Sawyer and Flynn were paroled. Sawyer, who had been promoted to major while in captivity, continued to serve in the 1st New Jersey until he was discharged. After the war he worked as a hotel manager and owner at Cape May, New Jersey, and Wilmington, Delaware. Sawyer died on October 16, 1893.[63]

Lieutenant Colonel Charles Smith, a teacher and law student who, with Colonel Douty missing, led the 1st Maine back from its spectacular charge at Fleetwood, was promoted and appointed to command of the regiment after Douty was killed at Aldie. Smith remained in command of the 1st Maine through the remainder of the war. After the end of hostilities, Smith returned to Maine where he served briefly in the state senate. Military life apparently suited Smith, and in 1866 he entered the regular army as colonel of the 27th Infantry Regiment (later the 19th Infantry). In 1867, Smith received two brevets: to brigadier for gallantry at Sayler's Creek in April 1865; and to major general for meritorious service throughout the war. Smith retired as colonel of his regiment in 1891— promotions were slow in the postwar army— and took up residence in Washington, D.C., where he remained active in veterans' affairs. In 1895, Smith was awarded the Congressional Medal of Honor for gallantry in action at St. Mary's Church on June 24, 1864. Smith died in Washington in 1902 and was buried at Arlington Cemetery.[64]

Two of the infantry regimental commanders served as general officers later in the war. Adin Underwood continued in command the 33rd Massachusetts Infantry when the regiment was sent to Tennessee with the XI Corps after Gettysburg. He was seriously wounded in October 1863, struck in the upper leg by a musket ball that shattered the femur. Contrary to the practice common at the time, doctors did not amputate the leg. However, when healed, the injured leg was four inches shorter than the healthy leg, leaving Underwood crippled for life. Because of his wound, Underwood never returned to field duty. Nonetheless, he was promoted to brigadier in November 1863, and breveted to major general in August 1865. After the war, Underwood served as the surveyor of the port of Boston until his death in 1888.[65] Colonel Hiram Burnham, 6th Maine, was promoted to brigadier general in April 1864, only to be killed on September 29, 1864, leading a probe against Fort Harrison in the defenses around Richmond.[66]

Three of the infantry commanders were honored with brevet promotions to brigadier general but never served in that grade. Lieutenant Colonel Martin Flood, 3rd Wisconsin, farmed and was active in politics after the war. From 1868 until 1871, he was employed as the President of the Board of Public Works in New Orleans, Louisiana. Flood died in Warsaw, Illinois in July 1873.[67] After the war, Colonel William Hoffman, 56th Pennsylvania, returned to Philadelphia and earned a living as a hosiery merchant while serving as a general in the Pennsylvania National Guard. He died in 1902.[68] Colonel A. Van Horne Ellis of the 124th New York, who commanded the detachments from the 124th and the 86th New York at Brandy Station, was shot through the head leading a charge on July 2 at Gettysburg. In official reports, he was characterized as "one of those dashing and chivalrous spirits that we frequently read of, but seldom encounter in real life." On February 20, 1869, he was posthumously honored with a brevet to brigadier general of volunteers. Ellis' promotion was the last official general officer brevet of the Civil War.[69]

In addition to Burnham and Ellis, three other infantry regimental commanders who fought at Brandy Station were killed later in the war. Lieutenant Colonel Edward Cross, the former editor and Mexican revolutionary — Cross had served briefly under Benito Juarez in Sonora before the Civil War — who commanded the 5th New Hampshire and a detachment from the 81st Pennsylvania, was killed at Gettysburg. Because of Cross's bravery at Fair Oaks and Antietam, the officers and men of the 5th New Hampshire had taken up a subscription and ordered a sword, watch, and pair of gold spurs for their commander. Unfortunately, the presentation items were delivered to the regiment after Cross' death. The sword, watch and spurs were instead presented to Cross' family.[70] In April 2004, the governor of New Hampshire posthumously promoted Cross to brigadier general in the state militia.[71] Lieutenant Colonel Charles Mudge also fell at Gettysburg, leading the 2nd Massachusetts in a charge against a Confederate breastwork on Culp's Hill during the third day of the battle. Major Henry Truefit, who in the absence of more senior officers was again serving in command of the 119th Pennsylvania, fell at the Bloody Angle at Spotsylvania on May 12, 1864.

Colonel William Robinson, the Mexican War veteran and former gold prospector in command of the 2nd Wisconsin, resigned his commission at Petersburg in July 1864. He returned to Wisconsin and farmed for ten years, and was then was appointed U.S. Consul to Madagascar, where he served for twelve years. Afterwards, Robinson returned to Wisconsin and went into the coal business. Robinson died on April 27, 1903 and was buried in the cemetery at Fort Lewis, Washington, where his son, Brigadier General William Robinson, Jr. (West Point, Class of 1869) was serving.[72] Lieutenant Colonel Francis M. Cummins, 124th New York, was wounded at Gettysburg, earning there a promotion to colonel of his regiment, a billet vacated by the death of A. Van Horne Ellis. Cummings was wounded again on May 6, 1864 at the Wilderness and subsequently discharged for disability on September 19, 1864.[73] Major Jacob Lansing, who commanded the 86th New York, was promoted to lieutenant colonel of his regiment in August 1863. He was wounded at the North Anna River on May 24, 1864, and the following month promoted to colonel. However, he was never mustered in that grade before being discharged in November 1864 at the end of his three-year enlistment.[74]

Two artillery officers who commanded batteries at Brandy Station were breveted to brigadier general in 1865. Captain William Graham, K Battery, 1st U.S. transferred to the volunteers and served as commander of the 2nd D.C. Infantry, earning his brevet more for service in that branch than the artillery (Graham was also the nephew of Major General Meade). Graham remained in the army after the war and was appointed major general of volunteers during the Spanish American War, retiring as a brigadier general of regulars in 1898. He died near Annapolis, Maryland in 1916 and was buried in Congressional Cemetery in the District of Columbia.[75] After Brandy Station, Captain Alexander C. M. Pennington, M Battery, 2nd U.S., whose fire struck down William Farley and M. C. Butler at Stevensburg, obtained a volunteer commission as colonel of the 3rd New Jersey Cavalry. He earned his brevet for distinguished service in command of a cavalry brigade late in the war. After the war, Pennington reverted to his regular grade, captain of artillery. After service in the Spanish American War, Pennington retired as a brigadier general in 1899. He died in November 1917 in New York City and was buried in the cemetery at West Point.[76] Finally, the artillery officer who saw the hardest fighting on June 9, Captain Joseph Martin, whose New York battery was overrun three times and finally lost its guns to Lomax's Virginians, continued to serve in command of his battery. Demonstrating that it was difficult to gain advancement in the artillery, Martin was mustered out in February 1865 at Harpers Ferry still holding the grade of captain.[77]

After Brandy Station, JEB Stuart continued to command the cavalry of the Army of Northern Virginia. His performance during the Gettysburg Campaign has been widely criticized. Many historians, notably including Douglas Southall Freeman, have since speculated that Stuart may have separated himself and his three most trusted brigades from Lee's infantry and embarked on a raid through Maryland and Pennsylvania in an effort to burnish a reputation that had been tarnished by the events of June 9.

While one can legitimately criticize the wisdom of Stuart's excursion leading from the suburbs of Washington to the Susquehanna, there is no doubt that he and his cavalry's collective performance at Aldie, Middleburg, and Upperville, was highly effective, as it was when covering the withdrawal of Lee's army from Gettysburg to safety in Virginia. Stuart demonstrated that he was a talented commander, and his subordinate leaders and men showed that they possessed considerable fighting skills.

Following the Gettysburg Campaign, Robert E. Lee finally approved the reorganization long recommended by Stuart. Two cavalry divisions were formed, Fitz Lee and Wade Hampton promoted to major general, and several deserving colonels were elevated to brigadier. However, Stuart, although now essentially a corps commander, was not promoted to lieutenant general. Since the Confederate War Department never formally created a cavalry corps, such a promotion for Stuart was not officially warranted. Additionally, Lee may have believed that cavalry command inherently carried less responsibility than comparable infantry command.[78] In any event, Stuart did not publicly express disappointment that he remained a major general, although privately he would have been pleased to receive a third star.[79]

Stuart was seriously wounded at Yellow Tavern near Richmond on May 11, 1864. He was sitting on his horse behind a fence, firing his pistol at a party of Michigan cavalrymen. A dismounted Union trooper, withdrawing from the fight, fired a shot from his pistol at the Confederate commander at a range of ten to fifteen yards. The ball struck Stuart in the abdomen. As Stuart was being carried off the field, he saw several of his own men retreating and reportedly exhorted them to return to the fight, shouting, "Go back! Go back! I had rather die than be whipped."[80] Although they prevailed on the field, later that afternoon General Philip Sheridan's forces turned away from their advance on Richmond.

The following day Stuart succumbed to his wound. He was thirty-one years old. Ever the cavalier, Stuart gave two of his horses to his closest staff officers, his gold spurs to a woman in Shepherdstown, today West Virginia, and a Confederate flag he had carried hidden in the lining of his hat to a woman in Columbia, South Carolina. Stuart left his sword to his son.[81] Upon his baby daughter he had previously bestowed the name Virginia Pelham, in honor of his state and his fallen artillery commander. The *Richmond Examiner*, which had excoriated Stuart after Brandy Station, eulogized him after death as "the model of Virginia cavaliers and dashing chieftain whose name was a terror to the enemy and familiar as a household word in two continents."[82]

Stuart and Brigadier General William E "Grumble" Jones never developed an effective professional relationship, perhaps because their personalities were simply too divergent — Stuart the ebullient versus Jones the irascible. In September 1863, a verbal altercation

In addition to the obelisk, the Stuart Plot in Richmond's Hollywood Cemetery contains grave markers for JEB and Flora Stuart (she died in 1923), JEB Stuart III, and several family members who died in childhood (Joseph W. McKinney).

occurred between the two generals. While the exact substance of their confrontation was kept secret and the details remain obscure, it was sufficiently serious for Stuart to order Jones arrested and to prefer charges against him. In October 1863, Jones' courts-martial board concluded that the dour general was not guilty of disobeying an order, nor of conduct to the prejudice of good order and military discipline. However, the court did find Jones guilty of behaving with disrespect to his commanding officer. The court recommended a lenient sentence — that Jones be privately reprimanded "in consideration of the reprimand contained in a circular to Brig. Gen. Jones by Maj. Gen. Stuart which solicited [Jones'] disrespectful communication."[83]

Top: On May 30, 1907, an equestrian statue honoring Stuart was unveiled on Monument Avenue in Richmond. The crowd was estimated at 50,000 people (Library of Congress). *Bottom*: The Stuart Monument today. In bronze, Stuart is facing toward the state capitol, not the enemy to the north (Joseph W. McKinney).

Robert E. Lee, who respected Jones' ability if not his discretion, reprimanded Jones and transferred him to southwest Virginia. Presumably, this satisfied Stuart and Jones, who once quipped, in a slap at Stuart, that he wished to be reassigned somewhere near a cobbler so that he "might mend his boots, worn out not by dancing, but in the service of his country."[84]

At Piedmont on June 5, 1864, Jones was shot and killed while attempting to rally a regiment of infantrymen in his front line. Jones' body was left on the field, abandoned by his men who fled in confusion. Advancing Union troops, under command of Major General David Hunter, a Union officer much-hated by Virginians, recovered the body and returned it to Jones' friends for burial.[85]

Shot in the thigh on Yew Ridge, Brigadier General W.H.F. "Rooney" Lee went to Hickory Hill in Hanover County, Virginia, the home of the Wickham family, to be nursed by his wife, Charlotte Wickham Lee. On June 26, a raiding party consisting of the 11th Pennsylvania Cavalry and part of the 12th Illinois Cavalry, supposedly on a mission to suppress a persistent band of smugglers, raided Hickory Hill. Finding Rooney there, the Union troopers took him prisoner.[86] Rooney was taken to Fort Monroe where he was held hostage to ensure proper treatment for two Union prisoners— Sawyer and Flynn — then being held at Libby Prison in Richmond. General Henry Halleck ordered Rooney Lee and one other Confederate officer to be held in close confinement under strong guard, and to be immediately hanged should the Confederates execute Sawyer and Flynn.[87] In a letter to his wife, Robert E. Lee characterized Rooney's capture and confinement as an "additional affliction" that the Lee family must bear with "fortitude and resignation."[88]

Rooney's physical condition continued to improve in captivity. By September, the elder General Lee had received word that his son was "up and able to walk about," although with a stiff leg. Rooney's improved health was perhaps due in part to a weekly basket of provisions delivered to him by several ladies who lived near Fortress Monroe.[89] However,

During the Spanish-American War, Fitz Lee obtained a brigadier general's commission, but hostilities ended before he could deploy to Cuba. Instead of fighting, Lee served in the occupation government of the island (Library of Congress).

as Rooney recovered, Charlotte's health deteriorated. By December she was gravely ill, prompting Rooney to request a forty-eight-hour pass so that he might visit her on her deathbed. Custis Lee, Rooney's elder brother, offered to stand-in for Rooney as hostage should Federal authorities approve the pass. Senior Union officials, however, peremptorily turned down the request. Charlotte Lee died in Richmond on December 26.

Prudently, the Confederate government did not execute Sawyer and the other captain, and Rooney Lee was finally exchanged in March 1864. He was promoted to major general — at the age of twenty-six, the youngest in Confederate service — the following month and was given command of a cavalry division, a position which he held for the remainder of the war.[90]

After hostilities, Lee took to farming and served as president of the Virginia Agricultural Society. He also was active in politics, serving four years in the state senate and four years in the U.S. Congress. Lee remarried in 1867, and with his second wife, Mary Tabb Bolling of Petersburg, had two sons. Rooney Lee died in 1891, toward the end of his second term in Congress.[91] He was initially buried at Ravensworth, his estate near Burke, Virginia, but his remains were later moved to the Lee mausoleum in Lexington, Virginia.[92]

Brigadier General Fitzhugh Lee, although incapacitated by rheumatism at Brandy Station, continued to serve actively with the cavalry throughout the war. Following the formation of the Cavalry Corps in September, Lee was promoted to major general and appointed to command of a division. In a confidential note, Stuart congratulated his favorite subordinate and observed that with Lomax, Chambliss, and Wickham as his brigadiers, Lee would be fortunate to have all "pulling smoothly and together," while he had "never had a team without at least one nag addicted to the 'Studs,'" most likely an allusion to past friction between Stuart and Hampton.[93] After Hampton was sent to South Carolina in January 1865, Lee commanded the Cavalry Corps until the surrender of the Army of Northern Virginia at Appomattox.

Following the war, Lee engaged in farming and was active in veterans' organizations and in politics. He was elected governor of Virginia in 1885, but failed in a bid for the U.S. Senate in 1893. Grover Cleveland appointed Lee consul-general to Havana, a post he held when the USS Maine exploded in Havana's harbor in 1898. Lee returned to the United States, was appointed Major General of Volunteers and given command of the VII Corps. However, the war ended before the corps could deploy to Cuba. Instead, Lee went to Cuba without his corps and served in the occupation government until November 1900, when he was transferred to Omaha, Nebraska as the commander of the Department of the Missouri. In recognition of his service, the Federal Government awarded Lee a commission as brigadier general in the regular army. Lee accepted the commission on March 2, 1901 and retired the following day, thus ending a career that began with his graduation from West Point forty-five years earlier. Lee died in April 1905 and was buried in Hollywood Cemetery in Richmond.[94]

Just more than three weeks after Brandy Station, Brigadier General Wade Hampton was wounded three times — saber blows to the head and a gunshot wound to the thigh — at Gettysburg.[95] Fortunately he recovered in time be promoted to major general and given command of a division upon the formation of the Cavalry Corps.

After Stuart's death, Hampton was given command of the corps, which he led for nine months during the fighting around Richmond and Petersburg. In September 1864, Hampton led his troops on the famous "Beefsteak Raid" upon which they seized more than two thousand four hundred head of cattle and captured more than three hundred prisoners. Hampton was present at a fight at Burgess Mill on the morning of October 27, 1864, when his youngest son, Preston, was shot off his horse. Hampton's oldest son, Wade, rode to the aid of his brother and was shot in the back as he tended to him. While young Wade recovered, the wound to Preston's groin proved fatal.[96]

In January 1865, Hampton was ordered (as he had requested) to his home state with part of the Cavalry Corps to support General Joseph Johnston against Sherman. In that capacity, Hampton performed credibly, generally besting Sherman's cavalry, which was under the command of Judson Kilpatrick. Shortly before the end of the war, Hampton was promoted to lieutenant general, one of only three — the others being Nathan Bedford Forrest and Richard Taylor — in the Confederate army who had no prewar military experience.[97]

Following the surrenders of Lee and Johnston, Hampton considered going to Texas and there continuing to fight. To that end he fled west in search of President Jefferson Davis. Yet instead of meeting Davis, Hampton fortuitously found his wife in Yorkville, South Carolina. She convinced Hampton to lay down his arms and go home.[98]

The Civil War ruined Hampton financially. So without vast estates to manage, he was free to devote most of his energies to politics. He was elected the first post-Reconstruction governor of South Carolina in 1876, was reelected in 1878, and served in the U.S. Senate from 1879 until 1891. Additionally, Hampton maintained his lifelong enthusiasm for hunting and fishing. On a hunting trip in the fall of 1878, he was thrown from a mule and suffered a compound fracture in his leg. The wound became infected and consequently the leg was amputated. Afterwards, many Carolinians erroneously assumed that Hampton's wooden leg was the result of one of his five war wounds.[99]

Hampton died on April 11, 1902, at the age of eighty-four. His last words reportedly were, "God bless all my people, black and white."[100]

Brigadier General Beverly Robertson's performance at Brandy Station did much to validate the low opinion of him held by both Robert E. Lee and JEB Stuart. Further, Robertson did little to improve his standing during the Gettysburg Campaign. He had been slow moving his brigade from the Shenandoah Valley into Pennsylvania, and during the withdrawal back to Virginia had failed to block a mountain pass when instructed to do so by Stuart.[101] On July 15, 1863, Robertson, fully aware that he was out of favor with his superiors, requested that General Lee reassign him, citing the fact that the strength of his brigade had dropped to about three hundred men. Robertson asked to be returned to command of three regiments he left behind in South Carolina in May, or to be given another position commensurate with his grade. Lee endorsed Robertson's request and sent it to the War Department, recommending that Robertson be given command of a camp (yet to be established) for the rest and recuperation of cavalry units.[102] Instead, the Secretary of War arranged for Robertson's assignment as the commander of the 2nd Military District in South Carolina, a command consisting of one company of scouts, three cavalry companies, two infantry companies, and one artillery battery.[103] Robertson remained in South Carolina until Sherman swept through the state in 1865.

After the war, Robertson moved to Chicago and became an insurance agent. Later, still selling insurance, he moved to Memphis and became a respected member of that community. On December 26, 1877, the *Memphis Weekly Appeal* wrote a sketch on Robertson, commenting that, "A gallant soldier, he is equally a gallant gentleman. ... highly respected and esteemed by the people of the city."[104] In 1881, Robertson moved to Washington, D.C., where he worked selling insurance and real estate. Robertson died in Washington on November 12, 1910, at the age of eighty-three. He was buried at his family home, The Oaks, in Amelia County, Virginia.[105]

Several of Stuart's regimental commanders continued to distinguish themselves in the army and as civilians after the war.

Colonel John Chambliss, 13th Virginia, who took command of Rooney Lee's Brigade when Lee was shot, continued to command the brigade while Lee was convalescing and then imprisoned at Fortress Monroe. Chambliss was promoted to brigadier effective December 19, 1863. He was killed on August 16, 1864, during a daylong engagement with Brigadier General David McM. Gregg's cavalry division along the Charles City Road on the outskirts of Richmond. Chambliss' body fell into Union hands but was recognized by Gregg, who sent it back to Confederate lines with a note of condolence for Chambliss' widow.[106]

Colonel R. L. T. Beale, the former U.S. Representative in command of the 9th Virginia, was shot in the leg as his regiment attempted to impede the Union's advance into Culpeper Courthouse on September 13, 1863. He was taken to Orange where the bullet was removed and then convalesced for close to a

Wade Hampton, his fortune lost during the war, became a successful politician. He served the people of South Carolina as both governor and U.S. Senator (Library of Congress).

month at the home of a sister in Charlottesville. Beale then went to recuperate at his own home in Westmoreland County before returning to duty on Christmas Day, 1863. In the fall of 1864, Beale took command of a brigade in Rooney Lee's division and was promoted to brigadier general, effective January 6, 1865. After the war Beale resumed the practice of law in his hometown of Hague, Virginia, and was again elected to the US. Congress. He died in April 1893.[107]

The 4th Virginia's debacle at Stevensburg did not greatly harm the reputation of Colonel Williams Wickham. Wickham was promoted to brigadier general effective September 1, 1863. Although he had been elected to the Confederate Congress as a representative from Virginia, Wickham remained with the army, serving with General Early in the campaigns of 1864. In November 1864, Wickham finally took up his seat in Richmond where he sponsored a bill to compensate cavalry soldiers for their horses that were abandoned or disabled from wounds or hard use. After the war, Wickham served as chairman of the Hanover County board of supervisors and in the Virginia Senate for the five years before his death. He was also successful in business, being the president of both the Virginia Central and Chesapeake and Ohio railroads. Wickham died in 1888. After his death, Wickham was honored with a statue on the grounds of the Virginia Capitol.[108]

Colonel Lunsford Lomax, who had only recently been placed in command of the 11th Virginia, was promoted to brigadier with a date of rank of July 23, 1863. He commanded a brigade in Fitz Lee's division during Grant's Overland Campaign during the spring and summer of 1864, was promoted to major general in August 1864, and then given command of Jubal Early's cavalry in the Valley. At Woodstock, he was captured, but made his escape after being held only three hours. At the end of the war, Lomax was serving as commander of the Valley District. After the war, Lomax initially turned to farming in Fauquier County, Virginia, then spent the bulk of his later years in public service. He worked in the office of the Clerk of the U.S. House of Representatives, was elected president of the Virginia Agricultural College (today Virginia Tech), spent six years helping in the compilation of the *Official Records*, and served as a commissioner of the Gettysburg National Military Park. At Gettysburg, Lomax was instrumental in the placement of the Virginia Monument on Seminary Ridge. Lomax died on May 13, 1913, outlived by only one Confederate Major General.[109]

On August 1, 1863, Colonel P. M. B. Young, commander of Cobb's Legion Cavalry, was shot in the chest with a pistol ball during the third cavalry battle at Brandy Station. Fortunately his lungs were not injured and he recovered quickly. In October 1863, Young was promoted to brigadier general and placed in command of a brigade. On May 30, 1864, Young was again shot in the chest during fighting around Ashland. In this instance, the wound was much more serious and Young was unable to return to duty until late August. In November 1864, Young was sent to Augusta, Georgia, with a small party of dismounted cavalry and the following month he was promoted to major general. For the remainder of the war Young fought against Sherman's forces in Georgia and South Carolina with limited success.[110]

After the war ended, Young returned to his family home in Cartersville, Georgia, with his sister and parents to find the plantation house in disrepair and occupied by squatters. Although the Youngs regained their plantation and began farming, they were nearly impoverished. Money, for P. M. B Young, was an almost constant concern for the remainder of his life. Like many Confederate veterans, Young became active in Democratic politics. He was a delegate to three national Democratic conventions, and was elected to three terms in the U.S. House of Representatives. While serving in Washington, Young was implicated in a real estate investment scandal, and although no compelling evidence of wrongdoing was presented, Young's reputation was tarnished. In 1885, Young was appointed consul-general to St. Petersburg, Russia, by President Grover Cleveland, but he resigned his post after only a year, concerned over the effects of a second Russian winter on his health. In 1893, Young was appointed (again by Cleveland) as U.S. envoy to Guatemala and Honduras. While serving in that position, his health failed. Having returned to the United States to recuperate, Young died unexpectedly in New York City on July 6, 1896.[111] He never married.

Colonel Laurence Baker led the 1st North Carolina to Gettysburg and was there placed in command of Hampton's brigade after the South Carolinian general was wounded at Rummel's farm. On July 13, 1863, Baker was promoted to brigadier general and given command of Robertson's brigade upon that general's voluntary relief. The brigade was increased in size by the addition of the 1st North Carolina from Hampton's brigade and the 2nd North Carolina from Rooney Lee's brigade. Thus, Stuart's division finally had a brigade of North Carolina regiments commanded by a North Carolinian. On August 1, 1863, Baker was severely wounded fighting against Buford's division along the Rappahannock. He was subsequently reassigned to command of a department in North Carolina. After the war, Baker returned to Virginia where he farmed and worked as a railroad station and telegraph agent in Suffolk. He died there in 1907.[112]

Despite the *Charleston Mercury*'s assessment that he was "down and *hors du combat* for the war," Colonel M.C. Butler recovered from his wound and returned to duty. About three months after the battle Butler, who was convalescing from the loss of his leg at his home in Edgefield, South Carolina, received a telegram from the War Department asking if he were fit to retake the field. Butler went outside, mounted his favorite mare, and jumped over a few fences. Convinced he was again ready for action, Butler responded affirmatively. His commission as brigadier of cavalry arrived in the next mail.[113] For the remainder of the war, Butler commanded a brigade, then a division under Hampton. Afterwards, like his mentor Hampton, Butler went into politics. In that endeavor, Butler was highly successful, being elected to three terms in the U.S. Senate. At the outbreak of hostilities with Spain, Butler, who by then had been voted out of office, received a major general's commission in the U.S. Volunteers. The war ended, however, before Butler's division could deploy. Butler, himself, was sent to Cuba as a member of a commission to arrange the evacuation of Spanish soldiers from the island, and afterward

Matthew Calbraith Butler's loss of a leg at Stevensburg did not hamper his post war career. He served three terms as U.S. Senator from South Carolina (Library of Congress).

served on a courts-martial board appointed to try the army's quartermaster general on charges of purchasing tainted meat. After leaving the army, Butler practiced law, most notably winning damages for the Cherokee Indians in a suit against the Federal Government. He died in South Carolina in April 1909 at the age of seventy-three.[114]

Major Thomas J. Lipscomb, who took command of the 2nd South Carolina Cavalry on June 9 after Butler and Frank Hampton were wounded, was eventually promoted to colonel of the regiment, which he led through the remainder of the war, mostly in the Carolinas. During reconstruction Lipscomb became active in politics (reportedly, Lipscomb's home was burned by radicals) and was elected mayor of Columbia, South Carolina, for one term. Afterward, Lipscomb worked for twelve years as the Superintendent of the South Carolina State Penitentiary. He died on November 4, 1908, and was buried in Newberry, South Carolina.[115]

Colonel Thomas T. Munford, an officer of much promise, was never promoted to brigadier general, although he was recommended for advancement on several occasions. Munford was always passed over for other officers (named above, and Thomas Rosser) as vacancies became available. In April 1864, Stuart wrote to Munford's father promising to nominate the younger Munford for promotion to replace Wickham, who planned to resign and take up his seat in the Confederate Congress. That commitment ended with Stuart's death less than three weeks later. Before leaving Virginia for South Carolina in January 1865, Wade Hampton recommended Munford be promoted but to no avail. Fitz Lee formally nominated Munford for promotion on March 20, 1865. Robert E. Lee endorsed the recommendation, which reached the War Department on March 29. No action was taken by the Confederate Government before it fled from Richmond in April.[116]

Munford, was a highly effective regimental commander, and as a senior colonel, frequently found himself in temporary command of his brigade, and on occasion, his division. However, he also had his share of disappointments, besides Brandy Station. In September 1864, Munford, in temporary command of Fitz Lee's Brigade, was sent to the Shenandoah Valley to support Jubal Early. In October, Thomas Rosser, who pompously called himself "the savior of the Valley," was placed in command of Early's cavalry.[117] Thus Munford found himself serving under Rosser, whom he detested and who was once a far junior officer (at First Manassas, Rosser was a lieutenant while Munford was a lieutenant colonel). During the campaign that followed, Rosser accused Munford of failing to support a raid into West Virginia, placed Munford under arrest, and preferred charges against him. The courts-martial board disagreed and acquitted Munford after minimal deliberation.[118]

At the end of March 1865, Fitz Lee's division was defending part of the Confederate lines south of Petersburg. Lee placed Munford in charge for an afternoon while he and Major General George Pickett, whose infantry division was nearby, left the front to attend a shad bake at the invitation of Rosser.[119] As the three generals dined on the fresh fish, Sheridan attacked the Confederate lines with three cavalry divisions and an infantry corps. The results were disastrous for the leaderless Confederates. After the war, both Munford and Rosser wrote extensively, each attempting to affix blame for the debacle on the other.

At Appomattox, Munford, still in temporary command of Fitz Lee's Division, refused to surrender and instead slipped away with his men. He planned to continue to fight in North Carolina, but upon learning that Johnston had surrendered to Sherman, disbanded the remnants of the division in Lynchburg. Munford then went home.[120]

After the war, Munford devoted most of his efforts to managing family farms in Virginia and Mississippi. Additionally, he served four years on the VMI board of visitors and as secretary of the Southern Historical Society. During his later life, Munford devoted considerable effort to convincing the Virginia governor and state legislature to alter the state seal.[121] Munford died in February 1918 at the home of his son in Uniontown, Alabama.[122]

Thomas Munford, though never officially promoted, assumed the grade of brigadier general after the war. Shown here in old age, he wears his uniform with the United Daughters of the Confederacy Southern Cross of Honor (VMI Archives).

Despite having never been promoted in life, Munford adopted the title "General," and is frequently listed as such in print. Munford's *alma mater*, VMI, includes him among its general officer graduates.

The Gettysburg campaign cost Stuart four of his regimental commanders. Colonel Peter Evans, whose 5th North Carolina played almost no role in the battle at Brandy Station, was wounded and captured at Middleburg, Virginia, on June 21. Evans died in a hospital in Washington, DC, on July 24 of "gunshot wound of back and dysentery."[123] Colonel James H. Drake, 1st Virginia, was mortally wounded — shot in the thigh, shoulder and chest — at Kearneysville, West Virginia, on July 16, 1863. He died that night.[124] After recovering from his saber wound, Asher Harmon returned to duty with the 12th Virginia, only to be captured near Harpers Ferry on July 14. He remained a prisoner until February 1865 and never returned to duty. After the war, Harmon worked as a railroad executive in Staunton, where he died in April 1895.[125] On July 6 near Williamsport, Pennsylvania, Colonel James Lucius Davis and his 10th Virginia were covering the Confederate withdrawal. Davis ordered a charge, and in the resulting action his horse was shot and fell. Davis was last seen afoot, defending himself with his saber as his men retreated.[126] Wounded and with his ankle injured in his fall, Davis was captured. After his exchange in March 1864, Davis returned to duty, serving with his regiment and at times in temporary command of Chambliss' brigade. Davis brigadier. Until his death in 1871, Davis served as Superintendent of Public Instruction in Buckingham County. The war had been hard on the Davis family. Colonel Davis' son, Lewellyn Catesby Davis, a private in the 10th Virginia, died of disease in July 1863. James Lucius Davis, Jr., also a private in the 10th, was mortally wounded — shot in the face — at Samaria Church in June 1864.[127]

Lieutenant Colonel Thomas Marshall, who with the 7th Virginia helped blunt Buford's attack at Beverly Ford, continued to serve with his regiment after its commander, Colonel Richard Dulaney, recovered from his wounds and returned to duty. Though not in command, Marshall continued to lead a dangerous life. He had horses killed at Fairfield, Pennsylvania in July, 1863, at Culpeper Courthouse in September, 1863, and at Trevillian Station in June 1864. Marshall, who had been wounded and captured earlier in the war, was wounded again (gunshot to the shoulder) at Ream's Station on August 25, 1864. He recovered from his wound and returned to duty in October. Again in temporary command of the regiment, Marshall was withdrawing from a Union force near Nineveh, Virginia, on November 12, 1864. Marshall remarked to the officer riding next to him that, when retreating, he always worried that he would be shot in the back, an undignified wound for a cavalry commander. A moment later, Marshall said, "There it is now" as a bullet struck him in the back and exited through his chest. The thirty-eight-year-old officer died on the spot. Marshall was initially buried in the University of Virginia cemetery, but in 1866 his remains were taken to Winchester and reburied next to the grave of Turner Ashby, the first commander of the 7th Virginia.[128]

Lieutenant Colonel James Watts, in command of the 2nd Virginia at Brandy Station while Munford commanded the brigade, was shot in the right forearm — his fourth wound of the war — at Aldie on June 17 and was permanently disabled. After four months' convalescence and ten months of commanding a camp at Liberty (today Bedford), Virginia, Watts returned to duty only to be wounded again at Opequon in September 1864. Although retired for his disability, Watts again went back to limited duty at Liberty. After Appomattox, Watts fled south, eventually surrendering to Federal forces in Augusta, Georgia. Afterwards, Watts moved with his brothers (one of whom also served in the regiment) to

Lynchburg, Virginia, and established a chain of hardware stores in that city and Roanoke, Salem, Bedford, and Danville. Until his death in 1906, Watts was active in local government and was a longtime member of the Lynchburg city council.[129]

Colonel Dennis Ferebee, commander of the 4th North Carolina, was wounded on October 13, 1863, shot in the foot in a cavalry engagement on John Minor Botts' farm near Brandy Station at the start of the Bristoe Campaign. After being furloughed until the spring of 1864, he returned to his regiment and remained in command until he resigned his commission in March 1865. For the last month of the war, Ferebee served on the staff of North Carolina's governor, Zebulon Vance. Immediately after the war, Ferebee served as a delegate the State Convention of 1865. Afterward, except for a term as sheriff, Ferebee remained in private life until his death in Camden County, North Carolina in April 1886.[130]

Lieutenant Colonel Joseph Frederick Waring continued in command of the Jeff Davis Legion for the remainder of the war. After the surrender of Joseph Johnston's army, Waring went to Greensboro, North Carolina, where he accepted his parole, and returned from there to his home in Savannah, Georgia. After the war, Waring was employed as a freight forwarding agent for the Central Railroad of Georgia. In 1872, Georgia received authority from the Federal government to reconstitute its militia, and Waring was elected captain of the new Georgia Hussars, the company he had commanded in Virginia eleven years earlier. Waring died in 1876.[131]

Colonel John Logan Black commanded the 1st South Carolina in Virginia and his home state through the remainder of the war. Once Black was wounded, and the surgeon offered him a drink of whiskey. Black, however, favored prohibition, and responded, "A drink of cold water please, Doctor."[132]

In 1881 his wife of twenty-seven years died, seven months after giving birth to Virginia, their tenth child, and Black's three young daughters were sent to live with his wife's sister. Two years later, Black remarried. However, his second marriage may have not been the most happy union. Black's new wife lived with relatives in Greenville, while Black lived near Blacksburg, South Carolina, where he worked as the vice president of the Magnetic Iron and Steel Ore Company, a mining company in which the family held an interest. On March 25, 1902, Black was dining at the home of a cousin in Blacksburg when he had a heart attack and died. Black was buried next to his first wife in Ridgeway, South Carolina.

In his spare time before his death, Black wrote his memoirs, prefacing them to his children, "Remarks, I have written this, all, all alone — I am here by myself. The time is not dull with me. I dream of the past. My children are all I care for anyway. It is for them and especially [daughter] Virginia I write. This is hers. I seldom see anyone in daylight and I have no neighbors who visit me at night. J. L. B.— December 14, 10 p.m."[133]

Thomas H. Owen, 3rd Virginia, remained in command of his regiment through the remainder of the war, coming through the fighting almost unscathed. Owen's only wound was incurred at Todd's Tavern on May 6, 1964. He was shot in the left hand, losing the second finger. After the war, Owen returned to his home in Halifax County and took up farming. Times were apparently hard for the VMI graduate and former engineer. When the equestrian statue of Robert E. Lee was dedicated in Richmond in 1890, many veterans of the 3rd Virginia attended the ceremony, Owen among them. However, Owen was unable to afford a horse to ride. Hearing of the situation, A. P. Hill's former chief of staff sent his horse to Owen, and the old colonel was again able to ride at the head of his regiment. Owen died in Halifax County in May 1894.[134]

Lieutenant Colonel Elijah Viers White, 35th Virginia Battalion, returned home to Loudoun County where he served as the county sheriff from 1866 until 1870. He continued to farm, became a prosperous merchant in Leesburg, and was president of the Peoples National Bank for fifteen years. White also found time to be active in veterans' affairs, serving as the commander of the local Confederate Veterans' Camp. He was also very active in religious affairs, serving as an elder and pastor in several Primitive Baptist churches. About the only activity White avoided was politics, although he was urged to run for office as a Democrat. White died on January 11, 1907, and was buried in Union Cemetery in Leesburg.[135]

In the absence of more senior officers, Major Cabell Flournoy, whose timely counterstroke at Beverly Ford disrupted Pleasonton's plan of attack, remained in command of the 6th Virginia through the Gettysburg Campaign.[136] Still, despite his performance at Brandy Station and continuing credible service — the 6th Virginia's Chaplain wrote that "Flournoy has conducted himself surprisingly well in the recent fight & altogether"— Flournoy was not formally appointed to command of the regiment.[137]

As the cavalry campaigned, the administrative actions resulting from the board of officers convened by General Jones at Harrisonburg in May continued to grind forward. On June 16, General Stuart endorsed the findings of the board with respect to Flournoy and John "Shac" Green, but recommend that Edward Dillon, a former lieutenant in the regular army, be appointed as colonel of the regiment. General Lee endorsed the board's findings on August 13, but disagreeing with Stuart, concurred with the board's recommendation that the Secretary of War reappoint former commander Colonel Julien Harrison to command of the regiment.[138]

Meanwhile, Flournoy had continued to lead the 6th Virginia. On September 13, 1863, the regiment aided in covering the withdrawal of Stuart's cavalry from Culpeper to safety on the south side of the Rapidan River. On September 14 near Rapidan Station, Union skirmishers on the north bank of the river were harassing Stuart's troopers on the south bank with long range fire. The 6th crossed to the north side of the river and, as Stuart watched, Flournoy led what one observer called "the most brilliant charge of the war." The following day Stuart recommended Flournoy for promotion to colonel for "extraordinary valor & skill" at Brandy Station, Culpeper and Rapidan Station. Further, Stuart noted that the men of the 6th had accepted Flournoy as their leader.[139] On September 28 Lee endorsed Stuart's recommendation but noted that while he was pleased with the performance of Flournoy, it was too late the "rectify the proceedings," since the action to reinstate Harrison was pending in Richmond. Apparently, unbeknownst to Stuart, the Secretary of War had on September 23 appointed Harrison, a position Harrison accepted on that same day.[140]

As it turned out, Harrison's appointment barely interrupted Flournoy's tenure as the *de facto* commander of the 6th Virginia Cavalry. Colonel Harrison returned to duty with the regiment at the end of September, but on October 10, 1863, he was shot in the thigh during a battle near Brandy Station. Harrison never returned to active service.[141]

Although Flournoy, quoting Napoleon, had reportedly quipped that "the bullet to kill me has yet been moulded," he was killed on May 31, 1864, shot as he stood on the breast works at Cold Harbor taunting Union troops to come out and fight.[142] Although Fitz Lee described the dead major as a "dashing, zealous officer," one trooper in the 6th Virginia was apparently more accurate in his observation that Flournoy "was a dashing young colonel, but not as prudent as an officer should be."[143]

In an ironic twist, in his report on the Overland Campaign, Major General Philip Sheridan wrote that his men killed the commander of the 6th Virginia, "Colonel Green." In reality, Lieutenant Colonel John Shackleford Green had been acquitted by courts-martial in September 1863 and after leading the regiment during the Bristoe and Mine Run Campaigns, resigned his commission. Following the war, Green lived in Norfolk, Virginia, dying there on January 1, 1891. When published in 1912, Benson Lossing's *Mathew Brady's Illustrated History of the Civil War* featured Green's photograph in a composite showing a "group of Confederate Generals," unofficially promoting the lackluster officer.[144]

Less than two weeks after the Battle at Brandy Station, Major Heros von Borcke was seriously wounded — shot off his horse by a Union sharpshooter at Upperville, Virginia. At the time, von Borcke was sitting next to Stuart observing the ongoing battle with Union cavalry. Since both officers were dressed alike, had ostrich plumes in their hats, and were well mounted, von Borcke suspected that the marksman had intended to kill the general.[145] Stuart shared that suspicion.

Von Borcke's convalescence was lengthy — the ball had entered his neck and lodged in his chest — and he never returned to active field service. In January 1864, von Borcke was honored by the Confederate Congress with a resolution thanking him for his services.[146] Additionally, Wade Hampton, who replaced Stuart as commander of the Cavalry Corps of the Army of Northern Virginia, officially recommended von Borcke for promotion to brigadier and command of a cavalry brigade. However, the nomination, though endorsed by Robert E. Lee, was never acted upon by the War Department. It is possible that von Borcke was not promoted because he was a foreigner, although incapacity from his wound is equally plausible.[147] Instead of being promoted to brigadier, von Borcke was promoted to colonel and in January 1865, sent on a diplomatic mission to Britain where he remained until the end of the war.[148]

After the end of the Civil War, von Borcke returned to his home in Germany where he regained his commission in the Prussian army and participated in Austro-Prussian War of 1866.[149] Von Borcke wrote two books about his experiences in the Confederacy.

In April 2002, Captain William Farley's remains were exhumed from Culpeper's Fairview Cemetery and transferred with military honors to his family cemetery in Laurens, South Carolina. After 139 years, Farley's wish to be sent home came true. The two Belgian draft horses drawing Farley's caisson are much larger than the teams that drew Beckham's artillery pieces (Joseph W. McKinney.

Characteristically, the urbane and ambitious Prussian gave himself more credit than due for some of Stuart's exploits—an effort at self-promotion that raised the ire of some of von Borcke's former Confederate comrades. Nevertheless, in 1884, von Borcke returned to the United States for a visit and was well received by his old friends. By that time, von Borcke was no longer a dashing cavalryman—his girth had expanded greatly and his weight was estimated at between four and five hundred pounds.[150]

Von Borcke married twice, having three sons by his first wife and a daughter, Caroline Virginia Magdalene, by the second. He died in Berlin in May 1895.[151]

Shortly after the war, the remains of Captain William Downs Farley were moved from under the grape arbor in the yard of the Ashby house to the Ashby/MacKall plot in Culpeper's Citizen's Cemetery.[152] There, Farley rested for more 138 years, causing speculation among local people that there had perhaps been a romantic relationship between Farley and one of Dr. Charles Ashby's daughters. On October 18, 2001, Farley's remains were disinterred from the cemetery, which had been renamed Fairview. Examination of the remains by forensic anthropologists from the Smithsonian Institution showed that Farley was not separated in death from his "old friend." His severed leg had been placed with him in his pine casket. However, no brass uniform buttons were found in the grave, which showed that Farley had not been buried in his dress coat.[153] In April 2002, Farley's remains were transferred to the Sons of Confederate Veterans and reinterred with honors in the Farley family plot in Laurens, South Carolina.[154] One hundred thirty-nine years after his death, Will Farley finally went home.

In December 1863, Major Henry B. McClellan obtained twenty days leave to travel to Cumberland County, Virginia, that he might marry Catherine Macon Matthews. They were wed on December 31, after which McClellan returned to duty. Over the course of their marriage the McClellans had nine children.

McClellan was the staff officer on whom fell the sad duty of executing Stuart's deathbed bequests. He was also the recipient of Stuart's bay horse; Stuart left his gray to Major Andrew R. Venable, another staff officer.

After Stuart's death, McClellan spent three months on Robert E. Lee's staff, and was then assigned to the staff of Wade Hampton. McClellan accompanied Hampton to the Carolinas and surrendered near Greensboro, North Carolina on April 26, 1865. McClellan had been promoted to lieutenant colonel shortly before the surrender, but the notice of the promotion did not reach him until after the war was over. Since he had never served in a higher grade, McClellan continued to call himself a major through the remainder of his life.

After the war, McClellan and his family lived for several years in Cumberland County. In 1869 they moved to Lexington, Kentucky, where McClellan accepted a teaching position at the Sayre Female Institute. He served as the principal of Sayre for thirty-four years. Until his death in 1904, McClellan kept busy with veterans' activities and writing.[155] During that time he wrote extensively for publication including his, *I Rode with JEB Stuart*, originally entitled *The Life and Campaigns of Major General J.E.B. Stuart*. In his writings, McClellan made great effort to defend Stuart's performance at Brandy Station and his abilities as a cavalry commander overall. When John Esten Cooke published his sketch of a rollicking Stuart as part of the *Annals of the War* series, McClellan penned in the margin of his personal copy: "Poor Stuart! He frequently expressed the fear that Cooke would 'take his life'— and now he has done it. Any intelligent reader will certainly wonder how such a mountebank as Cooke here describes, could have achieved the great things which certainly belong to Stuart's memory—and will perhaps conclude that in this picture Cooke has done an injustice to a great man. This is a caricature, not a likeness of Stuart. As a professional novelist

Cooke has seized upon one phase of his character and greatly exaggerated it.—H. B. McClellan."[156]

In February 1864, a frustrated Major Robert Beckham transferred to Hood's Army. Despite Stuart's urging, the War Department refused to authorize a lieutenant colonel's billet for the horse artillery, forcing Beckham to move to be promoted. In command of Lieutenant General S.D. Lee's guns, Beckham was mortally wounded by Union artillery fire on the approaches to Franklin, Tennessee, on November 29, 1864.[157]

As it turned out, Lieutenant Isaac Coles of the 6th Virginia had a lengthy time to ponder over whether he gave the best answer to his Irish captor on the road from Beverly Ford. He remained a prisoner until the end of the war. Coles was among the "Immortal 600," Confederate officers who were confined on Morris Island under the fire between Confederate guns in Charleston and Union guns ringing the city's harbor (the Confederates held a like number of Union officers under fire in Charleston itself). After the war, Coles returned home to farming in Pittsylvania County. His long imprisonment apparently did little harm to his constitution—he married, fathered six children, and lived until 1926, dying in his 92nd year.[158]

Lieutenant Robert H. Goldsborough, captured carrying a message from Stuart to Williams Wickham, continued to be plagued by bad luck. Instead of receiving a speedy exchange, he was confined in Union prisons until March 1865. Upon returning to Virginia, Goldsborough obtained a position as *aide de camp* to Custis Lee, Robert E. Lee's eldest son, assuming his duties just before the retreat from Richmond in April. At Sayler's Creek, Goldsborough was struck by shrapnel and mortally wounded, the last of Stuart's staff to be killed in the war. The content of the message Goldsborough was carrying when captured on June 9, 1863, was not recorded.[159]

Later in the war, Captain Charles O'Ferrall, who pistol-whipped a Union officer on Fleetwood and the next day recovered that officer's stolen watch, received authority to recruit a regiment of cavalry. Had O'Ferrall succeeded, he would have earned a promotion to colonel. Unfortunately, recruiting had become difficult, O'Ferrall failed, and he remained a captain in the 12th Virginia. After the war, O'Ferrall was charged with wartime depredations in the new state of West Virginia. However, West Virginia authorities' attempts to extradite O'Ferrall were not successful and he was never prosecuted. No longer welcome in what had been his home state, O'Ferrall remained in the Old Dominion. He studied law at Washington College in Lexington, Virginia, opened a practice in Harrisonburg, and went into politics. After several terms in the Virginia legislature, O'Ferrall was elected governor of Virginia, serving from 1894 to 1898. O'Ferrall died in 1905.[160]

After riding the black mare almost to his death on the road to Beverly Ford, and then almost being overtaken and captured at Fleetwood, Private John Opie secured a pass to go home and find a new horse. A year earlier he had purchased a "young blooded skeleton" for 150 dollars, and upon arrival in Staunton, Opie was pleased to find that in the care of his family, the "skeleton" had grown into the finest horse he had ever seen. Opie fondly recalled that the new horse could "run like the wind, was gentle as a lamb, and was frightened at no sound or object, and yet was full of life and spirit."[161] Within four days Opie had returned to the 6th Virginia and served with the regiment until he was wounded at Brandy Station on October 11, 1863. Opie's wound was serious—the ball from a Union carbine entered his arm at the wrist and exited at his elbow—and as a result, Opie was invalided out of active service.

Opie returned home to Staunton where, in June 1864, he raised a mounted company in response to the increased threat of a Union advance into the upper Shenandoah Valley.

Opie and his men, most of whom were equipped with infantry muskets and fought dismounted, served first under Jones at Piedmont, then under Breckinridge at Lynchburg, and marched and fought up and down the Valley with Early.[162]

On February 6, 1865, while on a scout in the lower Valley, Opie was captured by soldiers from the 12th Pennsylvania Cavalry near Charlestown. Opie was questioned by their commander, Colonel Marcus Reno, before being sent off to prison. After a short stint at Elmira, New York, Opie was paroled at City Point. He made his way by train to Lynchburg and from there to Staunton riding most of the way on a quartermaster mule. His war was over.[163]

After the war, Opie was active in Confederate veterans' organizations. He received a law degree from the University of Virginia in 1885, and went into Virginia politics, serving in the House of Delegates from 1882 to 1884 and in the Virginia Senate from 1896 to 1904. In 1899, Opie published his memoirs, *A Rebel Cavalryman with Lee, Jackson, and Stuart*, providing a colorful account of his exploits and memorializing the antics of his black mare. Opie died in Staunton in January 1906.[164]

Lieutenant Frank Robertson, who riding the blundering Bostona had barely escaped death or capture on Fleetwood Hill, almost came to grief during the Gettysburg Campaign. On a rainy night during the retreat from Gettysburg, Robertson, riding his favorite horse (a mare named Miranda), was galloping through the streets of Williamsport, Pennsylvania, carrying a message for Stuart. Without slowing, Robertson and the mare galloped off an abutment and into the Chesapeake & Ohio Canal that parallels the Potomac River at that point. Horse and rider fell roughly twenty-seven feet into the mud; neither was injured.[165]

After returning to Virginia, Robertson, whose health was always fragile, was forced to leave active service for a lengthy period of convalescence. At some point, Robertson provided a doctor's statement to Stuart verifying that he remained in poor health. In September 1863, Stuart responded to his former Assistant Engineer:

Dear Lieutenant

I deeply regret the continuance of your illness, for I had hoped by this time you would be able to join us. I know very well that you could not be kept from your post except by inexorable necessity. It needed no surgeon's certificate to satisfy me of it.

I am glad of the present opportunity of expressing to you my sense of the usefulness, the bravery, the devotion to duty and daring for which you were distinguished during your stay with me. I sent you through fiery ordeals at Chancellorsville and elsewhere from which I scarcely hoped to see you return, but rejoiced to see you escape. You will never forget those trials and I hope the kind Providence which so signally favored you will soon see you restored to the field and to your much attached comrades.

Present my kindest regards to your father's family and believe me

Your sincere friend

J. E. B. Stuart Major General[166]

In January 1864, Robertson returned to duty, serving first as a map-maker for Stuart, then on Fitz Lee's staff until the end of the war. Although he may not have been robust, Robertson lived for more than sixty years after the war, wishing that when his death came, it would be the result of a riding accident. Instead, Robertson succumbed to cancer in August 1926. As Stuart predicted, Robertson never forgot the trials he endured in the Cavalry Division. Shortly before his death, Robertson remarked that he would like the note from Stuart — which he kept secure, wrapped in a newspaper on the top shelf of his desk — to be buried with him. Robertson's grandson tucked Stuart's note into the old soldier's coffin, burying with him his finest memory of the war — the respect and loyalty of his commander.[167]

* * * * * *

Using a now-popular phrase, the cavalrymen who fought at Brandy Station were "bands of brothers" united in the comradery of men who fought together. Today they are scattered. A few are at West Point. Some are in Arlington or other national cemeteries. Most are now in church graveyards or family plots throughout the country. Many still lie beneath the grassy fields near Saint James Church, Fleetwood, and Yew Ridge, their graves unmarked. According to the refrain of the popular British song of World War I, made forever famous by General Douglas MacArthur in his farewell speech to Congress in 1951, "Old Soldiers never die; they just fade away." The old soldiers of Brandy Station, and all other Civil War Battles, are now long dead. Remarkably, however, the memory of them has yet to fade.

Thinking of the men who fought on June 9, 1863, evokes images of a different era — thundering masses of men on horses, flashing steel, bugle calls — a time when the outcome of battle depended as much on *elan* as discipline. That era is gone. Fortunately it is not forgotten.

After the war, Private John Opie returned to Staunton, obtained a law degree, and was active in state politics. In 1897 he wrote a book about his experiences as a soldier, including his exploits on the black mare (***A Rebel Cavalryman***).

Appendix A:
Order of Battle and Casualties

On June 9, 1863, the cavalry forces available to Brigadier General Alfred Pleasonton and Major General JEB Stuart were evenly matched in number. Each commanding general had roughly eight thousand sabers on the field. In artillery, Pleasonton, with six batteries, each with six guns, had numeric superiority over Stuart with five batteries, each with four guns. All Union artillery pieces were three-inch rifled ordnance guns. Stuart's batteries had a mix of weapons, Blakely and Whitworth rifled cannon, smoothbore Napoleons, and howitzers from six to twenty-four pounds.[1] Further, Joseph Hooker augmented Pleasonton with two brigades of fifteen hundred infantrymen each, giving the Federal commander a distinct advantage over Stuart, who had no infantry under his control.

During the day's fighting, the Union force suffered 865 documented casualties, of which 763 were within cavalry regiments. Although accurately compiling Confederate casualties is difficult, it appears that Pleasonton's corps inflicted significantly fewer casualties on Stuart's division (582, most within cavalry regiments). While the number of soldiers killed and mortally wounded was fairly evenly distributed between the opposing forces (89 Union to 72 Confederate), Pleasonton reported roughly 100 more men wounded and almost 200 more men missing than documented losses in those categories in Stuart's division. The disparity in the number of missing is not surprising since at the end of the day the Confederates held the field.[2]

This appendix provides details regarding both Union and Confederate order of battle and casualties.

Union

On paper, General Alfred Pleasonton had twenty-two cavalry regiments in the fight at Brandy Station on June 9, 1863. In addition, his force included one squadron of the 3rd West Virginia Cavalry and an independent cavalry company from the District of Columbia.[3] However, those figures are misleading, because significant portions of those twenty-two regiments—comprising at least twenty-one companies, the equivalent of almost two regiments—were detached for duty elsewhere on the day of the battle.

Nine companies were assigned as escorts and couriers at Army of the Potomac and corps headquarters. Two companies from the 6th Pennsylvania Cavalry were detached to the Provost Guard at Army Headquarters. One company from the 1st Maine was detached to Headquarters, 1st Corps. One company from the 1st New Jersey was detached to the Headquarters, 6th Corps, as was one company from the 1st Pennsylvania. Two companies from the 17th Pennsylvania were detached to the Headquarters, 5th Corps, and two companies from the 9th New York were detached to the Headquarters, 12th Corps.

Two regiments were not organized at their full strength of twelve companies. Two companies of the 1st U.S. Cavalry had remained in New Mexico when that regiment moved east at the beginning of the war. Eventually the two companies were disbanded. Not until October 1863 were two new regular cavalry companies organized and assigned to the regiment to bring it up to its authorized level of organization. One battalion of four companies from the 6th Ohio was sent to the far west for duty shortly after that regiment was organized in October 1861. The battalion was officially detached from that regiment in September 1862. Two replacement companies were raised during the winter of 1862–1863, but the final two companies of the 6th Ohio were not raised until the winter of 1863–1864.

Two regiments had battalions and squadrons detailed to duty outside the Army of the Potomac. One battalion of four companies from the 3d Indiana, although remaining on the regimental rolls, served continuously with the Army of the Cumberland in Tennessee. Additionally, one squadron of two companies from the 3rd Indiana was temporarily detailed as provost guard in Indianapolis, Indiana, in the summer of 1863. When the 1st Massachusetts moved from coastal South Carolina to Virginia in October 1862, it left four companies behind on the Carolina Sea Islands.

Additionally, many men assigned to the Cavalry Corps remained dismounted because of arduous duty during Stoneman's raid in May, and those troopers were left in camp when their regiments deployed to southern Fauquier in the lead-up to the battle. Five companies of the 9th New York had so many men dismounted that only five companies from that regiment (two of the regiment's companies were detailed as escorts) left camp on June 7 to join Buford near Catlett's Station. It is likely that entire companies in other regiments were also dismounted and did not participate in the battle, but documentation is lacking.

Union strength figures were aggregated for each of the three cavalry divisions and the Reserve Brigade. Those figures, taken from the *Official Records*, are provided in the table below. Presumably, those are the present-for-duty figures and do not include dismounted men left in camp, sick, or on other detail. The figures likely do not include men assigned to the four artillery batteries supporting the cavalry (number of guns, not men, is the more significant figure when tallying artillery).

The exact strength of the picked infantry brigades assigned to Pleasonton is unknown. Hooker tasked his corps commanders to furnish fifteen hundred infantrymen for each brigade, to which were added pack masters, ambulance attendants, a few brigade headquarters personnel, and an artillery battery. Consequently, the total strength of each brigade was probably between seventeen hundred and eighteen hundred men.

In summary, Pleasonton attacked across the Rappahannock with no more than 239 cavalry companies—the equivalent of 20 Union regiments—supported by six batteries of light artillery, and three thousand infantrymen.

Union casualties are tabulated by regiment in three categories: killed (KIA), wounded (WIA), missing/captured (MIA). Casualties documented in the *Official Records*, with few exceptions, are shown in the table below.[4]

Cavalry Corps, Army of the Potomac
Brigadier General Alfred Pleasonton

		STRENGTH	KIA	WIA	MIA	TOTAL
Cavalry Corps Totals		10981	83	394	392	869

Right Wing
Brigadier General John Buford

		STRENGTH	KIA	WIA	MIA	TOTAL
Right Wing Totals		5418	51	284	165	500

First Cavalry Division
Brigadier General John Buford

		STRENGTH	KIA	WIA	MIA	TOTAL
First Division Totals		2061	14	128	12[5]	154

First Brigade, First Division
Colonel Benjamin F. "Grimes" Davis (KIA)

REGIMENT	COMMANDER	STRENGTH	KIA	WIA	MIA	TOTAL
8th New York	Maj Edmund M. Pope		11	31	7	49
8th Illinois	Capt Alpheus Clark (Mortally Wounded)		1	46	3	50
3d Indiana (A-F only)[6]	Maj William S. McClure		1	23	0	24
9th New York (5 companies)[7]	Maj William B. Martin (Wounded)		0	15	1	16
3d West Virginia (A & C only)[8]	Capt Seymore B. Conger		0	3	0	3
B & L Btry, 2d U.S. Artillery[9]	Lt Albert O. Vincent		0	3	0	3
First Brigade			14[10]	121	11	146

Second Brigade, First Division
Colonel Thomas C. Devin

REGIMENT	COMMANDER	STRENGTH	KIA	WIA	MIA	TOTAL
6th New York	Maj William E Beardsley		0	4	0	4
17th Pennsylvania (-D & H)[11]	Col Josiah H. Kellogg		0	3	0	3
Second Brigade Totals			0	7	0	7

Reserve Brigade
Major Charles J. Whiting

REGIMENT	COMMANDER	STRENGTH	KIA	WIA	MIA	TOTAL
6th Pennsylvania (-E & I)[12]	Maj Robert Morris, Jr. (Captured)		5	25	78	108
1st U.S.(- D & G)[13]	Capt Richard S.C. Lord		1	1	0	2
2d U.S.	Capt Wesley Merritt		11	29	26	66
5th U.S.	Capt James E. Harrison		6	17	15	38
6th U.S.[14]	Capt George C. Cram		8	26	32	66
E, 4th U.S. Artillery	Lt Samuel S. Elder		0	0	0	0
Reserve Brigade Totals		1857	31	98	151	280

Attached Infantry Brigade
Brigadier General Adelbert Ames

REGIMENT	COMMANDER	STRENGTH	KIA	WIA	MIA	TOTAL
2d Massachusetts Lt Col Charles R. Mudge[15]	Lt Col Martin Flood	500	1	3	2	6
3d Wisconsin Maj Edwin L. Hubbard			1	14	0	15
33d Massachusetts	Col Adin B. Underwood	500	0	3	0	3
124th New York Lt Col Francis M. Cummins	Col A. Von Horne Ellis	500	2	12	0	14
86th New York Maj Jacob H. Lansing			2	24	0	26
K, 1st U.S. Artillery	Capt William M. Graham		0	2	0	2
Infantry Totals (Excluding artillery and support personnel)		1500	6	58	2	66

Left Wing
Brigadier General David McM. Gregg

	STRENGTH	KIA	WIA	MIA	TOTAL
Left Wing Totals	5563	32	110	227	369

Second Cavalry Division
Colonel Alfred N. A. Duffie

	STRENGTH	KIA	WIA	MIA	TOTAL
Second Division Totals	1893	5	11	13	29

UNIT	COMMANDER	STRENGTH	KIA	WIA	MIA	TOTAL
Battery M, 2d U.S. Artillery	Lt Alexander C.M. Pennington		0	0	0	0

First Brigade, Second Division
Colonel Luigi P. diCesnola

REGIMENT	COMMANDER	STRENGTH	KIA	WIA	MIA	TOTAL
1st Massachusetts (-I, K, L, M)[16]	Lt Col Greely S. Curtis		2	9	5	16
6th Ohio (-F & M)[17]	Maj William Stedman		1[18]	1	1	3
1st Rhode Island	Lt Col John L. Thompson		2	0	3	5
4th New York	Col Luigi diCesnola		On Other Duty			
First Brigade Totals			5	10	9	24

Second Brigade, Second Division
Colonel John Irvin Gregg

REGIMENT	COMMANDER	STRENGTH	KIA	WIA	MIA	TOTAL
3d Pennsylvania	Lt Col Edward Jones		0	0	0	0
4th Pennsylvania	Lt Col William E. Doster		0	1	4	5
16th Pennsylvania[19]	Maj William H Frye		0	0	0	0
Second Brigade Totals			0	1	4	5

Appendix A — Order of Battle and Casualties

Third Cavalry Division
Brigadier General David McM. Gregg

		STRENGTH	KIA	WIA	MIA	TOTAL
Third Division Totals[20]		2170	26	94	211	331

UNIT	COMMANDER	STRENGTH	KIA	WIA	MIA	TOTAL
6th Btry, New York Lt. Arty	Capt Joseph W. Martin		0	8	13	21

First Brigade, Third Division
Colonel Hugh Judson Kilpatrick

REGIMENT	COMMANDER	STRENGTH	KIA	WIA	MIA	TOTAL
1st Maine (-L)[21]	Col Calvin S. Douty		1	2	28	38[22]
2d New York	Lt Col Henry E. Davies		4	14	21	39
10th New York	Lt Col William Irvine (Captured)		3	18	61	82[23]
Orton's Co. (DC)	Capt William H. Orton		0	0	0	0
First Brigade Totals			8	34	117	159

Second Brigade, Third Division
Colonel Percy Wyndham (WIA)

REGIMENT	COMMANDER	STRENGTH	KIA	WIA	MIA	TOTAL
1st Maryland[24]	Lt Col James M. Deems		6	13	44	63
1st New Jersey (-L)[25]	Lt Col Virgil Broderick (Killed)		7	21	24	52
1st Pennsylvania (-H)[26]	Col John P. Taylor		5	18	12	35
12th Illinois	Colonel Arno Voss	On Other Duty				
Second Brigade Totals			18	52	80	150

Attached Infantry Brigade
Brigadier General David A. Russell

REGIMENT	COMMANDER	STRENGTH	KIA	WIA	MIA	TOTAL
7th Wisconsin	Col William Robinson	500	0	0	0	0
2d Wisconsin (A & I only)			0	0	0	0
56th Pennsylvania	Col J. William Hoffman		1	5	3	9
5th New Hampshire	Col Edward Cross (5th NH)	500	0	0	0	0
81st Pennsylvania			0	0	0	0
6th Maine	Col Hiram Burnham	500	0	0	0	0
119th Pennsylvania	Major Henry Truefit		0	0	0	0
C, 3rd U.S. Artillery	1st Lt William D. Fuller		0	0	0	0
Infantry Totals		1500	1	5	3	9

(Excluding artillery and support personnel)

Recapitulation by Arm of Service

Cavalry	7981	76	320	374	770
Infantry	3000	7	61	5	73
Artillery	Not Provided	0	13	13	26

Confederate

On June 9, JEB Stuart had available to blunt Pleasonton's attack no more than 188 cavalry companies—the equivalent of roughly 19 Confederate regiments or 16 Union regiments—supported by five batteries of artillery. Determining an accurate numeric strength of Stuart's force is problematic. Stuart's cavalry—at least those regiments in Culpeper County—was mustered on May 25, 1863, and the returns from that date provided the strength for those regiments in three categories: present effectively mounted; present not effectively mounted; absent. Several regiments were not mustered, including those of Jones' brigade, which had not moved to Culpeper from the Shenandoah Valley. Wickham's 4th Virginia, which was still on picket duty near Fredericksburg, also was not mustered. Various sources place Jones' effective strength at 1600 men, and Wickham's regiment was reportedly one of the stronger regiments in Stuart's division, perhaps numbering close to 600 effectives.

Doubtless, the status of the regiments in Culpeper improved during the two weeks between the May 25 muster and the battle on June 9, although probably not to the extent reported by Heros von Borcke who, known to exaggerate, recalled that "hundreds of men flocked in daily from their distant homes, bringing with them fresh horses."[27] However, during the Confederate cavalry's late-spring hiatus in Culpeper, dismounted troopers did have time to obtain remounts, while malnourished horses benefitted from rest and the opportunity to graze on late-spring grass.

Additionally, even the men who not were not effectively mounted were available to fight or perform other useful duties during the battle on June 9. Stuart, by dispatching Lieutenant Frank Robertson to Brandy Station with orders for General Hampton's dismounted men, revealed that he viewed the dismounted men as assets. Moreover, a party of dismounted men of the 2nd South Carolina fought with Major Lipscomb at Stevensburg. Consequently, is appropriate to aggregate the effectively mounted and not effectively mounted categories, as shown in the strength column in the table below. Strength figures, except where noted, are from the *Official Records*.

It is equally difficult to determine accurately the Confederate casualties. In the body of his official report, Stuart stated that his casualties in killed, wounded, and missing "amounted to about 480 total," a figure that is almost impossible to verify, and appears significantly understated.[28] Casualties for the fighting on June 9, submitted in tabular format after the Gettysburg Campaign, documented losses of seven officers killed and twenty-three officers wounded. A second table showed 51 enlisted killed, 250 enlisted wounded, and 132 missing.[29] It is more likely that the Confederates suffered close to 600 casualties on June 9. There are several reasons for the disparity.

The accounting of casualties by commanders at all levels does not appear to have been particularly accurate. It seems as if commanders made little effort, at least immediately following the battle, to gather and submit detailed information to their superior headquarters.

For example, Hampton's aggregate—fifteen killed, fifty-five wounded, and fifty missing—fails to correspond to the figures provided by his regimental commanders in their reports. Additionally, in their reports, both Jones and Lomax admitted that they did not know the exact number of their men who had been captured because some of their missing were "stragglers" who would presumably report back to duty in the days immediately following the battle.[30]

Regrettably, a few regimental commanders, including all those in Rooney Lee's brigade, either failed to file official reports or their reports were later lost and not included in the *Official Records*. Other commanders, including Elijah White and John Chambliss (filing a brigade report for the wounded Rooney Lee), appended casualty lists to their reports, and while the reports were included in the *Official Records*, the appended lists were apparently lost.

Even Stuart had problems accurately tallying and reporting his casualties. The table of officer casualties appended to Stuart's official report showed an aggregate of thirty officers killed and wounded, but does not show any officers captured by the enemy, of whom there were at least six, including one of Stuart's own *aides-de-camp*.[31] In the table of enlisted casualties, Stuart provided a total of 485, a figure that exceeded the sum of the killed, wounded, and missing by fifty-two. A marginal note explained this 10 percent variance: "No report from White's battalion (Thirty-fifth Virginia). Loss heavy. Total loss in this [Jones'] brigade, probably 200."[32]

Because of inaccuracies and omissions in the *Official Records*, the casualties provided in the table below are derived from a variety of sources. Information from commanders' official reports is provided when available and of reasonable accuracy. Other sources include letters and newspaper accounts. Casualty data derived from compiled service records (Louis Manarin for North Carolina Regiments and H.E. Howard's Virginia Regimental History Series) are also cited. However, there are limitations with compiled service record information, and casualty counts derived from them are likely understated. Unfortunately, we will never accurately know the casualties suffered by Stuart's division on June 9.

Because Confederate commanders frequently reported those mortally wounded, a separate column (MWIA) has been added. Confederate soldiers who were captured, captured and wounded, or listed as missing, are all carried in the MIA column.

Cavalry Division — Army of Northern Virginia
Major General JEB Stuart

	ESTIMATED STRENGTH Off./Enl.	KIA	MWIA	WIA	MIA	TOT.
Division Total	589/9725	71	17	269	226	582[33]

Jones' Brigade
Brigadier General William E. "Grumble" Jones

REGIMENT	COMMANDER	ESTIMATED STRENGTH	KIA	MWIA	WIA	MIA	TOT.
6th Virginia	Maj Cabell E Flournoy		6	6	11	29	52[34]
7th Virginia	Lt Col Thomas Marshall		2	2	18	2	24[35]
11th Virginia	Col Lunsford Lomax		5	0	13	4	22[36]
12th Virginia	Col Asher W. Harman (WIA)		6	1	31	21	59[37]
35th Battalion, Virginia Cavalry	Lt Col Elijah V. White) (WIA		8	0	39	66	113[38]
Brigade Totals		130/1600 (est.)	27	9	112	122	270

Rooney Lee's Brigade
Brigadier General William F. H. "Rooney" Lee (WIA)

REGIMENT	COMMANDER	REPORTED STRENGTH	KIA	MWIA	WIA	MIA	TOT.
2nd North Carolina	Col Solomon Williams (KIA)	28/236	4	2	14	10	30[39]

REGIMENT	COMMANDER	REPORTED STRENGTH	KIA	MWIA	WIA	MIA	TOT.
9th Virginia	Col Richard L. T. Beale	27/689	15	0	21	0	36[40]
10th Virginia (-D)	Col James Lucius Davis	28/331	4	2	37	16	59[41]
13th Virginia	Col John Chambliss	30/541	0	0	4	0	4[42]
15th Virginia	Maj Charles R. Collins	Picket Duty on Rappahannock below Fredericksburg					
Brigade Totals		113/1797	23	4	77[43]	29	129

Hampton's Brigade
Brigadier General Wade Hampton

REGIMENT	COMMANDER	REPORTED STRENGTH	KIA	MWIA	WIA	MIA	TOT.
Cobb's Legion (Georgia)	Col Pierce M. B. Young	32/492	6	0	22	16	44[44]
Phillips' Legion (Georgia) (A-F)	Col W. W. Rich	Picket Duty on Lower Rappahannock					
Jeff Davis Legion (Mississippi) (A-F)	Lt Col Joseph F. Waring	22/339	0	0	4	0	4[45]
1st South Carolina	Col John L. Black	39/519	3	1	8	5	17
2nd South Carolina	Col Matthew C. Butler (WIA)	38/405	0	1	1	15	17[46]
1st North Carolina	Col Laurence S. Baker	39/651	5	0	12	14	31[47]
Brigade Totals		170/2405	14	2	47	50	113

Fitzhugh Lee's Brigade
Colonel Thomas T. Munford

REGIMENT	COMMANDER	REPORTED STRENGTH	KIA	MWIA	WIA	MIA	TOT.
1st Virginia	Col James H. Drake	36/481	0	0	1	0	1[48]
2nd Virginia	Lt Col James O. Watts	31/637	5	0	12	0	17[49]
3rd Virginia	Col Thomas H. Owen	29/460	1	0	8	0	9[50]
4th Virginia	Col William C. Wickham	590 (est.)	0	1	1	26	28[51]
5th Virginia	Col Thomas L. Rosser	Picket duty on upper Rappahannock near Amissville					
Brigade Totals		96/2168 (incl. 4th VA)	6	1	22	26	55

Robertson's Brigade
Brigadier General Beverly H. Robertson

REGIMENT	COMMANDER	STRENGTH	KIA	MWIA	WIA	MIA	TOT.
4th North Carolina (A-H)	Col Dennis C. Ferebee	37/611	0	0	0	0	0
5th North Carolina (-E)	Col Peter G. Evans	35/625	0	0	0	0	0
Brigade Totals		72/1236	0	0	0	0	0

Stuart Horse Artillery
Major Robert F. Beckham

BATTERY	COMMANDER	STRENGTH	KIA	MWIA	WIA	MIA	TOT.
Hart's	Capt James F. Hart		0	0	1	0	1
Breathed's	Capt James Breathed		0	0	3	0	3
Chew's	Capt Roger P. Chew		0	0	3	0	3
Moorman's	Capt Marcellus Moorman		1	0	3	1	5
McGregor's	Capt William C. McGregor		0	0	0	0	0
Battalion Total		8/519[52]	1	0	10	1	12

Appendix B:
West Pointers at Brandy Station

Union

According to the U.S. Military Academy's Association of Graduates, 828 West Point graduates served in the Union Army during the Civil War. Of those, the twenty shown in the list below participated in the battle at Brandy Station. West Pointers suffered sixty battle-deaths in Union service during the Civil War. One of those, Colonel Benjamin F. "Grimes" Davis, was killed at Brandy Station. One other graduate who fought at Brandy Station, Major General David Russell, was killed later in the war. Captain Charles Canfield, who left West Point two years before his graduation, was also killed at Brandy Station.

Name	*Grade*	*Position*	*Class*	*Cullum #*[1]
Whiting, Charles J.	Major	Cdr, Reserve Bde	1835	789
Pleasonton, Alfred	Maj Gen	Cdr, Cavalry Corps	1844	1212
Russell, David A.	Brig Gen	Cdr, Infantry Bde	1845	1268
Buford, John	Brig Gen	Cdr, 1st Division	1848	1384
Davis, Benjamin F.	Colonel	Cdr, 1st Bde, 1st Div	1854	1662
Gregg, David McM.	Brig Gen	Cdr, 3rd Division	1855	1684
Lord, Richard S. C.	Captain	Cdr, 1st U.S. Cav.	1856	1750
Canfield, Charles W.	Captain	2nd U.S. Cav.	Ex. 1857	
McKee, Samuel	Captain	1st U.S. Cav.	1858	1810
Baker, Eugene	Bvt Maj	1st U.S. Cav.	1859[2]	1836
Kellogg, Josiah H.	Colonel	Cdr, 17th Pennsylvania Cav.	1860	1859
Pennington, Alex	1st Lt	Cdr, Brty M, 2nd Artillery	1860	1864
Merritt, Wesley	Captain	Cdr, 2nd U.S. Cav.	1860	1868
Ames, Adelbert	Brig Gen	Cdr, Infantry Bde	May 1861	1892
Kilpatrick, Judson	Colonel	Cdr, 1st Bde, 3rd Division	May 1861	1904
Leoser, Charles McK.	1st Lt	2nd U.S. Cav.	May 1861	1907
Noyes, Henry	1st Lt	2nd U.S. Cav.	June 1861	1955
Fuller, William D.	Bvt Capt	Cdr, Brty C, 3rd Artillery	June 1861	1957
Custer, George A.	Bvt Capt	*Aide de camp* to Gen Pleasonton	June 1861	1966
Mackenzie, Ranald S.	Bvt Capt	*Aide de camp*	1862	1967[3]
Hamilton, Thomas	Bvt 1st Lt	3rd Artillery	1862	1978

Two member of the Class of 1854 served on General Pleasonton's staff but were not present on the battlefield on June 9, 1863. Major Charles Sawtelle (#1668) served as Chief Quartermaster of the Cavalry Corps from January 24 until June 13, 1863, but was apparently attending to his duties elsewhere. George A. Gordon (#1660), a captain (Bvt Major) in the 2nd U.S. Cavalry, was detailed as Chief Ordnance Officer and Commissary of Musters for the Cavalry Corps during the spring of 1863, but was absent due to illness at the time of the battle.

Several other USMA graduates were assigned to regular cavalry regiments in the Reserve Brigade but were detailed to other duty on June 9. Marcus Reno (Class of 1857, #1779), later of Little Big Horn fame, was a captain in the 2nd Cavalry. Reno had been breveted to major for gallantry at Kelly's Ford on March 17, 1863, suffering a hernia during the fight. He was detached on recruiting duty during June 1863. Charles Norris (Class of 1851, #1517) was also a captain in the 2nd Cavalry, but was detailed as a mustering and disbursing officer in Indianapolis from December 1962 through June 1863.[4]

Additionally, Lieutenant James Lancaster (1862, #1981) was assigned to Fuller's battery, but Cullum did not document his presence on June 9. Is it likely that Lancaster was detailed elsewhere on that date.

At least one soldier who fought in the battle as an enlisted man later attended the Military Academy. Earl D. Thomas served an a corporal and sergeant in the 8th Illinois Cavalry for three years beginning in April 1862. He entered West Point in 1865 and graduated with the Class of 1869. Commissioned in the 5th Cavalry, Thomas fought in the Indian Wars and in Cuba before retiring in 1911 as a brigadier general.[5] Another former soldier, Edward E. Wood, Class of 1871, may have fought at Brandy Station. Wood enlisted in the 17th Pennsylvania Cavalry in September 1862 and rose to the rank of first lieutenant before being mustered out of the service in August 1865. After graduation from West Point, Wood was commissioned in the cavalry. He served in the West chasing Geronimo and as a professor of modern languages at West Point before retiring as a brigadier general in 1910.[6]

Many West Pointers served in leadership positions in Union volunteer cavalry regiments during the formative first year of the war. Most are noted in the narrative of Chapter 4. For example, Richard Rush (Class of 1846, #1297) raised the 6th Pennsylvania and served as the commander of that distinctive regiment until he was reassigned at the end of April 1863. Although Colonel Rush was not in the battle at Brandy Station, his regiment, "Rush's Lancers," continued to bear his name throughout the war.

Confederate

The Association of Graduates lists 303 West Pointers who served the Confederacy.[7] The Southern states drew extensively from that pool of potential officers to fill the senior leadership positions of their cavalry regiments. Twenty-two regiments of cavalry were assigned to Stuart's cavalry division on June 9, 1863. Fourteen of those regiments had been initially commanded by either a graduate of the Military Academy or a former cadet who resigned from the academy before his graduation. Among the Virginia regiments, the percentage was even greater: eleven of the thirteen Virginia regiments in the Cavalry Division of the Army of Northern Virginia were initially commanded by West Pointers.[8]

Two years into the war and many command changes later, academy-trained officers still filled a significant percentage of the colonel and general officer billets within Stuart's division. JEB Stuart was a West Pointer, as were three of his five brigade commanders: Beverly Robertson, William E. "Grumble" Jones, and Fitzhugh Lee. At the time of the battle, nine of Stuart's twenty-two regiments were still commanded by West Pointers, as was the division's horse artillery battalion. The eleven West Point officers who fought for the South at Brandy Station are shown in the following list.

Name	Grade	Position	Class	Cullum #
Davis, J. Lucius	Colonel	Cdr, 10th Virginia Cav.	1833	722
Jones, William E.	Brig Gen	Cdr, Bde	1848	1378
Robertson, Beverly	Brig Gen	Cdr, Bde	1849	1431
Baker, Laurence S.	Colonel	Cdr, 1st North Carolina Cav.	1851	1535
Chambliss, John R.	Colonel	Cdr, 13th Virginia Cav.	1853	1609
Stuart, J.E.B.	Maj Gen	Cdr, Cavalry Division	1854	1643
Black, John L.	Colonel	Cdr, 1st South Carolina Cav.	Ex. 1854	
Lomax, Lunsford L	Colonel	Cdr, 11th Virginia Cav.	1856	1731
Williams, Solomon	Colonel	Cdr, 2nd North Carolina Cav.	1858	1808
Beckham, Robert F.	Major	Cdr, Stuart Horse Artillery	1859	1830
Young, P.M.B.	Colonel	Cdr, Cobb's Legion Cav.	Ex. June 1861	

Three of Stuart's West Point commanders were not present on the field on June 9. On the day of the battle, Thomas Munford, a VMI graduate, replaced the ailing Fitz Lee (Class of 1856, #1755). Two of Stuart's regiments were on picket duty. Colonel Thomas Rosser (ex May 1861) and the 5th Virginia were guarding the upper Rappahannock near Amissville. Major Charles R. Collins (Class of 1859, #1827), in temporary command of the 15th Virginia, was on the lower Rappahannock below Fredericksburg (the regiment's colonel was on extended leave due to illness, and the regiment's lieutenant colonel had been recently captured). Collins, a highly capable officer, was appointed colonel of the regiment shortly before being killed at Todd's Tavern in May 1864.

Another West Pointer in Stuart's Cavalry Division was the lieutenant colonel of the 2nd North Carolina, William G. Robinson (Class of 1858, #1822). Robinson had been wounded and captured in April 1862. Although he had been paroled, he did not return to the regiment until after the Gettysburg Campaign.

Of the forty-five West Point graduates listed as Confederate battle deaths by the Association of Graduates, one, Solomon Williams, was killed at Brandy Station.[9] Four other graduates who fought at Brandy Station — Jones, Stuart, Chambliss, and Beckham — were killed later in the war.

Notes

Introduction

1. U.S. War Department, *War of the Rebellion: A Compilation of the Official Records of the Union and Confederate Armies* [hereafter *OR*] (Washington: Government Printing Office, 1880–1901), 25, II:516.
2. Eugene M. Scheel, *Culpeper: A Virginia County's History Through 1920* (Culpeper, VA: Culpeper Historical Society, 1982), 338.
3. J.H. Kidd, *Personal Recollections of a Cavalryman* (Ionia, MI: Sentinel press; reprint, New York: Time-Life, 1983), 426–428.
4. James L. Robertson, "War in Words," *Civil War Times Illustrated* 22 (September 1983), 39.

1—A Real Virginia Winter

1. Douglas Southall Freeman, *R. E. Lee*, 4 vols. (New York: Charles Scribner's Sons, 1949), 2:462.
2. Alexander Hunter, *Johnny Reb & Billy Yank* (New York: Neale, 1905; reprint ed., Konecky & Konecky), 326.
3. Post-war references to Jackson as a Roundhead are common, in contrast to JEB Stuart, the dashing Cavalier. Charles Minor Blackford, a captain in the 2nd Virginia Cavalry and the judge advocate on Longstreet's staff, referred to Jackson as a Roundhead because, unlike many Confederate generals, Jackson dressed shabbily. More in the essence of Roundhead-ism, Blackford went on to describe Jackson as an officer with no social life, who "divides his time between military duties, prayer, sleep, and solitary thought," all recognizable as Cromwellian characteristics. (Charles Minor Blackford and Susan Leigh Blackford, *Letters from Lee's Army*, edited by Charles Minor Blackford III [New York: Scribner's, 1947; reprint ed., Lincoln: University of Nebraska Press, 1998], 86, 89.)
4. Hooker had both privately and openly disparaged Burnside's abilities as an army commander. Burnside, in turn, demanded that Lincoln dismiss Hooker and several other generals for insubordination. Should Lincoln elect to do otherwise, Burnside offered to resign. Lincoln, forced to choose between the inept Burnside and the self-serving Hooker, selected the latter.
5. Edward J. Stackpole, *Chancellorsville*, 2nd ed. (Harrisburg, PA: Stackpole, 1988), 14–15. Hooker's chief of staff, Major General Daniel Butterfield, is generally credited with devising distinctive unit insignia. Butterfield, a man of many talents, also composed "Taps," the bugle call used to mark the end of the soldier's duty day.
6. *OR*, 25, II:59, 119–122, 148–149.
7. Stephen W. Sears, *Chancellorsville* (New York: Houghton Mifflin, 1996), 68–70. For a more detailed discussion of the formation of the Army of the Potomac's Bureau of Military Information, see Edwin C. Fishel, *The Secret War for the Union: The Untold Story of Military Intelligence in the Civil War* (New York: Houghton Mifflin, 1996).
8. Samuel M. Potter to Cynthia (wife), February 21, 1863, "Valley of the Shadow: Two Communities in the American Civil War," a project of the Virginia Center for Digital History, University of Virginia, Charlottesville, VA. Potter was a hospital orderly in the 16th Pennsylvania Cavalry. He died of chronic diarrhea on September 6, 1864. Potter, along with many other soldiers, both Union and Confederate, commented upon the informal truces arranged among pickets that they might gossip, trade, or bathe in the river. Such communications doubtlessly continued, although perhaps to a lesser extent, despite Hooker's ban.
9. Stackpole, *Chancellorsville*, 15–21.
10. Ernest B. Furguson, *Chancellorsville 1863: The Souls of the Brave* (New York: Alfred A Knopf, 1992), 34. This statement has also been attributed to other generals, both Union and Confederate.
11. *OR*, 25, II:51. To correct past problems with piecemealing the cavalry out to infantry corps and divisions, Hooker directed that cavalry details be limited to not more than a squadron (two companies) for each corps headquarters. The Headquarters of the Cavalry Corps, like the infantry corps, was also provided its own distinctive flag which featured a yellow field (the traditional color of the cavalry) with white crossed sabers (*OR*, 25, II:470).
12. *OR*, 24, II:65–66. The figures are from strength returns of February 10, 1863.
13. Ezra J. Warner, *Generals in Blue* (Baton Rouge: Louisiana State University Press, 1999), 481.
14. *OR*, 25, II:72.
15. Freeman, *R.E. Lee*, 2:490–496.
16. Robert E. Lee, *Wartime Papers*. 2 vols., edited by Clifford Dowdey (New York: Little, Brown, 1961; reprint ed., Pennington, NJ: Collectors Reprints, 1996), 1:385.
17. *Ibid.*
18. Confederate States War Department, *Regulations for the Army of the Confederate States, 1863* (Richmond, VA; reprint ed., Evansville, IN: Crescent City Sutler), 103. Through the first three months of 1863, the enlisted present-for-duty strength of the fifteen cavalry regiments

with the Army of Northern Virginia averaged fifty-eight percent of authorized strength (*OR*, 25, II:602, 650, 696).

19. Lee, *Wartime Papers*, 1:385. In his correspondence during the first few months of 1863, Lee expressed concern for the suffering of the army's horses on at least six occasions.

20. Janet Hewett et al., eds., *Supplement to the Official Records of the Union and Confederate Armies* (Wilmington, NC: Broadfoot, 1995–2000), II, 48:69. While perhaps of lesser concern, the lack of forage was also a problem for the horses in infantry regiments. In a letter to his wife dated March 15, Brigadier General Elisha F. Paxton wrote, "Many of our horses have died this winter for want of forage, and those that remain are much reduced in flesh and strength." (Elisha Franklin Paxton, "Memoir and Memorials: Elisha Franklin Paxton, Brigadier-General, C.S.A.; Composed of his Letters from Camp and Field While an Officer in the Confederate Army, with an Introductory and Connecting Narrative Collected and Arranged by his Son, John Gallatin Paxton." [Documenting the American South Collection, Academic Affairs Library, University of North Carolina, Chapel Hill, 1998], 93.) Leading the Stonewall Brigade, Paxton was killed at Chancellorsville on May 3, 1863 (Warner, *Generals in Gray*, 230).

21. *OR*, 25, II:695. Aware of Lee's pressing need for horses, the Confederate government made efforts to reduce shortages. Purchasing agents from as far away as Louisiana bought several hundred draft horses and mules for Lee's army, but those animals could not be brought to the Rappahannock until grass began to grow, otherwise they, too, would starve.

22. Freeman, *R.E. Lee*, 2:492.

23. *OR*, 25, II:711, 740.

24. William R. Carter, *Sabres, Saddles, and Spurs: The War Diary of Colonel William R. Carter, CSA*, edited by Walbrook D. Swank (Shippensburg, PA: Burd Street, 1998), 41; Robert Thruston Hubard, Jr. to his father, January 9, 1863, Robert Thruston Hubard Papers, 1811–1863 (#11556-a), Albert and Shirley Small Special Collections Library, University of Virginia, Charlottesville. Carter was the lieutenant colonel of the 3rd Virginia Cavalry. He was mortally wounded at Trevilian Station on June 11, 1864. Hubard was the adjutant of the 3rd Virginia Cavalry.

25. Sam Sweeney, Stuart's banjo player, was on the rolls of Company H, 2nd Virginia Cavalry, as a private. Sweeney died of smallpox at Orange Courthouse on January 13, 1864. (Robert J. Trout, *They Followed the Plume: The Story of J.E.B. Stuart and his Staff* [Mechanicsburg, PA: Stackpole, 1993], 322.)

26. JEB Stuart to Flora Stuart, February 8, 1864 (#7442), Albert and Shirley Small Special Collections Library, University of Virginia, Charlottesville. Flora may have had good cause to be concerned with her husband's conduct. Stuart's correspondence with Laura Ratcliff (more commonly spelled "Ratcliffe") in the winter of 1861–2 hints at a relationship that had evolved beyond flirting. In a lengthy letter from "Camp Laura" dated March 26, 1862, Stuart wrote, "Will you forget me? I am vain enough Laura to be flattered with the hope that *you* are among the few of mankind that neither time, place, or circumstances can alter — that your regard, which I so *dearly prize*, will not wane with yon moon that saw our last parting, but endure to the end." (Letters of JEB Stuart, 1861–1862, Miscellaneous Manuscripts Collection, Library of Congress, Washington, DC.) Laura Ratcliffe was a Southern sympathizer who lived in the Frying Pan area of Fairfax County, Virginia. Described as a "rather striking brunette," she on occasion passed information regarding Union troop movement to John S. Mosby and is today regarded as having been a spy for the Confederacy. (Virgil Carrington Jones, *Ranger Mosby* [Chapel Hill: University of North Carolina Press, 1944; reprint ed., McLean, VA: Elm, Nd.], 81–82, 146–147; John Bakeless, *Spies of the Confederacy* [New York: Lippincott, 1970], 62.).

27. The Rapidan River derived its name from Queen Ann ("rapid Anne"). The Rappahannock River above the Great Fork was known locally as Hedgeman's River. The "Little Fork" was upstream from the Great Fork at the confluence of the Rappahannock and the Hazel rivers.

28. Mary B. Daughtry, *Gray Cavalier: The Life and Wars of General W. H. F. "Rooney" Lee* (Cambridge, MA: Da Capo, 2002), 6, 13.

29. White House, the former homestead of Martha Washington, had been used by the Federals as a supply depot during the Peninsular Campaign the previous summer. Federal troops burned the house when they fled as Stuart made his famous ride around the Army of the Potomac. The original White House of Martha Washington's day had burned about thirty years before the war. (Freeman, *Lee's Lieutenants*, 3 vols. [New York: Scribner's, 1944], 1:634.)

30. G. W. Beale, *A Lieutenant of Cavalry in Lee's Army* (Boston, MA: Gorham, 1918; reprint ed., Baltimore, MD: Butternut and Blue, 1994), 220. G.W. Beale's father was R.L.T. Beale, who assumed command of the 9th Virginia upon Rooney Lee's promotion to brigadier general.

31. George W. Cullum, *Biographical Register of the Officers and Graduates of the U.S. Military Academy at West Point, N. Y. from Its Establishment in 1802, to 1890 with the Early History of the United States Military Academy*, 3 vols., 3rd ed. (New York: Houghton Mifflin, 1891), #1755. Lee ranked forty-fifth out of forty-nine graduates. (Harry Warren Radnour, doctoral dissertation, "General Fitzhugh Lee: A Biography" [University of Virginia, 1971], 20–22. The leader of the expedition to the Washita River was then-major Earl Van Dorn, later major general, C.S.A. Then-captain Kirby Smith, later general, C.S.A., was slightly wounded a few minutes before Lee was struck by the arrow.

32. Radnour, "General Fitzhugh Lee," 20–22.

33. Warner, *Generals in Gray*, 178. Inexplicably, Cullum's *Biographical Register* does not reflect Lee's assignment as a tactics instructor.

34. On only one known occasion did Stuart severely rebuke Fitz Lee. At the beginning of the Second Manassas Campaign, Lee dallied when moving his brigade to Orange County. On the night of August 17, 1862, Stuart, along with several of his staff officers, napped on the porch of a house in Vierdersville while awaiting Lee's arrival. Unexpectedly, a party of Union cavalry approached down the road leading to the small hamlet. Stuart escaped by leaping his horse over a picket fence around the back yard of the house, but in his haste he abandoned his plumed hat. To Stuart's chagrin, the hat was "captured" by the Yankees. In his official report, Stuart criticized Fitz Lee for arriving late and thus frustrating Robert E. Lee's plans for trapping Union Major General John Pope's army in Culpeper County. A week later, Stuart avenged the loss of his hat by raiding Pope's headquarters at Catlett's Station and making off with the coat from Pope's dress uniform. In jest, Stuart proposed that a cartel be formed to arrange an exchange of the "prisoners." Pope's coat and Stuart's hat were not exchanged, and instead Pope's coat was sent to Richmond and displayed at the Library of Virginia. (Douglas Southall Freeman, *Lee's Lieutenants*, 2:58, 72; Shelby Foote, *The Civil War: A Narrative*, 3 vols. [New York: Random House, 1974; reprint ed., New York: Vintage, 1986], 1:610.)

35. *New York Times*, March 22, 1863. Saint Patrick's Day activities included horse racing (both flat and steeplechasing), foot racing, leaping, vaulting, and a greased pig chase.

36. Henry B. McClellan, *I Rode with JEB Stuart: The Life and Campaigns of Major-General J.E.B. Stuart* (Bloomington: Indiana University Press, 1958; reprint ed., New York: Da Capo, 1994), 202–217. For a highly personal account of the fight at the ford, see R. H. Peck, *Reminiscences of a Confederate Soldier of Co. C, 2nd Va. Cavalry* (Fincastle, VA: Np., 1913).

37. *OR*, 25, I:50.

38. *OR*, 25, II:100–104.
39. Foote, *The Civil War: A Narrative*, 2:245–246. Although the coffee incident is imbedded in Civil War lore, the exact nature of the communications between Lee and Averell is open to question. On March 8, Charles Adams, Jr., a captain in the 1st Massachusetts Cavalry, wrote to his father that Fitz Lee "left us his compliments by the Widow Coakley" (Worthington, C. Ford, ed., *A Cycle of Adams Letters, 1861–1865*, 2 vols. [New York: Houghton Mifflin, 1920], 1:262–263). In his diary, Averell alluded to a taunt from his Confederate friend and may have mentioned the taunt to Hooker and President Lincoln (Eric J. Wittenberg, *The Union Cavalry Comes of Age: Hartwood Church to Brandy Station, 1863* [Washington, DC: Brassey's, 2003], 62, 117). However, Lee apparently did not cite the incident in his private papers, and Averell did not include an account of the incident in his memoir, *Ten Years in the Saddle*. Additionally, H. B. McClellan, who included descriptions of the Hartwood Church raid and the battle at Kelly's Ford in his book, *The Life and Campaigns of Major-General J.E.B. Stuart, Commander of the Cavalry of the Army of Northern Virginia*, did not include the taunt/coffee exchange.
40. Harry Gilmor, *Four Years in the Saddle* (New York: Harper & Brothers, 1866; reprint ed., Baltimore, MD: Butternut and Blue, Nd.), 64, 71–74. Gilmore was present when Pelham was wounded and assisted in taking the fatally wounded officer to the rear. A more popular, but probably embellished account of the incident described Pelham as galloping to the front, waving his sword and exhorting the men at the stone fence to attack, shouting, "Forward, Forward!" before being struck down (Freeman, *Lee's Lieutenants*, 2:463). Pelham was a true Southern hero, so it is not surprising that he was given a heroic death in Southern lore. For a detailed analysis of how Pelham "fell," see Robert J. Trout, *Galloping Thunder: The Stuart Horse Artillery Battalion* (Mechanicsburg, PA: Stackpole, 2002) 649–653.
41. Robert E. Lee to Charles Carter Lee, March 24, 1863 (#11424), Albert and Shirley Small Special Collections Library, University of Virginia, Charlottesville.
42. JEB Stuart to Flora Stuart (wife), November 2, 1863, Stuart Papers, 1833–1864 (St923 d 1–107), Virginia Historical Society, Richmond.
43. Sydney Smith Lee to Charles Carter Lee, March 28, 1863, Fitzhugh Lee Papers, 1731–1952 (Microfilm #1829–1931), Albert and Shirley Small Special Collections Library, University of Virginia, Charlottesville.
44. John J. Hennessy, "Lincoln Wins Back His Army," in *Civil War Times Illustrated* 34 (February 2001), 40.
45. Sears, *Chancellorsville*, 114–115.
46. David M. Gregg, "Brevet Major General David McMurtrie Gregg," Papers of David McMurtrie Gregg (MMC-0539), Library of Congress, Washington, DC, 183–185. After the review, Gregg sought out the owner of the horse and found him in his tent suffering from a broken arm, a result of having been thrown. Obviously, Gregg was not the first rider to encounter difficulty with the mount. Surprisingly, Gregg still bought the horse, but from that day forward he rode it with a more severe bit.
47. Hennessy, "Lincoln Wins Back his Army," 65.
48. *Ibid.*, 47. Commonly, the sight of a Lancer would provoke an infantryman to make a derisive gobbling sound (Sears, *Chancellorsville*, 115). However, it is likely that the foot soldiers curtailed their harassment of the distinctive troopers in the presence of the President.
49. *OR*, 25, I:1066.
50. Sears, *Chancellorsville*, 123–124. Confederates sent out from Culpeper captured about twenty-five of Davis' troopers while the crossing was being conducted.
51. *Ibid.*
52. For a more thorough description of the security measures employed successfully by Hooker, see Sears, *Chancellorsville*, 143–144.

53. Jacob Kent Langhorne Papers, Virginia Military Institute Library, Lexington.
54. Charles D. Walker, editor, *Memorial, Virginia Military Institute: Biographical Sketches of the Graduates and Eleves for the Virginia Military Institute Who Fell During the War Between the States* (Philadelphia, PA: Lippincott, 1875), 337–338. The *Memorial* provides biographical data on 170 VMI graduates or former cadets (the eleves) who died in Confederate service.
55. Extract of a letter from Mrs. Egbert Watson (Aunt Bettie) to Mrs. John A. Langhorne, June 16, 1863. Langhorne Family Papers (Mss 2 L26536, 7–8), Virginia Historical Society, Richmond.
56. Jacob Kent Langhorne to John Archer Langhorne (father), May 8, 1863, Jacob Kent Langhorne Papers, Civil War Collection, Virginia Military Institute Library, Lexington.
57. Cullum, *Biographical Register*, #1212; Warner, *Generals in Blue*, 373.
58. *OR*, 25, I:784. Major Pencock Huey, the commander of the 8th Pennsylvania, reported that his regiment was positioned to the right and front of Major General Sickles' division when he was ordered by Pleasonton to report to Major General Howard. In his official report, Huey made no mention of orders from Pleasonton to stop Jackson's corps "at all cost."
59. *OR*, 25, I:113.
60. Furguson, *Chancellorsville 1863*, 188–194.
61. Freeman, *Lee's Lieutenants*, 2:507.
62. The Confederates captured Little Sorrel from the Federals at Harpers Ferry in 1861 and Jackson purchased the small horse from the Confederate Quartermaster Department. Sorrel was recovered by the Confederates shortly after the Battle of Chancellorsville and given to Jackson's widow. She kept Sorrel at her home in North Carolina until 1883, when she presented the horse to VMI. Sorrel died there three years later at the age of thirty-six — extremely old for a horse. Sorrel's hide was preserved and is presently displayed over a plaster frame in the VMI Museum. In 1997 the horse's bones, which had been stored at the VMI Museum, were cremated and interred on the Institute's parade ground near Jackson's statue. (*Washington Post*, July 21, 1997, B1.)
63. Freeman, *Lee's Lieutenants*, 2:570–571; 582–583. Sandie Pendleton was the son of William Nelson Pendleton, Robert E. Lee's artillery chief. Sandie Pendleton was mortally wounded at Fisher's Hill in September 1864, just shy of his twenty-fifth birthday.
64. Upon Jackson's death, there was some speculation that Stuart would be promoted and appointed to command of the Second Corps. However, Lee chose to reorganize and elevate both Richard Ewell and Hill to corps command. One can surmise that Lee considered Stuart more valuable as his cavalry commander than as a commander of an infantry corps.
65. Freeman, *R. E. Lee*, 2:557.
66. *OR*, 25, II:464. Strength returns for May 10, 1863, showed 7,181 officers and 111,881 enlisted men present for duty.
67. *OR*, 25, II:437–438.
68. *OR*, 25, II:439.
69. *OR*, 25, II:463.

2 — Every Private Was a General

1. Roster data provided in H. E. Howard's Virginia Regimental History Series provides a wealth of readily accessible information regarding the men — at least the Virginians — who served in Stuart's cavalry.

2. Michael P. Musick, *6th Virginia Cavalry* (Lynchburg, VA: H.E. Howard, 1990), 108.

3. Papers of George Julian Pratt, 1861–1905 (#11283, 11283-a), Albert and Shirley Small Special Collections Library, University of Virginia, Charlottesville. Pratt, a University of Virginia student at the outbreak of the war, served initially in the "University Volunteers," Company G, 59th Virginia Infantry, and later as a lieutenant in the 18th Virginia Cavalry.

4. W. W. Lester and Wm. J. Bromwell, eds., *A Digest of the Military and Naval Laws of the Confederate States, from the Commencement of the Provisional Congress to the End of the First Congress Under the First Constitution* (Columbia, S.C.: Evans and Cogswell, 1864; Documenting the American South Collection, Academic Affairs Library, University of North Carolina, Chapel Hill), para. 62. While this law prescribed the organization of the cavalry regiment of the Confederacy's regular army, regiments provided by the states to the Provisional Army were similarly organized.

5. Woodford B. Hackley, *The Little Fork Rangers: A Sketch of Company "D" Fourth Virginia Cavalry* (Richmond, VA: Dirtz, 1927, reprint ed., Stephens City, VA: Commercial, 1999), 32–33.

6. Richard L. Armstrong, *11th Virginia Cavalry* (Lynchburg, VA: H. E. Howard, 1989), 119–120. Dulany Ball, whose four brothers enlisted in his company, was eventually promoted to lieutenant colonel of his regiment. Dulany's brother, Mottrom M. Ball, succeeded Dulaney in command of the company. Six of the ten members of the Ball family were wounded during the war, two of them mortally.

7. George Baylor, *Bull Run to Bull Run, or Four Years in the Army of Northern Virginia* (Richmond, VA: B. F. Johnson, 1900), 38, 39.

8. Charles Minor Blackford and Susan Leigh Blackford, *Letters from Lee's Army*, edited by Charles Minor Blackford III (New York: Scribner's, 1947; reprint ed., Lincoln: University of Nebraska Press, 1998), 1.

9. Hackely, *The Little Fork Rangers*, 26.

10. Robert Thruston Hubard, Jr., "Civil War Reminiscences of Robert Thruston Hubard, Jr.," Robert Thruston Hubard Papers, 1811–1863 (#11556-a), Albert and Shirley Small Special Collections Library, University of Virginia, Charlottesville.

11. Hackely, *The Little Fork Rangers*, 27–28, 33.

12. Confederate States War Department, *Regulations for the Army of the Confederate States, 1863* (Richmond, VA: J. W. Randolph, 1863; reprint ed., Evansville, IN: Crescent City Sutler, Nd.), 402–404.

13. Henry Woodhead, ed., *Arms and Equipment of the Confederacy* (Alexandria, VA: Time-Life Books, 1996), 82–85.

14. Confederate States War Department, *Regulations for the Army of the Confederate States, 1863*, 107.

15. Robert J. Trout, *They Followed the Plume: The Story of J.E.B. Stuart and his Staff* (Mechanicsburg, PA: Stackpole, 1993), 30–31.

16. The Union Sharps featured a patented primer system that automatically fed a paper primer disk into the breech in conjunction with the weapon's hammer fall. The Confederate version of the Sharps featured the more common and less complex nipple/percussion cap design.

17. The Union Army purchased about 146,000 Colt revolvers and 130,000 Remington revolvers in both army and navy models. The Remington revolvers were mostly issued later in the war after a fire damaged the Colt plant in Hartford, Connecticut. (Berkeley R. Lewis, *Notes on Cavalry Weapons of the American Civil War 1861–1865*, [Washington, D.C.: American Ordnance Association, 1961], 21).

18. Only about 1500 LeMat pistols were imported. Thus the LeMat, although popular, was not widely used.

19. Hackley, *The Little Fork Rangers*, 32.

20. W. A. Graham, "Nineteenth Regiment (Second Cavalry)," *Histories of the Several Regiments and Battalions from North Carolina in the Great War 1861–65: Witten by Members of the Respective Commands*, 5 vols., edited by Walter Clark (Raleigh, NC: E. M. Uzzell, 1901; reprint ed., Wendell, NC: Broadfoot's Bookmark, 1982), 2:82. Graham served as the commander of Company K, 2nd North Carolina Cavalry. His father was a former Governor of North Carolina (1840–43) and served as Secretary of the Navy (1845–49). After the war, the younger Graham became active in politics and served in both the North Carolina House and Senate.

21. Thomas T. Munford, "Reminiscences of Cavalry Operations," *Southern Historical Society Papers* 12 (1884), 348. Given the condition of Confederate cavalry at the end of the war, his observations are probably exaggerated.

22. At the time, it was relatively uncommon to refer to cavalry companies as troops, and units identified with a letter designation were always identified as companies.

23. Douglas Southall Freeman, *Lee's Lieutenants*, 3 vols. (New York: Charles Scribner's Sons), 1971), 1:701–702.

24. Douglas Southall Freeman, *R. E. Lee*, 4 vols. (New York: Charles Scribner's Sons, 1949), 2:26–27. Afterward, vacancies among lieutenants were to be filled by election from the ranks, while vacancies among captains and field grade officers were to be filled by promotion of qualified officers from within the regiment.

25. JEB Stuart to "My Dear Wifey," January 29, 1862, JEB Stuart Papers, 1851–1968 (Mss1 St 923d 19), Virginia Historical Society, Richmond.

26. Lee A. Wallace, Jr., *A Guide to Virginia Military Organizations 1861–1865* (Richmond: Virginia Civil War Commission, 1964), 46–68.

27. Bell I. Wiley, *The Life of Johnny Reb* (Baton Rouge: Louisiana State University Press, 1993), 327–329. Slaves were also employed by the Confederate army as teamsters, with payment for their services being given to their masters. See Ervin L. Jordan, Jr., *Black Confederates and Afro Yankees in Civil War Virginia* (Charlottesville: University Press of Virginia, 1995), Chapter 7, for a detailed description of body servants in the Confederate Army. A company officer was also authorized to detail a soldier as his "waiter" or orderly.

28. Robert T. Hubard, Jr., to Robert T. Hubard (father), January 9, 1863, Robert Thruston Hubard Papers, 1811–1863 (#11556-a), Albert and Shirley Small Special Collections Library, University of Virginia, Charlottesville. Matthews was probably George H. Matthews, Jr., a captain in the 3rd Virginia, who, like Hubard, was from Cumberland County, Virginia, and enlisted in Company G at the start of the war. Matthews was mortally wounded at Mitchell's Shop on May 9, 1864. He died four days later. (Thomas P. Nanzig, *3rd Virginia Cavalry*, [Lynchburg, VA: H.E. Howard, 1989], 118.) Ca Ira was the Cumberland County home of another of Hubard's messmates, Dr. Charles Palmore, the 3rd Cavalry's regimental surgeon. The name "Ca Ira" was taken from a French Revolutionary song; meaning "it will do," it was used as a rallying cry by the Federalists (Brewer, E. Cobham, *Dictionary of Phrase and Fable* [www.bartleby.com]).

29. Robert Scott Hudgins, II, *Recollections of an Old Dominion Dragoon: The Civil War Experiences of Sgt. Robert S. Hudgins II, Co. B, 3d Virginia Cavalry*, edited by Garland C. Hudgins and Richard B. Kleese (Orange, VA: Publisher's Press, 1993), 84–85.

30. Early in the war, some states provided horses for their cavalrymen. For example, troopers in the 1st and 2nd North Carolina Cavalry were issued horses by the state when those regiments were organized.

31. Confederate States War Department, *Regulations for the Army of the Confederate States, 1863*, 103.

32. William W. Blackford, *War Years with JEB Stuart* (New York: Scribner's, 1945; reprint ed., Baton Rouge: Louisiana State University Press, 1993), 89. William W. Blackford was the elder brother of Charles Minor Blackford, cited above.

33. The premier thoroughbred of the mid-1800s was

Lexington, a four-mile racer owned by Richard TenBroeck. TenBroeck was a New Yorker who, after leaving West Point in 1830 after only one year as a cadet, moved to Kentucky and began a long career as a race horse breeder and gambler. (Association of Graduates, USMA, *Register of Graduates*.) Cincinnati, U.S. Grant's favorite horse, was sired by Lexington. The foundation sire for the modern quarterhorse was Janus, a thoroughbred stallion that was imported from England in 1756.

34. Blackford, *War Years with JEB Stuart*, 21–23. Blackford's affection for his favorite mount, Comet, is obvious from his two-page description of the horse's appearance and mannerisms. Comet was wounded in the neck at Chantilly in August 1862 and Blackford retired him from service. After the war, Blackford had surgery performed on Comet's wound, which had not healed properly. After the surgery, Comet provided "good service" to Blackford for several more years (133–138).

35. Robert K. Krick, *9th Virginia Cavalry*, 4th ed. (Lynchburg, VA: H. E. Howard, 1982), 18.

36. John H. Ervine to Ellen Ervine, June 18, 1861 (#361), Civil War Collection, Virginia Military Institute Library, Lexington.

37. Hackley, *The Little Fork Rangers*, 31–32. If appraised value is an indication, the officers of the Little Fork Rangers were, on average, better mounted than the privates.

38. Thomas T. Hoskins to John T. Hoskins (father), June 10, 1863, Hoskins Family Papers (#H7935 a 2–11), Virginia Historical Society, Richmond. In August 1863, Thomas Hoskins wrote home and traded Little Peep for his father's horse, a large gray named Extra Billy (after former Virginia governor and Culpeper resident William "Extra Billy" Smith). The elder Hoskins admonished Thomas to take good care of Extra Billy because he was a valuable horse (John T. Hoskins to Thomas T. Hoskins, September 16, 1863). Thomas Hoskins was mortally wounded at Manassas on October 17, 1863. He died two days later at Catlett's Station.

39. George Julian Pratt to his mother, June 21, 1863, Papers of George Julian Pratt, 1861–1905 (#11283, 11283-a), Albert and Shirley Small Special Collections Library, University of Virginia, Charlottesville.

40. JEB Stuart to William Alexander Stuart, March 1, 1864, William Alexander Stuart Papers (St938 a 1–19), Virginia Historical Society, Richmond. Stuart's horses were ill with farcy, a bacterial infection better known today as glanders. The disease, now relatively rare, was formerly a serious problem when large numbers of horses and mules were used by armies during wartime.

41. Thomas T. Munford, "Reminiscences of Cavalry Operations," *Southern Historical Society Papers* 12 (January–December 1884), 347.

42. Richard L. Armstrong, *7th Virginia Cavalry* (Lynchburg, VA: H. E. Howard, 1992), 125.

43. William Clark Corson to Jennie (Mss1 C8184 a), Virginia Historical Society, Richmond. Corson's horse, Don, was appraised at five hundred dollars.

44. Most commonly, horses lose shoes by stepping on the heel of a front shoe with their hind toe. As a horse's hooves grow, the likelihood that the horse might pull a shoe increases. Shoes that are lost are commonly referred to as being "cast," "thrown," or "pulled."

45. Karl Douglas Butler, *Principles of Horseshoeing II: An Illustrated Textbook of Farrier Science and Craftsmanship* (Laporte, CO: Butler, 1983), 25–26. A portion of the Confederate Army's horse shoes were manufactured by blacksmiths under contract to the Quartermaster department or by blacksmiths working in Confederate armories. In the year ending in September 1863, the army issued 266,951 pounds of horse shoes to its units. (Jennings C. Wise, *The Long Arm of Lee: A History of the Artillery of the Army of Northern Virginia* [Lynchburg, VA: J. P. Bell, 1915; reprint ed., 2 vols., Lincoln: University of Nebraska Press, 1991], 1:49.)

46. Henry B. McClellan, *I Rode with Stuart: The Life and Campaigns of Major-General J.E.B. Stuart* (Bloomington: University of Indiana Press, 1958; reprint ed., New York: Da Capo, 1994), 261. Under many circumstances, one would expect the shoes on dead horses to be well-worn and hardly worth salvaging. In any event, it seems a trooper would be more likely to remove the shoes from the hoofs than the hoofs from the horse. Severing a horse's leg at the fetlock joint is a difficult task which, when completed, leaves the trooper with a cumbersome and messy bundle to sling over his saddle and carry away. On the other hand, using simple tools one can quickly and easily open a shoe's nail-clinches and then pry the shoe off of the hoof.

47. Thomas T. Munford, "Reminiscences of Cavalry Operations," *Southern Historical Society Papers* 12 (1884), 347.

48. JEB Stuart to Thomas Rosser, April 4, 1864 (#8482), Albert and Shirley Small Special Collections Library, University of Virginia, Charlottesville. Federal cavalrymen were also instructed to carry extra shoes and nails (Theodore F. Rodenbough, ed., *The Cavalry*, vol. 2 of *Photographic History of the Civil War* ed. Francis Trevelyan Miller [New York: Review of Reviews, 1911; reprint ed., Secaucus, NJ: Blue & Gray, 1987], 62).

49. William R. Carter, *Sabres, Saddles, and Spurs: The War Diary of Colonel William R. Carter, CSA*, edited by Walbrook D. Swank (Shippensburg, PA: Burd Street, 1998), 28–29. At the time, numerous cavalry horses were afflicted with scratches (an inflamation of the horse's skin above the hoofs) and sore tongues. R. E. Lee, when apprised of these problems, wrote Stuart: "The former [problem] I think by proper attention on the part of your men can be easily remedied, & the latter is probably occasioned or aggravated by feeding on the ground. I need not recommend to you to urge upon your officers & men strict attention to this matter." (Robert E. Lee, *Wartime Papers*, 2 vols., edited by Clifford Dowdey, [New York: Little, Brown, 1961; reprint ed., Pennington, NJ: Collectors Reprints, 1996], 1:329.)

50. The Union army established six major remount depots. The largest was at Giesboro Point in the District of Columbia (now the site of Bolling Air Force Base). Between January 1, 1864, and June 30, 1866, over 175,000 horses passed through Giesboro. (Rodenbough, *Photographic History of the Civil War*, vol. 4, *The Cavalry*, 334.)

51. Stephen S. Starr, "Cavalry Tactics in the American Civil War," Cincinnati Civil War Roundtable, 1997 (http://www.mmcwrt.org/2002/default0205.htm).

52. Ezra J. Warner, *Generals in Gray* (Baton Rouge: Louisiana State University Press, 1990), 62–63.

53. J. Lucius Davis, *The Trooper's Manual: or, Tactics for Light Dragoons and Mounted Riflemen ...* (Richmond, VA: A. Morris, 1861), preface, viii. Davis politely noted that in his haste to publish the manual, he failed to obtain permission for his book's revolver drill that had been written by a Captain Bell, U.S. Cavalry.

54. Jennings C. Wise, *Military History of Virginia Military Institute from 1861– 1865* (Lynchburg, VA: J. P. Bell, 1915), 55, 114–115. Gilham, an 1840 graduate of West Point, resigned his commission in 1846 to accept a position on the faculty at VMI.

55. Musick, *6th Virginia Cavalry*, 1.

56. Winston S. Churchill, *My Early Life* (London: Odhams, 1947), 64.

57. Hudgins, *Recollections of an Old Dominion Dragoon*, 39–41.

58. *OR*, 25, II:823.

59. On May 24, 1863, General Hooker sent a note to General Lee pointing out to the Southern commander his army's seine fishing on the south bank of the Rappahannock afforded opportunity for communication between the soldiers of the two armies — communications that Hooker was attempting to quash. Hooker wrote that he was bringing the matter to Lee's attention to avoid the needless shedding of blood. (*OR*, 25, I:521.)

60. Janet Hewett et al., eds., *Supplement to the Official Records of the Union and Confederate Armies* (Wilmington, NC: Broadfoot, 1995–2000), II, 69:684.
61. John N. Opie, *A Rebel Cavalryman with Lee Stuart and Jackson* (Chicago: W. B. Conkey, 1899; reprint ed., Dayton, Ohio, Morningside Bookshop, 1972), 158.
62. *OR*, 25, II:823.
63. Naturally one should not downplay other factors—deprivation, fear, fatigue, homesickness—that motivated soldiers to go AWOL. See Ella Lonn, *Desertion During the Civil War* (Gloucester, MA: Peter Smith, 1966), Chapter 1, for a detailed discussion of the causes of desertion among soldiers of the Confederacy.
64. Tom Garber to Addie Garber, April 15, 1863, "Valley of the Shadow: Two Communities in The American Civil War," a project of the Virginia Center for Digital History, University of Virginia, Charlottesville. Garber, a cousin to Colonel Asher Harman, the regimental commander, was killed at Upperville on June 21, 1863.
65. Musick, *6th Virginia Cavalry*, 8–9.
66. *Ibid*.
67. Musick, *6th Virginia Cavalry*, roster information.
68. Richard L. Armstrong, *7th Virginia Cavalry* (Lynchburg, VA: H. E. Howard, 1992), 222. Shands, a lawyer from Harrisonburg, was forty-two years old at the time he was shot.
69. Blackford and Blackford, *Letters from Lee's Army*, 137.
70. Blackford and Blackford, *Letters from Lee's Army*, 139. Captain William Steptoe replaced Charles Minor Blackford as commander of the Wise Troop.
71. Dennis E. Frye, *12th Virginia Cavalry*, 2nd ed. (Lynchburg, VA: H.E. Howard, 1988), 109.
72. *OR*, 25, II:836–837.

3—By Easy Marches

1. Even the Union army appreciated the quality of the grass in Culpeper County. On May 27, 1863, Hooker was informed by Colonel Starke, his intelligence chief, that Stuart's cavalry was in Culpeper being "constantly and rapidly recruited by spring grasses." Pleasonton, in a message to Hooker, further opined that Culpeper had the best grazing in Virginia. (*OR*, 25, II:528; *OR*, 27, III:30.)
2. Lord Culpeper, who spent only a few weeks in the colony he was charged with administering, devoted most of his energy to amassing vast estates in the Northern Neck region. Now remembered mostly for his avarice, Lord Culpeper died in 1689 in the bed of his mistress, with whom he had two daughters.
3. Raus McDill Hanson, *Virginia Place Names, Derivations, Historical Uses* (Verona, VA: McClure, 1969), 67. The Old Carolina Road was commonly called Rogues Road after the numerous highwaymen that preyed upon its travelers.
4. Eugene M. Scheel, *Culpeper: A Virginia County's History Through 1920* (Orange, VA: Green, 1982), 338; 408, n. 18. According to Scheel, this is the first known description of Brandy. There are other stories regarding the origin of the town's name. According to some sources, a group of soldiers passing down the Carolina Road during the War of 1812 stopped at the tavern. The soldiers became disgruntled when they exhausted the Herrings' supply of brandy. In protest, they supposedly scrawled "BRANDY" on the side of the tavern as they departed, from which the name of the community was later derived.
5. The engagement was fought between Brigadier General Beverly Robertson's brigade and a Union brigade commanded by Brigadier General George D. Bayard. Stuart, who observed the fight, reported Robertson's losses as three killed and thirteen wounded, with Union losses at several more killed and sixty-four captured. Stuart praised the conduct of Colonel William E. Jones, then the commander of the 7th Virginia Cavalry and serving under Robertson. (*OR*, 12, II:727–728.)
6. Parts from the grist mill machinery are now displayed as lawn sculpture at the Culpeper County Museum in Culpeper.
7. Scheel, *Culpeper: A Virginia County's History*, 346–347; Daniel E. Sutherland, *Seasons of War: The Ordeal of a Confederate Community* (New York: The Free Press, 1995), 12–13, 24; W.D. Gore, "Kelly's Ford and John Kelly's House," U.S. Government, Works Project Administration, "Virginia Historical Inventory," Library of Virginia, Richmond, 1936; U.S. Census Records for Culpeper County, 1860. For a view of Kellyville as it appeared in November 1863, see Robert Knox Sneeden, *Images from the Storm*, edited by Charles F. Bryan, Jr., and Nelson D. Lankford (New York: The Free Press, 2001), 176.
8. The vote in Culpeper County was 1051 to 0 in favor of secession.
9. John Minor Botts, *The Great Rebellion: Its Secret History, Rise, Progress, and Disastrous Failure* (New York: Harper & Brothers, 1866), 294, 301, 302, 305.
10. Margaret Jeffries, "Auburn," U.S. Government, Work Projects Administration, Virginia Historical Inventory, Library of Virginia, Richmond, 1937.
11. Scheel, *Culpeper: A Virginia County's History*, 201.
12. Botts, *The Great Rebellion*, 294. Culpeper County records indicate that Botts and Franklin Stearns, a Vermonter who moved to Culpeper before the war, purchased Auburn from Beckham for one hundred thousand dollars in December 1862. However, shortly after the war Beckham died and his heirs sued to regain possession of the property. The County Court ruled against the heirs, chiding them for presenting evidence that was not relevant and, further, was "declared by the law to be slanderous and which shock[ed] the sense of propriety of the court." The Beckham heirs promptly appealed. On November 25, 1875, the Virginia Supreme Court of Appeals set aside the decision of the lower court, finding that when James A. Beckham executed the deed transferring Auburn to Botts and Stearns, he was incapacitated by an attack of paralysis to the extent that he could only sign his name by making an "x." Consequently, the court nullified the December 1862 deed and returned Auburn to the Beckham family. (Culpeper County Deed Book # 14:543; Culpeper County Chancery Court Order Book #5: 253; Virginia Supreme Court of Appeals, Richmond Session, Order Book # 24:33.) The main house at Auburn was built in 1843 and still stands. It is visible to the north of Highway 29, ½ mile east of the Route Business 29 exit to Culpeper.
13. Scheel, *Culpeper: A Virginia County's History*, 202. The main house still stands on the north side of County Route 666 between Culpeper and Brandy Station.
14. See Robert J. Trout, *They Followed the Plume: The Story of J.E.B. Stuart and his Staff* (Mechanicsburg, PA: Stackpole, 1993) for a detailed description of the organization and personnel of Stuart's headquarters.
15. Blackford, *War Years with JEB Stuart* (New York: Scribner's, 1945; reprint ed., Baton Rouge: Louisiana State University Press, 1993), 156. Estimates of von Borcke's size vary. Other contemporaries referred to von Borcke as being six feet three inches or six feet four inches tall and weighing 230 or 240 pounds. All sources agree that von Borcke was a very large man.
16. Henry B. McClellan, *I Rode with JEB Stuart: The Life and Campaigns of Major-General J.E.B. Stuart* (Bloomington: Indiana University Press, 1958; reprint ed., New York: Da Capo, 1994), v–vii.
17. George W. Cullum, *Biographical Register of the Officers and Graduates of the U.S. Military Academy at West*

Point, N.Y. from its Establishment in 1802 to 1890 with the Early History of the United States Military Academy, 3 vols. (New York: Houghton Mifflin, 1891), #1261; Bruce S. Allerdice, *More Generals in Gray* (Baton Rouge: Louisiana State University Press, 1995), 171; Jeffry Wert, "Colonel Tom Munford: A Man of Achievement," *Civil War Times Illustrated* 24 (June 1985), 30. At VMI Munford roomed with George S. Patton, also a Confederate colonel and grandfather of the "Blood & Guts" general of World War II fame.

18. *OR*, 25, II:654.

19. James Ewell Brown Stuart, *Letters of Major General James E. B. Stuart*, edited by Adele H. Mitchell (Stuart-Mosby Historical Society, 1990), 217, 274–275; Henry B. McClellan, "Letters from Stuart's Headquarters," *Southern Historical Society* Papers 3 (January–June 1877), 191.

20. Jacob Kent Langhorne to Papa (John Archer Langhorne), May 11, 1863, Jacob Kent Langhorne Papers, Civil War Collection, Virginia Military Institute Library, Lexington. The identity of "Judge" is not clear.

21. Thomas P. Nanzig, *3rd Virginia Cavalry* (Lynchburg, VA: H. E. Howard, 1989), 8.

22. *Ibid.*, 13, 25.

23. *Ibid.*, 121. In April 1862, then-Captain Owen and another VMI graduate, Captain John Thornton, decided not to allow the popular vote to determine which of the two would serve as lieutenant colonel of the regiment. Instead they engaged in a fencing match. The winner of the match, Thornton, was promoted to lieutenant colonel and the loser, Owen, to major. Thornton was mortally wounded at Antietam and Owen was promoted to take his place. (*Ibid.*, 21–22.)

24. Before the Civil War, Pate had gone to Kansas and fought with the pro-slavery Missouri militia.

25. Stuart, *Letters of Major General James E. B. Stuart*, 275. Later in the war, Rosser was sent to support Jubal Early west of the Blue Ridge, an event that prompted Rosser to pompously proclaim himself the "Savior of the Valley." Shortly afterward, the erstwhile "Savior" was soundly thrashed by Sheridan's cavalrymen at Tom's Creek.

26. Millard K. Bushong and Dean M. Bushong, *Fightin' Tom Rosser, C. S. A.* (Shippensburg, PA: Beidel, Inc., 1983), 42–43; Thomas O. Beane, master's thesis, "Thomas Lafayette Rosser: Soldier, Railroad Builder, Politician, Businessman (1836–1910)" (University of Virginia, 1957), 24–25. The sources differ on the date of the wedding, one citing May 29, the other May 28. Reportedly, early in the war Rosser and several officers were riding through Hanover Courthouse. Seeing a young boy sitting on a fence, Rosser asked for a drink of water, promising that if the boy fetched it, he would return and marry the boy's sister. About a year later, Rosser was again passing through Hanover. He stopped at a house to borrow a pencil and paper. By chance, the same young boy answered the door, recognized Rosser, and ran into the house shouting, "Betty, Betty! Here is the man that said he was going to come back and marry you." Rosser and Elizabeth Winston were married several months later. The well-attended wedding was held at the Winstons' home, "Courtland."

27. There is some justification for Pate's accusation. Rosser was known to drink when unhappy, a practice that he endeavored to change after his marriage. On June 18, 1863, Rosser wrote to his wife that her influence had caused him to change his "moral condition," and that he was "growing a better man." (Thomas L. Rosser to Betty Rosser, June 18, 1863, Papers of Thomas Lafayette Rosser [Mss 1171], Albert and Shirley Small Special Collections Library, University of Virginia, Charlottesville.)

28. Robert J. Driver, Jr., *5th Virginia Cavalry* (Lynchburg, VA: H. E. Howard, 1997), 249. After Rosser was promoted to brigadier general in October 1863, Pate was appointed to command of the 5th Virginia and eventually promoted to colonel. Pate was killed at Yellow Tavern — shot in the head — while defending a position that Stuart had directed he "hold at all hazard." The *Richmond Examiner* reported that while relations between Stuart and Pate had been strained, the two shook hands and renewed their friendship shortly before each was shot. However, there is little evidence to corroborate this event. (Driver, *5th Virginia Cavalry*, 22–23, 67, 76, 241–242; *Richmond Examiner*, May 17, 1864.) Rosser ended the war as a major general. Afterwards he worked as a railroad executive and farmer near Charlottesville. He was appointed brigadier general of volunteers during the Spanish-American War and given command of an infantry brigade but did not see service overseas. Rosser later became a Republican and was appointed by Theodore Roosevelt as postmaster of Charlottesville, where he died in 1910.

29. Robert J. Driver, Jr., *1st Virginia Cavalry* (Lynchburg, VA: H. E. Howard, 1991), 1, 169.

30. *OR*, 25, II:499.

31. Alexander Hunter, *Johnny Reb & Billy Yank* (New York: Neale, 1905; reprint ed., Konecky & Konecky), 419. The name of the company was selected by the organization's first commander, John Scott, and derived from an old Saxon symbol, the white horse. Perhaps for originality, Scott decided to change the color of the horse from white to black. (Katherine Isham Keith, "The Record of the Black Horse Troop," *Bulletin of the Fauquier Historical Society* [July 1924]: 436.

32. Kenneth Stiles, *4th Virginia Cavalry*, 2d ed. (Lynchburg, VA: H.E. Howard, 1985), 10.

33. Ezra J. Warner, *Generals in Gray* (Baton Rouge: Louisiana State University Press, 1959), 335.

34. John Fortier, *15th Virginia Cavalry* (Lynchburg, VA: H. E. Howard, 1993), 30–31.

35. Fortier, *15th Virginia Cavalry*, 15–16; George W. Cullum, *Biographical Register*..., #1827. At the beginning of the war, Collins spent several weeks as a mustering officer in Elmira, New York, before he resigned his commission and went south.

36. Fortier, *15th Virginia Cavalry*, 33.

37. Collins turned out to be the leader who gave his men "chances in the field," but his promotion was delayed because both Ball and Critcher remained on the rolls of the regiment. Ball, although continuously absent, did not resign his commission until January 1864. For valor, Collins was given a temporary promotion to colonel in February 1864. Two months later he was killed leading his men at Todd's Tavern. After Collins' death Critcher returned to the command of the regiment, lasting only three weeks before being relieved on the field by Brigadier General Lunsford Lomax. After the war Critcher returned to the practice of law, became a judge, and served a term in the U.S. Congress. He died in 1901. Ball reportedly committed suicide shortly after the end of the war. (Fortier, *15th Virginia Cavalry*, 71, 75, 104, 106, 120, 127, 129.)

38. The two most notable extant examples of Johnson's architectural work are Staunton Hill, a Gothic mansion in Charlotte County, Virginia, and Berry Hill, a Greek revival plantation house in Halifax County. Both are on the National Register of Historic Places.

39. Robert Krick, *Lee's Colonels*, 2nd ed., revised (Dayton, OH: Morningside Bookshop, 1984), 192. Johnson later served as a volunteer *aide de camp* to Lieutenant General Richard Ewell.

40. Warner, *Generals in Gray*, 20–21.

41. Cullum, *Biographical Register*, #1609.

42. Robert J. Driver, Jr., *10th Virginia Cavalry* (Lynchburg, VA: H. E. Howard, 1992), 107–108. Bathurst M. Davis was a private in Companies E and G. James L. Davis, Jr., was a private in Companies E and A. Lewellyn Catesby Davis was a private in Company E.

43. Daniel T. Balfour, *13th Virginia Cavalry*, 2d ed. (Lynchburg, VA: H. E. Howard, 1986), 9–16.

44. Louis H. Manarin, *The Cavalry*. Vol. 2 of *North Carolina Troops 1861–1865, A Roster...* (Raleigh: North Carolina State Department of Archives and History, 1968), 98.

45. Janet Hewett et al., eds., *Supplement to the Official Records of the Union and Confederate Armies* (Wilmington, NC: Broadfoot, 1995–2000), II, 48, 56–57.

46. Cullum, *Biographical Register*, #1808.

47. Myrta Lockett Avery, ed., *A Virginia Girl in the Civil War 1861–1865: Being a Record of the Actual Experiences of the Wife of a Confederate Officer* (New York: D. Appleton, 1903), 245.

48. Manly Wade Wellman, *Giant in Gray: A Biography of Wade Hampton of South Carolina* (New York: Scribner's, 1949), 50–51.

49. Reportedly, Hampton personally killed thirteen opponents in battle, two with his sword (*Ibid.*, 331).

50. *Ibid.*, 99–101.

51. As a matter of policy, Jefferson Davis was reluctant to accept those holding general officer commissions from states for service in the Provisional Army of the Confederacy at that grade.

52. Bruce S. Allerdice, *More Generals in Gray* (Baton Rouge: Louisiana State University Press, 1995), 184. Phillips briefly returned to command the Legion in South Carolina, but ill health forced him to seek further medical treatment and led to his resignation in February 1863. Afterwards, Phillips operated the Marietta Paper Mills until they were destroyed by Sherman's forces in 1864.

53. Rich became ill with hepatitis in 1864 and resigned his commission in January 1865.

54. In 1864, four Alabama cavalry companies were added to the Phillips Legion Cavalry bringing it up to the regimental authorization of ten companies.

55. John Logan Black, *Crumbling Defenses or Memoirs and Reminiscences of John Logan Black, Colonel C. S. A. ..*, edited by Eleanor D. McSwain (Macon GA: Np., 1960), 13–14. Black was married in December 1853 to Mary Peay Black, his first cousin, so perhaps romantic interests prompted his resignation from the military academy. Then, as now, cadets were prohibited from marrying.

56. Hewett et al., *Supplement to the Official Records*, II, 64:42.

57. Warner, *Generals in Gray*, 40. After Butler's father died in 1849, Butler's maternal uncle, Commodore Matthew Calbraith Perry, offered to raise the young boy in Massachusetts. Instead, Butler chose to live with his fraternal uncle in South Carolina. (Samuel J. Martin, *Southern Hero: Matthew Calbraith Butler* [Mechanicsburg, PA: Stackpole, 2001], 5, 7).

58. Cullum, *Biographical Register*, #1535; Manarin, *North Carolina Troops*, vol. 2, *The Cavalry*, 1–3, 7. Baker's given name was changed from Laurence to Lawrence in his official file because of a clerical error (Warner, *Generals in Gray*, 14). The 1st North Carolina also contained two other noteworthy officers. First Lieutenant William P. Roberts was serving as first lieutenant of Company C. In February 1865, Roberts, then five months shy of his twenty-fourth birthday, became the youngest general in the Confederate army. Captain Rufus Barringer, a lawyer and politician, was related by marriage to generals D. H. Hill and Stonewall Jackson. Barringer raised a company, the Cabarrus Rangers, in June 1861, and had served as its captain ever since. However, in the coming year the forty-two year old officer would be promoted to major, lieutenant colonel, and then brigadier general.

59. Thomas Cobb was promoted to brigadier general in November 1862 and appointed to command of an infantry brigade. He was mortally wounded — a gunshot wound to the leg severed his femoral artery — while defending the sunken road at the base of Marye's Heights at Fredericksburg. (Douglas Southall Freeman, *Lee's Lieutenants* [New York: Scribner's, 1944], 2:361.)

60. Mustering-in of the final company was delayed, however, because the men lacked horses. In October 1863, an eleventh company (L Company) was raised. In July 1864, L Company was transferred to the Phillips Legion and Cobb's Legion Cavalry was redesignated the 9th Georgia Cavalry. (Joseph H. Crute, *Units of the Confederate States Army*, [Midlothian, VA: Derwent Books, 1987], 118; Hewett et al., *Supplement to the Official Records*, II, 7:244.)

61. Young's West Point class was originally scheduled to graduate in June 1862, but instead graduated in June 1861 because of the war. Later in life, Young inaccurately referred to himself as an academy graduate.

62. Lynwood M. Holland, *Pierce M. B. Young: The Warwick of the South* (Athens: University of Georgia Press, 1964), 52, 54–55, 67–68.

63. In 1864 four more companies from Alabama and Georgia were added to the Jeff Davis Legion to bring it up to regimental strength.

64. *Roll of Officers and Members of the Georgia Hussars and of the Cavalry Companies, of which the Hussars are a Continuation, with Historical Sketch Relating Facts Showing the Origin and Necessity of Rangers, or Mounted Men in the Colony of Georgia from the Date of Its Founding* (Savannah, GA: The Morning News, 1906), 228.

65. Michael P. Musick, *6th Virginia Cavalry* (Lynchburg, VA: H.E. Howard, 1990), 4; *Roll of Officers and Members of the Georgia Hussars* 271–272. Undoubtedly, the Georgians were influenced in their decision to join the 6th Virginia by the fact that Colonel Charles Field, the commander of the cavalry training camp at Ashland, Virginia, had been appointed to command that regiment.

66. Patrick A. Bowmaster, master's thesis, "Confederate Brig. Gen. B. H. Robertson and the Gettysburg Campaign" (Virginia Polytechnic Institute and State University, 1995), 5.

67. Warner, *Generals in Gray*, 259–260.

68. *OR*, 18:1088. In August 1862, Lee had sent Stuart to inspect Robertson's brigade, then in the Shenandoah Valley. Stuart reported that Robertson's brigade was "a fine body of Cavalry, well armed; discipline and instruction good." While giving Robertson credit for the condition of his organization, Stuart cautioned that he was "convinced of [Robertson's] deficiency in the qualities essential to a bold, vigorous and successful cav' commander in the ever-changing and extended operations of a campaign." (George Bolling Lee, Papers 1813–1924 [Mss1 L5114d; Reel C 278], Virginia Historical Society, Richmond.)

69. *OR*, 18:1071, 1075. In previous correspondence to Secretary of War Seddon, Hill had commented that his troops in North Carolina included the "wonderfully inefficient brigade of Robertson" (*OR*, 18: 891). Hill had proposed that Hampton be sent to North Carolina to replace Robertson, but Lee, who greatly appreciated Hampton's abilities, naturally did not support that idea.

70. Manarin, *North Carolina Troops*, vol. 2, *The Cavalry*, 263, 266. The regiment's ninth and tenth companies were not added until the spring of 1864.

71. *OR*, 28:19; Neil H. Raiford, *4th North Carolina Cavalry in the Civil War* (Jefferson, NC: McFarland, 2003), 17–20.

72. *Ibid.*, 2:367, 368, 372, 213. E Company of the 5th North Carolina remained in North Carolina and did not rejoin the regiment until April 1864.

73. Hewett et al., *Supplement to the Official Records*, II, 48:108, 121, 124, 133; *OR*, 25, II:823.

74. Jones' Brigade is today best known as the "Laurel Brigade." In April 1864, JEB Stuart endorsed a report by then-brigade commander Thomas Rosser, commenting that the brigade had earned "fresh laurels." Rosser, always with an eye toward self-promotion, then encouraged his men to pin a sprig of laurel to either their hats or their coats. (William N. McDonald, *A History of the Laurel*

Brigade, edited by Bushrod C. Washington, [Baltimore, MD: Mrs. Kate S. McDonald, 1907, reprint, ed.: Baltimore: Johns Hopkins University Press, 2002]), 5.

75. It was customary to travel by ship to Nicaragua, go overland across Central America, and then travel by ship up the West Coast.

76. " 'Grumble' Jones: A Personality Profile," *Civil War Times Illustrated* 7 (June 1968): 35–36; Thomas E. Colley, "Brig. Gen William E. Jones," *Confederate Veteran* 11 (June 1903), 266.

77. The Company, originally called the Washington Mounted Rifles (after Washington County, Virginia), was initially organized in 1859 by W. W. Blackford, who replaced Jones as company commander when Jones was elected lieutenant colonel of the 1st Virginia. Jones and Blackford later had a falling-out, Jones had Blackford briefly arrested, and Blackford eventually transferred to the Engineers and served on Stuart's staff. Perhaps Blackford's well known disdain for West Pointers stemmed from his experiences with Jones.

78. Warner, *Generals in Gray*, 167.

79. Stuart, *Letters of Major General James E. B. Stuart*, 272.

80. Envisioning the need for more cavalry, on May 16, Robert E. Lee sent a telegram to Major General Sam Jones, the Commander of the Department of West Virginia, directing that Grumble Jones and Imboden return with their commands to the Valley. By that time, both commanders had essentially completed their raiding. (*OR*, 25, II:807.)

81. *OR*, 25, II:819–820.

82. Cullum, *Biographical Register, #173*. McDonald continued to serve the Confederacy as he was able. He commanded artillery at Winchester, assisted Jackson at Romney, and afterward commanded a post at Lexington. The old soldier was wounded and captured fighting Hunter near Lexington in 1864 and afterward confined at Cumberland, Maryland, Wheeling, West Virginia, Washington, DC, and Point Lookout (for part of his confinement, McDonald was manacled in leg irons). He died in Richmond on December 1, 1864, three weeks after being exchanged. McDonald's son, William, was the author of the *History of the Laurel Brigade*. (Richard L. Armstrong, *7th Virginia Cavalry*, [Lynchburg, VA: H. E. Howard, 1992], 187).

83. The Upperville Horse and Colt Show is still held every June, and is the longest-running horse show in the United States.

84. Armstrong, *7th Virginia Cavalry*, 191.

85. Musick, *6th Virginia Cavalry*, 9. Commanding an infantry brigade, Field was seriously wounded at Second Manassas. After a lengthy convalescence he was promoted to major general and given command of Hood's old division, a position that he held until the end of the war. After the war, Field served for two years in the Egyptian Army. (Ezra J. Warner, *Generals in Gray*, 87–88.)

86. Musick, *6th Virginia Cavalry*, 11.

87. *Ibid.*, 115. Thomas Flournoy, who had served one term in the U.S. House of Representatives, was an unsuccessful candidate for governor of Virginia in the election of 1855 and again in 1863.

88. Frank M. Myers, *The Comanches: A History of White's Battalion, Virginia Cavalry, Laurel Brigade, Hampton's Div., A. N. V., C. S. A.* (Baltimore, MD: Kelly, Piet, 1871; reprint ed., Alexandria, VA: Stonewall House, 1985), 55(n).

89. *OR*, 19, II:3.

90. Richard T. Davis to Louisa M. Davis, September 23, 1863, Davis Preston Saunders Collection (#4951), Albert and Shirley Small Special Collections Library, University of Virginia, Charlottesville.

91. *OR*, 19, II:2, 4.

92. Richard T. Davis to Louisa M. Davis, September 23, 1863, Davis Preston Saunders Collection (#4951), Albert and Shirley Small Special Collections Library, University of Virginia, Charlottesville.

93. Another son of Thomas Flournoy, Henry, served in the 6th Virginia first as an orderly to his father and then as orderly to his brother, Cabell (Musick, *6th Virginia Cavalry*, 115).

94. Music, *6th Virginia Cavalry*, 23, 36.

95. Stephen French, *The Jones-Imboden Raid Against the B & O Railroad at Rowlesburg, Virginia, April 1863* (Danville, VA: Blue and Gray Education Society, 2001), 44–47. Private John Opie, who claimed to have overheard the discussion between Jones and Green, later contended that Jones gave conflicting orders to Green regarding the attack. Opie recalled that Jones first directed Green to charge, then instructed him to proceed with great caution (John Opie, *A Rebel Cavalryman with Lee, Stuart and Jackson*, [Chicago: W. B. Conkey, 1899; reprint ed., Dayton, OH: Morningside Bookshop, 1972], 121–122).

96. Daniel Grimsley, January 19, 1905, Virginia Department of Confederate Military Records, 1859–1996 (Subseries 2: Cavalry) (#27684), Box 15, Folder 23, Library of Virginia, Richmond.

97. Compiled Service Records, Lieutenant Colonel John S. Green.

98. Hopkins, *From Bull Run to Appomattox*, 190.

99. Opie, *A Rebel Cavalryman with Lee, Stuart and Jackson*, 94, 115.

100. Dennis E. Frye, *12th Virginia Cavalry*, 2nd ed. (Lynchburg, VA: H.E. Howard, 1988), 1–2, 134.

101. William McDonald later wrote that following the reorganization, either the elected officers were not recommended for promotion by Jackson or the election results were arbitrarily overruled by the War Department (McDonald, *A History of the Laurel Brigade*, 76).

102. Myers, *The Comanches*, introduction (by Lee W. Wallace, Jr.). White's Ferry, which today crosses the Potomac between Loudoun county, Virginia, and Montgomery County, Maryland, was originally operated by Elijah White's family.

103. John E. Devine, *35th Battalion Virginia Cavalry* (Lynchburg, VA: H. E. Howard, 1985), 1–2.

104. Wallace, *A Guide to Virginia Military Organizations*, 66–67.

105. Myers, *The Comanches*, introduction (by Lee W. Wallace, Jr.). A large part of the population of Loudoun County supported the Union throughout the war. The Loudoun Scouts and Cole's Maryland Cavalry were frequently active in the county and a Confederate presence was helpful in protecting the interests of Southern sympathizers.

106. Warner, *Generals in Gray*, 190–191; Richard L. Armstrong, *11th Virginia Cavalry* (Lynchburg, VA: H.E. Howard, 1989), 22, 160.

107. Armstrong, *11th Virginia Cavalry*, 143.

108. Wofford B. Hackley, *The Little Fork Rangers: A Sketch of Company "D" Fourth Virginia Cavalry* (Richmond, VA: Dietz, 1927; reprint ed., Stephens City, VA: Commercial, 1999), 47, 85. Hackley's primary source was the diary of Lieutenant John Holtzman.

4 — Pretty Well Used Up

1. Averell's division, seven regiments and thirty-four hundred men, was opposed by the 9th and 13th Virginia Cavalry regiments under the command of Rooney Lee.

2. Stephen W. Sears, *Chancellorsville* (New York: Houghton Mifflin, 1996), 299. The lieutenant colonel commanding the 16th Pennsylvania resigned his commission two weeks later.

3. *OR*, 25, I:1079.
4. *OR*, 25, I:1080.
5. *OR*, 25, I:1072–1073. Averell was given command of a cavalry brigade in Western Virginia where he performed credibly for the remainder of 1863 and through early 1864. However, Sheridan, who took command in the Shenandoah Valley in August 1864, was dissatisfied with Averell's lack of aggressiveness. In September 1864, Sheridan relieved Averell for failing to pursue Jubal Early's defeated force after the battle at Fisher's Hill (*OR*, 43, II:171). Until his death, Averell believed he was relieved to make way for a more favored junior officer, Brigadier General Alfred T.A. Torbert. After the war Averell engaged in the asphalt business and held minor government appointments. He died on February 3, 1900 (William W. Averell, *Ten Years in the Saddle: The Memoir of William Woods Averell*, edited by Edward K. Eckert and Nicholas J. Amato, [San Rafael, CA: Presidio, 1978], 398–417).
6. *OR*, 25, II:439.
7. *OR*, 25, II:463.
8. *OR*, 25, II:450. Stoneman's message, referred to by Hooker, is not in the *Official Records.*
9. *OR*, 25, II:468–469.
10. *OR*, 25, II:474.
11. *OR*, 25, II:475.
12. *OR*, 25, II:483.
13. *OR*, 25, II:484.
14. Pleasonton assumed command of the Cavalry Corps on May 22 (*OR*, 25, II:513). It was said that Hooker's first choice as Stoneman's replacement was Major General Winfield Scott Hancock, but Hancock instead took command of an infantry corps. Also, Hooker was reported to have preferred Buford for command of the cavalry corps, but instead stuck with Pleasonton, the more senior brigadier. (Eric J. Wittenberg, *The Union Cavalry Comes of Age: Hartwood Church to Brandy Station, 1863,* [Washington, DC: Brassey's, 2003], 237.)
15. Elias W. H. Beck, "Letters of a Civil War Surgeon," *Indiana Magazine of History* 27 (1931), 152.
16. Worthington C. Ford, ed., *A Cycle of Adams Letters, 1861–1865,* 2 vols. (New York: Houghton Mifflin, 1920), 2:8. *Bête noire,* French for "black beast," is used to denote someone who is particularly detested.
17. *OR*, 25, II, 533–534. Pleasonton reported that the corps had 6,677 serviceable horses, of which approximately 2,000 were with Kilpatrick at Gloucester Point or otherwise detached.
18. *Ibid.* On May 26, the Quartermaster Officer of the Cavalry Corps submitted his report on Stoneman's raid. He opined that the corps' horses started the raid in "generally fair condition" but that afterward they were all "weakened and exhausted by the march" and suffering from mud fever and sore backs, the latter a result of being kept saddled for extended periods and from having saddles too narrow at the withers. The quartermaster further reported that during the raid approximately one thousand horses were abandoned. The troopers had standing orders to shoot abandoned horses that they not fall into Rebel hands, but the Quartermaster believed that the order "was neglected in some cases." (*OR* 25, I:1069.)
19. George W. Cullum, *Biographical Register of the Officers and Graduates of the U.S. Military Academy at West Point, N.Y. from Its Establishment in 1802, to 1890 with the Early History of the United States Military Academy,* 3 vols., 3rd ed. (New York: Houghton Mifflin, 1891), #1384.
20. Cullum, *Biographical Register,* #1662; Catherine Ann Devereaux Edmondston, *Journal of a Secesh Lady: The Diary of Catherine Ann Devereaux Edmondston 1860–1866,* 2nd ed., edited by Beth G. Crabtree and James W. Patton (Raleigh: North Carolina Division of Archives and History, Department of Cultural Resources, 1979), 407.
21. Frederick H. Dyer, ed., *A Compendium of the War of the Rebellion,* 3 vols. (New York: Thomas Yoseloff, 1959), 3:1376. A number of New York cavalry regiments were organized as three battalions, each consisting of four companies. Each battalion was authorized its own lieutenant colonel and staff. Over time, the battalion organization fell into disuse.
22. Samuel J. Crooks was later appointed colonel of the 22nd New York Cavalry. He was captured, and while imprisoned ordered held in irons in retaliation for similar treatment meted out by Federal authorities to Colonel Angus McDonald, formerly commander of the 7th Virginia Cavalry, then a Union prisoner of war. However, Crooks' health was poor and Confederate authorities relented. (*OR*, Series 2, 7:669.)
23. Cullum, *Biographical Register,* #1313; Ezra J. Warner, *Generals in Blue* (Baton Rouge: Louisiana State University Press, 1999), 172–173; Henry Norton, *Deeds of Daring: A History of the Eighth New York Volunteer Cavalry* (Norwich, CT: Chenango Telegraph Printing House, 1899), 159. After he was exchanged, Gibbs, an 1846 graduate of West Point, was appointed to the command of the 130th New York Infantry. Later Gibbs commanded a cavalry brigade under Sheridan. He was promoted to brigadier general of volunteers and breveted to major general before the war's end. After the war, Gibbs reverted to major in the 7th Cavalry. He died suddenly at Fort Leavenworth in December 1868.
24. Norton, *Deeds of Daring,* 17.
25. *Ibid.,* 24.
26. Roger D. Hunt and Jack R. Brown, *Brevet Brigadier Generals in Blue* (Gaithersburg, MD: Olde Soldier, 1990), 486.
27. Dyer, *Compendium,* 3:1026.
28. Abner Hard, *History of the Eighth Cavalry Regiment Illinois Volunteers During the Great Rebellion* (Aurora, IL: Np., 1868), 35, 37–39.
29. *Ibid.*; Warner, *Generals in Blue,*149–150. Lieutenant Colonel David Clendinin and majors John Beveridge and William Medill were absent. During the battle at Brandy Station, Gamble was left in charge of the 1st Cavalry Division's camps (*OR*, 27, III:93). Gamble, an Irishman, had served as an enlisted man in the 1st Dragoons before the war. He was breveted to brigadier general in December 1864 and after the war he remained in the army, accepting an appointment as major of the 8th Cavalry, but his tenure in that position was brief. Gamble contracted cholera while en route with the regiment to the Pacific Coast. He died in Nicaragua on December 20, 1866. (Warner, *Generals in Blue,* 165–166.)
30. Dyer, *Compendium,* 3:1104–1105.
31. Beck, "Letters of a Civil War Surgeon," 153.
32. W. N. Pickerill, *History of the Third Indiana Cavalry* (Indianapolis, IN: Aetna, 1906), 9–13, 74; Warner, *Generals in Blue,* 80–81. Later in the war, Chapman was promoted to brigadier and breveted to major general. After the war he served as a judge in Marion County, Indiana, and in the Indiana state senate. He died in 1882.
33. James A. Goecker, "William S. McClure, Major, Third Indiana Cavalry" (unpublished manuscript).
34. Dyer, *Compendium,* 3:1376.
35. Newel Cheney, *History of the Ninth Regiment New York Volunteer Cavalry, War of 1861 to 1865* (Jamestown, NY: Martin Mertz, 1900), 22.
36. Cheney, *History of the Ninth Regiment New York Volunteer Cavalry,* 46–47.
37. Cullum, *Biographical Register,* #1094; Eric J. Wittenberg, *The Union Cavalry Comes of Age,* 28–30. After resigning, Beardsley worked as a trust agent, his occupation before the war. He died on February 18, 1900, at age eighty-nine, the oldest surviving member of his West Point class.
38. Cheney, *History of the Ninth Regiment,* 95, 97.
39. Janet Hewett, et al., eds., *Supplement to the Official Records* (Wilmington, NC: Broadfoot, 1995–2000), II, 73:779, 784, 788, 791, 793.

40. Warner, *Generals in Blue*, 123–124.
41. Dyer, *Compendium*, 3:1375.
42. Hillman A. Hall, *History of the Sixth New York Cavalry (Second Ira Harris Guard), Second Brigade—First Division—Cavalry Corps, Army of the Potomac, 1861–1865* (Worcester, MA: Blanchard, 1908), 3, 31.
43. Ibid., 37, 42.
44. See Wittenberg, *The Union Cavalry Comes of Age*, for a description of the fighting at Alsop's field.
45. Dyer, *Compendium*, 3:1566.
46. Cullum, *Biographical Register*, #1859.
47. *History of the Seventeenth Regiment Pennsylvania Volunteer Cavalry or One Hundred and Sixty-Second in the Line of Pennsylvania Volunteer Regiments* (Lebanon, PA: Sowers, 1911), 27–29.
48. Cullum, *Biographical Register*, #789. Whiting was originally appointed to the academy with the class of 1834, only to be rejected for being 1/4 inch below the minimum height requirement. During the following year, he grew sufficiently to gain admittance with the class of 1835. Reportedly, Whiting helped himself grow by hanging from a tree limb with bricks tied to his feet. (Francis Whiting Hatch, "Charles J. Whiting: Civil War Hero," *Castine Visitor: Castine Historical Society Newsletter* 11 [Spring 2001]: 7.
49. George F. Price, *Across the Continent with the Fifth Cavalry* (New York: Noble Offset Printers, 1883; reprint ed., New York: Antiquarian Press, 1959), 331; "The Star Spangled Life of Charles Jarvis Whiting" in *The Ellsworth American* (undated copy provided by the Castine Historical Society); Alice R. Trulock, *In the Hands of Providence: Joshua Chamberlain and the American Civil War* (Chapel Hill: University of North Carolina Press, 1997), 34–35. Chamberlain's father hoped the experience might "fit" his son for West Point. However, Chamberlain's mother did not favor a military career for her son, believing such a course of action would prove "narrowing and enervating." Chamberlain himself shied away from a career in the peacetime army, and instead studied divinity.
50. Cullum, *Biographical Register*, #789.
51. Ibid.; Price, *Across the Continent with the Fifth Cavalry*, 331–332.
52. Cullum, *Biographical Register*, #789.
53. Originally, the 6th Cavalry was to be designated the 3rd Cavalry. In addition, the army raised a seventh regiment of regular cavalry, but Congress failed to appropriate the funds necessary for its support. The regiment was instead designated a New York Volunteer regiment, the 2nd New York Cavalry, also known as the Harris Light.
54. There are only twenty-six documented cases of enlisted men in the regular army joining the Confederate forces (Robert M. Utley, *Frontiersmen in Blue: The United States Army and the Indian, 1848–1865*, [New York: Macmillan, 1967], 212, n.4).
55. Dyer, *Compendium*, 3:1689–1690.
56. Cullum, *Biographical Register*, #839. Other noteworthy members of the class of 1835 were Major General George Meade and Herman Haupt, who supervised Union military railroads.
57. Cullum, *Biographical Register*, #1750; John Taylor, *Bloody Valverde: A Civil War Battle on the Rio Grande, February 21, 1862* (Albuquerque: University of New Mexico Press, 1995), 90–92, 117; Theophilus F. Rodenbough, ed., *From Everglade to Canyon with the Second United States Cavalry: An Authentic Account of Service in Florida, Mexico, Virginia, and the Indian Country, 1836–1875* (New York: D. Van Nostrand, 1875; reprint ed., Norman: University of Oklahoma Press, 2000), 241.
58. Cullum, *Biographical Register*, #1517. Norris returned to command the regiment during the Gettysburg Campaign during which he earned a brevet to major for gallantry. In 1870 he was dismissed from the service after absenting himself from duty and being intoxicated. He worked as a tax collector in Texas until his death in 1875. (http://www.bufordsboys.com/NorrisBiography.htm.)
59. Cullum, *Biographical Register*, #1868.
60. *OR*, 25, I:1071–1072.
61. Don E. Alberts, *Brandy Station to Manila Bay: A Biography of General Wesley Merritt* (Austin, TX: Presidial, 1980), 38.
62. Warner, *Generals in Blue*, 244. Hunter, an 1822 graduate of the Military Academy, had a dismal war record, but still managed to earn the hatred of Virginians by burning the Virginia Military Institute in Lexington. Hunter is perhaps best remembered outside the Shenandoah Valley as the presiding officer at the military trial of the Lincoln conspirators.
63. W. H. Carter, *From Yorktown to Santiago with the Sixth U.S. Cavalry* (Baltimore, MD: Lord Baltimore, 1900), 17–18; Sidney Morris Davis, *Common Soldier, Uncommon War: Life as a Cavalryman in the Civil War*, edited by Charles F. Cooney (privately published, 1994), 51. Due to war-time shortages, initially only the men of one squadron, referred to as "flankers," were issued carbines.
64. Davis, *Common Soldier, Uncommon War*, 52, 53, 65.
65. Carter, *From Yorktown to Santiago with the Sixth U.S. Cavalry*, 18.
66. Warner, *Generals in Blue*, 142–143. Emory rose to major general of volunteers and commanded the XIX Corps during the Red River Campaign in Louisiana.
67. Carter, *From Yorktown to Santiago with the Sixth U.S. Cavalry*, 33–36; Cullum, *Biographical Register*, #1571. Williams' sister Martha, known as "Markie" within the family, was a confidant of Robert E. Lee. William's younger brother, William Orton Williams, Colonel C. S. A., who served briefly in the 5th U.S. Cavalry, was apprehended by Union forces in Tennessee on June 8, 1863, and accused of being a spy. Williams was executed by order of General William Rosecrans on the following day, June 9, 1863. Rosecrans' order was signed by his chief of staff, Brigadier General James A. Garfield, later the twentieth President of the United States. In December 1862, Orton Williams had proposed to Robert E. Lee's second daughter, Agnes, but Agnes rejected his entreaty. (*OR*, 23, II:397, 416; *New York Times*, June 10 and June 12, 1863; Carter, *From Yorktown to Santiago with the Sixth U.S. Cavalry*, 36–41; Charles Bracelen Flood, *Lee: The Last Years*, [Boston: Houghton Mifflin, 1981]), 6, 73–75. Flood, in error, places Lawrence Williams at Appomattox as a Union brigadier general. For a detailed account of Orton William's espionage activities, see George F. Price, *Across the Continent with the Fifth Cavalry* (New York: Noble, 1883; reprinted., New York: Antiquarian, 1959), 489–493.
68. Warner, *Generals in Blue*, 419–420. Sanders was promoted to brigadier general of volunteers a month before he was killed at Knoxville, Tennessee, in November 1863. Sanders' three brothers fought for the Confederacy.
69. Davis, *Common Soldier, Uncommon War*, 348.
70. Price, *Across the Continent with the Fifth Cavalry*, 26–27, 95; Robert M. Utley, *Frontiersmen in Blue*, 211–212. William Emory, the Colonel of 6th Cavalry, was, along with Hardee, one of the two majors of the 2nd U.S. Cavalry.
71. Price, *Across the Continent with the Fifth Cavalry*, 358–359; U.S. Coast Guard, "The Coast Guard at War" (www.uscg.mil), 3; George W. Martin, editor, "Collections of the Kansas State Historical Society, 1911–1912," vol. 12, Topeka, KS, State Printing Office, 1912 (KSGENWEB Internet Genealogical Society). The Marine Revenue Service was the predecessor of the present U.S. Coast Guard.
72. Dyer, *Compendium*, 3:1560; Thomas W. Smith, *"We Have It Damn Hard Out Here": The Civil War Letters of Sergeant Thomas W. Smith, 6th Pennsylvania Cavalry*, edited by Eric J. Wittenberg (Kent, OH: Kent State University Press, 1999) 26.
73. Cullum, *Biographical Register*, #1297.
74. S. L. Gracey, *Annals of the Sixth Pennsylvania*

Cavalry (Philadelphia: E. H. Butler, 1868; reprint ed., Lancaster, OH: Vanberg, 1996), 34. The lances were manufactured after an Austrian design and featured a Norway fir shaft capped with an eleven-inch three-sided blade.

75. *Ibid.*, 135, 154. During the war, the Union army procured 4301 lances and manufactured an additional 266 in Federal arsenals. That small number, when compared to the purchases of pistols, carbines, and sabers, is an indication that most senior officers shared the trooper's view regarding the lance's impracticality (Berkeley R. Lewis, *Notes on Cavalry Weapons of the American Civil War 1861–1865*, [Washington, D.C.: American Ordnance Association, 1961], 28).

76. *Ibid.*, 90–91; Samuel P. Bates, *Martial Deeds of Pennsylvania* (Philadelphia, PA: T. H. Davis, 1876), 556; Wittenberg, *The Union Cavalry Comes of Age*, 138; Theophilus F. Rodenbough, *The Cavalry*, vol. 2 of *The Photographic History of the Civil War*, ed. Francis Trevelyan Miller (New York: Review of Reviews, 1911; reprint ed., Secaucus, NJ: Blue & Gray Press, 1987), 56; Gracey, *Annals of the Sixth Pennsylvania Cavalry*, 300–301.

77. Cullum, *Biographical Register*, #1684.

78. Kilpatrick was described as being about 5 feet 7 inches tall and weighing about 140 pounds.

79. Warner, *Generals in Blue*, 267; Samuel J. Martin, *"Kill-Cavalry": Sherman's Merchant of Terror: The Life of Union General Hugh Judson Kilpatrick* (Teaneck, NJ: Fairleigh Dickinson University Press, 1996), 26.

80. Cullum, *Biographical Register*, #1904. Kilpatrick's commission was in the artillery.

81. Warner, *Generals in Blue*, 267.

82. Cullum's biographical sketch of Kilpatrick excused some of his conduct, noting that "the severest criticism ever made of Kilpatrick was that he did not take proper care of his horses, and the sufficient answer to this is that neither he nor anyone else could have done any better under the system then in vogue." (Cullum, *Biographical Register*, #1904.)

83. Martin, *"Kill-Cavalry,"* 33–34, 54, 57–58; Willard Glazier, *Three Years in the Federal Cavalry* (New York: R. H. Ferguson, 1874), 139. Glazier was the officer of the guard on the day of an altercation between the two cooks. He noted that the women mostly struck each other with their heads and that the "blows they dealt upon each other were most terrible, reminding one of the battering rams of old." Given the social mores of the time, the fact that both women were black added to the scandalous nature of Kilpatrick's sexual escapades.

84. In December 1863, Orton's Company was assigned to the 1st Maryland Cavalry as that Regiment's Company M (Daniel C. Toomey and Charles A. Earp, *Marylanders in Blue: The Artillery and the Cavalry* [Baltimore, MD: Toomey, 1999], 101).

85. Glazier, *Three Years in the Federal Cavalry*, 24, 25, 27; Wittenberg, *The Union Cavalry Comes of Age*, 19–21. The French tried Duffié in absentia, and the courts-martial board sentenced him to five years confinement and a dishonorable discharge.

86. Henry Davies was also the nephew of Brigadier General Thomas A. Davies, an 1829 West Point graduate who in 1863 was serving in district command, first in Columbus, Kentucky, and then in Rolla, Missouri (Warner, *Generals in Blue*, 114).

87. Dyer, *Compendium*, 3:1377; Noble D. Preston, *History of the Tenth Regiment of Cavalry New York State Volunteers, August, 1861, to August, 1865* (New York: D. Appleton, 1892), 12.

88. George A. Rummel III, *72 Days at Gettysburg: Organization of the 10th New York Volunteer Cavalry* (Shippensburg, PA: White Mane, 1997), 123–124.

89. *Ibid.*, 150–151. The regiment was initially issued some muskets, but there is no evidence that the men ever fired the obsolete weapons. Officers purchased their own side arms.

90. Rummel, *72 Days at Gettysburg*, 54–55, 185–187; Preston, *History of the Tenth Regiment of Cavalry*, 270. Preston wrote that Colonel Lemmon was thrown from his horse. In Rummel's account, Lemmon's ambulance was attacked by a small party of Rebels. While fleeing, the ambulance overturned, and Lemmon injured his knee. To avoid capture, Lemmon ordered the hospital orderly to exchange uniform jackets with him before the two emerged from the wrecked wagon. After the accident, Lemmon was hospitalized in Washington for several months before he resigned his commission. After the war, Lemmon worked as a clerk in the treasury department until his death in 1875.

91. Edward P. Tobie, *History of the First Maine Cavalry, 1861–1865* (Boston, MA: Emery & Hughes, 1887), 4. The regiment mustered into the service on November 5, 1861 (Dyer, *Compendium*, 3:1215).

92. *Memoirs and Services of Three Generations* (Rockland, ME: Np., 1909), 9. Cilley, who was quickly promoted to captain of Company B, was wounded three times during the war, rose to lieutenant colonel commanding the regiment, and was breveted to brigadier general (Tobie, *History of the First Maine Cavalry*, 455–456).

93. Tobie, *History of the First Maine Cavalry*, 25. According to Cullum, Hight resigned his volunteer commission on March 14, 1862. He commanded a squadron in the 2nd Cavalry during the Peninsular Campaign where he was captured. After a period of absence without leave, Hight resigned his regular commission in April 1863. In 1864, Hight served briefly as the commander of the 31st Maine Infantry. From 1864 until his death in 1867, Hight worked as a druggist in Portland, Maine. (Cullum, *Biographical Register*, #1587.)

94. Tobie, *History of the First Maine Cavalry*, 13–17.

95. *Ibid.*, 27.

96. Edward G. Longacre, "Sir Percy Wyndham," *Civil War Times Illustrated* 8 (December 1968): 12–15.

97. J. H. Kidd, *A Cavalryman with Custer* (Iona, Michigan: Sentinel, 1908; reprint ed., New York: Bantam, 1991), 35. Kidd was in error with respect to Wyndham's peerage and parentage.

98. *OR*, 25, II:858.

99. Whether the slap-on-the-bottom story was true or not, Stoughton's reputation never recovered. An 1859 graduate of West Point, Stoughton was the youngest general in the army and an officer of much promise. However, when Stoughton was exchanged two months after his capture, no effort was made to give him a command or reappoint him in grade (his commission had expired). Stoughton returned to New York to practice law. He died on Christmas Day in 1868. (Warner, *Generals in Blue*, 482–483; Cullum, *Biographical Register*, #1841.)

100. Thomas P. Lowry, *Tarnished Eagles: The Courts-Martial of Fifty Union Colonels and Lieutenant Colonels* (Mechanicsburg, PA: Stackpole, 1997), 25–27. Halsted is also spelled Halstead in some accounts. The regimental chaplain, in an account written after the war, charitably observed that Halsted, "in the midst of a throng of duties, all strange and peculiar in their character, found himself unable to concentrate his attention upon any one," and that he was "called to labor constantly beyond his strength, harassed by responsibilities for which he was unprepared by military experience." (Henry R. Pyne, *Ride to War: The History of the First New Jersey Cavalry*, edited by Earl S. Miers, [New Brunswick, NJ: Rutgers University Press, 1961], 6.)

101. Pyne, *Ride to War*, 124.

102. Dyer, *Compendium*, 3:1228; Cullum, *Biographical Register*, #1396; L. Allison Wilmer, J. H. Jarnett, and Geo. W. F. Vernon, *History and Roster of Maryland Volunteers, War of 1861–65* (Baltimore, MD: Guggenheim, Weil, 1899), 1:704; Hunt and Brown, *Brevet Brigadier Generals in Blue*, 155.

103. William P. Lloyd, *History of the First Reg't Pennsylvania Reserve Cavalry, from Its Organization, August, 1861, to September 1894, with a List of Names of All Officers and Enlisted Men Who Have Ever Belonged to the Regiment and Remarks Attached to Each Name Noting Change &c* (Philadelphia, PA: King and Baird, 1864), 9–12.

104. The major leading the charge reported that only seventy-one troopers returned to Union lines. However, most of the men must have made their way back later, since the official tally of casualties was five killed, twenty-five wounded, and four missing. For a detailed description of the 1st Pennsylvania's charge, see Robert K. Krick, *Stonewall Jackson at Cedar Mountain* (Chapel Hill: University of North Carolina Press, 1990), 232–250.

105. Lloyd, *History of the First Reg't Pennsylvania Reserve Cavalry*, 138. At Fredericksburg, Bayard was struck in the thigh by an artillery shell fragment and mortally wounded, causing much sorrow among his former troopers.

106. Bates, *Martial Deeds of Pennsylvania*, 929.

107. Dyer, *Compendium*, 3:1029. Companies K, L, and M were not organized until December 1863 — January 1864.

108. Wittenberg, *The Union Cavalry Comes of Age*, 208; *OR*, 25, I:1087. Voss resigned in August 1863 and Davis was promoted to fill the vacancy. The May 5, 1863, edition of the *Richmond Examiner* reported the Colonel Davis was very "chatty," and that he claimed to have originally been from King George County, that he was related to Jefferson Davis, and that he had many times fox hunted over the land about Ashland, Virginia.

109. Wittenberg, *The Union Cavalry Comes of Age*, 19–21. Wittenberg's account of Duffié's French service is based upon examination of Duffié's military records in the French archives.

110. DiCesnola claimed to have met General George McClellan in the Crimea, where McClellan, then a captain, served as an observer for the U.S. Army (Luigi diCesnola to Hiram Hitchcock, May 28, 1863, Luigi diCesnola Papers [Ms 68], Rauner Special Collections Library, Dartmouth College Library, Hanover, NH.)

111. Elizabeth McFadden, *The Glitter and the Gold: A Spirited Account of the Metropolitan Museum of Art's First Director, the Audacious and High-handed Luigi Palma diCesnola* (New York: Dial, 1971), 5–11.

112. Ibid., 25–35.

113. Frederick Phisterer, *New York in the War of Rebellion, 1861–1865*, 5 vols. with index (Albany, NY: Weed and Parsons, 1890), 1:806.

114. Ibid., 41–44.

115. Luigi diCesnola to Hiram Hitchcock, May 24, 1863, Luigi diCesnola Papers (Ms 68); Dyer, *Compendium*, 1:325. In letters of May 24 and May 28, also in the Rauner Collection, diCesnola failed to mention that he had been given command of his brigade, which could cause one to speculate that the appointment was made on paper only.

116. Cullum, *Biographical Register*, #1512.

117. Benjamin W. Crowinshield, *A History of the First Regiment of Massachusetts Cavalry Volunteers* (Boston, MA: Houghton Mifflin 1891; reprint ed., Baltimore, MD: Butternut and Blue, 1995), 41–43. Crowninshield admitted, though, that many of the horses in the regiment's initial draw later turned out to be excellent cavalry mounts.

118. Ibid., 289.

119. Ibid., 47.

120. Ibid., 48.

121. Ford, *A Cycle of Adams Letters*, 1:98.

122. The four companies left in South Carolina were assigned to the 4th Massachusetts Cavalry when that regiment was formed in December 1863.

123. For meritorious service, Williams was breveted to brigadier general in March 1865. After the war he continued to serve in the Adjutant General's office, eventually rising to brigadier general and serving as the army's Adjutant General before his retirement in 1893. (Cullum, *Biographical Register*, #1512.)

124. Ford, *A Cycle of Adams Letters*, 1:206. The "John" mentioned in the letter is Charles' older brother, John Quincy Adams, who served on the staff of Governor Andrew. At one point, Sargent placed Charles Francis Adams, Jr., under arrest for briefly leaving camp to visit a friend in another regiment. Perhaps that event colored Adams' opinion of Sargent's abilities as a commander.

125. Ibid., 1:16.

126. Whitelaw Ried, *Ohio in the War: Her Statesmen, Generals, and Soldiers*, 2 vols. (Cincinnati, OH: Robert Clarke, 1895), 2:790–791; William G. Burnett, *Better a Patriot Soldier's Grave: The History of the Sixth Ohio Volunteer Cavalry*, [Np, 1982], 6–9. Paddy McManus was named after his owner, Private Miles McManus. The dog went missing after a year with the regiment. Miles McManus (or McMannis) was captured at Fayetteville, Virginia, on November 21, 1863. He was killed in the explosion of the steamer *Sultana* on April 27, 1865 (211).

127. *Report of the Forty-Ninth Annual Reunion of the Sixth Ohio Volunteer Cavalry Association* (Warren, OH: Wm. Ritezel, 1914), 31. Newly raised companies B and E joined the regiment while recruiting for companies F and M continued.

128. Ried, *Ohio in the War*, 2:788; Richard J. Staats, *Life and Times of Colonel William Stedman of the 6th Ohio Cavalry* (Volume 4, *Grassroots History of the American Civil War*, [Bowie, MD: Heritage Books, 2003]), 24, 27, 42, 61, 357. Stedman's seventeen-year-old son, Eddie, enlisted as a private in the 6th Ohio in August 1862 and on May 1, 1863, was appointed chief bugler. Eddie left the army due to poor health in December 1863. Charlie, another of Stedman's sons, enlisted in the 6th Ohio in March 1864 and served until the end of the war.

129. Frederick Denison, *Sabres and Spurs: The First Regiment Rhode Island Cavalry in the Civil War, 1861–1865* (Central Falls, RI: E. L. Freeman, 1876), 30–34.

130. Dyer, *Compendium*, 3:1627.

131. Ibid., 37.

132. George N. Bliss, "Duffié and the Monument to his Memory," in *Personal Narratives, 4th Series* (Providence, RI: Soldiers & Sailors Historical Society of Rhode Island, 1889–1890), 8–9.

133. New Hampshire Division of Historical Resources (www.state.nh.us/nhdhr/warheroes).

134. James M. McPherson, ed., *Encyclopedia of Civil War Biographies*, 3 vols. (Armonk, NY: M. E. Sharpe, 2000), 2:308.

135. Dyer, *Compendium*, 3:1558; *History of the Third Pennsylvania Cavalry Sixtieth Regiment Pennsylvania Volunteers in the American Civil War 1861–1865* (Philadelphia: Franklin, 1905), 5, 11.

136. Warner, *Generals in Blue*, 100. At Winchester in 1864, McIntosh was wounded, resulting in the amputation of his right leg. He was breveted to brigadier and major general in both volunteer and regular services. After the war, he reverted to lieutenant colonel of the 42nd Infantry. McIntosh retired in 1870 as a brigadier.

137. Dyer, *Compendium*, 3:1559.

138. Samuel P. Bates, *History of the Pennsylvania Volunteers, 1861–1865* (Harrisburg, PA: B. Singerly, 1869–1871), 2:522–523.

139. Ibid., 524, 531.

140. Samuel P. Bates, *Martial Deeds of Pennsylvania* (Philadelphia, PA: T. H. Davis & Co., 1876), 786–787.

141. Dyer, *Compendium*, 3:1566.

142. Bates, *Martial Deeds of Pennsylvania*, 849–849.

143. Bates, *History of the Pennsylvania Volunteers*, 4:956.

5 — Stirring Events

1. David G. Douglas, *Boot Full of Memories: Captain Leonard Williams, 2nd S.C. Cavalry* (Camden, SC: Gray Fox, 2003), 211. Captain Leonard Williams made the observations on Culpeper in a letter to his older brother, Henry, dated May 16, 1863. Timothy is a type of high-quality grass.

2. Confederate States War Department, *Regulations for the Army of the Confederate States, 1863* (Richmond, VA: J. W. Randolph, 1863; reprint ed., Evansville, IN: Crescent City Sutler, Nd.) 54–55. As an alternative to picketing the horses in front of the tents, troopers sometimes tied their horses to a rope stretched between two trees. Semi-permanent winter camps, in which the men built crude huts for shelter, differed greatly from the camp design set forth in Confederate regulations.

3. Jacob Kent Langhorne to Margaret Kent Langhorne (mother), May 19, 1863, Jacob Kent Langhorne Papers, Civil War Collection, Virginia Military Institute, Lexington.

4. Jacob Kent Langhorne to John A. Langhorne (father), June 1, 1863, Jacob Kent Langhorne Papers, Civil War Collection, Virginia Military Institute Library, Lexington.

5. Henry B. McClellan, *I Rode with JEB Stuart* (Bloomington: Indiana University Press, 1958; reprint ed., New York: Da Capo, 1994), 261. Robert E. Lee, then in Fredericksburg, heard of the May 22 review in a letter from his daughter-in-law, Charlotte, the wife of Rooney Lee. The elder Lee observed that ink must have been scarce in Culpeper since Charlotte's letter was written in pencil (R. E. Lee to Mary Lee, May 31, 1863, *Wartime Papers*, 2 vols., edited by Clifford Dowdey [New York: Little, Brown, 1961; reprint ed., Pennington, New Jersey, Collectors Reprints, 1996], 2:498). In a separate letter, the elder Lee advised Rooney that he should soon send Charlotte home, because "soldiers complain of officers wives visiting them & theirs cannot." (Robert E. Lee to "My dear Fitzhugh," undated, George Bolling Lee Papers 1813–1924 [Mss1 L5114d; Reel C 278], Virginia Historical Society, Richmond.

6. William G. Deloney to Rosa (wife), May 23, 1863, William Gaston Deloney Family Papers (Ms 184), Hargrett Library, University of Georgia, Athens, Georgia. Because he was writing to his wife, Deloney may have downplayed some of the enjoyable aspects of the ball. A much respected officer, Deloney was mortally wounded at Jack's Shop in September 1863.

7. J. J. Shoemaker, *Shoemaker's Battery, Stuart Horse Artillery, Pelham's Battalion, Army of Northern Virginia* (Memphis, TN: S. C. Toof, Nd.; reprint ed., Gaithersburg, MD: Butternut, Nd.), 37. Smith earned his nickname from the manner in which he finagled additional payments from the government while carrying mail between Washington and Milledgeville, Georgia, during the Jackson administration. After a lackluster performance at Gettysburg, perhaps reflecting his advanced age (he was born in September 1797), Smith resigned his commission. After receiving an honorific promotion to major general, Smith was inaugurated in January 1864. After Richmond was captured by the Federals in April 1865, Smith eluded capture for two months, despite a $25,000 reward that had been offered on him. Smith eventually surrendered, was paroled, and lived in Warrenton until his death in 1887. ("'Extra Billy' Smith," *Civil War Times Illustrated* 2 [December 1963]): 38–41; Ezra J. Warner, *Generals in Gray*, [Baton Rouge: Louisiana State University Press, 1999], 285.)

8. William W. Blackford, *War Years with JEB Stuart* (New York: Scribner's, 1945; reprint ed., Baton Rouge: Louisiana State University Press, 1993], 211.

9. Heros von Borcke, *Memoirs of the Confederate War*, 2 vols. (New York: 1866; reprint ed., New York: Peter Smith, 1938), 2:264.

10. Ibid.

11. Blackford, *War Years with JEB Stuart*, 211.

12. Myrta Lockett Avary, editor, *A Virginia Girl in the Civil War 1861–1865: Being a Record of the Actual Experiences for the Wife of a Confederate Officer* (New York: D. Appleton, 1903), 240. Myrta Lockett Avary is perhaps best known to readers today as the editor of the 1905 edition of Mary Chesnut's *Diary from Dixie*. In *A Virginia Girl*, Avary purports to represent the recollections of a close friend that were told to her over the course of time. Avary does not name her friend, instead falsely identifying the woman as Nellie Grey, the wife of cavalry officer named Dan Grey.

13. Leiper Moore Robinson, Memoir, Virginia Historical Society, Richmond. Robinson's memoir begins with his enlistment in Company H, 9th Virginia Cavalry, in October 1863. This extract, which is filed with the Robinson memoir, was written by an anonymous "youngster," temporarily with the 5th Virginia Cavalry. It is not clear whether the "youngster" was Robinson.

14. Robert Scott Hudgins, II, *Recollections of an Old Dominion Dragoon: The Civil War Experiences of Sgt. Robert S. Hudgins II, Co. B, 3d Virginia Cavalry*, edited by Garland C. Hudgins and Richard B. Kleese (Orange, VA: Publisher's Press, 1993), 75.

15. Von Borcke, *Memoirs of the Confederate War*, 2:265.

16. Randolph contracted tuberculosis and died in 1867 at the age of 49. He was buried in the Jefferson family cemetery at Monticello (Warner, *Generals in Gray* 252). John Jones, the War Clerk diarist, had little regard for Randolph. In his diary entry for November 17, 1862, Jones opined that Randolph's friends would make it appear that Randolph's resignation was a consequence of Davis's undue restrictions, but the resignation was actually either a "a silly caprice" or intended to avoid a "cloud of odium he [Randolph] knew must sooner or later burst around him." (John B. Jones, *A Rebel War Clerk's Diary*, 2 vols. [Philadelphia: Pa: J. B. Lippincott, 1866; reprint ed., New York: Time-Life, 1982]), 1:189–191.)

17. J. C. Swayze, *Hill & Swayze's Confederate Rail-Road & Steam-Boat Guide....* (Griffin, GA: Hill & Swayze, Publishers, 1862; Electronic edition, University of North Carolina, Chapel Hill), 33. In 1863 there was daily train service between Culpeper and Gordonsville. The trip required three hours with stops at Mitchells, Rapidan, Orange and Madison Run.

18. Von Borcke, *Memoirs of the Confederate War*, 2:264.

19. D. Giraud Wright, *A Southern Girl in '61: The War-Time Memories of a Confederate Senator's Daughter* (New York: Doubleday, 1905), 136. Mrs. Wright was the daughter of Louis T. Wigfall, who at the beginning of the Civil War was a fire-eating U.S. Senator from Texas. After resigning from the Senate, Wigfall served in the Confederate army and briefly commanded Hood's Texas Brigade before taking a seat in the Confederate Congress. Mrs. Wright spent part of the summer of 1863 in Orange. Since she did not arrive there from Richmond until the end of June, it is unlikely that she attended the ball. Her brother, Francis Halsey Wigfall, was a lieutenant in Chew's battery of the Stuart Horse Artillery. During the war, Culpeper's Court House building, the site of the ball, fell into disrepair (for a time it was even used as a jail when Union forces occupied the county). On September 18, 1868, the *Culpeper Observer* editorialized: "The Court House is now in a dreadful condition, and a disgrace to the town and County.... The building should be repaired and altered to answer the demands of justice and the comfort and convenience of the Bench, Bar, Jury, and audience, and should be done at once. Nothing gives strangers so good an opinion of a community as for it to have good, substantial and ornamental public buildings...." The county tore down the old building in 1870 and build a new, and ornamental, Court House two blocks west on Davis Street.

20. Von Borcke, *Memoirs of the Confederate War*, 2:264–265.

21. Robert J. Trout, *They Followed the Plume: The Story of J.E.B. Stuart and his Staff* (Mechanicsburg, PA: Stackpole, 1993), 114.

22. Douglas Southall Freeman, *Lee's Lieutenants*, 3 vols. (New York: Scribner's, 1944), 3:5. To estimate the height of the corn, Freeman consulted with Dr. Thomas Hughes, whose family owned a farm nearby. Hughes' farm records from 1863 were used by Freeman to estimate the condition of the crops at Auburn at the time of the review.

23. Daniel A. Grimsley, *Battles in Culpeper County, Virginia, 1861–1865* (Culpeper, Virginia: Raleigh Travers Green, 1900; reprint ed., Orange, Virginia: Green Publishers), 8. Grimsley served in the 6th Virginia Cavalry throughout the war, rising to the rank of major. After the war, he became an attorney and served as a judge in Culpeper County. Today the State Police Division Headquarters building between Old Brandy Road and Highway 29 is located on the approximate site of the Grand Review. Freeman, apparently relying upon Grimsley's description of the review, estimated the length of the furrow at 1½ miles, which was almost certainly too short (Freeman, *Lee's Lieutenants*, 3:2). That frontage would accommodate approximately 3300 troopers in two ranks with standard intervals between squadrons and regiments.

24. Douglas, *Boot Full of Memories*, 217. John W. Peyton, *Eyewitness to War in Virginia, 1861–1865: The Civil War Diary of John William Peyton.*, edited by Walbrook D. Swank (Shippensburg, PA: Burd Street, 2003), 68, 71. In a letter to his wife dated June 8, Captain Williams wrote, "It is remarkably cool, almost enough so for a frost." In his diary, Peyton, a resident of Rapidan, usually recorded the day's weather and the passing of trains to and from Culpeper on the O&A Railroad.

25. McClellan estimated that eight thousand troopers passed in review (McClellan, *I Rode with JEB Stuart*, 261). Grimsley wrote of "nearly ten thousand sabres flashing in the sun light" (*Battles in Culpeper County*, 8). Freeman wrote, "For the ladies, the gallop, the excitement, the foxhunters' call from nearly 10,000 throats were overwhelming" (*Lee's Lieutenants*, 3: 3). Blackford observed that "these 12,000 mounted men [in the review] produced the effect of three times their number of infantry" (*War Years with JEB Stuart*, 212).

26. H. B. McClellan, "The Battle of Fleetwood," in *Annals of the War, Written by Leading Participants North and South* (Philadelphia, PA: Times, 1879; reprint ed., Edison, NJ: Blue & Gray, 1996), 393.

27. Grimsley, *Battles in Culpeper County*, 8. One account of the review (Leiper Moore Robinson, "Civil War Experiences, 1863–1865" [R5642:1], Virginia Historical Society, Richmond, 2) indicated that the Cavalry Division was drawn up in three parallel lines, with roughly two hundred yards between each line. Such a formation would be inconsistent with standard cavalry drill. Other accounts indicate that Stuart's division was formed in the standard formation: a single line with two ranks of troopers.

28. Samuel S. Cooper, *A Concise System of Instructions and Regulations for the Militia and Volunteers of the United States* (Philadelphia: Robert P. Desilver, 1836, pt.2: 7, 8); Philip St. George Cooke, *Cavalry Tactics or, Regulations for the Instruction, Formations and Movements of the Cavalry of the Army and Volunteers of the United States* (Philadelphia: J. B. Lippincott, 1862), 39.

29. George W. Cullum, *Biographical Register of the Officers and Graduates of the U.S. Military Academy at West Point, N. Y. From Its Establishment in 1802, to 1890 with the Early History of the United States Military Academy*, 3 vols., 3rd ed. (New York: Houghton Mifflin, 1891), #1830. Classmates included Union Brigadier General Edwin Stoughton, who was captured by then-Lieutenant John Mosby in a raid on Fairfax Courthouse in March 1863, and Lieutenant General Joseph Wheeler, who rose to command of the cavalry of the Army of Tennessee. Some sources (Grimsley, *Battles in Culpeper County, Virginia*, 8; George M. Neese, *Three Years in the Confederate Horse Artillery* [New York: Neale, 1911], 168) place only four batteries and sixteen guns at the review.

30. Robert J. Trout, *They Followed the Plume*, 60.

31. Wayne Austerman, "Case Shot and Canister, Field Artillery in the Civil War," *Civil War Times Illustrated* 26 (September 1987): 22.

32. U. R. Brooks, *Butler and His Cavalry, 1861–1865* (Columbia, SC: The State Co., 1909) 151. Brooks confirms that Hampton, whose promotion to brigadier general dated to May 23, 1862, was positioned on the right. Robertson was next senior with his promotion dated to June 9, 1862, followed by Fitz Lee (July 24, 1862) and his cousin Rooney Lee (September 15, 1862). Jones was junior among the brigadiers, having been promoted four days after Rooney Lee (Warner, *Generals in Gray*, 122, 260, 178, 184, 167).

33. Cooper, *A Concise System of Instructions and Regulations*, pt. 2:20; Cooke, *Cavalry Tactics*, 6.

34. Grimsley, *Battles in Culpeper County*, 8.

35. John Esten Cooke, *Wearing of the Gray* (New York: E. B. Treat, 1867; reprint ed., Baton Rouge: Louisiana State University Press, 1997), 226–227. Several memoirs written after the war, most notably those of John Esten Cook and W. W. Blackford, place Hood's Division at a review held on June 8, discussed later. However, other sources indicate that instead Hood and his division attended the review on June 5. These sources include Thomas Ware and John West of Hood's division, George Neese and Charles McVicar of Chew's battery, and William Carter of the 3rd Virginia Cavalry. H. B. McClellan, an accurate observer, did not comment on the presence of Hood's Division at either review. In *Lee's Lieutenants*, Douglas Southall Freeman concluded that Neese was in error and, using Cooke's depiction of events, placed Hood and his infantrymen at the June 8 review. Because the diaries of Ware, Carter and McVicar were written contemporaneously, as were West's letters, the evidence is more persuasive that Hood's division attended the June 5 review as described here.

36. Blackford, *War Years with JEB Stuart*, 212. For descriptions of cavalry reviews, see Gillham's *Manual of Instruction for the Volunteers and Militia*, drawing facing page 42 and 604–606, and Cooke's *Cavalry Tactics*, 15–18.

37. Cooper, *A Concise System of Instructions and Regulations*, pt. 2:9; Cooke, *Cavalry Tactics*, 38–39. Both manuals prescribed the speeds for the gaits used by cavalry. Cooper set the walk between 3½ and 4 miles per hour; the trot at 8½ miles per hour; and the gallop at 11 miles per hour. Cooke set the paces at 3¾ miles per hour at the walk, 7½ miles per hour at the trot, and 10 miles per hour at the gallop. At Cooke's rates, a cavalryman would cover ½ mile at the walk in 8 minutes, at the trot in 4 minutes, and at the gallop in 3 minutes.

38. Neese, *Three Years in the Confederate Horse Artillery*, 167.

39. Avary, *A Virginia Girl in the Civil War*, 241–242.

40. Hudgins, *Recollections of an Old Dominion Dragoon*, 76.

41. Marching in a column of fours and coming on-line only when approaching the reviewing party simplified the review. Maneuvering cavalry on-line was one of the more difficult drills in the cavalry manual, particularly wheeling movements, which required the man at the pivot point to remain almost stationary while those on the outside of the line increased their speed so that the movement was made with the rank in a straight line. Additionally, those on the outside of the line had to maintain the proper distance from the pivot point — one yard per man in the rank — otherwise "the arc of circle; if it is too great, the files are made to open and disunite, and the wheel becomes longer; if it is too small, the files are crowded, there is confusion, and

the pivot is forced." (Cooke, *Cavalry Tactics*, 198–200.) Squadron drill specified practicing wheeling initially at the walk, then at the trot, and finally at the gallop; the faster the pace, the more difficult the maneuver.

42. William N. McDonald, *A History of the Laurel Brigade*, edited by Bushrod C. Washington (Baltimore, MD: Mrs. Kate S. McDonald, 1907), 131.

43. Alexander Hunter, *Johnny Reb & Billy Yank* (New York: Neale, 1905; reprint ed., Konecky & Konecky), 419.

44. Most likely, after passing the reviewing party, the squadrons continues straight ahead for almost mile before breaking from their line to the left in a column of fours. They then marched in a column of fours, made a left turn, proceeded along the furrow, made another left turn, then came on-line to the left and passed the reviewing party a second time.

45. Neese, *Three Years in the Confederate Horse Artillery*, 169. Neese wrote that his gun fired 10 rounds during the review.

46. Francis Smith Robertson, "Reminiscences, 1861–1865" (Mss5:1 R5462:1), Virginia Historical Society, Richmond. 14.

47. John N. Opie, *A Rebel Cavalryman with Lee Stuart and Jackson* (Chicago: W. B. Conkey Company, 1899; reprint ed., Dayton, Ohio, Morningside Bookshop, 1972), 146.

48. Avary, *A Virginia Girl in the Civil War*, 241.

49. Blackford, *War Years with JEB Stuart*, 212.

50. Robinson, Memoir, Virginia Historical Society, Richmond.

51. Mark Nesbitt, *35 Days to Gettysburg, the Campaign Diary of Two American Enemies* (Harrisburg, PA: Stackpole, 1992), 31. The information is taken from a diary entry by Thomas Ware, a soldier in Hood's division, for June 5.

52. John C. West, *A Texan in Search of a Fight* (Waco, TX: J. S. Hill, 1901; reprint ed., Waco, TX: Texian, 1969), 72.

53. McClellan, *I Rode with JEB Stuart*, 261.

54. Opie, *A Rebel Cavalryman with Lee Stuart and Jackson*, 145. Opie, writing well after the war, described only a single review — that for R.E. Lee, who was present only on June 8. However, the events Opie described in his account are those of June 5.

55. Von Borcke, *Memoirs of the Confederate War*, 2:266–267.

56. *OR*, 27, III:9.

57. *OR*, 27, III:14.

58. Opie, *A Rebel Cavalryman with Lee Stuart and Jackson*, 145.

59. Not all Southerners were hostile toward Botts. One trooper in the 6th Virginia Cavalry, recalling that he and other soldiers bought fresh milk from Botts at the very reasonable price of twenty-five cents per quart, later wrote "all of us had a good word to say for Mr. Botts and his family even if they were Unionists." (Luther W. Hopkins, *From Bull Run to Appomattox, A Boy's View*, [Baltimore, MD: Fleet-McGinley, 1908], 116.) For a more detailed and sympathetic sketch of Botts, see Hunter, *Johnnie Reb & Billy Yank*, 433–438.

60. Avary, *A Virginia Girl in the Civil War*, 238–239.

61. Ibid., 240.

62. Jones, *A Rebel War Clerk's Diary*, 1:364. The letter is noted in Jones' diary entry for June 29, 1863, indicating that Botts did not hesitate in writing to the War Department with his grievance. While Botts may have not received any compensation for the trampled corn, he outlived both Stuart and the Confederate government and thus had last word on the issue. In his book, Botts described in detail the mistreatment he suffered from the Confederacy in general and from Stuart in particular. Botts claimed that Stuart and his cavalrymen turned their horses loose to graze in every field, killed his hogs, drove off portions of his cattle, and stole horses worth $50,000 in Confederate money. Botts asserted that he "had neither peace nor rest, day nor night" until the arrival of Union troops under General Meade in November 1863. (John Minor Botts, *The Great Rebellion: Its Secret History, Rise, Progress, and Disastrous Failure*, [New York: Harper & Brothers, Publishers, 1866], 294.)

63. For example, at about the same time Botts was complaining to the Confederate War Department, John Peyton Dulaney, of Loudoun County, Virginia, was filing a similar petition with Union authorities. In a letter dated July 22, 1863, to the Provost Marshal General of the Army of the Potomac, Dulaney claimed that Union troops had deprived him of "nearly all my meat (7000–8000 pounds), 200–300 sheep, 100–180 hogs, many cattle, cows, calves, forage of every kind." Dulaney added that his house had been "entered and swept of all supplies of groceries and other conveniences of life." However, in a separate letter to his son, Dulaney advised that he had been able to hide several horses in the mountains where he hoped they would be safe. The son, Colonel Richard Henry Dulaney, was the commander of the 7th Virginia Cavalry who at the time was convalescing in Charlottesville from a wound received on the Jones-Imboden Raid. (Margaret Ann Vogtsberger, *The Dulaneys of Welbourne: A Family in Mosby's Confederacy* [Berryville, VA: Rockbridge Publishing Company, 1995], 47, 102–4).

64. McClellan, *I Rode with JEB Stuart*, 261.

65. *OR*, 25, II:844.

66. R. E. Lee to Mary Lee, May 31, 1863, *Wartime Papers*, 2:500. In this letter, Lee refers to a letter he received from his son, Rooney, that apparently mentioned the review. In his personal correspondence, Lee referred to his son, Rooney, as "Fitz," not to be confused with his nephew, Fitzhugh.

67. Ewell's Corps had left Fredericksburg for Culpeper the week before. Longstreet's Corps was also en route to Culpeper from south of the James River where it had been sent during the winter.

68. *OR*, 27, II:293. Although Lee stated that he left Fredericksburg in the evening of June 6, Brigadier General Pendleton indicated in his report that Lee left for Culpeper soon after midday (*OR*, 27, II:347).

69. McClellan, *I Rode with JEB Stuart*, 261.

70. *OR*, 27, III:865–866.

71. *OR*, 27, III:865.

72. Neese, *Three Years in the Confederate Horse Artillery*, 169–170. In his diary, John Peyton noted of the weather, "Cool enough for a fire today" (*Eyewitness to War in Virginia*, 71).

73. Susan Pendleton Lee, *Memoirs of William Nelson Pendleton* (Philadelphia, PA: J. B. Lippincott, 1893), 277. In a letter to his wife dated June 10, Brigadier General Pendleton estimated that the distance Lee covered during his inspection of the troops was six miles "at a full run for our horses."

74. Robinson, Memoir, Virginia Historical Society, Richmond.

75. Robertson, "Reminiscences of 1861–1865," 15. Robertson was able to locate the supine General Jones by recognizing Jones' "claybank" horse. A claybank is a light colored dun (that is, a sandy or light-reddish colored horse) with a black dorsal stripe. Claybanks are relatively uncommon. General Jones was not the only member of the Laurel Brigade taking his ease. After Lee and his party completed their ride up and down the line of troops, Reverend Richard T. Davis, the Chaplain of the 6th Virginia, dismounted and commenced writing a letter to his wife. However, as soon as he dated his paper, the order came to mount-up. Chaplain Davis had to "scuffle smartly" to put away his writing materials away and climb into the saddle. (Richard T. Davis to his wife, June 8, 1863, Davis Preston Saunders Collection [#4951], Albert and Shirley Small Special Collections Library, University of Virginia, Charlottesville.)

76. McClellan, *I Rode with JEB Stuart*, 262.
77. Lee, *Memoirs of William Nelson Pendleton*, 277.
78. G. Moxley Sorrel, *Recollections of a Confederate Staff Officer* (New York: Neale, 1905; reprint ed., New York: Bantam, 1992), 129.
79. Richard T. Davis to his wife, June 8, 1863, Davis Preston Saunders Collection [#4951], Albert and Shirley Small Special Collections Library, University of Virginia, Charlottesville.
80. Robert E. Lee to Mary Lee, June 9, 1863, *Wartime Papers*, 2:507.
81. Les Jenson, "Comfort for Man and Horse. McClellan's Saddle," *Civil War Times Illustrated* 21 (January 1983), 30–31. The Jenifer saddle was particularly hard on a horse's withers as the horse lost weight on campaign. The Confederacy replaced the Jenifer with the McClellan saddle in 1863. The Jenifer was patented in 1860 by then-Lieutenant Walter Jenifer. Jenifer, who entered West Point with the class of 1845 but did not graduate, had served in Mexico and in the west with dragoons and the 2nd Cavalry. At the beginning of the Civil War, Jenifer resigned his Federal commission and entered Confederate service as commander of the 8th Virginia Cavalry. However, he was not reelected in the reorganization of April 1862. Later in the war, Jenifer served as an inspector of cavalry in Mobile, Alabama. After the war, Jenifer found employment for a year as an inspector of cavalry for the Khedive of Egypt. He died in 1878 (*Register of Graduates*; William B. Hesseltine and Hazel C. Wolf, *The Blue and the Gray on the Nile* [Chicago: University of Chicago Press, 1961], 256).
82. Berkeley R. Lewis, "Notes on Cavalry Weapons of the American Civil War 1861–1865" (Washington, D.C.: American Ordnance Association,1961), 17. The Richmond Sharps was the most common Confederate-manufactured breech loading weapon. Approximately 5000 Richmond Sharps were manufactured between 1862 and the end of the war. (*Arms and Equipment of the Confederacy*, [Alexandria, VA: Time-Life, 1996], 48–49) Although more crudely made than the Union original, the Richmond Sharps was a credible copy of that weapon. The Union Army issued linen cartridges that did not leak powder and thus did not experience problems with flashing during firing.
83. Robert E. Lee to Colonel Josiah Gorgas, June 8, 1863, *OR*, 27, III:872–873.
84. In August 1863, Colonel John Chambliss wrote a memorandum echoing Lee's sentiments regarding cavalry weapons and saddles. In part, Chambliss stated: "The superiority of the enemy's cavalry armament [breech-loading carbines], coupled with their better ammunition, is a point demanding prompt attention.... The sabers issued by the Department are miserably inferior weapons, estimated at so low a value by the solider, and really of so little account, that they are soon lost or cast away as worthless.... The saddles issued by the Ordnance Department are dreaded, ridiculed, and avoided by officers and men, and are used only through necessity, seldom without proving ruinous to the backs of horses." Colonel Gorgas noted Chambliss' complaints, but equivocated over possible corrective actions. The Chief of Ordnance responded that some officers favored muzzle-loading carbines over breech loaders, and that until recently, the cavalry had been happy with the Jenifer saddle. (*OR*, Series IV, 2:718–721.)
85. McClellan, *I Rode with JEB Stuart*, 262.
86. Ibid.
87. Margaret Jeffries, "Beauregard," U.S. Government, Work Projects Administration, "Virginia Historical Inventory," Library of Virginia, Richmond, 1937. The mansion, built in 1850, is located about six tenths of a mile west of Brandy Station and is visible from Highway 29.
88. McClellan, *I Rode with JEB Stuart*, 262.
89. Ibid.
90. Blackford, *War Years with JEB Stuart*, 212.
91. Von Borcke, *Memoirs of the Confederate War*, 1:239; 2:267.
92. Frank M. Myers, *The Comanches, A History of White's Battalion, Virginia Cavalry* (Baltimore, MD: Kelly, Piet, 1871; reprint ed., Alexandria, VA: Stonewall House, 1985), 181.

6—What Dispositions Should Be Made?

1. Emory M. Thomas, *Bold Dragoon: The Life of J.E.B. Stuart* (New York: Harper & Row, 1986), 195–200.
2. *OR*, 25, III:514. On the same day, Robert E. Lee wrote Stuart that while he did not wish to discourage Stuart from striking a blow, he thought it better for his cavalry commander to devote his attention to "the organization and recuperation" of his command (*OR*, 25, II 820).
3. Stahel was a Hungarian who had served in the Austrian army before joining the Hungarian independence movement. After the independence movement failed, he went into exile and in 1859 emigrated to the United States.
4. *OR*, 25, III:515–516.
5. *OR*, 25, III:516.
6. *OR*, 25, II:527.
7. The bulk of the Army of the Potomac's supplies were transported by ship to Aquia Landing and then moved by rail on the Richmond, Fredericksburg, and Petersburg line to depots supporting the various corps.
8. *OR*, 25, III:520–521.
9. *OR*, 23, II:271, 289. Meigs attributed part of Rosecrans' shortage of horses to mismanagement. He ended one message to the Tennessee commander by asking, "Is efficiency gained by service which breaks down horses, tasking them beyond their strength? Three cavalry regiments have been broken down by long return marches, without necessity marching 50 miles a day returning to camp."
10. *OR*, 25, II:533, 530.
11. *OR*, 25, II:522. In a policy similar to Pleasonton's, Stuart on April 23, 1863, directed that the enlisted men in his cavalry division carry on their horses only one blanket and a change of underclothes (*OR*, 25, II:859).
12. Apparently the need to travel light was a difficult lesson to learn. A new recruit in the 1st Massachusetts Cavalry recalled being inspected before moving from winter encampment in 1864. Inspecting officers discarded the recruit's calfskin shoes, two shirts, two boxes of paper collars, one vest, one neck scarf, one bed quilt, one feather pillow, one soft felt hat, one folding camp stool, one blacking brush, two cans preserves, one bottle cologne, one pair slippers, one pair buckskin mittens, one pair saddlebags, one tin pan, one bottle hair oil, one looking glass, one haversack with victuals from home, one checkerboard, one hammer, and a peck of walnuts. The recruit's account, written from memory, was probably exaggerated. (Stanton P. Allen, *Down in Dixie: Life in a Cavalry Regiment in the War Days, from the Wilderness to Appomattox*, [Boston, MA: D. Lothrop, 1892].)
13. Worthington C. Ford, ed., *A Cycle of Adams Letters, 1861–1865*, 2 vols. (New York: Houghton Mifflin, 1920), 2:15. Captain Charles Francis Adams, Jr., complained of the unhealthy conditions of the camps in Stafford County where "the whole country for miles about that vicinity is full of decaying animal matter and one lives in an atmosphere of putrifaction" (21).
14. Samuel P. Bates, *History of the Pennsylvania Volunteers*, 1861–1865 (Harrisburg, PA: B. Singerly, 1869–1871), 4:951; Jonah. Yoder, Diary, "Valley of the Shadow: Two

Communities in the American Civil War," Project of the Virginia Center for Digital History, University of Virginia, Charlottesville. (http://etext.virginia.edu/etcbin/ot2www-cwdiaries?specfile=/web/data/civilwar/valley/cwdiaries.o2w&act=text&offset=2556141&textreg=2&query=yoder). In his diary, Private Jonah Yoder recorded that the saddles and horses were condemned on June 3. The condemned saddles may have been the result of either poor quality or neglect. The regiment had been with the army only a little more than six months.

15. Ford, *A Cycle of Adams Letters*, 2:15.
16. *OR*, 25, I:1116.
17. *OR*, 25, II:857. Stuart's proposed title for the organization never caught on.
18. *OR* 25, II:538–539. Hooker advised the navy that there was a good wharf at Urbanna and on the opposite bank of the river was suitable beach for landing with three feet of water and a gravel bottom.
19. *OR*, 25, II:528. Jones had only a single battery of artillery (Chew's), although three other batteries (Jackson's, Griffin's, and McClanahan's) were in the Valley (Robert J. Trout, *Galloping Thunder: The Stuart Horse Artillery Battalion* (Mechanicsburg, PA: Stackpole Books, 2002) 171, 172.
20. *OR*, 25, II:534, 536.
21. *OR*, 25, II:536.
22. *OR*, 25, II 537, 538. The obvious question is why Pleasonton, with two of his division and the Reserve Brigade operating near Bealeton, did not personally take charge of the operations along the upper Rappahannock and the Orange & Alexandria Railroad. At the time Pleasonton was "dual hatted," commanding both the 1st Cavalry Division and the Cavalry Corps, and perhaps did not have confidence that Colonel Benjamin Davis, his senior colonel, could command the division in his absence. However, given Davis' experience, that seems unlikely. It appears more probable that Pleasonton simply desired to remain near Hooker's headquarters. Later, at Gettysburg, Pleasonton remained near Meade's headquarters while his cavalry divisions ranged afield.
23. *OR* 25, II:572. Bealeton had insufficient sources of water which made it necessary for Buford to move his base while remaining close to the rail line.
24. Apparently at a loss for a title, Buford addressed his messages from "Headquarters, Cavalry Forces." At Warrenton Junction a spur from the O&A Railroad led to Warrenton. Today the small hamlet is known as Calverton and the rail spur to Warrenton has been abandoned. Instead, the spur now terminates at a nearby rock quarry.
25. *OR*, 25, II:593. Sulphur Springs was also know as White Sulphur Springs and Fauquier Springs. A pre-war spa, once visited by George Washington, was located at the site. Today it is the site of the Fauquier Springs County Club.
26. William R. Carter, *Sabres, Saddles, and Spurs*, edited by Walbrook D. Swank (Shippensburg, PA: Burd Street, 1998), 65; Ford, *A Cycle of Adams Letters*, 2:26–27; *OR*, 27, I:902; Benjamin W. Crowninshield, *A History of the First Regiment of Massachusetts Cavalry Volunteers* (Boston, MA: Houghton, Mifflin, 1891; reprint ed., Baltimore, MD: Butternut and Blue, 1995), 125–127. Gleason returned to the regiment's camp the following day. Pleasonton commended the lieutenant for his gallantry.
27. *OR*, 25, II:542–543. Stahel's division, unlike those of the Cavalry Corps, was relatively fresh. Its strength was listed as 220 officers and 3392 enlisted men.
28. *OR*, 25, II:543.
29. *OR*, 25, II 543–544. Meigs had solicited reports from the various quartermaster officers in the Army of the Potomac regarding the Chancellorsville Campaign. In his report back to Meigs, Ingalls commented that there was no complaint of overly long marches or lack of forage during Stoneman's raid. In Ingalls' opinion, half of the Cavalry Corps' horses were rendered unserviceable because the troopers carried too much weight, the horses were not unsaddled, the horses were not properly groomed, and the intervals between feeding and watering were irregular. (*OR*, 25, II:547.)
30. *OR*, 27, III:10.
31. *OR*, 27, I:30–31, 32.
32. *OR*, 27, I:33.
33. *OR*, 27, III:24–25.
34. Newel Cheney, *History of the Ninth Regiment New York Volunteer Cavalry, War of 1861 to 1865* (Jamestown, NY: Martin Mertz, 1900), 95; Janet Hewett et al., eds., *Supplement to the Official Records of the Union and Confederate Armies* (Wilmington, NC: Broadfoot, 1995–2000), II, 57:459.
35. *OR*, 27 III:33. Further complicating matters was a change in commanders. During Stoneman's Raid, the regiment had been led by its lieutenant colonel, Hasbrouck Davis. Upon returning from Gloucester Point, the regiment's colonel, Arno Voss, who had been absent due to illness, resumed command.
36. Ford, *A Cycle of Adams Letters*, 2:28–29.
37. *OR*, 27, III:12–14. In his message to Buford, Hooker was characteristically concerned with denying the Confederates information regarding the upcoming attack on Stuart. He directed that Buford shut off all communications across the upper Rappahannock for the next three days.
38. While in enemy territory for the day, the division's sole casualty was one horse that was shot in a skirmish.
39. Ford, *A Cycle of Adams Letters*, 2:29.
40. Walter F. Beyer and Oscar F. Keydel, eds., *Deeds of Valor: How America's Civil War Heroes Won the Congressional Medal of Honor* (reprint ed., New York: Smithmark, 2000), 6–7.
41. Ezra J. Warner, *Generals in Blue* (Baton Rouge: Louisiana State University Press, 1999), 5, 6.
42. Warner, *Generals in Blue*, 434–435.
43. Warner, *Generals in Blue*, 416–417.
44. *OR*, 27 III: 15.
45. *OR*, 27 III: 29.
46. *OR*, 27, III:15. Hooker's dispatch to the Chief of Artillery only directed the detachment of a battery for Ames. Pleasonton, apparently concerned at this possible oversight, sent a dispatch to Army headquarters asking whether Russell would also have a battery. Hooker's response was tart: "I informed you this morning that General Russell would have a horse battery with him, which you will have to provide for. I suppose you have received my dispatch before this." (*OR*, 27, III: 30).
47. Daniel Oakey, *History of the Second Massachusetts Regiment of Infantry: Beverly Ford, A Paper Read at the Officers' Reunion in Boston, May 12, 1884* (Boston, MA: Geo. H. Ellis, 1884), 3.
48. Hewett et al., *Supplement to the Official Records* II, 75: 161. A and I companies were selected for the mission.
49. The regimental events list revealed that the 5th New Hampshire provided 10 officers and 136 men for the operation (Hewett et al., *Supplement to the Official Records*, II, 39:203).
50. The 119th Pennsylvania provided two hundred sixty men for the operation (Larry B. Maier, *Rough and Regular: A History of Philadelphia's 119th Regiment of Pennsylvania Volunteer Infantry, The Gray Reserves*, [Shippensburg, PA: Burd Street Press, 1997], 67).
51. *OR*, 27, III:15–16, 29. While Hooker made a great effort to conceal the details of the plan, word leaked out that a major operation was pending. A soldier in the 124th New York recalled that on June 6, a man from the 86th New York who had been on duty as a headquarters clerk said that he had copied orders for three small picked brigades to accompany a large body of cavalry on a secret mission (Charles

H. Weygant, *History of the One Hundred Twenty-Fourth Regiment, N. Y. S. V.,* [Newburgh, NY: Journal Printing House, 1877], 139. Charles Wainwright, the Chief of Artillery in Reynolds' corps, obtained more accurate information. In his diary entry of June 7, Wainwright recorded: "The cavalry, I hear, are to make a grand reconnaissance or demonstration toward Culpeper today, and two brigades of picked infantry have been sent up to aid them, while the Third Corps is said to have moved up as far as Kelly's Ford in support...." (Charles S. Wainwright, *A Diary of Battle: The Personal Journals of Colonel Charles S. Wainwright, 1861–1865,* edited by Alan Nevins (New York: Harcourt, Brace, & World, 1962), 217.

52. *OR,* 27, I:822. However, during two days of marching, Ames' regiments covered between thirty and forty miles in their assembly and approach to the Rappahannock. The 33rd Massachusetts reportedly traveled forty-five miles, but that is almost certainly an overestimate (Adin B. Underwood, *The Three Years Service of the Thirty-Third Mass. Infantry Regiment, 1862–1865* [Boston, MA: A. Williams & Co., 1881], 106).

53. Weygant, *History of the One Hundred Twenty-Fourth Regiment,* 142.

54. Edwin E. Bryant, *History of the 3rd Regiment of Wisconsin Volunteer Infantry* (Madison, WI: Democrat, 1891), 165.

55. William R. Ray, *Four Years with the Iron Brigade,* edited by Lance Herdegen and Sherry Murphy (Cambridge, MA: Da Capo, 2002), 178.

56. *OR,* 27, III:28. Sweitzer had two regiments positioned at Kelly's Ford. His other three regiments were downstream guarding Kemper's Ford, Ellis' Ford, and Skinker's Ford. (*OR* 25, II:572.)

57. *OR,* 27, III:27.

58. *OR,* 24, II:517–518.

59. *OR,* 27, III:27–28.

60. *OR,* 27, III:31, 34–35. Hooker apparently never received a response regarding his requests—made on at least three occasions—for assistance from Stahel. On June 8, Hooker asked Halleck to inform him whether he would receive any assistance for his attack against Stuart. No response is recorded in the *Official Records.*

61. *OR,* 27, III: 37.

62. *OR,* 27, III:34.

63. *OR,* 27, III: 27.

64. *Ibid.* The soldiers of the cavalry corps were almost universal in their desire to take the offensive against their Rebel counterparts. For example, in a letter to his sister on April 15, 1863, Daniel Peck wrote, "Our Regt. has drawn some horses & expect more soon. I hope they will mount us soon for we all want a chance at the Rebs and active service. Laying about camp I don't like." (Daniel Peck, *Dear Rachel: The Civil War Letters of Daniel Peck,* edited by Martha Gerber Stanford, [Freeman, SD: Pine Hill, 1993], 42])

7—Success Was Dearly Bought

1. An early landowner in the local area was Carter Beverley. Following common practice, the crossing site on his property was originally known as Beverley's Ford. The first bridge over the Rappahannock River in Culpeper County was built at that site in 1798, but the bridge was washed away in the flood of 1810 and never rebuilt. (Eugene M. Scheel, "The Historical Site Survey and Archaeological Reconnaissance of Culpeper, County, Virginia" [(Culpeper County Government, November 1992–April 1994], REM-18.) Over time, the third "e" in "Beverley" was dropped from the name of the ford. While some Civil War participants referred to the ford as "Beverly's," most omitted the possessive, a convention followed here.

2. *OR,* 27, III:15.

3. William R. Ray, *Four Years with the Iron Brigade,* edited by Lance Herdegen and Sherry Murphy (Cambridge, MA: DaCapo, 2002), 178.

4. *OR,* 27, I:1043, 1047; Janet Hewett et al, eds., *Supplement to the Official Records of the Union and Confederate Armies* (Wilmington, NC: Broadfoot, 1995–2000), I, 5:227. This is Buford's report of the battle which was not included in the *Official Records.*

5. Jeffry D. Wert, *Custer: The Controversial Life of George Armstrong Custer* (New York: Simon & Schuster, 1996), 77–78; Lynn Hopewell, "The Bravest of the Brave," 61 (http://www.blackhorsecavalry.org/files/ROSTER%20August%202002%20special.pdf). Rappahannock Station's name was changed to Remington in 1890. (*Fauquier County Virginia, 1759–1959,* [(Warrenton: Virginia Publishing, 1959], 82).

6. Henry N. Comey, *A Legacy of Valor: The Memoirs and Letters of Captain Henry Newton Comey, 2nd Massachusetts Infantry,* edited by Lyman Richard Comey (Knoxville: University of Tennessee Press, 2004), 127.

7. Sidney Morris Davis, *Common Soldier, Uncommon War: Life as a Cavalryman in the Civil War,* edited by Charles F. Cooney (Privately published, 1994), 391.

8. It is difficult to determine the exact timing of events during Civil War battles. Time-keeping was sketchy and imprecise. There was no easy way for an officer to ensure that his watch—if he had a watch—kept accurate time. Further, it was not a common practice for commanders to "synchronize" their watches before an operation. The probability that the time kept by commanders—either on the same side or opposing—would agree is highly remote. Solar events (e.g: sunrise, daybreak, noon, sunset, dark) were commonly used to describe when activities occurred, but were highly subjective. On the morning of June 9, Buford noted that his column was in motion about 4:00 a.m. and that the ford was seized by 4:30. (Hewett et al., *Supplement to the Official Records,* I., 5: 227). Pleasonton later wrote that troops began crossing the river at 5:00 a.m. (Alfred Pleasonton, *The Campaign of Gettysburg,* in *Annals of the War, Written by Leading Participants North and South,* [(Philadelphia: Times 1879; reprint ed., Edison, NJ: Blue & Gray, 1996], 449). Other accounts stated that the march to the ford commenced at 4:30 a.m. (*OR,* 27, I:1047) and 5:00 a.m. (*Daily Union and Advertiser,* Rochester, NY, June 18, 1863). In one account, the *New York Times* reported that the battle started at dawn, while another account indicated that the battle began at 5:00 a.m. (*New York Times,* June 11 & 12). Of course, different regiments began marching and fighting at different times, adding to the complexity of determining the specific timing and sequencing of events.

9. Daniel Oakey, *History of the Second Massachusetts Regiment of Infantry: Beverly Ford, A Paper Read at the Officers' Reunion in Boston, May 12, 1884* (Boston, MA: Geo. H. Ellis, Printer, 1884), 5; Henry N. Comey, *A Legacy of Valor,* 121–122. The company, under command of Captain Comey, had scouted the route at 3:00 a.m. and remained hidden in the bushes along the north bank of the river until the cavalry began crossing.

10. *OR,* 27, I:1047; Hewett et al, *Supplement to the Official Records,* I, 5:227.

11. Hewett et al., *Supplement to the Official Records,* I,5:227. For military operational purposes, daylight begins and ends with nautical twilight. Nautical twilight occurs when the center of the sun is twelve degrees below the horizon, which under clear atmospheric conditions provides sufficient light to see objects on the ground. On June 9, 1863, the Beginning of Morning Nautical Twilight (BMNT) was at 3:36 a.m. with sunrise at 4:47 a.m. Sunset was at 7:35 p.m. with the End of Evening Nautical Twilight

(EENT) following at 8:46 p.m. Thus, on the day of the battle there were a little over seventeen hours of daylight for fighting. (All times are in Eastern Standard Time, a modern convention). (U.S. Naval Observatory, http://aa.usno.navy.mil/cgi-bin/aa_rstable.pl)

12. F. C. Newhall, "The Battle of Beverly Ford" in *Annals of the War, Written by Leading Participants North and South* (Philadelphia, PA: Times, 1879; reprint ed., Edison, NJ: Blue & Gray, 1996), 139. Newhall was an *aide de camp* to Pleasonton at the time of the battle.

13. Alfred Pleasonton, "The Campaign of Gettysburg," in *Annals of the War*, 449. At the ford, the steep banks of the Rappahannock had been dug away to allow entry and exit from the river. Additionally, the riverbed — sand in most places — had been firmed up at places with thousands of small stones so that wagons would not bog down when crossing.

14. Various accounts have the troopers moving through the water either single file or two abreast. (Davis, *Common Soldier, Uncommon War*, 391; Abner Hard, *History of the Eighth Cavalry Regiment Illinois Volunteers During the Great Rebellion*, [Aurora, IL: Np., 1868], 243).

15. Newhall, "The Battle of Beverly Ford" in *Annals of the War*, 139.

16. Custer graduated last in his West Point class in June 1861 after only four years at the academy (the five-year curriculum for Custer's class was curtailed by one year due to the war). A first lieutenant on the rolls of the 5th Cavalry, Custer had been breveted to captain in June 1862 while serving as an *aide de camp* to Major General George B. McClellan. (George W. Cullum, *Biographical Register of the Officers and Graduates of the U.S. Military Academy at West Point, N. Y. From its Establishment in 1802 to 1890 with the Early History of the United States Military Academy*, 3 vols., 3rd ed., [New York: Houghton Mifflin, 1891], #1966).

17. Newhall, "The Battle of Beverly Ford" in *Annals of the War*, 139. Newhall may have erred in placing MacKenzie at Beverly Ford. Cullum's *Biographical Register* does not include the battle at Beverly Ford in MacKenzie's service record. At the time MacKenzie was officially serving as an Engineer officer under Gouverneur Warren, but it is possible that he was present with Pleasonton in an unofficial capacity. By the end of the war, MacKenzie had earned seven brevets at the expense of six wounds, was in command of a cavalry division, and had gained the respect of Ulysses Grant, who regarded him "as the most promising young officer in the army." Afterwards, MacKenzie commanded the 4th U.S. Cavalry Regiment and campaigned effectively against hostile Indians throughout the West, where in 1871 he was again wounded. Sadly, for all his promise, MacKenzie went insane and was forced to retire in 1884. There is speculation that his condition was a result of syphilis. MacKenzie died in January 1889 and is buried at West Point. Mackenzie's family name was actually Slidell, but at age thirty-four Mackenzie's father adopted his mother's maiden name. Confederate diplomat John Slidell, best known for the international incident that ensued after he and James Mason were taken off the British steamer *Trent* in international waters in the fall of 1861, was Ranald MacKenzie's uncle. (Michael D. Pierce, *The Most Promising Young Officer: A Life of Ranald Slidell MacKenzie*, [Norman: University of Oklahoma Press, 1993], 6, 30–31, 225–226; Warner, *Generals in Blue*, 302.)

18. A second of Hooker's *aides*, Captain E. Cadwalader, was also present as part of Pleasonton's party (*OR*, 27, I:1044).

19. John W. Peake, "Recollections of a Boy Cavalryman," *Confederate Veteran*, 34 (July 1926), 261.

20. According to one Union account, Gibson and his men were surprised at breakfast with their horses unsaddled. Reportedly, several of the Confederates, in their haste, failed to tighten their girths and two of Gibson's men were captured "owing to the turning of their saddles." (*Daily Union and Advertiser*, Rochester, NY, June 18, 1863.) It is likely that Gibson's men would have loosened their horses' girths when in camp. In the excitement of the moment, several may have forgotten to tighten their girths before mounting up, accounting for some "turning" of saddles." However, Confederate accounts, perhaps out of embarrassment at such slapstick, do not mention any captures resulting from that oversight.

21. *OR*, 27, I:1047.

22. Luther W. Hopkins, *From Bull Run to Appomattox: A Boy's View* (Baltimore, MD: Fleet McGinley, 1908), 90. It is likely that Hopkins, in his memory, compressed the timing of events.

23. Peake, "Recollections of a Boy Cavalryman," 261.

24. Henry Norton, *Deeds of Daring: A History of the Eighth New York Volunteer Cavalry* (Norwich, CT: Chenango Telegraph, 1899), 65; Frederick. Phisterer, *New York in the War of Rebellion, 1861–1865*, 5 vols. (Albany, NY: Weed and Parsons, 1890), II:895. Some sources, including *The New York Herald* in its casualty list of June 11, list Cutler as a member of Company A.

25. Hopkins, *From Bull Run to Appomattox*, 89–91.

26. *OR*, 27, II:754. Popular accounts that some men of the 6th Virginia rode to battle bareback should be treated with some skepticism. Troopers who in their haste failed to saddle-up knew that their individual effectiveness was greatly reduced and they faced increased odds that they would end up unhorsed and captured.

27. John N. Opie, *A Rebel Cavalryman with Lee Stuart and Jackson* (Chicago: W. B. Conkey, 1899; reprint ed., Dayton, OH: Morningside Bookshop, 1972), 148–149. Opie, apparently in error, recalled that the horse he mounted belonged to a Lieutenant Morton of H Company. Muster rolls do not list such an officer, although there was a Captain Morton in I Company. Morton survived Brandy Station only to be killed at Tom's Brook in October 1864. Additionally, no officers in H company were reported killed at Brandy Station. (Michael P. Musick, *6th Virginia Cavalry*, [Lynchburg, VA: H.E. Howard, 1990], 140.)

28. John N. Opie, "How Major J. N. Opie Led a Charge: A Graphic Story of a Dash Through the Federal Cavalry at Brandy Station" in *Southern Historical Society Papers*, 19 (1891), 253.

29. Isaac Coles, Memoir, "Recollections of 1861–65" (Pocket Plantation Papers, 1720–1923, Albert and Shirley Small Special Collections Library, University of Virginia, Charlottesville), 6. In his memoir, Coles wrote, apparently in error, that his company was on picket duty and cut off by advancing Union troops. However, before being detailed as acting adjutant, Coles was a member of the Pittsylvania Dragoons, Company E, 6th Virginia. (Hewett et al., *Supplement to the Official Records*, II, 69: 773.) Consequently, it seems more likely that Coles was captured as presented here.

30. Thomas D. Gold, *History of Clarke County, Virginia, and Its Connection with the War Between the States* (Berryville, VA: Np., 1914; reprint ed, Berryville, VA: Chesapeake Book, 1962), 268–269. Several accounts of the Davis-Allen encounter — some more dramatic than others — have been recorded. Some reported that Allen had taken refuge in the woods because his horse had been wounded. Others wrote that Allen had only one load remaining in his pistol when he rode onto the road to confront Davis. The *New York Times* in its June 12 edition reported: "Col. Davis, who was gallantly leading the advance, turned to rally [the 8th New York], and waving his sword to the Eighth Illinois, shouted, 'Come on boys,' when a rebel rode out in front of him, and fired three shots from his pistol at him, the last one taking effect in his forehead, and inflicting a mortal wound. Quick as thought, Lieut. Parsons, acting A.[ssistant] A.[djutant] General to

Col. Davis, was at the side of the rebel, and raising in his stirrups, with one well-directed blow of his sabre, he laid his head open midway between the eyes and chin, and the wretch fell dead in the dust at his horse's feet." The soldier struck down by Lieutenant Parson's blow was apparently Sergeant John B. Stone, of Company H., 6th Virginia Cavalry, not Lieutenant Allen (Musick, *6th Virginia Cavalry*, 40). While the details may vary, the most significant outcome of the encounter is always the same: Davis lay dead in the road.

31. *OR*, 27, I:902. The time on Pleasonton's telegram, which may or may not have been accurate, indicated that it was written at 6:00 a.m.

32. Hewett et al., *Supplement to the Official Records*, I, 5:228.

33. In a letter written the day after the battle, Elias Beck, the surgeon of the 3d Indiana, told his wife that "...Davis was a Regular, a Mississippian by Birth — a proud tyranical devil — & had the ill will of his whole Command. & Il bet was Killed by his own Men.... General rejoicing among our Brigade that Davis was Killed he was such a Tyrant." (Elias W. H. Beck, "Letters of A Civil War Surgeon," Indiana Magazine of History 27 (1931): 154–155.) Beck was a veteran of the Mexican War who, in addition to his patriotism, joined the Union army to earn enough money to pay his debts and buy a house.

34. On the evening of June 9, Brigadier General Marsena Patrick, Hooker's Provost Marshal General, recorded in his diary that the battle had cost the life of the army's best cavalry officer (Marsena Patrick Journal, 1862–1865, Miscellaneous Manuscripts Collection, Library of Congress).

35. Marguerite Merington, ed., *The Custer Story: The Life and Intimate Letters of General Custer and His Wife Elizabeth* (New York: Devin-Adair, 1950), 58; Edward G. Longacre, *Lincoln's Cavalrymen: A History of the Mounted Forces of the Army of the Potomac, 1861–1865* (Mechanicsburg, PA: Stackpole, 2000), 155; Jeffry D. Wert, *Custer: The Controversial Life of George Armstrong Custer* (New York: Simon & Schuster, 1996), 78. Some accounts indicate that Custer's horse bolted and ran away with him during the battle.

36. Newhall, "The Battle of Beverly Ford," in *Annals of the War*, 139. Forsyth, who began the war as a private in the Chicago Dragoons, ended the war as a brevet brigadier general of volunteers. Afterwards he remained in the army, initially serving in the west with the 9th Cavalry, one of the two regiments of "Buffalo Soldiers." In 1868 Forsyth commanded a detachment of scouts that was besieged by Roman Nose, a noted Comanche chief, on Beecher's Island, Colorado. Roman Nose was killed during the fighting and Forsyth was subsequently breveted to Brigadier General, U.S. Army, for his actions during that engagement. Forsyth retired from the Army in 1890 and died in 1915.

37. Norton, *Deeds of Daring*, 65. According to an account in the *New York Times*, a Confederate skirmisher fired three shots at Captain Foote, the third striking Foote's horse. Foote dismounted to check the severity of the horse's wound, and as he was remounting, the Confederate shot him in the back. As Foote fell dead, a nearby private named Carruthers reportedly shot and killed Foot's assailant. (*New York Times*, June 14, 1863).

38. *OR*, 27, I:1047.

39. Hewett et al., *Supplement to the Official Records*, I, 5:227, 233; James M, McPherson, ed., *Encyclopedia of Civil War Biographies*. 3 vols. (Armonk, NY: M.E. Sharpe, 2000), 1:195. Devin had been appointed to the command of the Second Brigade only a day earlier.

40. Although the land was owned by James Barbour, the Miller family, who had agreed to purchase the surrounding land, occupied the house. After the war the Millers and the Barbours had a falling-out, the Barbours claiming that the Millers had not paid the agreed-upon purchase price.

To resolve the dispute, the court ordered the house and 1400 acres sold at auction. The house and property went to auction on February 14, 1867. (Culpeper Chancery Court Order Book 5, 235; *Culpeper and General Advertiser*, January 25, 1867.)

41. Francis Smith Robertson, "Reminiscences, 1861–65" (R5462:1), Virginia Historical Society: Richmond, 15.

42. *OR*, 27, II:772. Breathed's battery had been detached with one section supporting Rooney Lee's brigade near the Wellford House, and the other section supporting Fitz Lee's brigade farther up the Rappahannock and across the Hazel River at Oak Shade.

43. *OR*, 27, II:772.

44. Page B. Mitchell, "History of Saint James and Christ Episcopal Churches, 1840–1986," in *Early Churches of Culpeper County, Virginia: Colonial and Ante-Bellum Congregations*, edited by Arthur Dicken Thomas, Jr. and Angus McDonald Green (Culpeper, VA: The Culpeper Historical Society, 1987), 261. Saint James was founded in 1840 with a congregation of eleven members. At the beginning of the Civil War, the congregation had grown to twenty-eight members who were in the process of raising three thousand dollars to build a parsonage. The church measured approximately thirty-five feet by forty-five feet and was constructed of red brick that had been fired on the site by slaves. The interior was well appointed, with carpet and cushioned pews. St James, like many Southern churches, featured an upstairs "gallery" where slaves sat during services. Unfortunately, no photographs of Saint James are known to exist. (Douglas W. Olwsley et al., *History and Archeology of St. James Episcopal Church, Brandy Station, Virginia*, [Np., Nd.] 1, 5.)

45. *OR*, 27, II:772; James P. Hart, "Battle of Brandy Station," *Philadelphia Weekly Times* 4 (June 26, 1880); George M. Neese, *Three Years in the Confederate Horse Artillery* (New York: Neale, 1911), 171.

46. *OR*, 27, II:748, 862.

47. Neese, *Three Years in the Confederate Horse Artillery*, 170–171.

48. *OR*, 27, II:582, 772.

49. *OR*, 27, II:754.

50. *OR*, 27, II:757.

51. *OR*, 27, I:1045.

52. For example, in a column of fours Buford's cavalry would have extended for approximately three miles with standard intervals of one yard between each rank and ten yards between regiments and squadrons. Moving at a walk, the cavalry would have required close to an hour to simply pass by a given point (now known as "pass time" in movement planning). Crossing a river, perhaps in single file or two abreast, in a wooded area under combat conditions would in all likelihood have considerably increased the cavalry's pass time.

53. *OR*, 27, I:1043.

54. Charles H. Weygant, *History of the One Hundred Twenty-Fourth Regiment, N. Y. S. V.* (Newburgh, NY: Journal Printing House, 1877), 145.

55. Hewett et al., *Supplement to the Official Records*, I, 5:229.

56. Eugene M. Scheel, "The Historical Site Survey and Archaeological Reconnaissance of Culpeper, County, Virginia." Culpeper County Government, November 1992 — April 1994, REM 17; Richard. S. Ewell, *The Making of a Soldier: Letters of General R. S. Ewell*, edited by Percy G. Hamlin (Richmond, VA: Whittet & Shepperson, 1935) 110. Elkwood was finally burned by Union troops in 1864.

57. Saint James Church survived the engagement that was fought around it on June 9 only to be torn down the following November by Union soldiers who used its timbers and brick as construction materials for their winter huts. The church was never rebuilt — the parish instead moved to Brandy Station. In 1913, Christ Church in Brandy

Station sued the Federal Government and the following year received $1575 in compensation for the destruction of Saint James (Scheel, "The Historical Site Survey and Archaeological Reconnaissance of Culpeper, County, Virginia," REM-15). Christ Church still owns the two acre plot deeded to the parish by the Cunningham family where Saint James once stood (Olwsley et al., *History and Archeology of St. James Episcopal Church*, 25).

58. John S. Mosby, *Stuart's Cavalry in the Gettysburg Campaign* (New York: Mofat, Yard, & Co., 1908), 18; George H. Moffet, "Battle of Brandy Station," *Confederate Veteran*, 14 (February 1906),74.

59. The most direct road between Rappahannock Station and Brandy Station, the Old Carolina Road, crossed the Rappahannock River at Norman's Ford, about a mile downstream from the O&A bridge. The Old Carolina Road converged with a road from Kelly's Ford and the O&A Railroad about 2_ miles south of the river—today the hamlet of Elkwood (named for the Cunningham farm) on U.S. Highway 29.

60. *OR*, 27, II:727; *The Sentinel*, Richmond, VA, June 17, 1863. The information regarding a squadron of 1st South Carolina being dispatched to support the pickets was contained in a letter to the newspaper written by "*Veritas*."

61. *OR*, 27, II:680.

62. Frank Robertson Reade, "*In the Saddle with Stuart*:" *The Story of Frank Smith Robertson of Jeb Stuart's Staff*, edited by Robert J. Trout. (Gettysburg, PA: Thomas, 2004), 76.

63. John Logan Black, *Crumbling Defenses, or Memoirs and Reminiscences of John Logan Black, Colonel C. S. A.*, edited by Eleanor D. McSwain (Macon, GA: Privately Published, 1960), 19.

64. *OR*, 27, II:721.

65. In 1859, JEB Stuart patented a metal hook that allowed troopers to more quickly and easily unhook their sabers from their belts and attach their sabers to their saddles. The War Department paid Stuart $5000 for use of the patented hook. Stuart also received a royalty for each hook purchased. (Emory M. Thomas, *Bold Dragoon: The Life of J.E.B. Stuart* (New York: Harper & Row, 1986), 54.

66. *History of the Seventeenth Regiment Pennsylvania Volunteer Cavalry or One Hundred and Sixty-Second in the Line of Pennsylvania Volunteer Regiments* (Lebanon, PA: Sowers Printing Co, 1911), 45.

67. *OR*, 27, I:1047.

68. *OR*, 27, I:1048; John B. Inglis, Diary (SC 22716) (New York State Library, Albany), entry for June 9.

69. Charles H. Weygant, *History of the One Hundred Twenty-Fourth Regiment, N. Y. S. V.*, 148–151.

70. *OR*, 27, II:680, 721.

71. *OR*, 27, II:737.

72. Ibid.

73. *OR*, 27, I:1046; Hewett et. al., *Supplement to the Official Records*, I, 5:229; Hard, *History of the Eighth Cavalry Regiment Illinois Volunteers During the Great Rebellion*, [Aurora, IL: Np., 1868], 246); Warner, *Generals in Blue*, 148–150.

74. *New York Times*, June 14, 1863. In the same day's edition, the *Times* also reported that a black servant from the 6th New York Cavalry "got a gun and fought gallantly in a line of skirmishers."

75. Heros von Borcke, *Memoirs of the Confederate War for Independence* (Edinburgh, UK: W. Blackwood and Sons, 1866; reprint ed., Nashville, TN: J. S. Sanders, 1999), 415–416.

76. *OR*, 27, II:749.

77. Charles T. O'Ferrall, *Forty Years of Active Service* (New York: Neale, 1904) 65. O'Ferrall was the commander of Company I, 12th Virginia.

78. Wesley Merritt, *Personal Recollections—Beverly Ford to Mitchell's Station (1863)* in *From Everglade to Canyon with the Second United States Cavalry: An Authentic Account of Service in Florida, Mexico, Virginia, and the Indian Country, 1836–1875*, edited by Theodore F. Rodenbough (New York: D. Van Norstrand, 1875; reprint ed., Norman: University of Oklahoma Press, 2000) 286–287. Buford tactfully wrote in his official report that the 2nd Cavalry, before clearing the woods, "received different orders." (Hewett et al., *Supplement to the Official Records*, I, 5:228).

79. Buford placed a positive spin on the brigade's piecemeal effort by recording in his official report: "The brigade was somewhat delayed in getting out of the woods, and in the eagerness for the advance the column became somewhat lengthened." (Hewett et al., *Supplement to the Official Records*, I, 5:228.)

80. Henry C. Whelan, "A Race for Life at Brandy Station," edited by Edward G. Longacre in *Civil War Times Illustrated* 17 (January 1979): 34; Hewett et al., *Supplement to the Official Records*, I, 5:239.

81. Hewett et al., *Supplement to the Official Records*, I, 5:239.

82. Neese, *Three Years in the Confederate Horse Artillery*, 172.

83. *OR*, 27, II:768.

84. Frank M. Myers, *The Comanches: A History of White's Battalion, Virginia Cavalry* (Baltimore, MD: Kelly, Piet, 1871; reprint ed., Alexandria, VA: Stonewall House, 1985), 182. Afterwards, the men of the 35th Battalion adopted the Indian tribe's name as the battalion nickname.

85. W. H. Carter, *From Yorktown to Santiago with the Sixth U.S. Cavalry* (Baltimore, MD: Lord Baltimore, 1900), 85. Carter noted that the 6th U.S. "promptly charged the enemy who had just successfully resisted the Sixth Pennsylvania." A total of twelve officers and two hundred fifty-four enlisted men of the 6th U.S. fought in the battle.

86. Whelan, "A Race for Life at Brandy Station," 36. Whelan observed that he was only pinned in the gate for a few minutes, but it seemed like "hours of horror" with the expectation that at any moment he would be shot or stabbed by pursuing rebels.

87. Whelan, "A Race for Life at Brandy Station," 35–37.

88. Ibid., 33–34.

89. *OR*, 27, II:680.

90. Robert J. Trout, *With Pen and Saber: The Letters and Diaries of J.E.B. Stuart's Staff Officers* (Mechanicsburg, PA: Stackpole, 1995), 209.

91. *OR*, 27, III:38. The time on Pleasonton's message was 7:40 a.m.

92. Information is sparse regarding the time that Gregg's wing reached Brandy Station. In his official report, Lieutenant J. Wade Wilson, leader of the trailing section of the 6th Independent New York Light Artillery Battery, noted that he heard a rapid cannonading at Brandy Station at about 10:30 a.m. (*OR*, 27 I:1026.)

8—A Small Affair

1. *OR*, 27, III:41–42; Worthington C. Ford, ed., *A Cycle of Adams Letters, 1861–1865*, 2 vols. (New York: Houghton Mifflin, 1920), 2:31. Adams wrote that his regiment did not begin its march to Morrisville until 5:00 p.m. and went into camp near Morrisville at 11:00 p.m. In his official report, Duffié wrote that his command reached Morrisville at 7:00 p.m. (*OR*, 27, I: 961). While some of his men may have reached Morrisville at the earlier hour, Duffié's report is almost certainly incorrect with respect to the bulk of his division.

2. On that day, about two dozen dismounted cavalrymen manning rifle pits on the south bank of the river contested the crossing by Averell's division. Duffié's brigade,

which was in the lead, was delayed for about ninety minutes and lost three killed and seven wounded before securing the ford (Henry B. McClellan, *I Rode with JEB Stuart: The Life and Campaigns of Major-General J.E.B. Stuart*, [Bloomington: Indiana University Press, 1958; reprint ed., New York: Da Capo, 1994], 207–209). According to one account, Duffié's horse was shot as he attempted to ride through the ford with the first wave of troopers from his brigade (R. H. Peck, *Reminiscences of a Confederate Soldier of Co. C, 2nd Va. Cavalry*, [Fincastle, VA: Np., 1913], 22).

3. William Child, *A History of the Fifth Regiment New Hampshire Volunteers, in the American Civil War, 1861–1865* (Bristol, NH: R. W. Musgrove, 1893), 200–201.

4. Ford, ed., *A Cycle of Adams Letters, 1861–1865*, 2:31. Adams related that the march to the ford took five hours to cover as many miles.

5. *OR*, 27, I:950.

6. *OR*, 27, III: Duffié's written orders were dated June 9, 1863.

7. Elizabeth McFadden, *The Glitter and the Gold: A Spirited Account of the Metropolitan Museum of Art's First Director, the Audacious and High-Handed Luigi Palma di Cesnola* (New York: Dial, 1971), 5–11.

8. *OR*, 27, I:974. Although diCesnola is listed in the *Official Records* as the commander of Duffié's 1st Brigade at the time of the battle, it is likely that he was on duty elsewhere on June 9. In his official report, Duffié described the orders he gave directly to the regiments of the 1st Brigade and made no mention of diCesnola, a telling omission. Also, unofficial accounts of the battle also make no mention of diCesnola's role in events. Further, diCesnola apparently filed no report on the battle. Finally, diCesnola's regiment, the 4th New York, did not participate in the battle.

9. William R. Ray, *Four Years with the Iron Brigade*, edited by Lance Herdegen and Sherry Murphy (Cambridge, MA: DaCapo, 2002), 178–179.

10. *OR*, 27, I:608–609. Sweitzer's brigade also included the 9th Massachusetts, the 32nd Massachusetts, the 4th Michigan, and the 62nd Pennsylvania Infantry regiments.

11. Ray, *Four Years with the Iron Brigade*, 179; Noble D. Preston, *History of the Tenth Regiment of Cavalry New York State Volunteers, August, 1861, to August, 1865* (New York: D. Appleton, 1892), 89.

12. *OR*, 27, II:28.

13. Justin Wintle, ed., *Dictionary of War Quotations* (New York: The Free Press, 1989), 280.

14. Butler, in later accounts of the battle, wrote that while waiting in Brandy Station, he was advised by a courier from one of his company commanders that Union troopers had entered Stevensburg (one of Butler's companies was picketing near Carrico's Mill, three miles southeast of Brandy Station). Butler recalled that "not having time to communicate with either Hampton or Stuart, there was nothing left for me to do but move [there] without orders as rapidly as our horses could carry us...." (Ulysses R. Brooks, *Butler and his Cavalry in the War of Secession, 1861–1865*, [Columbia, SC: The State, 1909], 152). Stuart and Hampton, in their official reports written immediately after the battle, each stated that he ordered Butler to Stevensburg.

15. Wickham's men had anticipated receiving orders to join their brigade near Oak Shade. They were surprised to march out of camp in the opposite direction. (Wofford B. Hackley, *The Little Fork Rangers: A Sketch of Company "D" Fourth Virginia Cavalry*, [Richmond, VA: Dirtz, 1927, reprint ed., Stephens City, VA: Commercial, 1999], 85.)

16. After crossing Mountain Run, the country road taken by both Duffié and Gregg splits. The left fork leads to Madden's Tavern where it intersects with Ely's Ford Road. The right fork leads more directly to Stevensburg. Henry McClellan later determined that both columns veered to the left and marched to Madden's where Duffié turned right onto Ely's Ford Road and Gregg made a more acute right onto the old Fredericksburg Plank Road (McClellan, *The Life and Campaigns of Major-General J.E.B. Stuart*), map). It seems more likely that after crossing Mountain Run, both divisions would take the right fork of the country road, saving each about two miles of marching. Many Union cavalrymen were familiar with the area from operations in the summer of 1862 and raids earlier in 1863. Madden's was a well known landmark and was not mentioned by either Gregg or Duffié in their official reports. In addition, Major Thomas Lipscomb, 2nd South Carolina, reported that Duffié's column approached Stevensburg from Carrico's, a mill on Mountain Run to the northeast of the town. An approach from Carrico's Mill would be consistent with having veered right at the fork in the country road. (*OR*, 27, II:729.)

17. *OR*, 27, I: 961. Duffié indicated that he received word from Stanhope at about 8:30 a.m. that the town was unoccupied. Stanhope was mortally wounded eight days later at Aldie, Virginia (*OR*, 27, II:972).

18. Eugene M. Scheel, "The Historical Site Survey and Archaeological Reconnaissance of Culpeper County, Virginia" (Culpeper County Government, November 1992–April 1994, CE 33; J. P. Thompson, "Proposed University Site," U.S. Government, Works Project Administration, "Virginia Historical Inventory," Library of Virginia, Richmond, 1937). In May 1782, the Virginia Assembly officially changed the name of the town to honor Brigadier General Edward Stevens, a local Revolutionary War hero.

19. Before the war, Butler had challenged Lipscomb to a duel after the two got into an argument over precedence on the floor at a dance. Fortunately the two future officers reconciled their differences before resorting to arms. (Samuel J. Martin, *Southern Hero: Matthew Calbraith Butler*, [Mechanicsburg, PA: Stackpole, 2001] 9–10).

20. Given the timing of events, it is likely that Stanhope began withdrawing his battalion from Stevensburg before Duffié's courier arrived with the order to hold his position.

21. There is a second explanation for the area's name. According to some, highwaymen would hide in the rocks on Hansbrough Ridge. When travelers would pass by on the road, "the devils would jump out" and rob them. In the winter of 1863–64, the 5th New York Cavalry camped at the Devil's Jump. During the encampment, the regimental chaplain began a temperance drive that met with some success—over two hundred troopers signed the pledge to refrain from drinking. To commemorate the drive, the chaplain and Mr. Doggett, who was apparently on good terms with the Federal occupiers, renamed the area "Temperance Hill." Not surprisingly, the new name was forgotten once the Union army moved on in May 1864. (Louis N. Beaudry, *War Journal of Louis N. Beaudry, Fifth New York Cavalry*, edited by Richard E. Beaudry [Jefferson, NC: McFarland, 1996], 109.

22. Kenneth Styles, *4th Virginia Cavalry*, 2d ed. (Lynchburg, VA: H.E. Howard, 1985) 27.

23. Ezra J. Warner, *Generals in Gray* (Baton Rouge: Louisiana State University Press, 1999), 40, 355.

24. Wickham and Butler had no face-to-face communications that morning.

25. Norman's Mill was operated by Thomas Norman from 1798 until 1838. Norman's daughter, Lucy, married a man named David Stanton and moved to Ohio. Their son, Edwin, became Lincoln's Secretary of War. (J. P. Thompson, "The Norman Place," U.S. Government, Works Project Administration, "Virginia Historical Inventory," Library of Virginia, Richmond, 1936).

26. *OR*, 27, II:961. Butler, writing well after the war, timed the approach of the main body of Duffié's division at a little after 11:00 a.m.

27. John Burden Weston, *Picket Pins and Sabers: The Civil War Letters of John Burden Weston*, edited by Robert

W. Frost and Nancy D. Frost (Ashland, KY: Economy Printers, 1971), 48–49.

28. Well after the war, M.C. Butler wrote to H. B. McClellan advising that his orders to Hampton were to "fly [retreat] in the face of anything that came up the road." Butler wrote that he suspected that Hampton was in doubt as to whether he should follow that order since Wickham, a more senior colonel, was on the scene. Butler thought Hampton had hesitated to withdraw and, consequently, was overrun on the road at Dogett's. To Wickham, McClellan wrote, "I have thought it best to say in my narrative as little as possible on this point." (H. B. McClellan to Williams Wickham, July 12, 1883, Wickham Family Papers 1754–1977 [MssW6326cFA2], Virginia Historical Society, Richmond.) In his book, *The Life and Campaigns of Major General JEB Stuart*, McClellan inexplicably wrote that Hampton's orders were "to charge anything that might assail him." McClellan further wrote that Hampton ordered his men to mount in preparation for falling back on Wickham's Virginians so that together they might charge the Federals advancing up the road. However, the Federals advanced more rapidly than anticipated. In danger of being overrun before he could move to the rear, Hampton ordered his troopers to execute a "right-about wheel" to face the Union charge. As Hampton's men were trying to turn-about to face the attack, they were overwhelmed by the 1st Massachusetts. Hampton, who managed to avoid capture, succumbed to his wound that night at the home of Jack Barbour, about a mile west of Stevensburg. According to a friend, who sat with Hampton until his death, the South Carolinian never uttered a complaint (John Cheves Haskell, "Reminiscences of the Confederate War, 1861–1865" [Mss7:3 E605 H2738:1], Virginia Historical Society, Richmond, 66). Throughout the remainder of his life, Wade Hampton blamed his younger brother's death on the disgraceful conduct of the 4th Virginia that day.

29. Crowninshield, *A History of the First Regiment of Massachusetts Cavalry Volunteers*, Boston: Houghton Mifflin, 1891; reprint ed. Baltimore: Butternut and Blue, 1995, 133.

30. John F. Murray to "My Own Dear Wife," June 12, 1863, Murray Family Papers, 1861–1863, 1866, Nd. (#27084), Library of Virginia, Richmond. The circumstances of the 4th Virginia's embarrassing rout were subject to some dispute. H. B. McClellan went to great length to rationalize the flight of the 4th Virginia, attributing its conduct to, among other factors, the circuitous route around Stevensburg which resulted in its being mal-positioned, as well as its soldiers overhearing and misinterpreting Hampton's orders to his small party of South Carolinians. (H. B. McClellan, *I Rode with JEB Stuart*, 287–289.) It is likely that much of McClellan's explanation for the 4th Virginia conduct came from Wickham, since Stuart's former adjutant consulted with Wickham regarding the events, and even provided Wickham a copy of his draft for review. (H. B. McClellan to Williams Wickham, July 12, 1883, Wickham Family Papers 1754–1977 [MssW6326cFA2], Virginia Historical Society, Richmond.) A Union veteran, probably with some accuracy, characterized McClellan's explanation for the 4th Virginia's rout as an attempt "to throw a little dust in the eyes of the reader." (Crowninshield, *A History of the First Regiment of Massachusetts Cavalry Volunteers*, 132.) Wickham, in his report of the engagement, laid some of the blame for the 4th Virginia's conduct on the 2nd South Carolina, writing that a rush of fleeing South Carolinians "demoralized" his men. Butler found that Wickham's explanation lacked credulity, later writing, "How twenty-eight or thirty men could 'run over' as large a regiment as the Fourth Virginia was, mounted, it is difficult to understand." (Ulysses R. Brooks, *Butler and his Cavalry in the War of Secession, 1861–1865*, [Columbia, SC: The State Co., 1909], 153).

31. Haskell, "Reminiscences of the Confederate War, 1861–1865," 66.

32. Wickham reported losses of fifteen wounded and twenty-seven missing (*OR*, 27, II:743). Examination of muster roll data reveals that one trooper of the 4th Virginia was mortally wounded (gunshot to the throat), two wounded, and twenty-six captured, one of whom was also wounded (Kenneth Stiles, *4th Virginia Cavalry*, 2d ed., [Lynchburg, VA: H.E. Howard, 1985], Muster roll data). Apparently most of those reported as wounded by Wickham were only slightly injured. Duffié reported that his division captured one officer and fifty-seven enlisted men at Stevensburg (*OR*, 27, I:961). Naturally, some of those captured may have been from the 2nd South Carolina.

33. Ford, *A Cycle of Adams Letters*, 32.

34. Crowninshield, *A History of the First Regiment of Massachusetts Cavalry Volunteers*, 133.

35. *Ibid.*

36. McClellan in his map to accompany *The Life and Campaigns of Major-General J.E.B. Stuart, Commander of the Cavalry of the Army of Northern Virginia* (New York, Houghton Mifflin, 1885) placed Butler's final position along the north bank of Jonas Run, a smaller stream that parallels Mountain Run approximately one mile to the north toward Brandy Station. That location is supported by Scheel in "The Historical Site Survey and Archaeological Reconnaissance of Culpeper County, Virginia," based upon information provided to him by a descendant of a participant in the battle. It seems much more likely that the 2nd South Carolina's subsequent position was just north of Mountain Run. Most first-hand accounts of the battle, including Butler's, indicate that the 2nd South Carolina took up positions along Mountain Run after withdrawing from Stevensburg. Little or no mention is made of Jonas Run. Additionally, Confederate positions along Jonas Run would be beyond the effective range of the light artillery supporting Duffié's division. Finally, high ground between Jonas Run and Mountain Run masks Jonas Run from the heights to the east of Stevensburg.

37. *OR*, 27, II:730.

38. Janet Hewett et al., eds., *Supplement to the Official Records of the Union and Confederate Armies* (Wilmington, NC: Broadfoot, 1995–2000), I, 5:280.

39. Brooks, *Butler and his Cavalry*, 169.

40. *Ibid.*, 155.

41. (Hewett et. al., eds., *Supplement to the Official Records*, I, 5:282–283). Pennington made no mention of specifically firing at Butler in his official report, although he wrote that his two guns engaged the enemy "with good effect." During the day, Pennington's gunners fired a total of thirty-three rounds with their three-inch rifled guns, mostly from Stevensburg. The battery was stocked with Schenkl ammunition — the round featured a paper maché sabot that gripped the lands and grooves in the rifled barrel to impart spin to the projectile (Berkeley R. Lewis, *Notes on Ammunition of the American Civil War 1861–1865*, Washington, D.C., American Ordnance Association, 1959). Butler later wrote that the Union artillery projectile, after doing its damage, dropped into the road near Farley's horse (Brooks, *Butler and his Cavalry*, 155). However, given the laws of physics, it is more likely that the projectile, which had sufficient velocity to pass through two horses and cleanly sever Farley's leg, traveled a considerable distance farther.

42. Brooks, *Butler and his Cavalry*, 155, 156, 160. One of the men first on the scene and to provide aid was Captain John Chesnut, brother-in-law of Mary Chesnut, the Richmond diarist.

43. *Ibid.*, 169. There are at least two first-hand accounts that support the story of Farley and his severed leg. Butler recalled that when brought the limb, Farley "took it in his arms and embraced it with some affection" (Brooks, *Butler and his Cavalry*, 156).

44. Douglas W. Owsley, Malcolm L. Richardson, and William E. Hanna, "Bioarcheological Investigation and Exhumation of the Remains of Captain William Downs Farley, CSA," March 2002, 22–23. Doctor Jones was perhaps James Farish Jones, a veteran of the Brandy Rifles who had left the army to return to the practice of medicine. Doctor Ashby had died a few months before the battle. Shortly after Farley's death, his younger brother, Captain Henry Saxon Farley, joined Stuart's staff as an aide. Henry Farley, a member of the West Point class of 1862, was reportedly the first cadet to resign from the academy in response to the secession crisis. (Robert J. Trout, *They Followed the Plume: The Story of J.E.B. Stuart and His Staff*, [Mechanicsburg, PA: Stackpole, 1993], 103.

45. *Ibid.*, 156. Butler asked his surgeon if he had spoken while under anesthesia, perhaps in fear that he had disclosed personal indiscretions (Butler was reportedly fond of attractive women). The surgeon informed Butler that he had only "strongly admonished W. C. Swaffield to keep his little sorrel mare under better control in line while drilling." (Brooks, *Butler and his Cavalry*, 170.)

46. *Ibid.*

47. *OR*, 27. 1:950, 962, 975. None of the principal participants recorded the time that Duffié received Gregg's orders and started his movement to Brandy Station. Captain Charles Francis Adams, Jr. wrote that "about noon" the division was recalled (Ford, *A Cycle of Adams Letters*, 32).

48. In his official report of the battle, General Pleasonton was critical of Duffié, commenting that General Gregg "would have achieved more had Colonel Duffié, commanding the Second Division, brought up his command to [Gregg's] assistance in the time he should have done." (*OR*, 27, I:1045.) Pleasonton fails to mention that he sent Duffié's division to accomplish a mission that, in Hooker's estimate, required only a regiment.

49. Brooks, *Butler and his Cavalry*, 171. Brooks wrote that the 2nd South Carolina took two hundred forty men into the battle on June 9, and the next day reported about two hundred men present for duty.

50. Crowninshield, *A History of the First Regiment of Massachusetts Cavalry Volunteers*, 142.

9—Fight Like Gentlemen!

1. There is some confusion over the type of gun that Carter withdrew to Fleetwood. McClellan wrote that it was a six-pound howitzer, although a report in February 1863 indicated that Chew's battery had only two British Blakely's and a twenty-four pounder, with a Napoleon (12-pounder) expected shortly. Perhaps Carter's piece was the Napoleon. (Robert J. Trout, *Galloping Thunder: The Stuart Horse Artillery Battalion*, [Mechanicsburg, PA: Stackpole, 2002], 696, n. 30.)

2. Robert J. Trout, *They Followed the Plume: The Story of J.E.B. Stuart and His Staff* (Mechanicsburg, PA: Stackpole, 1993), 200–201. Apparently, McClellan was considered for appointment to Stuart's staff even before the death of Channing Price. In a letter dated April 6, 1863, Fitzhugh Lee advised Stuart: "In reply to your inquiries about McClellan, I have to say that from observation and inquiry I am of the opinion that he will make an excellent a. a. g. [assistant adjutant general]." (George Bolling Lee, Papers 1813–1924 [Mss1 L5114d; Reel C 278], Virginia Historical Society, Richmond.)

3. Washington Roebling, who earned fame as an engineer officer at Gettysburg and later as the builder of the Brooklyn Bridge, had served earlier in the 6th New York Light as a lieutenant.

4. David McMurtrie Gregg, "The Second Cavalry Division, Army of the Potomac, in the Gettysburg Campaign" (Handwritten Manuscript, Ac. 4536, Add. 3), Papers of David McMurtrie Gregg (MMC-0539), Library of Congress, Washington, DC, 6–7. In his published account, Gregg commented that his advance did not reach Brandy Station for some hours after Buford's attack "owing to the number of miles to be marched and obstructions met in the roads (David McMurtrie Gregg, *The Union Cavalry at Gettysburg*, in *Annals of the War, Written by Leading Participants North and South*, [Philadelphia: Times, 1879; reprint ed., Edison, NJ: Blue & Gray, 1996], 376). Significantly, obstacles in the road were not mentioned by either Gregg or other Union commanders in their official reports of the battle.

5. David Douglas, *A Boot Full of Memories: Captain Leonard Williams, 2nd S.C. Cavalry* (Camden, SC: Gray Fox, 2003), 224.

6. Henry B. McClellan, *The Life and Campaigns of Major-General J.E.B. Stuart, Commander of the Cavalry of the Army of Northern Virginia*. New York: Houghton Mifflin, 1885. Republished as *I Rode with JEB Stuart: The Life and Campaigns of Major-General J.E.B. Stuart*. Bloomington: Indiana University Press, 1958; reprint ed., New York: Da Capo, 1994, 269; *OR*, 27, II:733; *OR*, 27, II:734; Robert E. L. Krick, *Staff Officers in Gray* (Chapel Hill: University of North Carolina Press, 2003), 310.

7. McClellan, *I Rode with JEB Stuart*, 269–270.

8. *OR*, 27, II:965. Wyndham, in his official report, mistakenly identified the Miller House on Fleetwood as the Barbour House, which sits on a hill about ½ mile to the northwest of the Miller House.

9. Janet Hewett et al., eds., *Supplement to the Official Records of the Union and Confederate Armies* (Wilmington, NC: Broadfoot, 1995–2000), I, 5:281.

10. McClellan, *I Rode with JEB Stuart*, 270. Lieutenant Moses Clark, in his report, wrote that "in the short space of fifteen minutes, we had silenced their artillery and compelled them to assume a new position from which they were again driven." (Hewett et al., eds., *Supplement to the Official Records*, I, 5:281).

11. Frank M. Myers, *The Comanches: A History of White's Battalion, Virginia Cavalry* (Baltimore, MD: Kelly, Piet, 1871; reprint ed., Alexandria, VA: Stonewall House, 1985), 183.

12. McClellan, *I Rode with JEB Stuart*, 271; Douglas Southall Freeman, *Lee's Lieutenants*, 3 vols. (New York: Scribner's, 1944), 3:9; James P. Hart "Battle of Brandy Station" *Philadelphia Weekly Times* (June 26, 1880). Deane had been detailed to Stuart's headquarters from the 4th Virginia Cavalry (Trout, *They Followed the Plume*, 305).

13. Francis Smith Robertson, "Reminiscences, 1861–65" (R5462:1), Virginia Historical Society, Richmond, 16–17.

14. The trot, an energy-conserving pace for the horses, is generally preferable to the canter or the gallop for traveling a significant distance. Columns of troops, both mounted and dismounted, experience a disagreeable "accordion effect" when their pace changes. The column extends as the pace increases and contracts as the pace slows. Those at the rear of the column are most affected by the accordion effect and frequently find themselves waiting as the column gets underway and then hurrying to catch up, even after those at the front of the column have halted.

15. Wyndham reported that the strength of the 1st Maryland was little more than that of a squadron. Additionally, one company of the regiment had been left north of the Rappahannock to guard the wagon train. The 1st New Jersey went into the battle with 18 officers and 281 enlisted men (*OR*, 27, II:1055).

16. Hewett et al., eds., *Supplement to the Official Records*, I, 5:281.

17. For a succinct discussion of Stuart's view of cavalry tactics, see his General Order Number 26, dated July 30, 1863 (*OR, 27, III:1054–1055.*)

18. See John Keegan, *The Face of Battle* (New York: Viking, 1976) for an insightful discussion of cavalry vs. cavalry engagements. While Keegan analyzes the cavalry of Wellington and Napoleon at Waterloo, the characteristics of mounted combat were much the same a half century later. Naturally, as an alternative to the pattern described, one side might panic and flee, as had occurred with the 4th Virginia at Stevensburg earlier that morning.

19. Hewett et al., eds., *Supplement to the Official Records*, I, 5:249.

20. George Baylor, *Bull Run to Bull Run, or Four Years in the Army of Northern Virginia* (Richmond, VA: B. F. Johnson, 1900), 143.

21. Hewett et al., eds., *Supplement to the Official Records*, I, 5:281; Trout, *Galloping Thunder: The Stuart Horse Artillery Battalion*, 687, n.45.

22. *OR, 27, II:768–769.*

23. William P. Lloyd, *History of the First Reg't Pennsylvania Reserve Cavalry, from Its Organization, August 1861, to September 1894, with a List of Names of all Officers and Enlisted Men Who have Ever Belonged to the Regiment and Remarks Attached to Each Name Noting Change & (c)* (Philadelphia: King and Baird, 1864), 50, 56. Lloyd's *History* includes Taylor's official report, which was not included in the *Official Record*. Taylor, like Wyndham, confused the Miller House on Fleetwood with the Barbour House.

24. Dennis E. Frye, *12th Virginia Cavalry*, 2nd ed. (Lynchburg, VA: H.E. Howard, 1988), 39.

25. *Ibid.*

26. Charles T. O'Ferrall, *Forty Years of Active Service* (New York: Neale, 1904), 67.

27. Frye, *12th Virginia Cavalry*, 39.

28. *OR, 27, II:755.*

29. *OR, 27, II:754–755.* Because of the severity of his wound, Allen never returned to active service. He was paroled on April 15,1865, at Winchester and died there in August 1918. (Musick, *6th Virginia Cavalry*, 41, 92.) Allen's two younger brothers died in Confederate service. David H. Allen, also a lieutenant in Company D, 6th Virginia, was mortally wounded at First Manassas. A. S. Allen was mortally wounded at Chancellorsville. (Thomas D. Gold, *History of Clarke County, Virginia, and Its Connection with the War Between the States* [Berryville, VA: Np., 1914; reprint ed, Berryville, VA: Chesapeake, 1962], photo caption facing page 195.)

30. John W. Peake, "Recollections of a Boy Cavalryman," *Confederate Veteran*, 34 (July 1926): 261.

31. John N. Opie, *A Rebel Cavalryman with Lee, Stuart and Jackson* (Chicago: W. B. Conkey, 1899; reprint ed., Dayton: Morningside Bookshop, 1972), 153, 154.

32. Henry R. Pyne, *Ride to War: The History of the First New Jersey Cavalry*, edited by Earl S. Miers (New Brunswick, NJ: Rutgers University Press, 1961), 120. As an indication of the confused nature of the fighting on Fleetwood, Major Hugh Janeway, in his report to the Governor of New Jersey, wrote that accounts regarding Lieutenant Colonel Broderick and Major Shelmire (also killed), who were initially believed wounded and captured, were so conflicting that he deferred making any statement until more could be learned (*OR, 27, I:1054*).

33. Samuel Toombs, *New Jersey Troops in the Gettysburg Campaign from June 5 to July 31, 1863* (Orange, NJ: Evening Mail, 1888), 56–57. Kitchen was later promoted to Lieutenant Colonel of the 2nd New Jersey Cavalry. He resigned on June 30, 1864.

34. Presumably, Stuart ordered the company of the 6th Virginia to support White's Battalion.

35. Toombs, *New Jersey Troops in the Gettysburg Campaign*, 58; *OR, 27, II:769; OR, 27, I:1024–1025.*

36. Toombs, *New Jersey Troops in the Gettysburg Campaign*, 58.

37. Heros von Borcke, *Memoirs of the Confederate War for Independence* (Edinburgh, UK: W. Blackwood and Sons, 1866; reprint ed., Nashville, TN: J. S. Sanders, 1999), 416–418; Robertson, "Reminiscences, 1861–65," 17. White, although still suffering from his wound, participated in the Gettysburg campaign. Afterward, Stuart detailed White, whose wound had not properly healed, to the cavalry division's horse hospital southwest of Charlottesville. (Robert J. Trout, *They Followed the Plume: The Story of J.E.B. Stuart and his Staff* (Mechanicsburg, PA: Stackpole Books, 1993), 281–282.)

38. Robertson, "Reminiscences, 1861–65," 17; Robert J. Trout, *With Pen and Saber: The Letters and Diaries of J.E.B. Stuart's Staff Officers* (Mechanicsburg, PA: Stackpole Books, 1995), 210. Turning about in place can be achieved by either turning on the forehand (the horse's hindquarters pivot about its stationary front legs), or by circling on the haunches (the horse pivots about its stationary hindquarters). Both moves were taught in the School of the Trooper. Bostona was apparently not proficient in either technique.

39. *Ibid.* For two accounts of Robertson's accounts of the battle, one recorded in a letter in 1863, the other before Robertson's death in 1926, see Reade's *In the Saddle with Stuart: The Story of Frank Smith Robertson of Jeb Stuart's Staff*, edited by Robert J. Trout (Gettysburg: Thomas, 1998), 56–62.

40. Chiswell Dabney to Father (John B. Dabney), June 14, 1863, Saunders Family Papers (Mss1 Sa878 a), Virginia Historical Society, Richmond. Dilbert was apparently not a particularly accomplished rider. Several days earlier, he had injured himself in a fall from a horse he was trying to ride without Dabney's knowledge. Fortunately, Dilbert only suffered a sprain.

41. William W. Blackford, *War Years with JEB Stuart* (New York: Scribner's, 1945; reprint ed., Baton Rouge: University of Louisiana Press, 1993), 217.

42. *OR, 27, II:685*; Blackford, *War Years with JEB Stuart*, 216, 217; Trout, *They Followed the Plume*, 146.

43. Noble D. Preston, *History of the Tenth Regiment of Cavalry New York State Volunteers, August, 1861, to August, 1865* (New York: D. Appleton, 1892), 84. Similarly, one member of the 1st Maine recalled that while the regiment halted before moving up into line, "Many a man tightened the girth of his saddle, examined his carbine, and tried the edge of his sabre on the ball of his thumb (Samuel H. Merrill, *The Campaigns of the First Maine and the First District of Columbia Cavalry*, [Portland, ME: Bailey & Noyes, 1866], 106).

44. If Hampton's brigade withdrew directly to their rear, after ½ mile they would have reached the railroad in the vicinity of modern day Elkwood, Virginia.

45. Gregg, "The Second Cavalry Division, Army of the Potomac, in the Gettysburg Campaign," 7.

46. *OR, 27, II:1026.*

47. Robert J. Trout, *Galloping Thunder: The Stuart Horse Artillery Battalion* [Mechanicsburg, PA: Stackpole], 2002, 229.

48. Noble D. Preston, *History of the Tenth Regiment of Cavalry New York State Volunteers, August, 1861, to August, 1865* (New York: D. Appleton, 1892), 86.

49. Frederick Poughkeepsie, Pension Application, National Archives, Washington, D.C. (Provided to the Brandy Station Foundation by Allan J. Zellnock.) Poughkeepsie's hernia proved a more significant long-term disability than the shrapnel wound, the gunshot wound, or the broken toe.

50. Wiley C. Howard, *Sketch of Cobb Legion Cavalry and Some Incidents and Scenes Remembered: Presented and Read under Appointment of Atlanta Camp 159, United Confederate Veterans, August 19, 1901* (Np. Nd.), 7. Roughly translated, *nolens volens* means "willing or not." Howard ended the war as a First Lieutenant in command of Company C.

51. Preston, *History of the 10th Regiment*, 87–88. Contrary to first-hand accounts, Kilpatrick wrote that each of his regiments left the field after numerous charges and counter charges with its "organization preserved" (*OR*, 27, I:986). Some accounts written after the war (James Moore), *Kilpatrick and Our Cavalry: Comprising a Sketch of the Life of General Kilpatrick, with an Account of the Cavalry Raids, Engagements, and Operations under His Command, from the Beginning of the Rebellion to the Surrender of Johnston,* New York: W.J. Widdleton, 1865.; Glazier, *Three Years in the Federal Cavalry,* New York: R.H. Ferguson, 1874.) ascribe a significant role to Kilpatrick in rallying the 10th New York and the Harris Light after their initial set-backs. However, other first-hand accounts fail to describe much rallying at all after the two New York regiments were driven back across the railroad tracks in disorder.

52. *Ibid.,* 86–87. Fox's *Regimental Casualties* indicated that Robb was sabered while pinned beneath his horse because he would not surrender (59). However, accounts in Preston's *History of the 10th Regiment* indicated that Robb was not pinned to the ground when stabbed. One witness wrote that after being stabbed, Robb clung to his horse as it scrambled out of the ditch and traveled fifty to one hundred feet before falling to the ground.

53. Lieutenant Colonel Henry E. Davies, Jr., the commander of the 2nd New York, recorded that "on reaching the railroad, by reason of an order improperly given, as is alleged, the head of the column was turned to the left and proceeded some distance down the railroad, where it crossed, and charged another body of the enemy" (*OR,* 27, I:997). The regiment, by turning to its left, was moving toward Brandy Station and away from the advancing 1st South Carolina.

54. *OR,* 27, I:997.

55. John Logan Black, *Crumbling Defenses, or Memoirs and Reminiscences of John Logan Black, Colonel C. S. A.,* edited by Eleanor D. McSwain (Macon, GA: Privately Published, 1960), 20.

56. *OR,* 27, II:1027.

57. *OR,* 27, II:722.

58. According to some accounts, Kilpatrick "dashed to the head of this regiment, shouting 'Men of Maine! You must save the day! Follow me!'" (Moore, *Kilpatrick and our Cavalry,* 59; Glazier, *Three Years in the Federal Cavalry,* 219). Kilpatrick gave a similar account in a speech to the veterans of the regiment in 1885 (Edward P. Tobie, *History of the 1st Maine Cavalry, 1861–1865,* [Boston: Emery & Hughes, 1887], 156).

59. Tobie, *History of the First Maine Cavalry,* 148–149. Although Kilpatrick had developed a reputation as a fierce raider, there is little evidence that he exhibited exceptional personal courage at Brandy Station. Unlike Wyndham, who led his brigade into the fight, Kilpatrick sent his regiments forward. In his report, Kilpatrick wrote that "with the First Maine [he] swept to the right and charged the enemy in the flank." However, if Kilpatrick did join the 1st Maine's charge, he must have dropped out early, since other accounts do not comment on his presence.

60. *Ibid.,* 150. Horses are herd animals, and it is possible that some of the Confederates' horses chose to join the 1st Maine's charge despite the desires of their riders.

61. Colonel Douty rejoined his regiment later in the day.

62. Torlief S. Holmes, *Horse Soldiers in Blue* (Gaithersburg, MD: Butternut, 1985), 86.

63. Donald C. Pfanz, *Richard S. Ewell: A Soldier's Life* (Chapel Hill: University of North Carolina Press, 1998), 281. Ewell, an 1840 graduate of West Point, had served almost his entire career with the dragoons in the Southwest before resigning to join the Confederacy. He had distinguished himself as a brigade and division commander under Jackson and lost a leg at Brawner's Farm during Second Manassas. Elevated to corps command after the death of Jackson, he was untested in that capacity.

64. McClellan, *I Rode with JEB Stuart,* 295; *OR,* 27, II:439–440, 565, 592.

65. *OR,* 27, II:564, 592. According to Donald Pfanz, Rodes had anticipated the order to support Stuart and had already began moving his brigades toward the fighting. Daniel was an 1851 graduate of West Point who resigned his commission in January 1858 to manage his family plantation in Louisiana. He was mortally wounded in the "Mule Shoe" at Spotsylvania in May 1864. O'Neal was an attorney from Alabama with no military experience prior to the Civil War. He commanded Rodes's old brigade at Chancellorsville and through the Gettysburg Campaign, earning a recommendation from Robert E. Lee for promotion to Brigadier. However, Lee later withdrew his recommendation and the promotion was cancelled by Jefferson Davis. After the war, O'Neal served two terms as governor of Alabama. (Ezra J. Warner, *Generals in Gray,* [Baton Rouge: Louisiana State University Press, 1999], 67; 226.)

66. Blackford, *War Years with JEB Stuart,* 216; *OR,* 27, II: 374. Earlier in the day, Lee had advised Stuart that he had issued warning orders to both Ewell and Longstreet to enter the fight if needed (Robert E. Lee, *Wartime Papers,* 2 vols., edited by Clifford Dowdey, [New York: Little, Brown & Co., 1961; reprint ed., Pennington, NJ: Collectors Reprints, 1996], 2:505–506). Mount Pony, a prominent hill between Culpeper and Stevensburg, frequently served as a signal site and observation post for both Union and Confederate armies. Today, a facility dug into the slopes of Mount Pony and formerly used by the Federal Reserve, is being upgraded to serve as the film repository for the National Archives.

67. Today Chestnut Forks is known as Catalpa.

68. Mary S. Jones and Mildred C. Jones, eds., *Historic Culpeper* (Culpeper, VA: Culpeper Historical Society, 1972), 29. In 1861 James Barbour, at the request of Major Roberdeau Wheat, the commander of the "Louisiana Tigers," renamed his farm Beauregard in honor of the hero of First Manassas. Wheat was convalescing from wounds at the time. The farm is still known as Beauregard today. The Barbour House stands about ½ mile north of the intersection of U.S. Highway 29 and County Route 663 at Brandy Station. The cupola was removed from the house in the early 1900s.

69. Jedediah Hotchkiss, *Make Me a Map of the Valley: The Civil War Journal of Stonewall Jackson's Topographer* (Dallas, TX: Southern Methodist University Press, 1973), 150. Upon the death of Jackson, Hotchkiss served as Ewell's topographer.

70. *OR,* 27, II:772; Trout, *Galloping Thunder,* 230

71. *OR,* 27, II:763; George H. Moffett, "Battle of Brandy Station," *Confederate Veteran* 14 (February 1906), 75. Moffett wrote that the Union guns were supported by a party of New York cavalry, most likely the squadron of the Harris Light that had become separated from the regiment during Davies' attack.

72. H. S. Thomas, an officer of the 1st Pennsylvania Cavalry detailed to Gregg's staff, presented a contradictory account of the loss of Martin's guns. He recalled that after Wynham's first charge up Fleetwood had been blunted, Martin's drivers fled with their limbers. The 1st Maryland, which were positioned to protect the guns, was ordered elsewhere. With no support available, Thomas wrote that he ordered the gunners to abandon their pieces, which they did reluctantly, with some of the men in tears. Thomas recalled that Martin's guns were overrun only once, not three times. (*Philadelphia Weekly Times,* November 10, 1877.)

73. *OR,* 27, I:1025. Two of the three abandoned guns were found to be serviceable. Martin's guns fired fifteen rounds of cannister in their own defense during the day's fighting.

74. *OR,* 27, I:966.

75. *OR*, 27, II:749–750; 763. Lomax indicated that he sent a squadron to Stevensburg. Jones reported that Lomax went himself to that location.
76. *OR*, 27, I:962. Duffié, since he was criticized for not moving to Gregg's assistance in a timely manner, may have exaggerated the number of stragglers he encountered and the amount of time he lost.
77. *OR*, 27, I:609. "*Et id genus omni*" translates roughly as "and everything of that sort."
78. *OR*, 27, II:722.
79. *Ibid.*
80. The reports of Confederate infantry moving to Brandy by train were false. There were no trains sent from Culpeper to Brandy Station with infantry. It is possible, however, that Gregg's men did detect the movement brigades from McLaws's and Rodes's divisions, despite the men's efforts to remain out of sight.
81. Gregg, "The Second Cavalry Division, Army of the Potomac, in the Gettysburg Campaign" (A645 36 Add 3), Papers of David McMurtrie Gregg (MMC-0539), Library of Congress, Washington, DC, hand written note on the back of page 5 of typescript.

10—Hurrah for Hell, Wade In!

1. Janet Hewett et al., eds., *Supplement to the Official Records of the Union and Confederate Armies* (Wilmington, NC: Broadfoot, 1995–2000), I, 5:234.
2. *Ibid.*
3. *Ibid.* 229.
4. *OR*, 27, I:1043.
5. *OR*, 27, I:902. In a message written at 11:00 a.m., Pleasonton informed Hooker that he heard Gregg's guns in Stuart's rear.
6. *OR*, 27, I:1045.
7. *OR*, 27, I: 903.
8. *Ibid.* In addition to keeping Hooker informed of the situation, Pleasonton was also in communication with General Junius Stahel, then at Catlett's Station. In one message to Stahel, Pleasonton asked for rail cars to be sent to Bealeton for his wounded. In another message, Pleasonton warned Stahel that Stuart might attempt to cross the Rappahannock above Beverly Ford before Buford and Gregg could join forces. At the time, such an aggressive course of action was completely beyond the capability of the hard-pressed Confederate commander.
9. *OR*, 27, III:39.
10. Wesley Merritt later wrote that Buford had earlier wished to press the attack on his right, but Buford implied that he had been restrained from doing so by orders from Pleasonton (Wesley Merritt, *Personal Recollections—Beverly Ford to Mitchell's Station (1863)* in *From Everglade to Canyon with the Second United States Cavalry: An Authentic Account of Service in Florida, Mexico, Virginia, and the Indian Country, 1836–1875*, edited by Theodore F. Rodenbough, [New York: D. Van Norstrand, 1875; reprint ed., Norman: University of Oklahoma Press, 2000], 287).
11. Well after the war, Union writers pointed out that at Brandy Station, Stuart enjoyed the advantage of "interior lines." In geometric terms, Stuart could reinforce Fleetwood from Saint James by sending his regiments along a chord, while to reinforce Gregg, Pleasonton's forces had to follow a more lengthy arc. In reality, however, Pleasonton made no effort to have Buford move to Gregg's support, nor to have Gregg move to Buford's. On the contrary, Buford moved away from Fleetwood during the afternoon's fighting.
12. Culpeper County Deed Record Book 15, 231; Eugene M. Scheel, *Culpeper: A Virginia County's History Through 1920* (Orange, VA: Green, 1982), 341–342. This entry in the Deed Books includes a plat of the Cunningham farm from 1866.
13. Culpeper County Deed Record Book 9, 449–451; Eugene M. Scheel, "The Historical Site Survey and Archaeological Reconnaissance of Culpeper County, Virginia" (Culpeper County Government, November 1992—April 1994), BS-55.
14. Culpeper County Deed Record Book 9, 443–445; Scheel, "The Historical Site Survey and Archaeological Reconnaissance of Culpeper County, Virginia," BS-55.
15. Margaret Jeffries, "Farley," U.S. Government (Work Projects Administration, "Virginia Historical Inventory," Library of Virginia, Richmond, 1937; Scheel, *Culpeper: A Virginia County's History Through 1920*, 342–343; Scheel, "The Historical Site Survey and Archaeological Reconnaissance of Culpeper County, Virginia," BS-57–58. A stone monument, reportedly marking William Carter's grave (Carter died in 1832), stands in a field approximately one half mile northeast of the Wellford House. The house, today again known as Farley, served as General John Sedgewick's VI Corps headquarters during the winter of 1863–1864.
16. The origins of the name "Yew Hills" and "Yew Ridge" are obscure, but obviously refer to the terrain and its vegetation. An extensive band of trees, known as the Schoolhouse Woods, stood at the intersection of the Green, Thompson, and Wellford farms. At least one yew grew in the Schoolhouse Woods, since it was cited in a survey as a boundary marker in the Green farm property line. (Culpeper County Deed Book 9, 550, 552.) One map in the Library of Congress collection, prepared by topographical engineers of the Army of the Potomac in 1863, depicts a terrain feature named "YEW MT" just west of Beverly Ford (Call number "G 3880 svar 1863 U5 CW 483.5" with map title "Culpeper [sic] C.H. and vicinity—annotated in pencil." The map is tenth in a series of fifteen under that call number). Since Yew Mountain does not appear on other Union maps, nor on the map prepared by Stuart's engineer, Major William W. Blackford, it is likely that the names Yew Ridge, Yew Hills, or Yew Mountain were not in wide use during the Civil War.
17. W. A. Graham, *Nineteenth Regiment (Second Cavalry)* in *Histories of the Several Regiments and Battalions from North Carolina in the Great War 1861–65: Written by Members of the Respective Commands*, 5 vols., edited by Walter Clark (Raleigh, NC: E. M. Uzzell, 1901; reprint ed., Wendell, NC: Broadfoot's Bookmark, 1982), 2:90–91. Captain John G. Blasingame died on June 11. Captain S. Jay Andrews was shot in the foot, which was later amputated. (Roger H. Harrell, *2nd North Carolina Cavalry*, [Jefferson: McFarland, 2004], 394–395.)
18. Thomas Toliaferro Hoskins to "Papa," June 10, 1863, Hoskins Family Papers (Mss1 H7935 a 2–11), Virginia Historical Society, Richmond. Charles Ward was a private in Company F (Robert K. Krick, *9th Virginia Cavalry*, 4th ed., [Lynchburg, VA: H.E. Howard, 1982] Muster roll data).
19. Whelan, Henry C. "A Race for Life at Brandy Station," edited by Edward G. Longacre. *Civil War Times Illustrated* 17 (January 1979): 36–37; Hewett et al., eds., *Supplement to the Official Records*, 239.
20. *Ibid.*
21. Abner Hard, *History of the Eighth Cavalry Regiment Illinois Volunteers During the Great Rebellion* (Aurora, IL: Np., 1868; reprint ed., Dayton, OH: Morningside Bookshop, 1996), 244.
22. Edwin E Bryant, *History of the 3rd Regiment of Wisconsin Volunteer Infantry* (Madison, WI: Democrat, 1891), 171; Daniel Oakey, *History of the Second Massachusetts Regiment of Infantry: Beverly Ford, A Paper Read at the Officers' Reunion in Boston, May 12, 1884* (Boston: Geo. H. Ellis, 1884), 10–12. In a contradictory account, the Chaplain of the 10th Virginia, writing in the June 15 edition of the *Richmond Sentinel*, reported that his regiment, dismounted as

sharpshooters, held its position until withdrawn, "though exposed to an incessant and galling fire from the 5th U.S. Regulars, who were snugly ensconced behind a stone fence."

23. *OR*, 27, II:681.

24. The serviceability rates for various Union fuses ranged from 53 to 85 percent. The corresponding failure rates thus ranged from 47 to 15 percent. Confederate fuses were generally inferior in quality to Union fuses. Additionally, sabots, used with several types of projectiles to grip the lands and grooves in a rifled gun's barrel and impart spin, tended to separate after the projectile left the muzzle of the piece. Shards from separated sabots also presented a hazard to friendly troops under the gun-target line. (Berkeley R. Lewis, "Notes on Ammunition of the American Civil War 1861–1865" [Washington, D.C., American Ordnance Association, 1959]).

25. Rodenbough, only slightly wounded at Brandy Station, lost an arm a year later while commanding the regiment at Trevilian Station. Breveted to brigadier general of volunteers, Rodenbough was retired from the service in December 1870 due to disability resulting from his Civil War wounds. After leaving the army, he wrote a history of the 2nd U.S. Cavalry and the volume on cavalry as part of the *Photographic History of the Civil War*. In 1893, Rodenbough was awarded the Medal of Honor for his gallantry at Trevilian. After six weeks convalescence, Leoser returned to duty with the regiment. Appointed to command after Rodenbough's capture at Trevilian, Leoser was himself taken prisoner by the Confederates the following day. After being exchanged in September 1864, Leoser served on detached duty until he resigned his commission in October 1865. Shortly after Brandy Station, O'Keefe was exchanged and he returned to duty with his regiment, the 2nd New York Cavalry. Rising to the grade of major, O'Keefe was mortally wounded leading a dismounted attack at Five Forks. For his gallantry, O'Keefe was breveted posthumously to lieutenant colonel. (Theophilus F. Rodenbough, ed., *From Everglade to Canyon with the Second United States Cavalry: An Authentic Account of Service in Florida, Mexico, Virginia, and the Indian Country, 1836–1875*, [New York: D. Van Norstrand, 1875; reprint ed., Norman: University of Oklahoma Press, 2000], 288, 328, 465–467; U.S. Army Center for Military History, "Medal of Honor Recipients," http://www.army.mil/cmh-pg/mohciv2.htm; *OR*, 66, I:1115.)

26. Wesley Merritt, *Personal Recollections—Beverly Ford to Mitchell's Station (1863)* in *From Everglade to Canyon with the Second United States Cavalry: An Authentic Account of Service in Florida, Mexico, Virginia, and the Indian Country, 1836–1875*, edited by Theophilus F. Rodenbough, 289.

27. Graham, *Nineteenth Regiment (Second Cavalry)*, 2:91, 92.

28. James McClure Scott, "War Record" (Mss7:1 Sco845:1), edited by Sarah Travers Lewis Scott Anderson (Virginia Historical Society, VA), 10; Robert J. Driver, Jr., *10th Virginia Cavalry* (Lynchburg, VA: H. E. Howard, 1992), 156, 162.

29. Merritt, *Personal Recollections*, 288; Scott, "War Record" (Mss7:1 Sco845:1), edited by Sarah Travers Lewis Scott Anderson, 10. Scott asserted that his sword saved his head. Dewees was identified by Scott as Lieutenant "Derves" from Philadelphia (Dewees was born in Pennsylvania). Dewees was captured and held as a prisoner until exchanged in 1864.

30. Merritt, *Personal Recollections*, 289. The regular regiments had a significant number of Irish immigrants in their ranks.

31. *Ibid.*; Harrell, *2nd North Carolina Cavalry*, 395.

32. Graham, *Nineteenth Regiment (Second Cavalry)*, 2:91, 92; Mrs. Pegram to James W. Pegram, June 19, 1863, Pegram Family Papers (Mss1 P3496c 81–115), Virginia Historical Society, Richmond.

33. Graham, *Nineteenth Regiment (Second Cavalry)*, 2:91–92.

34. Daniel T. Balfour, *13th Virginia Cavalry*, 2d ed. (Lynchburg, VA: H. E. Howard, 1986), 17, 93. Only a week earlier, Phillips had been convicted at courts-martial for being absent without leave. Because of mitigating circumstances, Phillips merely received a private reprimand as his punishment. Because of his wounds, Phillips did not return to duty until November 1863. In 1864, he was promoted to colonel and appointed to command of the 13th Virginia Cavalry.

35. *OR*, 27, II:771.

36. *OR*, 27, I:1045; *OR*, 27, III:39. Pleasonton, in a message timed at 2:40 p.m., notified Stahel that he would withdraw that evening.

37. Lieutenant Ellis recovered from his wound and in 1864 was promoted to captain and served on the staff of Brigadier General Torbert.

38. F. C. Newhall, *The Battle of Beverly Ford*, in *Annals of the War, Written by Leading Participants North and South* (Philadelphia: Times, 1879; reprint ed., Edison, NJ: Blue & Gray, 1996), 142–144.

39. It is interesting to speculate whether Buford, had he continued to press his attack, would have succeeded in turning Stuart out of his position on Fleetwood Hill near the Miller House. With only four regiments available on Yew Ridge, Buford's force was matched by Rooney Lee's brigade of four regiments. Additionally, Stuart had dispatched the 1st South Carolina to support Lee. Consequently, it is doubtful that Buford would have made much more headway. In any event, the eventual arrival of Munford with his three fresh regiments would have likely prompted Buford to break off the attack and withdraw.

40. Oak Shade, just off Highway 229, is the site of the Little Fork Episcopal Church which was built in 1776. The churchyard contains a monument to the Little Fork Rangers, Company D, 4th Virginia Cavalry.

41. *OR*, 27, II:737. Fitz Lee's message was signed by First Lieutenant Henry C. Lee, an *aide de camp* to his brother, General Fitzhugh Lee (Robert Krick, *Staff Officers in Gray*, [Chapel Hill: University of North Carolina Press], 199). Stuart's message was signed by Lieutenant R. H. Goldsborough, brand-new to the staff and in his first battle as a cavalryman that day.

42. William R. Carter, Diary, Carter Family Papers, 1817–1892 (#33886) (Library of Virginia, Richmond), 95. H. B. McClellan charitably wrote that Munford was delayed by the "perplexing ambiguity" of his orders. (*I Rode with JEB Stuart*, 283). Doubtless, Munford heard the early morning cannon fire from Saint James. It is surprising that he did not, of his own initiative, march to the sound of the guns.

43. *OR*, 27, II:737–738.

44. St. George T. Brooke, Autobiography, 1907 (#25146) (Library of Virginia, Richmond), 27. A surcingle is a strap that passes over the seat of the saddle and under the horse's belly.

45. *Ibid.*; *OR*, 27, II:738.

46. Hewett et al., eds., *Supplement to the Official Records of the Union and Confederate Armies*, I, 5:240–241. Lord reported that his regiment first came under fire at 2:00 p.m., estimate that seems a little early in the day.

47. *OR*, 27, I:962, 975.

48. Larry B. Maier, *Rough and Regular: A History of Philadelphia's 119th Regiment of Pennsylvania Volunteer Infantry, The Gray Reserves* (Shippensburg, PA: Burd Street Press, 1997), 69.

49. William R. Ray, *Four Years with the Iron Brigade*, edited by Lance Herdegen and Sherry Murphy (Cambridge, MA: DaCapo, 2002).

11—Few Will Exult

1. *OR*, 27, III:46. The *New York Times* reported that Stuart responded to Pleasonton's offer by saying that the dead had been buried, the wounded well cared for, and the prisoners sent to Richmond (with no list of their names retained in Culpeper). Consequently, there was no need for a flag of truce. (*New York Times*, June 14, 1863.)

2. JEB Stuart to Flora Stuart (wife), June 12, 1863, Virginia Historical Society, Richmond. For the most part, horse carcasses were left to rot in the fields. Burying them required extensive effort and burning them required significant fuel. It is likely that people, using teams of horses or mules, dragged some carcasses to out-of-the-way places where they, and the flies and buzzards they attracted, would be less offensive.

3. Robert E. Lee, *Wartime Papers*, edited by Clifford Dowdey (New York: Little, Brown & Co., 1961; reprint ed., Pennington, NJ: Collectors Reprints, 1996), 2:511. The Hill Mansion, which today is privately owned, is located at 501 S. East Street, adjacent to the Culpeper National Cemetery.

4. Mary Chesnut, *A Diary from Dixie*, edited by Isabella D. Martin and Myrta Lockett Avary (New York: Portland House, 1905; reprint ed., New York: Random House Value Publishing, 1997), 236. James Chesnut had served two years in the U.S. Senate immediately before the secession of South Carolina, which perhaps explained his selection as an *aide* to the President of the Confederacy. Mary Chesnut made no entries in her journal from August 1862 through October 1863, filling in events from that period from memory when she began converting her journal into book form in 1875. Thus, one might question the verbatim accuracy of the conversation she recalled. (See the introduction of C. Vann Woodward's, *Mary Chesnut's Civil War* [New Haven, CT: Yale University Press, 1982] for details regarding the drafting of Mary Chesnut's "diary.")

5. Janet Hewett et al., eds., *Supplement to the Official Records of the Union and Confederate Armies* (Wilmington, NC: Broadfoot, 1995–2000), I, 5:51; *New York Times*, June 12, 1863. Union Assistant Surgeon Benjamin Howard reported that twenty percent of the wounds he treated were saber slashes. He reported treating one soldier who had five such wounds.

6. Berkeley G. Calfee, *Confederate History of Culpeper County: Culpeper County in the War Between the States, Together with a Complete Roster of the Confederate Soldiers from this County* (Culpeper, VA: Np., 1948; reprinted, Culpeper, VA: Np., 1994), 7. The land for the Glebe was bought in 1788 by the parish of St. Mark's Episcopal Church (Mary S. Jones and Mildred C. Jones, eds., *Historic Culpeper*, [Culpeper, VA: Culpeper Historical Society, 1972], 29). Today the Glebe is an active dairy farm. The pre–Civil War farmhouse sits to the south of Route 663, about one and one half miles from that road's juncture with Route 29 at Brandy Station.

7. Culpeper County Deed Book 16, 165–166. The property on which the frame building sat was owned at the time by James S. Barbour. In 1862, Stone paid Barbour $112.50 per acre for the three-acre lot, and the title to the property was finally transferred from Barbour to Stone in 1869.

8. The former hospital is now known as the "Graffiti House." The building serves as the visitor's center for the Brandy Station Foundation and the Brandy Station battlefield. Marshall's signature, along with inscriptions and drawings from other Confederate and Union soldiers, are visible on the walls of the second floor. While it is not certain that Marshall inscribed his name on the wall while recovering from wounds incurred on June 9, it seems likely that he did so at that time. Marshall was a grand-nephew of John Marshall, the fourth Chief Justice of the U.S. Supreme Court.

9. Early in the battle, Pleasonton sent a message to General Stahel asking him to send trains south to evacuate the wounded (*OR*, 27, III:38).

10. Rappahannock Station, today known as Remington, was the first station on the Orange and Alexandria north of the Rappahannock River.

11. Charles T. O'Ferrall, *Forty Years of Active Service* (New York: Neale, 1904), 68–69. According to O'Ferrall, he and the Union officer exchanged addresses and corresponded after the war. Perhaps O'Ferrall visited his wounded men in the Graffiti House. At least one soldier from the 12th Virginia, in addition to Lieutenant Marshall, inscribed his name on the upstairs wall of the building.

12. In his official report, Stuart noted that Union dead were "buried on different parts of the field before an opportunity was afforded to count them" (*OR*, 27, II:684). Although a Confederate cemetery was established in Culpeper Courthouse in 1861, no known casualties from the battle at Brandy Station were among the 357 Confederate soldiers that were buried in it. Over time, the wooden grave markers were lost, some apparently burned for firewood by Union troops in 1863–1864. The loss of the markers made identification of the individual graves difficult, if not impossible. In 1880 the remains in the Confederate cemetery were disinterred and buried in a mass grave in the Culpeper Citizen's Cemetery. On July 2, 1881, a local veterans' group dedicated "a very neat shaft" costing one thousand dollars on the site to commemorate those Confederate dead. (Daniel Grimsley, *Battles in Culpeper County, Virginia*, [Culpeper, VA: Raleigh Travers Green, 1900; reprint ed., Orange, VA: Green, Nd.], 46; *Confederate Veteran* 11, 2 [February 1903], 69). Today, the obelisk still stands in the cemetery, now known as Fairview. At least one Union soldier, Thomas Needham of Massachusetts, is buried in the Confederate mass grave. Needham was wounded and captured at First Manassas and taken to the Confederate hospital in Culpeper where he died. Later, his home state was mistakenly recorded as Mississippi. In 1867, the Federal Government established a National Cemetery in Culpeper. In one section rest 912 unidentified dead whose remains were moved from nearby battlefields, including Brandy Station. Three officers killed at Brandy Station (Lieutenant Colonel Virgil Broderick and Major John Shelmire, both of the 1st New Jersey Cavalry, and Lieutenant Isaac Ward, 6th U.S. Cavalry) are now buried in the Officer's Circle about the flagpole in Culpeper National Cemetery.

13. Reportedly, the ground near the church was covered with Confederate graves, each marked with a wooden post with the soldier's name and regiment (Douglas W. Owsley et al. *History and Archeology of St. James Episcopal Church, Brandy Station, Virginia*, [Np., Nd.], 19).

14. Myrta Lockett Avary, *A Virginia Girl in the Civil War 1861–1865: Being a Record of the Actual Experiences of the Wife of A Confederate Officer* (New York: D. Appleton, 1903), 251; Mrs. Pegram to James W. Pegram, June 19, 1863, Pegram Family Papers (Mss1 P3496c 81–115), Virginia Historical Society, Richmond. Williams's new bride was Mrs. Pegram's daughter and Lieutenant Pegram's sister.

15. Chesnut, *A Diary From Dixie*, 237; Woodward, ed., *Mary Chesnut's Civil War*, 452, 457. As previously described, a gunshot to the stomach was the mortal, albeit less visible, wound that Hampton received at Stevensburg.

16. Ulysses R. Brooks, *Butler and His Cavalry in the War of Secession, 1861–1865* (Columbia, SC: The State Co., 1909), 186. The location for Farley's initial burial site is from an account by his body servant, Calvin Harper, who later said that Farley was buried in Dr. Thomas's vineyard. Dr. Jones, who treated Farley, was perhaps occupying the Ashby House and Jones had a brother named Thomas, perhaps causing Harper to err regarding ownership of the property. (See Douglas W. Owsley, Malcolm L. Richardson, and William

E. Hanna, "Bioarcheological Investigation and Exhumation of the Remains of Captain William Downs Farley, CSA," [March 2002], 22–23, for a discussion of the genealogical linkage among Dr. Ashby, Dr. Jones, and Dr. Thomas.)

17. Robert J. Trout, *Galloping Thunder: The Stuart Horse Artillery Battalion* (Mechanicsburg, PA: Stackpole, 2002), 235.

18. Langhorne Family Papers (Mss2: L 26536 7–8), Virginia Historical Society, Richmond. Shawsville is a small town on US Highway 11 about halfway between Roanoke and Radford, Virginia.

19. Langhorne Family Papers, Virginia Historical Society, Richmond. After the war, Colonel Thomas T. Munford prepared a roster of the 2d Virginia Cavalry on which he again noted that Langhorne was killed on June 9, 1863 near Brandy Station in "his first fight." (Virginia Department of Confederate Military Records, 1859–1996, [Subseries 2: Cavalry] [#27684]. Library of Virginia, Richmond.) While Steptoe's resolution portrays Langhorne's death in a sanguine manner, another soldier assigned to Company B who knew Langhorne later wrote that he was told Langhorne died the night of the battle "in agony." (St. George T. Brooke, "Autobiography, 1907," [#25146], Library of Virginia, Richmond). Langhorne's obituary appeared in the *Lynchburg Daily Virginian* on June 27, 1863. Captain Steptoe's resolution on the death of the young soldier apparently was not published in the *Daily Virginian*.

20. OR, 27, II:720. Stuart's chief of ordnance was Captain John Esten Cooke, a fiction writer today best known for his post-war book, *Wearing of the Gray*. Cooke was related to Stuart by marriage (his uncle, Phillip St. George Cooke, was Stuart's father-in-law).

21. Grimsley, *Battles in Culpeper County, Virginia*, 12.

22. OR, 27, II:750.

23. *Richmond Examiner*, June 11, 1863. The prisoners arrived the previous evening (June 10) by train from Gordonsville.

24. Ervin L. Jordan, Jr., *Black Confederates and Afro Yankees in Civil War Virginia* (Charlottesville: University of Virginia Press, 1995), 191.

25. John N. Opie, *A Rebel Cavalryman with Lee, Stuart and Jackson* (Chicago: W. B. Conkey, 1899; reprint ed., Dayton, OH: Morningside Bookshop, 1972), 159; Compiled Service Records.

26. Heros Von Borcke, *Memoirs of the Confederate War*, 2 vols. (Initially published 1866; reprint ed., New York: Peter Smith, 1938), 2: 239, 2:267–280.

27. Additionally, some wounded horses may have been sent to the army's horse infirmary between Charlottesville and Lynchburg. There is little documentation on this subject, but since there were roughly two thousand horses in the horse infirmary by mid–July, it seems likely that a few wounded at Brandy Station might have been sent there to recuperate. (Robert J. Trout, *They Followed the Plume: The Story of J.E.B. Stuart and His Staff*, [Mechanicsburg, PA: Stackpole, 1993], 282.)

28. Frank Robertson Reade, *In the Saddle with Stuart: The Story of Frank Smith Robertson of Jeb Stuart's Staff*, edited by Robert J. Trout (Gettysburg, PA: Thomas, 2004), 62. Robertson did not record what happened to the sorrel horse, but certainly it quickly died.

29. OR, 27, II:771.

30. OR, 27, II:683, 734.

31. OR, 27 II:733–736. Robertson wrote his initial report on June 12, 1863, and in response to endorsements from Stuart, supplemented it on June 13, and again on June 15.

32. OR, 27, II:683, 737.

33. OR, 27, II:737–738. Douglas Southall Freeman pointed out that various accounts of the battle erred with respect to the location of Wellford's Ford on the Hazel River and on Munford's route to the battlefield (*Lee's Lieutenants* 3 vols, New York: Scribner's, 1944, 3: 16–17). However, the distance from Oak Shade, where Fitz Lee's brigade was camped, to Wellford's Ford, is a little farther than five miles, an easy one-hour march for cavalry. Freeman observed that there was little regarding the battle in Munford's voluminous papers, and concluded that "Munford manifestly was not ashamed of his conduct at Brandy, but neither was he proud of it." (*Lee's Lieutenants*, III:16, n. 84.)

34. OR, 27, II:721–723.

35. OR, 27, II:729–731.

36. OR, 27, II:744.

37. OR, 27, II,748–750. Neither Major Flournoy nor Lieutenant Colonel Marshall reported receiving orders to attack Buford's division, which at the time was advancing up the road from Beverly Ford.

38. OR, 27, II:680–681, 683.

39. OR, 27, II:680–681.

40. OR, 27, II:679–686. Stuart also singled out Major Robert Beckham, as a "daring and efficient officer" who "deserves the highest praise."

41. OR, 27, II:687. The fighting on June 9 warranted only a single paragraph in Robert E. Lee's report of the Gettysburg Campaign.

42. OR, 27, I:1024–1025. Martin's battery was equipped with three-inch rifled guns. The fourth gun in the two sections supporting Wyndham was disabled when a projectile became lodged in its bore. That gun was withdrawn and thus not captured when Martin and Lieutenant Clark's sections were overrun for the third and final time by Lunsford Lomax and the 11th Virginia. Although the three lost guns were spiked, Stuart's men were able to quickly restore two to a serviceable condition. The strength and casualty figures provided by Martin in his report were inconsistent.

43. OR, 27, I:961–962. There is no evidence that Duffié considered fighting through the 2nd South Carolina to approach Brandy Station on the Old Carolina Road.

44. There is no evidence that Gregg considered leading with his 3rd Division to better keep the advance of his wing on schedule. There appears to have been little tactical advantage — improved flank security only — to having Duffié's division lead the Left Wing's advance.

45. OR, 27, I:949–952.

46. Hewett et al., eds. *Supplement to the Official Records*. I, 5:227–231.

47. OR, 27, I: 903.

48. OR, 27, I:904. Pleasonton was apparently not aware that the batteries in the Stuart Horse Artillery contained a mix of weapons.

49. OR, 27, I:1044–1046. Inaccuracies in Pleasonton's official report exceed the exaggerations and omissions frequently found in Civil War reporting. There were no infantry approaching Brandy Station by train. Gregg did not seize Stuart's headquarters and all of its documents. There is no documented basis for the claim that Rooney Lee's officers resorted to shooting and sabering their own men to keep them in the fight on the Yew Hills. Moreover, as seen from subsequent events, Stuart's division was hardly crippled.

50. Ibid.

51. Ibid.

52. Von Koerber's sketch map was not included in the *Official Records*. It, and his maps of the battles at Aldie and Upperville, are in the Albert and Shirley Small Special Collections Library at the University of Virginia (MSS 5447).

53. OR, 27, II:161. Schenk, a "political general" from Ohio who displayed military competence as a brigade and division commander, was wounded at Second Manassas and disabled from further field service. He resigned his commission in December 1863 to take up a seat in Congress, where he served until 1870, whereupon he was appointed as United States Ambassador to Great Britain. (Warner, *Generals in Blue*, 423.)

54. Marsena Patrick, "Marsena Patrick Journal,

1862–1865," Miscellaneous Manuscripts Collection, Library of Congress, Washington, DC.

55. Several other Northern newspapers printed excerpts from the *New York Times* article.

56. *New York Times*, June 12, 1863. The correspondent went on to describe the intelligence information that had been obtained, including an order from Stuart directing his command to be ready to move on fifteen minute's notice.

57. *New York Herald*, June 11, 1863; *American and Commercial Advertiser*, Baltimore, MD, June 11, 1863.

58. *New York Herald*, June 11, 1863.

59. *Richmond Examiner*, June 10, 1863.

60. *Ibid.*, June 11, 1863. In a notable inaccuracy, the *Examiner* reported that a Union general named John Smith, identified as possibly the commander of the Union force, had been captured during the battle. There was no Union general named Smith in the battle at Brandy Station, nor were any Union generals captured during the engagement.

61. There were two well established fords on the Rappahannock between Kelly's and Beverly: Norman's, near the Orange and Alexandria Railroad Bridge; and Wheatley's, about a mile upstream from Kelly's (Eugene M. Scheel, "The Historical Site Survey and Archaeological Reconnaissance of Culpeper County, Virginia," [Culpeper County Government, November 1992–April 1994], REM-10). On the morning of June 9, 1863, Federal troopers used neither Norman's nor Wheatley Ford, nor any other crossing sight unknown to the Confederates. In an apparent attempt to stifle criticism, a Confederate censor excised remarks about Stuart being surprised from a telegraphic report by a correspondent from the *Mobile Register* (Brayton Harris, *Blue & Gray in Black & White: Newspapers in the Civil War*, [Dulles, VA: Batsford Brassey, 1999], 257.) The effort to restrict the flow of embarrassing information proved futile.

62. *Richmond Examiner*, June 12, 1863. The *Examiner* discounted the Union claim that General Lee's plans had been found in Stuart's camp because, "General Lee's plans are known only to himself, his Lieutenant Generals, and the Heads of the Government in Richmond."

63. *Ibid.*, June 12, 1863. This editorial, which had been summarized by other authors, is included here in its entirety.

64. *Daily Virginian*, Lynchburg, VA, June 13, 1863.

65. *Charleston Mercury*, June 12, 1863, June 15, 1863.

66. JEB Stuart to "My Darling Wife," June 12, 1863, Stuart Papers, 1833–1864 (St923 d 1–107), Virginia Historical Society, Richmond. On May 26, a newspaper reporter arrived at Stuart's Headquarters to accompany the Cavalry Division on the pending campaign. Stuart sent the reporter away. However, Stuart noted that the reporter was due to return the following day "with a flea in his ear." Stuart anticipated that the reporter would try and abuse him. It is possible that Stuart believed that the reporter might be the source of the *Examiner*'s animosity. (JEB Stuart to "Dearest One," May 26, 1863, Stuart Papers, 1833–1864 [St923 d 1–107], Virginia Historical Society, Richmond.)

67. *Ibid.*

68. JEB Stuart to "My Dear Friend," June 15, 1863, Stuart Papers, 1833–1864 (St923 d 1–107), Virginia Historical Society, Richmond.

69. *Richmond, Sentinel*, June 13, 1863.

70. *Ibid.*, June 17, 1863.

71. *Richmond Examiner*, June 18, 1863.

72. *Ibid.*, June 24, 1863.

73. *Ibid.*, June 24, 1863.

74. John B. Jones, *A Rebel War Clerk's Diary*, 2 vols. (Philadelphia, PA: J. B. Lippincott, 1866; reprint ed., Time-Life, 1982), 1:161–162.

75. Joseph A. Waddell, Diary, Albert and Shirley Small Special Collections Library, University of Virginia, Charlottesville.

76. Charles Minor Blackford and Susan Leigh Blackford *Letters from Lee's Army*, edited by Charles Minor Blackford III (New York: Scribner's, 1947; reprint ed., Lincoln: University of Nebraska Press, 1998), 175.

77. Thomas Rosser to Betty (sister), June 12, 1863, Papers of Thomas Lafayette Rosser [Mss 1171], Albert and Shirley Small Special Collections Library, University of Virginia, Charlottesville. In a letter to his wife on June 18, Rosser provided a hint of additional criticism regarding the fighting at Brandy Station. Writing about the previous day's battle at Aldie, Rosser told his wife, "Had it not been for me, there would have been another *surprise*" [emphasis in the original].

78. Michael J. Welton, ed. *My Heart Is So Rebellious: The Caldwell Letters, 1861–65*, 189–90. Susan Caldwell's husband, Lycurgus, was in Richmond working for the Confederate Government. Her letter was begun on May 31, but not completed until June 12.

79. Catherine Ann Devereaux Edmondston, *Journal of A Secesh Lady: The Diary of Catherine Ann Devereaux Edmondston 1860–1866*, second ed., edited by Beth G. Crabtree and James W. Patton (Raleigh, NC: Division of Archives and History, Department of Cultural Resources, 1979), 404–405.

80. *Ibid.* Catherine Edmondston's husband, Patrick Edmondston, had been appointed to West Point in 1837 but did not graduate.

81. Edmondston, *Journal of A Secesh Lady*, 407. Mrs. Edmondston mistakenly attributed the claim about fox-hunting to Grimes Davis, not Lieutenant Colonel Hasbrouck Davis, 12th Illinois Cavalry. Also, Wyndham was not particularly well-born.

82. Guy R. Everson and Edward H. Simpson, eds., "*Far, Far from Home": The Wartime Letters of Dick and Tally Simpson, Third South Carolina Volunteers* (New York: Oxford University Press, 1994), 245.

83. William Hartwell Perry to father, June 14, 1863, Papers of William Hartwell Perry, 1860–65 (#7786-d), Albert and Shirley Small Special Collections Library, University of Virginia, Charlottesville.

84. Henry Brainerd McClellan, Papers (M1324 b), Southern Historical Society, Richmond, VA.

85. Douglas Southall Freeman, *Lee's Lieutenants*, 3:52. The letter did not reach Stuart until after he crossed into Pennsylvania during the Gettysburg Campaign.

12 — Old Soldiers Never Die

1. In his private correspondence to John Farnsworth, former commander of the 8th Illinois and brigadier general who had left the army to take a seat in Congress, Pleasonton expressed his disdain for foreigners. In a letter dated June 23, 1863, in which he railed against Major General Stahel, then commanding the cavalry around Washington, Pleasonton wrote, "Tell the President from me that I will sacrifice my life to support his Government & save the country, but that I will not *fight* under the orders of a *Dutchman*." (Alfred Pleasonton Papers, Miscellaneous Manuscript Collection,, Library of Congress, Washington, DC).

2. George W. Cullum, *Biographical Register of the Officers and Graduates of the U.S. Military Academy at West Point, N. Y. from its Establishment in 1802 to 1890 with the Early History of the United States Military Academy*, 3 vols., 3rd ed. (New York: Houghton Mifflin, 1891), #1868, #1966; Ezra J. Warner, *Generals In Blue* (Baton Rouge: Louisiana State University Press, 1999), 149. In a marginal note to his June 23 letter to John Farnsworth (cited above), Pleasonton wrote "I want [Captain Elon] Farnsworth to command the *old* brigade! Have him made!" John Farnsworth was the

uncle of Elon Farnsworth, and thought to be influential in the government.

3. Edward G. Longacre, *General John Buford, a Military Biography* (Conschocken, PA: Combined Books, 1995), 177–178.

4. Alfred Pleasonton Papers, Miscellaneous Manuscript Collection, Library of Congress, Washington, DC. Snicker's Gap is where present-day U.S. Route 7 crosses the Blue Ridge between Berryville and Round Hill.

5. Edward G. Longacre, "Alfred Pleasonton: The Knight of Romance," *Civil War Times Illustrated* 13 (December 1974): 19–21; Cullum, *Biographical Register*, #1844.

6. *Ibid*., 22. In 1888 Pleasonton was reinstated in the Army and retired as a major.

7. *Ibid*., 23. See also the biography of Pleasonton at www.bufordboys.com for additional information regarding Pleasonton's later life.

8. Robert E. Lee to James A. Seddon, *Wartime Papers*, 2:678. Dahlgren was killed by a party from the 9th Virginia Cavalry that had been posted east of Richmond in King William County. The officer leading the party turned Dahlgren's documents over to Colonel R. L. T. Beale (G. W. Beale, *A Lieutenant of Cavalry in Lee's Army*,[Boston, MA: Gorham, 1918; reprint ed., Baltimore, MD: Butternut and Blue, 1994], 138–139).

9. Jeffry D. Wert, *Custer: The Controversial Life of George Armstrong Custer* (New York: Simon & Schuster, 1996), 78; Cullum, *Biographical Register*, #1966. Various authors have asserted that Custer, acting as an observer for Pleasonton, assumed *de facto* command of the 1st Brigade after Davis was killed (e.g: Thom Hatch, *Clashes of Cavalry: The Civil War Careers of George Armstrong Custer and Jeb Stuart*, [Mechanicsburg, PA: Stackpole, 2001], 77–78). While he may have played an active role in the fighting near the ford, the documentary record fails to reveal that Custer exercised any actual command over troops during the battle.

10. Longacre, *General John Buford*, 243–247; Cullum, *Biographical Register*, #1384.

11. Warner, *Generals in Blue*, 124. After the war, Colonel Thomas Devin would have been senior to Pleasonton in the cavalry had Pleasonton remained in the army.

12. George F. Price, *Across the Continent with the Fifth Cavalry* (New York: Noble Offset, 1883; reprint ed., New York: Antiquarian, 1959), 333.

13. Francis Whiting Hatch, "Charles J. Whiting: Civil War Hero," *Castine Visitor: Castine Historical Society Newsletter* 11 (Spring 2001), 9; Cullum, *Biographical Register*, #789. Regarding Whiting's life in the nineteen years after he left the army and before his death, his *Cullum* entry states "Unknown, no authentic information having been received." Whiting's obituary appeared in West Point's *Annual Reunion* of 1891. It also provided no information regarding Whiting's life after he left the Army.

14. Ralph Kishner, *The Class of 1861* (Carbondale: Southern Illinois University Press, 1999), 97, 102–103. Blanch Butler Ames maintained her residence in Lowell, MA.

15. *Ibid*., 97, 105–106.

16. Ezra J. Warner, *Generals In Blue*, 6.

17. Edward G. Longacre, *Lincoln's Cavalrymen: A History of the Mounted Forces of the Army of the Potomac, 1861–1865* (Mechanicsburg, PA: Stackpole, 2000), 322–323. Longacre, citing a conversation overhead by the surgeon of the 6th Ohio Cavalry, speculates that Gregg resigned because after more than three years of combat he had lost his nerve. However, one must view the recollection of the surgeon, made public well after the war and uncorroborated by other evidence, with a healthy degree of skepticism.

18. James M. McPherson, ed., *Encyclopedia of Civil War Biographies*, 3 vols. (Armonk, NY: M.E. Sharpe, 2000) 2:122–123; Warner, *Generals in Blue*, 188, 623 (n. 150); Cullum, *Biographical Register*, #1684.

19. Edward G. Longacre, "Sir Percy Wyndham," *Civil War Times Illustrated*. 8 (December 1968), 18. At the time, Giesboro was a major, and costly, activity.

20. Henry R. Pyne, *Ride to War: The History of the First New Jersey Cavalry*, edited by Earl S. Miers (New Brunswick, NJ: Rutgers University Press, 1961), xvi.

21. *Ibid*.

22. William R. Carter, *Sabres, Saddles, and Spurs*, edited by Walbrook D. Swank (Shippensburg, PA: Burd Street Press, 1998), 97.

23. Warner, *Generals in Blue*, 267.

24. Samuel J. Martin,*"Kill-Cavalry"— Sherman's Merchant of Terror: The Life of Union General Hugh Judson Kilpatrick* (Teaneck, NJ: Fairleigh Dickinson University Press, 1996), 221–222.

25. Warner, *Generals in Blue*, 267.

26. Martin, *"Kill-Cavalry,"* 7, 243, 247. Kilpatrick's first wife died at West Point on November 22, 1863 (Warner, *Generals in Blue*, 145).

27. *OR*, 27, I:962–964; George N. Bliss, *The First Rhode Island Cavalry at Middleburg, Va., June 17 and 18, 1863* in *Personal Narratives, 4th Series* (Providence: Soldiers & Sailors Historical Society of Rhode Island, 1889–1890), 14, 16–17, 28. Duffié was later criticized, with some justification, for not extricating his regiment under the cover of darkness. However, as at Stevensburg, the Frenchman apparently felt it necessary to rigidly comply with his orders. Those orders, given with perhaps the expectation that Duffié could link up with Kilpatrick at Middleburg, were of questionable tactical acumen.

28. James J. Williamson, *Mosby's Rangers* (New York: Ralph B. Kenyon, 1896; reprint ed. Time-Life, 1982), 281–283.

29. George N. Bliss, *Duffié and the Monument to his Memory* in *Personal Narratives, 4th Series* (Providence: Soldiers & Sailors Historical Society of Rhode Island, 1889–1890), 62–64. The largest donation was three hundred dollars from the Rhode Island government. The veterans also raised $6.10 soliciting on the city's "horse cars."

30. McPherson ed., *Encyclopedia of Civil War Biographies*, 2:308.

31. Walter F. Beyer and Oscar F. Keydel, eds., *Deeds of Valor: How America's Civil War Heroes Won the Congressional Medal of Honor* (reprint ed., New York: Smithmark, 2000), 211–212.

32. Frederick Phisterer, *New York in the War of Rebellion, 1861–1865*, 5 vols. with index (Albany, NY: Weed and Parsons, 1890), I:806. The 4th New York Cavalry, with its large proportion of immigrants, was never a well regarded regiment. On September 16, 1863, the regiment allowed one of its squadrons to be captured by Confederates (diCesnola was in Libby Prison at the time). On September 17, 1863, General Pleasonton published a general order prohibiting the regiment from displaying a color or guidon until their performance improved. The order was read at every regiment in the Cavalry Corps. (*OR*, 29, I:114.)

33. Elizabeth McFadden, *The Glitter and the Gold: A Spirited Account of the Metropolitan Museum of Art's First Director, the Audacious and High-handed Luigi Palma di Cesnola* (New York: Dial, 1971), 127.

34. *Ibid*., 229.

35. *Ibid*., 245.

36. *Ibid*., 248–249.

37. *OR*, 29, I:190.

38. Don E. Alberts, *Brandy Station to Manila Bay: A Biography of General Wesley Merritt* (Austin, TX: Presidial Press, 1980), 138, 275.

39. *Ibid*., 157.

40. *Ibid*., 215–217.

41. *Ibid*., 276–278, 281–283. Throughout his military career, Merritt stressed the need for the professional development of the Army's officer corps. He was a founding member of the U.S. Cavalry Association, wrote extensively in

professional journals, and with British and French co-authors, wrote a book surveying the armies of major nations.
42. *Ibid.*, 314, 317–318.
43. *Ibid.*, 322, 323.
44. *OR*, 27, II:948; W. H. Carter, *From Yorktown to Santiago with the Sixth U.S. Cavalry* (Baltimore, MD: Lord Baltimore Press, 1900), 97, 313.
45. Price, *Across the Continent with the Fifth Cavalry*, 360–361.
46. Cullum, *Biographical Register*, #1750.
47. Cullum, *Biographical Register*, #1859.
48. Samuel P. Bates, *Martial Deeds of Pennsylvania* (Philadelphia: T. H. Davis, 1876), 576.
49. Eric J. Wittenberg, *The Union Cavalry Comes of Age: Hartwood Church to Brandy Station, 1863* (Washington, DC: Brassey's, 2003), 262.
50. *OR*, 43, I:505.
51. Warner, *Generals in Blue*, 113.
52. Richard J. Staats, *Life and Times of Colonel William Stedman of the 6th Ohio Cavalry*, Volume 4, *Grassroots History of the American Civil War*, [Bowie, MD: Heritage, 2003], 228, 323, 337, 360, 371. Later, there was a controversy because Stedman's personal effects, including money he had reportedly taken with him to Cuba, were never returned to his family. Old Put recovered from the wound to his nose, returned to Ohio with Stedman, and lived to be thirty-five.
53. William E. Doster, *A Brief History of the Fourth Pennsylvania Cavalry* (Pittsburgh: Np., 1891; reprint ed., Hightstown, NJ: Longstreet House, 1997), v.
54. Bates, *Martial Deeds of Pennsylvania*, 787–788; Roger D. Hunt and Jack R. Brown, *Brevet Brigadier Generals in Blue* (Gaithersburg, MD: Olde Soldier, 1990), 619.
55. Daniel C. Toomey and Charles A. Earp, *Marylanders in Blue: The Artillery and the Cavalry* (Baltimore: Toomey Press, 1999); Hunt and Brown, *Brevet Brigadier Generals in Blue*, 155.
56. Hunt and Brown, *Brevet Brigadier Generals in Blue*, 606. Taylor's brevet was dated August 4, 1865.
57. *Ibid.*, 309; George A. Rummell, III, *72 Days at Gettysburg: Organization of the 10th New York Volunteer Cavalry* (Shippensburg, PA: White Mane, 1997), 55–56.
58. Frederick Phisterer, *New York in the War of Rebellion*, 2:1106–1107. The 26th New York Cavalry lost three men to disease during its five months of service. Willard Glazier, formerly of the Harris Light and a prolific post-war writer, served as first lieutenant of Company L, 26th New York.
59. *Ibid.*, 2:913; John B. Inglis, Diary (SC 22716), New York State Library, Albany, entry for June 9, 1863.
60. James A. Goecker, manuscript, "William S. McClure, Major, Third Indiana Cavalry."
61. S.L. Gracey, *Annals of the Sixth Pennsylvania Cavalry* (Philadelphia: E. H. Butler, 1868; reprint ed. Lancaster, OH: Vanberg, 1996), 301–302. There is scant information documenting Whelan's command of the regiment. However, in the absence of Colonel Richard Rush (who held his commission until September 29, 1863), the continual detail of Lieutenant Colonel C. Ross Smith to Cavalry Corps Headquarters, and the capture and imprisonment of Major Robert Morris, Jr., Whelan was the senior officer present for duty.
62. William G. Burnett, *Better a Patriot Soldier's Grave: The History of the Sixth Ohio Volunteer Cavalry* (Np.: 1982), 23, 90.
63. Henry R. Pyne, *Ride to War: The History of the First New Jersey Cavalry*, xx–xxiv, 270 (n. 52, 53).
64. Torlief S. Holmes, *Horse Soldiers in Blue* (Gaithersburg, MD: Butternut, 1985), 3, 227–228.
65. Warner, *Generals in Blue*, 519, 667 (n. 702).
66. *Ibid.*, 55–56.
67. Hunt and Brown, *Brevet Brigadier Generals in Blue*, 208. Hoffman's brevet was dated August 1, 1864.
68. Hunt and Brown, *Brevet Brigadier Generals in Blue*, 288.
69. *OR*, 27, I:494; Hunt and Brown, *Brevet Brigadier Generals in Blue*, 191.
70. New Hampshire Department of Historic Resources (www.state.nh.us/nhdhr/warheroes.html).
71. *Hanover Evening Sun*, April 26, 2004 (http://www.eveningsun.com/Stories/~2109474,00.html).
72. Alan T. Nolan, *The Iron Brigade: A Military History*. Bloomington: Indiana University Press, 1994, 27, 276, 376 (n. 47); The Seventh Wisconsin Website (http://www.7thwisconsin.com/original/fieldstaff-photos.html)
73. Phisterer, *New York in the War of Rebellion, 1861–1865*, 4:3470.
74. *Ibid.*, 4:2963.
75. Hunt and Brown, *Brevet Brigadier Generals in Blue*, 240.
76. *Ibid.*, 476; Cullum, *Biographical Register*, #1864.
77. Phisterer, *New York in the War of Rebellion*, 2:1575.
78. Douglas Southall Freeman, *Lee's Lieutenants*, 3:212.
79. In actuality, all Confederate colonels and general officers wore three stars on their collars.
80. Henry B. McClellan, *I Rode with JEB Stuart: The Life and Campaigns of Major-General J.E.B. Stuart* (Bloomington: Indiana University Press, 1958; reprint ed., New York: Da Capo, 1994), 415; Freeman, *Lee's Lieutenants*, III:761. Wounds such as that suffered by Stuart were almost always fatal, and certainly Stuart and those around him knew immediately that he had little hope of recovery. For a detailed discussion of the cause of Stuart's death, see Freeman, *Lee's Lieutenants*, 3:761–763.
81. *Ibid.*, 415–416.
82. *Richmond Daily Examiner,* May 17, 1864.
83. General Order dated October 8, 1863, William Edmondson Jones Papers, 1845–1968 (Mss2J7286b), Virginia Historical Society, Richmond.
84. James B. Avirett, *The Memoirs of General Turner Ashby and his Compeers* (Baltimore, MD: Shelby & Dulany, 1867), 303.
85. Ezra J. Warner, *Generals In Gray* (Baton Rouge: Louisiana State University Press, 1999), 167.
86. *OR*, 27, II: 794–796; William Henry Redman, "History of the 12th Illinois Cavalry," Memoir (#7415-b), Albert and Shirley Small Special Collections Library, University of Virginia, Charlottesville; Douglas Southall Freeman, *R. E. Lee*, 4 vols. (New York: Scribner's, 1949), 3:139. See Robert E. Lee, *Recollections and Letters of General Robert E. Lee, by His Son Capt. Robert E. Lee* (New York: Doubleday, Page, 1904; reprint ed., Garden City, NY: Garden City Publishing, 1926), 98–101, for a description of Lee's capture. Robert Lee, the son, was present at Hickory Hill at the time Rooney Lee was captured.
87. Series II *OR*, 6:69, 118.
88. R.E. Lee to Mary Lee, July 7, 1863, Robert E. Lee, *Wartime Papers*, 2 vols., edited by Clifford Dowdey (New York: Little, Brown, Inc., 1961; reprint ed., Pennington, NJ: Collectors Reprints, 1996), 2:542.
89. R. E. Lee to Mildred Lee, September 10, 1863; Lee, *Wartime Papers*, 2:598.
90. Warner, *Generals In Gray*, 184. Contrary to expectations, Major General Benjamin "Beast" Butler, the Union commander at Fort Monroe, had been kind to his prisoner and reportedly even returned Rooney's horse upon his release (Mary Chesnut, *A Diary From Dixie*, edited by Isabella D. Martin and Myrta Lockett Avary, [New York, Portland House, 1905; reprint ed., New York: Random House Value Publishing, 1997], 300).
91. Lyon Gardiner Tyler, ed., *Encyclopedia of Virginia Biography* (New York: Lewis Historical, 1915), 772.
92. Ravensworth burned in 1925. The estate was later obliterated by development—a shopping center now stands on the site of the house. (Mary B. Daughtry, *Gray Cavalier: The Life and Wars of General W. H. F. "Rooney" Lee*, [Cambridge, MA: DaCapo, 2002], 303.)

Notes — Chapter 12

93. JEB Stuart to Fitzhugh Lee, Fitzhugh Lee Papers, 1731–1952 (#8494), Albert and Shirley Small Special Collections Library, University of Virginia, Charlottesville.

94. Harry Warren Radnour, Doctoral dissertation, "General Fitzhugh Lee: A Biography," University of Virginia, 1971, 249–267.

95. Edward G. Longacre, *Gentleman and Soldier: The Extraordinary Life of Wade Hampton*. Nashville, TN: Rutledge Hill, 2003. 148, 154.

96. Manly Wade Wellman, *Giant in Gray: A Biography of Wade Hampton of South Carolina* (New York: Scribner's, 1949), 161–2. The younger Wade Hampton died of malaria in Mississippi on December 22, 1879 (Wellman, *Giant In Gray*, 307).

97. Warner, *Generals In Gray*, 123.

98. Wellman, *Giant In Gray*, 188–189.

99. *Ibid.*, 301–303, 307.

100. *Ibid.*, 333.

101. Freeman, *Lee's Lieutenants*, 3:208.

102. *OR*, 27, III:1006, 1007.

103. *OR*, 28, II:467.

104. Patrick A. Bowmaster, master's thesis, "Confederate Brig. Gen. B. H. Robertson and the Gettysburg Campaign" (Virginia Polytechnic Institute and State University, 1995), 101.

105. *Ibid.*

106. Warner, *Generals in Gray*, 47; R. L. T. Beale, *History of the Ninth Virginia Cavalry in the War Between the States* (Richmond, VA: B. F. Johnson, 1899), 140.

107. Warner, *Generals in Gray*, 21.

108. *Ibid.*, 336; Confederate House Bill # 323, January 5, 1865. A similar bill had been proposed in 1864.

109. Warner, *Generals in Gray*, 190–191; "Maj. Gen. L. L. Lomax," *Confederate Veteran* 21 (September 1915), 450.

110. Lynwood M. Holland, *Pierce M. B. Young: The Warwick of the South* (Athens: University of Georgia Press, 1964), 74, 77, 83, 88.

111. *Ibid.*, 105, 161, 193, 201, 217; Ezra J. Warner, *Generals In Gray*, 348. The nature of Young's medical condition is somewhat clouded. On July 7, the *Atlanta Constitution* reported that hospital authorities "were rather reticent as to the nature of General Young's illness" saying only that he had a "medical condition." The *Constitution* added that Young "desired the greatest retirement and [Young] instructed the superintendent of the hospital to say in answer to all inquiries that he wished to rest in quiet." The following day in an article on funeral arrangements, the *Constitution* devoted two paragraphs to Young's long-term health problems, and ended by mentioning that Young died from the effects of Bright's Disease (kidney failure). Holland, in his biography of Young, apparently honored Young's desires and omitted the cause of the general's death.

112. Warner, *Generals in Gray*, 15; Cullum, *Biographical Register*, #1535.

113. *Charleston Mercury*, June 15, 1863; J. W. Ward, "General M. C. Butler of South Carolina," *Confederate Veteran* 3 (February 1895), 42.

114. Warner, *Generals in Gray*, 40–41; Samuel J. Martin, *Southern Hero: Matthew Calbraith Butler* (Mechanicsburg, PA: Stackpole, 2001), 298, 308. While Butler was serving as a major general of volunteers during the Spanish-American War, the people of New York purchased for him a fine thoroughbred named Admiral Dewey — undoubtedly a more refined animal than Old Bench Legs, his horse that was killed at Stevensburg.

115. Ulysses R. Brooks, *Butler and His Cavalry in the War of Secession, 1861–1865* (Columbia, SC: The State Co., 1909), 546; South Carolina Department of Corrections (http://www.state.sc.us/scdc/AgencyHistory/Agency History4.hrml).

116. Jeffry Wert, "His Unhonored Service: Colonel Tom Munford — A Man of Achievement," *Civil War Times Illustrated* 24 (June 1985), 33.

117. *Ibid.*

118. Freeman, *Lee's Lieutenants*, 3:596, 667.

119. *Ibid.*, 3:667–668.

120. Bruce S. Allardice, *More Generals in Gray* (Baton Rouge: Louisiana State University Press, 1995), 171.

121. Lyon Gardiner Tyler, ed., *Encyclopedia of Virginia Biography*, 3:77–78.

122. VMI's Civil War Generals, Virginia Military Institute Archives, Preston Library, Lexington, VA. (http://www.vmi.edu/archives/Civil_War/munfordt.html)

123. Louis H. Manarin, *The Cavalry*, vol. 2 of *North Carolina Troops 1861–1865, A Roster ...* (Raleigh: North Carolina State Department of Archives and History, 1968), 372.

124. *OR*, 27, II:706; Robert J. Driver, Jr., *1st Virginia Cavalry* (Lynchburg, VA: H. E. Howard, 1991) 169.

125. Dennis E. Frye, *12th Virginia Cavalry*, 2d ed., (Lynchburg: H.E. Howard, 1988), 134..

126. R.L.T. Beale, *History of the Ninth Virginia Cavalry in the War Between the States*, (Richmond, VA: B.F. Johnson Publishing Co., 1899), 92. Davis had that morning borrowed the horse of his regimental surgeon, his own horse being worn out. (Archibald Atkinson Jr., "Memoir of Archibald Atkinson, Jr.," Special Collections Department. Virginia Polytechnic Institute and State University Library, Blacksburg, VA, 53.) (http://spec.lib.vt.edu/civwar/memoirs.htm)

127. Driver, Jr., *10th Virginia Cavalry*, (Lynchburg, VA: H.E. Howard 1992) 42–43, 107–108; U.S. Military Academy, *Annual Reunion*, June 17, 1871, 30–31.

128. Richard Armstrong, *7th Virginia Cavalry* (Lynchburg, VA: H. E. Howard, 1992), 191.

129. Driver, Jr., *2nd Virginia Cavalry*, 282; Lyon Gardiner Tyler, ed., *Encyclopedia of Virginia Biography*, 4 vols. (New York: Lewis Historical, 1915), 4:31–32. Watts was wounded early in the war at Flint Hill in Rappahannock County, took eight saber cuts at 2nd Manassas, and was wounded in the groin at Occoquan in December 1862.

130. Louis H. Manarin, *The Cavalry*, 266; Neil H. Raiford, *4th North Carolina Cavalry in the Civil War* (Jefferson, NC: McFarland, 2003), 92.

131. Michael P. Musick, *6th Virginia Cavalry* (Lynchburg, VA: H.E. Howard, 1990), 163; *Roll of Officers and Members of the Georgia Hussars and of the Cavalry Companies, of which the Hussars are a Continuation, with Historical Sketch Relating Facts Showing the Origin and Necessity of Rangers, or Mounted Men in the Colony of Georgia from the Date of Its Founding*. Savannah, GA: The Morning News, 1906, 324.

132. "Col. John Logan Black, of South Carolina," *Confederate Veteran* 35 (June 1927), 214.

133. John Logan Black, *Crumbling Defenses, or Memoirs and Reminiscences of John Logan Black, Colonel C. S. A.*, edited by Eleanor D. McSwain (Macon, GA: Privately Published, 1960). Virginia Black was born on September 5, 1880.

134. Thomas P. Nanzig, *3rd Virginia Cavalry*, 90, 121.

135. Frank M. Myers, *The Comanches: A History of White's Battalion, Virginia Cavalry, Laurel Brigade, Hampton's Div., A. N. V., C. S. A.* (Baltimore, MD: Kelly, Piet, 1871; reprint ed., Alexandria, VA: Stonewall, 1985).

136. A report dated July 31, 1863, mistakenly listed Lieutenant Colonel J. "Shac" Green as commander of the 6th Virginia. At the time, Green was absent pending courts-martial for disobedience of orders and breech of arrest. (*OR*, 27, III:1062).

137. Richard T. Davis to his wife, June 28, 1863, Davis Preston Saunders Collection (#4951), Albert and Shirley Small Special Collections Library, University of Virginia, Charlottesville.

138. Musick, *6th Virginia Cavalry*, 49–50.

139. *Ibid.*

140. *Ibid.* Harrison's appointment, which was contrary to army regulations, prompted the regiment's major, John

A. Throckmorton, to angrily submit his resignation. Throckmorton's resignation was accepted on December 6, 1863 (Musick, *6th Virginia Cavalry*, 159).

141. Ibid., 51, 122. Harrison served on courts-martial duty briefly in 1865. He died on July 17, 1877.

142. Luther W. Hopkins, *From Bull Run to Appomattox, A Boy's View* (Baltimore, MD: Fleet-McGinley, 1908), 190. Flournoy's comment is questionable since the account was written well after the war and the quotation is commonly attributed to Napoleon.

143. Ibid., 168, 190; Musick, *6th Virginia Cavalry*, 91.

144. *OR*, 36, I:780; Musick, *6th Virginia Cavalry*, 119; Bruce S. Allardice, *More Generals in Gray* (Baton Rouge: Louisiana State University Press, 1995), 248. The photograph of Green appears on page 360 of *Brady's Illustrated History*.

145. Heros von Borcke, *Memoirs of the Confederate War for Independence* (Edinburgh, UK: W. Blackwood and Sons, 1866; reprint ed., New York: Peter Smith, 1938), 2 vols. 293.

146. *OR*, 27, II:712.

147. Ella Lonn, *Foreigners in the Confederacy* (Gloucester, MA: Peter Smith, 1965), 174. Von Borcke personally believed that his nationality was the reason he was not elevated to the ranks of the general officer corps (von Borcke, *Memoirs of the Confederate War*, 2:302).

148. von Borcke, *Memoirs of the Confederate War for Independence*, 447.

149. Lonn, *Foreigners in the Confederacy*, 175.

150. William W. Blackford, *War Years with JEB Stuart* (New York: Scribner's, 1945; reprint ed.: Baton Rouge: University of Louisiana Press, 1993), 160, 220.

151. Robert J. Trout, *They Followed the Plume: The Story of J.E.B. Stuart and His Staff* (Mechanicsburg, PA: Stackpole, 1993), 279–280.

152. Douglas W. Owsley, Malcolm L. Richardson, and William E. Hanna, "Bioarcheological Investigation and Exhumation of the Remains of Captain William Downs Farley, CSA" (March 2002), 22–23. Although Farley may have had time for romance in Culpeper during the spring of 1863, no evidence has been found to support that hypothesis.

153. Ibid., 14, 18. The only remains that had not dissolved were several of Farley's teeth, but discoloration of the soil in the grave revealed that Farley's severed leg had been placed in the casket below its stump. Three porcelain buttons, a brass clasp for adjusting the waist of his trousers, and a fragment of a leather strap, perhaps used as a tourniquet, were also found in the grave.

154. *Culpeper Star-Exponent*, Culpeper, VA, April 7, April 28, May 5, 2002.

155. Henry B. McClellan, *The Life and Campaigns of Major-General J.E.B. Stuart, Commander of the Cavalry of the Army of Northern Virginia*. New York: Houghton Mifflin, 1885. Republished as *I Rode with JEB Stuart: The Life and Campaigns of Major-General J.E.B. Stuart*. Bloomington: Indiana University Press, 1958; reprint ed., New York: De Capo Press, Inc., 1994. McClellan's biography is contained in Burke Davis' introduction to the University of Indiana Press edition.

156. Henry B. McClellan, Papers (M1324a) Virginia Historical Society, Richmond.

157. Trout, *They Followed the Plume*, 62.

158. *OR*, Series II, 7:683, 826–827. Mauriel Joslyn, *Biographical Roster of the Immortal 600* (Shippensburg, PA: White Mane Publishing Co., Inc., 1992), 74.

159. Trout, *They Followed the Plume*, 148–149.

160. Charles T. O'Ferrall, *Forty Years of Active Service* (New York: Neale, 1904), 155–158. In addition to Fitz Lee and O'Ferrall, a third officer who fought at Brandy Station was elected governor of Virginia. Captain Philip W. McKinney, a lawyer from Farmville, Virginia, commanded Company K of the 4th Virginia. He was severely wounded at Stevensburg and incapacitated from further field duty. In 1864, McKinney resigned his commission to take a seat in the Virginia legislature representing Buckingham County. In 1889 McKinney defeated the Republican gubernatorial candidate, former major general William Mahone, and served as governor from 1890 to 1894. McKinney died in 1899. (*Encyclopedia of Virginia*, [New York: Somerset, 1992], 183.)

161. John N. Opie, *A Rebel Cavalryman with Lee Stuart and Jackson* (Chicago: W. B. Conkey, 1899; reprint ed., Dayton, OH: Morningside Bookshop, 1972), 159.

162. Ibid., 197–200, 218, 258.

163. Ibid., 309–312, 326–333, 318–323; Compiled Service Records.

164. Musick, *6th Virginia Cavalry*, 143.

165. Ibid., 238–239. While in Pennsylvania, Robertson "swapped" Bostona for a horse he found concealed in the woods and tied to a tree. Apparently the horse's owner had attempted — unsuccessfully — to hide the animal from Stuart's marauding cavalrymen.

166. Frank Robertson Reade, "In the Saddle with Stuart: The Story of Frank Robertson of Jeb Stuart's Staff" (#7566), Albert and Shirley Small Special Collections Library, University of Virginia, Charlottesville, 1–2.

167. Ibid.

Appendix A — Order of Battle and Casualties

1. Jennings Wise, in *The Long Arm of Lee*, wrote that the Stuart Horse Artillery Battalion had twenty-four guns at Brandy Station: three batteries of four guns and two batteries of six guns. Other sources, contemporaneous and otherwise, indicate that Stuart had twenty guns available on June 9. It appears that the lower number is the more accurate. While some artillery officers felt that a mix of weaponry was an advantage, it appears that any benefit to the Confederates during the fighting around Brandy Station was marginal at best.

2. Pleasonton reported capturing 297 Confederates in his official report. That figure is almost certainly exaggerated. From information in various Confederate sources, it appears that Stuart's division lost 194 missing/captured as a result of the day's fighting. The *New York Times* reported that Federals captured 200 Confederates, a figure that coincides closely with the Confederate tally. (*New York Times*, June 11, 1863.) With respect to Federals who fell into Confederate hands, Pleasonton's and Stuart's numbers almost match. Pleasonton reported 382 men missing/captured. Stuart reported that his division captured ten officers and 363 enlisted men.

3. *OR*, 27, III:33. Two additional regiments which might have been available, the 4th New York Cavalry and the 12th Illinois Cavalry, did not participate in the battle. The 4th New York was relieved from picket duty at Fayetteville, a small hamlet between Bealeton and Sulphur Springs on June 8 (Janet Hewett et al., eds., *Supplement to the Official Records of the Union and Confederate Armies*, [Wilmington, NC: Broadfoot, 1995–2000], II, 56:657). The location and activities of the 4th New York Cavalry on June 9, 1863, however, are not documented in official records. One battalion of the 12th Illinois Cavalry, a regiment of only nine companies, remained in Gloucester Point and was unavailable to Pleasonton on June 9. As previously mentioned, the other battalion of the regiment failed to join the Cavalry Corps at Catlett due to misunderstanding on the part of the regimental commander, Colonel Arno Voss.

4. *OR*, 27,I:168–170, 905–906.

5. This figure includes one division staff officer missing/captured.

6. G, H, I, and K Companies were assigned to the Army

of the Cumberland. L and M Companies were detailed to provost guard duty at Indianapolis, Indiana. (Hewett et al., eds., *Supplement to the Official Records of the Union and Confederate Armies*, II, 15:228–229, 233).

7. D and L Companies were detached as escorts for Major General Slocum (*Ibid.*, II, 41:388, 424). Additionally, B, C, E, G, and I Companies were awaiting remounts at Stafford Courthouse (Newel Cheney, *History of the Ninth Regiment New York Volunteer Cavalry, War of 1861 to 1865*, [Jamestown, NY: Martin Mertz, 1900], 95).

8. Hewett et al., eds., *Supplement to the Official Records*, II, 73:779, 784, 788, 791, 793.

9. The *Official Records* show B&L Batteries, 2nd U.S. Artillery, combined as a single battery starting with the Peninsular Campaign in June 1862, and continuing through the end of the war.

10. Colonel Davis is included in the brigade KIA figure and not among the 8th New York Cavalry casualties as in the *Official Records*.

11. Hewett et al., eds., *Supplement to the Official Records*, II, 57:485, 502.

12. *OR*, 25, II:515; *OR*, 27, I:155.

13. Frederick H. Dyer, editor, *A Compendium of the War of the Rebellion*, 3 vols. (New York: Thomas Yoseloff, 1909; reprint ed., Sagamore), 3:1689.

14. The 6th U.S. Cavalry entered the battle with ten companies. The remaining squadron, under the command of Captain James S. Brisbin, had been detached the previous day. However, Brisbin's squadron rejoined the regiment at about noon on June 9. (Hewett et al., eds., *Supplement to the Official Records*, I, 5:245.)

15. The strength of the 2nd Massachusetts Infantry at Brandy Station was 21 officers and 285 enlisted men (*OR*, 27, I:1043).

16. I and M Companies were on duty at Hilton Head, South Carolina, while K and L Companies were at Beaufort, South Carolina (Hewett et al., eds., *Supplement to the Official Records*, II, 27:107,114).

17. *Report of the Forty-Ninth Annual Reunion of the Sixth Ohio Volunteer Cavalry Association* (Warren, OH: Wm. Ritezel, 1914), 31.

18. One of the men reported as wounded in the *Official Records*, First Sergeant John Dunlap, Company G, died of his wound on June 19, 1863 (Wells A. Bushnell, *Sixth Regiment Ohio Volunteer Cavalry Memoir, 1861–1865* (21) 52A Microfilm Edition, [Western Reserve Historical Society, Cleveland, OH], 178). Consequently, one of the two reported wounded in the 6th Ohio has been moved to the killed column.

19. The 16th Pennsylvania was assigned the mission of securing the 2nd Cavalry Division's wagon train, which Duffié had been ordered to bring with him on the previous day's march to Morrisville, and played no significant part in the battle (Samuel Bates, *History of the Pennsylvania Volunteers, 1861–1865*, 5 vols., [Harrisburg, PA: B Singerly, 1869–1871], 4:951.)

20. Includes one division staff officer missing.

21. Hewett et al., eds., *Supplement to the Official Records*, II, 25:6.

22. Edward P. Tobie, *History of the First Maine Cavalry, 1861–1865* (Boston, MA: Press of Emery & Hughes, 1887), 671–672. The 1st Maine's casualties in the *Official Records* were ten wounded and twenty-five missing. In his history of the 1st Maine, Tobie accounted for the casualties shown here by name. All of those in the MIA column were captured, and seven of the thirty-five were also wounded.

23. A post-war account indicated that the 10th New York suffered six killed, two mortally wounded, sixteen wounded, and sixty-one missing, for a total of eighty-five (Frederick Phisterer, *New York in the War of Rebellion, 1861–1865*, 5 vols. with index [Albany, NY: Weed and Parsons, 1890], 2:921). Because Phisterer did not list his casualties by name, those from the *Official Records* are shown here.

24. Part of Company A was on picket duty and did not participate in the battle (Hewett et al., eds., *Supplement to the Official Records*, II, 26: 136).

25. *OR*, 25 II:580; *OR*, 27, I:162. Major Hugh Janaway, in a separate report to the governor of New Jersey, wrote that the regimental strength at the time of the battle was 299 men (*OR*, 27, I:1055).

26. *OR*, 25, II:580; *OR*, 27, I:162.

27. Heros von Borcke, *Memoirs of the Confederate War for Independence* (Edinburgh, UK: W. Blackwood and Sons, 1866; reprint ed., Nashville, TN: J.S. Sanders, 1999), 410.

28. *OR*, 27, II:684.

29. *OR*, 27, II:718–719. Stuart also reported fifteen horses killed and fourteen wounded, figures that appear extremely low.

30. *OR*, 27, II:750, 763.

31. *OR*, 27, II:718. The officers captured include: Lieutenant Goldsborough, division headquarters; Captain Rich, Cobb's Legion Cavalry; Lieutenant Coles, 6th Virginia; Captains Anderson and Graybill, both of White's Battalion; and Lieutenants Rouss and Rust, both of the 12th Virginia Cavalry.

32. *OR*, 27, II:719.

33. Casualties include: Captain Farley, mortally wounded; Captain White, wounded; Lieutenant Goldsborough, captured.

34. Michael P. Musick, *6th Virginia Cavalry* (Lynchburg, VA: H.E. Howard, 1990), muster roll data. Flournoy reported casualties of five killed, twenty-five wounded, and twenty-four missing, for a total of fifty-four. Four officers (two killed and two wounded) may have been included in Flournoy's figures. Flournoy did not mention the capture of Lieutenant Coles. (*OR*, 27, II:754.)

35. *OR*, 27, II:758. Analysis of compiled service records indicates that the 7th Virginia suffered an aggregate of twenty-two casualties on June 9, 1863 (Richard L. Armstrong, *7th Virginia Cavalry* [Lynchburg, VA: H. E. Howard, 1992], 54). Given Confederate record keeping, it is likely that the two additional casualties reported by Marshall were never mustered in the regiment.

36. Richard L. Armstrong, *11th Virginia Cavalry* (Lynchburg, VA: H. E. Howard, 1989), 43. In the *Official Records*, the casualties for the 11th Virginia were listed as five killed, eleven wounded, and six missing, for a total of twenty-two. However, in his official report, Colonel Lomax, who reported five killed and eleven wounded, wrote that he was not certain how many of his were captured, but the number did not exceed five or six (*OR*, 27, II:762).

37. Dennis, E. Frye, *12th Virginia Cavalry*, 2nd ed. (Lynchburg, VA: H.E. Howard, 1988), 40. Frye arrived at his figures by analyzing the compiled service records for the officers and men in the companies of the 12th Virginia. Colonel Harmon has been added to the wounded tallied by Frye. Lieutenant Colonel Thomas Massie, who prepared the official report instead of the wounded Harmon, wrote that the regiment suffered fifty-five casualties on June 9. However, to his report, Massie appended a table accounting for only fifty-three casualties: six killed; thirty-four wounded; thirteen missing. (*OR*, 27, II:766).

38. John E. Devine, *35th Battalion Virginia Cavalry* (Lynchburg, VA: H.E. Howard, 1985), 28, 29. Devine arrived at his figures by analyzing compiled service records of soldiers assigned to the 35th Battalion. Frank M. Myers wrote that the 35th suffered ninety casualties on June 9: four killed; twenty-seven wounded; fifty-nine missing (*The Comanches: A History of White's Battalion, Virginia Cavalry*, [Baltimore, MD: Kelly, Piet, 1871; reprint ed., Alexandria, VA: Stonewall, 1985], 186–187). It is possible that Myers's figures were those reported by White after the battle.

39. Louis H. Manarin, *The Cavalry*, Vol. 2 of *North

Carolina Troops 1861–1865, A Roster... (Raleigh: North Carolina State Department of Archives and History, 1968), muster roll data; Roger H. Harrell, *2nd North Carolina Cavalry* (Jefferson, NC: McFarland, 2004), 126, 394–395.

40. Robert K. Krick, *9th Virginia Cavalry*, 4th ed. (Lynchburg, VA: H.E. Howard, 1982), 21. Well after the battle, Colonel Beale wrote that the regiment lost about ten men killed and "many" wounded during the battle (R. L. T. Beale, *History of the Ninth Virginia Cavalry in the War Between the States*, [Richmond, VA: B. F. Johnson, 1899], 70).

41. *Richmond Sentinel*, Richmond, VA, June 15, 1863. An account of the battle accompanied by a list of casualties was provided by the regimental chaplain in a letter to the *Sentinel*. D Company was listed as being on detached service in the chaplain's account.

42. Daniel T. Balfour, *13th Virginia Cavalry*, 2d ed. (Lynchburg, VA: H. E. Howard, 1986), muster roll data.

43. Includes W.H.F. "Rooney" Lee.

44. William Delony to Rosa (wife), June 12, 1863, William Gaston Deloney Family Papers (Ms 184), Hargrett Library, University of Georgia, Athens. In a letter to Rosa dated June 10, Deloney, the lieutenant colonel of Cobb's Legion, wrote that the regiment lost three killed, twenty-six wounded, and twenty-one missing. In his letter of June 12, he amended his casualty figures. The amended figures are shown here and coincide with the aggregate figure provided by Colonel PMB Young in his report of the battle (*OR*, 27, II:729). Presumably, in the two days between Deloney's letters, three of the wounded died and several stragglers returned to the ranks.

45. *OR*, 27, II, 733. Lieutenant Colonel Waring reported two privates slightly wounded, his ordnance sergeant seriously wounded in both legs, and one private severely wounded.

46. In his report, the only casualties cited by Major Lipscomb were Colonel Butler and Lieutenant Colonel Hampton, prompting him to write, "Our loss, though small in number, is deeply felt..." (*OR*, 27, II:731). U. R. Brooks, writing well after the war, commented that the 2nd South Carolina went into the fighting at Stevensburg with 240 men and the next day could only muster 200 (*Butler and His Cavalry in the War of Secession, 1861–1865*, [Columbia, SC: The State Co., 1909], 171). In a letter to his wife dated June 11, 1863, Captain Leonard Williams, who commanded a detachment of videttes near Carrico's Mill on the day of the battle, characterized the loss of privates in the regiment as "trifling, some 15 or 20 missing." (David Douglas, *A Boot Full of Memories: Captain Leonard Williams, 2nd S.C. Cavalry*, [Camden, SC: Gray Fox, 2003], 225). Because most of the fighting was done by Hampton's small detachment, and in view of Lipscomb's comment, Williams's contemporaneous figure appears more reasonable than Brooks's.

47. Manarin, *The Cavalry*, muster roll data. Illustrating some of the complexity in analyzing casualty data is the case of Private C. Cox of K Company. On June 9, Cox received a gunshot wound and was captured. He died in captivity on June 24, 1863. Cox is carried in this table as mortally wounded. Colonel Baker reported five killed, twelve wounded, and fourteen missing, for a total of thirty-one. Presumably, Colonel Baker accounted for Cox in the MIA figure provided in his report.

48. *OR*, 27, II 739. These casualties were reported by Munford in his report for Fitz Lee's Brigade.

49. Robert Driver, Jr., *2nd Virginia Cavalry* (Lynchburg, VA: H. E. Howard, 1995), 179. Munford reported losses of two killed and nine wounded in his official report of the battle (*OR*, 27, II:739).

50. *OR*, 27, II:739. These casualties were reported by Munford in his report for Fitz Lee's Brigade.

51. Kenneth L. Stiles, *4th Virginia Cavalry* (Lynchburg, VA: H.E. Howard, 1985), 27, muster roll data. Wickham reported that he had fifteen men wounded and twenty-seven men missing (*OR*, 27,II:744). His count of the wounded is excessive since the regiment ran away instead of fighting.

52. Robert J. Trout, "In Pelham's Shadow: The Commanders of the Horse Artillery of the Army of Northern Virginia After Major John Pelham," *Civil War Quarterly* 11 (1987), 49.

Appendix B—West Pointers at Brandy Station

1. Each West Point graduate is numbered consecutively in order of graduation. Thus, Joseph Swift and Simon McGruder, who were the only members of the Class of 1802, are numbered 1 and 2, while George Armstrong Custer, the last graduate in the Class of June 1861, is number 1966. Those numbers are known as "Cullum Numbers" after George W. Cullum, Class of 1833, # 709, who devised the system for use in his *Biographical Register of the Officers and Graduates of the U.S. Military Academy at West Point, N. Y.*

2. Jefferson Davis, when serving as Secretary of War, expanded the course of instruction at the Military Academy by one year. The youngest twenty-two cadets from the Class of 1858 were held over for a fifth year of study to comprise the Class of 1859. The Classes of 1860, 1861, and 1862 were also five-year classes, although the class of 1862 graduated a year early, in June 1861, because of the necessities of the war. The class that graduated in June 1862, and those afterward, reverted to a four-year curriculum.

3. The source for Mackenzie's presence at Beverly Ford is Newhall's "The Battle of Beverly Ford" in *Annals of the War*. Newhall's account, written well after the war, may be inaccurate since Cullum's *Biographical Register* indicates that MacKenzie was in command of an engineer company at the time.

4. Norris was dismissed from the service in 1870 after being convicted by a court-martial for drunkenness.

5. George F. Price, Across the Continent with the Fifth Cavalry (New York: Noble Offset, 1883; reprint ed., New York: Antiquarian, 1959), 526.

6. Cullum, Biographical Register, #2317. Wood's biographical entry indicates that he was captured on December 27, 1862 at Occoquan, Virginia, exchanged in May 1863, and served in all the operations of the 1st Cavalry division thereafter. Consequently, he may have been present at Brandy Station. The classes of 1867 through 1873 included sixty-five graduates who were Civil War veterans. From Cullum biographies, it appears that none, other than Thomas and perhaps Wood, were at Brandy Station.

7. Gerard Patterson in *Rebels from West Point* states that 306 academy graduates served the Confederacy, of whom sixty-nine died while in service. Cullum did not compile Confederate service data for those graduates who were disloyal to the Union. The presence of the Confederate officers listed in this appendix is amply verified by other sources.

8. The two non–West Point commanders were Colonel Asher Harmon of the 12th Virginia, and Colonel William Ball of the 15th Virginia. One Virginia regiment was initially commanded by a Naval Academy graduate, Charles Thornburn, USNA 1853. That regiment, the 14th Virginia, was assigned to Jenkins's Brigade and not normally attached to the Army of Northern Virginia.

9. Lieutenant Colonel William Robinson, Solomon Williams's classmate, was appointed colonel of the 2nd North Carolina shortly after Williams was killed. In early 1864, Robinson resigned his commission to accept a position with the Confederate Navy.

Select Bibliography

*Books, Articles, and Other Published Sources**

Alberts, Don E. *Brandy Station to Manila Bay: A Biography of General Wesley Merritt.* Austin, TX: Presidial Press, 1980.
Alexander, Edward Porter. *Fighting for the Confederacy: The Personal Recollections of General Edward Porter Alexander.* Edited by Gary W. Gallagher. Chapel Hill: University of North Carolina Press, 1989.
Allardice, Bruce S. *More Generals in Gray.* Baton Rouge: Louisiana State University Press, 1995.
Allen, Stanton, P. *Down in Dixie: Life in a Cavalry Regiment in the War Days, from the Wilderness to Appomattox.* Boston: D. Lothrop, 1892.
"April 6th Memorial Service Scheduled for Captain Will Farley, C.S.A." Brandy Station Foundation Bulletin, 12 (Spring 2002), 2–3.
Armstrong, Richard L. *11th Virginia Cavalry.* Lynchburg, VA: H. E. Howard, 1989.
_____. *7th Virginia Cavalry.* Lynchburg, VA: H. E. Howard, 1992.
Austerman, Wayne. "Case Shot and Canister, Field Artillery in the Civil War." *Civil War Times Illustrated* 26 (September 1987): 16–29, 43–48.
Avary, Myrta Lockett, ed. *A Virginia Girl in the Civil War 1861–1865: Being a Record of the Actual Experiences of the Wife of a Confederate Officer.* New York: D. Appleton, 1903. (This work is also available online in the Documenting the American South Collection, Academic Affairs Library, University of North Carolina, Chapel Hill. [http://docsouth.unc.edu/early/menu.html]).
Averell, William W. *Ten Years in the Saddle: The Memoir of William Woods Averell.* Edited by Edward K. Eckert and Nicholas J. Amato. San Rafael, CA: Presidio, 1978.
Avirett, James B. *The Memoirs of General Turner Ashby and His Compeers.* Baltimore, MD: Selby & Dulany, 1867.
Bakeless, John. *Spies of the Confederacy.* New York: J. B. Lippincott, 1970.
Balfour, Daniel T. *13th Virginia Cavalry*, 2d ed. Lynchburg, VA: H. E. Howard, 1986.
Barringer, Rufus. *The First North Carolina, A Famous Cavalry Regiment.* Np, Nd.
_____. *Ninth Regiment (First Cavalry).* In *Histories of the Several Regiments and Battalions from North Carolina in the Great War 1861–65: Written by Members of the Respective Commands*, 5 vols. Edited by Walter Clark. Raleigh: E. M. Uzzell, 1901; reprint ed., Wendell, NC: Broadfoot's Bookmark, 1982.
"Barringer, Gen. Rufus." Obituary. *Confederate Veteran* 9 (February 1901): 69–70.
Bartholomees, J. Boone. *Buff Facings and Gilt Buttons: Staff and Headquarters Operations in the Army of Northern Virginia.* Columbia: University of South Carolina Press, 1998.
Baylor, George. *Bull Run to Bull Run, or Four Years in the Army of Northern Virginia.* Richmond: B. F. Johnson, 1900.
Beach, William H. *First New York Lincoln Cavalry, April 19, 1861–July 7, 1865.* Milwaukee, WI: Burdick & Allen, 1902.
Beale, G. W. *A Lieutenant of Cavalry in Lee's Army.* Boston: Gorham, 1918; reprint ed., Baltimore, MD: Butternut and Blue, 1994.
_____. "The Greatest Cavalry Battle of Modern Times, at Brandy Station June 9, 1863." *Times Dispatch.* Richmond, VA, August 4, 1912.
Beale, R. L. T. *History of the Ninth Virginia Cavalry in the War Between the States.* Richmond, VA: B. F. Johnson, 1899.
"Beau Sabreur of Georgia." *Southern Historical Society Papers* 25 (1987): 146–151.
Beaudry, Louis N. *War Journal of Louis N. Beaudry, Fifth New York Cavalry.* Edited by Richard E. Beaudry. Jefferson, NC: McFarland, 1996.
Beck, Elias W. H. "Letters of a Civil War Surgeon." *Indiana Magazine of History* 27 (1931): 132–163.

*And see page 311 for unpublished sources, 314 for newspapers, and 314 for online sources.

Beyer, Walter F. and Oscar F. Keydel, eds. *Deeds of Valor: How America's Civil War Heroes Won the Congressional Medal of Honor*. Detroit, MI: Perrien-Keydel, 1903; reprint ed., New York: Smithmark, 2000.

Black, John Logan. *Crumbling Defenses, or Memoirs and Reminiscences of John Logan Black, Colonel C. S. A.* Edited by Eleanor D. McSwain. Macon, GA: Privately Published, 1960.

"Black, Col. John Logan of South Carolina." Obituary. *Confederate Veteran* 35 (June 1927): 214.

Blackford, Charles Minor and Susan Leigh Blackford. *Letters from Lee's Army*. Edited by Charles Minor Blackford III. New York: Scribner's, 1947; reprint ed., Lincoln: University of Nebraska Press, 1998.

Blackford, William W. *War Years with JEB Stuart*. New York: Scribner's, 1945; reprint ed., Baton Rouge: University of Louisiana Press, 1993.

Bliss, George N. *Duffié and the Monument to His Memory* in *Personal Narratives, 4th Series*. Providence: Soldiers & Sailors Historical Society of Rhode Island, 1889–1890.

———. *The First Rhode Island Cavalry at Middleburg, Va., June 17 and 18, 1863* in *Personal Narratives, 4th Series*. Providence: Soldiers & Sailors Historical Society of Rhode Island, 1889–1890.

Boies, Andrew J. *Record of the Thirty-third Massachusetts Volunteer Infantry, from Aug. 1862 to Aug. 1865*. Fitchburg, MA: Sentinel, 1880.

Bolton, Horace W. *Personal Reminiscences of the Late War*. Chicago: H. W. Bolton, 1892.

Botts, John Minor. *The Great Rebellion: Its Secret History, Rise, Progress, and Disastrous Failure*. New York: Harper & Brothers, 1866.

Bowmaster, Patrick. "An Examination of Gen. Robertson's Conduct in the Great Cavalry Battle." *Blue & Gray Magazine* 15 (October 1996): 22–33.

A Brief History of the Fourth Pennsylvania Veteran Cavalry, Embracing Organization, Reunions, Dedication of Monument at Gettysburg and Address of General W. E. Doster, Venango County Battalion, Reminiscences, Etc. Pittsburgh, PA: Ewens & Eberle, 1891.

Brooks, Ulysses R. *Butler and His Cavalry in the War of Secession, 1861–1865*. Columbia, SC: The State, 1909; reprint ed., Camden, SC: J. J. Fox, Nd.

Bryant, Edwin E. *History of the 3rd Regiment of Wisconsin Volunteer Infantry*. Madison, WI: Democrat, 1891.

Burnett, William G. *Better a Patriot Soldier's Grave: The History of the Sixth Ohio Volunteer Cavalry*. Np, 1982.

Bushong, Millard K, and Dean M. Bushong. *Fightin' Tom Rosser, C.S.A*. Shippensburg, PA: Beidel, 1983.

Butler, Karl Douglas. *Principles of Horseshoeing II: An Illustrated Textbook of Farrier Science and Craftsmanship*. Laporte, CO: Butler, 1983.

Calfee, Berkeley G. *Confederate History of Culpeper County: Culpeper County in the War Between the States, Together with a Complete Roster of the Confederate Soldiers from this County*. Culpeper, VA: Np., 1948; reprint ed., Culpeper, VA: Np., 1994.

Calvert, Mary Renier. *The First Maine Cavalry*. Monmouth, ME: Monmouth, 1997.

Campbell, William. "Autobiographical Sketch." *William & Mary Quarterly*, 2nd Series 9 (1929): 88–109.

Carter, Robert G. *Four Brothers in Blue, or Sunshine and Shadows of the War of the Rebellion, A Story of the Great Civil War from Bull Run to Appomattox by Captain Robert Goldthwaite Carter*. Washington, DC: Gibson Brothers, 1913; reprint ed., Austin: University of Texas Press, 1978; reprint ed., Norman: University of Oklahoma Press, 1999.

Carter, Samuel, III. *The Last Cavaliers: Confederate and Union Cavalry in the Civil War*. New York: St. Martin's, 1979.

Carter, W. H. *From Yorktown to Santiago with the Sixth U.S. Cavalry*. Baltimore, MD: Lord Baltimore, 1900.

Carter, William R. *Sabres, Saddles, and Spurs*. Edited by Walbrook D. Swank. Shippensburg, PA: Burd Street, 1998.

Cheney, Newel. *History of the Ninth Regiment New York Volunteer Cavalry, War of 1861 to 1865*. Jamestown, NY: Martin Mertz, 1900.

Chesnut, Mary. *A Diary from Dixie*. Edited by Isabella D. Martin and Myrta Lockett Avary. New York: Portland, 1905; reprint ed., New York: Random House Value, 1997.

Child, William. *A History of the Fifth Regiment New Hampshire Volunteers, in the American Civil War, 1861–1865*. Bristol, NH: R. W. Musgrove, 1893.

Clark, Walter, ed. *Histories of the Several Regiments and Battalions from North Carolina in the Great War 1861–65: Written by Members of the Respective Commands*, 5 vols. Raleigh: E. M. Uzzell, 1901; reprint ed., Wendell, NC: Broadfoot's Bookmark, 1982.

Coffman, Richard M. "A Vital Unit, Being a Brief and True History of 10,000 Volunteers, Phillips Legion." *Civil War Times Illustrated* 20 (January 1982): 40–45.

Colley, Thomas E. "Brig. Gen. William E. Jones." *Confederate Veteran* 11 (June 1903): 266–267.

Comey, Henry N. *A Legacy of Valor: The Memoirs and Letters of Captain Henry Newton Comey, 2nd Massachusetts Infantry*. Edited by Lyman Richard Comey. Knoxville: University of Tennessee Press, 2004.

Confederate States War Department. *Regulations for the Army of the Confederate States, 1863*. Richmond, VA: J. W. Randolph, 1863; reprint ed., Evansville, IN: Crescent City Sutler, Nd.

Cooke, John Esten. *General Stuart in Camp and Field*. In *Annals of the War, Written by Leading Participants North and South*. Philadelphia: Times, 1879; reprint ed., Edison, NJ: Blue & Gray, 1996.

———. *Wearing of the Gray*. New York: E. B. Treat, 1867; reprint ed., Baton Rouge: Louisiana State University Press, 1997.

Cooke, Phillip St. George. *Cavalry Tactics: or, Regulations for the Instruction, Formations and Movements of the Cavalry of the Army and Volunteers of the United States*. Philadelphia: J. B. Lippincott, 1862; reprint ed., Union City, TN: Pioneer, 1997.

Cross, Edward E. *Stand Firm and Fire Low: The Civil War Writings of Colonel Edward E. Cross*. Edited by Walter Holden, William E. Ross, and Elizabeth Slomba. Hanover: University of New Hampshire Press, 2003.
Crouch, Richard E., *Brandy Station: A Battle Like No Other*. Westminster, MD: Willow Bend, 2002.
Crowninshield, Benjamin W. *A History of the First Regiment of Massachusetts Cavalry Volunteers*. Boston: Houghton Mifflin, 1891; reprint ed., Baltimore, MD: Butternut and Blue, 1995.
Crute, Joseph H. Jr. *Units of the Confederate States Army*. Midlothian, VA: Derwent, 1987.
Cullum, George W. *Biographical Register of the Officers and Graduates of the U.S. Military Academy at West Point, N.Y. from its Establishment in 1802, to 1890 with the Early History of the United States Military Academy*, 3 vols., 3rd ed. New York: Houghton Mifflin, 1891.
Daughtry, Mary B. *Gray Cavalier: The Life and Wars of General W. H. F. "Rooney" Lee*. Cambridge, MA: Da Capo, 2002.
Davis, J. Lucius. *The Trooper's Manual: or, Tactics for Light Dragoons and Mounted Riflemen. Compiled, abridged and arranged, by Col. J. Lucius Davis, Graduate of the United States Military Academy, West Point, Formerly an Officer of the United States Army; and for Many Years Commander and Instructor of Volunteer Cavalry*. Richmond, VA: A. Morris, 1861.
Davis, Jefferson. *Rise and Fall of the Confederate Government*, 2 vols. New York: D. Appleton, 1881.
Davis, Sidney Morris. *Common Soldier, Uncommon War: Life as a Cavalryman in the Civil War*. Edited by Charles F. Cooney. Baltimore, MD: John H. Davis, Jr., 1994.
Denison, Frederick. *Sabres and Spurs: The First Regiment Rhode Island Cavalry in the Civil War, 1861–1865*. Central Falls, RI: E. L. Freeman, 1876.
Devine, John E. *35th Battalion Virginia Cavalry*. Lynchburg, VA: H. E. Howard, 1985.
diCesnola, Luigi Palma. *Ten Months in Libby Prison*. Np., 1865.
Dickenson, Jack L. *8th Virginia Cavalry*. Lynchburg, VA: H. E. Howard, 1986.
Dickerson, Frank. *Dearest Father: The Civil War Letters of Lt. Frank Dickerson, A Son of Belfast Maine*. Edited by H. Draper Hunt. Unity, ME: North Country, 1992.
Doster, William E. *A Brief History of the Fourth Pennsylvania Cavalry*. Pittsburgh, PA: Np., 1891; reprint ed., Hightstown, NJ: Longstreet, 1997.
_____. *Lincoln and Episodes of the Civil War*. New York: G. P. Putman's Sons, 1915.
Doubleday, Abner. *Chancellorsville and Gettysburg*. New York: Scribner's, 1886; reprint ed., Wilmington, NC: Broadfoot, 1989.
Douglas, David G. *A Boot Full of Memories: Captain Leonard Williams, 2nd S.C. Cavalry*. Camden, SC: Gray Fox, 2003. (Although fiction, this book contains the wartime letters Captain Williams wrote to his wife.)
Douglas, Henry Kyd. *I Rode with Stonewall*. Chapel Hill: University of North Carolina Press, 1940; reprint ed., New York: Premier, 1961.
Downey, Fairfax. *Clash of Cavalry: The Battle of Brandy Station*. New York: David McKay, 1959.
Driver, Robert J. Jr. *5th Virginia Cavalry*. Lynchburg, VA: H. E. Howard, 1997.
_____. *1st Virginia Cavalry*. Lynchburg, VA: H. E. Howard, 1991.
_____. *14th Virginia Cavalry*, 2nd ed. Lynchburg, VA: H. E. Howard, 1988.
_____. *2nd Virginia Cavalry*. Lynchburg, VA: H. E. Howard, 1995.
_____. *10th Virginia Cavalry*. Lynchburg, VA: H. E. Howard, 1992.
Dyer, Frederick H., ed. *A Compendium of the War of the Rebellion*, 3 vols. Des Moines, IA: Dyer, 1908; reprint ed., New York: Thomas Yoseloff, 1959.
Edmonds, Amanda V. *Journal of Amanda Virginia Edmonds: Lass of Mosby's Confederacy, 1857–1867*. Edited by Nancy Chappelear Baird. Stephens City, VA: Commercial, 1984.
Edmondston, Catherine Ann Devereaux. *Journal of a Secesh Lady: The Diary of Catherine Ann Devereaux Edmondston 1860–1866*, 2nd ed. Edited by Beth G. Crabtree and James W. Patton. Raleigh, NC: Division of Archives and History, Department of Cultural Resources, 1979.
Elliot, Ellsworth, Jr. *West Point in the Confederacy*. New York: G.A. Baker, 1941.
Encyclopedia of Virginia. New York: Somerset, 1992.
Esposito, Vincent J. *The West Point Atlas of American Wars*, 2 vols. New York: Frederick A. Praeger, 1959.
Everson, Guy R. and Edward H. Simpson, eds. *"Far, Far from Home": The Wartime Letters of Dick and Tally Simpson, Third South Carolina Volunteers*. New York: Oxford University Press, 1994.
Ewell, Richard S. *The Making of a Soldier: Letters of General R. S. Ewell*. Edited by Percy G. Hamlin. Richmond, VA: Whittet & Shepperson, 1935.
"'Extra Billy' Smith." *Civil War Times Illustrated* 2 (December 1963): 38–41
Fauquier County Virginia, 1759–1959. Warrenton: Virginia, 1959.
Fishel, Edwin C. *The Secret War for the Union: The Untold Story of Military Intelligence in the Civil War*. New York: Houghton Mifflin, 1996.
Flood, Charles Bracelen. *Lee: The Last Years*. Boston: Houghton Mifflin, 1981.
Foote, Shelby. *The Civil War: A Narrative*, 3 vols. New York: Random House, 1974; reprint ed., New York: Vintage, 1986.
Ford, Worthington, C., ed. *A Cycle of Adams Letters, 1861–1865*, 2 vols. New York: Houghton Mifflin, 1920.
Fortier, John. *15th Virginia Cavalry*. Lynchburg, VA: H. E. Howard, 1993.
Foster, Alonzo. *Reminiscences and Record of the 6th New York V. V. Cavalry*. Np., 1892.
Freeman, Douglas Southall. *Lee's Lieutenants*, 3 vols. New York: Scribner's, 1944.
_____. *R. E. Lee*, 4 vols. New York: Scribner's, 1949.

French, Stephen. *The Jones-Imboden Raid Against the B & O Railroad at Rowlesburg, Virginia, April 1863*. Danville, VA: Blue and Gray Education Society, 2001.
Frye, Dennis, E. *12th Virginia Cavalry*, 2nd ed. Lynchburg, VA: H.E. Howard, 1988.
Furgurson, Ernest B. *Chancellorsville 1863: The Souls of the Brave*. New York: Alfred A. Knopf, 1992.
Gallaher, DeWitt Clinton. *A Diary Depicting the Experience of DeWitt Clinton Gallaher in the War Between the States While Serving in the Confederate Army*. Edited by DeWitt Clinton Gallaher, Jr. Np., 1945.
Galloway, John M. *Sixty-third Regiment (Fifth Cavalry)* in *Histories of the Several Regiments and Battalions from North Carolina in the Great War 1861–65: Written by Members of the Respective Commands*, 5 vols. Edited by Walter Clark. Raleigh: E. M. Uzzell, 1901; reprint ed., Wendell, NC: Broadfoot's Bookmark, 1982.
Garnett, Theodore Stanford. *Riding with Stuart: Reminiscences of an Aide-de-Camp*. Edited by Robert J. Trout. Shippensburg, PA: White Mane, 1994.
Garrison, Web. *Encyclopedia of Civil War Usage*. Nashville, TN: Cumberland, 2001.
Gilham, William. *Manual for the Instruction of Volunteers and Militia of the United States: with Numerous Illustrations*. Philadelphia: Charles Desilver, 1861.
Gilmor, Harry. *Four Years in the Saddle*. New York: Harper & Brothers, 1866; reprint ed., Baltimore, MD: Butternut and Blue, Nd.
Glazier, Willard. *Battles for the Union*. Hartford, CT: Dustin Gilman, 1875.
_____. *Three Years in the Federal Cavalry*. New York: R. H. Ferguson, 1874.
Gold, Thomas D. *History of Clarke County, Virginia, and Its Connection with the War Between the States*. Berryville, VA: Np., 1914; reprint ed, Berryville, VA: Chesapeake, 1962.
Goldy, James. "I Have Done Nothing to Deserve This Penalty." *Civil War Times Illustrated* 26 (March 1987): 17–21.
Gracey, S.L. *Annals of the Sixth Pennsylvania Cavalry*. Philadelphia: E. H. Butler, 1868; reprint ed. Lancaster, OH: Vanberg, 1996.
Gragg, Rod. "Southern Soldiers' Tales." *Civil War Times Illustrated* 27 (October 1988): 34–36.
Graham, W. A. *Nineteenth Regiment (Second Cavalry)* in *Histories of the Several Regiments and Battalions from North Carolina in the Great War 1861–65: Written by Members of the Respective Commands*, 5 vols. Edited by Walter Clark. Raleigh: E. M. Uzzell, 1901; reprint ed., Wendell, NC: Broadfoot's Bookmark, 1982.
Gregg, David McMurtrie. *The Union Cavalry at Gettysburg*. In *Annals of the War, Written by Leading Participants North and South*. Philadelphia: Times, 1879; reprint ed., Edison, NJ: Blue & Gray, 1996.
Grimsley, Daniel A. *Battles in Culpeper County, Virginia, 1861–1865*. Culpeper: Raleigh Travers Green, 1900; reprint ed., Orange, VA: Green, Nd.
"'Grumble' Jones: A Personality Profile." *Civil War Times Illustrated* 7 (June 1968): 35–41.
Hackley, Woodford B. *The Little Fork Rangers: A Sketch of Company "D" Fourth Virginia Cavalry*. Richmond, VA: Dirtz, 1927; reprint ed., Stephens City, VA: Commercial, 1999.
Hall, Clark B. "'The Army Is Moving': Lee's March to the Potomac, 1863, Rodes Spearheads the Way." *Blue & Gray Magazine* 21 (Spring 2004): 6–22, 44–52.
_____. "Long and Desperate Encounter: Buford at Brandy Station." *Civil War* 24 (1990): 12–17, 66–67.
Hall, Hillman A. *History of the Sixth New York Cavalry (Second Ira Harris Guard), Second Brigade — First Division — Cavalry Corps, Army of the Potomac, 1861–1865*. Worcester, MA: Blanchard, 1908.
"Hampton's Duel." *Southern Historical Society Papers* 22 (1894): 124–125.
Hanson, Raus McDill. *Virginia Place Names, Derivations, Historical Uses*. Verona, VA: McClure, 1969.
Hard, Abner. *History of the Eighth Cavalry Regiment Illinois Volunteers During the Great Rebellion*. Aurora, IL: Np., 1868; reprint ed., Dayton, OH: Morningside Bookshop, 1996.
Harrell, Roger H. *2nd North Carolina Cavalry*. Jefferson, NC: McFarland, 2004.
Harris, Brayton. *Blue & Gray in Black & White: Newspapers in the Civil War*. Dulles, VA: Batsford Brassey, 1999.
Hart, James P. "Battle of Brandy Station." *Philadelphia Weekly Times* (June 26, 1880).
Hatch, Francis Whiting. "Charles J. Whiting: Civil War Hero." *Castine Visitor: Castine Historical Society Newsletter* 11 (Spring 2001): 7–9.
Hatch, Thom. *Clashes of Cavalry: The Civil War Careers of George Armstrong Custer and Jeb Stuart*. Mechanicsburg, PA: Stackpole, 2001.
Henderson, William D. *The Road to Bristoe Station*, 2nd ed. Lynchburg, VA: H. E. Howard, 1987.
Hennessy, John L. "Lincoln Wins Back His Army." *Civil War Times Illustrated* 34 (February 2001): 34–42, 65.
Henry, Robert Selph. *The Story of the Confederacy*. Indianapolis, IN: Bobbs-Merrill, 1931.
Hesseltine, William B and Hazel C. Wolf. *The Blue and the Gray on the Nile*. Chicago: University of Chicago Press, 1961.
Hewett, Janet, et al., eds. *Supplement to the Official Records of the Union and Confederate Armies*. Wilmington, NC: Broadfoot, 1995–2000.
Hinkley, Julian Wisner. *Service with the Third Wisconsin Infantry*. Wisconsin History Commission, 1912.
History of the Seventeenth Regiment Pennsylvania Volunteer Cavalry or One Hundred and Sixty-Second in the *Line of Pennsylvania Volunteer Regiments*. Lebanon, PA: Sowers, 1911.
History of the Third Pennsylvania Cavalry Sixtieth Regiment Pennsylvania Volunteers in the American Civil War 1861–1865. Philadelphia: Franklin, 1905.
Hodge, Robert A. *A Death Roster of the Confederate General Hospital at Culpeper, Virginia*. Fredericksburg, VA: Np., 1977.
Holland, Lynwood M. *Pierce M. B. Young: The Warwick of the South*. Athens: University of Georgia Press, 1964.
Holmes, Torlief S. *Horse Soldiers in Blue: First Maine Cavalry*. Gaithersburg, MD: Butternut, 1985.

Hopkins, Donald A. *The Little Jeff: The Jeff Davis Legion, Cavalry, Army of Northern Virginia*. Shippensburg, PA: White Mane, 1999.
Hopkins, Luther, W. *From Bull Run to Appomattox: A Boy's View*. Baltimore, MD: Fleet-McGinley, 1908.
Hotchkiss, Jedediah. *Make Me a Map of the Valley: The Civil War Journal of Stonewall Jackson's Topographer*. Dallas, TX: Southern Methodist University Press, 1973.
_____. *Virginia*. Vol. 3 of *Confederate Military History*. Edited by Clement A. Evans. Atlanta, GA: Confederate Publishing Co., 1899; reprint, ed., Secaucus, NJ: Blue and Grey, Nd.
Howard, Oliver Otis. *The Campaign and Battle of Gettysburg*. In *Battles and Leaders of the Civil War*, vol. 5. Edited by Peter Cozzens. Urbana: University of Illinois Press, 2002.
Howard, Wiley C. *Sketch of Cobb Legion Cavalry and Some Incidents and Scenes Remembered: Presented and Read under Appointment of Atlanta Camp 159, United Confederate Veterans, August 19, 1901*. Np., Nd. (This work is also available online in the Documenting the American South Collection, Academic Affairs Library, University of North Carolina, Chapel Hill, NC (http://docsouth. unc.edu/howard/menu.html).)
Hudgins, Robert Scott II. *Recollections of an Old Dominion Dragoon: The Civil War Experiences of Sgt. Robert S. Hudgins II, Co. B, 3d Virginia Cavalry*. Edited by Garland C. Hudgins and Richard B. Kleese. Orange, VA: Publisher's, 1993.
Hunt, Henry J. *The First Day at Gettysburg*. In *Battles and Leaders of the Civil War*, 4 vols, edited by Robert Underwood Johnson and Clarence Clough Buel. New York: E. P. Dutton, 1887–88; reprint ed., New York: Thomas Yoseloff, 1956.
Hunt, Roger D. and Jack R. Brown. *Brevet Brigadier Generals in Blue*. Gaithersburg, MD: Olde Soldier, 1990.
Hunter, Alexander. *Johnny Reb & Billy Yank*. New York: Neale, 1905; reprint ed., Konecky & Konecky, Nd.
Hyndman, William. *History of a Cavalry Company: A Complete Record of Company A, 4th Pennsylvania Cavalry*. Philadelphia: Jas. B. Rodgers, 1870.
Jenson, Les. "Comfort for Man and Horse: McClellan's Saddle." *Civil War Times Illustrated* 21 (January 1983): 30–31.
Johnson, Elisabeth and C. E. Johnson, Jr. *Rappahannock County, Virginia: A History*. Orange, VA: Green, 1981.
Jones, John B. *A Rebel War Clerk's Diary*. 2 vols. Philadelphia: J. B. Lippincott, 1866; reprint ed., Richmond, VA: Time-Life, 1982.
Jones, Mary S. and Mildred C. Jones, eds. *Historic Culpeper*. Culpeper, VA: Culpeper Historical Society, 1972.
Jordan, Ervin L. Jr. *Black Confederates and Afro Yankees in Civil War Virginia*. Charlottesville: University of Virginia Press, 1995.
Joslyn, Mauriel. *Biographical Register of the Immortal 600*. Shippensburg, PA: White Mane, 1992.
Keegan, John. *The Face of Battle*. New York: Viking, 1976.
Keith, Katherine Isham. "The Record of the Black Horse Troop." *Bulletin of the Fauquier Historical Society* (July 1924): 434–460.
Kennedy, Francis H., ed. *The Civil War Battlefield Guide*. Boston: Houghton Mifflin, 1990.
Kerksis, Sidney C. and Thomas S. Dickey. *Field Artillery Projectiles in the Civil War, 1861–1865*. Atlanta: Phoenix, 1968.
Kester, Donald E. *Cavalryman in Blue: Colonel John Wood Kester of the First New Jersey Cavalry in the Civil War*. Hightstown, NJ: Longstreet, 1997.
Kidd, J. H. *Personal Recollections of a Cavalryman with Custer's Michigan Brigade in the Civil War*. Ionia, MI: Sentinel, 1908; reprint ed., Time-Life, 1983. Republished and abridged as *A Cavalryman with Custer*, New York: Bantam, 1991.
Kishner, Ralph. *The Class of 1861*. Carbondale: Southern Illinois University Press, 1999.
Klein, Maury. "J.E.B. Stuart's Life: What Should We Think of the General?" *Civil War Times Illustrated* 25 (September 1986): 20–21, 47, 50.
Krick, Robert K. *Conquering the Valley: Stonewall Jackson at Port Republic*. New York: William Morrow, 1996.
_____. *Lee's Colonels*, 2nd ed., revised. Dayton, OH: Morningside Bookshop, 1984.
_____. *9th Virginia Cavalry*, 4th ed. Lynchburg, VA: H.E. Howard, 1982.
_____. *Staff Officers in Gray*. Chapel Hill: University of North Carolina Press, 2003.
_____. *Stonewall Jackson at Cedar Mountain*. Chapel Hill: University of North Carolina Press, 1990.
Krolick, Marshall D. "The Battle of Brandy Station." *Civil War Quarterly* 7 (1987): 52–65.
Lamb, John. "The Confederate Cavalry: Its Wants, Travails, and Heroism." *Southern Historical Society Papers* 26 (1898): 359–365.
Lee, Robert E. *Recollections and Letters of General Robert E. Lee, by His Son Capt. Robert E. Lee*. New York: Doubleday Page, 1904; reprint ed., Garden City, NY: Garden City, 1926.
_____. *Wartime Papers*. 2 vols. Edited by Clifford Dowdey. New York: Little, Brown, 1961; reprint ed., Pennington, NJ: Collectors Reprints, 1996.
Lee, Susan Pendleton. *Memoirs of William Nelson Pendleton*. Philadelphia: J. B. Lippincott, 1893.
Lewis, Berkeley R. "Notes on Ammunition of the American Civil War 1861–1865." Washington, D.C. American Ordnance Association, 1959.
_____. "Notes on Cavalry Weapons of the American Civil War 1861–1865." Washington, D.C. American Ordnance Association, 1961.
Lloyd, William P. *History of the First Reg't Pennsylvania Reserve Cavalry, from Its Organization, August 1861, to September 1894, with a List of Names of All Officers and Enlisted Men Who Have Ever Belonged to the Regiment and Remarks Attached to Each Name Noting Change &c*. Philadelphia: King and Baird, 1864.
"Lomax, Maj. Gen. L. L." Obituary. *Confederate Veteran* 21 (September 1913): 450.

Longacre, Edward G. "Alfred Pleasonton: The Knight of Romance." *Civil War Times Illustrated* 13 (December 1974): 10–23.
_____. *The Cavalry at Gettysburg: A Tactical Study of Mounted Operations during the Civil War's Pivotal Campaign, 9 June–14 July 1863.* Rutherford, NJ: Fairleigh Dickenson University Press, 1986.
_____. *General John Buford: A Military Biography.* Conschocken, PA: Combined Books, 1995.
_____. *Gentleman and Soldier: The Extraordinary Life of Wade Hampton.* Nashville, TN: Rutledge Hill, 2003.
_____. *Lee's Cavalrymen: A History of the Mounted Forces of the Army of Northern Virginia, 1861–1865.* Mechanicsburg, PA: Stackpole, 2002.
_____. *Lincoln's Cavalrymen: A History of the Mounted Forces of the Army of the Potomac, 1861–1865.* Mechanicsburg, PA: Stackpole, 2000.
_____. "Sir Percy Wyndham." *Civil War Times Illustrated* 8 (December 1968): 12–19.
Lonn, Ella. *Desertion During the Civil War.* Gloucester, MA: Peter Smith, 1965.
_____. *Foreigners in the Confederacy.* Gloucester, MA: Peter Smith, 1965.
Lowry, Thomas P. *Tarnished Eagles: The Courts-Martial of Fifty Union Colonels and Lieutenant Colonels.* Mechanicsburg, PA: Stackpole, 1997.
Maier, Larry B. *Rough and Regular: A History of Philadelphia's 119th Regiment of Pennsylvania Volunteer Infantry, The Gray Reserves.* Shippensburg, PA: Burd Street, 1997.
Manakee, Harold R. *Maryland in the Civil War.* Baltimore: Maryland Historical Society, 1961.
Manarin, Louis H. *The Cavalry,* vol. 2 of *North Carolina Troops 1861–1865, A Roster.* Raleigh: North Carolina State Department of Archives and History, 1968.
Martin, Samuel J. *"Kill-Cavalry": Sherman's Merchant of Terror: The Life of Union General Hugh Judson Kilpatrick.* Teaneck, NJ: Fairleigh Dickinson University Press, 1996.
_____. *Southern Hero: Matthew Calbraith Butler.* Mechanicsburg, PA: Stackpole, 2001.
Mays, Samuel Elias. "Sketches from the Journal of a Confederate Soldier." *Tyler's Quarterly Magazine* 5 (July 1923). Reprinted by Kraus Reprint Corp., New York, 1967.
McClellan, H. B. *The Battle of Fleetwood.* In *Annals of the War, Written by Leading Participants North and South.* Philadelphia: Times, 1879; reprint ed., Edison, NJ: Blue & Gray, 1996.
_____. "Letters from Stuart's Headquarters." *Southern Historical Society Papers* 3 (January-June 1877): 190–192.
_____. *The Life and Campaigns of Major-General J.E.B. Stuart, Commander of the Cavalry of the Army of Northern Virginia.* New York: Houghton Mifflin, 1885. Republished as *I Rode with JEB Stuart: The Life and Campaigns of Major-General J.E.B. Stuart.* Bloomington: University of Indiana Press, 1958; reprint ed., New York: Da Capo, 1994.
McDonald, William N. *A History of the Laurel Brigade.* Edited by Bushrod C. Washington. Baltimore, MD: Mrs. Kate S. McDonald, 1907; reprint ed. Baltimore, MD: Johns Hopkins, 2002.
McFadden, Elizabeth. *The Glitter and the Gold: A Spirited Account of the Metropolitan Museum of Art's First Director, the Audacious and High-handed Luigi Palma di Cesnola.* New York: Dial, 1971.
McPherson, James M., ed. *Encyclopedia of Civil War Biographies.* 3 vols. Armonk, NY: M.E. Sharpe, 2000.
Memoirs and Services of Three Generations. Rockland, ME: Np., 1909. (This pamphlet provides information on Jonathan P. Cilley, an officer in the 1st Maine Cavalry.)
Merington, Marguerite, ed. *The Custer Story: The Life and Intimate Letters of General Custer and His Wife Elizabeth.* New York: Devin-Adair, 1950.
Merrill, Francis L. "A Georgia Henry of Navarre." *Confederate Veteran* 23 (August 1915): 363. (This is a biographical sketch of Lieutenant Colonel William Deloney, Cobb's Legion.)
Merrill, Samuel H. *The Campaigns of the First Maine and the First District of Columbia Cavalry.* Portland, ME: Bailey & Noyes, 1866.
Merritt, Wesley. *Personal Recollections — Beverly Ford to Mitchell's Station (1863)* in *From Everglade to Canyon with the Second United States Cavalry: An Authentic Account of Service in Florida, Mexico, Virginia, and the Indian Country, 1836–1875.* Edited by Theophilus F. Rodenbough. New York: D. Van Norstrand, 1875; reprint ed., Norman: University of Oklahoma Press, 2000.
Mitchell, Page B. *History of Saint James and Christ Episcopal Churches, 1840–1986.* In *Early Churches of Culpeper County, Virginia: Colonial and Ante-Bellum Congregations.* Edited by Arthur Dicken Thomas, Jr., and Angus McDonald Green. Culpeper: Culpeper Historical Society, 1987.
Moffett, George H. "Battle of Brandy Station." *Confederate Veteran* 14 (February 1906): 74–75.
Moore, James. *Kilpatrick and Our Cavalry: Comprising a Sketch of the Life of General Kilpatrick, with an Account of the Cavalry Raids, Engagements, and Operations under His Command, from the Beginning of the Rebellion to the Surrender of Johnston.* New York: W. J. Widdleton, 1865.
Moore, Robert A. *A Life for the Confederacy.* Edited by James W. Silver. Jackson, TN: McCowat-Mercer, 1959.
Moore, Robert H., II. *Chew's Ashby, Shoemaker's Lynchburg, and the Newtown Artillery.* Lynchburg, VA: H. E. Howard, 1995.
_____. *The 1st and 2nd Stuart Horse Artillery.* Lynchburg, VA: H. E. Howard, 1985.
Mosby, John S. *The Memoirs of Colonel John S. Mosby.* New York, Little, Brown, 1917; reprint ed., Nashville, TN: J. S. Sanders, 1995.
_____. *Stuart's Cavalry in the Gettysburg Campaign.* New York: Mofat, Yard, 1908.
Munford, Thomas T. "Reminiscences of Cavalry Operations." *Southern Historical Society Papers* 12 (1884): 342–350; and 13 (1885): 133–145.

Musick, Michael P. *6th Virginia Cavalry.* Lynchburg, VA: H.E. Howard, 1990.
Myers, Frank M. *The Comanches: A History of White's Battalion, Virginia Cavalry, Laurel Brigade, Hampton's Div., A.N.V., C.S.A.* Baltimore, MD: Kelly, Piet, 1871; reprint ed., Alexandria, VA: Stonewall, 1985.
Nanzig, Thomas P. *3rd Virginia Cavalry.* Lynchburg, VA: H.E. Howard, 1989.
Neese, George M. *Three Years in the Confederate Horse Artillery.* New York: Neale, 1911.
Nesbitt, Mark. *Saber and Scapegoat.* Mechanicsburg, PA: Stackpole, 1994
____. *35 Days to Gettysburg: The Campaign Diary of Two American Enemies.* Harrisburg, PA: Stackpole, 1992.
Newhall, F. C. *The Battle of Beverly Ford.* In *Annals of the War, Written by Leading Participants North and South.* Philadelphia: Times, 1879; reprint ed., Edison, NJ: Blue & Gray, 1996.
Nichols, James L. *General Fitzhugh Lee — A Biography.* Lynchburg, VA: H.E. Howard, 1989.
Nielson, John M., ed. "The Prettiest Cavalry Fight You Ever Saw." *Civil War Times Illustrated* 17 (July 1978): 6–12, 42–43. (Originally in the Sitka, Alaska *Post,* November 5, 1876.)
Nolan, Alan T. *The Iron Brigade: A Military History.* Bloomington: Indiana University Press, 1994.
Norton, Henry. *Deeds of Daring: A History of the Eighth New York Volunteer Cavalry.* Norwich, CT: Chenango Telegraph, 1899.
Nye, W. S. "Brandy Station, June 9: Stuart vs. Pleasonton." *Civil War Times Illustrated* 2 (July 1963), 24.
Oakey, Daniel. *History of the Second Massachusetts Regiment of Infantry: Beverly Ford, A Paper Read at the Officers' Reunion in Boston, May 12, 1884.* Boston: Geo. H. Ellis, 1884.
O'Ferrall, Charles T. *Forty Years of Active Service.* New York: Neale, 1904.
"O'Ferrall, Gov. Charles T." Obituary. *Confederate Veteran* 13 (November 1905): 514.
Opie, John N. "How Major J. N. Opie Led a Charge: A Graphic Story of a Dash through the Federal Cavalry at Brandy Station." *Southern Historical Society Papers* 19 (1891): 251–253.
____. *A Rebel Cavalryman with Lee, Stuart and Jackson.* Chicago: W. B. Conkey, 1899; reprint ed., Dayton, OH: Morningside Bookshop, 1972.
Owsley, Douglas W., et al. *History and Archeology of St. James Episcopal Church, Brandy Station, Virginia.* Np., Nd.
Patterson, Gerard A. *Rebels from West Point.* Mechanicsburg, PA: Stackpole, 2002.
Peake, John W. "Recollections of a Boy Cavalryman." *Confederate Veteran,* 34 (July 1926): 260–262.
Peck, Daniel. *Dear Rachel: The Civil War Letters of Daniel Peck.* Edited by Martha Gerber Stanford. Freeman, SD: Pine Hill, 1993.
Peck, R. H. *Reminiscences of a Confederate Soldier of Co. C, 2nd Va. Cavalry.* Fincastle, VA: Np., 1913.
Peterson, Harold L. "Notes on Ordnance of the American Civil War 1861–1865." Washington, D.C. American Ordnance Association, 1959.
Peyton, John W. *Eyewitness to War in Virginia, 1861–1865: The Civil War Diary of John William Peyton.* Edited by Walbrook D. Swank. Shippensburg, PA: Burd Street, 2003.
Pfanz, Donald C. *Richard S. Ewell: A Soldier's Life.* Chapel Hill: University of North Carolina Press, 1998.
Phisterer, Frederick. *New York in the War of Rebellion, 1861–1865,* 5 vols. with index. Albany, NY: Weed and Parsons, 1890.
Pickerill, W. N. *History of the Third Indiana Cavalry.* Indianapolis, IN: Aetna, 1906.
Pierce Michael D. *The Most Promising Young Officer: A Life of Ranald Slidell MacKenzie.* Norman: University of Oklahoma Press, 1993.
Pleasonton, Alfred. *The Campaign of Gettysburg.* In *Annals of the War, Written by Leading Participants North and South.* Philadelphia: Times, 1879; reprint ed., Edison, NJ: Blue & Gray, 1996.
Preston, Noble D. *History of the Tenth Regiment of Cavalry New York State Volunteers, August, 1861, to August, 1865.* New York: D. Appleton, 1892.
Price, George F. *Across the Continent with the Fifth Cavalry.* New York: Noble Offset, 1883; reprint ed., New York: Antiquarian, 1959.
Pride, Mike and Mark Travis. *My Brave Boys: To War with Colonel Cross and the Fighting Fifth* [New Hampshire Infantry]. Hanover, NH: University Press of New England, 2001.
Pyne, Henry R. *Ride to War: The History of the First New Jersey Cavalry.* Edited by Earl S. Miers. New Brunswick, NJ: Rutgers University Press, 1961.
Quint, Alonzo H. *The Record of the Second Massachusetts Infantry, 1861–65.* Boston: James P. Walker, 1867.
Raiford, Neil H. *4th North Carolina Cavalry in the Civil War.* Jefferson, NC: McFarland, 2003.
Ray, William R. *Four Years with the Iron Brigade.* Edited by Lance Herdegen and Sherry Murphy. Cambridge, MA: Da Capo, 2002.
Reade, Frank Robertson. *In the Saddle with Stuart: The Story of Frank Smith Robertson of Jeb Stuart's Staff.* Edited by Robert J. Trout. Gettysburg, PA: Thomas, 2004.
Register of Graduates, Association of Graduates, United States Military Academy, West Point, NY, 2000. (The Register of Graduates, published annually, contains abbreviated biographical data regarding USMA graduates. The 2000 edition also contains statistics on USMA graduate battle deaths.)
Reid, Whitelaw. *Ohio in the War: Her Statesmen, Generals, and Soldiers,* 2 vols. Cincinnati: Robert Clarke, 1895.
Report of the Forty-Ninth Annual Reunion of the Sixth Ohio Volunteer Cavalry Association. Warren, OH: Wm. Ritezel, 1914.
Rhodes, Charles D. *History of the Cavalry of the Army of the Potomac, Including That of the Army of Virginia (Pope's),*

and also the History of the Operations of the Federal Cavalry in West Virginia During the War. Kansas City, MO: Hudson-Kimberly, 1900.

Robertson, James. "The War in Words." *Civil War Times Illustrated* 22 (September 1983), 39.

Rodenbough, Theophilus F., ed. *The Cavalry*, vol.2 of *Photographic History of the Civil War*. New York: Review of Reviews, 1911; reprint ed., Secaucus, NJ: Blue & Gray, 1987.

———., ed. *From Everglade to Canyon with the Second United States Cavalry: An Authentic Account of Service in Florida, Mexico, Virginia, and the Indian Country, 1836–1875.* New York: D. Van Norstrand, 1875; reprint ed., Norman: University of Oklahoma Press, 2000.

Roll of Officers and Members of the Georgia Hussars and of the Cavalry Companies, of Which the Hussars Are a Continuation, with Historical Sketch Relating Facts Showing the Origin and Necessity of Rangers, or Mounted Men in the Colony of Georgia from the Date of Its Founding. Savannah: Morning News, 1906.

Rowland, Thomas, "Letters of Major Thomas Rowland, C.S.A., from the Camps at Ashland and Richmond, Virginia, 1861." *William and Mary Quarterly Historical Magazine*, 24 (January 1916), 145–153; (April, 1916), 232–238.

Rummel George A., III. *72 Days at Gettysburg: Organization of the 10th New York Volunteer Cavalry.* Shippensburg, PA: White Mane, 1997.

Scheel, Eugene M. *Culpeper: A Virginia County's History Through 1920.* Orange, VA: Green, 1982.

Scheibert, Justus. *Sieben Monate in den Rebellion Staaten.* Stettin, Germany: Np., 1868.

Sears, Stephen W. *Chancellorsville.* New York: Houghton Mifflin, 1996.

Shaw, W. P. *Fifty-Ninth Regiment (Fourth Cavalry)* in *Histories of the Several Regiments and Battalions from North Carolina in the Great War 1861–65: Written by Members of the Respective Commands,* 5 vols. Edited by Walter Clark. Raleigh: E. M. Uzzell, 1901; reprint ed., Wendell, NC: Broadfoot's Bookmark, 1982.

Shoemaker, J. J. *Shoemaker's Battery, Stuart Horse Artillery, Pelham's Battalion, Army of Northern Virginia.* Memphis, TN: S. C. Toof, Nd.; reprint ed.: Gaithersburg, MD: Butternut, Nd.

Sifakis, Stewart. *South Carolina and Georgia*, vol. 9 of *Compendium of the Confederate Armies.* New York: Facts on File, 1995.

Smith, Thomas W. *"We Have It Damn Hard Out Here": The Civil War Letters of Sergeant Thomas W. Smith, 6th Pennsylvania Cavalry.* Edited by Eric J. Wittenberg. Kent, OH: Kent State University Press, 1999.

Sneeden, Robert Knox. *Eye of the Storm.* Edited by Charles F. Bryan, Jr. and Nelson D. Lankford. New York: Free, 2000.

———. *Images from the Storm.* Edited by Charles F. Bryan, Jr. and Nelson D. Lankford. New York: Free, 2001.

Sorrel, G. Moxley. *Recollections of a Confederate Staff Officer.* New York: Neale, 1905; reprint ed., New York: Bantam, 1992.

Stackpole, Edward J. *Chancellorsville*, 2nd ed. Harrisburg, PA: Stackpole, 1988.

Starr, R. F. S. "A Prussian for Virginia: Heros von Borcke." *Civil War Times Illustrated* 19 (February 1981): 32–39.

Starr, Stephen Z. *The Union Cavalry in the Civil War*, 3 vols. Baton Rouge: Louisiana State University Press, 1979.

Statts, Richard J. *Life and Times of Colonel William Stedman of the 6th Ohio Cavalry,* vol 4 of *Grassroots History of the American Civil War.* Bowie, MD: Heritage, 2003.

Stern, Philip van Doren, ed. *Soldier Life.* Greenwich, CT: Fawcett, 1961.

Stiles, Kenneth. *4th Virginia Cavalry,* 2d ed. Lynchburg, VA: H.E. Howard, 1985.

Stuart, James Ewell Brown. *Letters of Major General James E. B. Stuart,* edited by Adele H. Mitchell. Stuart-Mosby Historical Society, 1990.

Suhr, Robert, "Lee's October 63 Move on Meade." *Military Heritage* (October 2000): 78–85.

Sutherland, Daniel E. *Seasons of War.* New York: Free, 1995.

Taylor John. *Bloody Valverde: A Civil War Battle on the Rio Grande, February 21, 1862.* Albuquerque: University of New Mexico Press, 1995.

Taylor, Nelson. *Saddle and Saber: The Letters of Civil War Cavalryman Corporal Nelson Taylor.* Edited by Gray N. Taylor. Bowie, MD: Heritage, 1993.

Thomas, Emory M. *Bold Dragoon: The Life of J.E.B. Stuart.* New York: Harper & Row, 1986.

———. "The Real J.E.B. Stuart." *Civil War Times Illustrated.* 28 (November/ December 1981): 34–41, 75–77.

Thomason, John. *JEB Stuart.* New York: Scribner's, 1930.

Tobie, Edward P. *History of the First Maine Cavalry, 1861–1865.* Boston: Press of Emery & Hughes, 1887.

Toombs, Samuel. *New Jersey Troops in the Gettysburg Campaign from June 5 to July 31, 1863.* Orange, NJ: Evening Mail, 1888.

Toomey, Daniel C. and Charles A. Earp. *Marylanders in Blue: The Artillery and the Cavalry.* Baltimore, MD: Toomey, 1999.

Trout, Robert J. *Galloping Thunder: The Stuart Horse Artillery Battalion.* Mechanicsburg, PA: Stackpole, 2002.

———. "In Pelham's Shadow: The Commanders of the Horse Artillery of the Army of Northern Virginia After Major John Pelham." *Civil War Quarterly* 11 (1987): 47–59.

———. *They Followed the Plume: The Story of J.E.B. Stuart and His Staff.* Mechanicsburg, PA: Stackpole, 1993.

———. *With Pen and Saber: The Letters and Diaries of J.E.B. Stuart's Staff Officers.* Mechanicsburg, PA: Stackpole, 1995.

Trulock, Alice R. *In the Hands of Providence: Joshua Chamberlain and the American Civil War.* Chapel Hill: University of North Carolina Press, 1997.

Tyler, Lyon Gardiner, ed. *Encyclopedia of Virginia Biography*, 5 vols. New York: Lewis Historical, 1915.
Underwood, Adin B. *The Three Years Service of the Thirty-Third Mass. Infantry Regiment, 1862–1865*. Boston: A. Williams, 1881.
U.S. War Department. *Atlas to Accompany the Official Records of the Union and Confederate Armies*. Washington: Government Printing Office, 1891–1895; reprinted as *The Official Military Atlas of the Civil War*. New York: Gramercy, 1983.
U.S. War Department. *War of the Rebellion: A Compilation of the Official Records of the Union and Confederate Armies*. 70 vols. in 128 books and index. Washington, DC: Government Printing Office, 1880–1901. Unless otherwise noted, all citations are from Series I (reports and correspondence relating to operations in the field).
Utley, Robert M. *Frontier Regulars: The United States Army and the Indian, 1866–1891*. New York: Macmillan, 1973.
_____. *Frontiersmen in Blue: The United States Army and the Indian, 1848–1865*. New York: Macmillan, 1967.
"*Virginia Calendar of State Papers*, vol. 11 (January 1, 1836–April 15, 1869). Edited by H. W. Flournoy. Richmond, VA: Np., 1893; reprint ed., New York: Kraus Reprint Corp, 1968.
Vogtsberger, Margaret Ann. *The Dulaneys of Welbourne: A Family in Mosby's Confederacy*. Berryville, VA: Rockbridge, 1995.
von Borcke, Heros. *Memoirs of the Confederate War for Independence*. Edinburgh, UK: W. Blackwood and Sons, 1866; reprint ed., New York: Peter Smith, 1938; reprint ed., Nashville, TN: J. S. Sanders, 1999.
von Borcke, Heros and Justus Scheibert. *The Great Cavalry Battle of Brandy Station*, trans. by Stuart T. Wright and F. D. Bridgewater. Winston-Salem, NC: Palaemon, 1976.
Wagner, Margaret E., et al, eds. *The Library of Congress Civil War Desk Reference*. New York: Simon & Schuster, 2002.
Wainwright, Charles S. *A Diary of Battle: The Personal Journals of Colonel Charles S. Wainwright, 1861–1865*. Edited by Alan Nevins. New York: Harcourt, Brace, & World, 1962.
Wakelyn, Jon L. *Biographical Dictionary of the Confederacy*. Westport, CT: Greenwood, 1977.
Walker, Charles D., ed. *Memorial, Virginia Military Institute: Biographical Sketches of the Graduates and Eleves for the Virginia Military Institute Who Fell During the War Between the States*. Philadelphia: J. B. Lippincott, 1875.
Wallace, Lee A., Jr. *A Guide to Virginia Military Organizations 1861–1865*. Richmond: Virginia Civil War Commission, 1964. (This work was later published by H. E. Howard, Richmond.)
Ward, J. W. "General M. C. Butler of South Carolina." *Confederate Veteran* 3 (February 1895): 42.
Warner, Ezra J. *Generals In Blue*. Baton Rouge: Louisiana State University Press, 1999.
_____. *Generals In Gray*. Baton Rouge: Louisiana State University Press, 1999.
Warthen, Harry J. Jr., ed. "Family Ties: Letters from JEB Stuart." *Civil War Times Illustrated* 22 (October 1983): 34–35.
Watson, Thomas Jackson. "Was with 'JEB' Stuart When He Was Shot." *Confederate Veteran* 11 (December 1903): 553.
Waugh, John C. *Class of 1846*. New York: Warner, 1994.
Wellman, Manly Wade. *Giant in Gray: A Biography of Wade Hampton of South Carolina*. New York: Scribner's, 1949.
Welton, J. Michael, ed. *My Heart Is So Rebellious: The Caldwell Letters 1861–1865*. Warrenton, VA: Fauquier National Bank, 1991.
Wert, Jeffry D. *Custer: The Controversial Life of George Armstrong Custer*. New York: Simon & Schuster, 1996.
_____. "His Unhonored Service: Colonel Tom Munford — A Man of Achievement." *Civil War Times Illustrated* 24 (June 1985): 28–34.
West, John C. *A Texan in Search of a Fight*. Waco: J. S. Hill, 1901; reprint ed., Waco: Texian, 1969.
Weston, John Burden. *Picket Pins and Sabers: The Civil War Letters of John Burden Weston*. Edited by Robert W. Frost and Nancy D. Frost. Ashland, KY: Economy, 1971.
Weygant, Charles H. *History of the One Hundred Twenty-Fourth Regiment, N.Y.S.V.* Newburgh, NY: Journal, 1877.
Whelan, Henry C. "A Race for Life at Brandy Station." Edited by Edward G. Longacre. *Civil War Times Illustrated* 17 (January 1979): 32–38.
Wiley, Bell Irwin. *The Life of Billy Yank*. Baton Rouge: Louisiana State University Press, 1952; reprint ed., Baton Rouge: Louisiana State University Press, 1978.
_____. *The Life of Johnny Reb*. Baton Rouge: Louisiana State University Press, 1943
Willard, Van R. *With the 3rd Wisconsin Infantry: The Living Experience of the Civil War through the Journals of Van R. Willard*. Edited by Steven S. Raub. Mechanicsburg, PA: Stackpole, 1999.
Williamson, James J. *Mosby's Rangers*. New York: Ralph B. Kenyon, 1896; reprint ed. Time-Life, 1982.
Wilmer, L. Allison, J. H. Jarnett, and Geo. W. F. Vernon. *History and Roster of Maryland Volunteers, War of 1861–65*. Baltimore: Guggenheim, Weil, 1899. (This work is also available online at Maryland State Archives Online.)
Wintle, Justin, ed. *Dictionary of War Quotations*. New York: Free, 1989.
Wise, Jennings C. *The Long Arm of Lee: A History of the Artillery of the Army of Northern Virginia*. Lynchburg, VA: J. P. Bell, 1915; reprint ed., 2 vols., Lincoln: University of Nebraska Press, 1991.
_____. *Military History of Virginia Military Institute from 1861–1865*. Lynchburg, VA: J. P. Bell, 1915.
Wittenberg, Eric J. *The Union Cavalry Comes of Age: Hartwood Church to Brandy Station, 1863*. Washington, DC: Brassey's, 2003.
Woodhead, Henry, ed. *Arms and Equipment of the Confederacy*. Alexandria, VA: Time-Life, 1996.
Woodward, C. Vann, ed. *Mary Chesnut's Civil War*. New Haven, CT: Yale University Press, 1982.
Wormser, Richard. *The Yellowlegs: The Story of the United States Cavalry*. Garden City, NY: Doubleday, 1966.
Young, T. J. "Battle of Brandy Station." *Confederate Veteran* 23 (April 1915): 171–172.

Manuscripts and Other Unpublished Sources

Alexander, Charles. Letters. Gustavus Brown Alexander Papers, 1800–1890 (#4800). Albert and Shirley Small Special Collections Library, University of Virginia, Charlottesville.
Barringer, Rufus C. Manuscript. Papers of the Barringer Family, 1828–1963 (#2588). Albert and Shirley Small Special Collections Library, University of Virginia, Charlottesville.
Beane, Thomas O. Master's thesis. "Thomas Lafayette Rosser: Soldier, Railroad Builder, Politician, Businessman (1836–1910)." University of Virginia, 1957.
Blackford, Gay. Manuscript. Papers of William Willis Blackford (#5017). Albert and Shirley Small Special Collections Library, University of Virginia, Charlottesville.
Blackford, William W. Annotations by W. W. Blackford (Mss 5859). Albert and Shirley Small Special Collections Library, University of Virginia, Charlottesville.
Botts, John Minor. Papers, 1842–1863 (#38840). Library of Virginia, Richmond.
Bowman, Ephriam. Diary. Bowman Family Papers, 1861–1900 (#7643). Albert and Shirley Small Special Collections Library, University of Virginia, Charlottesville.
Bowmaster, Patrick A. Master's thesis. "Confederate Brig. Gen. B. H. Robertson and the Gettysburg Campaign." Virginia Polytechnic Institute and State University, 1995.
Brooke, St. George T. Autobiography, 1907 (#25146). Library of Virginia, Richmond.
Brumback, Jacob H. Diary (537 THL, Box 1). Handley Regional Library, Winchester, VA.
Bushnell, Wells A. Sixth Regiment Ohio Volunteer Cavalry Memoir, 1861–1865 (2152A Microfilm Edition). Western Reserve Historical Society, Cleveland.
Carter, William R. Diary and Letters. Carter Family Papers, 1817–1892 (#33886). Library of Virginia, Richmond. (This diary, edited by Walbrook D. Swank, is published as *Sabres, Saddles, and Spurs*.)
Cartmell, Thomas K. Letters and Documents. Thomas K. Cartmell Collection, 1740–1949 (164 WTCH). Handley Regional Library, Winchester, VA.
Chewing, Charles R. "The Journal of Charles R. Chewing, Company E, 9 Virginia Cavalry, C.S.A" (900 THL). Edited by Richard B. Armstrong. Handley Regional Library, Winchester, VA.
Coles, Isaac. "Recollections of 1861–65." Pocket Plantation Papers, 1720–1923 (#2027, 2027a). Albert and Shirley Small Special Collections Library, University of Virginia, Charlottesville.
Collins, John Overton. Diary (Mss1 C6944a Microfilm). Virginia Historical Society, Richmond.
Compiled Service Records, National Archives, Washington, DC. (Compiled Service Records for personnel who served in Virginia units are available on microfilm at the Library of Virginia, Richmond.)
Corson, William Clark. Letters (Mss1 C8184 a). Virginia Historical Society, Richmond. (Corson's war-time letters to his future wife are contained in *My Dear Jennie*, edited by Blake W. Corson, Jr. . Richmond: Dietz, 1982.)
Culpeper County Chancery Court Order Books. County Courthouse, Culpeper, VA.
Culpeper County Deed Record Books. County Courthouse, Culpeper, VA.
Dabney, Chiswell. Letters. Saunders Family Papers (Mss1 Sa878 a, Microfilm). Virginia Historical Society, Richmond.
Davis, Eugene. Letters. Papers of Eugene Davis, 1744–1925 (#2483 & 2483a). Albert and Shirley Small Special Collections Library, University of Virginia, Charlottesville.
Davis, Richard T. Reverend. Letters. Davis-Preston-Saunders Collection (#4951). Albert and Shirley Small Special Collections Library, University of Virginia, Charlottesville.
Deloney, William G. Letters. William Gaston Deloney Family Papers (Ms 184). Hargrett Library, University of Georgia, Athens.
diCesnola, Luigi Palma. Letters. Luigi diCesnola Papers (Ms-68). Rauner Special Collections Library. Dartmouth College, Hanover, NH.
Donahue, John C. Civil War Diary, 1861–1865 (#28589), Library of Virginia, Richmond.
Freeman, Douglas Southall. Letters and Manuscript. Papers of Douglas Southall Freeman (#5220). Albert and Shirley Small Special Collections Library, University of Virginia, Charlottesville.
Goecker, James A. Manuscript. "William S. McClure, Major, Third Indiana Cavalry." Provided by its author.
Gregg, David McMurtrie. Manuscripts. Papers of David McMurtrie Gregg (MMC-0539). Library of Congress, Washington, DC.
Halsey, J. J. Letters. Morton-Halsey Papers ca. 1786–1938 (#3995). Albert and Shirley Small Special Collections Library, University of Virginia, Charlottesville.
Haskell, John Cheves. "Reminiscences of the Confederate War, 1861–1865." (Mss7:3 E605 H2378:1). Virginia Historical Society, Richmond.
Hawse, Jasper. Manuscript. "Diary of Jasper Hawse, 1861–1864" (Microfilm, #5188 & 5188a). Albert and Shirley Small Special Collections Library, University of Virginia, Charlottesville. (A typescript of the diary of Jasper Hawse, prepared by Marjorie Plumpton in 1956 (53 WFCHS), is available at the Handley Regional Library, Winchester, VA.)
Hennessee, John W. Master's thesis. "The Battle of Brandy Station." George Washington University, February 1958.
Holland, Mark. Letters. Papers of Asa Holland, 1820–1890 (#902). Albert and Shirley Small Special Collections Library, University of Virginia, Charlottesville.
Holliday, B. T. Manuscript. "The Account of My Capture" (#4121). Albert and Shirley Small Special Collections Library, University of Virginia, Charlottesville.
Hoskins, Thomas Toliaferro. Letters. Hoskins Family Papers (Mss1 H7935 a 2–11). Virginia Historical Society, Richmond.

Hubard, Robert Thruston, Jr. Letters and Manuscript. Robert Thruston Hubard Papers, 1811–1863 (#11556-a). Albert and Shirley Small Special Collections Library, University of Virginia, Charlottesville.
_____. "Notebook of Robert Thruston Hubard, 1860–1866" (#10522). Albert and Shirley Small Special Collections Library, University of Virginia, Charlottesville.
Hubbard, John L. Letter (208WFCHS, Box 2). Handley Regional Library, Winchester, VA.
Inglis, John B. Diary (SC 22716). New York State Library, Albany.
Jones, William Edmonson. Papers, 1845–1968 (Mss2J7286b). Virginia Historical Society, Richmond.
Kearns, Watkins. Diary (Mss5:1 K2143: 1–3). Virginia Historical Society, Richmond.
Lee, Fitzhugh. Letters. Fitzhugh Lee Papers, 1731–1952 (Microfilm #1829–1931). Albert and Shirley Small Special Collections Library, University of Virginia, Charlottesville.
Lee, George Bolling. Papers 1813–1924 (Mss1 L5114d; Reel C 278). Virginia Historical Society, Richmond.
Lee, Robert E. Correspondence, 1861–1865 (#25786). Library of Virginia, Richmond.
_____. Letter to Charles Carter Lee, March 23, 1863 (#11424). Albert and Shirley Small Special Collections Library, University of Virginia, Charlottesville.
McClellan, Henry Brainard. Letters and papers (1 M1324 a-b). Virginia Historical Society, Richmond.
McVicar, Charles William. Diary, Accounts, and Reminiscences, 1862–1865 (#29910). Library of Virginia, Richmond.
Murray, John F. Letters. Murray Family Papers, 1861–1863, 1866, Nd. (#27084). Library of Virginia, Richmond.
Oviatt, Martin. Diary. Papers of Martin Oviatt, 1863 -1995 (MMC — 3644). Library of Congress, Washington, DC.
Owsley, Douglas W., Malcolm L. Richardson and William E. Hanna. "Bioarcheological Investigation and Exhumation of the Remains of Captain William Downs Farley, CSA." March 2002.
Patrick, Marsena. Marsena Patrick Journal, 1862–1865. Miscellaneous Manuscripts Collection, Library of Congress, Washington, DC.
Pegram Family Papers (Mss1 P3496c 81–115). Virginia Historical Society, Richmond.
Perry, William Hartwell. Letters. Papers of William Hartwell Perry, 1860–65 (#7786-d). Albert and Shirley Small Special Collections Library, University of Virginia, Charlottesville.
Pleasonton, Alfred. Letters. Miscellaneous Manuscript Collection. Library of Congress, Washington, DC.
Pratt, George Julian. Letters. Papers of George Julian Pratt, 1861–1905 (#11283, 11283-a). Albert and Shirley Small Special Collections Library, University of Virginia, Charlottesville.
Radnour, Harry Warren. Doctoral dissertation. "General Fitzhugh Lee: A Biography." University of Virginia, 1971.
Reade, Frank Robertson. "In the Saddle with Stuart: The Story of Frank Robertson of Jeb Stuart's Staff" (#7566). Albert and Shirley Small Special Collections Library, University of Virginia, Charlottesville. (This manuscript, edited by Robert J. Trout, is published as *In the Saddle with Stuart*, Gettysburg, PA: Thomas, 1998.)
Redman, William Henry. "History of the 12th Illinois Cavalry" (#7415-b). Albert and Shirley Small Special Collections Library, University of Virginia, Charlottesville.
Reed, Thomas J. "A Profile of Brig. Gen Alfred N.A. Duffié." Manhattan, KS: MA/AH Publishing, Kansas State University, 1982.
Robertson, Francis Smith. "Reminiscences, 1861–65" (R5462:1). Virginia Historical Society. Richmond.
Robinson, Leiper Moore. "Civil War Experiences, 1863–1865" (R5642:1). Virginia Historical Society, Richmond.
Rosser, Thomas L. Papers of Thomas Lafayette Rosser (Mss 1171). Albert and Shirley Small Special Collections Library, University of Virginia, Charlottesville.
Scheel, Eugene M. "The Historical Site Survey and Archaeological Reconnaissance of Culpeper County, Virginia." Culpeper County Government, November 1992–April 1994.
Scott, James McClure. "War Record" (Mss7:1 Sc0845:1). Edited by Sarah Travers Lewis Scott Anderson. Virginia Historical Society, Richmond.
Scott, John Zachary H. Manuscript (Mss2 Sc0843). Virginia Historical Society, Richmond.
Sheridan, Philip. Philip Sheridan Papers. Miscellaneous Manuscripts Collection. Library of Congress, Washington, DC.
Sneeden, Robert Knox. Diary 1861–1865 (Mss5:1 SN237:1) Virginia Historical Society, Richmond.
Steptoe, William. Resolution of Sympathy. Langhorne Family Papers, 1843–1863 (L2653 a 85–98). Virginia Historical Society, Richmond.
Stuart, James Ewell Brown. Letters. Stuart Papers, 1833–1864 (St923 d 1–107). Virginia Historical Society, Richmond.
_____. Letter, 1863, June 15 (St922 a 14). Virginia Historical Society, Richmond.
_____. Letters to his Wife, Flora Cook Stuart (#7442). Albert and Shirley Small Special Collections Library, University of Virginia, Charlottesville.
_____. Newspaper Clippings. Stuart Papers, 1851–1864 (St 923 a 19–46). Virginia Historical Society, Richmond.
_____. Letter to Thomas L. Rosser, 1864 (#8482). Albert and Shirley Small Special Collections Library, University of Virginia, Charlottesville.
_____. Letters. William Alexander Stuart Collection (St938 a 1–19). Virginia Historical Society, Richmond.
_____. Letters. JEB Stuart Letters, 1861–1862. Miscellaneous Manuscripts Collection. Library of Congress, Washington, DC.
Taylor, Charles Elisha. Letters. Charles Elisha Taylor Papers, 1849–1874 (#3091, a-c). Albert and Shirley Small Special Collections Library, University of Virginia, Charlottesville.
U.S. Government. Census Records, Culpeper County, 1860. Culpeper County Library, Culpeper, VA.
van Leyden, Maurice. Letters (#12182). Albert and Shirley Small Special Collections Library, University of Virginia, Charlottesville.
"Vicinity of Brandy Station, Culpeper Co., Va.: Showing Battlefield of June 9, 1863." Cincinnati, OH: Strobridge &

Co., Lithographers, 1863. Library of Virginia, Richmond. (This map, which is also available on the Internet at the Library of Congress website, is misdated. It was prepared to accompany H. B. McClellan's *Life and Campaigns of Major General J.E.B. Stuart*, which was published in 1885.)
Virginia Department of Confederate Military Records, 1859–1996, (Subseries 2: Cavalry) (#27684). Library of Virginia, Richmond.
Virginia Supreme Court of Appeals, Richmond City, Order Books 23 and 24, Library of Virginia, Richmond.
von Koerber, V. E. "Maps of Cavalry Engagements at Aldie, Brandy Station, and Upperville, 1863" (#5477). Albert and Shirley Small Special Collections Library, University of Virginia, Charlottesville.
Walker, Sam A. Letters. Walker Family Papers, 1753–1873 (#1532). Albert and Shirley Small Special Collections Library, University of Virginia, Charlottesville.
Wallace, Charles. Letters. Wallace Family Papers, 1799–1920 (#2689). Albert and Shirley Small Special Collections Library, University of Virginia, Charlottesville.
Watkins, Richard Henry. Letters (Mss1 W3272 a Microfilm). Virginia Historical Society, Richmond.
Whitehead, Irving P. "The Campaigns of Munford and the 2d Virginia Cavalry" (Microfilm, #910). Albert and Shirley Small Special Collections Library, University of Virginia, Charlottesville.
Wickham, Williams. Letters. Wickham Family Papers, 1754–1977 (Mss1 W6326cFA2). Virginia Historical Society, Richmond.
Wise, John. Letters. Papers of Michael Wise, 1743–1903 (#6741). Albert and Shirley Small Special Collections Library, University of Virginia, Charlottesville.
Wynkoop, Guy. Letters (1862–1863) (SC 19402). New York State Library, Albany.
Young, George C. Letters. Civil War Correspondence of George C. and I. A. Young (#3676). Albert and Shirley Small Special Collections Library, University of Virginia, Charlottesville.

Newspapers

American and Commercial Advertiser, Baltimore, MD: June 11–12, 1863.
Atlanta Constitution, Atlanta, GA: July 7–8, 1896.
Boston Daily Advertiser, Boston, MA: June 11–13, 1863.
Charleston Mercury, Charleston, SC: June 12–13, 15–16, 22, 1863.
Chicago Tribune, Chicago, IL: June 10–11, 1863.
Culpeper Observer and General Advertiser, Culpeper, VA: June 24, 1859; March 9, 1860; February 21, 1863; January 25, 1867; September 18, 1868.
Culpeper Star-Exponent, Culpeper, VA: April 7–8, 2002; May 5, 2002.
Daily Examiner, Richmond, VA: May 5, 1863; June 6, 9–13, 15, 18, 24, 1863; May 14, 17, 1864.
Daily National Intelligencer, Washington, DC: June 11–12, 1863.
Daily Union and Advertiser, Rochester, NY: June 18, 1863.
Daily Virginian, Lynchburg, VA: June 12–13, 16–17, 23, 27, 1863; July 1, 1863.
Ellsworth American, Ellsworth, ME (Undated copy of an article by Francis W. Hatch, "The Star Spangled Life of Charles Jarvis Whiting," provided by the Castine, Maine Historical Society).
Hanover Evening Sun, Hanover, NH: April 26, 2004.
New York Herald, New York: June 10–11, 1863.
New York Times, New York: March 22, 1863; June 10–12, 14, 1863.
Philadelphia Weekly Times, Philadelphia, PA: November 10, 1877; June 26, 1880.
The Sentinel, Richmond, VA: June 11, 13, 15, 17, 1863.
The Sun, Baltimore, MD: June 11–12, 1863.
Times-Dispatch, Richmond, VA: August 4, 1912.
Washington Post, Washington, DC: July 21, 1997.
Weekly Banner, Athens, GA: May 2, 1983.
The Whig, Richmond, VA: June 10–12, 1863.
Worcester Aegis and Transcript, Worcester, NY: June 13, 1863.

Online Sources

Atkinson, Archibald, Jr. "Memoir of Archibald Atkinson, Jr." Special Collections Department. Virginia Polytechnic Institute and State University Library, Blacksburg. (http://spec.lib.vt.edu/civwar/memoirs.htm)
Bates, Samuel P. *History of the Pennsylvania Volunteers, 1861–1865*, 5 vols. Harrisburg, PA: B Singerly, 1869–1871. (http://www.rootsweb.com/~pamercer/PA/Military/CivilWar/bates.htm)
_____. *Martial Deeds of Pennsylvania*. Philadelphia: T. H. Davis, 1876. USGenWeb Pennsylvania Archives. (http://www.rootsweb.com/~usgenweb/pa/1pa/1picts/bates/mdeedspa.htm)
"Coast Guard at War." U.S. Coast Guard. (www.uscg.mil)
Collis, Septima M. *Woman's War Record 1861–1865*. New York: G. P. Putnam, Knickerbocker, 1889. Documenting

the American South Collection, Academic Affairs Library, University of North Carolina, Chapel Hill. (http://docsouth.unc.edu/collis/menu.html)

Cooper, Samuel S. *A Concise System of Instructions and Regulations for the Militia and Volunteers of the United States....* Philadelphia: Robert P. Desilver, 1836. The Drill Network. (http://home.att.net/~Rebmus/Cooper.htm# SiteNav)

Early, Jubal Anderson. *Autobiographical Sketch and Narrative of the War Between the States.* Notes by R. H. Early. Philadelphia: J. B. Lippincott, 1912. Documenting the American South Collection, Academic Affairs Library, University of North Carolina, Chapel Hill. (http://docsouth.unc.edu/early/ menu.html)

Eggleston, George Cary. *A Rebel's Recollections.* Cambridge, MA: Riverside, 1875. Documenting the American South Collection, Academic Affairs Library, University of North Carolina, Chapel Hill. (http://docsouth.unc.edu/eggleston/menu.html)

Ervine, John H. Letters. Civil War Collection. Virginia Military Institute Library, Lexington. (http://www.vmi.edu/archives/Manuscripts/ms331trn.html)

Gallaher, William B. Letters. "Valley of the Shadow: Two Communities in the American Civil War." Virginia Center for Digital History, University of Virginia, Charlottesville. (http://valley.vcdh.virginia.edu/personalpapers/collections/augusta/gallaher.html)

Garber, Thomas. Letters. "Valley of the Shadow: Two Communities in the American Civil War." Virginia Center for Digital History, University of Virginia, Charlottesville. (http://valley.vcdh.virginia.edu/personalpapers/collections/augusta/garber.html)

Graham, Kurt. "Lt. Col William Wofford Rich." (http://www.angelfire.com/ga2/PhillipsLegion/rich. html)

Hopewell, Lynn. "The Bravest of the Brave." (http://www.blackhorsecavalry.org/)

Langhorne, Jacob Kent. Letters. Civil War Collection. Virginia Military Institute Library, Lexington. (http://www.vmi.edu/archives/Manuscripts/ms361.html)

Leon, Louis. *Diary of a Tar Heel Confederate Soldier.* Charlotte, NC: Stone, 1913. Documenting the American South Collection, Academic Affairs Library, University of North Carolina, Chapel Hill. (http://docsouth.unc.edu/leon/menu.html)

Lester, W. W. and Wm. J. Bromwell, eds. *A Digest of the Military and Naval Laws of the Confederate States, from the Commencement of the Provisional Congress to the End of the First Congress Under the First Constitution.* Columbia, S.C.: Evans and Cogswell, 1864. Documenting the American South Collection, Academic Affairs Library, University of North Carolina, Chapel Hill. (http://docsouth.unc.edu/digest/menu.html)

Memoir of Captain Samuel Brown Coyner. "Valley of the Shadow: Two Communities in the American Civil War." Virginia Center for Digital History, University of Virginia, Charlottesville. (http://valley.vcdh.virginia.edu/personal/coyner.html)

Message from the Execttive [sic] *of the Commonwealth, with Accompanying Documents, Showing the Military and Naval Preparations for the Defense of the State of Virginia, &c. &c.* Richmond, VA, June 17, 1861. Documenting the American South Collection, Academic Affairs Library, University of North Carolina, Chapel Hill. (http://docsouth.unc.edu/message/menu.html)

National Register of Historic Places. (http://www.nationalregisterofhistoricplaces.com/welcome. html)

Paxton, Elisha Franklin. "Memoir and Memorials: Elisha Franklin Paxton, Brigadier-General, C.S.A.; Composed of his Letters from Camp and Field While an Officer in the Confederate Army, with an Introductory and Connecting Narrative Collected and Arranged by his Son, John Gallatin Paxton." Documenting the American South Collection, Academic Affairs Library, University of North Carolina, Chapel Hill, 1998. (http://docsouth.unc.edu/paxton/menu.html)

Potter, Samuel M. Letters. "Valley of the Shadow: Two Communities in the American Civil War." Virginia Center for Digital History, University of Virginia, Charlottesville. (http://valley.vcdh.virginia.edu/personalpapers/documents/franklin/p2potterletters.html)

Royall, William L. *Some Reminiscences.* New York: Neale, 1909. Documenting the American South Collection, Academic Affairs Library, University of North Carolina, Chapel Hill. (http://docsouth. unc.edu/royall/menu.html)

Starr, Stephen Z. "Cavalry Tactics in the American Civil War." Cincinnati Civil War Roundtable, 1997. (http://www.mmcwrt.org/2002/default0207.htm)

Stubbs, Mary Lee and Stanley Russell Connor. *Armor-Cavalry Part 1: Regular Army and Army Reserve.* Office of the Chief of Military History, U.S. Army, Washington, D.C.: 1969. (http://www.army.mil/cmh-pg/books/Lineage/arcav/arcav.htm)

Swayze, J. C. *Hill & Swayze's Confederate States Rail-road & Steam-boat Guide, Containing the Time-Tables, Fares, Connections and Distances on all the Rail-roads of the Confederate States; also, the Connecting Lines of Rail-roads, Steam-boats and Stages. And Will Be Accompanied by a Complete Guide to the Principal Hotels, with a Large Variety of Valuable Information, Collected, Compiled, and Arranged by J. C. Swayze.* Griffin, GA: Hill & Swayze, 1862. Documenting the American South Collection, Academic Affairs Library, University of North Carolina, Chapel Hill. (http://docsouth. unc.edu/imls/swayze/menu.html)

U.S. Army Center for Military History, "Medal of Honor Recipients." (http://www.army.mil/cmh-pg/moh1.htm).

U.S. Government, Works Project Administration. "Virginia Historical Inventory." Library of Virginia, Richmond. http://www.lva.lib.va.us/whatwehave/mab/vh.about.htm (tm) (Virginia Historical Inventory listings for Culpeper County are also available on microfilm in the Culpeper County Library.)

U.S. Naval Observatory (Solar and Lunar Data), Washington, D.C. (http://www.usno.navy.mil/)

Waddell, Joseph Addison. Diary, 1855–1865. "Valley of the Shadow: Two Communities in the American Civil War." Virginia Center for Digital History, University of Virginia, Charlottesville. (http://valley.vcdh.virginia.edu/personalpapers/collections/augusta/waddell.html)

Wainwright, R. P. Page. "First Regiment of Cavalry." In *Excerpts from the Army of the United States: Historical Sketches of Staff and Line with Portraits of Generals-in-Chief.* Edited by T. F. Rodenbough and William L. Haskin. New York: Maynard, Merrill, 1896. Extracted in U.S. Regulars Civil War Archives. (http://www.usregulars.com/library.htm)

Wright, Mrs. D. Giraud. *A Southern Girl in '61: The War-Time Memories of a Confederate Senator's Daughter.* New York: Doubleday, Page, 1905. Documenting the American South Collection, Academic Affairs Library, University of North Carolina, Chapel Hill. (http://docsouth.unc.edu/wright/ menu.html)

Yoder, Jonah. Diary. "Valley of the Shadow: Two Communities in the American Civil War." Virginia Center for Digital History, University of Virginia, Charlottesville. (http://etext.lib.virginia.edu/etcbin/toccer-valley?id=FD1013&tag=public&images=images/modeng/F&data=/texts/english/ civilwar/diaries&part=0)

Index

Adams, Charles Francis, Jr. Capt., U.S. 57, 58, 74, 96, 98, 101, 266n39, 277n124, 281n13, 286n1, 287n4, 289n47
Adams, John 66, 69
Afton (Bradford Farm) 40, 80, 81, 83, 89, 90, 93
Alabama 48, 58, 200, 291n65
Albemarle County 17, 33
Aldie 218, 225, 227, 230, 232, 233, 235, 245, 287n17, 295n52, 296n77
Alexander, A.J., Lt. Col., U.S. 181
Alexandria 66, 94, 199
Allen, A.S., C.S. 290n29
Allen, David, Lt., C.S. 290n29
Allen, R.O., Lt., C.S. 114, 115, 116, 163, 216, 284n30, 290n29
Allen, Samuel, Maj., U.S. 69, 70
Alsop, Hugh 63
Amelia County 240
American & Commercial Advertiser 210
Ames, Adelbert, Brig. Gen., U.S.: early career 101–102, 103, 104, 108, 125, 181, 183, 195; later life 223–224, 256, 262, 282n46; *see also* Ames' Brigade
Amhurst 45
Amissville 11, 42, 86, 264
Anderson, Capt., C.S. 301n31
Andrew, John A. 277n124
Andrews, S. Jay, Capt., C.S. 292n17
Annals of the War 249
Annapolis, MD 64, 74, 234
Antietam, MD (including Battle of and Campaign) 68, 70, 72, 65, 67, 230, 234, 271n23
Appleton (Thompson Farm) 182, 187, 188, 189, 292n16
Appomattox 219, 239, 244, 245, 275n67
Aquia Landing 5, 101, 281n7
Arab (British ship) 70
Arkansas 226, 230
Arlington (Lee/Custis Home) 65

Arlington National Cemetery 233, 252
Artillery: Blakley rifled gun 45, 253, 289n1; fuses, problems with 293n24; guns available to Cavalry Corps and Stuart Horse Artillery 253, 300n1; type projectiles fired by Union batteries 205, 288n41, 289n1; Whitworth rifled gun 253
Ashby, Charles, Dr. 151, 249, 289n44
Ashby, Turner, Brig. Gen., C.S. 28, 48, 49, 50, 51, 245
Ashby House 201, 249, 295n16
Ashby's Gap 51
Ashland (including Camp of Cavalry Instruction) 17, 34, 41, 51, 242, 272n65, 277n108
Atlanta Constitution 299n111
Atzerodt, George 231
Auburn (Botts Farm) 40, 84–85, 88, 89, 91, 93, 176, 198, 246, 270n12, 279n22
Augusta, GA 242, 245
Augusta, ME 69, 70
Austria 73
Austrian Army 281n3
Austro-Prussian War 248
Averell, William W., Brig. Gen., U.S.: at Chancellorsville and relief of 55–56, 58, 72, 74, 75, 76, 78, 216, 230; at Kelly's Ford 11–13, 266–267n39; later life 274n5

Babbitt, Charles, Lt. Col., U.S. 59
Baker, Eugene, Bvt. Maj., U.S. 262
Baker, Laurence S., Col., C.S.: early career 47, 272n58, 49; later life 242, 260, 264, 302n47; *see also* 1st North Carolina Cavalry Regiment
Ball, Dulaney M., Capt., C.S. 21, 22, 268n5
Ball, Mottrom M., Capt., C.S. 268n5

Ball, William B., Col., C.S. 43, 271n37, 302n8
Ball's Bluff 53
Baltimore and Ohio Railroad 50, 52
Baltimore, MD 2, 71, 94, 209, 231
Banks, Nathaniel, Maj. Gen., U.S. 59, 70, 71
Banks' Ford 97
Barbour, Jack 288n28
Barbour, James S. 145, 176, 285n40, 291n68
Barbour House *see* Beauregard
Barringer, Rufus, Capt., C.S. 272n58
Barwell, Billy 80
Bayard, George D., Brig. Gen., U.S. 71, 270n5, 277n105
Beale, G.W., Lt., C.S. 266n30
Beale, Richard L.T., Col., C.S.: early career 44, 187, 188, 189; later life 241, 260, 266n30, 297n8, 302n40; *see also* 9th Virginia Cavalry Regiment
Bealeton 97, 98, 101, 103, 104, 106, 108, 282n22, n23, 292n8
Beardsley, John, Col., U.S. 60, 274n37
Beardsley, William E., Maj., U.S. 63, 232, 255; *see also* 6th New York Cavalry Regiment
Beaufort, SC 301n16
Beauregard (Barbour House) 4, 172, 173, 175, 176, 281n87, 289n8, 290n3; how named 291n68
Beauregard, P.G.T, Gen., C.S. 93, 291n68
Beck, Elias, surgeon, U.S. 57, 285n33
Beckham, Coleman 176
Beckham, James A. 40, 270n12
Beckham, Robert F., Maj., C.S.: early career 86, 93, 120, 129, 132, 157, 175, 178, 216, 261; later life 250, 264, 295n40; *see also* Stuart Horse Artillery Battalion

317

Index

Bedford (Liberty) 245, 246
Beecher's Island, CO 285n36
"Beefsteak Raid" 239
Bell, _____, Capt., U.S. 269n53
Bell Isle 202
Berlin, Germany 76, 249
Bernstein, _____ 69
Berry Hill 271n38
Berryville 297n4
Bertie County, NC 45
Bethlehem, PA 231
Beveridge, John, Maj., U.S. 274n29
Beverley, Carter 122, 283n1
Beverly Ford 1, 4, 93, 100, 104, 107, 108, 110–111, 114, 122, 123, 126, 132, 139, 182, 192, 193, 220, 230, 245, 247, 250, 283n1, 284n17, 292n8, 296n61, 302n3
Beverly Ford Road: plat showing route of 109, 112, 117, 119, 120, 121, 122, 125, 126, 127, 164, 167, 177, 183, 196, 250, 295n37
Big Bethel, Battle of 67
Billings, Henry, Capt., C.S. 37–38
Birney, David, Maj. Gen., U.S. 103
Black, John L., Col., C.S.: early career 47, 272n55, 123, 124, 125, 139, 166, 171, 178; later life 246, 260, 264; see also 1st South Carolina Cavalry Regiment
Black, Mary Peay (Mrs. John L. Black) 272n55
Black, Virginia 246, 299n133
Blackford, Charles Minor, Capt., C.S. 37, 213, 265n3, 270n70
Blackford, William W., Capt., C.S. 29, 166, 175, 205, *206*, 208, 269n34; early career 273n77, 277n25
Blacksburg, SC 246
Blackwater River, NC 49
Bladensburg, MD 65
Blakley rifled gun 45, 253, 289n1
Blasingame, John G., Capt., C.S. 292n17
Bloody Angle 234; see also Spotsylvania
Blue Ridge Mountains 39, 50, 51, 54, 140, 143, 209, 271n25, 297n4
Bolling Air Force Base 269n50; see also Giesboro
Borcke, Caroline Virginia Magdalene 249
Borcke, Heros von, Maj., C.S. 24, 40 82, 83, 92 126, 127, 165, 202; later life 248, 249, 258, 270n15, 300n147
Boston, MA 74, 75, 231, 233
Botts Farm see Auburn
Botts, John Minor 85, 89, 90, 246, 270n12, 280n59, n62, n63
Bowen, William, Sr. 108
Bowenville see Rappahannock Station
Bradford, Samuel 40
Bradford Farm see Afton
Brady, Mathew 248
Bragg, Braxton, Gen., C.S. 47
Brandy House (Herring's Tavern) 39

Brandy Station (Brandy, Crossroads) 1, 2, 3, 4, 39, 40, 80, 81, 85, 93, 106, 107, 114, 115, 119, 123, 124, 129, 132, 135, 138, 139, 140, 148, 151, 152, 153, 154, 155, 156, 157, 158, 162, 166, 167, 168, 171, 175, 176, 177, 178, 179, 181, 192, 195, 196, 197, 199, 201, 203, 205, 207, 208, 209, 210, 212, 213, 214, 218, 219, 223, 224, 226, 228, 230, 231, 233, 234, 235, 239, 240, 244, 245, 246, 247, 248, 249, 250, 252, 253, 262, 263, 264, 270n4, 270n13, 274n29, 281n87, 285n57, 286n59, n92, 287n14, 288n36, 289n47, n4, 291n53, n59, n68, 292n80, n11, 293n25, 294n8, n12, 295n19, n27, n33, n43, n49, 296n60, n77, 300n160, n1, 302n6
Brandy Station Foundation 294n8
Brawner Farm 291n63; see also Second Manassas
Breathed, James, Capt., C.S. 261; see also Brethead's Battery
Breckinridge, John C., Maj. Gen., C.S. 251
Brennan, Peter, Pvt., U.S. 76
Brisbin, James S., Capt., U.S. 301n14
Bristoe Campaign 225, 246, 247
Britain 183, 248; see also Great Britain
Broderick, Virgil, Lt. Col., U.S. 71, 164, 165, 257, 290n32, 294n12; see also 1st New Jersey Cavalry Regiment
Brooke, St. George T., Pvt., C.S. 195
Brooklyn Bridge 289n3
Brooks' Station 101
Brown, John 21, 33, 53
Buckingham County 245, 300n160
"Buckland Races" 225
Buffalo, NY 69
"Buffalo Soldiers" 228
Buford, John, Brig. Gen., U.S. 57; early career 58, 61, 63, 64, 90, 97, 98, 100, 101, 106, 107, 108, 109, 116, 117, 119, 121, 122, 123, 125, 126, 127, 132, 133, 135, 139, 156, 180, 181, 183, 185, 186, 187, 189, 191, 192, 193, 195, 196, 204, 207, 208, 220; later life 222–223, 230, 245, 255, 274n14, 282n23, n24, n37, 283n4, 286n78, n79, 289n4, 292n8, n9, 293n39, 294n6; see also 1st Cavalry Division
Bunker Hill 226
Bureau of Military Information 6, 97, 265n7
Burgess Mill 239
Burke (Burke Station) 94, 239
Burmese government 224
Burnham, Hiram, Col., U.S. 233–234, 257
Burnside, Ambrose, Maj. Gen., U.S. 5, 6, 26, 233, 265n4
Burnside Carbine 26
Butler, Benjamin, Maj. Gen., U.S. 223, 298n90

Butler, Blanche (Mrs. Adelbert Ames) 223, 297n14
Butler, Matthew Calbraith., Col., C.S.: early career 47, 272n57, 49, 139, 140, 141, 143, 144, 145, 148, 150, 151, 155, 204, 211, 225, 234; later life 242–243, 260, 287n14, n19, n24, n26, 288n28, n30, n36, n41, n43, 289n45, 299n114, 301n46; see also 2nd South Carolina Cavalry Regiment
Butterfield, Daniel, Maj. Gen., U.S. 56, 57, 95, 103, 104, 181, 229, 264n5

Ca Ira (Hubard Farm) 28, 268n28
Cadiz, Spain 226
Cadwalader, Charles E., Capt., U.S. 284n18
Calcutta, India 224
Caldwell, John C., Brig. Gen., U.S. 103
Caldwell, Lycurgus 296n78
Caldwell, Susan 213, 296n78
California 49, 63, 230
Calverton see Warrenton Junction
Cambridge, MA 11
Camden County, SC 49, 246
Camp Farley 198
Camp Laura 266n26
Camp of Cavalry Instruction see Ashland
Camp Scott, NY 61
Campbell, David, Col., U.S. 77
Canada 232
Canby, Edward, Col., U.S. 64
Canfield, Charles, Capt., U.S. 262
Cape May, NJ 233
Carlisle, PA 48
Carrico's Mill 124, 155, 287n14, n16, 302n46
Carruthers, Pvt., U.S. 285n37
Carter, John, Lt., C.S. 153, 155, 156, 157, 289n1
Carter, Scott, Col., U.S. 59, 60
Carter, William 182, 292n15
Carter, William R., Lt. Col., C.S. 266n24
Cartersville, GA 242
Caskie, Mr and Mrs. James 198
Castine, MA 223
Catlett's Station (Catlett, Catlett's) 97, 98, 101, 107, 133, 215, 254, 266n34, 292n8, 300n3
Cavalry Bureau, Washington, DC 230
Cedar Creek, Battle of 3
Cedar Mountain, Battle of 70, 71
Cedar Run 56, 57
Cemetery Ridge, PA 222; see also Gettysburg
Central America 273n75
Central Railroad of Georgia 246
Centreville 226
Cesnola, Luigi P. di, Col., U.S.: early career 73, 136, 219; later life 226–228, 256, 277n110, n115; perhaps not present during battle 287n8, 297n32

Chain Bridge (over the Potomac at Washington) 94
Chamberlain, Joshua, Maj. Gen., U.S. 63, 275n49
Chambersburg Turnpike 222
Chambliss, John R., Col., C.S.: death of 241, 259, 260, 264, 281n84; early career 45, 48, 191, 203, 239; *see also* 13th Virginia Cavalry Regiment
Chancellorsville (Battle of and Campaign) 17–19, 39, 41, 42, 45, 49, 55, 57, 63, 75, 78, 80, 102, 153, 215, 266n20, 267n52, 282n29, 291n65
Chapman, George H. Col., U.S. 60; later life 274n32
Charles I, King of England 20
Charles City 231
Charles City Road 241
Charleston Mercury 211, 212
Charleston, SC 66, 250
Charlestown, WV 251
Charlotte County 271n38
Charlottesville 51, 81, 140, 241, 271n28, 280n63, 290n37, 295n27
Cheat River, WV 52
Cherokee Indians 243
Chesapeake & Ohio Canal 251
Chesapeake & Ohio Railroad 241
Chesapeake Bay 143
Chesnut, James, Col., C.S. 198, 200, 294n4
Chesnut, John, Capt., C.S. 198, 200, 288n42
Chesnut, Mary 278n12, 288n42, 294n4
Chestnut Forks 176
Chew, Roger P., Capt., C.S. 153, 261; *see also* Chew's Battery
Chicago, IL 72, 76, 231, 240
Childs, James, Col., U.S. 77
Chile 225
Christ Church, Brandy Station 285n57
Christianburg 16
Churchill, Winston: comment on cavalry tactics 34., 276n92
Cilley, Jonathan P., Capt., U.S. 69
Citizen's Cemetery *see* Culpeper Citizen's Cemetery
City Point 251
Clapsaddle, Byrd, Capt./Pvt., C.S. 31
Clark, Alpheus, Maj., U.S. 59, 117, 126, 220; death of 230, 255; *see also* 8th Illinois Cavalry Regiment
Clark, Moses, Lt., U.S. 156, 157, 158, 159, 161, 163, 165, 289n10, 295n42
Clark County 53
Clendinin, David, Lt. Col., U.S. 274n29
Cleveland, Grover, Pres. 239, 242
Cobb, Thomas, Brig, Gen., C.S. 47, 272n59
Cold Harbor 247
Coles, Isaac, Lt., C.S. 115, 250, 284n29, 301n31, 301n34
Cole's Hill 141

Collins, Charles, R., Maj., C.S.: death of 271n37; early career 43–44, 271n35, 260, 264
Colorado 229
Colt rifle and revolver 26, 201
Columbia, South Carolina 200, 235, 243
Columbus, KY 276n86
Comanche Indians 11
Comey, Henry N, Capt., U.S. 283n9
Commodore Perry (U.S. ship) 49
Confederate Cavalry: blacksmith and farrier services 31–32; camp layout and routine 79–80; characteristics of recruits 20–21; commonmedical problems 37; horse hospital established 33; organizing regiments 26–27; personnel shortages 35–36; providing horses for 29–31; raising companies 21–22; selecting officers for 27–28; slaves and servants with 28–29; training and drill manuals 33–35; uniforms 22–25; weapons 25–27
Confederate Cemetery, Culpeper *see* Culpeper Confederate Cemetery
Confederate Congress 241, 278n19
Confederate military organizations: *1st Battalion, South Carolina Cavalry* 47; *1st North Carolina Cavalry Regiment* 46; (organization of) 47, 139, 171, 178, 242; (strength and casualties) 260, 302n47, 264, 268n30, 272n58; *1st South Carolina Cavalry Regiment* 46; (organization of) 47, 123, 138, 139, 166, 169, 171, 173, 178, 212, 246; (strength and casualties) 260, 264, 286n60, 291n53, 293n39; *1st Virginia Cavalry Regiment* 11, 22, 28, 30; (organization of) 42–43, 50, 51, 86, 193, 245; (strength and casualties) 260, 302n49, 273n77; *2nd Military District, South Carolina* 240; *2nd North Carolina Cavalry Regiment (Colonel Spruill's Cavalry)* 8, 26; (organization of) 45, 124, 185, 189, 191, 199, 214, 243, 258; (strength and casualties) 259, 264, 268n20, 268n30, 302n8; *2nd South Carolina Cavalry Regiment* 46; (organization of) 47, 79, 124, 139, 140, 143, 144, 145, 152, 155, 177, 204, 207, 243, 243; (strength and casualties) 260, 302n46, 288n30, n32, n36, 289n49, 295n43; *2nd Virginia Cavalry Regiment* 26, 28, 32, 36; (organization of) 41, 80, 93, 193, 195, 201, 203, 216, 245; (strength and casualties) 260, 266n25, 295n19; *3rd North Carolina Cavalry Regiment* 49; *3rd Virginia Cavalry Regiment* 28, 29, 31, 34; (organization of) 41–42, 81, 98, 153, 193, 225, 246; (strength and

casualties) 260, 266n4; *4th Battalion, South Carolina Cavalry* 47; *4th North Carolina Cavalry Regiment* (organization of) 49, 246; (strength and casualties) 260; *4th Virginia Cavalry Regiment* 27, 28; (organization of) 43, 48, 54, 86, 93, 139, 143, 144, 145, 148, 152, 177, 191, 204, 215, 241, 258; (strength and casualties) 260, 302n51, 287n15, 288n30, n32, 289n12, 300n160; *5th North Carolina Cavalry Regiment* (organization of) 49, 139, 216, 245; (strength and casualties) 260; *5th Virginia Cavalry Regiment* 13, 41; (organization of) 42, 45, 213; (strength and casualties) 260, 264, 271n28, 278n13; *5th Virginia Infantry Regiment* 53; *6th Virginia Cavalry Regiment* 20, 27, 28, 34, 36, 38, 48, 50; (organization of) 51–53, 88, 92, 111, 114, 115, 117, 121, 122, 123, 124, 132, 163, 164, 165, 202, 204, 216, 247, 250; (strength and casualties) 259, 301n34, 272n65, 273n93, 279n23, 280n59, n75, 284n26, 285n30, 290n29, n34, 299n136; *7th Virginia Cavalry Regiment* 28, 36; (organization of) 50–51, 53, 54, 120, 121, 123, 132, 177, 199, 204, 216, 245; (strength and casualties) 259, 301n35, 270n5, 274n22, 280n63; *8th Virginia Cavalry Regiment* 281n81; *9th Georgia Cavalry Regiment* 272n60 (*see also* Cobb's Legion); *9th Virginia Cavalry Regiment* 30, 31; (organization of) 44, 185, 187, 188, 189, 193, 195, 203, 241; (strength and casualties) 260, 302n40, 266n30, 273n1, 278n13, 297n8; *10th Virginia Cavalry Regiment* 2, 28; (organization of) 44, 189, 191, 245; (strength and casualties) 260, 321n41, 264, 271n42, 293n22; *11th Virginia Cavalry Regiment* 28, 50; (organization of) 54, 123, 176, 177, 241; (strength and casualties) 259, 301n36, 264, 295n42; *12th Virginia Cavalry Regiment* 22, 28, 36, 37, 38, 50; (organization of) 53, 54, 123, 127, 128, 157, 158, 161, 162, 163, 165, 166, 199, 202, 250; (strength and casualties) 259, n31, n37, 294n11, 301, 302n8; *13th Virginia Cavalry Regiment* 28; (organization of) 45, 191, 241; (strength and casualties) 260, 264, 293n34; *14th Virginia Cavalry Regiment* 27, 302n8; *15th Virginia Cavalry Regiment* (organization of) 43–44, 86, 260, 264, 302n8; *18th North Carolina Infantry Regiment* 18; *18th Virginia Cavalry Regiment* 20, 31, 267n3; *20th*

North Carolina Infantry Regiment 45; *30th Virginia Mounted Infantry Regiment* 41; *35th Battalion, Virginia Cavalry (White's Battalion, the "Comanches")* 50; (organization of) 53–54, 123, 128, 129, 157, 158, 161, 166, 246; (strength and casualties) 259, 301n38, 286n84, 290n34, 301n31; *39th Battalion, Virginia Cavalry* 166; *41st Virginia Infantry Regiment* 45; *Army of Northern Virginia* 15, 16, 19, 39, 46, 48, 49, 78, 119, 210, 235, 239; (average strength of cavalry regiments) 265n18, 302n8; *Army of East Tennessee* 54; *Army of Tennessee* 279n29; *Ashby's Cavalry* 54 (see also 7th Virginia Cavalry Regiment); *Baylor Light Horse (Company B, 12th Virginia Cavalry)* 22, 161; *Black Horse Troop (Company H, 4th Virginia Cavalry)* 27, 43, 88, 108, 215; (how named) 271n31; *Brandy Rifles (Company E, 13th Virginia Infantry)* 199, 289n44; *Breathed's Battery* 186, 188, 195, 203; (casualties) 261, 285n42; *Cabarrus Rangers (Company F, 1st North Carolina Cavalry)* 272n58; *Cavalry Corps, Army of Northern Virginia* 239, 240, 248; *Cavalry Division, Army of Northern Virginia (Stuart's Division)* 2, 81, 85, 89, 91, 133, 135, 138, 166, 176, 187, 201, 209, 213, 215, 245, 253; (strength and casualties) 258–261, 301n33, 263, 264, 277n27, 295n49, 296n66, 300n2; *Chambliss' Brigade* 245; *Chew's Company/Battery* 51, 86, 87, 91, 119, 153; (casualties) 261, 278n19, 282n19, 289n1; *Clarke County Cavalry (Company D, 6th Virginia Cavalry)* 27; *Cobb's Legion (Cobb's Legion Cavalry, 9th Georgia Cavalry)* 2, 46; (organization of) 47–48, 80, 124, 139, 169, 170, 171, 173, 176, 178, 232; (strength and casualties) 260, 302n44, 264, 301n31; *Cumberland Light Dragoons (Company G, 3rd Virginia Cavalry)* 22; *Daniels' Brigade* 175, 176; *Edgefield Hussars (I Company, 2nd South Carolina Cavalry)* 47; *Ewell's Corps (II Corps)* 175, 209, 280n67; *Fitzhugh Lee's Brigade* (composition of) 41–43, 93, 98, 126, 143, 193, 244; (strength and casualties) 260, 285n42, 295n33, 302n48, n50; *Fitzhugh Lee's Division* 241, 244; *Georgia Hussars (Company E, 6th Virginia Cavalry, Company F, Jeff Davis Legion)* 48, 52, 246, 272n65; *Gibson's Company (Company A, 6th Virginia Cavalry, Loudoun Dragoons)* 119; *Governor's House Guard (Company A, Phillips Legion)* 22; *Griffin's Battery* 282n19; *Halifax Troop (Company G, 6th Virginia Cavalry)* 20; *Hampton's Brigade (including Hampton's Legion)* (composition of) 45–48, 93, 129, 168, 178, 242; (strength and casualties) 260, 290n44; *Hanover Light Dragoons (Company G, 4th Virginia)* 43; *Hart's Battery* 119, 121, 176; (casualties) 261; *Hill's Corps (III Corps)* 91; *Hood's Brigade* 278n19; *Hood's Division* 89, 273n85, 279n35; *Imboden's Command* 50, 273n80; *Jackson's Battery* 282n19; *Jackson's Corps* 18, 267n58, 267n64; *Jeff Davis Legion* 46; (organization of) 48, 52, 124, 139, 171, 178, 246; (strength and casualties) 260, 302n45, 272n63; *Jenkins' Brigade* 54, 302n8; *Jones' Brigade (Laurel Brigade)* (composition of) 49–54, 91, 93, 100, 120, 156, 157, 170, 176, 212, 213, 258; (strength and casualties) 259, 280n75; *Kershaw's Brigade* 214; *Lee's Light Horse (Company C, 9th Virginia)* 44; *Little Fork Rangers (Company D, 4th Virginia Cavalry)* 21, 23, 26, 30, 43, 293n40; *Longstreet's Corps (I Corps)* 209, 213, 214, 280n67; *Loudoun Light Horse (Company H, 1st Virginia Cavalry)* 22; *Louisiana Tigers* 291n68; *Maryland Exiles (Company B, 35th Battalion Virginia Cavalry)* 22; *McClanahan's Battery* 282n19; *McClaws' Division* 176, 292n8; *McGregor's Battery* 119, 157, 170, 176; (casualties) 261; *Mebane's Company (Company C, 5th Virginia Cavalry)* 22; *Moorman's Battery* 119, 148, 150, 201; (casualties) 261; *Mosby's Battalion (43rd Battalion, Virginia Cavalry, Partisan Rangers)* 215; *Newtown Light Dragoons (Company A, 1st Virginia Cavalry)* 22, 42; *O'Neal's Brigade* 175, 176; *Phillips' Legion (Phillips Legion Cavalry)* (organization of) 46, 260, 272n52, 272n54, 272n60; *Pittsylvania Dragoons (Company E, 6th Virginia Cavalry)* 52, 284n29; *Prince William Cavalry (Company A, 4th Virginia Cavalry)* 22; *Richmond Howitzers* 82; *River Rangers (Company K, 1st Virginia Cavalry)* 22; *Robertson's Brigade* (composition of) 48–49, 134, 138, 139, 216, 242; (strength and casualties) 260, 272n68, 272n69; *Rodes' Division* 292n80; *Rooney Lee's Brigade* (composition of) 43–45, 177, 183, 185, 192, 193, 195, 241, 242, 258; (strength and casualties) 260, 285n42, 293n39; *Stonewall Brigade* 53, 266n20; *Stuart Horse Artillery Battalion (Beckham's Battalion)* 13, 86, 88, 119, 121, 123, 124, 126, 127, 128, 129, 139, 201, 204, 208, 209, 216, 253, 300n1; (strength and casualties) 261, 264, 295n48; *Texas Irregulars* 59; *University Volunteers (Company G, 59th Virginia Infantry)* 267n3; *Valley District* 242; *Washington Mounted Rifles (Company D, 1st Virginia Cavalry)* 273n77; *White's Rebels (Company A, 35th Battalion Virginia Cavalry)* 22, 53; *Wildcat Company (Company A, 11th Virginia Cavalry)* 22; *Wise Legion* 44; *Wise Troop (B Company, 2nd Virginia Cavalry, Steptoe's Company)* 22, 37, 41, 80

Congdon, John, Pvt., U.S. 69
Conger, Seymore, B., Capt., U.S. 61; death of 230, 255; see also 3rd West Virginia Cavalry Regiment
Congressional Cemetery, Washington, DC 222, 234
Connecticut 68
Cooke, Flora see Stuart, Flora Cooke
Cooke, John Esten, Capt., C.S. 249, 240, 295n20
Cooke, Phillip St. George, Brig. Gen., U.S. 48, 64, 66, 159, 295n20
Cooke's Cavalry Tactics 86
Cooper, Samuel, Gen., C.S. 33, 213
Cooper House 175
Cooper's Volunteer Manual 33, 86
Corbin, William, Capt., C.S. 233
Corson, William, Pvt., C.S. 31
Courtland (Winstonhome) 271n26
Cox, C., Pvt., C.S. 302n47
Cram, George C., Capt., U.S. 65, 229; later life 230, 255; see also 6th U.S. Cavalry Regiment
Craun, Samuel, Pvt. C.S. 35
Crews, Ephriam, Pvt., C.S. 20
Crimea (Crimean War) 73, 277n110
Critcher, John R., Lt. Col., C.S. 43, 271n37
Crockett-Kent Graveyard 201
Crooks, Samuel, Col., U.S. 59, 274n22
Cross, Edward E., Col., U.S. 234, 257; see also 5th New Hampshire Infantry Regiment
Cross Keys 75
Crossroads 39; see also Brandy Station
Cub Run 43
Cuba 239, 243, 263, 298n52
Cullum, George W., Brig. Gen., U.S. 302n1
Culpeper, Lord Thomas 39, 270n2
Culpeper Citizen's Cemetery (Fairview) 249, 294n12

Index

Culpeper Confederate Cemetery 294n12
Culpeper County 1, 21, 23, 39, 40, 41, 43, 46, 49, 50, 54, 55, 56, 74, 79, 80, 81, 86, 91, 92, 94, 95, 97, 98, 99, 100, 101, 103, 104, 106, 107, 119, 120, 140, 182, 209, 210, 212, 213, 214, 219, 220, 247, 258, 266n34, 270n1, 270n8, 270n12, 270n13, 278n1, n5, 279n23, 280n67, n68, 283n1, 294n1
Culpeper County Museum 270n6
Culpeper Courthouse 1, 11, 13, 15, 39, 40, 42, 79, 80, 81, 82, 83, 85, 87, 97, 100, 107, 126, 134, 135, 136, 137, 138, 140, 151, 152, 153, 175, 177, 178, 192, 193, 198, 200, 207, 208, 251, 245, 267n50, 269n38, 270n6, 270n12, 278n17, n19, 279n24, 283n51, 291n66, 292n80, 294n12, 300n152.
Culpeper National Cemetery 200, 294n3, n12
Culpeper Observer 278n19
Culp's Hill 222, 234
Cumberland County 41, 249, 268n28
Cumberland, MD 273n82
Cummins, Francis M., Lt. Col., U.S. 234, 256; *see also* 124th New York Infantry Regiment
Cunningham, Richard H. 122, 181, 182
Cunningham Farm *see* Elkwood
Curtis, Greely S., Lt. Col., U.S. 75, 231, 256; *see also* 1st Massachusetts Cavalry Regiment
Custer, Elizabeth 222
Custer, George A., Bvt. Capt., U.S. 3, 96, 109, 117, 220, 221; later life and Elizabeth's comments on 222, 224, 228, 262, 284n16, 285n35, 297n9, 302n1
Cutler, Henry C., Lt., U.S. 112, 114, 284n24
Cyprus 227

Dabney, Chiswell, Lt., C.S. 123, 166, 290n40
Dahlgren, John, Adm., U.S. 104
Dahlgren, Ulrich, Capt., U.S. 104, 111, 127, 222, 297n8
Dahlgren Raid 221, 222, 223, 225, 297n8
Daily Virginian 211
Daniel, Junius, Brig. Gen., C.S. 175, 176, 291n65
Danville 52, 226, 246
Davies, Henry, E., Lt. Col., U.S. 68, 169, 230, 231, 257, 276n86, 291n53, n70; *see also* 2nd New York Cavalry Regiment
Davies, J. Mansfield, Col., U.S. 68
Davies, Thomas A., Brig. Gen., U.S. 276n86
Davis, Bathurst M., Pvt., C.S. 271n42
Davis, Benjamin F. "Grimes," Col., U.S. 16; death of 115–116, 163, 200, 207, 214, 232, 255, 262, 267n50, 281n30, 282n22, 285n33, 296n81, 297n9, 301n10; early career 58, 59, 61, 71, 72, 108, 112, 114, *see also* 1st Brigade, 1st Cavalry Division
Davis, Hasbrouck, Lt. Col., U.S. 72, 277n108, 280n35, 296n81
Davis, James Lucius, Col., C.S. 2, 33; early career 44, 189; later life 245, 260, 264, 269n53, 299n126; *see also* 10th Virginia Cavalry Regiment
Davis, James Lucius, Jr., Pvt., C.S. 245, 271n42
Davis, Jefferson 2, 27, 46, 58, 82, 92, 198, 214, 215, 218, 222, 240, 272n51, 277n108, 278n16
Davis, Lewellyn Catesby, Pvt., C.S. 245, 271n42
Davis, Matthew, Col., C.S. 45
Davis, Richard, Chaplain, C.S. 52, 280n75
Davis, Sidney, Pvt., U.S. 65
Deane, Francis, Pvt., C.S. 157, 289n12
Deems, James M., Lt. Col., U.S. 2; early career 71, 162; later life 231, 257; *see also* 1st Maryland Cavalry Regiment
Deep Bottom 226
Delony, William G., Maj., C.S. 80, 81, 278n6, 302n44
Devil's Jump 143, 287n21; *see also* Hansbrough Ridge
Devin, Thomas, C., Col., U.S.: early career 61–62, 108, 117, 119, 120, 122, 180, 192; later life 223, 255, 297n11; *see also* 2nd Brigade, 1st Cavalry Division
Dewees, Thomas, Lt., U.S. 189, 293n24
Dickel, Christian, Col., U.S. 73
Dillon, Edward, Col., C.S. 247
Doggett, _____ 287n21
Doggett House (Dogget's) 143, 144, 204, 288n28
Dornin, Anthony, Cpl., C.S. 201
Doster, William E., Lt. Col., U.S.: early career 77; later life 231, 256; *see also* 4th Pennsylvania Cavalry Regiment
Douty, Calvin S., Col., U.S.: death of 230, 233, 257, 291n61; early career 70, 171, 173, 175; *see also* 1st Maine Cavalry Regiment
Dover, ME 173
Drake, James H., Col., C.S.: death of 245, 260; early career 42–43; *see also* 1st Virginia Cavalry Regiment
Duffié, Alfred N., Brig. Gen., U.S.: early career 68, 72–73, 72, 75, 76, 90, 97, 100, 101, 106, 107, 108, 133, 135, 137, 139, 140, 141, 143, 144, 145, 148, 150, 151, 152, 155, 166, 177, 178, 192, 195, 196, 203, 205, 207, 216, 276n85; later life 226–226, 227, 256, 277n109, 286n1, 287n6, n8, n16, n17, n20, 288n32, 289n47, n48, 291n65, 295n43, 297n27, 301n19; *see also* 1st Rhode Island Cavalry Regiment and 2nd Cavalry Division
Dulaney, John Peyton 280n63
Dulaney, Richard, Col., C.S. 28; early career 51, 245, 280n63
Dumfries 97
Dunlap, John, 1st Sgt, U.S. 301n18

Early, Jubal, Maj. Gen., C.S. 81, 223, 226, 228, 241, 242, 244, 251, 271n25, 274n5
Edgefield, SC 243
Edmonston, Catherine Ann Devereaux 213, 214, 296n80
Edmonston, Patrick 296n80
Egypt (including Army of and Khedive of) 275n85, 281n81
Elder, Samuel S., Lt., U.S. 185, 255; *see also* E Battery, 4th U.S. Artillery
Elk River *see* Hazel River
Elkwood (Elk Wood, Cunningham Farm) 122, 126, 127 181, 182, 183, 285n56, 286n59, 292n12
Ellis, A. Van Horne, Col., U.S. 125; death of 233–234, 256; *see also* 124th New York Infantry Regiment
Ellis, Rudolph, Lt., U.S. 192, 293n37
Ellis' Ford 283n56
Ellsworth, ME 63., 287n16
Elmira, NY 69, 251, 271n35
Ely's Ford 55, 78, 104, 137, 143, 287n16
Emory, William H., Brig. Gen., U.S. 65, 275n66, 275n70
Enfield Rifle/Musket 26, 45, 124, 143, 171
England 26, 269n33, 296n53; *see also* Great Britain
English Channel 70
Esposito, Vincent 1
Essex County 8
Europe 228
Evans, Peter G., Col., C.S.: death of 245, 260; early career 49; *see also* 5th North Carolina Cavalry Regiment
Ewell, Richard, Lt. Gen., C.S. 175, 176, 291n63, n66, n69; *see also* Ewell's Corps

Fair Oaks 234
Fairfax County 21, 39, 94, 266.n26,
Fairfax Courthouse 62, 106
Fairfield, PA 218, 229, 245
Falmouth 12, 14, 97, 101
Farley *see* Wellford House
Farley, Henry Saxon, Capt., C.S. 289n44
Farley, William D., Capt., C.S. 83, 119, 139, 143, 144, 148; burial of 249, 294–295n16, 300n152, n153, 288n41, n43, 301n33; mortal wounding of 150–151, 201, 211, 213, 234, 248
Farmville 300n160

Farnsworth, Elon, Capt., U.S. 126, 181, 220, 224, 297n2
Farnsworth, John F., Brig. Gen., U.S. 59, 126, 220, 296n1, 297n2
Fauquier County 16, 23, 39, 43, 51, 81, 96, 98, 107, 133, 183, 251, 216, 220, 242, 254
Fauquier Sulphur Springs (White Sulphur, Sulphur Springs) 16, 98, 100, 101, 106, 282n25
Fayetteville, NC 225, 277n126
Ferebee, Dennis C., Col., C.S.: early career 49; later life 246, 260; *see also* 4th North Carolina Cavalry Regiment
Ferneyhough, George, Capt., C.S. 161, 162
Field, Charles, Brig. Gen., C.S. 34, 51, 272n65; later life 273n85
First Manassas (Battle of, Campaign) 11, 43, 45, 47, 53, 66, 93, 102, 244, 291n68, 294n12
Fisher's Hill 267n62, 274n5
Fitzhugh, Mrs _____ 151
Five Forks 220, 293n25
Fleetwood (Fleetwood Hill, Miller House, Miller House Hill) 1, 2, 4, 93, 119, 123, 124, 126, 138, 139, 148, 153, 155, 156, 157, 158, 159, 161, 162, 163, 164, 165, 166, 167, 168, 169, 170, 171, 173, 175, 176, 177, 178, 179, 181, 183, 187, 188, 192, 195, 198, 199, 204, 205, 207, 208, 209, 217, 230, 232, 233, 250, 241, 252, 289n1, n8, 290n3, n32, 291n72, 292n11, 293n39
Flint Hill 29n129
Flood, Martin L., Lt. Col., U.S.: later life 233, 256; *see also* 3rd Wisconsin Infantry Regiment
Florida 18, 224
Flournoy, Cabel, Maj., C.S.: board action regarding 52–53, 114, 115, 119, 120, 122, 123, 124, 132, 163, 216; early career 52; later career and death of 247, 259, 273n93, 295n37, 300n142, 301n34; *see also* 6th Virginia Cavalry Regiment
Flournoy, Henry, Pvt., C.S. 273n93
Flournoy, Thomas S., Col., C.S. 51, 52, 273n87, n93
Flynn, John, Capt., U.S. 233, 238
Foote, Benjamin F, Capt., U.S. 117, 285n37
Ford, Charles, Lt., C.S. 176
Forrest, Nathan B., Lt. Gen. C.S. 240
Forsyth, George, Capt., U.S. 117, 126, 220; later life 285n36
Fort Harrison 233
Fort Leavenworth, KS 7, 64, 274n23
Fort Lewis, WA 231
Fort Pulaski, GA 46
Fort Steilacoom, WA 66
Fortress Monroe 238, 241, 298n90
Fought, Joseph, Pvt., U.S. 117
France 33
Frederick County 42

Fredericksburg 5, 7, 15, 16, 18, 19, 39, 43, 46, 54, 56, 62, 70, 86, 90, 91, 97, 100, 102, 111, 139, 258, 264, 272n59, 277n105, 278n5, 280n67, n68
Fredericksburg Plank Road 139, 153, 177, 287n16
Freeman, Douglas S. 3, 235, 295n33
Fremont, John C., Maj. Gen., U.S. 75
French Revolution of 1848 70
Frye, William, Maj., U.S. 78, 232, 256; *see also* 16th Pennsylvania Cavalry Regiment
Frying Pan 266n26
Fuller, William D, Bvt. Capt., U.S. 257, 262; *see also* C Battery, 3rd U.S. Artillery
Funston, Oliver O. Jr, Lt. Col., C.S. 54

Gaines' Mill 3, 63, 66
Gamble, William, Col., U.S. 59; later life 274n29
Garber, Thomas, Sgt, C.S. 36, 270n64
Garfield, James, Brig. Gen., U.S. (later President) 225, 231, 275n67
Garibaldi, Giuseppe 70, 224
Gee House 114, 122, 124
Georgia 46, 47, 48, 225, 242
Germanna Ford 104, 137
Geronimo 263
Gettysburg National Military Park 242
Gettysburg, PA (including Battle of and Campaign) 1, 29, 69, 218, 220, 222, 223, 224, 225, 228, 229, 230, 231, 232, 233, 235, 239, 240, 242, 245, 247, 251, 258, 264, 275n58, 278n7, 282n22, 289n3, 290n37, 291n65, 295n41
Gibbs, Alfred, Brig. Gen., U.S. 59; later life 274n23
Gibson, Bruce, Capt., C.S. 111, 112, 114, 216, 284n20
Giesboro, DC 30, 224, 269n50, 297n19
Gilham, William 33, 269n54
Gilham's Manual 33
Gilmor, Harry, Maj., C.S. 267n40
Glazier, Willard, Capt., U.S. 276n83, 298n58
Gleason, Daniel, Lt., U.S. 98, 282n26
The Glebe (Wagner Farm) 199, 294n6
Gloucester County 97
Gloucester Point 56, 67, 72, 97, 101, 274n17, 282n35, 300n3
Goddard, John Col., U.S. 69
Goldsborough, Robert H., Lt., C.S. 41, 166; later life 250, 293n41, 301n31, n33
Goode, Thomas, Col., C.S. 42
Gordon, George A., Capt., U.S. 263
Gordonsville 15, 16, 45, 82, 92, 278n17, 295n23
Gorgas, Josiah, Col., C.S. 281n84

Graffiti House (John Stone House) 154, 154, 294n8, n11
Graham, W.A., Capt., C.S. 268n20
Graham, William M., Capt., U.S. 234, 256; *see also* K Battery, 1st U.S. Artillery
Grand Army of the Republic 2
Grant, Ulysses S., Lt. Gen., U.S. (later President) 218, 223, 224, 226, 228, 231, 268–269n33, 284n17
Graybill, Capt., C.S. 301n31
Great Britain 26, 183, 248, 269n33, 296n53
Great Fork 10, 39, 266n27
Green, Daniel S. 182
Green, John Shackelford, Lt. Col., C.S.: later life 247–248, 273n95, 299n136; wounded at Paris 51–52, 53
Green Farm 183, 185, 187, 292n16
Greenland Gap, WV 31
Greensboro, NC 246, 249
Greenville, SC 246
Gregg, David, McM., Brig. Gen., U.S.: early career 67, 68, 70, 76, 97, 100, 106, 107, 108, 124, 132, 133, 134, 135, 136, 137, 138, 139, 152, 153, 155, 156, 161, 166, 168, 175, 177, 178, 179, 180, 181, 192, 195, 203, 205, 207, 208, 216, 219; at Falmouth review 14–15, 267n46; later life 224, 241, 256, 257, 262, 286n92, 287n16, 289n47, n48, n4, 291n65, n72, 292n80, n5, n8, n11, 295n44, n49, 297n17; *see also* 3rd Cavalry Division
Gregg, John I., Col., U.S.: early career 76, 78, 136; later life 226; *see also* 2nd Brigade, 2nd Cavalry division
Gregg, Maxy, Col., C.S. 143
Gregg, T.J., Lt., U.S. 207
Grier, William, Lt. Col., U.S. 64
Grimsley, Daniel, Maj., C.S. 279n23, n25
Guadaloupe-Hidalgo, Treaty of 63
Guatemala 242
Guerry, Legrand, Pvt., C.S. 176

Hagerstown, MD 222
Hague 241
Halifax County, NC 213, 246, 271n38
Halleck, Henry, Maj. Gen. U.S. 1, 58, 94, 95, 96, 99, 100, 226, 238, 283n60
Hall's Carbine 25, 26, 59
Halsted, William, Col., U.S. 70, 71, 276n100.
Hamilton (U.S. ship) 66
Hamilton, Thomas, Lt., U.S. 262
Hampshire County, WV 91
Hampton, Frank, Lt. Col., C.S. 141, 143, 144, 145, 200, 201, 204, 211, 232, 243, 288n28, n30, 294n15, 301n46
Hampton, Preston, Capt., C.S. 239, 240

Hampton, Wade, Brig. Gen., C.S. 4, 9, 11; early life and career 45–46, 79, 86, 97, 123, 124, 125, 129, 138, 139, 141, 157, 163, 165, 167, 169, 171, 175, 178, 180, 181, 192, 203, 204, 205, 214, 215, 230, 235; later life 239–240, 241, 243, 248, 249, 258, 260, 272n49, 272n69, 279n32, 287n14
Hampton, Wade, IV, Capt., C.S. 239, 240, 299n96
Hancock, Winfield Scott, Maj. Gen., U.S. 103, 224, 274n14
Hanover County 198, 214, 238, 241
Hanover Courthouse 230, 271n26
Hanover, PA 218
Hansbrough Ridge 140, 141, 143, 148, 287n21; see also Devil's Jump
Hardee, William, Lt. Gen., C.S. 66, 275n70
Harman, Asher, Col., C.S.: early career 53, 127, 157, 158, 161, 162, 163; later life 245, 259, 270n64, 301n37, 302n8; see also 12th Virginia Cavalry Regiment
Harper, Calvin 294n16
Harpers Ferry, WV 21, 42, 59, 70, 71, 72, 99, 234
Harris, Ira 68
Harrisburg, PA 63, 71, 78
Harrison, James E., Capt., U.S. 62; early career 66; later life 230, 255; see also 5th U.S. Cavalry Regiment
Harrison, Julien, Col., C.S. 51, 52, 53, 247, 300n140, n141
Harrisonburg 50, 51, 247, 250, 270n68
Hart, James F., Capt., C.S. 120, 157, 169, 170, 261; see also Hart's Battery
Hart, Jimmy, Sgt, U.S. 98
Hartford, CT 268n17
Hartwood Church 12, 98, 102, 103, 107, 108, 215
Harvard University 10, 76, 77
Haupt, Herman, Brig. Gen., U.S. 275n56
Havana, Cuba 239
Hazel River (Elk River) 93, 101, 126, 129, 181, 182, 193, 195, 266n27, 285n42, 295n33
Hedgeman's River see Rappahannock River
Heidelberg, University of 77
Heintzleman, Samuel P., Maj. Gen., U.S. 104
Herring, Hannah 39
Herring, Isaac 39
Herring's Tavern see Brandy House
Hickory Hill (Wickham Farm) 198, 199, 238, 298n86
Hight, Thomas, Lt. Col., U.S. 69; later life 276n93
Hill, Ambrose, P., Lt. Gen., C.S. 18, 71, 91, 198, 267n64; see also Hill's Corps
Hill, D.H., Maj. Gen., C.S. 48, 49, 272n58, 272n69
Hillsborough 201

Hilton Head, SC 74, 301n16
History of the Laurel Brigade 273n82
Hoffman, J. William, Col., U.S. 233, 257; see also 56th Pennsylvania Infantry Regiment
Hollywood Cemetery 239
Holtzman, John, Lt., C.S. 273n108
Honduras 242
Hood, John Bell, Maj. Gen., C.S. 42, 66, 87; see also Hood's Division
Hooker, Joseph, Maj. Gen., U.S. 5, 6, 7, 11, 12, 14, 15, 16, 17, 19, 55, 56, 57, 58, 60, 76, 89, 94, 95, 96, 97, 98, 99, 100, 101; plan for battle 104, 106, 107, 116, 119, 132, 133, 135, 137, 138, 181, 208, 209, 215, 222, 253, 254, 265n4, n5, n7, n8, n11, 267n52, 269n59, 270n1, 274n14, 282n18, n22, n37, n46, n51, 283n60, 284n18, 292n5, n8; plans for infantry support 102–103
Hopkins, W.M., Lt., C.S. 204
horses 9, 30; breeds used 29, 75, Confederate horse hospital established 33, 290n37, 295n27; diseases of 269n40, n49; disposal of carcasses 294n2; horse shoeing 269n44, n45, n46, n48; Union horse shortages prior to battle 95–96
horses and mules (named): Admiral Dewey (Col. M.C. Butler) 299n114; Bill (Chaplain Richard Davis) 52; Bostona (Lt. Frank Robertson) 165, 166, 202, 203, 251, 290n38, 300n165; Cincinnati (Maj. Gen. U.S. Grant) 268–269n33; Clodhopper (Col. Robert Williams) 74; Comet (Capt W.W. Blackford) 29, 269n34; Dixie (Pvt. Daniel Gleason) 98; Don (Pvt. William Corson), Extra Billy (Pvt. Thomas Hoskins) 269n38; Gray Eagle (Brig. Gen John Buford) 109; Janus 269n33; Kitt (Heros von Borcke) 93, 126, 127; Lancer (Maj. Henry Whelan) 129, 185; Lexington (Richard Ten Broeck) 268n33; Little Peep (Pvt. Thomas Hoskins) 31, 269n38; Little Sorrel (Lt. Gen T.J. Jackson) 18, 267n62; Maggie (Pvt. Jacob K. Langhorne) 80; Magic (Capt W.W. Blackford) 29; Manassas (Capt W.W. Blackford) 29; Miranda (Lt. Frank Robertson) 251; Old Bench Legs (Col. M.C. Butler) 150, 299n114; Old Bill (Chaplain Richard Davis) 52; Putman (Maj. William Stedman) 231, 298n52; Romeo (Pvt. St. George Brooke) 195; Traveler (Gen. Robert E. Lee) 91
Hoskins, Charles, Pvt., C.S. 185
Hoskins, Thomas T., Pvt., C.S. 269n39

Hotchkiss, Jedediah, Maj., C.S. 291 269
Hotchkiss projectiles 205
Howard, Benjamin, Surgeon, U.S. 294n5
Howard, H.E. 259, 267n1
Howard, Oliver O., Maj. Gen., U.S. 18, 267n58; see also 11th Corps
Howard, Wiley, Pvt., C.S. 170, 171, 291n50
Hubard, Robert Thruston, Jr., Lt., C.S. 22, 28
Hubard Farm see Ca Ira
Hubbard, Edwin L., Maj., U.S. 256; see also 3rd Wisconsin Infantry Regiment
Hudgins, Robert S., Sgt, C.S. 29, 81
Hudson River, NY 60
Huey, Pencock, Maj., U.S. 267n58
Hughes, Thomas, Dr. 279n22
Hunchback (U.S. ship) 49
Hunter, David, Maj. Gen., U.S. 64, 65, 238, 273n82, 275n62
Hunton, Eppa, Col., C.S. 53

I Rode with JEB Stuart 249
Illinois 230
Illustrated History of the Civil War 248
Imboden, John, Brig. Gen., C.S. 50, 91, 273n80; see also Imboden's Command
"Immortal 600" 250
Indianapolis, IN 64, 254, 263, Ingalls, Rufus, Brig. Gen., U.S. 95
Invalid Corps 67
Irvine, William, Lt. Col., U.S.: early career 69, 168, 170; later life 232, 257; see also 10th New York Cavalry Regiment
Italy 73, 234

Jack's Shop 278n6
Jackson, Andrew, Pres. 278n7
Jackson, Thomas J., Lt. Gen., C.S.: death of 18, 19, 20, 42, 48, 53, 55, 59, 70, 72, 75, 267n62, 267n64, 272n58, 273n82, 273n101, 291n60, n69; as roundhead 5, 6, 265n3, 10, 17; see also Jackson's Corps
James, Bob, Pvt., C.S. 111
James, Fleet, Pvt., C.S. 111
James River 9, 41, 86, 104, 280n67
Janaway, Hugh, Maj., U.S. 290n32, 301n25
Jefferson, Thomas, Pres. 82
Jeffersonton 21, 23, 99, 100, 101, 106, 152
Jenifer, Walter, Col., C.S. 281n81
Jenifer Saddle 25, 92, 201, 281n81, 301 25
Jenkins, Albert G., Brig. Gen., C.S.: 54, 91; see also Jenkins' Brigade
John Stone House see Graffiti House
Johnson, Andrew, Pres. 225
Johnson, John E., Col., C.S. 44, 271n39, n39

Johnston, Albert S., Gen., C.S. 65
Johnston, Joseph, Gen., C.S. 11, 42, 54, 240, 244, 246
Johnston, Philip P. Lt., C.S. 186
Johnston, Robert, Col., C.S. 41, 42
Jonas Run 288n36
Jones, James F., Dr. 151, 289n44, 295n16
Jones, Edward, Lt. Col., U.S. 76, 232, 256; *see also* 3rd Pennsylvania Cavalry Regiment
Jones, John B. 213, 278n16
Jones, Owen, Col., U.S. 71
Jones, Samuel, Brig. Gen., C.S. 273n80
Jones, Thomas ("Dr. Jones") 295n16
Jones, William E., Brig. Gen., C.S. 28; death of 238, 247, 251, 258, 259, 263, 264, 270n5, 272n74, 273n77, n80, n95, 279n32, 280n75, 282n19, 292n75; early career 49–50; later life 235–238; Stuart's opinion of 50, 51, 52, 53, 81, 92, 97, 119, 122, 123, 124, 126, 127, 128, 129, 139, 156, 157, 176, 177, 181, 187, 201, 204, 205, 208, 213, 216; *see also* Jones' Brigade
Jones-Imboden Raid 280n63
Jones, NC 45
Juarez, Benito 234

Kanawha River (including Kanawha Valley Campaign) 46
Kansas 11, 43, 54, 226, 229271n24
Kearneysville, WV 245
Keegan, John 290n18
Kellogg, Josiah H., Col., U.S.: early career 63, 126; later life 230, 255, 262; *see also* 17th Pennsylvania Cavalry Regiment
Kelly, John P. 40
Kelly's Ford: Battle of 11–13, 45, 55, 56, 72, 73, 75, 78, 86, 93, 97, 103, 104, 107, 123, 124, 129, 133, 134, 136, 138, 139, 177, 197, 199, 205, 207, 211, 213, 216, 263, 283n51, n56, 286n59, 291n56
Kellyville 40, 137, 270n7
Kemper's Ford 283n56
Kentucky 48, 51, 233, 268n33
Kerr, James, Col., U.S. 77
Kettle Run 106
Kidd, James A., Bvt. Brig. Gen., U.S. 3
Kielmansegge, Eugene, Col., U.S. 71,
Kilpatrick, Hugh Judson, Col., U.S. 56; early career 67–68, 72, 101, 137, 166, 167, 168, 169, 175, 204, 209; later life 224–245, 240, 257, 262, 274n17, 276n78, n82, n83, 291n51, n58, n59, 297n26, n27; *see also* 1st Brigade, 3rd Cavalry Division
King George County 61, 277n108
King William County 297n8
Kirtley Road 140, 144
Kitchen, Marcus, Lt., U.S. 164, 165, 290n33

Knoxville, TN 274n68
Koerber, V.E. von, Capt., U.S. 208, 295n52
Kramer, William K., Pvt., C.S. 36, 48

Lancaster, James, Lt., U.S. 263
Lane, James, Col., C.S. 18
Langhorne, Jacob Kent, Pvt., C.S. 4, 16, 17, 41, 53, 79, 195, 196; resolution to 201, 203, 295n19
Lansing, Jacob H., Maj., U.S. 234, 260
Laurens, SC 831, 249
Lawton, Robert, Col., U.S. 75
Lee, Charlotte Wickham (Mrs. Rooney Lee) 43, 198, 238, 239, 278n5
Lee, Custis, Brig. Gen., C.S. 7, 215, 239, 250
Lee, Fitzhugh, Brig. Gen., C.S. 9; at Chancellorsville 28, 41, 42, 50, 55, 63, 87, 92, 97, 106, 126, 153, 181, 193, 203; early career 11, 12, 266n31, n33, n34; at Kelly's Ford 12–13, 17, 266–267n39; later life 235, 238, 239, 243, 247, 251, 260, 263, 264, 279n32, 289n1, 293n41, 300n160; *see also* Fitz Lee's Brigade
Lee, Henry, Capt., C.S. 293n41
Lee, Mary Custis (Mrs. Robert E. Lee) 65, 198, 199
Lee, Mary Tabb Bolling (Mrs. Rooney Lee) 239
Lee, Robert, Capt., C.S. 298n86
Lee, Robert E., Gen., C.S. 1, 2, 3, 5, 6; concern for the condition of the army's horses 7–9, 10, 11, 265n19, 266n21; on death of Pelham 13, 15, 16, 17, 19, 29, 38, 39, 47, 48, 49, 50, 65, 66, 90, 91, 92, 99, 100, 106, 107, 165, 177, 181, 186, 187, 188, 189, 191, 198, 199, 203, 205, 219, 220, 222, 224, 235, 238, 240, 244, 246, 247, 248, 249, 250, 266n34, 267n64, 269n49, n59, 272n68, n69, 273n80, 275n67, 278n5, 280n54, n68, n73, n75, 281n84, n2, 291n65, n66, 293n39, 295n41, 296n62
Lee, William H.F. "Rooney," Brig. Gen., C.S. 9; early career 10–11, 12, 16, 43, 44, 45, 65, 92, 93, 97, 106, 122, 124, 125, 126, 127, 129, 233; later life 239–239, 241, 259, 266n30, 273n1, 278n5, 279n32, 295n49, 298n86, n90, 302n43; *see also* Rooney Lee's Brigade
Lee/Custis Home *see* Arlington
Leesburg 246
LeMat revolver 26, 268n18
Lemmon, John C., Col., U.S. 68, 69, 276n90
Lexington 16, 53, 239, 249, 250, 273n82, 275n62
Libby Prison 202, 222, 227, 230, 233, 238, 297n32
Liberty *see* Bedford

Life and Campaigns of Major General JEB Stuart 249
Lincoln, Abraham, Pres.: visit to the Army at Falmouth 14–15, 16, 95, 96, 100, 102, 220, 223, 227, 265n4, 275n62
Lincoln, Mary 14
Lincoln, Tad 14
Lipscomb, Thomas J., Maj., C.S. 141, 143, 148, 150, 151, 152, 204, 243, 258, 287n16, n19, 301n46
Little Big Horn, MT 213
Little Fork 266n27
Little Fork Episcopal Church 293n40
Lloyd, William R., Col., U.S. 75
Loeser, Charles McK., Lt., U.S. 188, 262, 293n25
Lomax, Lunsford, Col., C.S.: early career 54, 123, 176, 178; later life 241–242, 258, 259, 264, 271n37, 292n75, 295n42, 301n36; *see also* 12th Virginia Cavalry Regiment
London, United Kingdom 66
Longstreet, James, Lt. Gen., C.S. 5, 37, 91, 92, 145, 175, 176, 265n3, 291n66; *see also* Longstreet's Corps
Lord, Richard, S.C., Capt., U.S. early career 64, 195; later life 230, 255, 260, 262, 293n46; *see also* 1st U.S. Cavalry Regiment
Lossing, Benson J. 248
Loudoun County 53, 54, 225, 246, 273n102, n105, 280n63
Louisiana 226, 275n66, 291n65
Lowell, MA 297n14
Lynchburg 9, 22, 37, 41, 80, 201, 211, 295n27
Lynchburg Daily Virginian 211, 295n19

MacArthur, Douglas, Gen., U.S. 252
MacDonald, Angus, Col., C.S. 28; early career 50–51; later life 273n82, 274n22
MacDonald, William, Capt., C.S. 273n82, 273n101
Mackenzie, Ranald, S., Bvt. Capt., U.S. 111, 262, At Beverly ford and Later life 284n17, 302n3
Macklin, James, Pvt., U.S. 59
Mack's Mill 37
MacLaws, Lafayette, Maj. Gen., C.S. 176
Madagascar 234
Madden, Willis 40
Madden's Tavern 40, 287n16
Madison, IN 59, 60, 232
Madison Run 278n17
Magnetic Iron & Steel Ore Company 246
Magruder, John Bankhead, Maj. Gen., C.S. 47
Mahone, Maj. Gen., C.S. 300n160
Maine 63, 233
Maine (U.S. ship) 239
Malvern Hill, Battle of 59, 67
Manarin, Louis 259

Index

Manassas 23, 47, 225; *see also* First Manassas and Second Manassas
Mandalay 224
Manila, Philippine Islands 229
Marias de Cygnes, KS 221
Marietta Paper Mills 272n52
Marion County, IN 274n32
Marshall, James, Lt., C.S. 51, 199, 294n8, 294n11
Marshall, John 294n8
Marshall, Richard, Pvt., C.S. 51
Marshall, Thomas, Lt. Col., C.S. 51, 120, 122, 177, 217; death of 245, 259, 295n37; *see also* 7th Virginia Cavalry Regiment
Martin, Joseph W., Capt., U.S. 137, 153, 159, 163, 165, 171, 177, 178, 205, 207; later life 235, 257, 295n42; *see also* 6th New York Independent Light Artillery Battery
Martin, William T., Brig. Gen., C.S. 48
Martin, William B., Maj., U.S. 125, 180, 232, 255
Martinsburg, WV 72
Marye's Heights 272n59
Maryland 1, 18, 47, 94, 161, 166, 208, 209, 210, 226, 235
Maryland Campaign *see* Antietam
Mason, James 274n17
Massachusetts 63, 74, 153, 223, 224
Massanutten Mountain 50
Massie, Thomas, Lt. Col., C.S. 301n37
Matthews, Catherine M. (Mrs. H.B. McClellan) 249
Matthews, George H., Capt., C.S. 268n28
Maynard's Carbine 25–26
McClellan, George B., Maj. Gen., U.S. 6, 7, 43, 44, 66, 227, 277n110, 284n16, 288n30
McClellan, Henry B., Maj., C.S. 32, 41, 153, 155, 156, 158, 205; later life 249–250, 267n39, 267n39, 279n25, 287n16, 288n28, n36, 289n1, n2, 293n42, 300n155
McClellan Saddle 201, 281n81
McClure, William S., Maj., U.S. 60, 117, 122, 125, 180; later life 232, 255; *see also* 3rd Indiana Cavalry Regiment
McDowell, Irving, Maj. Gen., U.S. 43
McGraw, T.G., Capt., C.S. 233
McGregor, William C., Capt., C.S. 157, 261; *see also* McGregor's Battery
McGruder, Simon 302n1
McIntosh, John, Col., U.S. 76, 220, 277n136
McKee, Samuel, Capt., U.S. 262
McKinney, Phillip W., Capt., C.S. 300n160
McManus, Miles, Pvt., U.S. 277n126
McVicar, Charles, Pvt., C.S. 279n35

McVicar, Duncan, Lt. Col., U.S. 63
Meade, George C., Maj. Gen., U.S. 89, 103, 181, 219, 220, 221, 234, 275n56, 280n62, 282n22; *see also* 5th Corps
Meagher, Thomas F., Brig. Gen., U.S. 11
Mecklenburg County 42
Medill, William, Maj., U.S. 274n29
Memphis, TN 240
Merritt, Charles 228–229
Merritt, Wesley, Capt., U.S. 3; early career 64, 180, 186, 189, 192, 220, 224; later life 228–229, 230, 255, 262, 292n29, 298n41; *see also* 2nd U.S. Cavalry Regiment
Mexico (including Mexican War) 6, 18, 41, 46, 57, 60, 72, 76, 102, 234, 281n81, 285n33
Middleburg 216, 218, 225, 226, 235, 245, 297n27
Middlesex County 97
Miegs, Montgomery C., Brig. Gen., U.S. 94, 95, 99, 281n9, 282n29; *see also* Quartermaster Department
Milledgeville, GA 278n7
Miller, Andrew, Col., U.S. 71
Miller Family 285n40
Miller House/Miller House Hill *see* Fleetwood
Milroy, Robert H., Maj. Gen., U.S. 31, 50, 61, 100
Mine Run Campaign 232
Mississippi 45, 46, 48, 58, 200, 223, 224, 230, 244, 294n12
Mississippi Rifle 26
Missouri 221, 271n24
Mitchell's (Mitchell's Station) 278n17
Mitchell's Shop 268n28
Mobile, AL 281n81
Monroe County, NY 59
Montgomery County, MD 53, 273n101
Monticello 278n16
Moorefield, WV 230
Moorman, Marcellus, Capt., C.S. 205, 261; *see also* Moorman's Battery
Morris, Robert 67
Morris, Robert, Jr., Maj., U.S. 67, 127, 128, 129, 185; death of 230, 232, 255, 298n61; *see also* 6th Pennsylvania Cavalry Regiment
Morris Island, SC 250
Morrisville 106, 107, 108, 133, 280n1, 301n19
Morton, William J. Capt., C.S. 284n27
Mosby, John, Capt., C.S. 70, 96, 97, 98, 226, 266n26, 279n29
Mount Pony 145, 176, 291n66
Mountain Run 136, 137, 139, 140, 141, 144, 148, 150, 151, 152, 204, 287n16, 288n36

"Mud March" 5–6
Mudge, Charles R., Lt. Col., U.S. 234, 256; *see also* 2nd Massachusetts Infantry Regiment
"Mule Shoe" 291n65; *see also* Spotsylvania
Munford, Thomas T., Col., C.S. 26, 31, 32; early career 41, 43, 93, 124, 126, 129, 193, 195, 203; later life 243–244, 245, 260, 270–271n17, 293n39, n42, 295n19, n33, 302n48, n49, n50; *see also* 2nd Virginia Cavalry Regiment
Munich, Germany 76

Napoleon Bonaparte 207, 247, 290n18, 300n142
Napoleon smoothbore cannon 253, 289n1
Natchez, MS 48
National Archives 3
Natural Bridge 229
Naval Academy, Annapolis, MD 27
Nebraska 54
Needham, Thomas, Pvt., U.S. 294n12
Neese, George, Sgt, C.S. 87, 91
New Berne, NC 26
New Hampshire 75, 76, 234
New Jersey 2, 67, 68, 76, 161
New Market 36, 97
New Mexico 59, 64, 223, 254
New Orleans, LA 233
New York 53, 60, 61, 68, 72, 73, 74, 223, 232
New York City 224, 228, 231, 235, 242, 276n99, 299n114
New York Herald 202, 210
New York Metropolitan Museum of Art 227
New York Militia 61, 102
New York Times 199, 209, 211, 283n8, 284n30, 294n1, 296n55, 300n2
New York Tribune 202
Newberry, SC 243
Newby's Shop 137
Newhall, Frederick C., Capt., U.S. 192, 193, 195, 284n12, 284n17
Newport, RI 54
Nicaragua 273n75, 274n29
Nineveh 245
Norfolk 247
Norman, Lucy 287n25
Norman, Thomas 287n25
Norman's Ford 286n59, 295n61
Norman's Mill 144, 150, 287n25
Norris, Charles, Capt., U.S. 64, 263; later life 275n58, 302n4
North Africa 72
North Anna River 234
North Carolina 8, 48, 49, 81, 100, 242, 244, 246, 267n62, 272n69, n72
Northern Neck 44, 96, 97
Northern Virginia 65
Noyes, Henry, Lt., U.S. 262

Index

Oak Shade 93, 126, 193, 285n42, 287n15, 293n40, 295n33
Oakey, Daniel, Capt., U.S. 108, 186, 187
The Oaks (Robertson Home) 240
Occoquan 299n129, 302n6
O'Ferrall, Charles, Capt., C.S. 127, 163, 199, 250, 294n11, 300n160
Officials Records 254, 258, 259, 295n52, 301n9, 10, n18
Ohio 53, 230, 231, 233, 287n25, 295n53, 298n52
Ohio River 60
O'Keefe, Joseph, Capt., U.S. 188, 293n25
Oklahoma Land Rush 229
Old Capitol Prison, Washington, D.C. 67
Old Carolina Road (Rogue's Road) 39, 123, 140, 177, 270n3, n4, 293n43
Omaha, NE 239
O'Neal, Edward A., Col., C.S. 175, 176, 291n65
Opequon Creek 228, 245
Opie, John, Pvt., C.S. 53, 88, 89, 90, 114, 115, 117, 164, 202, 252; later life 250–251, 273n95, 284n27
Orange and Alexandria (O & A) Railroad 1, 39, 82, 85, 87, 88, 95, 96, 97, 107, 108, 119, 122, 123, 124, 138, 167, 169, 170, 215, 279n24, 282n22, n24, 286n59, 294n10, 295n61
Orange County 41, 42, 43, 45, 213, 241, 266n34
Orange Courthouse 17, 51, 100, 266n35, 278n17, n19
Orlean 98
Orton, William H., Capt., U.S. 257
Overland Campaign 224, 241, 247
Owen, Thomas H., Col., C.S.: early career 42, 98; later life 246, 260, 271n23; *see also* 3rd Virginia Cavalry Regiment

Pacific Coast/Northwest 64, 66, 102, 226, 273n75, 274n29
Paddy McManus (Mascot of 6th Ohio Cavalry) 75, 277n126
Palmore, Charles, Lt., C.S. 268n28
Pamunkey River 11
Paoli Mill 136, 137, 139
Paris 51, 52, 53, 76, 229
Parsons, E.B., Lt., U.S. 284n30
Pate, Henry C., Lt. Col., C.S. 13, 271n24, n28; controversy with T. Rosser 42n27
Patrick, Marsena, Brig. Gen., U.S. 209, 285n34
Patton, George S., Col., C.S. 271n17
Pautucket, RI 75
Paxton, Elisha F., Brig. Gen., C.S. 265–266n20
Payne, Lewis 231
Payne, William H.F., Lt. Col., C.S. 45, 143, 191

Peck, Daniel, Pvt., U.S. 283n64
Pegram, John, Lt., C.S. 191, 200, 294n14
Pelham, John, Maj., C.S.: death of 13, 267n40, 42, 86
Pender, Dorsey, Brig. Gen., C.S. 19
Pendleton, Alexander, Lt. Col., C.S. 18, 267n63, 280n68, n73
Pendleton, Willliam Nelson, Brig. Gen., C.S., 267n63
Peninsula of Virginia (including Peninsular Campaign) 7, 18, 45, 47, 60, 62, 64, 65, 66, 67, 76, 102, 266n29, 276n93, 301n9
Pennington, Alexander C.M., Capt., U.S. 136, 149, 150; later life 234–235, 256, 262, 288n41; *see also* M Battery, 2nd U.S. Artillery
Pennsylvania 1, 43, 54, 67, 68, 90, 91, 98, 136, 210, 218, 220, 224, 235, 240, 300n165
Pennsylvania Militia/National Guard 76, 233
Pensacola, FL 47
People's National Bank, Leesburg 247
Perry, Matthew Calbraith, Commodore 272n57
Perry, William H., Lt. Col., C.S. 214
Perryville, MD 62
Petersburg 45, 189, 200, 219, 228, 234, 239, 244, 245
Peyton, John W 279n24, 280n72
Phelps, Charles, Lt., C.S. 201
Philadelphia, PA 41, 232, 233, 293n29
Philippine Islands (Philippines) 229
Phillips, Jefferson, Lt. Col., C.S. 191, 293n34
Phillips, William, Col., C.S. 46, 272n52
Pickett, George, Maj. Gen., C.S. 66, 244
Piedmont, Battle at 238, 251
Piedmont Region of Virginia 79
Pinkerton agents (Pinkerton's) 6
Piscataquis County, ME 70
Pittsburgh, PA 60, 64, 71
Pittsylvania County 250
Plank Road 18
Pleasonton, Alfred, Brig. Gen., U.S. 1, 2, 17, 220; assigned to command of Cavalry Corps 57–58, 60, 64, 78, 95, 96, 97, 98, 100, 101, 103, 104, 106, 107, 108, 109, 111, 116, 117, 119, 121, 122, 126, 127, 132, 133, 135, 137, 138, 139, 175, 178, 180, 181, 191, 192, 198, 199, 202, 205, 207, 208, 209, 210, 215; at Chancellorsville 18 & 267n58; early career 18; later life 221–222, 225, 232, 247, 253, 254, 256, 258, 262, 270n1, 274n14, n17, 281n11, 282n22, n26, n46, 284n12, n17, n18, 285n30, 289n48, 292n5, n8, n9, n11, 293n36, 294n1, n9, 295n48, n49,

296n1, 297n2, n6, n7, n9, n11, n32, 300n2, n3; reorganizes Cavalry Corps 219–220
Poinsett, Joel 33
Point Lookout, MD 273n82
Pope, Edmund, M., Maj., U.S. 59, 180, 231, 255; *see also* 8th New York Cavalry Regiment
Pope, John, Maj. Gen., U.S. 40, 71, 90, 122, 266n34
Port Royal 10
Portage County, OH 75
Porter, B.B., Lt., U.S. 170
Porter, Fitz John, Maj. Gen., U.S. 66
Porter, Peter B. 69
Portland, ME 223, 230, 276n93
Potomac River 59, 94, 97, 273n102
Potter, Samuel M., Hosp. Orderly, U.S. 265n8
Poughkeepsie, Frederick, Capt., U.S. 170, 290n49
Prague, Czech Republic 224
Pratt, George J., Lt., C.S. 20, 267n3
Preston, James K., Pvt., C.S. 203
Price, Channing, Maj., C.S. 41, 153, 289n2
Price, Sterling, Maj. Gen., C.S. 221
Prince William County 97, 106
Providence, RI 226
Provisional Army of the Confederacy (PACS) 23, 26, 27, 86, 268n4
PrussianArmy 248
Purcellville 225

"Q Company" 36, 202
Quartermaster (General, Department, Army of the Potomac, Cavalry Corps) 26, 28, 65, 202, 274n18
Quartermaster Department (Confederate) 7, 8, 201, 267n62, 69n45
Queen Anne of England 266n27
Quirk, Paul, Lt., U.S. 189

Racoon Ford 104
Radford, Richard C.W., Col., C.S. 41, 295n16
Randolph, George W., Brig. Gen., C.S. 82, 278n16
Randolph, OH 231
Rangoon Gazette 224
Ransom, Robert, Brig. Gen., C.S. 47
Rapidan River 10, 55, 56, 140, 219, 247, 266n27
Rapidan Station 39, 247, 278n17, 279n24
Rappahannock County 11, 51, 299n129
Rappahannock (Hedgeman's) River 4, 5, 6, 9, 10, 11, 13, 15, 16, 19, 23, 35, 39, 40, 42, 43, 44, 55, 56, 57, 72, 86, 89, 90, 91, 92, 93, 95, 96, 97, 98, 100, 101, 103, 104, 106, 107, 108, 119, 124, 136, 137, 140, 179, 181, 182, 185, 191, 195, 199,

Index

202, 205, 207, 208, 210, 211, 213, 215, 218, 222, 228, 230, 242, 254, 264, 265n3, 266n27, 269n59, 282n22, n37, 283n52, n1, 284n13, 285n42, 286n52, 289n15, 292n8, 294n10, 296n61
Rappahannock Station (Bowenville, Remington) 15, 16, 56, 90, 97, 108, 123, 192, 196, 197, 199, 207, 219, 228, 283n5, 286n59, 294n10
Ratcliffe, Laura: relationship with JEB Stuart 266n26
Ravensworth (Rooney Lee Home) 239, 299n92
Ray, William, Pvt., U.S. 137
Readville, MA 74
Ream's Station 245
Rebel Cavalryman with Lee, Stuart, and Jackson 251
Red River Campaign 275n66
Remington *see* Rappahannock Station
Remington revolver 268n17
Reno, Marcus, Capt., U.S. 251, 263
reviews: Lincoln's review of the Army of the Potomac at Falmouth 14–15; purposes of 80, Stuart's grand reviews 80, 84, 86–89, 91–92
Reynolds, John F., Maj. Gen U.S. *see also* 1st Corps 103
Rhode Island 75, 297n29
Rich, Capt., C.S. 301n31
Rich, William W., Col., C.S. 46, 260; later life 272n53
Richards' Ford (ferry) 137
Richmond 15, 16, 19, 34, 36, 40, 48, 56, 63, 67, 82, 91, 92, 104, 198, 200, 202, 212, 213, 214, 220, 221, 222, 226, 230, 233, 235, 238, 239, 241, 244, 246, 247, 250, 266n34, 273n82, 278n7, n19, 294n1, 296n62, n78, 297n8, n32
Richmond Arsenal 25
Richmond Examiner 202, 210, 211, 212, 213, 218, 235, 271n28, 277n108, 296n66
Richmond, Fredericksburg & Potomac (RF&P) Railroad 281n7
Richmond Sentinel 212
Richmond Sharps Carbine 25, 92, 268n16, 281n82
Ridgeway, SC 246
Rio Grande River 64
Rixeyville 101
Rixeyville Road 175
Roanoke 246, 295n18
Robb, William J., Lt., U.S. 170, 171, 271n52
Roberts, William P., Lt., C.S. 272n58
Robertson, Beverly H., Brig. Gen., C.S. 43, 48, 49, 97, 124, 138, 139, 153, 155, 156, 205, 208; later life 240, 260, 263, 264, 270n5, 272n69, 279n32, 295n31; *see also* Robertson's Brigade
Robertson, Francis S. Lt., C.S. 124,

129, 157, 165, 166, 202, 203, 251, 258, 290n39, 295n28, 300n165
Robinson, Leiper M., Pvt., C.S. 278n13
Robinson, William, Col., U.S. 234, 257
Robinson, William G., Lt. Col., C.S. 45, 264, 302n8
Robinson, William, Jr., Brig. Gen., U.S. 234
Rochester, NY 59
Rock Creek, PA 69
Rockingham County 37
Rockville, MD 1
Rodenbough, Theophilus, Capt., U.S. 188, 293n25
Rodes, Robert, Maj. Gen., C.S. 175, 291n65
Roebling, Washington, Lt., U.S. 289n3
Rogers, Lorenzo, Lt. Col., U.S. 78
Rogue's Road *see* Old Carolina Road
Rolla, MO 276n86
Roman Nose 285n36
Romney, WV 91
Roosevelt, Theodore, Pres. 271n28
Rosecrans, William, Maj. Gen., U.S. 95, 99, 281n9
Rosser, Joseph Travis, Maj., C.S. 189
Rosser, Thomas L., Col., C.S. 32; controversy with T.T. Munford 244, 271n27, 260, 264, 271n25, n26, n28, 272n74, 296n77; early career and controversy with H.C. Pate 42, 213, 243; *see also* 5th Virginia Cavalry Regiment
Round Hill 297n4
Roundhead, Jackson as 265n3
Rouss, Milton, Lt., C.S. 301n31
Rowlesburg, WV 52
Ruffins Run 182, 183
Rummel's Farm 242
Rush, Benjamin 66
Rush, Richard, Col., U.S. 66, 67, 263, 298n61
Russell, Charles, Maj., U.S. 161
Russell, David A., Brig. Gen., U.S. 102, 103, 104, 107, 135, 137, 138, 178, 203, 209; later life 228, 257, 262, 282n46; *see also* Russell's Brigade
Rust, John R., Lt., C.S. 301n31
Rutgers University 230

Sackett, William, Col., U.S. 60, 61
Saddles *see* Jenifer Saddle and McClellan Saddle
St. Charles, IL 59
St. Cyr, France 73
Saint James Church 119, 121, 122, 123, 124, 126, 129, 131, 132, 139, 153, 155, 156, 157, 158, 161, 165, 166, 167, 175, 176, 177, 180, 181, 187, 192, 193, 200, 204, 207, 208, 209, 222, 230, 252, federal compensation for destruction of 285n57, 292n11, 293n42; history of 285n44

Saint James Church Road 182, 188, 189
St. Mark's Episcopal Church 294n6
St. Mary's Church 233
Saint Petersburg, Russia 242
Salem 246
Samaria Church 245
San Diego, CA 7
San Francisco, CA 232
Sanders, William P., Capt., U.S. 65, 275n68
Santa Fe, MN 229
Santiago, Cuba 231
Sardinian Army 73
Sargent, Horace, Col., U.S. 74, 75, 277n124
Satan 143
Savannah, GA 246
Sawtelle, Charles, Maj., U.S. 262
Sawyer, Henry, Capt., U.S. 176, 233, 238, 239
Sayler's (Sailor's) Creek 233, 250
Sayre Female Institute 249
Schenck, Robert, Maj. Gen., U.S. 209, 295n53
Schenkl projectile 288n41
Schoolhouse Woods 292n16
Scott, James, Pvt., C.S. 189
Scott, John, Capt., C.S. 293n29
Second Manassas (Battle and Campaign) 40, 48, 58, 68, 70, 71, 111, 266n34, 273n85, 291n63, 295n53, 299n129
Seddon, James A. 50
Sedgwick, John, Maj. Gen., U.S. 91, 103, 292n15; *see also* 6th Corps
Seminary Ridge 242
Seminole Indians 18, 60, 63
Seven Day's Battles 47, 48
Shaler, Alexander, Brig. Gen., U.S. 102
Shands, Everton, Capt., C.S. 37, 270n68
Sharpe, George H., Col., U.S. 6, 97, 270n1
Sharps Carbine 25, 26, 67, 201, 268n16
Shawsville 201, 295n18
Shelmire, John, Maj., U.S. 164, 176, 290n32, 294n12
Shenandoah River 29
Shenandoah Valley (including Valley Campaign) 16, 39, 42, 48, 49, 50, 54, 59, 70, 71, 75, 81, 86, 91, 93, 97, 106, 119, 175, 209, 220, 226, 228, 240, 242, 244, 250, 258, 272n68, 273n80, 274n5, 275n62, 282n19
Shepherdstown, WV 235
Sheridan, Philip, Maj. Gen., U.S. 218, 223, 224, 226, 228, 231, 235, 244, 247, 271n25, 274n5
Sherman, A.A., Sgt, U.S. 145
Sherman, William T., Maj. Gen., U.S. 138, 225, 240, 242, 244, 272n52
Shumate, G.G., Lt., C.S. 114
Sickles, Daniel, Maj. Gen., U.S. 103, 267n58; *see also* 3rd Corps

Sigel, Franz, Maj. Gen., U.S. 231
Simpson, Tally, Cpl., C.S. 214
Sioux Indians 18
Skinker's Ford 283n56
slaves/servants (named): Albert (W.W. Blackford) 29; Calvin Harper (William Farley) 294n16; Dilbert (Chiswell Dabney) 166, 290n40; Gilbert (W.W. Blackford) 29; Henry (Heros von Borcke) 202; Jim (Robert Hudgins) 29, 81; Jim Smith (Robert T. Hubard) 28, Overton 202; Robert (Robert T. Hubard) 28; Thruston (Robert T. Hubard) 28; Tom 202
Slidell, John 284n17
Slocum, Henry W., Maj. Gen., U.S. 103, 301n7; *see also* 12th Corps
Smith, C. Ross, Lt. Col., U.S. 67, 298n61
Smith, Charles H., Lt. Col., U.S. 175, 233
Smith, John, Pvt., C.S. 189
Smith, John, Brig. Gen., U.S. 296n60
Smith, Kirby, Gen., C.S. 65, 266n31
Smith, William "Extra Billy," Brig. Gen., C.S. 81, 268n38, 278n7
Smithsonian Institution 249
Snicker's Gap 220, 297n4
Socorro, NM 48
Sons of Confederate Veterans 249
Sonora, Mexico 234
South Amboy, NJ 60
South Anna River 64
South Carolina 45, 48, 201, 213, 214, 239, 240, 242, 243, 254, 272n52, n57, 294n4
South Carolina State Penitentiary 243
Southern Historical Society 244
Spain 243
Spanish-American War 224, 229, 234, 235, 271n28, 299n114
Spotsylvania: Bloody Angle at 234; Mule Shoe at 291n65
Spotted Tavern 102, 103, 108
Sprague, William 73
Springfield, IL 72
Spruill, Stephen, Col., C.S. 45
Stafford County 43, 63, 95, 107, 281n13
Stafford Courthouse 101, 301n7
Stahel, Julius, Maj. Gen., U.S. 94, 98, 99, 100, 106, 127, 281n3, 283n60, 292n8, 293n36, 294n9, 296n1; *see also* Stahel's Division
Stanhope, Benjamin C., Maj., U.S. 140, 141, 143, 232, 287n17, n20
Stanton, David 287n25
Stanton, Edwin M. 1, 19, 56, 94, 95, 96, 99, 209, 222, 287n25
Starke's Ford 193
Starr, Samuel H., Maj., U.S. 229
Staten Island, NY 62, 72
Staunton 53, 82, 202, 213, 250, 251
Staunton Hill 271n31
Stearns, Franklin 182, 270n12

Stedman, Charlie, Pvt., U.S. 277n128
Stedman, Eddie, Pvt., U.S. 277n128
Stedman, William, Maj., U.S.: early career 75, 140; later life 231, 256, 277n128, 298n52; *see also* 6th Ohio Cavalry Regiment
Steptoe, William, Capt., C.S. 41, 80, 201, 270n70, 295n19
Stevens, Edward 287n18
Stevensburg (York) 39, 93, 104, 106, 123, 135, 136, 137, 139, 140, 141, 143, 144, 145, 147, 148, 150, 152, 153, 155, 166, 198, 204, 205, 214, 241, 258, 287n14, n16, n20, 288n30, n32, n41, 291n66, 292n75, 294n15, 299n114, 300n160, 302n46
Stevensburg Road 177
Stevenson, George W., Capt., U.S. 186, 187
Stone, John 285n30
Stoneman, George, Maj. Gen., U.S. 6, 7, 8, 15, 16, 56–57, 58, 60, 64, 66, 99, 222, 274n14
Stoneman's Raid (Raiders) 15, 19 41, 43, 45, Hooker's dissatisfaction with 55–57, 60, 61, 64, 67, 70, 71, 72, 75, 78, 95, 101, 211, Condition of horses after 274n18, 282n29, n35
Stoughton, Edwin H, Brig. Gen., U.S. 70, 276n99, 279n29
Strasburg 91
Strother, David, Col., U.S. 61
Stuart, Flora Cooke (Mrs. JEB Stuart) 48, 235, 266n26
Stuart, J.E.B., Maj. Gen., C.S. 1, 2, 5, 9, 10, 13, 14, 15, 16, 17, 266n26; at Chancellorsville 18–19, 20, 23, 25, 26, 27, 28, 29, 30, 31, 32, 33, 34, 35, 36, 38, 39, 40, 41, 42, 44, 46, 47, 48, 50, 52, 53, 54, 55, 58, 70, 78, 79, 80, 81, 82, 83, 86, 87, 88, 89, 90, 91, 92, 93, 94, 96, 97, 98, 99, 100, 101, 104, 106, 107, 119, 120, 123, 124, 126, 129, 132, 137, 138, 139, 143, 148, 152, 153, 155, 156, 157, 158, 161, 163, 165, 166, 169, 175, 176, 177, 178, 179, 180, 181, 187, 188, 189, 193, 198, 202, 203, 204, 205, 208, 210, 211, 212, 213, 214, 215, 216, 218, 225, 227, 228, 235, 236, 237, 238, 239, 240, 243, 245, 247, 248, 249, 250, 251, 253, 258, 263, 264, 266n29, 266n34, 267n64, 269n49, 270n5, 271n28, 272n68, n74, 273n77, 280n62, 281n2, n11, 282n17, n37, 283n60, 286n65, 287n14, 289n44, n1, 290n17, n34, n37, 291n66, 292n5, n8, n11, 293n39, n41, 294n1, 295n20, n31, n40, n49, 296n56, n61, n62, n66, 298n80, 300n1, n2, 301n29; *see also* Cavalry Division, Army of Northern Virginia
Stuart, Virginia Pelham 13, 235
Suffolk 242

Sulfur Springs *see* Fauquier Sulfur Springs
Sulley, Edward, Pvt., C.S. 176
Sultana (U.S. ship) 277n126
Susquehanna River 69, 235
Swaffield, W.C., Pvt., C.S. 289n45
Sweeney, Sam, Pvt., C.S. 40, 266n25
Sweitzer, Jacob, Col., U.S. 103 136, 137, 177, 283n56
Swift, Joseph 302n1

"Taps" 255n4
Tatum, Pinkney, Capt., C.S. 191
Taylor, John P., Col., U.S.: early career 72, 162, 177; later life 231–232, 257, 290n23, 298n86; *see also* 1st Pennsylvania Cavalry Regiment
Taylor, Richard, Lt. Gen., C.S. 240
TenBroeck, Richard 268n33
Tennessee 48, 95, 233, 254275n67
Terre Haute and Cincinnati Railroad 222
Tewksbury, J.L., Capt., U.S. 145
Texas 11, 49, 66, 223, 228, 240, 275n58, 278n19
Texas Rangers 44
Thomas, Earl D., Sgt, U.S. 263, 302n6
Thomas, George, Maj. Gen., U.S. 66
Thomas, H.S., Lt., U.S. 291n72
Thomas, Samuel, Pvt., C.S. 36
Thompson, George G. 182
Thompson, John L., Lt. Col., U.S.: early career 76; later life 231, 256; *see also* 1st Rhode Island Cavalry Regiment
Thompson Farm *see* Appleton
Thornburn, Charles, Col., C.S. 27, 302n8
Thornton, John, Lt. Col., C.S. 271n23
Thoroughfare Gap 225
Throckmorton, JohnA., Maj., C.S. 300n140
Tidewater 45
Todd's Tavern 246, 271n37
Tom's Creek 271n25, 284n27
Torbert, Alfred T.A., Brig. Gen., U.S. 274n5, 293n37
Trent (British ship) 284n17
Trevilian Station 245, 293n25
Trooper's Manual 33
Truefit, Henry, Maj., U.S.: later life 234, 257; *see also* 119th Pennsylvania Infantry Regiment
Twigg, David, Brig. Gen., U.S. 66

Underground Railroad 75
Underwood, Aidin, B., Col., U.S. 233, 256
Union Cemetery, Leesburg, VA 247
Union military organizations (Federal [including post-war] and Volunteer): *1st Brigade (Davis'), 1st Cavalry Division*; (composition of) 59–61 140, 216, 222, 232; (strength and casualties)

Index

255, 262, 297n9; *1st Brigade, 1st Division (Wadsworth's), 1st Corps* 103; *1st Brigade, 1st Division (Caldwell's), 2nd Corps* 103; *1st Brigade (di Cesnola's), 2nd Cavalry Division*; (composition of) 73–76, 108, 119, 121, 125, 126, 136, 152, 219; (strength and casualties) 256, 287n8; *1st Brigade (Kilpatrick's), 3rd Cavalry Division*; (composition of) 68–70, 97, 137, 173, 178; (strength and casualties) 257, 262; *1st Cavalry Division (Buford's)*; (composition of) 59–67, 100, 101, 108, 119, 122, 139, 167, 168, 176, 180, 185, 219, 223, 242; (strength and casualties) 255, 262, 274n29, 282n22, 285n52, 295n37, 302n6; *1st Corps (I Corps, Reynolds' Corps)* 15, 102, 103, 222, 254, 283n51; *1st Dragoons* 63, 64, 274n29 (*see also* 1st U.S. Cavalry Regiment); *1st Illinois Light Artillery* 76; *1st Maine Cavalry Regiment* 14, 68; (organization of) 69–70, 137, 167, 169, 173, 175, 176, 233, 254; (strength and casualties) 257, 301n22, 290n43, 291n59, n60; *1st Maryland Cavalry Regiment* 2, 59, 70; (organization of) 71, 137, 156, 158, 161, 162, 208, 231; (strength and casualties) 257, 301n24, 301n16, 276n84, 289n15, 291n72; *1st Massachusetts Cavalry Regiment* 57; (organization of) 74–75, 98, 136, 144, 145, 152, 231, 254; (strength and casualties) 256, 266n39, 281n12, 288n28; *1st Michigan Infantry Regiment* 137; *1st New Hampshire Cavalry* 231; *11st New Jersey Cavalry Regiment (Halsted's Horse)*: (organization of) 70–71, 137, 156, 158, 161, 164, 176, 233, 253; (strength and casualties) 257, 301n25, 289n15, 294n12; *1st New York Cavalry Regiment* 61; *1st Pennsylvania Cavalry Regiment* 70; (organization of) 71–72, 137, 158, 162, 177, 231, 254; (strength and casualties) 257, 277n104, 291n72; *1st Rhode Island Cavalry Regiment (1st New England Cavalry)* 73; (organization of) 75–76, 136, 144, 225, 226, 231; (strength and casualties) 256; *1st U.S. Cavalry Regiment* 63 (*see also* 1st Dragoons); (organization of) 64, 106, 127, 195, 230, 254; (strength and casualties) 255, 262; *1st Vermont Cavalry Regiment* 225; *2nd Brigade (Devin's), 1st Cavalry Division*; (composition of) 61–63, 108, 116, 126; (strength and casualties) 255, 285n39; *2nd Brigade, 1st Division (Wadsworth's), 1st Corps* 103; *2nd Brigade, 1st Division (Birney's)*, *3rd Corps* 103; *2nd Brigade (Gregg's), 2nd Cavalry Division*; (composition of) 76–78, 136, 152; (strength and casualties) 256; *2nd Brigade, 2nd Division (Steinwehr's), 11th Corps* 103; *2nd Brigade (Wyndham's), 3rd Cavalry Division*; (composition of) 70–72, 101, 133, 135, 137, 139, 153, 192, 195, 207; (strength and casualties) 257; *2nd Cavalry Division (Averell's/Duffié's)*; (composition of) 72–78, 100, 107, 108, 219, 232; (strength and casualties) 256, 273n1, 286n2, 287n26, 288n32, n36, 289n48, 295n44, 301n19; *2nd Corps (II Corps, Couch's Corps)* 15, 102, 103; *2nd D.C. Infantry Regiment* 234; *2nd Dragoons* 48, 58, 64, 126 (*see also* 2nd U.S. Cavalry Regiment); *2nd Massachusetts Infantry Regiment* 103, 108, 186, 234; (strength and casualties) 256, 301n15; *2nd New York Cavalry Regiment (Harris Light, 7th U.S. Cavalry)* 67; (organization of) 68, 73, 75, 137, 167, 168, 169, 171, 231; (strength and casualties) 257, 275n53, 291n51, n53, n70, 293n25, 298n58; *2nd U.S. Cavalry Regiment* 7, 11, 34, 63 (*see also* 2nd Dragoons); (organization of) 64, 65, 66, 69, 76, 127, 180, 186, 187, 188, 189, 191, 228; (strength and casualties) 255, 262, 263, 275n70, 276n93, 281n81, 286n78; *2nd Wisconsin Infantry Regiment* 103, 234; (strength and casualties) 257; *3rd Brigade, 1st Division (Williams'), 12th Corps* 103; *3rd Brigade, 1st Division (Wright's), 6 Corps* 103, 228; *3rd Cavalry Division (Gregg's Division)* 15, 16,; (composition of) 67–72, 100, 107, 108, 133, 139, 151, 153, 171, 173, 180, 192, 195, 196, 205, 207, 219; (strength and casualties) 257, 262, 295n44; *3rd Corps (III Corps, Sickles' Corps)* 15, 102, 103, 282n51; *3rd Indiana Cavalry Regiment* 57; (organization of) 59–60, 96, 117, 125, 180, 232, 254; (strength and casualties) 255, 301n6, 285n33; *3rd New Jersey Cavalry Regiment* 234, 29n33; *3rd Pennsylvania Cavalry Regiment (Kentucky Light Cavalry)* (organization of) 76, 136, 220, 232; (strength and casualties) 256; *3rd U.S. Cavalry Regiment* 223 (*see also* Regiment of Mounted Rifles); *3rd West Virginia Cavalry Regiment* (organization of) 61, 230, 253; (strength and casualties) 255; *3rd Wisconsin Infantry Regiment* 103, 186, 233; (strength and casualties) 256; *4th Massachusetts Cavalry Regiment* 277n122; *4th Michigan Infantry Regiment* 287n10; *4th New York Cavalry Regiment (Dickel's Mounted Rifles)* (organization of) 73, 219, 227, 256, 297n32, 300n3; *4th Pennsylvania Cavalry Regiment* 15; (organization of) 76–77, 136, 152, 231; (strength and casualties) 256; *4th U.S. Cavalry Regiment* 230, 284n17; *4th U.S. Infantry Regiment* 66, 102; *5th Corps (V Corps, Meade's Corps)* 16, 97, 103, 181, 254; *5th Kentucky Cavalry Regiment* 65; *5th New Hampshire Infantry Regiment* 103, 133, 234; (strength and casualties) 257, 282n49; *5th Pennsylvania Cavalry Regiment* 77; *5th New York Cavalry Regiment* 287n20; *5th U.S. Cavalry Regiment* 63, 64; (organization of) 65–66, 76, 127, 187, 230; (strength and casualties) 255, 263, 275n67, 293n22; *6th Corps (VI Corps, Sedgewick's Corps)* 15, 100, 102, 103, 254, 292n16; *6th Maine Infantry Regiment* 103, 233; (strength and casualties) 257; *6th New York Cavalry Regiment (2nd Ira Harris Guard)* (organization of) 61–62, 63, 108, 111, 123, 153, 232; (strength and casualties) 255, 286n74; *6th New York Independent Light Artillery Battery (Martin's)* 137, 156, 163, 166, 168, 205, 234; (strength and casualties) 257, 286n92, 289n3, 291n72, n73, 295n42; *6th Ohio Cavalry Regiment* (organization of) 75, 136, 14, 144, 231, 232, 254; (strength and casualties) 256, 301n18, 297n17; *6th Pennsylvania Cavalry Regiment (Rush's Lancers, First Philadelphia Light Cavalry)* 63; (organization of) 66–67, 127, 128, 129, 185, 187, 188, 192, 207, 222, 230, 232, 253, 263; (strength and casualties) 255, 267n48, 286n85; *6th U.S. Cavalry Regiment* 63; (organization of) 64–65, 275n53, 67, 76, 127, 129, 187, 223, 224, 229; (strength and casualties) 255, 301n14, 275n70, 286n85, 294n12; *7th (VII) Corps (during Spanish-American War)* 239; *7th Massachusetts Infantry Regiment* 102; *7th U.S. Cavalry Regiment* 68, 274n23; *7th Wisconsin Infantry Regiment* 103, 137, 197; (strength and casualties) 257; *8th Illinois Cavalry Regiment* (organization of) 59, 112, 113, 117, 125, 126, 181, 186, 220, 230; (strength and casualties) 255, 263, 284n30, 296n1; *8th New York Cavalry Regiment* (organization of) 59, 108, 112, 113, 116, 117, 125, 180, 231;

(strength and casualties) 255, 284n30, 301n10; *8th Pennsylvania Cavalry Regiment* 18, 61, 67, 267n58; *8th U.S. Cavalry Regiment* 223, 226, 274n29; *9th Indiana Cavalry Regiment* 232; *9th Massachusetts Infantry Regiment* 287n10; *9th New York Cavalry Regiment* (organization of) 60–61, 63, 125, 180, 232, 254; (strength and casualties) 255, 301n7; *9th U.S. Cavalry Regiment* 228, 285n63; *10th New York Cavalry Regiment (Porter Guard)* (organization of) 68–69, 137, 166, 167, 168, 170, 177, 178, 207; (strength and casualties) 257, 301n23, 291n51; *10th U.S. Infantry Regiment* 65; *11th Corps (XI Corps, Howard's Corps)* 15, 17, 18, 102, 103, 233; *11th New York Cavalry Regiment* 73; *11th Pennsylvania Cavalry Regiment* 238; *11th U.S. Infantry Regiment* 76; *12th Corps (XII Corps, Slocum's Corps)* 15, 102, 103, 254; *12th Illinois Cavalry Regiment* 59, 70; (organization of) 72, 101, 238, 257, 296n81, 300n3; *12th Pennsylvania Cavalry Regiment* 251; *16th Pennsylvania Cavalry Regiment* 55, 76; (organization of) 78, 96, 136, 232; (strength and casualties) 256, 301n19, 264n7; *17th Pennsylvania Cavalry Regiment* 61; (organization of) 63, 126, 230, 254, 263; (strength and casualties) 255, 262; *18th Pennsylvania Cavalry Regiment* 222; *19th (IXX) Corps* 275n66; *19th U.S. Infantry Regiment* 233; *20th Maine Infantry Regiment* 102; *24th U.S. Infantry Regiment* 223; *26th New York Cavalry Regiment* 232, 298n58; *27th U.S. Infantry Regiment* 233; *31st Maine Infantry Regiment* 276n93; *32nd Massachusetts Infantry Regiment* 287n10; *33rd Massachusetts Infantry Regiment* 103, 233; (strength and casualties) 256, 283n52; *42nd U.S. Infantry* 277n136; *47th New York Infantry Regiment* 143; *51st Indiana Infantry Regiment* 233; *56th Pennsylvania Infantry Regiment* 103, 233; (strength and casualties) 257; *81st Pennsylvania Infantry Regiment* 103, 133, 234; (strength and casualties) 257; *86th New York Infantry Regiment* 103, 125, 233, 234; (strength and casualties) 256, 282n51; *119th Pennsylvania Infantry Regiment* 103, 196, 234; (strength and casualties) 257, 282n50; *124th New York Infantry Regiment (Orange Blossoms)* 103, 125, 233, 234; (strength and casualties) 256, 282n51; *130th New York Infantry Regiment* 274n23; *Ames' Brigade*; (composition of) 102–103, 108, 119, 122, 132, 208; (strength and casualties) 256, 283n52; *Army of the Cumberland* 223, 254; *Army of the Potomac* 1, 5, 6, 11, 16, 17, 19, 48, 55, 58, 59, 62, 66, 70, 73, 74, 75, 76, 77, 94, 95, 99, 102, 103, 133, 135, 153, 180, 181, 192, 195, 207, 216, 219, 220, 221, 226, 254, 265n6, 266n29; (strength after Chancellorsville) 267n66, 280n63, 281n7, 282n29; *B & L Battery (Vincent's), 2nd U.S. Artillery Regiment* 95, 122; (strength and casualties) 255, 301n9; *C Battery (Fuller's), 3rd U.S. Artillery Regiment* (strength and casualties) 257, 262, 263; *Cavalry Corps, Army of the Potomac* 2, 6, 14, 15, 16, 61, 63, 67, 72, 78, 94, 95, 96, 100, 101, 106, 107, 219, 220, 221, 228, 253, 254; (strength and casualties) 255–257, 262, 263, 265n11, 274n14, 282n22, n27, n29, 297n32, 298n61, 300n3; *Chicago Dragoons* 285n36; *Cole's Maryland Cavalry* 273n105; *Department of the Missouri (in 1900)* 239; *Department of West Virginia* 226; *E Battery (Elder's), 4th U.S. Artillery Regiment* (strength and casualties) 255; *First Philadelphia Light Cavalry see 6th Pennsylvania Cavalry Regiment;* "Irish Brigade" 11; "Iron Brigade" 103; *K Battery (Graham's), 1st, U.S. Artillery Regiment* 234; (strength and casualties) 256; *Loudoun Scouts* 273n105; *M Battery (Pennington's), 2nd U.S. Artillery Regiment* 234, 256; (strength and casualties) 262; "Mormon Battalion" 7; *Orton's Company, D.C. Cavalry* 68, 253; (strength and casualties) 257, 276n84; *President's Mounted Guard (Company D, 3rd Pennsylvania Cavalry)* 76; *Regiment of Mounted Rifles (see also 3rd U.S. Cavalry Regiment)* 75; *Reserve Brigade*; (composition of) 63–67, 97, 100, 101, 108, 119, 122, 126, 127, 219, 223, 228, 254; (strength and casualties) 255, 262, 263, 282n22, 286n79; *Russell's Brigade*; (composition of) 103, 135, 137, 138; (strength and casualties) 257; *Stahel's Division* 195, 282n27; *Sweitzer's Brigade* 136, 137, 287n10

Uniontown, AL 244
United Confederate Veterans 2
United States Cavalry Association 298n41
United States Ford 97
United States Military Academy *see* West Point

United States Naval Academy 302n8
United States Volunteers (Spanish-American War) 243
Upperville 218, 225, 235, 248, 270n64, 295n52
Upperville Colt and Horse Show 51, 273n83
Urbanna 97
Utah 43, 58, 64, 126
Ute Indians 229

Val Verde, NM, Battle of 64
Valley Pike 226
Van Buren, Martin, Pres. 43
Vance, Zebulon 246
Van Dorn, Earl, Maj. Gen., C.S. 54, 266n31
Venable, Andrew R., Maj., C.S. 249
Vicksburg, MS 218, 220, 223
Victor Emmanuel, King of Italy 2, 70
Vierdersville 266n34
Vincent, Albert O., Lt., U.S. 255; *see also* B & L Battery; 2nd U.S. Artillery
Virginia 11, 29, 43, 47, 48, 54, 59, 63, 68, 72, 74, 75, 81, 95, 153, 211, 222, 235, 238, 239, 240, 241, 242, 243, 244, 246, 251, 254, 263, 270n1, 274n5
Virginia Agricultural College (Virginia Tech) 242
Virginia Agricultural Society 239
Virginia Central Railroad 43, 82, 241
Virginia, Library of 266n34
Virginia Military Institute (VMI) 16, 33, 34, 41, 42, 53, 195, 244, 245, 267n54, 267n62, 269n54, 270–271n17, 271n23, 275n62
Virginia Militia 44
Virginia Supreme Court of Appeals 270n12
Virginia, University of 39, 43, 51, 140, 143, 245, 251, 267n3
Voss, Arno, Col., U.S. 72, 101, 257, 277n108, 282n35, 300n3

Waddell, Joseph 213
Wadsworth, James S., Brig. Gen., U.S. 103
Wagner, Mrs Charles 199
Wagner Farm *see* The Glebe
Wainwright, Charles, Col., U.S. 283n51
War Department, Confederate 90, 235, 273n101
War Department, Federal 33, 59, 60, 61, 68, 95, 286n65
War of 1812 20
Ward, Charles, Pvt., C.S. 185, 292n18
Ward, George, Pvt., U.S. 185
Ward, Issac, Lt., U.S. 294n12
Ware, Thomas, Pvt., C.S. 279n35
Waring, J. Frederick, Lt. Col., C.S.: early career 48, 246, 260; *see also* Jeff Davis Legion

Warren, Gouverneur, Maj. Gen., U.S. 284n17, 301n54
Warrenton 23, 81, 97, 98, 213, 215, 278n7
Warrenton Junction (Calverton) 98, 101, 103, 107, 108, 282n24
Warsaw, IL 233
Washington, George, Pres. 282n25
Washington, Martha 266n29
Washington College 250
Washington County 273n77
Washington, DC 1, 16, 18, 43, 59, 60, 62, 63, 64, 65, 67, 68, 70, 71, 73, 76, 94, 95, 99, 101, 104, 202, 220, 222, 223, 224, 226, 229, 231, 233, 235, 240, 242, 245, 273n82, 276n90, 278n7, 284n16
Washington Navy Yard 104
Washington Territory 67
Washita River, KS 266n31
Waterloo 23, 39, 98, 290n18
Watts, James O., Lt. Col., C.S. 245–246, 260, 299n129; *see also* 2nd Virginia Cavalry Regiment
Welbourne (Dulaney Farm) 51
Wellford, William 182
Wellford House/Farm (Farley) 126, 182, 183, 188, 189, 193, 194, 195, 285n42, 292n15, n16
Wellford's Ford 112, 119, 126, 193, 195, 295n35
Wellford's Ford Road 119, 182
Wellington, Arthur Wellesley, Duke of 290n18
West, John, Capt., C.S. 279n35
West Point, NY (United States Military Academy at) 1, 6, 7, 11, 12, 18, 27, 28, 33, 41, 42, 43, 44, 45, 47, 48, 49, 50, 51, 54, 58, 60, 61, 63, 64, 65, 66, 67, 69, 71, 74, 86, 102, 111, 127, 136, 200, 207, 223, 225, 229, 230, 234, 235, 239, 252, 262, 263, 264, 268n33, 269n54, 272n55, n61, 274n23, 275n48, n49, n62, 276n86, n99, 281n81, 284n17, 289n44, 291n63, n65, 296n80, 297n13, n26, 302n1, n2
West Virginia 44, 50, 51, 52, 53, 54, 230, 244, 250
Westmoreland County 44, 241
Westport, KS 221
Wheat, Roberdeau, Maj. C.S. 291n68
Wheatley's Ford 295n61

Wheeler, Joseph, Lt. Gen., C.S. 48, 279n29
Wheeling, WV 60, 75
Whelan, Henry C., Maj., U.S. 129, 185, 232, 286n86, 298n61; *see also* 6th Pennsylvania Cavalry Regiment
White, Benjamin, Capt., C.S. 165, 290n37, 301n33
White, Elijah V, Lt. Col., C.S. early career 53, 128, 157, 158, 161, 162, 163, 165; later life 246–247, 259, 273n102, 302n38; *see also* 35th Battalion, Virginia Cavalry
White House on the Pamunkey 11, 65, 266n29
White Sulphur Springs *see* Fauquier Sulphur Springs
Whitehead (U.S. ship) 49
White's Ferry 273n102
Whiting, Charles J., Maj., U.S. 62; early career 64, 275n48, 66, 127, 129, 187, 191, 192; later life 223, 255, 262, 297n13; *see also* Reserve Brigade
Whitworth rifled gun 253
Wickham, Williams C., Col., C.S.: early career 43, 54, 139, 143, 144, 145, 148, 152, 166, 204, 239; later life 241, 243, 250, 258, 260, 284n24, 288n28, n30, n32, 302n51; *see also* 4th Virginia Cavalry Regiment
Wickham Farm *see* Hickory Hill
"Widow" Coakley 266n39
Wigfall, Francis H., Lt. C.S. 278n19
Wigfall, Louis T. 278n19
Wilderness, Battle of 228, 234
Williams, George 39
Williams, Lawrence, Maj., U.S. 65, 275n67
Williams, Leonard, Capt., C.S. 278n1, 279n24, 302n46
Williams, Martha ("Markie") 275n67
Williams, Robert, Col., U.S. 74
Williams, Solomon, Col., C.S.: early career 45, 185, 189, 191, 200, 214, 259, 264, 294n14, 302n8 *see also* 2nd North Carolina Cavalry Regiment
Williams, William Orton, Col., C.S. 275n67
Williams College 41, 153

Williamsburg (Battle of) 43, 64
Williamsport, PA 245, 251
Wilmington, DE 233
Wilson, Wade, Lt., U.S. 168, 171, 286n92
Wiltshire, _____, Mr. (Cunningham's Overseer) 122
Winchester 50, 61, 226, 228, 245, 273n82, 277n136, 290n29
Winder, John H., Brig. Gen., C.S. 33, 44, 233
Winston, Elizabeth (Mrs. Thomas Rosser) 271n26
Winston Home *see* Courtland
Wisconsin 234
Wise, Henry, Brig. Gen., C.S. 44
Wise, Jennings 300n1
Wood, Edward E., Lt., U.S. 263
Woods, James, Pvt., U.S. 164, 165, 302n6
Woodstock 242
Worthington, William N., Capt., C.S. 155
Wright, D. Giraud 278n19
Wyndham, Percy, Col., U.S. 2; early career 70, 71, 137, 156, 157, 158, 159, 161, 163, 166, 167, 177, 209, 214, 220; later life 224, 257, 276n97, 289n8, n15, 290n3, 291n59, n72, 295n42; *see also* 2nd Brigade, 3rd Cavalry Division

Yager, _____ (Union Spy) 106
Yale University 77
Yellow Tavern 228, 235, 271n28
Yew Hills (including Yew Ridge and Yew Mountain) 4, 183, 187, 189, 191, 192, 193, 195, 203, 220, 229, 238, 252, Source of name 292n16, 295n49
Yoder, Jonah, Pvt., U.S. 282n14
York *see* Stevensburg
York, PA 62
York River 97
Yorktown 34, 41, 97
Yorkville, SC 240
Young, Pierce M.B., Col., C.S. 2; early career 47–48, 272n61, 80, 169, 171, 178; later life 242, 260, 264, 299n111, 301n44; *see also* Cobb's Legion
Young, William, Col., U.S. 76

www.ingramcontent.com/pod-product-compliance
Lightning Source LLC
Chambersburg PA
CBHW081537300426
44116CB00015B/2669